FEDERAL INCOME TAXATION OF PARTNERSHIPS AND S CORPORATIONS

FOURTH EDITION

by

PAUL R. MCDANIEL
Professor of Law and
James J. Freeland Eminent Scholar in Taxation
University of Florida

MARTIN J. MCMAHON, JR.
Clarence J. TeSelle Professor of Law
University of Florida

DANIEL L. SIMMONS
Professor of Law
University of California at Davis

FOUNDATION PRESS

2006

© 1991, 1997, 1999 FOUNDATION PRESS
© 2006 By FOUNDATION PRESS
        395 Hudson Street
        New York, NY 10014
        Phone Toll Free 1–877–888–1330
        Fax (212) 367–6799
        foundation–press.com
Printed in the United States of America

ISBN–13: 978–1–58778–835–2
ISBN–10: 1–58778–835–7

TEXT IS PRINTED ON 10% POST CONSUMER RECYCLED PAPER

PREFACE

This book covers the federal income taxation of partnerships and S corporations. It is excerpted from our larger work, *Federal Income Taxation of Business Organizations, 4d Ed.* (Foundation Press, 2006), for use in courses that cover only partnership taxation, and possibly S corporation taxation, separately from the study of taxation of C Corporations. In a course, or coordinated sequence of courses, covering partnerships, S corporations, and C corporations, *Federal Income Taxation of Business Organizations* should be used for comprehensive coverage. Chapters 1-9 of this volume are identical to the corresponding chapters in *Federal Income Taxation of Business Organizations*, and Chapter 10, covering S corporations is identical to Chapter 18 of that work (with the exception of the elimination of some cross references).

Because the significant structural changes in the income tax effected in the Tax Reform Act of 1986 altered the manner in which businesses are organized and transactions are structured, over the past decade and a half important issues have to some extent changed and new issues have emerged. The importance of partnerships and limited liability companies has significantly increased, and commensurately so has the detail in Subchapter K and the Treasury Regulations under Subchapter K. The detailed nature of the statutory and regulatory provisions and number of fact specific cases and rulings preclude encyclopedic analysis, particularly where largely historical issues are concerned. Accordingly, both students and instructors must bear in mind that the cases and rulings discussed in connection with any particular issue in many instances are only examples of a much larger body of law.

This book is suitable for courses on Partnership and Subchapter S taxation at either the J.D. or LL.M. level. We recognize that teachers approach their courses with different objectives in mind and use different techniques for handling the materials. In selecting and organizing the materials, we have attempted to maximize the usefulness of these materials for whatever approach the teacher wishes to adopt—an intensive technical analysis, a problem oriented method, a consideration of the policies that underlie the technical tax structure, or a survey of the principal elements of the federal income taxation of partnerships and S corporations. While the selection of principal cases and the numerous examples discussed in the Illustrative Material can, in effect, serve as problems for students and class discussion, many instructors choose to cover partnership and S corporations taxation by using a series of detailed problems for class discussion. We have published an accompanying separately bound set of Class Discussion Problems keyed to the materials in this volume, together with an accompanying teacher's manual.

Like the earlier editions and its companion volumes, this book charts a course between those books that employ primarily textual explanation and those that rely for the most part on cases. Most chapters and sections of chapters are introduced by a textual discussion or outline of the basic issues and structure of the statute governing treatment of the particular item or transaction covered in the chapter or section. Principal cases have been included to illustrate key concepts not governed by a detailed statutory provision, as well as to illustrate how the courts have utilized the technical tools at their disposal. We have recognized, however, that the dramatic changes in the statutory structure in the past two decades, particularly those in the Tax Reform Act of 1986—the changing magnitude of the capital gain preference, the flattening of the personal income tax rates, and the passive activity loss rules—have changed dramatically the important issues. As a result, many cases long used in teaching materials are no longer helpful to students, even though they remain valid precedents. Thus, the statutory changes have made it impossible to include a judicial decision as a principal case to illustrate the application of a significant number of Code provisions. Accordingly, in many chapters the "principal case" is an excerpt from a congressional committee report or a Revenue Ruling, which helps the student understand the reasons underlying changes in the statute, as well as providing a road map to assist in mastering the detailed statutory provisions.

In the Illustrative Material, which follows the principal cases, we have attempted to provide sufficient discussion of rulings and cases to give an insight into the endless variety of factual situations to which the highly technical provisions of the Internal Revenue Code governing partnership taxation must be applied. The Illustrative Material also provides important historical background and discussion of sequential amendments to particular sections of the Code and regulations necessary to understand the significance of the current Code provisions. The breadth and detail of the Illustrative Material is such that many instructors may wish to assign only portions of it depending on the scope of the particular course. To assist in selective use of Illustrative Material, we have endeavored generally to arrange the Illustrative Material from the general to the more specific as the outline format progresses.

Of course, the Internal Revenue Code and Treasury Regulations are the centerpiece of any course in federal taxation. This text is intended to be used in conjunction with either a complete set of the Code and regulations or one of the several available edited versions of the Code and regulations. The statutory and regulatory references at the head of each topic are not intended to be exhaustive. Rather, they represent only the essential sections of the Code and regulations which the student must understand to obtain the framework for the cases and materials under the particular topic. We have not undertaken completely to explain the operation of the Code and regulations in the textual notes and Illustrative Material. The student must work with the statute and regulatory material before undertaking the examination of its application in the materials in this volume.

As to editorial matters, the statutory references throughout are to the 1986 Code, except where the text expressly indicates otherwise. References in the cases and other primary sources to the 1954 and 1939 Codes and prior statutes have been edited to conform them to the 1986 Code. Generally the practice is to omit the earlier citation and instead refer to the matter as "the former version," or "the predecessor," or to give the current relevant 1986 Code section if there has been no significant change in the statutory language. But if a significant change has occurred, that fact is noted and the prior language is given. Footnotes in cases and materials frequently have been omitted. Where retained the original numbering of the footnotes has been kept so that, in many instances, the footnote numbers are not consecutive. Editorial footnotes for cases and materials are so designated and are indicated by an asterisk. References to Tax Court Memorandum decisions are to the number assigned by the Tax Court and not to any particular commercial publication. In general, references to the Code, regulations, cases and rulings are current as of December 31, 1998.

We are indebted to Teena Enneking, Doug Holland, Scott Little, Chad McCormick, and Karen Reschley, all of whom are graduates of the University of Florida College of Law Graduate Tax Program, for research and editorial assistance.

PAUL R. MCDANIEL
MARTIN J. MCMAHON, JR.
DANIEL L. SIMMONS

April, 2006

*

SUMMARY OF CONTENTS

*

TABLE OF CONTENTS

*

TABLE OF INTERNAL REVENUE CODE SECTIONS

xvii

TABLE OF TREASURY REGULATIONS

*

TABLE OF CASES AND RULINGS

Principal cases are in bold type. Non-principal cases are in roman type. References are to Pages.

FEDERAL INCOME TAXATION OF PARTNERSHIPS AND S CORPORATIONS

*

PART I

Taxation of Partners and Partnerships

CHAPTER 1

Introduction to Partnership Taxation

Section 1. Introduction to Subchapter K

The extraordinary flexibility of the partnership form of doing business makes it a popular vehicle for conducting closely held business, whether large or small. Many individuals who join together in a professional practice form a partnership rather than a corporation, as do many other service oriented businesses. The partnership format is not limited to service businesses, however, and many other businesses are conducted in partnership form. Almost all rental real estate businesses are conducted in partnership form. The pattern of taxation of partnerships also has encouraged their use. Since the partnership is treated as a conduit for tax purposes, profits are taxed only once, in contrast to the taxation of corporate profits, first, when earned by the corporation, and again, when distributed to shareholders. In addition, when the enterprise realizes losses, the partners may deduct the losses currently on their own returns, while losses at the corporate level may not be deducted by shareholders.

In addition to general partnerships and limited partnerships,[1] most limited liability companies (LLCs) are taxed as partnerships. The Internal Revenue Code does not provide a taxing regime for LLCs. It generally

---

1. In general, this text refers only to general and limited partnerships and does not separately discuss the limited liability partnership and the limited liability limited partnership variations.

1

treats all business organizations with two or more owners as either a partnership or a corporation, and an LLC must be classified for federal income tax purposes as one of those two types of entities. Indeed, the rules governing partnership taxation were the impetus for the creation of the LLC concept in the 1980s.

Until 1988, all forms of partnership activity were treated under the same set of rules. The partnership provisions covered a wide variety of situations, ranging from small service or business partnerships involving two or three members, to large accounting and law partnerships with hundreds of members, to tax shelter and investment partnerships, which may involve as many owners as publicly held corporations. For taxable years after 1987, however, § 7704 generally treats limited partnerships and LLCs with publicly traded interests as corporations.[2]

The rules for taxing partnerships and partners are found in Subchapter K of the Internal Revenue Code. The provisions of Subchapter K are highly interrelated. Few, if any of its provisions can be studied or wholly understood in isolation. For example, when the statute allows the partners to affect the current tax liability of one partner through the shaping of the partnership agreement—which Subchapter K does with surprising frequency—there generally will be an offsetting effect on other partners or the affected partner in a later year. Often the offsetting effect is found in the operation of a different provision than that governing the first transaction, one that may be invoked by a seemingly unrelated future transaction. With this in mind, a brief overview of the basic statutory pattern of Subchapter K may be helpful before studying its particular provisions in depth.

A partnership does not pay income tax as such, although it must file a partnership return. I.R.C. §§ 701, 6031. Instead, the separate partners are liable in their individual capacities to pay tax on their shares of the partnership's income. But the partnership is an accounting entity for purposes of computing the partnership's taxable income, which is then taxed to the partners as individuals according to the manner in which it is divided among them; hence the need for a partnership return, which also acts as an information return.[3] A partnership return is more than just an information return, however, because audits and adjustments with respect to partnership items must be conducted at the partnership level, not the

---

2. Because of their essential nature under state law, general partnership interests, including the general partnership interest in a limited partnership, cannot be publicly traded.

3. For 2002, approximately 2.24 million partnership returns, with 14.3 million partners, were filed. These returns reflected aggregate net income less deficits of approximately $271 billion. Broken down between general and limited partnerships and LLCs, general partnerships in the aggregate realized about $96.9 billion of net income and

$18.6 billion of deficits, limited partnerships realized about $146.8 billion of net income and $54.3 billion of deficits, LLCs realized about $135.9 billion of net income and $87.3 billion of deficits and limited liability partnerships realized about $31.3 billion of net income and $2.7 billion of deficits. Foreign partnerships realized $13.9 billion of net income and $3.2 billion of deficits. T. Wheeler and M. Parsons, Partnership Returns 2002, 24 I.R.S. S.O.I. Bulletin, No. 2, 34–55.

individual partner level, except in the case of certain small partnerships. I.R.C. §§ 6221–6233.

The central theoretical issue in partnership taxation, which leads to most of the difficulties in actual practice, is when and for what purposes a partnership should be treated as an entity separate from the partners or merely as the aggregate of the partners, a conduit. Subchapter K resolves this dilemma by adopting entity treatment for some purposes and aggregate treatment for other purposes. Generally, this approach has been successful, although problems sometimes arise when the two approaches apply to different aspects of the same transaction, and incongruities occur.

Following an entity model, taxable income of a partnership is computed following the same rules that govern the computation of the taxable income of any individual engaged in business, with a few specific modifications. See I.R.C. § 703(a)(2); Treas. Reg. § 1.703–1(a)(2). Sections 702(a) and 703(a)(1) and Treas. Regs. §§ 1.703–1(a), 1.702–1(a)(1)–(8) require certain items entering into the computation of an individual's income tax liability to be segregated and separately stated on the partnership return. This rule applies to items whose taxable status is affected by the tax situation of the individual partner. Aggregate partnership taxable income or loss, exclusive of the separately stated items and nonallowable deductions, is computed under the general rules regarding gross income and deductions. In this regard, the partnership has its own accounting period and accounting methods, although § 706(b) restricts the partnership's ability to choose a taxable year that does not coincide with the taxable year of a majority of its partners. Although partnership business income generally is computed on an entity basis, because of the passive loss limitations of § 469, it may be necessary for a partnership to state separately the net income or loss from each separate business "activity" that it conducts; and this segregation is always required for limited partnerships. Nevertheless, it is fair to describe the approach so far as more of an entity approach than an aggregate approach.

Once the taxable income of the partnership is computed, aside from the special modifications treating the partnership itself as an accounting entity, the approach shifts. The entity approach to computing taxable income yields to treatment of the partnership as a conduit through which the individual partners are regarded as receiving the income so computed as if they had earned it individually. Each partner is liable for the tax attributable to his distributive share of the separately stated items and the remaining partnership taxable income, whether or not it is distributed. This result is accomplished by requiring the partner to include his share of income, deductions, or losses on his own return along with the rest of his taxable income. This is so even in the extreme case where the partner reports on the cash method and the partnership uses the accrual method but has not actually received payment of the income item. Likewise, because each partner is entitled to his distributive share of separately stated deduction items and credits, as well as a residual loss, if any, deduction items accrued by the partnership, even if not paid, affect the taxation of a cash method partner. Finally, § 702(c) includes a partner's distributive share of partnership gross income in the partner's gross income whenever it is necessary to determine gross income to apply any Code provision.

This quantitative "fragmentation" of the partnership income among the several partners is accompanied by a further "qualitative" division under which all specially treated items retain their qualitative identity when allocated to the several partners. I.R.C. § 702(b). This qualitative division permits the different items of income and deduction derived from the partnership to be joined with their counterparts derived from the nonpartnership activities of the respective individual partners. But the partnership as an accounting entity still affects aspects of this allocation of distributive shares, such as the time of inclusion of those shares. Since the partnership income is computed on the basis of the partnership's accounting period, the attribution to the partners is normally made only at the end of that period. Accordingly, the individual partners must include their share of partnership income for the taxable year of the partnership ending with or within the individual partner's taxable year. I.R.C. § 706(a). However, as a result of special rules governing the use of fiscal taxable years, a partner and the partnership will usually have the same taxable year. I.R.C. § 706(b). Moreover, in general, elections affecting the computation of taxable income derived by a partnership must be made by the partnership.

This divergent treatment of a partnership—an accounting entity on the one part, an aggregation of separate individuals on the other—avoids on the one hand the confusion that would result from a computation of income based on the different accounting methods of the partners and, on the other, the tax avoidance and tax liability problems that would result from taxing the partnership on its income and postponing taxation of the partners until actual distribution of the income. But this conduit approach does introduce some accounting complexities in requiring the separate computation of the various special items of partnership income, gain, loss or credit, and more importantly, creates the difficult problem of determining the amount and character of the partners' distributive shares of each of the various items. Determining the character of income can be important because § 1(h) provides a preferential rate for capital gains. For taxpayers in the 15 percent marginal tax bracket, the maximum rate on capital gains is generally five percent, and for all other taxpayer's the maximum rate on capital gains generally is 15 percent.[4] Thus, a partner who is otherwise subject to tax at the higher marginal tax rates receives a significant advantage when capital gains realized by the partnership retain that character when taxed to the partner.

---

4. The 2003 Act reduced the preferential rates on long-term capital gain from 10 and 20 percent to five and 15 percent. The provisions of the 2003 Act sunset on December 31, 2008. P.L. 108–27 § 303. Unless Congress extends the lower rates, rates will return to the previous levels for taxable years beginning after 2008.

Significant tax difficulties arise in those aspects of partnership operation in which the choice of the entity as against the aggregate approach would produce material differences. These situations involve the formation of the partnership, the disposition of partnership assets, the distribution of partnership assets to partners, the dissolution of a partnership, sales by a partner of his partnership interest to other partners or outsiders, and so on. Increasingly, the use of detailed statutory and regulatory rules governing most partnership transactions largely resolve the issues as to the aggregate and entity view of the partnership, but these rules in turn introduce an intricate framework engendering its own complexity and difficulties.

SECTION 2. DEFINITION OF A PARTNERSHIP

Since subchapter K does not apply at all unless a partnership exists, the logical starting point is an examination of the definition of a partnership for tax purposes. The remainder of this chapter will deal with that issue. Succeeding chapters deal with the formation, operation and liquidation of partnerships, and the transfer of partnership interests by sale or death.

There are two levels of inquiry prerequisite to the application of Subchapter K. First, to be a partnership, the joint activity of two or more investors must be classified as a joint business enterprise. Secondly, that joint business entity must be classified as a partnership rather than as an association taxable as a corporation.

A. PARTNERSHIP VERSUS OTHER BUSINESS ARRANGEMENT

INTERNAL REVENUE CODE: Sections 761(a); 7701(a)(2).

REGULATIONS: Sections 1.761–1(a), (b), 2(a); 301.7701–1, –2(a), (b)(1)–(7), –3(a), (b)(1).

Sections 761(a) and 7701(a)(2) each define the term "partnership" in virtually identical, sparse language. The regulations expand upon this sparse statutory language. As discussed in the next section of this chapter, Treas. Reg. § 301.7701–2 provides that a business entity with two or more members is classified as either a partnership or a corporation. For this purpose the term "business entity" is very broad, as reflected by the provisions of Treas. Reg. § 301.7701–1(a)(2), which includes "financial operations," "ventures," and "trades and businesses" from which the participants divide the profits as activities that may be treated as entities separate from their individual owners. Entities that are listed in Treas. Reg. § 301.7701–2(b), such as an entity incorporated under the laws of one of the United States, are automatically classified as corporations. A "business entity" that is not listed in Treas. Reg. § 301.7701–2(b) is classified as a partnership. Treas. Reg. § 301.7701–3(a) and (b). An entity that is classified as a partnership may elect to be taxed as a corporation, Treas.

Reg. § 301.7701–3(a), but if no election is made, the entity is by default classified as a partnership. Treas. Reg. § 301.7701–3(b). For these classification rules to apply, an entity that is to be classified as a partnership must represent a business or joint enterprise engaged in an endeavor for profit. Treas. Reg. § 301.7701–4 distinguishes businesses, financial operations, and ventures taxed as partnerships from trusts established for the protection and conservation of property (which may include a trade or business operated by the trust as a sole proprietor). The regulations, however, provide only limited guidance in respect to the types of agreements other than formal partnership agreements, LLC agreements, and articles of incorporation that create an entity separate and distinct from the person or persons conducting a business or owning property in the first place. The classification issue in these cases has been resolved largely by case law and revenue rulings.

Madison Gas and Electric Co. v. Commissioner

United States Court of Appeals, Seventh Circuit, 1980.
633 F.2d 512.

■ CUMMINGS, CIRCUIT JUDGE.

This is an action under 26 U.S.C. § 7422 for the refund of federal income taxes. The question is whether certain training and related expenses incurred by a public utility in the expansion of its generating capacity through the joint construction and operation of a nuclear plant with two other utilities are deductible as ordinary and necessary expenses in the years of payment or are non-deductible pre-operating capital expenditures of a new partnership venture. The Tax Court in an opinion reported at 72 T.C. 521 held that they are non-deductible capital expenditures. We affirm.

I

All relevant facts have been stipulated by the parties (App. 8–41) and found and set forth at length by the Tax Court. We find it necessary to summarize them only briefly. Taxpayer Madison Gas and Electric Co. (MGE), a Wisconsin corporation, is an operating public utility which has been engaged since 1896 in the production, purchase, transmission and distribution of electricity and the purchase and distribution of natural gas. MGE is subject to the jurisdiction and regulation of the Public Service Commission of Wisconsin (PSC) and the Nuclear Regulatory Commission. The Federal Energy Regulatory Commission (FERC) also has or may have jurisdiction over MGE.

MGE is required to furnish reasonably adequate service and facilities within its service area at rates found reasonable and just by the PSC. During 1969 and 1970, the tax years here in issue, MGE rendered service to some 73,000 residential and commercial customers in a service area of approximately 200 square miles in Dane County, Wisconsin. MGE also sells a small percentage of its electrical power to other utilities in Wisconsin. Its primary responsibility, however, is to its customers in the service area. The number of customers within that area has grown rapidly and continuously during the past 25 years, and the customer demand for electricity has increased with the expansion of commercial and industrial accounts, the substitution of electricity for other forms of energy, and the increasing prevalence of high-energy devices such as air-conditioning units. Thus at the time of trial MGE was servicing almost 90,000 residential, commercial and industrial customers.

MGE has over the years kept pace with the increasing demand for electrical power and provided it at reasonable rates by expanding the generating capacity of its facilities, contracting for the purchase and sale of excess electrical power, interconnecting transmission facilities with those of other Wisconsin utilities, and finally by building and operating additional facilities in conjunction with other utilities. Expenses incurred in connection with one of these joint ventures is the subject of the present suit.

On February 2, 1967, MGE entered into an agreement, entitled "Joint Power Supply Agreement" (Agreement)(App. 42–59), with Wisconsin Public Service Corporation (WPS) and Wisconsin Power and Light Co. (WPL) under which the three utilities agreed, *inter alia,* to construct and own together a nuclear generating plant now known as the Kewaunee Nuclear Power Plant (Plant). Under the Agreement, the Plant is owned by MGE, WPS and WPL as tenants-in-common with undivided ownership interests of 17.8%, 41.2% and 41.0% respectively. Electricity produced by the Plant is distributed to each of the utilities in proportion to their ownership interests. Each utility sells or uses its share of the power as it does power produced by its own individually owned facilities, and the profits thereby earned by MGE contribute only to MGE's individual profits. No portion of the power generated at the Plant is offered for sale by the utilities collectively, and the Plant is not recognized by the relevant regulatory bodies as a separate utility licensed to sell electricity. Each utility also pays a portion of all expenditures for operation, maintenance and repair of the Plant corresponding exactly to its respective share of ownership. Under utility accounting procedures mandated by the PSC and the FERC, these expenses are combined with and treated in the same manner by MGE as expenses from its individually owned facilities. The ownership and operation of the Plant by MGE, WPS and WPL is regarded by the PSC and the FERC as a tenancy-in-common. It was the intention of the utilities to create only a co-tenancy and not a partnership and to be taxed as co-tenants and not as partners.

In its 1969 and 1970 taxable years, MGE incurred certain expenses relating to the nuclear training of WPS employees, the establishment of internal procedures and guidelines for plant operation and maintenance, employee hiring activities, nuclear field management, environmental activities and the purchase of certain spare parts (App. 116–126). MGE had to incur these expenses in order to carry out its Plant activities. Pursuant to order of the PSC, MGE was required to amortize training expenses, net of income taxes, over a 60–month period from the date of commercial operation of the Plant, a date occurring after those in issue here, and the other non-construction expenses associated with the Plant, net of income taxes, over a three-year period beginning January 1, 1978. MGE did not deduct the expenses described above on its tax returns for 1969 and 1970, but in the Tax Court claimed a deduction for them by amendment to its refund petition in the total amounts of $33,418.45 and $114,434.27 for 1969 and 1970 respectively.

MGE's position was, and is, that the claimed expenses were currently deductible under Section 162(a) of the Internal Revenue Code of 1954 (Code) as ordinary and necessary business expenses. The Commissioner's position was, and is, that the claimed expenses were non-deductible capital expenditures. The Tax Court agreed with the Commissioner, holding that the operation of the Plant by MGE, WPS and WPL is a partnership within the meaning of Section 7701(a)(2) of the Code, that the expenses in question were incurred not in the carrying out of an existing business but as part of the start-up costs of the new partnership venture, and that the expenses were therefore not currently deductible but must be capitalized under Section 263(a) of the Code. MGE appeals from this judgment, arguing that its arrangement with WPS and WPL is not a partnership within the meaning of the Code and, alternatively, that even if it is a partnership the expenses are currently deductible.

II

The threshold issue is whether MGE's joint venture with WPS and WPL is a tax partnership. The Commissioner concedes that if it is not, the expenses are currently deductible under Section 162(a). A partnership for federal tax purposes is defined by the Code in Section 7701(a)(2), which provides in pertinent part:

> "The term 'partnership'—includes a syndicate, group, pool, joint venture, or other unincorporated organization, through or by means of which any business, financial operation, or venture is carried on, and which is not, within the meaning of this title, a trust estate or a corporation."

MGE's arrangement with WPS and WPL in connection with the Plant clearly establishes an unincorporated organization carrying on a "business, financial operation, or venture" and therefore falls within the literal statutory definition of a partnership. The arrangement is, of course, not taken out of this classification simply because the three utilities intended to be taxed only as a co-tenancy and not as a partnership. While it is well-settled that mere co-ownership of property does not create a tax partnership, see, e.g., Estate of Appleby v. Commissioner, 41 B.T.A. 18 (1940), co-owners may also be partners if they or their agents carry on the requisite "degree of business activities." Powell v. Commissioner, 26 T.C.M. 161 (1967); Hahn v. Commissioner, 22 T.C. 212 (1954).

MGE's argument is that a co-tenancy does not meet the business activities test of partnership status unless the co-tenants anticipate the earning and sharing of a single joint cash profit from their joint activity.

Because its common venture with WPS and WPL does not result in the division of cash profits from joint marketing, MGE contends that the venture constitutes only a co-tenancy coupled with an expense-sharing arrangement and not a tax partnership. The Tax Court held that the Code definition of partnership does not require joint venturers to share in a single joint cash profit and that to the extent that a profit motive is required by the Code it is met here by the distribution of profits in kind. We agree.

The definition of partnership in Section 7701(a)(2) was added to the Code by Section 1111(a) of the Revenue Act of 1932 and first appeared in Section 3797(a)(2) of the 1939 Code. The Congressional Reports accompanying the 1932 Act make clear, in largely identical language, that Congress intended to broaden the definition of partnership for federal tax purposes to include a number of arrangements, such as joint ventures, which were not partnerships under state law. H.P.Rep. No. 708, 72d Cong., 1st Sess., 53 (1932); S.Rep. No. 665, 72d Cong., 1st Sess., 59 (1932). In so doing, they briefly discuss the advantages of requiring a partnership return for joint venturers rather than leaving the sole responsibility for reporting annual gains and losses on the individual members. MGE invites us to infer from these discussions that Congress contemplated inclusion only of those joint ventures that are capable of producing joint cash gains and losses. But even if we were inclined to narrow the statutory language on the basis of such slender evidence, the subsequent legislative history would dissuade us from reaching MGE's suggested construction.

In Bentex Oil Corp. v. Commissioner, 20 T.C. 565 (1953), the Tax Court held that an unincorporated organization formed to extract oil under an operating agreement which called for distribution of oil in kind was a partnership within the meaning of Section 3797(a)(2) of the 1939 Code. The Bentex joint venture is not distinguishable from that presented here in any meaningful way. The co-owners there, as here, shared the expenses of production but sold their shares of the production individually. Following *Bentex,* Congress reenacted the definition of partnership in Section 3797(a)(2) of the 1939 Code without change as Section 7701(a)(2) of the 1954 Code. In addition, it repeated the definition verbatim in Section 761(a), which permits certain qualifying organizations to elect to be excluded from application of some or all of the special Subchapter K partnership provisions. A qualifying corporation is one which is used

> "(1) for investment purposes only and not for the active conduct of a business, or

> "(2) for the joint production, extraction, or use of property, but not for the purpose of selling services or property produced or extracted, if the income of the members of the organization may be adequately determined without the computation of partnership taxable income."

In short, Section 761(a) allows unincorporated associations such as the Bentex venture and the one in issue here, which fall within the statutory definition of partnership, to elect out of Subchapter K.[2] The Section has generally been interpreted, in the absence of any legislative history, as approving the *Bentex* decision while providing relief from certain resulting hardships. * * * This interpretation is surely correct for, as the Tax Court observed:

> "[i]f distribution in kind of jointly produced property was enough to avoid partnership status, we do not see how such distribution could be used as a test for election to be excluded from the partnership provisions of subchapter K" (72 T.C. at 563).

MGE also relies on Treasury Regulation Sections 301.7701-3 and 1.761-1(a) (26 C.F.R.) to support its argument that joint marketing is a *sine qua non* of partnership status. These Sections state in identical language that tenants in common

> "may be partners if they actively carry on a trade, business, financial operations, or venture and divided the profits thereof."

In addition, MGE cites to us case law referring to a joint profit motive as a characteristic of partnerships.[3] See, e.g., Commissioner v. Tower, 327 U.S. 280, 286, 66 S.Ct. 532, 535, 90 L.Ed. 670 ("community of interest in the profits and losses"); Ian Allison v. Commissioner, 35 T.C.M. 1069 (1976)("an agreement to share profits"). Neither the above-quoted Treasury Regulations Sections nor the case law distinguish between the division of cash profits and the division of in-kind profits, and none of the cited cases involved in-kind profits. Moreover, while distribution of profits in-kind may be an uncommon business arrangement, recognition of such

---

2. MGE argues that in enacting Section 761(a) Congress had in mind only oil, gas and mineral ventures acting under operating agreements and that therefore the Section should not be automatically construed to include an operating agreement for the production of electricity. In support of this position, MGE inexplicably cites Taubman, Oil and Gas Partnerships and Section 761(a), 12 Tax L.Rev. 49 (1956), in which the author expressly states:

> "Congress thus attempted to establish a workable formula which would be valid not only for oil and gas, but all types of operating agreements, as well as the related and equally difficult field of investment." 12 Tax L.Rev. 49, 67.

The three utilities here in fact did file a partnership return and election-out of Subchapter K (App. 19, 41). The Tax Court held that the filing of a partnership return and election-out under Section 761(a) are not admissions of partnership status (72 T.C. at 558). MGE did not argue below that election-out caused the organization not to be a partnership for non-Subchapter K tax purposes,

and the Tax Court declined to decide this possible issue (72 T.C. at 559 n. 9). In its alternative position here, however, MGE contends that the holding below is "inconsistent with the purpose" of Section 761(a)(Br. 41). This argument is indistinguishable from an argument that election-out under Section 761(a) negates partnership status except where the Code explicitly provides to the contrary. Since the issue was not raised and decided below, we do not address it here. We note, however, that Section 7701(a)(2) explicitly states that an organization which is a partnership as defined in that Section is a partnership for the purposes of the entire Code, whereas Section 761(a) provides only for election-out of Subchapter K.

3. The Commissioner takes the position that the presence of a joint profit motive is merely one factor to be considered in determining partnership status, while MGE argues that it is a necessary element. Because we find a joint profit motive here, albeit for in-kind profits, we need not resolve this dispute.

arrangements as tax partnerships is not novel. See, e.g., *Bentex,* supra; Luckey v. Commissioner, 334 F.2d 719 (9th Cir.1964); Bryant v. Commissioner, 46 T.C. 848, affirmed, 399 F.2d 800 (5th Cir.1968).[4]

The practical reality of the venture in issue here is that jointly produced electricity is distributed to MGE and the other two utilities in direct proportion to their ownership interest for resale to consumers in their service areas or to other utilities. The difference between the market value of MGE's share of that electricity and MGE's share of the cost of production obviously represents a profit. Just as obviously, the three utilities joined together in the construction and operation of the Plant with the anticipation of realizing these profits. The fact that the profits are not realized in cash until after the electricity has been channeled through the individual facilities of each participant does not negate their joint profit motive nor make the venture a mere expense-sharing arrangement.[5] We hold therefore that MGE's joint venture with WPS and WPL constitutes a partnership within the meaning of Sections 7701(a)(2) and 761(a) of the Code.

III

On the ultimate issue in this case, the Tax Court held that the claimed expenses were incurred as pre-operational costs of the partnership venture and therefore under settled law were non-deductible capital expenditures. See Richmond Television Corp. v. United States, 345 F.2d 901 (4th Cir. 1965), vacated on other grounds, 382 U.S. 68.

MGE argues that this holding elevates form over substance in that even if the operating arrangement is technically a tax partnership, the claimed expenses were in actuality simply ordinary and necessary expenses of expanding its existing business. MGE asks us therefore to ignore the partnership entity as lacking economic substance.

* * *

Here MGE, WPS and WPL are engaged in the joint production of electricity for resale, a joint venture for profit. Because they were each already in the business of selling electricity, it can, of course, be argued that the partnership venture itself is an extension or expansion of their existing businesses. It does not follow from this though that we should

---

4. See generally, McKee, Nelson & Whitmire, Federal Taxation of Partnerships and Partners, par. 3.02, pp. 3–8, in which the authors conclude: "A partnership may result from a joint extraction or production agreement among co-owners of mineral property or production facilities, even though the co-owners separately take and sell (or reserve the right to take and sell) their shares of production. * * * Despite the absence of an objective to earn a joint cash profit, these ventures are generally considered partnerships" (footnotes omitted).

5. Treasury Regulation Sections 301.7701[–1(a)(2)] and 1.761–1(a) (26 C.F.R.) state that a "joint undertaking merely to share expenses is not a partnership," and go on to give the example of neighboring landowners who jointly construct a ditch "merely to drain surface water from their properties." We agree with the Tax Court that the venture here is "in no way comparable to the joint construction of a drainage ditch" (72 T.C. at 560).

ignore the partnership as lacking economic substance. Such reasoning would lead to the absurd conclusion that any partnership established to do collectively what its participants formerly did individually or continue to do individually outside the partnership lacks economic substance and should not be treated as a partnership for tax purposes.

At bottom, MGE's position is that it is not sound policy to treat the entity here as a partnership. But we are not free to rewrite the tax laws, whatever the merits of MGE's position. Under the Internal Revenue Code the joint venture here is a partnership and the expenses were non-deductible, pre-operational start-up costs of the partnership venture. Accordingly, the judgment of the Tax Court is affirmed.

ILLUSTRATIVE MATERIAL

1. THE NATURE OF THE INQUIRY

1.1. *In General*

A partnership is broadly defined in § 761(a) as any "syndicate, group, pool, joint venture or other unincorporated organization through or by means of which any business, financial operation, or venture is carried on, and which is not * * * a corporation, or a trust or estate." In an important case decided before the enactment of Subchapter K, but which related to a year in which the statutory predecessor of § 761(a) appeared in the Code, the Supreme Court held that the test for determining the existence of a partnership is whether the parties by their actions intended to join together to conduct a business and share in the profits and losses, regardless of how they characterized the relationship. Commissioner v. Culbertson, 337 U.S. 733 (1949).

Although the reported cases cite numerous factors that are considered in determining whether persons have entered into a partnership, the single most important factual question in all cases is whether the parties are acting as co-proprietors. See, e.g, Harlan E. Moore Charitable Trust v. United States, 9 F.3d 623 (7th Cir.1993) (sharecropping arrangement including sharing some expenses was not a partnership because the rent was not a percentage of profits).

No single factor is talismanic. The following passage from Luna v. Commissioner, 42 T.C. 1067, 1077–78 (1964), which involved the question of whether a particular arrangement was a partnership for tax purposes or an employment relationship, discusses some of the relevant factors:

> The following factors, none of which is conclusive, bear on the issue * * *: The agreement of the parties and their conduct in executing its terms; the contributions, if any, which each party has made to the venture; the parties' control over income and capital and the right of each to make withdrawals; whether each party was a principal and coproprietor, sharing a mutual proprietary interest in the net profits and having an obligation to share losses, or whether one party was the agent or employee of the other, receiving for his services contingent

compensation in the form of a percentage of income; whether business was conducted in the joint names of the parties; whether the parties filed Federal partnership returns or otherwise represented to respondent or to persons with whom they dealt that they were joint venturers; whether separate books of account were maintained for the venture; and whether the parties exercised mutual control over and assumed mutual responsibilities for the enterprise.

1.2. *Relevance of State Law*

Characterization of an arrangement under state law is not controlling for federal income tax purposes; Internal Revenue Code standards control. Treas. Reg. § 301.7701–1(a)(1), (b); Commissioner v. Culbertson, 337 U.S. 733 (1949); Kahn's Estate v. Commissioner, 499 F.2d 1186 (2d Cir.1974). Thus, Rev.Rul. 77–137, 1977–1 C.B. 178, held that an assignee of a limited partnership interest, who under state law was not admitted to the partnership by virtue of the assignment but who was entitled to distributions of partnership profits, nevertheless would be taxed as the owner of the partnership interest for federal income tax purposes. While local law may distinguish a partnership from a joint venture for some purposes, the latter generally being formed for a single business purpose in contrast to the formation of a partnership to conduct an ongoing business, the distinction is not relevant for tax law; a joint venture is treated the same as a partnership. See Podell v. Commissioner, 55 T.C. 429 (1970). Local law is controlling, however, in determining the rights and responsibilities of the participants that are taken into account in determining the existence of a partnership applying tax law standards.

A partnership conducting a professional business may exist for tax purposes between a member of a licensed profession and a person who does not hold a license even though it could not legally exist under local law. See Nichols v. Commissioner, 32 T.C. 1322 (1959) (finding that a partnership for the practice of medicine existed between a physician and nonphysician, an arrangement that would be proscribed under state law); Rev.Rul. 77–332, 1977–2 C.B. 484 (partnership between CPAs and non-CPA "principals" in accounting firm; state law prohibits non-CPA partners).

1.3. *Husband and Wife Partnerships*

Rev. Proc. 2002–69, 2002–2 C.B. 831, deals with the classification of partnerships, including limited liability companies (LLCs) taxed as partnerships, that are wholly owned by a husband and wife *as community property* in community property law states. If for federal tax purposes the husband and wife treat the entity as a disregarded entity with a single owner under Treas. Reg. § 301.7701–1(a)(4) and –2(a), the Service will accept the position that the entity is a disregarded entity for federal tax purposes. On the other hand, if the husband, wife, and the entity treat the entity as a partnership for federal tax purposes and file appropriate partnership returns, the Service will accept the position that the entity is a partnership for federal tax purposes. (A change in reporting position will be treated for federal tax purposes as a conversion of the entity.) Nothing in the revenue procedure allows husbands and wives who wholly-own an LLC or partnership in a common law property state to avoid entity characterization under Treas. Reg. § 301.7701–2(a).

1.4.   *State Law Partnership with Wholly–Owned LLC*

Suppose a state law partnership, the AL Partnership, has two partners, individual A and L, a limited liability company (LLC) of which A is the sole member. Is the AL Partnership a partnership for federal tax purposes? Unless L has elected under Treas. Reg. § 301.7701–3(c) to be taxed as a corporation, under the default rule of Treas. Reg. § 301.7701–3(b)(1), L is disregarded as an entity separate from its owner, A. Because L is disregarded, A is treated as owning all of the interests in AL. Because AL has only one owner for federal tax purposes, AL cannot be classified as a partnership under § 7701(a)(2). It is disregarded as an entity separate from A. The same analysis would apply if AL were an LLC in which A and L were the only members. AL would be disregarded.

2.   PARTNERSHIP VERSUS CO–OWNERSHIP OF PROPERTY

2.1.   *General*

Determining whether co-owners of property are engaged in business as partners is important for a variety of reasons beyond the requirement in § 6031 that a partnership file a return.[5] For example, if the arrangement is a partnership, all tax accounting elections, including cost recovery methods under § 168, must be made by the partnership, not by the individual co-owners. Other provisions whose proper application cannot be determined without first determining if a partnership exists include § 453, governing installment sales, § 1031, governing like kind exchanges (undivided interests in property are subject to § 1031; partnership interests are not), § 1033, dealing with involuntary conversions, and § 1221 defining capital assets. Also, if ownership is a cotenancy rather than a partnership, deductions, other than depreciation, attributable to the enterprise do not reduce the individual owners' bases in the property, whereas deductions that flow through to partners reduce their bases in their partnership interests. See I.R.C. § 705(a)(2)(A).

Despite the broad definition of a partnership in § 761(a), the Regulations provide that a joint undertaking to share expenses or the mere co-ownership of property that is maintained, kept in repair, and leased does not constitute a partnership. However, co-ownership will be treated as a partnership if active business operations are carried on, such as providing services for a tenant either directly or through an agent. Treas. Reg. § 301.7701–1(a)(2).

2.2.   *Cases Finding Partnership*

In Levine v. Commissioner, 72 T.C. 780 (1979), aff'd on other issues, 634 F.2d 12 (2d Cir.1980), the taxpayer and his son owned various

---

5.   For the importance of filing partnership returns, see Simons v. United States, 89–1 U.S.T.C. 57 9238 (S.D.Fla.1989) (up-   holding $1,000 per year failure to file penalty under § 6698).

commercial real estate properties that they leased to tenants. No partnership returns were filed, and the taxpayers reported the income or loss from the properties pro rata on their individual returns. The issue in the case was whether the gain from the disposition of a particular property was properly reportable by the taxpayer in 1968 or in 1969; if a partnership existed, the gain was properly reportable in 1969, rather than 1968.[6] Even though the parties did not characterize their relationship as a partnership, the Tax Court found that they were partners because they engaged in an active business by leasing the properties to tenants, providing property management services to the tenants, and sharing the gains and losses. These factors were found more indicative of a partnership business than "a mere passive investment." In Rothenberg v. Commissioner, 48 T.C. 369 (1967), co-owners of apartment buildings were found to be partners rather than tenants in common because the operation of the buildings constituted the active conduct of a rental business, and they held themselves out as partners and filed partnership tax returns. As a result, the partnership and not the individuals was the proper taxpayer to make the election under § 453 regarding installment method reporting of gains. In Underwriters Insurance Agency of America v. Commissioner, T.C. Memo. 1980–92, the taxpayer sold its interests in tuna fishing boats and claimed a § 1231 ordinary loss on the sale of depreciable property. The Commissioner asserted that the taxpayer was a partner in the fishing boat business and sold a partnership interest, resulting in a capital loss. The court held that the taxpayer was a partner, even though boats were registered and transferred in individual names as co-owners rather than in partnership name, because the boats were operated through employees or agents, not leased, and partnership returns were filed for some vessels for some years. Alhouse v. Commissioner, T.C. Memo. 1991–652, held that co-owners who leased property under a net lease and for whom property was managed under a management agreement nevertheless were partners; because they did not retain the right separately to convey their interests they had a joint profit motive. Accordingly, special rules relating to audits of partnerships applied.

In Bergford v. Commissioner, 12 F.3d 166 (9th Cir.1993), the taxpayers purchased an undivided fractional interest in computer equipment that was then leased back to the seller. Whether the Tax Court had jurisdiction to review the deficiency notice turned on whether the taxpayer was a co-owner or a partner. In deciding that the taxpayers had entered into a partnership with the other owners of undivided interests in the equipment as well as with the "manager" of the leasing operation, the court reasoned as follows:

> [T]he Tax Court found that the economic benefits to the individual participants were not derivative of their co-ownership of

---

6. Section 706, discussed at page 173, requires partners to report their shares of partnership income in their taxable year during or with which the partnership's taxable year ends. Thus, if the partnership uses a different taxable year than the partner, the proper year for reporting an item can depend on whether or not the item is a partnership item.

the computer equipment, but rather came from their joint relationship toward a common goal. It also held that taxpayers' ability to partition out an interest, judicially if needed, was illusory. We cannot say it erred. Taxpayers acted together with AmeriGroup Management in a long-term venture to finance, lease, and remarket the computer equipment. In reality, the participants have an interest in the CSE Program, not just in the equipment. As a practical matter, they must act in concert to buy the equipment and finance it, and none could sell, lease, or encumber the equipment without the consent of other participants. Although any participant has the right voluntarily to withdraw or assign his interest, consent of the manager must be obtained. In addition, the manager has the right to remarket the participants' interests and is to receive a remarketing fee regardless of whether a participant has terminated the management agreement. Termination does not, accordingly, affect the manager's economic interest in the value of the equipment. While taxpayers are correct that they have a right to partition the property, there is no indication that an individual unit interest has any appreciable value. Finally, at least to some extent the manager shares in the risk of gain and loss. Although the management agreement does not require the manager to loan money to participants if rental income fails to meet the anticipated return, the arrangement is structured to make advances available as needed. As the Tax Court presumed, the manager must have intended to honor that commitment and thus to undertake financial risk if necessary. Because the manager has the right to a remarketing fee regardless of whether a participant exercises the right to terminate the management agreement, the manager, as well as each other participant, has a continuing interest in the residual value of the equipment. These facts suffice to justify the Tax Court's conclusion that taxpayers, other participants, and the manager evidenced an intent to join together in a transaction in order to share profits and losses.

2.3. *Cases Finding Co-ownership*

In McShain v. Commissioner, 68 T.C. 154 (1977), no partnership existed where co-owners leased unimproved land to a single tenant, who was required to pay rent, all taxes, assessments, utility bills and other assessments relating to the land. The only activities of the lessors were collecting rent and signing applications for permits and licenses. Accordingly, when the land was condemned, § 1033 applied to the co-owners individually.

Revenue Ruling 75–374, 1975–2 C.B. 261, provides some examples of maintenance and repair activity that allow co-owners to avoid partnership status. Co-owners of an apartment building hired an unrelated management corporation to manage, operate and maintain the property. The management company negotiated and executed leases, collected rents and other payments from tenants, paid taxes, assessments and insurance premiums with respect to the property, and performed all other customary services to maintain and repair the property on behalf of and at the expense of the co-owners. Services provided to the tenants by the co-owners through the management company included heat, air conditioning, hot and cold water, unattended parking, trash removal, and cleaning of public areas. The management company also provided to tenants *on its own behalf* additional services such as attendant parking, cabanas, gas, and other utilities. The Ruling held that the co-owners were not partners between themselves, and implies that they were not partners with the management company. Since the Regulations apply the same standard whether services are provided directly or through an agent, the result in the Ruling should not have differed if the co-owners had provided maintenance and repairs directly. Those services provided by the management company on its own behalf, however, appear to have gone beyond maintenance and repair and, if the management company had provided those services on behalf of the co-owners or if the co-owners had provided those services directly, they probably would have been found to be partners.

Madison Gas and Electric turned on whether the joint profit motive requisite for finding a partnership could be satisfied if the venture was organized to produce a product of value that would be divided among the parties to the venture with each party, in turn, independently selling or using its share of the product. This issue was also raised in an earlier case, Allison v. Commissioner, T.C. Memo. 1976–248. In that case X Corporation, which was in the business of arranging financing for commercial property development, entered into an agreement with Y Corporation under which X Corporation would arrange to secure the financing necessary for Y Corporation to purchase and subdivide a tract of land; upon completion of the subdivision, Y Corporation was to deed X Corporation 75 of the subdivided lots. X Corporation claimed that the lots were received in a tax free liquidation of a joint venture; the Commissioner asserted that they were received as compensation for services. Emphasizing that there was no agreement to resell the subdivided lots jointly, the court found that there was no joint profit motive and thus no partnership. In addition, the court noted that no partnership books were kept and no partnership tax returns filed. The different result in this case might be reconciled with *Madison Gas and Electric* because the *Allison* case involved a venture of limited scope and duration rather than the ongoing conduct of a business, but the distinction is quite tenuous.

2.4. *Internal Revenue Service Ruling Policy*

In Rev. Proc. 2002–22, 2002–1 C.B. 733, the Service described conditions required for it to issue a private letter ruling that an undivided fractional interest in rental real property is not an interest in a business entity, which is a prerequisite to partnership status. The revenue procedure addresses sponsored co-ownership interests in property that is subject to a master lease which are sold to investors primarily as a vehicle to facilitate § 1031 exchanges of real estate. (Section 1031 is not applicable to an exchange of a partnership interest.) The revenue procedure identifies the following conditions, among others, for obtaining a ruling that a co-ownership arrangement is not a business entity:

(1) The co-owners must hold title to the property as tenants in common under local law.

(2) There may not be more than 35 co-owners (except that husband and wife and all persons who acquire an interest by inheritance will be treated as single co-owner).

(3) The co-ownership may neither designate itself nor conduct business as a partnership, corporation, or other business entity. Also the co-owners may not have held title to the property in a corporation or partnership prior to formation of the co-ownership.

(4) In general, each co-owner must have the rights to transfer, partition, and encumber the co-owner's undivided interest in the property without the agreement or approval of any person. However, the co-owners may enter into an agreement that requires any co-owner to offer the co-ownership interest to the other co-owners before exercising rights to partition the co-ownership interest and that certain actions regarding the co-ownership interests require a vote of 50 percent of the ownership interests.

(5) Certain actions such as a sale, lease, or re-lease of a portion or all of the property, any negotiation or renegotiation of indebtedness secured by a blanket lien, the hiring of any manager, or the negotiation of any management contract must require unanimous approval of the co-owners. Other actions may be taken by a vote of persons holding 50 percent of the undivided interests in the property.

(6) If the Property is sold, any debt secured by a blanket lien must be satisfied and the remaining sales proceeds must be distributed to the co-owners.

(7) All profits, expenses, losses, and indebtedness must be shared in proportion to co-ownership interests.

(8) A co-owner may issue an option to purchase the co-owner's undivided interest (call option) as long as the purchase price reflects the fair market value of the co-ownership interest. A co-owner is not allowed to hold an option to sell the co-owner's interest (a put option) to the sponsor, the lessee, the lender, or another co-owner (or to any related person).

(9) The co-ownership may not engage in the conduct of an active trade or business. Thus, the co-owners' activities must be limited to those customarily performed in connection with the maintenance and repair of rental real property. See Rev. Rul. 75–374, page 16.

2.5. *Election Out of Partnership Status*

Section 761(a) authorizes regulations under which members of "an unincorporated organization" may elect to be excluded from the operation of subchapter K if the organization is availed of (1) for investment purposes rather than the active conduct of a business; (2) for the joint production, extraction or use of property, but not for the purpose of selling services or property produced or extracted; or (3) by securities dealers engaged in a short term venture to underwrite, sell or distribute a particular issue of securities, provided in all cases that the members' incomes can adequately be determined without the computation of partnership taxable income.[7] See Treas. Reg. § 1.761–2 for further details and the manner for making the election. When a valid § 761 election is made, no partnership return need be filed. In addition, the election overrides § 703(b), which requires that all elections (with specified exceptions) be made by the partnership, and thereby permits co-owners to make inconsistent elections with respect to the accounting treatment of items relating to the property. See Rev. Rul. 83–129, 1983–2 C.B. 105 (election to capitalize and amortize mine development expenses under § 616). But where a provision of the Code outside of subchapter K specifically refers to the treatment of partnerships wholly apart from Subchapter K, a § 761 election has no effect. See Bryant v. Commissioner, 399 F.2d 800 (5th Cir.1968) (investment credit limitation under § 48(c)(2)(d) of 1954 Code applied to partnership that made 761 election); Rev. Rul. 65–118, 1965–1 C.B. 30 (same). Section 1031(a), however, specifically provides that an exchange of an interest in a partnership that has elected out of subchapter K will be treated as an exchange of the underlying assets of the partnership for purposes of determining the extent to which the exchange qualifies as a tax-free like-kind exchange under § 1031.

3. PARTNERSHIP VERSUS EMPLOYMENT OR AGENCY AGREEMENT

A partnership does not exist if the relationship between the parties is an employment, agency or independent contractor arrangement. See Rev. Rul. 75–43, 1975–1 C.B. 383 (no partnership where a corporate feedlot owner entered into a service agreement with individual cattle owners to raise cattle for the owners). This issue has arisen most frequently with respect to classifying receipts as ordinary income from compensation or gain from the sale of a capital asset. See Luna v. Commissioner, 42 T.C. 1067 (1964) (taxpayer was found to be an employee of an insurance company rather than a party to a joint venture; hence a lump sum payment to him was taxable as compensation and not as capital gain on the sale of a partnership interest).

In determining whether an arrangement is a partnership or an employment, agency, or contractor arrangement, the same standards used to determine if co-owners are partners apply. But because employees, agents, and independent contractors frequently are compensated on the basis of a percentage of the employer's profits, the sharing of profits aspect of the test may be more difficult to apply; sharing of losses, which is not common in employment or similar relationships may be more significant, but is not

---

7. See McMahon, The Availability and Effect of Election Out of Partnership Status   Under Section 761(a), 9 Va. Tax Rev. 1 (1989)

always necessary. The essential factual inquiry is whether the persons are "coproprietors" of the business. In Wheeler v. Commissioner, T.C. Memo. 1978–208, the taxpayer entered into an agreement with Perault to develop specific tracts of land. The taxpayer contributed "know-how" and Perault provided the financing, with the profits to be split 25 percent to the taxpayer and 75 percent to Perault. Although title to all properties was held in Perault's name, the parties did business under the name "Perault and Wheeler." The taxpayer had total authority to manage the day-to-day affairs of the business, but he could not borrow on behalf of the venture. Perault, however, was entitled to receive all of the operating income until he received back his entire investment plus six percent interest and was to bear all losses; consistently, he reported all of the operating income and expenses. Upon the sale of properties, however, Perault reported only his share of gains; he did not report the full gain and claim a deduction for compensation paid to the taxpayer. The Tax Court held that Wheeler and Perault were partners. Accordingly, Wheeler's share of the gains was taxable to him as capital gains, rather than being treated as compensation for services taxable as ordinary income. See also Rev. Rul. 54–84, 1954–1 C.B. 284 (holding properties in one partner's name and absence of loss sharing did not prevent partnership status).

Dorman v. United States, 296 F.2d 27 (9th Cir.1961), involved an agreement for a ranching venture under which the taxpayer, who contributed no capital, was to be an equal partner, but his interest was not "vested" until he fully paid promissory notes representing his capital contribution to the partnership. The notes, which were for an amount equal to one half of the other venturer's capital contribution, were payable only out of the taxpayer's share of profits from the venture. In the interim, the taxpayer received a salary. The taxpayer was found to be merely an employee with an executory right to become a partner. Therefore, he was not permitted to deduct any portion of the net operating loss incurred by the venture. See also Smith's Estate v. Commissioner, 313 F.2d 724 (8th Cir.1963)(purported partnership between investment advisors and investors in commodities in which investors contributed all of the capital and bore all of the losses, but shared trading profits with investment advisors, was not recognized; investment advisors realized income from compensation).

4. PARTNERSHIP VERSUS LOAN

Occasionally, a transaction otherwise denominated as a loan may be recharacterized as a partnership. This may occur in the case of an unsecured nonrecourse debt that is to be repaid only out of profits from a venture. See Hartman v. Commissioner, T.C. Memo. 1958–206. Even if there is security for the loan, if it is inadequate, the loan may be recharacterized as an equity investment when the debt is convertible into an equity investment. See Rev. Rul. 72–350, 1972–2 C.B. 394.

Characterization of a transaction as a loan on the one hand or as a partnership on the other hand is significant not only for the purpose of characterizing payments from the "borrower" to the "lender" as interest or as a payment by a partnership to a partner, but also for purposes of determining who is entitled to claim losses incurred by the venture, the treatment of the parties if the "loan" is not repaid, and the "lender's" treatment if he sells his interest.

In 70 Acre Recognition Equipment Partnership v. Commissioner, T.C. Memo. 1996–547, a bank (State Savings) promised to lend approximately $6,500,000 to a corporation (BCI) to provide a cash downpayment on a $14,000,000 real estate purchase. The balance of the purchase price was financed by a nonrecourse note back to the seller. The interest on the bank loan was 14 percent per annum, plus 50 percent of net profits from resale of the land. On the same day that the purchase was closed, BCI sold a portion of the land for approximately $7,000,000, using the proceeds to pay closing costs and the downpayment. State Savings never made the loan, but subsequently lent BCI additional funds, on a nonrecourse basis, to develop the property. BCI and State Savings filed a partnership return allocating the profit on the sale equally, but the Commissioner asserted that no partnership had been formed and that the entire gain was allocable to BCI. Even though the entire transaction had been documented as a loan and BCI had taken and conveyed title in its own name, the court found that an oral partnership had been formed and upheld the taxpayer's treatment of the transaction.

Even though it is well accepted that interest need not be a fixed rate, but may be a specified portion of the borrower's profits, see Dorzback v. Collison, 195 F.2d 69 (3d Cir.1952), participating loans and shared appreciation mortgages still raise the question of whether the purported lender and borrower are instead partners. Under certain circumstances, the Internal Revenue Service will treat a shared appreciation mortgage entirely as a loan. Rev. Rul. 83–51, 1983–1 C.B. 48, treats as interest contingent interest equal to a fixed percentage of the appreciation in value of the borrower's personal residence over the term of the loan. In the commercial context, the Service will not rule in advance on whether a shared appreciation mortgage creates a true loan. Rev. Proc. 85–22, 1985–1 C.B. 550. Cf. Rev. Rul. 76–413, 1976–2 C.B. 213 (certain contingent interest on a mortgage loan made to a real estate developer by a trust was "interest on obligations secured by real property" under § 856(c), relating to real estate investment trusts, rather than profits from active participation in the operation of the property; the result of the Ruling was changed by amendment of § 856, but the analysis appears to continue to be relevant).

5. PARTNERSHIP VERSUS LEASE

In Form Builders, Inc. v. Commissioner, T.C. Memo. 1990–75, a group of individuals and a corporation controlled by the individuals' parents formed a "partnership" to engage in the business-form printing business, using equipment owned by the individuals with the work to be performed by the corporation. Under the written "partnership agreement" the individuals and the corporation were to share gross receipts in specified percentages. The court held that although the venture was conducted with a profit motive, because the parties shared gross receipts rather than net income there was no "joint profit motive." Accordingly, the arrangement was recharacterized as a lease of the equipment from the individuals to the corporation, and all of the gross income was attributed to the corporation, which was allowed a deduction for a reasonable rental to the individuals.

Rev. Rul. 92–49, 1992–1 C.B. 433, dealt with whether an arrangement between the owner of coin operated amusements and the owner of business premises constitutes a partnership when the coin operated amusements are placed on the business premises and the receipts are split between the two owners on a percentage basis. The Ruling provides that whether the arrangement is a lease or a partnership depends on all of the facts and circumstances, but that such an arrangement generally is a lease. Under the Ruling, if the owner of the amusements in good faith treats it as a lease for the information reporting requirements of § 6041 and files Form 1099 with respect to payments to the property owner, the Service will not challenge the treatment. Conversely, if the parties treat the arrangement as a joint venture and file a partnership tax return, the Service likewise generally will not challenge the reporting position.

6. SHAM PARTNERSHIPS

In Duhon v. Commissioner, T.C. Memo. 1991–369, the Tax Court held that the existence of a purported partnership should not be respected. The taxpayer was a partner in a partnership with a corporation, Pernie Bailey Drilling Company, and other individuals, all of whom (including the taxpayer) were either shareholders or employees of the corporation. The only capital contribution to the partnership was $1,000 provided by the corporation, which sold an oil drilling rig to the partnership on an installment note for the full purchase price of $2,250,000. The corporation then operated the drilling rig on behalf of the partnership, having all management responsibility, and agreed to assume all risks associated with its operation. Disallowing individual partner's loss deductions attributable to the partnership's depreciation deductions on the drilling rig, the court found the partnership "was merely a paper conduit operated by Pernie Bailey in such manner that it was merely carrying on the corporate business." Accord Merryman v. Commissioner, 873 F.2d 879 (5th Cir.1989) (involving another partner in the same partnership).

7. ESTATE PLANNING PARTNERSHIPS

In recent years the use of partnerships to hold assets solely for estate planning purposes has been significant. The purpose of these partnerships is to facilitate inter vivos gifts of partial interests in property without surrendering control and to reduce the valuation for estate tax purposes of the retained interest. To achieve these objectives, the taxpayer will transfer business or investment assets previously owned solely by the taxpayer to a newly formed partnership in which the objects of the bounty of the taxpayer are the other partners. The other partners receive their partnership interests as gifts (or for nominal consideration). If the taxpayer retains voting control of the partnership and the partnership is respected for tax purposes, the value of the partnership assets that would be received by the other partners in liquidation of the partnership has been eliminated from the taxpayer's estate (although a gift tax usually is payable to achieve this goal). Furthermore, if the partnership is respected, under normal valuation rules the value of the retained partnership interest will be found to be less than the proportionate value of the underlying assets. For example, a 50 percent partnership interest in a partnership holding a parcel of land worth $1,000,000 will be found to be worth substantially less than $500,000. This planning technique has given rise to a number of cases in which the question of whether a formally organized partnership would be respected for tax purposes.

Shortly before his death, the decedent in Estate of Strangi v. Commissioner, 115 T.C. 478 (2000), formed a family limited partnership for the purpose of reducing the valuation of the decedent's assets for estate tax purposes. He transferred financial assets, real estate, and interests in other partnerships to the family limited partnership in exchange for a 99 percent interest as a limited partner. A corporation, owned 47 percent by decedent and 53 percent by his wife, as trustee, held a one percent general partnership interest. Soon after the decedent limited partner's death, the partnership distributed a substantial portion of it assets. The issue was whether the entity would be respected, which would be the asset to be valued for estate tax purposes, or whether the partnership's assets would be directly included in the decedent's estate (the value of the assets far exceeded the value of the partnership interest due to a substantial discount applicable to the interest). Although the court found as matters of fact that the entity was not a joint investment vehicle, that the entity was not formed for the purpose of managing assets, and that it conducted no active business, the entity was nevertheless recognized as a partnership. The crucial reasoning of the court was as follows.

> SFLP [the partnership] was validly formed under State law. The formalities were followed, and the proverbial "i's were dotted" and "t's were crossed." The partnership, as a legal matter, changed the relationships between decedent and his heirs and decedent and actual and potential creditors. Regardless of subjective intentions, the partnership had sufficient substance to be recognized for tax purposes. Its existence would not be disregarded by potential purchasers of decedent's assets, and we do not disregard it in this case.

A concurring opinion by Judge Laro would have limited the holding to the estate and gift taxes because he believed that the majority's opinion's broader reasoning could cause mischief in income tax cases. On appeal, the Fifth Circuit affirmed the Tax Court's conclusions regarding recognition of the partnership, but remanded the case to the Tax Court to consider the Commissioner's arguments regarding estate tax provisions. Estate of Strangi v. Commissioner, 293 F.3d 279 (5th Cir. 2002). The Commissioner was upheld on remand, T.C. Memo. 2003–145.

Knight v. Commissioner, 115 T.C. 506 (2000), another family limited partnership valuation case, also upheld the validity of the limited partnership's existence solely on the ground that it was a valid partnership under state law.

B.   PARTNERSHIP VERSUS CORPORATION

INTERNAL REVENUE CODE: Sections 761(a); 7701(a)(2), (3); 7704.

REGULATIONS: Sections 301.7701–1(a) and (b), –2(a), (b)(1)–(7), –3(a), (b)(1), (c)(1)(i)–(iv). See also section 301.7701–3(b)(3)(i).

A business may be conducted by an entity that under the law of the state or foreign nation in which the entity is organized as neither a corporation nor a partnership. An entity might so closely resemble a corporation in its structure and operation that it might be treated as a corporation for tax purposes. Limited liability companies are one such form of business organization. Any such entity generally must be classified as either a partnership or a corporation for federal income tax purposes. Additional classification issues arise because not all partnerships are the same. The substantive rights and liabilities of the partners, as well as the organizational structure of general partnerships and the limited partnerships are quite different. Furthermore, in recent years exotic new forms of partnership, such as the limited liability partnership (LLP), a hybrid between a general partnership and a limited partnership have emerged.

Both limited liability companies (LLCs) and limited partnerships have many characteristics in common with corporations. The resemblance to corporations of these forms of business organization raises the question whether they should be taxable as partnerships or as corporations. Although the Internal Revenue Code provides that the corporate tax applies not only to organizations that are "corporations" under state law, but to any organization that is an "association" as defined in § 7701(a)(3), the statutory definition of "association" is not particularly helpful. The courts and the Internal Revenue Service were forced to grapple with the definition of an "association" through years of litigation and administrative action. The Service ultimately abandoned the quest with regulations that provide an election for any business entity not formally organized as a corporation under governing laws.

Rules and Regulations, Department of the Treasury, Internal Revenue Service, Simplification of Entity Classification Rules

T.D. 8697, 1997–1 C.B. 215.

Explanation of Provisions

Section 7701(a)(2) of the Code defines a partnership to include a syndicate, group, pool, joint venture, or other unincorporated organization, through or by means of which any business, financial operation, or venture is carried on, and that is not a trust or estate or a corporation. Section 7701(a)(3) defines a corporation to include associations, joint-stock companies, and insurance companies.

The existing regulations for classifying business organizations as associations (which are taxable as corporations under section 7701(a)(3)) or as partnerships under section 7701(a)(2) are based on the historical differences under local law between partnerships and corporations. Treasury and the IRS believe that those rules have become increasingly formalistic. This document replaces those rules with a much simpler approach that generally is elective.

As stated in the preamble to the proposed regulations, in light of the increased flexibility under an elective regime for the creation of organizations classified as partnerships, Treasury and the IRS will continue to monitor carefully the uses of partnerships in the international context and will take appropriate action when partnerships are used to achieve results that are inconsistent with the policies and rules of particular Code provisions or of U.S. tax treaties.

A. *Summary of the Regulations*

Section 301.7701–1 provides an overview of the rules applicable in determining an organization's classification for federal tax purposes. The first step in the classification process is to determine whether there is a separate entity for federal tax purposes. The regulations explain that certain joint undertakings that are not entities under local law may nonetheless constitute separate entities for federal tax purposes; however, not all entities formed under local law are recognized as separate entities for federal tax purposes. Whether an organization is treated as an entity for federal tax purposes is a matter of federal tax law, and does not affect the rights and obligations of its owners under local law. For example, if a domestic limited liability company with a single individual owner is disregarded as an entity separate from its owner under § 301.7701–3, its individual owner is subject to federal income tax as if the company's business was operated as a sole proprietorship.

An organization that is recognized as a separate entity for federal tax purposes is either a trust or a business entity (unless a provision of the Code expressly provides for special treatment, such as the Qualified Settlement Fund rules (§ 1.468B) or the Real Estate Mortgage Investment Conduit (REMIC) rules, see section 860A(a)). The regulations provide that trusts generally do not have associates or an objective to carry on business for profit. The distinctions between trusts and business entities, although restated, are not changed by these regulations.

Section 301.7701–2 clarifies that business entities that are classified as corporations for federal tax purposes include corporations denominated as such under applicable law, as well as associations, joint-stock companies, insurance companies, organizations that conduct certain banking activities, organizations wholly owned by a state, organizations that are taxable as corporations under a provision of the Code other than section 7701(a)(3), and certain organizations formed under the laws of a foreign jurisdiction (including a U.S. possession, territory, or commonwealth).

* * *

Any business entity that is not required to be treated as a corporation for federal tax purposes (referred to in the regulation as an eligible entity) may choose its classification under the rules of § 301.7701–3. Those rules provide that an eligible entity with at least two members can be classified as either a partnership or an association, and that an eligible entity with a single member can be classified as an association or can be disregarded as an entity separate from its owner. * * *

In order to provide most eligible entities with the classification they would choose without requiring them to file an election, the regulations provide default classification rules that aim to match taxpayers' expectations (and thus reduce the number of elections that will be needed). The regulations adopt a passthrough default for domestic entities, under which a newly formed eligible entity will be classified as a partnership if it has at least two members, or will be disregarded as an entity separate from its owner if it has a single owner. The default for foreign entities is based on whether the members have limited liability. Thus a foreign eligible entity will be classified as an association if all members have limited liability. A foreign eligible entity will be classified as a partnership if it has two or more members and at least one member does not have limited liability; the entity will be disregarded as an entity separate from its owner if it has a single owner and that owner does not have limited liability. Finally, the default classification for an existing entity is the classification that the entity claimed immediately prior to the effective date of these regulations. An entity's default classification continues until the entity elects to change its classification by means of an affirmative election.

An eligible entity may affirmatively elect its classification on Form 8832, Entity Classification Election. The regulations require that the election be signed by each member of the entity or any officer, manager, or member of the entity who is authorized to make the election and who represents to having such authorization under penalties of perjury. An election will not be accepted unless it includes all of the required information * * *.

Taxpayers are reminded that a change in classification, no matter how achieved, will have certain tax consequences that must be reported. For example, if an organization classified as an association elects to be classified as a partnership, the organization and its owners must recognize gain, if any, under the rules applicable to liquidations of corporations.

B. *Discussion of Comments on the General Approach and Scope of the Regulations*

Several comments requested clarification with regard to the rules for determining when an owner of an interest in an organization will be respected as a bona fide owner for federal tax purposes. Some commentators * * * relying on Rev. Rul. 93–4, 1993–1 C.B. 225, suggested that if two wholly-owned subsidiaries of a common parent were the owners of an organization, those owners would not be respected as bona fide owners and the organization would be treated as having only one owner (the common parent). Although the determination of whether an organization has more than one owner is based on all the facts and circumstances, the fact that some or all of the owners of an organization are under common control does not require the common parent to be treated as the sole owner. Consistent with this approach, Rev. Rul. 93–4 treated two wholly owned subsidiaries as associates and then classified the foreign entity based on the four corporate characteristics under section 7701. While these four factors will no longer apply with the adoption of the regulations, determining whether the subsidiaries are associates continues to be an issue.

* * *

C. *Discussion of Comments Relating to the Elective Regime*

Most of the commentators agreed that the default rules included in the proposed regulations generally would match taxpayers' expectations. * * *

Some commentators requested that taxpayers be allowed to make classification elections with their first tax returns. The regulations retain the requirement that elections be made at the beginning of the taxable year. Treasury and the IRS continue to believe that it is appropriate to determine an entity's classification at the time that it begins its operations. Taxpayers can specify the date on which an election will be effective, provided that date is not more than 75 days prior to the date on which the election is filed (irrespective of when the interest was acquired) and not more than 12 months after the date the election was filed. * * *

The regulations limit the ability of an entity to make multiple classification elections by prohibiting more than one election to change an entity's classification during any sixty month period. * * * [T]he regulations permit the Commissioner to waive the application of the sixty month limitation by letter ruling. However, waivers will not be granted unless there has been more than a fifty percent ownership change. The sixty month limitation only applies to a change in classification by election; the limitation does not apply if the organization's business is actually transferred to another entity.

* * *

ILLUSTRATIVE MATERIAL

1. LIMITED LIABILITY ENTITIES

1.1. *Limited Partnerships*

For many years prior to 1997, under a prior version of Treas. Reg. § 301.7701–2 (the "*Kintner*" regulations), six characteristics were taken into account as the criteria for distinguishing corporations from other organizations: (1) the presence of associates; (2) an objective to carry on business and divide the gains therefrom; (3) continuity of life, i.e., the death, resignation, etc. of a member does not cause the dissolution of the organization; (4) centralization of management, i.e., fewer than all the members have exclusive authority to make management decisions; (5) limited liability; and (6) free transferability of interests. To be classified as an association taxable as a corporation, the organization must have had more corporate than noncorporate characteristics. The corporate characteristics common to the types of organizations being compared were ignored, and since the presence of associates and an objective to carry on a business for profit are common to both corporations and partnerships, the determination whether an organization is an association taxable as a corporation or is a partnership was made with reference only to the other four characteristics.

The test of the prior regulations virtually always resulted in classification of a limited partnership as a partnership, but the route to that end was somewhat torturous. A limited partner is liable for partnership debts only to the extent of his capital contribution plus any additional amounts that he has agreed to contribute. Thus there is a strong resemblance to the limited liability of corporate shareholders. On the other hand, all limited partnerships must have at least one general partner who is fully liable for debts of the partnership.

Limited partners have no right to participate in the day-to-day management of the partnership's business; that is the responsibility of the general partner. The limited partners are entitled to examine the partnership's books, receive accountings, and vote on changes in the partnership agreement, rights similar to the rights of corporate shareholders. While general partnership interests, because they represent an agency relationship, are not freely transferable—they cannot be sold and bought like corporate stock—limited partnership interests may or may not be transferable, subject to some statutory limitations, depending on the terms of the partnership agreement.

Finally, the death or withdrawal of a limited partner does not terminate the partnership; both the entity and its business continue. The death, bankruptcy, or withdrawal of a general partner, however, generally terminates the formal existence of the legal entity under state law, even if the partnership agreement provides that the business will be continued in a newly constituted successor partnership without interruption.

For many years, all of these attributes of limited partnerships made this form of business organization a popular vehicle for assembling groups of investors who desired limited liability, transferable interests, and professional management of the business, while avoiding treatment as a corporation for tax purposes. In addition, limited partnerships historically enjoyed great popularity as the organization of choice for tax shelters because of the flow through of tax losses. Although amendments to the Internal Revenue Code enacted in the Tax Reform Act of 1986, most particularly the restrictions on deductions from passive activities under § 469, discussed at page 258, generally reduced the availability of tax shelters, these changes did not totally eliminate the desirability of organizing ventures that will produce tax losses in the limited partnership form. After 1986, the limited partnership found a new role, providing a substitute for the corporate form of conducting profitable businesses. The changes in the rate structure introduced by the Tax Reform Act of 1986 increased the relative tax burden on retained corporate profits by establishing a corporate tax rate higher than the individual rate. In addition, certain technical changes were made in the taxation of gain at the corporate level that increased the tax burden on corporate distributions. This increased taxation of profits realized through the corporate form of business organization made the limited partnership form of investment attractive for potentially profitable operations.

1.2. *Limited Liability Companies*

The first modern limited liability company (LLC) statute was enacted in Wyoming in the mid–1980s. The Wyoming statute was carefully crafted to produce partnership classification under the *Kintner* regulations. Rev. Rul. 88–76, 1988–2 C.B. 360, dealt with classification under the Wyoming statute. Under state law the limited liability company could be managed either by the members, in proportion to their capital contributions, or by a designated manager. The limited liability company in the Ruling was managed by three designated managers. Under the governing statute, members of the limited liability company could transfer their interests only with the unanimous consent of all other members. If consent was not granted, the assignee could not participate in management, but was entitled to share in profits and a return of contributions. State law provided for the dissolution of the limited liability company upon (1) the expiration of its charter, (2) unanimous consent of the members, or (3) the death, retirement, resignation, expulsion, bankruptcy, or other termination of the membership of a member, unless under a provision in the articles of organization all remaining members consented to continue the business. The Service ruled that the limited liability company lacked continuity of life because consent to continue the business upon withdrawal of a member was not assured. Free transferability of interests did not exist because the members did not have the right to transfer all of the attributes of their membership interest without the consent of the other members. Accordingly, even though the entity had limited liability and centralized management, it was classified as a partnership.

The rest of the states enacted LLC statutes in the following decade. Some statutes, like the Wyoming statute, were so called "bullet-proof" statutes, that is, partnership classification was inevitable because two of the three remaining determinative factors under the *Kintner* regulations always would be noncorporate characteristics. Other statutes were flexible. They permitted the organizers to choose to provide centralized management, free transferability of interests, and continuity of life if they so desired, although all of the flexible LLC statutes were constructed to provide default rules regarding these characteristics that were noncorporate. Thus, the typical flexible LLC statute would provide that (1) the LLC was to be managed by all the members, (2) interests were not transferable, and (3) the organization would "dissolve" upon the death, incompetence, or bankruptcy of any member, but the LLC statute would permit the members to vary any of these terms by agreement.

As the states successively enacted limited liability company statutes, the Service published a string of "cookie cutter" rulings with respect to classification under each state's statute. In every case the ruling either held that the limited liability company was a partnership under the Regulations because it was formed pursuant to a bullet-proof statute or could be classified as either a corporation or a partnership, depending on how the LLC was organized. See, e.g., Rev. Rul. 93–5, 1993–1 C.B. 227 (Virginia LLC was a partnership because pursuant to statute the LLC dissolved upon the death, resignation, expulsion, bankruptcy or dissolution of any member unless the business was continued by unanimous consent, and an assignee of a member's interest does not become a substituted member with all of the assignee's rights unless the remaining members approved); Rev. Rul. 93–49, 1993–2 C.B. 308 (Illinois limited liability company could be either a partnership or a corporation, depending upon its structure); Rev. Rul. 93–53, 1993–2 C.B. 312 (Florida limited liability company could be either a partnership or a corporation).

In addition to the limited partnership and LLC, a number of states have enacted "limited liability partnership" statutes. A limited liability partnership (LLP) is a general partnership in which the traditional joint and several liability of general partners in tort, particularly for professional malpractice, has been eliminated.

1.3.   *Policy Issues*

The proliferation of new forms of business organization, particularly the LLC, was the result of how easily all of the important attributes of a closely held corporation could be achieved under state law while obtaining partnership status for tax purposes under the *Kintner* regulations. For nontax purposes most LLCs in all meaningful respects are virtually indistinguishable from closely held corporations, even though they could be structured to be taxed as partnerships. The cascade of "cookie-cutter" rulings dealing with the status of LLCs under various state statutes, all of which permit substantially the same combination of tax and nontax attributes, indicates that no significant policy goal is served by requiring closely held unincorporated organizations to meet formalistic tests to avoid classification as a corporation. Accordingly, in 1997 the Internal Revenue Service and Treasury amended Treas. Reg. §§ 301.7701–1 through 301.7701–4 to simplify the classification of business organizations for federal tax income purposes. These new rules, which are colloquially referred to as the "check-a-box" regulations, apply to all unincorporated business entities, including limited partnerships, LLCs, business trusts, and sole proprietorships.

Transcending these technical issues is the broader policy question of the circumstances in which business profits should be subject to a "double" level of tax, once at the entity level and again when made available to the participants. When Congress focused on the question in 1987, it found publicly traded interests to be one specific situation in which the corporate taxing pattern should be applicable regardless of the form of business organization. But this obviously is not the only approach that could be taken. The Treasury Department has recommended to Congress on a number of occasions that limited partnerships with more than 35 partners be taxed as corporations. In connection with the 1987 legislation, Congress instructed the Treasury to prepare a report and recommendations on the appropriate tax treatment of all partnerships that "significantly resemble" corporations. The "check-a-box" classification rules in Treas. Regs. § 301.7701–1 through –3, however, represent a movement in the other direction.

2.   PUBLICLY TRADED PARTNERSHIPS

2.1.   *General*

Section 7704 generally treats as a corporation any partnership the interests in which are traded on an established securities market or are readily tradable on a secondary market or a substantial equivalent of a secondary market. Because under state law general partnership interests cannot be traded, the provision in fact only applies to limited partnerships and limited liability companies. The legislative history explains that a secondary market exists if prices are regularly quoted by brokers or dealers who are making a market for such interests. Occasional accommodation trades of partnership interests, a buy-sell agreement between the partners (without more), or the occasional repurchase or redemption by the partnership or acquisition by a general partner of partnership interests will not be treated as a secondary market or the equivalent thereof. However, if the partners have regular and ongoing opportunities to dispose of their interests, the interests are tradable on the equivalent of a secondary market. Meaningful restrictions imposed on the right to transfer partnership interests may preclude classification as a corporation, even if some interests are actually traded. See H.Rep. 100–495, 100th Cong., 1st Sess. 943–950 (1987).

2.2.   *Meaning of "Publicly Traded"*

Treas. Reg. 301.7704–1(b) provides definitions of the statutory terms "established securities market" and "readily tradable on a secondary market or the substantial equivalent of a secondary market." Established securities markets include not only exchanges, but also inter-dealer quotation systems. A secondary market or a substantial equivalent of a secondary market exists if the partners are readily able to buy, sell, or exchange their interests in a manner that is economically comparable to trading on an established securities market. Interests are readily tradable on a secondary market or its equivalent if (1) firm quote trading exists, even if only one person makes available bid or offer quotes; (2) the holder of an interest has a readily available, regular and ongoing opportunity to sell or exchange such interest through a public means of obtaining or providing information of offers to buy, sell, or exchange interests; or (3) buyers and sellers have the opportunity to buy, sell, or exchange interests in a time frame and with the regularity and continuity that the existence of a market maker would provide. Interests are not readily tradable, however, unless the partnership participates in establishing the market or recognizes transfers by admission of purchasers to the partnership or recognizes their rights as transferees. Treas. Reg. § 301.7704–1(d). A redemption or repurchase plan can result in partnership interests being publicly traded.

The regulations provide several "safe harbors." Treas. Reg. § 301.7704–1(e) disregards transfers in which the transferee has a transferred basis, transfers at death, transfers between family members, transfers pursuant to certain redemption agreements, and certain other transfers in determining whether there is public trading of the partnership interests. The most broadly applicable safe harbor excludes from the definition of publicly traded partnership so-called "private placements"—that is, any partnership whose interests were not registered under the Securities Act of 1933—but only if the partnership does not have more than 100 members. Treas. Reg. § 301.7704–1(h).

In addition, a partnership will not be considered to be traded on the substantial equivalent of a secondary market for any year in which no more than two percent of the total interests in partnership capital or profits is sold or disposed of in transactions other than private transfers, qualifying redemptions, or certain other safe harbors. Treas. Reg. § 301.7704–1(j). It is clear from § 7704(f), dealing with the effect of a partnership becoming a corporation, that § 7704 contemplates the possibility that a partnership that is initially recognized as such might in a subsequent year become a corporation under § 7704. The "lack of actual trading" safe harbor, which applies on a year-by-year basis, suggests further that a partnership might be considered to be a corporation in one year and a partnership in the next, when it meets the safe harbor. This result could give rise to a constructive liquidation of the "corporation" with tax consequences to the entity and the investors or, conversely, the constructive formation of a new corporation.

2.3. *Exceptions*

A broad exception in § 7704(c) allows publicly traded limited partnerships more than ninety percent of whose gross income is from certain "passive sources" to continue to be treated as partnerships. Qualified income for this purpose, with some narrow exceptions, includes interest, dividends, real property rents, gain from the sale of real property, and income and gains from the exploration, development, extraction, processing, refining, etc. of oil and gas or any other natural resource. While the legislative history is silent as to the reason for this exception, it presumably is based on the historic use of limited partnerships in organizing such ventures and the availability of conduit taxation for other entity forms (e.g., real estate investment trusts) making investments of this type.

An additional exception permits publicly traded partnerships that were in existence on December 31, 1987 to continue to be treated as partnerships as long as they do not add a "substantial new line of business." See I.R.C. § 7704(g).

3.   FOREIGN BUSINESS ENTITIES

Treas. Reg. § 301.7701–2(b)(8) lists certain foreign business entities (including entities organized in U.S. possessions, territories, and commonwealths) that are classified as *per se* corporations. The listed organizations are limited liability entities, such as the British Public Limited Company, the French Societe Anonyme, and the German Aktiengesellschaft. Other foreign entities can elect under Treas. Reg. § 301.7701–3(a) whether to be treated as a partnership or as a corporation. In contrast to the partnership default classification rules for domestic organizations, under Treas. Reg. § 301.7701–3(b)(2) the default rule for foreign entities is based on whether the members have limited liability. A foreign entity is classified as an association if all members have limited liability, but it is classified as a partnership if it has two or more members and at least one member does not have limited liability. If a foreign entity has only one owner, who does not have limited liability, the entity is disregarded.

SECTION 3.   ANTI-ABUSE REGULATIONS

REGULATIONS: Section 1.701–2(a)–(c).

Treas. Reg. § 1.701–2 provides sweeping "anti-abuse" rules with respect to the application of Subchapter K. Under these provisions a transaction can be recast at the Commissioner's behest "even though the transaction may fall within the literal words of a particular statutory or regulatory provision." Among the possible consequences are: (1) the purported partnership may be disregarded and its assets and activities considered to be owned and conducted by one or more of the purported partners; (2) one or more of the purported partners may not be treated as a partner; (3) accounting methods may be adjusted to reflect clearly the partnership's or the partner's income; (4) the partnership's items of income, gain, loss, deduction, or credit may be reallocated; or (5) the claimed tax treatment may be otherwise adjusted or modified. Treas. Reg. § 1.704–1(b).

The premise of these anti-abuse rules is that "Subchapter K is intended to permit taxpayers to conduct joint business activities through a flexible economic arrangement without incurring an entity-level tax." Implicit in this intent are requirements that a partnership be bona fide and that each partnership transaction or series of related transactions have been entered into for a substantial business purpose; the form of partnership transaction should be respected after applying substance over form principles; and the tax consequences to the partnership and to each partner must accurately reflect the partners' economic agreement and clearly reflect each partner's income. The regulations acknowledge, however, that certain provisions of Subchapter K and the regulations thereunder have been adopted for administrative convenience and that the proper application of those provisions in some circumstances produce tax results that do not properly reflect income. In such cases, the clear reflection of income requirement is deemed to have been satisfied; see Treas. Reg. § 1.701–2(d), Ex. (11).

Treas. Reg. § 1.701–2(c) provides that whether a partnership was formed of availed of with a purpose to reduce substantially the partners' tax liabilities in a manner inconsistent with the intent of subchapter K is determined with reference to all of the facts and circumstances, including the purported business purpose for the transaction and the claimed tax benefits. The regulations list seven illustrative factors that may be taken into account, but disclaim any presumption based on the presence or absence of any of the factors. In addition, thirteen examples illustrate various applications of the factors. The examples include transactions that are consistent with the intent of Subchapter K as well as transactions that are inconsistent with the intent of Subchapter K.

Treas. Reg. § 1.701–2(e)(1) specifically provides that a partnership may be treated as the aggregate of the partners rather than as a separate entity if necessary to carry out the purpose of any provision of the Internal Revenue Code unless a provision of the Code or regulations prescribes entity treatment *and* the ultimate tax results are "clearly contemplated" by the provision. This provision is grounded on the Treasury's conclusion that there is significant potential for abuse "in the inappropriate treatment of a partnership as an entity in applying rules outside of subchapter K to transactions involving partnerships." T.D. 8588, 1995–1 C.B. 109. Treas. Reg. § 1.702–2(f) provides some examples of the application of this rule. In an abundance of caution, the regulations specifically state that the examples "do not delineate the boundaries of either permissible or impermissible types of transactions," and that changing any facts in the examples may change the results.

Because of the generality of the anti-abuse regulations, the secrecy of the taxpayers and tax practitioners structuring the transactions to which the regulations presumably are intended to be applied, and the relative dearth of case law laying a groundwork for the regulations, it is difficult for an observer to suggest hypothetical transactions to which these provisions will be applied. Although the Service has provided some examples of transactions to which the anti-abuse rules will be applied, as well as transactions to which they will not be applied, it is not possible to extrapolate a broad picture of the ambit of the anti-abuse regulations from these examples. The best that be said is that these rules might be intended to serve primarily as an *in terrorem* device to deter taxpayers and their advisors from planning too close to the edge.

CHAPTER 2

FORMATION OF THE PARTNERSHIP

SECTION 1. CONTRIBUTIONS OF MONEY OR PROPERTY

INTERNAL REVENUE CODE: Sections 721; 722; 723; 704(c)(1)(A); 1223(1) and
(2); 1245(b)(3). See also § 168(i)(7).

REGULATIONS: Sections 1.721–1; 1.722–1; 1.723–1. See also Sections 1.704–
1(b)(2)(iv)(a) through –1(b)(2)(iv)(d)(2).

When individuals (or corporations, which may enter into partnerships
with either individuals or other corporations) form a partnership, the
starting point for determining the partners' substantive interests in the
partnership's assets upon liquidation is the fair market value of the money
or other property contributed by each partner. The fair market value of
each partner's contribution should be recorded in the partner's "capital
account," and the partnership's "book value" for each asset, the starting
point for determining the partnership's accounting profit or loss with
respect to the asset, likewise will be its fair market value. Suppose, for
example, that A, B, and C form a partnership to which A contributes
$100,000 in cash, B contributes Whiteacre, for which B paid only $40,000
but which is worth $100,000, and C contributes Blackacre, for which C paid
$150,000 but which is worth only $100,000. Notwithstanding the different
cash outlays by B and C sometime in the past to purchase the property
currently being contributed to the partnership, each of A, B and C will be
treated as having contributed $100,000 to the partnership. For partnership
accounting purposes, but not for tax purposes, the partnership's "cost" or
book value of Blackacre and Whiteacre will be $100,000. Immediately after
the formation of the ABC partnership, its balance sheet at book value is
follows:

Assets		Partners' Capital Accounts	
Cash	$100,000	A	$100,000
Whiteacre	$100,000	B	$100,000
Blackacre	$100,000	C	$100,000
	$300,000		$300,000

This method of book accounting gives B credit for the $60,000 of apprecia-
tion in Whiteacre between the time he purchased it and the time he
contributed it to the partnership; likewise book accounting imposes on C
the burden of the $50,000 of depreciation in the value of Whiteacre
between the time she bought it and the time she contributed it to the
partnership. This treatment reflects the economic bargain between the
parties, but does not directly relate to the income tax consequences of
formation of the partnership.

From a tax perspective, the rules are somewhat different. Sections 721–723 provide that no gain or loss is recognized by the partnership or partners on a contribution of property to a partnership in exchange for a partnership interest, that a partner's basis for his partnership interest is equal to the sum of the adjusted basis for the contributed property, and any cash contributed, and that the partnership's basis for the contributed property is equal to its adjusted basis in the hands of the contributing partner. The nonrecognition rule of § 721 overrides the rule of § 1001(c), which generally requires that realized gains and losses be recognized. Section 722 prescribes the partner's basis in his partnership interest, which is a separate and distinct asset from the underlying property owned by the partnership. The contributing partner's basis in his partnership interest as determined under § 722 is commonly referred to in tax jargon as "outside basis." Section 723 prescribes the partnership's basis in the assets contributed by the partners. The partnership's basis in the contributed property as determined under § 723 (as well as the partnership's basis in property acquired by purchase) is commonly called "inside basis."

Applying these tax rules to the ABC Partnership, the results are that B does not recognize the $40,000 gain realized on the exchange of Whiteacre for his partnership interest, and C does not recognize the $50,000 loss realized on the exchange of Blackacre for her partnership interest. Instead, the gain and loss are preserved through the substituted basis rules. B's basis in his partnership interest is $40,000; C's basis in her partnership interest is $150,000. The ABC Partnership's basis in Whiteacre is $40,000, and its basis in Blackacre is $150,000.

The differences between partnership book accounting and partnership tax accounting can be illustrated by expanding the balance sheet of the ABC Partnership created above to include assets and partners' capital accounts at both book value and tax basis.

| | Assets | | | Partners' Capital Accounts | |
	Book	Tax Basis		Book	Tax Basis
Cash	$100,000	$100,000	A	$100,000	$100,000
Whiteacre	$100,000	$ 40,000	B	$100,000	$ 40,000
Blackacre	$100,000	$150,000	C	$100,000	$150,000
	$300,000	$290,000		$300,000	$290,000

As a result of the basis provisions in §§ 722 and 723, the gain that goes unrecognized under § 721 does not permanently escape taxation; it is deferred until a later recognition event occurs. Unrecognized losses are similarly deferred. If B were to sell his partnership interest for $100,000, its fair market value, B would recognize a gain of $60,000—the amount of gain realized but not recognized on the exchange of Whiteacre for the partnership interest. Similarly, if C were to sell her partnership interest for $100,000, she would recognize a loss of $50,000—the amount of the loss that was realized but not recognized on the exchange of Blackacre for the partnership interest. The transferred basis rule of § 723 would result in the partnership recognizing a $60,000 gain for tax purposes on the sale of Whiteacre for $100,000, even though it would have no profit for book accounting purposes; and on a sale of Blackacre for $100,000, the partnership would recognize a loss of $50,000 for tax purposes, even though it would have no loss for book accounting purposes.

The deferral mechanisms do not work perfectly, however, and in some instances, subsequent events may cause nonrecognition of gain or loss to become permanent. Conversely, because these provisions give rise to two bases in two distinct assets, there may be a double recognition of gain or loss in the future. The various basis adjustment provisions of Subchapter K generally prevent these occurrences as long as partnership interests are not bought and sold or otherwise transferred after the initial formation, but these problems nevertheless frequently do arise when partnership interests have been transferred.

Sections 721–723 apply both to contributions to an existing partnership as well as to contributions to a newly formed partnership. Application of these rules is fairly straightforward where only money and unencumbered property are contributed to the partnership, whether the partnership is already in existence or just being formed. However, if contributed property is encumbered by liens, the partnership otherwise assumes debts of a contributing partner, or cash or other property is distributed to a contributing partner in connection with the contribution, the tax treatment of the transaction is more complicated. In these cases some of the rules governing taxation of the operation of partnerships also come into play.

Nonrecognition under § 721 is accorded only to contributions of *property* in exchange for a partnership interest. If a partnership interest is received in exchange for services rendered to the partnership or to a partner, § 721 does not apply. Treas. Reg. § 1.721–1(b)(2). Such a transaction generally will be taxable under either § 83 or the general principles of § 61.

ILLUSTRATIVE MATERIAL

1. PARTNERS' CAPITAL ACCOUNTS

Treas. Reg. § 1.704–1(b)(2)(iv) provides detailed rules regarding the maintenance of partners' capital accounts, which for practical reasons generally must be followed throughout the life of the partnership. In applying these rules, a partner who has more than one interest in the partnership is treated as having a single capital account that reflects all of the partner's interests, even if one interest is as a general partner and the other is as a limited partner, without regard to the time or manner of acquisition of the interests. Because capital accounts are maintained with reference to the fair market value of property contributed to the partnership and property distributed by the partnership, a partner's capital account generally is not the same as his basis in his partnership interest.

A partner's initial capital account is the sum of the amount of any money contributed to the partnership by the partner, plus the fair market value (not the basis) of any property contributed by the partner. A partner's capital account will be increased in a like manner for any subsequent contributions by the partner to the partnership and by the amount of partnership income allocated to the partner; the capital account will be decreased by the amount of any money distributed to the partner and by the partner's share of partnership losses. If property is distributed to a partner, the partner's capital account must be reduced by the fair market value of the property. Treas. Reg. § 1.704–1(b)(2)(iv)(*e*).

Upon liquidation of the partnership, all capital accounts must be adjusted to reflect appreciation and depreciation of partnership property. In addition, partners' capital accounts may (but are not required to) be increased or decreased to reflect a revaluation of the partnership's property on the happening of certain events, such as the admission of a new partner, the distribution of property, or the liquidation of a partner's interest. Treas. Reg. 1.704–1(b)(2)(iv)(*f*). In general, the partners' determination of the fair market value of property will be accepted by the Internal Revenue Service if the value is arrived at in arm's length negotiations in which the partners have sufficiently adverse interests. Treas. Reg. 1.704–1(b)(2)(iv)(*h*).

2.   THE MEANING OF PROPERTY

2.1.   *General*

In addition to tangible property and cash, a variety of intangible property rights, such as patents, may qualify as property, even if those rights were created by the personal efforts of the person who contributed them. Thus, "property" includes business goodwill, Rev. Rul. 70–45, 1970–1 C.B. 17, secret processes and formulae, even if not patented, Rev. Rul. 64–56, 1964–1 (Part 1) C.B. 133, and contracts to acquire property, Ambrose v. Commissioner, T.C. Memo. 1956–125. The line between services and self created intangible property is not always easy to ascertain. See page 50.

The problem of identifying "property" that qualifies an exchange for nonrecognition under § 721 also arises in determining whether stock received in exchange for a contribution to a corporation is eligible for nonrecognition under § 351, which governs transfers to a corporation for stock, although § 351 has some additional requirements not imposed by § 721. Accordingly, the precedents may be applied interchangeably, at least insofar as the issue is determining the meaning of "property."

2.2.   *Accounts Receivable and Installment Obligations*

Installment obligations are specifically designated as eligible property in Treas. Reg. 1.721–1(a). Moreover, § 453B does not require recognition of gain upon a transfer of an installment obligation to a partnership. See Treas. Reg. § 1.453–9(c)(2). Accounts receivable from performing services for persons other than the partnership also constitute property for purposes of §§ 721–723. See Hempt Bros., Inc. v. United States, 490 F.2d 1172 (3d Cir.1974) (receivables are property for purposes of § 351). Under § 704(c), however, the remaining deferred gain on an installment obligation or the amount realized upon collection of a cash method account receivable must be allocated to the contributing partner when it is recognized.

At one time, before the application of § 704(c) was mandatory, the Internal Revenue Service sometimes raised the assignment of income doctrine when accounts receivable were contributed to a partnership. In Schneer v. Commissioner, 97 T.C. 643 (1991), a cash method lawyer joined a preexisting law partnership and assigned to his new partnership amounts owed or to become owing to him from his former law firm with respect to clients he had originated for the former firm. The court held that any amounts that had not accrued (hypothetically applying the accrual method) prior to the assignment were not considered to have been "earned" prior to the time they were contributed, even though the incoming partner may have fully performed all required services prior to the assignment. Accordingly, the fees from the former law firm remitted to the new partnership were not taxable directly to the taxpayer. On the other hand, amounts that would have been includable under the accrual method prior to the assignment were considered to have been "earned" when accrued, and the court taxed those amounts directly to the taxpayer. According to the court, a key factor was that the income was from services "within the ambit of the partnership business." The court distinguished situations in which the services and income were unrelated to the partnership's business, suggesting that all such receivables would have been taxable to the transferor under the assignment of income doctrine. This issue appears to be mooted by the current version of § 704(c).

2.3. *Partners' Promissory Notes*

A partner's personal promissory note contributed to the partnership in exchange for a partnership interest meets the definition of property, and the rules of §§ 721 through 723 govern. In this situation, however, Bussing v. Commissioner, 88 T.C. 449 (1987), held that the contributing partner has no basis in the promissory note, and therefore his initial basis in his partnership interest under § 722 is zero (plus the amount of any money and the basis of other property contributed). As payments are made on the note his basis will be increased pro tanto. Treas. Reg. § 1.704–1(b)(2)(iv)(d)(2) provides that in such a case the partner's capital account is to be increased only as payments are made on the note or upon disposition of the note. What is the partnership's basis in the note if it sells the note before any payments have been made?

2.4. *Contribution of Debt to a Partnership*

Section 108(e)(8) provides that when a partnership transfers a partnership interest to a creditor in satisfaction of partnership debt, the partnership must recognize cancellation of indebtedness income in the amount that would have been recognized if the debt had been satisfied with money equal to the fair market value of the partnership interest. When a creditor of an existing partnership contributes to the partnership a debt owed to the creditor by the partnership in exchange for a partnership interest (or an increased interest if the creditor already is a partner) the debt is extinguished. Thus there is a question whether there has been a contribution of property, because there is a potential conflict between the nonrecognition rules of § 721 and the rules requiring recognition of cancellation of indebtedness income under §§ 61(a)(12) and 108. Under § 108(e)(8), if a debt of $1,000 is contributed to the partnership in exchange for a partnership interest worth $1,000, no cancellation of indebtedness income arises. But if the creditor contributes a debt of $1,000 in exchange for a partnership interest worth only $700, then the partnership must recognize $300 of cancellation of indebtedness income. Any such cancellation of indebtedness income is allocated solely among the partners who held interests in the partnership immediately prior to the satisfaction of the debt.

On a related but slightly different point, Mas One Limited Partnership v. United States, 390 F.3d 427 (6th Cir. 2004), held that the payment of a partnership's debt to a creditor by a withdrawing partner, one day after the partner's withdrawal, for the purpose of obtaining a discharge from the partner's guarantee of certain partnership obligations was gross income to the partnership, rather than a contribution resulting in nonrecognition to the partnership under § 721. The court reasoned that the former partner's payment of the partnership's obligation was governed by Old Colony Trust Co. v. Commissioner, 279 U.S. 716 (1929), holding that the payment of a third party's payment of the taxpayer's debt results in gross income.

3. BUILT–IN GAINS AND LOSSES

Under the general rules of § 704, governing the allocation of items of income and deduction among partners, the gain or loss inherent in an asset at the time it is contributed to a partnership would be allocated among the partners according to their general profit sharing ratios. Thus, if A and B formed an equal partnership to which A contributed $10,000 cash and B contributed land with a fair market value of $10,000 and a basis of $3,000, and the land were sold for $10,000, the $7,000 gain would be recognized equally by A and B, $3,500 each. Section 704(c) prevents this result, however, by requiring built-in gains and losses at the time of contribution to be allocated for tax purposes to the partner who contributed the property, even though the gains and losses may be allocated otherwise for partnership accounting purposes. See Treas. Reg. § 1.704–1(b)(5), Ex. (13)(i). Section 704(c) is discussed in greater detail at page 154.

4. CHARACTER AND HOLDING PERIOD

4.1. *Treatment of Partner*

A partnership interest is a capital asset in the hands of a partner, even though it may have been acquired in exchange for assets that would produce ordinary income upon sale, such as inventory. I.R.C § 741. But if a partnership's property consists of inventory or unrealized accounts receivable, § 751 may require the recognition of ordinary income on a sale of the partnership interest notwithstanding its classification as a capital asset. Section 751 is discussed in Chapter 8.

As a consequence of the exchanged basis rule of § 722, if the contributed property was a § 1231 asset or a capital asset, pursuant to § 1223(1) a partner's holding period for his partnership interest includes the period for which he held the contributed property. If the property was an ordinary income asset, however, the holding period commences when the partnership interest is received. But if a mix of assets is contributed each with a different holding period, the computation of the holding period of the partnership interest is unclear; fragmentation of the partnership interest, which appears to be the most logical answer, is inconsistent with the general treatment of a partnership interest as a single unitary asset.[1]

4.2.   *Treatment of Partnership*

Except as provided in § 724, property contributed to a partnership in a transaction subject to §§ 721–723 is characterized as a capital asset, § 1231 asset, or ordinary income asset (e.g., inventory) according to the purpose for which the partnership holds the property. Treas. Reg. § 1.702–1(b). Section 724 provides three special rules designed to prevent the manipulation of the character of gains and losses by contributing property to a partnership that would hold the property for a purpose different than the purpose for which it was held by the contributing partner. Unrealized receivables contributed by a partner, such as a cash method service provider's accounts receivable, retain their ordinary income character permanently. Inventory items contributed by a partner retain their ordinary character for five years, even though not held as inventory by the partnership. Finally, property with a built-in capital loss at the time of the contribution retains its character as a capital asset, to the extent of the built-in loss, for five years even though the partnership holds the asset as an ordinary income asset.

Because § 723 gives the partnership a transferred basis in property contributed to it, § 1223(2) provides that the partnership's holding period for the property includes the period for which the contributing partner held the property. Thus, § 1231 property contributed to a partnership for use in its trade or business retains its character as § 1231 property even though the partnership has not independently met the holding period requirements specified in § 1231.

5.   CONVERSION INTO A PARTNERSHIP OF A SINGLE MEMBER LLC TREATED AS A DISREGARDED ENTITY

Rev. Rul. 99–5, 1999–1 C.B. 434, addresses the sale of an interest in a single-member limited liability company to another person. The ruling treats the transaction as if the selling member sells a partial interest in

---

1. The same question arises where property is contributed in exchange for corporate stock in a transaction governed by § 351. In that case the fragmentation theory has been applied. See Runkle v. Commissioner, 39 B.T.A. 458 (1939).

each of the limited liability company's assets to the purchasing member, followed immediately by a contribution of the assets to a partnership. No gain or loss is recognized on the contribution under § 721. The selling member recognizes gain on the asset sale. The selling member's basis in the limited liability company membership interest will be the same as the member's basis in the contributed portion of the limited liability company assets. I.R.C. § 722. The purchasing member's basis in the limited liability company membership interest will be the same as the purchase price of the assets deemed to have been contributed. I.R.C. §§ 1012 and 722. If, rather than purchasing an interest in a single member limited liability company, the new member contributes cash to the limited liability company, Rev. Rul. 99–5 treats the transaction as the formation of a new partnership by both the continuing member, who is deemed to contribute the assets of the existing limited liability company, and the new member who contributes cash. The contributions are nonrecognition transactions under § 721, with transferred and exchange basis under §§ 722 and 723. This treatment results in § 704(c) controlling post-sale allocations of built-in gain and loss and depreciation.

6. "SWAP FUND" PARTNERSHIPS

Suppose three investors each own a single block of stock in three different corporations and wish to diversify their investments on a tax free basis. Under § 721 as originally enacted, they could each contribute their stock to a newly formed partnership and each would then have an undivided one-third interest in the stock of the three corporations. They would have thus obtained a diversification of investment with no current tax. This basic technique was used on a larger scale for the establishment of so-called "swap funds" under which a number of investors wishing to diversify their investment portfolios entered into a partnership formed by an investment manager. Typically, the manager and the potential investor both had the right to withdraw from the transaction before it was consummated if the resulting "mix" of investments was not satisfactory to the manager or the investors. The Internal Revenue Service originally issued private rulings that such funds could in fact achieve diversification on a tax free basis, but in 1976 Congress put an end to the practice by enacting § 721(b). That section withdraws the nonrecognition of gain treatment under § 721(a) for transfers of property to a partnership which involve a diversification of investment. Because the contribution of property to a swap fund partnership is a recognition event if gain is realized, § 722 permits the contributing partner to increase his basis in his partnership interest by the recognized gain.

Section 721(b) is intended to apply the same constraints on diversification transfers to partnerships as apply to transfers to corporations or trusts. However, § 721(b) on its face withdraws nonrecognition only if a gain is realized and § 722 adjusts a partner's basis only with respect to recognized gains. Thus, if a loss is realized on a contribution to a swap fund the nonrecognition rules apply and no deduction is allowed currently.

7. PARTNERSHIP ORGANIZATION AND SYNDICATION EXPENSES

Section 709(a) disallows any deduction for partnership organization and syndication expenses. Section 709(b) then allows a deduction for up to $5,000 of organizational expenses, but not syndication expenses. If organizational expenses exceed $50,000, the deduction is reduced dollar for dollar (and is completely eliminated if organization expenses equal or exceed $55,000). Any organizational expenses that are not deductible must be capitalized and are amortizable over a 180–month period beginning with the month in which the partnership commences business. Syndication expenses are not amortizable. For the differences between the expenses, see Aboussie v. United States, 779 F.2d 424 (8th Cir.1985); Diamond v. Commissioner, 92 T.C. 423 (1989). If the partnership is liquidated before the end of the 180–month period, the partnership is allowed a loss deduction under § 165 for the unamortized deferred deduction. But if a § 709(b) election has not been made, the partnership is never allowed a loss deduction for organization expenses regardless of when the partnership is liquidated. Rev.Rul. 87–111, 1987–2 C.B. 160. Because the unamortized organization expenses are reflected in the partners' bases for their partnership interests, however, an amount equal to those expenses will be taken into account to reduce gain or increase loss on the liquidation of the partnership or to increase the basis of property distributed to the partners in the liquidation. See page 338. Organizational expenses are defined in § 709(b)(2) and Treas. Reg. § 1.709–2(a) to include items such as legal and accounting fees incident to the negotiation and drafting of the partnership agreement and establishing an accounting system, and filing fees. Expenses to acquire partnership assets are not organization fees.

Syndication fees, as defined in Treas. Reg. § 1.709–2(b), are never amortizable or deductible upon liquidation of the partnership. Such fees encompass brokerage fees incurred to sell partnership interests, legal fees in connection with an underwriting, securities laws registration fees, accounting fees connected with offering materials, printing costs of a prospectus, placement memorandum, or promotional material, etc. Rev. Rul. 85–32, 1985–1 C.B. 186. See also Rev. Rul. 88–4, 1988–1 C.B. 264 (attorneys' fees for tax opinion letter included in prospectus of syndicated partnership are syndication fees); Rev. Rul. 89–11, 1989–1 C.B. 179 (no § 165 loss deduction allowed for syndication expenses incurred in an unsuccessful effort to establish a partnership); Martyr v. Commissioner, T.C. Memo. 1990–558 (expense of tax opinion letter included in private placement memorandum for limited partnership offering is a nondeductible syndication expense). Driggs v. Commissioner, 87 T.C. 759 (1986) (§ 709 applied to a so-called "sponsor's fee" paid by a limited partnership to its promoter).

8. NONCOMPENSATORY PARTNERSHIP OPTIONS

Prop. Reg. § 1.721–2 (2003) addresses the issuance of noncompensatory partnership options, including convertible debt and convertible equity interests. Under the proposed regulations, the issuance of an option would not be governed by § 721, but rather by general tax principles under which it is an open transaction for the issuer and an investment by the holder. Neither the grant nor the exercise of an option generally would result in the recognition of gain or loss to either the partnership or the option holder. If, however, the holder uses appreciated or depreciated property to acquire the option, the holder would recognize gain or loss.

Upon exercise, the option holder would be treated as contributing property to the partnership in exchange for the partnership interest; the contributed property would be the original premium, the exercise price, and the option privilege.[2] Section 721 would apply even if the exercise resulted in a shift of capital from the old partners to the option holder. Section 721 would not apply to the lapse of an option; the lapse of an option results in recognition of income by the partnership and the recognition of loss by the former option holder. To deal with the fact that the option holder generally receives a partnership interest with a value that is greater or less than the sum of the option premium and exercise price, i.e., there is a capital shift, the Treasury Department has proposed amending the regulations under § 704 to allocate a disproportionate share of gross income, without a corresponding allocation of book income, to any partner or partners who have benefited from such a capital shift. This aspect of the treatment of partnership options under the proposed regulations is discussed at page 171.

Section 2. Contributions of Encumbered Property

Internal Revenue Code: Sections 705(a); 722; 723; 731(a) and (b); 733; 752(a)–(c).

Regulations: Sections 1.704–1(b)(2)(iv)(d)(1); 1.722–1, Ex. (2); 1.752–1(a)–(g) (omit Ex. (2)); 1.752–2(a), (b)(1), (2), (5), (f) Ex. (2); 1.752–3(a), (b)(1); 1.1245–4(c)(4), Ex. (3).

When property subject to liabilities is contributed to a partnership or the partnership assumes a partner's liabilities in connection with the contribution of property, analysis of the tax consequences of formation of a partnership is more complex. Subchapter K has no single provision dealing with this event. Instead, the results must be determined by piecing together the rules governing contributions to partnerships in §§ 721–723, treatment of debt in § 752, partnership distributions in §§ 731 and 733, and partners' basis in their partnership interests in § 705. Gain, but not loss, may be recognized upon the contribution of encumbered property to the partnership.

---

2. The conversion right in convertible debt or convertible equity would be taken into account for tax purposes as part of the underlying instrument. (The proposed regulations do not deal with the consequences of a right to convert partnership debt into an interest in the issuing partnership to the extent of any accrued but unpaid interest on the debt.) A proposed amendment to Treas. Reg. § 1.1272–1(e) would treat partnership interests as stock for purposes of the special OID rules for convertible debt instruments. Prop. Reg. § 1.1272–1(e) (2003).

The starting point is §§ 721–723. Upon contribution of the property the contributing partner takes a basis in his partnership interest equal to his basis in the property, without regard to the amount of the debt. By virtue of the transfer, however, the contributing partner has been relieved from the debt in his individual capacity and all of the partners have indirectly assumed the debt in their capacity as partners. Section 752(b) provides that any decrease in a partner's share of liabilities is to be treated as a distribution of money to the partner. Section 752(a) provides that an increase in a partner's share of liabilities by reason of a partnership transaction is to be treated as a contribution of cash to the partnership by the partners. If a partner's share of the liabilities is both increased and decreased in the same transaction, only the net increase or decrease is taken into account. Treas. Reg. § 1.752–1(f). This rule applies when a partner contributes encumbered property to a partnership because the partner is simultaneously relieved of all the liabilities in his individual capacity but becomes liable for a share of the liabilities in his capacity as a partner.[3] Thus, the amount of the deemed distribution to the contributing partner is equal to the portion of the debt for which the other partners bear the economic risk of loss. Under §§ 731 and 733, distributions of money reduce the partner's basis in the partner's partnership interest and are treated as gain to the extent that the distribution exceeds basis. The deemed cash contribution by the other partners increases their basis in their partnership interests under § 722.

As a consequence of these provisions, the contribution of encumbered property to a partnership by a partner will reduce the contributing partner's basis in the partnership interest to the extent of the share of the liability assumed by the other partners and will result in recognized gain to the contributing partner to the extent that amount exceeds the contributing partner's basis in the partner's partnership interest. Each noncontributing partner's basis in the partner's partnership interest will be increased to the extent of the noncontributing partner's share of the liability.

Under § 752(c), the same results are achieved even if the partnership merely takes the property subject to the debt and does not assume it. Assuming that either the partnership agreement or controlling state law treats the noncontributing partners as assuming ultimate liability for a share of the debt, the net effect for the contributing partner is the receipt of a deemed cash distribution.

The manner in which partners share the economic risk of loss for partnership debt is determined under Treas. Reg. § 1.752–2 for debt that is

---

3. Partners' shares of partnership indebtedness are determined under Treas. Regs. §§ 1.752–2 and 1.752–3, discussed in Chapter 5.

For purposes of § 752 the term "liability" is defined in Treas. Reg. § 1.752–1(a)(4) as limited to debts that: (1) create or increase basis (including cash balances); (2) give rise to a deduction (e.g., accrual method accounts payable); or (3) give rise to a nondeductible expenditure not chargeable to a capital account (under § 263 or § 263A). Thus, cash method accounts payable are not liabilities for purposes of § 752 and do not increase the partners' bases in their partnership interests.

with recourse to either the partnership or any partner, and under Treas. Reg. § 1.752–3 for debts which are without recourse to the partnership or any partner.[4] However, Treas. Reg. § 1.752–1(g), Ex. provides that there is no deemed distribution if the contributing partner retains ultimate liability to repay an indebtedness encumbering the contributed property.

Pursuant to §§ 731 and 733 (and § 705), the deemed distribution created by § 752 reduces the contributing partner's basis in his partnership interest and, to the extent that the deemed distribution exceeds the basis in his partnership interest, the excess is treated as gain from the sale or exchange of his partnership interest. Section 741 directs that this gain be treated as capital gain,[5] subject to certain exceptions provided in § 751. The other partners also are treated by § 752(a) as having contributed cash to the partnership in an amount equal to their respective shares of the debt assumed by the partnership, and they increase their bases in their partnership interests accordingly.

The following examples illustrate the above rules:

(1) Partner D contributes to the new DEF Partnership Greenacre, property with a fair market value of $1,100 and a basis of $1,000, subject to a recourse mortgage of $900, which is assumed by the partnership. (It is not relevant whether the lien is a purchase money mortgage or one that was placed on the property to secure a loan unrelated to its acquisition.) E and F each contribute $200 in cash and D, E and F are equal partners. The book value of D's contribution is the same as the book value of E's and F's contributions because D's contribution is measured by the *net* value of the contributed property, i.e., its fair market value minus the mortgage. D's basis for his partnership interest would be $400, i.e., the original $1,000 basis minus the $600 of the indebtedness that was, in effect, assumed by the other partners. E and F each would increase his basis by $300, from $200 to $500. The DEF partnership's balance sheet, at both book value and tax basis would then be as follows:

Assets			Debts and Partners' Capital Accounts		
	Book	Tax Basis		Book	Tax Basis
Cash	$ 400	$ 400	Mortgage	$ 900	
Greenacre	$1,100	$1,000	D	$ 200	$ 400
			E	$ 200	$ 500
			F	$ 200	$ 500
	$1,500	$1,400		$1,500	$1,400

4. A "recourse liability" is any liability "to the extent * * * that any partner or related person bears the economic risk of loss for that liability." Treas. Reg. § 1.752–1(a)(1) Partnership indebtedness is nonrecourse debt only to the extent that no partner (or any person related to a partner under Treas. Reg. § 1.752–4(b)) bears the economic risk of loss on the liability. Treas. Reg. § 1.752–1(a)(2).

5. However, Treas. Reg. § 1.1245–4(c)(4), Ex. (3) provides that such gain will be ordinary income to the extent that there is any depreciation recapture inherent in the contributed asset. This result conflicts with the statutory mechanics of Subchapter K, which treat the gain as realized on the sale or exchange of the partnership interest.

(2) If the mortgage amount in Example (1) were $1,800 (regardless of the fair market value of the property), D would recognize a gain of $200, i.e., the excess of the $1,200 of indebtedness that was in effect assumed by the other partners over the original $1,000 basis. D's basis in his partnership interest is reduced to zero as a result of these computations. E and F each increase their basis again, this time by $600. Realistically, if the mortgage were $1,800 and D, E and F are to be equal partners, the fair market value of Greenacre in all likelihood would be $2,000, resulting in the net value of each partner's contribution again being $200. In this case the partnership's balance sheet immediately after formation would be as follows:

		Assets		Debts and Partners' Capital Accounts		
		Book	Tax Basis		Book	Tax Basis
Cash		$ 400	$ 400	Mortgage	$1,800	
Greenacre		$2,000	$1,000	D	$ 200	$ 0
				E	$ 200	$ 800
				F	$ 200	$ 800
		$2,400	$1,400		$2,400	$1,600

In this case the partners' aggregate basis for their partnership interests (outside basis) exceeds the partnership's aggregate basis in its assets (inside basis) by an amount equal to the $200 gain recognized by D. Note that if DEF were a pre-existing partnership and D's outside basis were at least $200 before the contribution, he would not have recognized any gain on the contribution of the encumbered property.

(3) If D were personally liable for the $900 debt in Example (1) and the partnership merely took the property subject to the indebtedness without the partnership, E, or F agreeing to indemnify D for any repayment of the debt, the debt would be a nonrecourse debt of the partnership which was recourse with respect to D. In this case D bears the entire economic risk of loss. Therefore, D would be treated as receiving a distribution of $900 under § 752(b) and making a contribution of $900 under § 752(a). Since only the net contribution or distribution is taken into account, see Treas. Reg. § 1.752–1(f), D's basis for his partnership interest remains $1,000. See Treas. Reg. § 1.752–1(g), Ex. Applying this rule, D would recognize no gain even if the mortgage were $1,800 as in Example (2).

(4) If the $900 mortgage debt in Example (1) were a nonrecourse debt as to D, upon the contribution of the property to the partnership, the partnership would be treated by § 752(c) and Treas. Reg. § 1.752–1(e) as assuming the debt. Because the debt is a nonrecourse debt, under Treas. Reg. § 1.752–3(a)(2), D will be allocated an amount of the debt equal to the gain which would have been allocated to D under § 704(c) if the property had been conveyed to the lender in satisfaction of the mortgage; the balance of the debt generally will be allocated among the partners accord-

ing to their profit sharing ratios.[6] Since the basis of the property is $1,000 and the debt is only $900, no gain would be realized if the property were conveyed to the lender in satisfaction of the mortgage and hence there is no initial allocation to D. Thus, $300 of the $900 debt will be allocated to each of D, E, and F, because they share profits equally. As a result, D's basis in his partnership interest is $400 (the original $1,000 basis minus the $600 of debt in effect assumed by each of E and F), and, as in Example (1), E and F each increase their basis by $300. The partnership's balance sheet would be the same as in Example (1).

(5) If in Example (4) the nonrecourse mortgage amount were $1,800, however, under § 704(c), $800 of gain ($1,800 amount realized minus $1,000 basis) would be allocated to D if the property were transferred to the lender in satisfaction of the mortgage. Accordingly, $800 of the nonrecourse debt initially would be allocated to D. The remaining $1,000 of the debt generally would be allocated among the partners equally, because they share profits equally. Thus, a total of $1,133.33 of the indebtedness is allocated to D, and $333.33 is allocated to each of E and F. D's basis for his partnership interest is 333.33 (the original $1,000 minus the $666.66 of debt allocated to E and F), and E and F each increase their basis by $333.33. Assuming, as in Example (2), that the fair market value of Greenacre were $2,000 and that E and F each contributed $200, the partnership's balance sheet immediately after formation would be as follows:

Assets			Debts and Partners' Capital Accounts		
	Book	Tax Basis		Book	Tax Basis
Cash	$ 400	$ 400	Mortgage	$1,800	
Greenacre	$2,000	$1,000	D	$ 200	$ 333.33
			E	$ 200	$ 533.33
			F	$ 200	$ 533.33
	$2,400	$1,400		$2,400	$1,400.00

The rule allocating to the contributing partner an amount of nonrecourse debt equal to the excess of the nonrecourse debt over the basis of the property avoids recognition of gain on the contribution of the property to the partnership. The rationale for permitting the contributing partner to avoid recognizing any gain in this case, in contrast to Example (2) where gain was recognized with respect to property encumbered by a recourse mortgage, is twofold. First, none of the other partners actually has assumed a risk of loss where the mortgage on the contributed property is nonrecourse. Second, under the rules of § 704 governing allocations of partnership income, the contributing partner will be taxed on any partnership income applied to repay the portion of the nonrecourse debt that exceeds the basis of the property. See page 148.

---

6. In fact, the partners will be allowed some options with respect to both the operation of § 704(c) and in determining exactly how the remaining portion of the debt is allocated. See Treas. Reg. § 1.752–3(b)(3).

The assumption by a partnership of the accounts payable of a cash method sole proprietor who is contributing her business to the partnership presents a special problem. If accounts payable of a cash method partnership were taken into account as liabilities under § 752, a cash method partner who contributed equal amounts of receivables, which have a zero basis, and payables of a previously conducted sole proprietorship, and no other property, would be required to recognize gain. This result generally would adversely affect the formation of personal service partnerships. Section 357(c) specifically addresses this problem in the formation of corporations by providing that cash method accounts payable will not be considered liabilities assumed by the corporation. Subchapter K contains an analogous, albeit somewhat vague, provision in § 704(c)(3). For purposes of § 752, the term "liability", as defined in Treas. Reg. § 1.752–1(a)(4), is limited to debts that: (1) create or increase basis (including cash balances); (2) give rise to a deduction (e.g., accrual method accounts payable); or (3) give rise to a nondeductible expenditure not chargeable to a capital account (under § 263 or § 263A). Thus, the assumption of a cash method partner's accounts payable gives rise to neither a constructive distribution to the contributing partner under § 752(b) nor a constructive contribution by the other partners under § 752(a). See Rev. Rul. 88–77, 1988–2 C.B. 128, which rules that cash method accounts payable, which are not deductible until paid and do not give rise to basis in any asset, should not be treated as liabilities for purposes of § 752. In contrast, accrual method accounts payable are subject to the generally applicable principles of § 752.

SECTION 3. CONTRIBUTION OF PROPERTY VERSUS CONTRIBUTION OF SERVICES

A. TREATMENT OF THE PARTNER RECEIVING A PARTNERSHIP INTEREST IN EXCHANGE FOR SERVICES

INTERNAL REVENUE CODE: Sections 83(a)–(d); 721(a).

REGULATIONS: Sections 1.83–1(a), –3(e), –4(b)(2), (b); 1.721–1(b); 1.722–1.

PROPOSED REGULATIONS: Sections 1.83–3(e) and (*l*) (2005); 1.721–1(b) (2005).

Section 721 does not apply to provide nonrecognition if a partner receives a partnership interest in exchange for services. When a partnership interest received for services includes an interest in partnership capital, i.e., property contributed by other partners, Treas.Reg. § 1.721–1(b)(1) provides that the fair market value of the partnership interest is includable under §§ 61 and 83 as compensation for services. Treas. Reg. § 1.722–1 provides that any income so recognized increases the partner's basis in the partnership interest. In addition, § 83 provides comprehensive rules regarding the year in which the value of the partnership interest must be included in income if the interest is subject to a risk of forfeiture or other restrictions that prevent the interest from being fully vested. This aspect of § 83 applies, for example, if a partner is required to render services to the partnership for a certain period of time before the interest vests. In such a case taxation is deferred, but the amount includable is the value of the partnership interest at the time the restrictions lapse rather than on the earlier date when the partnership interest was first received. As a corollary of the receipt of income by the service partner, the partnership either deducts or capitalizes the same amount, depending on the nature of the services, in the year the partner recognizes the income.

Although the basic rules that apply when a service partner receives an interest in partnership capital are clear, receipt of an interest in exchange for services that entitles the service partner only to a share of future profits is more problematic.

Since nonrecognition under § 721 extends only to the receipt of a partnership interest in exchange for "property," a crucial issue in the formation of a partnership is whether a partner's contribution is "property" or services. Neither the Code nor the Regulations define the word "property," and this issue must be resolved on a case by case basis.

ILLUSTRATIVE MATERIAL

1. PROPERTY CREATED BY PERSONAL EFFORTS

The difference between services, which do not qualify under § 721, and self-created intangible property, which does qualify under § 721, sometimes presents problems. The leading cases on this point are United States v. Frazell, 335 F.2d 487 (5th Cir.1964), and United States v. Stafford, 727 F.2d 1043 (11th Cir.1984). In *Frazell* the taxpayer was a geologist who entered into a joint venture agreement with the N.H. Wheless Oil Company and W.C. Woolf. Under the agreement, Frazell was to identify potentially productive oil and gas properties, which he would recommend to Wheless and Woolf. With their approval, he would attempt to acquire the properties in the names of Wheless and Woolf, who paid all costs and expenses. In locating properties, Frazell used several oil maps that he had previously acquired. Frazell's ownership of these maps and other geological data and information was an important factor in Wheless' and Woolf's decision to enter into the agreement with Frazell. Under the agreement, Frazell was to receive "a monthly salary or drawing account," and, after Wheless and Woolf had recovered their costs and expenses for the properties, a specified interest in the properties. In 1955, after Wheless and Woolf had recovered their costs, an interest worth $91,000 was vested in Frazell. The court held that Frazell realized ordinary income to the extent that his interest was received in exchange for his services, but that to the extent that the interest in the venture was received in exchange for the oil maps, the nonrecognition rule of § 721 applied. The court remanded the case to the District Court for further proceedings because from the record it was unclear whether Frazell contributed ownership of the maps to the joint venture or retained ownership of the maps as his separate property and merely used them in rendering the services for which the interest was received.

In *Stafford*, the taxpayer obtained from an insurance company a "letter of intent" proposing to lend to the taxpayer or his designee a substantial sum of money on very favorable terms. Although the parties expected that a loan would be made pursuant to the letter of intent, it was not legally enforceable by the taxpayer. After obtaining the letter of intent in his own name, the taxpayer formed a limited partnership of which he was the sole general partner. He contributed $200,000 cash in exchange for two limited partnership shares, and, as required by the partnership agreement, he contributed the letter of intent in exchange for a third limited partnership share. The government asserted that § 721 did not apply to the limited partnership share received in exchange for the letter of intent because the interest was in fact received in consideration of services rendered to the partnership by the taxpayer in negotiating the loan to the partnership. First, the court concluded that the taxpayer owned the letter of intent, since he was working on his own behalf at the time he acquired it. Turning to the question of whether the letter was "property" within the meaning of § 721, the court concluded that the unenforceability of the letter was no bar to property status, citing Rev.Rul. 64–56, page 38. Because the taxpayer transferred all of his rights in the letter the contribution was a transfer of property. However, because the record on appeal contained insufficient evidence to determine whether the third limited partnership interest was received in exchange for the letter, or for services to be rendered to the partnership, or for both, the court remanded the case, with directions that if the value of the letter was less than $100,000, the difference between that amount and the value of the letter represented taxable compensation.

2. RECOGNITION OF INCOME UPON OF RECEIPT OF A CAPITAL INTEREST FOR SERVICES

2.1. *Generally*

When § 721 does not apply because a person exchanges services for a partnership capital interest, the amount includable in income is the fair market value of the partnership interest received. In some cases, however, the value of the partnership interest may be determined indirectly. In Hensel Phelps Construction Co. v. Commissioner, 74 T.C. 939 (1980), aff'd, 703 F.2d 485 (10th Cir.1983), the Tax Court valued an interest in partnership capital received in exchange for past services with reference to the fair market value of the services provided. Regardless of the valuation method employed, the service partner's basis for his partnership interest is the amount included in income, plus any money and the basis of other property contributed to the partnership. Treas. Reg. § 1.722–1.

2.2. *Partnership Interest Subject to Risk of Forfeiture*

If a partnership interest received for services is subject to a substantial risk of forfeiture, pursuant to § 83(a), the service partner's recognition of income is deferred until the interest vests. As a result, he will be taxable on any increase in the value of the partnership interest, whether or not attributable to services performed by the partner for the partnership, at the time the substantial risk of forfeiture lapses. For the meaning of "substantial risk of forfeiture," see I.R.C. § 83(c)(1); Treas. Reg. § 1.83–3(c). Johnston v. Commissioner, T.C. Memo. 1995–140, held that a partnership capital interest received in consideration of a combination of both past and future services must be valued on the date of the transfer where the right to the partnership interest was not conditioned on actually performing the future services.

Furthermore, under Treas. Reg. § 1.83–1(a), the transferee is not treated as the owner of the property until the risk of forfeiture lapses. Thus, although the recipient of the partnership interest may be a partner under state law, for federal income tax purposes, he is not a partner for tax purposes during this period.

A service provider who receives property, including a partnership interest, subject to a substantial risk of forfeiture may elect under § 83(b) to include the value in income in the year of receipt. If the partner makes a § 83(b) election, any increase in the of the partnership interest between the date the service partner is admitted to the partnership will not be taxed as compensation when the restriction lapses, but instead will be converted into capital gain realized at a later time.

3.   RECEIPT OF A PROFITS-ONLY PARTNERSHIP INTEREST IN EXCHANGE FOR SERVICES

3.1.   The *Diamond* Case

While the exchange nature of a transfer of in interest in partnership capital for services is relatively clear, and the tax consequences are determinable, the receipt of a partnership profits-only interest for services raises more complex questions that have not been susceptible of easy resolution. Before the decision in Diamond v. Commissioner, 492 F.2d 286 (7th Cir. 1974), it had been generally accepted that the receipt of a partnership *profits* interest for services was not currently taxable. See Rev. Rul. 70–435, 1970–2 C.B. 100, modifying Rev. Rul. 60–31, 1960–1 C.B. 174 (holding that receipt of future income interest in a joint venture is not taxable). The court in *Diamond* questioned this accepted wisdom and held that a receipt of a profits-only interest for services was a taxable event. Subsequent case law and Internal Revenue Service ruling policy generally accepted the position that the receipt of a profits-only interest was taxable, but the authorities found ways to defer immediate taxation. As discussed below, the Treasury Department has recently proposed regulations that deal comprehensively with both the receipt of a partnership capital interest and profits-only interest in exchange for services.

The tax consequence of receipt of a profits-only interest in a partnership in exchange for services can only be understood by examining the seminal opinion in *Diamond*. The taxpayer in *Diamond* was a mortgage broker. Diamond was approached by Philip Kargman who had acquired buyer's rights in a contract for the sale of an office building. Diamond received a 60 percent share in the profits of a partnership in exchange for obtaining a mortgage loan for the full $1,100,000 purchase price of the building. Kargman contributed the contract rights to acquire the building, which he had purchased for $25,000, and slightly more than $78,000 of cash required for the purchase beyond the loan proceeds. Under the partnership agreement, on sale of the building proceeds would first be applied to repay the money contributed by Kargman, then profits would be divided 40 percent to Kargman and 60 percent to Diamond. Shortly after the building was acquired by Kargman and Diamond, Diamond sold his partnership interest for $40,000 in a transaction by which a third party became a 50 percent partner with Kargman. The acquisition of the building and Diamond's transfer of his interest occurred in the same taxable year. Diamond reported the transaction as a sale of a partnership interest resulting in the recognition of $40,000 of capital gain. The Tax Court held that Diamond recognized ordinary income on the receipt of a partnership interest for services. 56 T.C. 530 (1971). The Seventh Circuit affirmed.[7]

Treas. Reg. § 1.721–1(b)(1) provides that, "To the extent that any of the partners gives up any part of his right to be repaid his contributions (as distinguished from a share in partnership profits) in favor of another partner as compensation for services (or in satisfaction of an obligation), section 721 does not apply." The taxpayer in *Diamond* asserted the widely held view that the first parenthetical phrase in Treas. Reg. § 1.721–1(b)(1) meant that a profits interest for services was not taxable. As quoted in the opinion of the Seventh Circuit, Professor Arthur Willis, who chaired an advisory group in 1956 that reviewed the regulations under Subchapter K, wrote in his treatise of the time (Willis on Partnership Taxation 84–85 (1971)):

> However obliquely the proposition is stated in the regulations, it is clear that a partner who receives only an interest in future profits of the partnership as compensation for services is not required to report the receipt of his partnership interest as taxable income. The rationale is twofold. In the first place, the present value of a right to participate in future profits is usually too conjectural to be subject to valuation. In the second place, the service partner is taxable on his distributive share of partnership income as it is realized by the partnership. If he were taxed on the present value of the right to receive his share of future partnership income, either he would be taxed twice, or the value of his right to participate in partnership income must be amortized over some period of time.

The double taxation referred to by Professor Willis occurs because the recipient of a profits interest for services would be taxed first on the receipt of the value of the interest, and secondly on the partner's share of profits as they are derived. Nonetheless, the Seventh Circuit concluded that, "In the present case, taxpayer's services had all been rendered, and the

---

7. The Tax Court analyzed the case treating the venture as a partnership. The Court of Appeals refused to consider suggestions that the relationship may have been an employment or other relationship on the grounds that no such findings had been made by the Tax Court. See Cowan, The Diamond Case, 27 Tax Law Review 161 (1972).

prospect of earnings from the real estate under Kargman's management was evidently very good. The profit-share had determinable market value." The court addressed the issue of double taxation as follows:

> Each partner determines his income tax by taking into account his distributive share of the taxable income of the partnership. 26 U.S.C.A. § 702. Taxpayer's position here is that he was entitled to defer income taxation on the compensation for his services except as partnership earnings were realized. If a partner is taxed on the determinable market value of a profit-share at the time it is created in his favor, and is also taxed on his full share of earnings as realized, there will arguably be double taxation, avoidable by permitting him to amortize the value which was originally treated as income. Does the absence of a recognized procedure for amortization militate against the treatment of the creation of the profit-share as income?

> Do the disadvantages of treating the creation of the profit-share as income in those instances where it has a determinable market value at that time outweigh the desirability of imposing a tax at the time the taxpayer has received an interest with determinable market value as compensation for services?

> We think, of course, that the resolution of these practical questions makes clearly desirable the promulgation of appropriate regulations, to achieve a degree of certainty. But in the absence of regulation, we think it sound policy to defer to the expertise of the Commissioner and the Judges of the Tax Court, and to sustain their decision that the receipt of a profit-share with determinable market value is income. * * *

The *Diamond* case presented the court with an appealing situation in which to tax the receipt of a profits interest received for services. The profits interest in that case was easily valued, was paid for past services, and was sold shortly after receipt. Nevertheless, even if the court in the *Diamond* case had accepted the taxpayer's argument that the receipt of the interest in future partnership profits was not a taxable event, the subsequent disposition of the partnership interest could nonetheless generate ordinary income. See Hale v. Commissioner, T.C. Memo. 1965–274, so holding, relying on Hort v. Commissioner, 313 U.S. 28 (1941).

3.2.   *The* Diamond *Progeny*

The principle, but not the result, of *Diamond*, bolstered by the application of § 83, was reaffirmed in Campbell v. Commissioner, 943 F.2d 815 (8th Cir.1991), rev'g T.C. Memo. 1990–162. In that case the taxpayer received a profits-only partnership interest in several syndicated tax shelter limited partnerships in consideration of services in organizing the partnerships and selling interests to investors. Both the Tax Court and the Court of Appeals held that the receipt of a profits-only partnership interest in exchange for services was a taxable event. The Tax Court valued the interest in future partnership profits by computing the discounted value of the stream of income and tax benefits expected to be received by the services partner, but the Court of Appeals reversed as clearly erroneous the Tax Court's holding that the partnership interest in question in that case had anything more than speculative value. Similarly, in Vestal v. United States, 498 F.2d 487 (8th Cir.1974), the taxpayer contracted with certain limited partners of a partnership, the sole asset of which was oil and gas rights in a then unproductive but proven field, for the transfer of a portion of their partnership interests after they had recovered their original capital investment in exchange for his services in organizing the partnership. The court held that no income was realized in the year the contract rights were received because the value was speculative. On rehearing, this decision was held to be consistent with *Diamond*. The crucial difference between *Diamond* and the opinions in *Campbell* and *Vestal* is that in *Diamond* the Tax Court's finding that the partnership interest had a "determinable market value" was upheld, possibly because of the rather unique fact pattern—the taxpayer's sale of the partnership interest soon after receipt was highly probative direct evidence of its fair market value.

Other cases approached the receipt of a profits-only interest by focusing on the service partner's interest in partnership capital, as measured by the service partner's capital account. In St. John v. United States, 84–1 U.S.T.C. ¶ 9158 (C.D.Ill.1983), the taxpayer received a current partnership interest entitling him only to future profits in exchange for services. The court held that § 83 applied to the receipt of an interest in partnership profits, but that the value of the interest was zero, because if the partnership were liquidated immediately after receipt of the interest, the taxpayer would have received nothing. Applying this analysis to the *Diamond* case suggests that perhaps Diamond in fact received an interest in partnership capital to the extent that the value of the building exceeded the value assigned to it by the partners upon formation of the partnership.[8] Similarly, in Mark IV Pictures, Inc. v. Commissioner, T.C. Memo. 1990–571, aff'd, 969 F.2d 669 (8th Cir.1992), the Tax Court, without any discussion of *Campbell*, found it necessary to determine whether a partnership interest received for services was a profits-only interest or an interest in capital. Presumably, if the court had followed *Campbell*, this determination would have been unnecessary and only the value of the interest received for services would have been at issue. Because the partnership agreement provided that the services partner, who received a general partnership interest, had a right to receive 50 percent of the liquidation proceeds after repayment to the limited partners of their capital contributions, the court found that a capital interest had been received. In affirming the Tax Court's decision in *Mark IV Pictures, Inc.*, the Court of Appeals held that the test to determine whether the interest received is an interest in partnership capital is an examination of the effect of a hypothetical liquidation immediately after the partnership was formed. If the partner

---

8. The Court of Appeals in *Diamond* refused to consider the Commissioner's argument that Diamond received more than a future profits interest because the value of the property may have been greater than its purchase price because no such findings had been made by the Tax Court.

would receive a distribution, the interest is an interest in capital, not a profits interest

3.3. *Personal Service Partnerships*

The rule of *Diamond* probably cannot be applied to partnership interests in personal services partnerships. The value of an interest as a newly admitted partner in any partnership in which a partner's income is determined largely with reference to income from personal services to be rendered in the future cannot be readily ascertained. Consider the implications of the *Diamond* holding if an associate in a law firm is admitted to a partnership and thus becomes entitled to a certain percentage of future profits. Should she realize income at that time? While both the associate and Diamond have received a "profits" interest in the sense that they have an interest in a partnership which does not involve a right to be paid out of the capital contributions of the other partners, the two situations intuitively seem quite different. Are the differences substantive or matters of valuation? If the former, are the differences sufficient to support tax distinctions between types of "profits" interests? Should it matter whether the partnership interest is received in exchange for past or future services? If this distinction is to be determinative, are there objective tests which can be used to determine on which side of the line a particular transaction falls? If the value of a partnership interest in future profits received in exchange for future services is taxable in the year of receipt, is the partner also taxable on the income as received in future years? How can double taxation be avoided? The Internal Revenue Service recognized these valuation problems in Rev. Proc. 93–27, 1993–2 C.B. 343, where it indicated that the Service will not treat the receipt of a profits-only interest in a partnership for services as a taxable event except in circumstances where it is possible to ascertain the value of the profits-only interest.

4. SECTION 83

Diamond involved tax years before the enactment of § 83. The rules concerning the treatment of a partner who receives a partnership interest as compensation for services must be coordinated with the rules under § 83, which in general are controlling as to the taxability of property transferred in connection with the performance of services. Section 83 requires that the fair market value of the "property" transferred be included in income. However, under § 83 there is a statutory issue whether an interest in partnership profits constitutes "property." Treas. Reg. § 1.83–3(e) defines "property" comprehensively and excludes only "an unfunded and unsecured promise to pay money in the future." The regulations appear to cover any kind of an interest in a partnership, including a profits interest of the type involved in *Diamond*. There is no significant difference between an unsecured and unfunded promise to pay money in the future, which is not covered by § 83, and a partnership interest in future profits. Applying § 83 to a profits only partnership interest in exchange for services raises the same valuation problems as in the *Diamond* case. Campbell v. Commissioner, supra, held that a profits only partnership interest constitutes property for purposes of § 83, although, as discussed above, the Eighth Circuit opinion concluded that the interest could not be valued for purposes of including an amount in gross income.

If § 83 is applied, should it matter whether the services must be performed continuously or only for a specified period of time? If property is received for services and the taxpayer's rights to the property are forfeitable or subject to substantial restrictions on transfer, the value of the property is not includable under § 83 until the property vests or the restrictions lapse. The value of the property is includable at its fair market value at that time. In such a case the service partner might consider an election under § 83(b) to include the value of the property at the time it is received, particularly if the value at the time of receipt is zero. (The Service might then, contrary to *Diamond*, seek to take the position that there was no "transfer" of "property" for § 83 purposes.)

5. INTERNAL REVENUE SERVICE RULING POSITION

In Rev. Proc. 93–27, 1993–2 C.B. 343, the Internal Revenue Service adopted the valuation approach of *Campbell* by announcing that it would treat a partner who performs services "in a partner capacity" in exchange for a profits-only partnership interest as realizing income upon receipt of the partnership interest only in the following three specific situations: (1) the partnership's profits are derived from a substantially certain and predictable stream of income, such as from high quality debt or a net lease; (2) the partner disposes of the partnership interest within two years of its receipt; or (3) the interest is a limited partnership interest in a publicly traded limited partnership as defined in § 7704(b), discussed at page 31. As a practical matter, this position eliminated the issue of whether a partner must recognize income upon receipt of profits-only interest in most circumstances, but the Revenue Procedure imposed certain other conditions that raised interpretative issues. The safe harbor applied only if the services for which the partnership interest has been received were rendered "to or for the benefit of the partnership" rather than to or for the benefit of another partner. The Revenue Procedure added, however, that services may be rendered "in anticipation of being a partner," as well as in the capacity of being a partner. Nevertheless, it was unclear whether receipt of a future profits interest in consideration of past services to another person, where the receipt creates a two person partnership, is within the safe harbor. There is no logical reason to distinguish this case from receipt of a future profits interest in a preexisting partnership.

Some of the technical problems raised by Rev. Proc. 93–27 were clarified by Rev. Proc. 2001–43, 2001–2 C.B. 191, which provides that classification of a partnership interest received for services will be determined at the time the interest is granted, even if the interest is not vested. Where the requirements of Rev. Proc. 93–27 are met, the Service will treat neither the grant of the interest, nor its vesting, as a taxable event to the recipient. Rev. Proc. 2001–43 requires that the service provider be treated as the owner of the partnership interest from the date of its grant. Therefore, the service provider is required to account for the appropriate share of all partnership items. The Revenue Procedure also states that neither the partnership nor any of the partners can claim a deduction for the cost of the services at either the time the interest is granted or at the time the profits only partnership interest becomes vested. The treatment of the service provider and the partnership upon vesting presumably is based on the fact that the service provider would have no capital account balance at that time and would, therefore receive nothing upon liquidation of the partnership.

6. PROPOSED REGULATIONS

The Court of Appeals in *Diamond* stated: "We think, of course, that the resolution of these practical questions makes clearly desirable the promulgation of appropriate regulations, to achieve a degree of certainty." Over thirty years later, the Treasury Department has proposed such regulations, which when finalized, will comprehensively deal with the treatment of partnership interests received for services. Prop. Regs. § 1.83–3(e) and (*l*) (2005) and § 1.721–1(b) (2005).

The preamble to the proposed regulations, Partial Withdrawal of Notice of Proposed Rulemaking Notice of Proposed Rulemaking, and Notice of Public Hearing, Partnership Equity for Services, REG–105346–03, 70 F.R. 29675 (May 23, 2005), explains the proposed rules as follows:

1. Application of Section 83 to Partnership Interests

[T]he proposed regulations [Prop. Reg. § 1.83–3(e) (2005)] provide that a partnership interest is property within the meaning of section 83, and that the transfer of a partnership interest in connection with the performance of services is subject to section 83.

The proposed regulations apply section 83 to all partnership interests, without distinguishing between partnership capital interests and partnership profits interests. * * * [T]he Treasury Department and the IRS do not believe that there is a substantial basis for distinguishing among partnership interests for purposes of section 83. All partnership interests constitute personal property under state law and give the holder the right to share in future earnings from partnership capital and labor. Moreover, * * * taxpayers may exploit any differences in the tax treatment of partnership profits interests and partnership capital interests. * * * Therefore, all of the rules in these proposed regulations and the accompanying proposed revenue procedure (described below) apply equally to partnership capital interests and partnership profits interests. * * *

Section 83(b) allows a person who receives substantially non-vested property in connection with the performance of services to elect to include in gross income the difference between: (A) the fair market value of the property at the time of transfer (determined without regard to a restriction other than a restriction which by its terms will never lapse); and (B) the amount paid for such property. Under section 83(b)(2), the election under section 83(b) must be made within 30 days of the date of the transfer of the property to the service provider.

Consistent with the principles of section 83, the proposed regulations provide that, if a partnership interest is transferred in connection with the performance of services, and if an election under section 83(b) is not made, then the holder of the partnership interest is not treated as a partner until the interest becomes substantially vested. If a section 83(b) election is made with respect to such an interest, the service provider will be treated as a partner. * * *

These principles differ from Rev. Proc. 2001–43 [2001–2 C.B. 191]. Under that revenue procedure, if a partnership profits interest is transferred in connection with the performance of services, then the holder of the partnership interest may be treated as a partner even if no section 83(b) election is made, provided that certain conditions are met.

Certain changes to the regulations under both subchapter K and section 83 are needed to coordinate the principles of subchapter K with the principles of section 83. Among the changes that are proposed in these regulations are: (1) conforming the subchapter K rules to the section 83 timing rules * * *. In addition, Rev. Procs. 93–27 (1993–2 C.B. 343), and 2001–43 (2001–2 C.B. 191), which generally provide for nonrecognition by both the partnership and the service provider on the transfer of a profits interest in the partnership for services performed for that partnership, must be modified to be consistent with these proposed regulations. Accordingly, in conjunction with these proposed regulations, the IRS is issuing Notice 2005–43 (2005–24 I.R.B.). That Notice contains a proposed revenue procedure that, when finalized, will obsolete Rev. Procs. 93–27 and 2001–43. * * *

5. Valuation of Compensatory Partnership Interests

* * * Section 83 generally provides that the recipient of property transferred in connection with the performance of services recognizes income equal to the fair market value of the property, disregarding lapse restrictions. * * * However, some authorities have concluded that, under the particular facts and circumstances of the case, a partnership profits interest had only a speculative value or that the fair market value of a partnership interest should be determined by reference to the liquidation value of that interest. See section 1.704–1(e)(1)(v); Campbell v. Commissioner, 943 F.2d 815 (8th Cir. 1991); St. John v. U.S., 1984–1 USTC 9158 (C.D. Ill. 1983). But see Diamond v. Commissioner, 492 F.2d 286 (7th Cir. 1974) (holding under pre-section 83 law

that the receipt of a profits interest with a determinable value at the time of receipt resulted in immediate taxation); Campbell v. Commissioner, T.C. Memo 1990–162, aff'd in part and rev'd in part, 943 F.2d 815 (8th Cir. 1991).

The Treasury Department and the IRS have determined that, provided certain requirements are satisfied, it is appropriate to allow partnerships and service providers to value partnership interests based on liquidation value. [Prop. Reg. § 1.83–3(*l*).] This approach ensures consistency in the treatment of partnership profits interests and partnership capital interests, and accords with other regulations issued under subchapter K, such as the regulations under section 704(b).

In accordance with these proposed regulations, the revenue procedure proposed in Notice 2005–43 (2005–24 I.R.B.) will, when finalized, provide additional rules that partnerships, partners, and persons providing services to the partnership in exchange for interests in that partnership would be required to follow when electing under section 1.83–3(*l*) of these proposed regulations to treat the fair market value of those interests as being equal to the liquidation value of those interests. For this purpose, the liquidation value of a partnership interest is the amount of cash that the holder of that interest would receive with respect to the interest if, immediately after the transfer of the interest, the partnership sold all of its assets (including goodwill, going concern value, and any other intangibles associated with the partnership's operations) for cash equal to the fair market value of those assets, and then liquidated.

For the most part, from the perspective of the partner receiving an interest in a partnership in exchange for services, these proposed regulations effect little substantive change.

B. TREATMENT OF THE PARTNERSHIP ISSUING A PARTNERSHIP INTEREST IN EXCHANGE FOR SERVICES

INTERNAL REVENUE CODE: Sections 83(h); 721(a).

REGULATIONS: Sections: 1.83–6(a)(4), (b); 1.721–1(b); 1.722–1.

PROPOSED REGULATIONS: Sections 1.83–3(e) and (*l*) (2005); 1.721–1(b) (2005).

The treatment of a partnership issuing a partnership capital interest in exchange for services has been more opaque than the treatment of the partner who receives the interest in exchange for services. It is clear that § 83(h) allows the partnership a deduction or capitalized cost of acquiring an asset (tangible or intangible) equal to the amount includable by the partner under § 83(a). See Treas. Reg. § 1.83–6(a). Logically, the service partner should not be entitled to any part of this deduction and a provision in the partnership agreement pursuant to § 704(b) allocating it to the other partners should be respected. Any deduction allowed would then reduce the outside bases of the other partners under § 705.

A more difficult question, however, is whether the partnership—that is to say, the other partners—recognize any gain of loss as a result of the transaction. Section 721(a), which provides nonrecognition to a partner who receives a partnership interest in exchange for property, but which does not provide nonrecognition to a partner who receives a partnership interest in exchange for services, is also the section providing that the partnership itself does not recognize gain of loss when it issues a partnership interest in exchange for property. This statutory structure suggests that the partnership that issues a partnership interest in exchange for property also should recognize gain or loss on the admission of a new partner in exchange for services.

McDougal v. Commissioner

Tax Court of the United States, 1974.
62 T.C. 720.

■ Fay, Judge:

* * *

FINDINGS OF FACT

* * *

F.C. and Frankie McDougal Maintained Farms at Lamesa, Tex., where they were engaged in the business of breeding and racing horses. Gilbert McClanahan was a licensed public horse trainer who rendered his services to various horse owners for a standard fee. he had numbered the McDougals among his clientele since 1965.

On February 21, 1965, a horse of exceptional pedigree, Iron Card, had been foaled at the Anthony Ranch in Florida. Title to Iron Card was acquired in January of 1967 by one Frank Ratliff, Jr., who in turn transferred title to himself, M. H. Ratliff, and John V. Burnett (Burnett). The Ratliffs and Burnett entered Iron Card in several races as a 2-year-old; and although the horse enjoyed some success in these contests, it soon became evident that he was suffering from a condition diagnosed by a veterinarian as a protein allergy.

When, due to a dispute among themselves, the Ratliffs and Burnett decided to sell Iron Card for whatever price he could attract, McClanahan (who had trained the horse for the Ratliffs and Burnett) advised the McDougals to make the purchase. He made this recommendation because, despite the veterinarian's prognosis to the contrary, McClanahan believed that by the use of home remedy Iron Card could be restored to full racing vigor. * * *

The McDougals purchased Iron Card for $10,000 on January 1, 1968. At the time of the purchase McDougal promised that if McClanahan trained and attended to Iron Card, a half interest in the horse would be his once the McDougals had recovered the costs and expenses of acquisition. This promise was not made in lieu of payment of the standard trainer's fee; for from January 1, 1968, until the date of the transfer, McClanahan was paid $2,910 as compensation for services rendered as Iron Card's trainer.

McClanahan's home remedy proved so effective in relieving Iron Card of his allergy that the horse began to race with success, and his reputation consequently grew to such proportion that he attracted a succession of offers to purchase, one of which reached $60,000. The McDougals decided, however, to keep the horse and by October 4, 1968, had recovered out of their winnings the costs of acquiring him. It was therefore on that date that they transferred a half interest in the horse to McClanahan in accordance with the promise which McDougal had made to the trainer. * * *

Iron Card continued to race well until very late in 1968 when, without warning and for an unascertained cause, he developed a condition called "hot ankle" which effectively terminated his racing career. From 1970 onward he was used exclusively for breeding purposes. That his value as a stud was no less than his value as a racehorse is attested to by the fact that in September of 1970 petitioners were offered $75,000 for him; but after considering the offer, the McDougals and McClanahan decided to refuse it, preferring to exploit Iron Card's earning potential as a stud to their own profit.

On November 1, 1968, petitioners had concluded a partnership agreement by parol to effectuate their design of racing the horse for as long as that proved feasible and of offering him out as a stud thereafter. Profits were to be shared equally by the McDougals and the McClanahans, while losses were to be allocated to the McDougals alone.[4]

Though the partnership initially filed no return for its first brief taxable year ended December 31, 1968, petitioners did make the computations which such a return would show and reported the results in their individual returns. The partnership was considered to have earned $1,314, against which was deducted depreciation in the amount of $278. Other deductions left the partnership with taxable income for the year of $737 * * *.

On their joint return for the year 1968 the McDougals reported, inter alia, gross income of $22,891 from their Lamesa farms. Against this income they deducted $1,390 representing depreciation on Iron Card for the first 10 months of 1968 and $9,213 in training fees.[5] The McDougals appear, however, to have initially claimed no deduction by reason of the transfer to McClanahan of the half interest in Iron Card.

---

4. The oral agreement was reduced to writing in April of 1970. * * *

5. Presumably this included $3,175 paid to McClanahan both before and after the transfer of Oct. 4, 1968, as compensation for the training of Iron Card.

In addition to their distributive share of partnership income referred to above, the McClanahans reported $5,000 of gross income which they identified as [an] interest in a racehorse.

[By an amended return for 1968, filed in 1970, the McDougals claimed] to have transferred the half interest in Iron Card to McClanahan as compensation for services rendered and thus to be entitled to a $30,000 business expense deduction, computed by reference to the last offer to purchase Iron Card received prior to October 4, 1968. Furthermore, the McDougals acknowledged that they had recognized a gain on the aforesaid transfer. By charging the entire depreciation deduction of $1,390 against the portion of their unadjusted cost basis allocable to the half interest in Iron Card which they retained, the McDougals computed this gain to be $25,000 and characterized it as a long-term capital gain under section 1231(a) of the Internal Revenue Code of 1954.

The McClanahans simultaneously increased their income arising out of the transfer from $5,000 to $30,000. They could thus claim to have a tax cost basis of $30,000 in their half interest in the horse. Finally, purporting to have transferred the horse to a partnership in concert on November 1, 1968, petitioner computed the partnership's basis in the horse to be $33,610 under section 723.[8] This increase in basis led the partnership to claim a depreciation deduction of $934 for 1968 instead of $278 and to report only $81 of taxable income for that year. The McDougals thereupon reduced their distributive share of partnership income for 1968 from $405 to $40, while the McClanahans reduced their share from $332 to $41. For the year 1969 the partnership claimed a deduction for depreciation on Iron Card in the amount of $5,602, closing the year with a loss of $8,911. This loss was allocated in its entirety to the McDougals, pursuant to the partnership agreement.

* * *

OPINION

Respondent contends that the McDougals did not recognize a $25,000 gain on the transaction of October 4, 1968, and that they were not entitled to claim a $30,000 business expense deduction by reason thereof. He further contends that were Iron Card to be contributed to a partnership or joint venture under the circumstances obtaining in the instant case, its basis in Iron Card at the time of contribution would have been limited by the McDougals' cost basis in the horse, as adjusted. Respondent justifies these contentions by arguing * * * that at some point in time no later than the transfer of October 4, 1968, McDougal and McClanahan entered into a

---

8. Having charged the entire amount of the depreciation which they had claimed ($1,390) against their unadjusted cost basis of $5,000 in the half interest in Iron Card which they retained, the McDougals considered themselves to have an adjusted basis of $3,610 in that retained half. The McClana-hans claimed a $30,000 tax cost basis in the half interest which they had just received. Under sec. 723 the contribution of the two halves to a partnership would therefore result in the partnership's having a basis of $33,610 in Iron Card.

partnership or joint venture[10] to which the McDougals contributed Iron Card and McClanahan contributed services. Respondent contends that such a finding would require our holding that the McDougals did not recognize a gain on the transfer of October 4, 1968, by reason of section 721, and that under section 723 the joint venture's basis in Iron Card at the time of the contribution was equal to the McDougals' adjusted basis in the horse as of that time.

* * *

A joint venture is deemed to arise when two or more persons agree, expressly or impliedly, to enter actively upon a specific business enterprise, the purpose of which is the pursuit of profit; the ownership of whose productive assets and of the profits generated by them is shared; the parties to which all bear the burden of any loss; and the management of which is not confined to a single participant [citations omitted].

While in the case at bar the risk of loss was to be borne by the McDougals alone, all the other elements of a joint venture were present once the transfer of October 4, 1968, had been effected. Accordingly, we hold that the aforesaid transfer constituted the formation of a joint venture to which the McDougals contributed capital in the form of the horse, Iron Card, and in which they granted McClanahan an interest equal to their own in capital and profits as compensation for his having trained Iron Card. We further hold that the agreement formally entered into on November 1, 1968, and reduced to writing in April of 1970, constituted a continuation of the original joint venture under section 708(b)(2)(A). Furthermore, that McClanahan continued to receive a fee for serving as Iron Card's trainer after October 4, 1968, in no way militates against the soundness of this holding. See sec. 707(c), and sec. 1.707–1(c), example 1, Income Tax Reg. However, this holding does not result in the tax consequences which respondent has contended would follow from it. See sec. 1.721–1(b)(1), Income Tax Regs.

When on the formation of a joint venture a party contributing appreciated assets satisfies an obligation by granting his obligee a capital interest in the venture, he is deemed first to have transferred to the obligee an undivided interest in the assets contributed, equal in value to the amount of the obligation so satisfied. He and the obligee are deemed thereafter and in concert to have contributed those assets to the joint venture.

The contributing obligor will recognize gain on the transaction to the extent that the value of the undivided interest which he is deemed to have transferred exceeds his basis therein. The obligee is considered to have realized an amount equal to the fair market value of the interest which he receives in the venture and will recognize income depending upon the character of the obligation satisfied.[12] The joint venture's basis in the assets

10. By reason of sec. 761(a) joint ventures and partnerships have an identical effect on the determination of income tax liability.

12. For example, if the obligation arose

will be determined under section 723 in accordance with the foregoing assumptions. Accordingly, we hold that the transaction under consideration constituted an exchange in which the McDougals realized $30,000, United States v. Davis, 370 U.S. 65 (1962) * * *.

In determining the basis offset to which the McDougals are entitled with respect to the transfer of October 4, 1968, we note the following: that the McDougals had an unadjusted cost basis in Iron Card of $10,000; that they had claimed $1,390 in depreciation on the entire horse for the period January 1 to October 31, 1968; and that after an agreement of partnership was concluded on November 1, 1968, depreciation on Iron Card was deducted by the partnership exclusively.

* * * Consistent with their intent and with our own holding that a joint venture arose on October 4, 1968, we now further hold that the McDougals were entitled to claim depreciation on Iron Card only until the transfer of October 4, 1968. Thereafter depreciation on Iron Card ought to have been deducted by the joint venture in the computation of its taxable income.

In determining their adjusted basis in the portion of Iron Card on whose disposition they are required to recognize gain, the McDougals charged all the depreciation which they had taken on the horse against their basis in the half in which they retained an interest. This procedure was improper. As in accordance with section 1.167(g)–1, Income Tax Regs., we have allowed the McDougals a depreciation deduction with respect to Iron Card for the period January 1 to October 4, 1968, computed on their entire cost basis in the horse of $10,000; so also do we require that the said deduction be charged against that entire cost basis under section 1016(a)(2)(A).[13]

As the McDougals were in the business of racing horses, any gain recognized by them on the exchange of Iron Card in satisfaction of a debt would be characterized under section 1231(a) provided he had been held by them for the period requisite under section 1231(b) * * *. [T]hey had held him for a period sufficiently long to make section 1231(a) applicable to their gain on the transaction. * * *

The joint venture's basis in Iron Card as of October 4, 1968, must be determined under section 723 in accordance with the principles of law set forth earlier in this opinion. In the half interest in the horse which it is

out of a loan, the obligee will recognize no income by reason of the transaction; if the obligation represents the selling price of a capital asset, he will recognize a capital gain to the extent that the amount he is deemed to have realized exceeds his adjusted basis in the asset; if the obligation represents compensation for services, the transaction will result in ordinary income to the obligee in an amount equal to the value of the interest which he received in the joint venture.

13. The depreciation on Iron Card to which the McDougals are entitled, their adjusted basis in the horse as of Oct. 4, 1968, and the gain recognized by them by reason of the transaction on that date remain to be determined in accordance with the decision under Rule 155, Tax Court Rules of Practice and Procedure.

deemed to have received from the McDougals, the joint venture had a basis equal to one-half of the McDougals' adjusted cost basis in Iron Card as of October 4, 1968, i.e., the excess of $5,000 over one-half of the depreciation which the McDougals were entitled to claim on Iron Card for the period January 1 to October 4, 1968. In the half interest which the venture is considered to have received from McClanahan, it can claim to have had a basis equal to the amount which McClanahan is considered to have realized on the transaction, $30,000. The joint venture's deductions for depreciation on Iron Card for the years 1968 and 1969 are to be determined on the basis computed in the above-described manner.

When an interest in a joint venture is transferred as compensation for services rendered, any deduction which may be authorized under section 162(a)(1) by reason of that transfer is properly claimed by the party to whose benefit the services accrued, be that party the venture itself or one or more venturers, sec. 1.721–1(b)(2), Income Tax Regs. Prior to McClanahan's receipt of his interest, a joint venture did not exist under the facts of the case at bar; the McDougals were the sole owners of Iron Card and recipients of his earnings. Therefore, they alone could have benefited from the services rendered by McClanahan prior to October 4, 1968, for which he was compensated by the transaction of that date. Accordingly, we hold that the McDougals are entitled to a business expense deduction of $30,000, that amount being the value of the interest which McClanahan received. * * *

ILLUSTRATIVE MATERIAL

1. EFFECT OF ADMISSION OF SERVICE PARTNER WITH A CAPITAL INTEREST

1.1. *Does a Partnership Recognize Gain or Loss on the Admission of a Service Partner?*

If the principles of *McDougal* are applied to an existing partnership rather than only to transfers of an interest in property in consideration of past services where the transfer results in the initial formation of a partnership, the partnership would recognize gain or loss on the admission of the service partner. See Treas. Reg. § 1.83–6(b). Under this model the partnership is treated as transferring an undivided portion of each of its assets to the service partner as payment for services, with gain and loss being recognized on the constructive transfer. The service partner then partnership constructively recontributes the property to partnership, which takes a basis equal to the service partner's "tax cost" basis, i.e., fair market value, in the property under § 723.

Some commentators and many tax practitioners, however, have long advanced an alternative theory—"cash-out-cash-in"—for dealing with the partnership's side of the transaction. Under the cash-out-cash-in theory, the partnership—that is, the other partners—are treated as if the partnership paid cash to the service partner equal to the value of the partnership interest, following which the service partner immediately contributed the cash back to the partnership in a transaction subject to § 721. Under this model the partnership recognizes no gain and the basis of its assets remains unchanged. Although the cash-out-cash-in model is not a wholly implausible alternative theory, it found no support in prior judicial decisions or administrative rulings.

Prop. Reg. § § 1.721–1(b)(2) (2005) would produce results for the partnership issuing a partnership interest in exchange for services that is identical to the results under the cash-out-cash-in model, although the proposed regulations do not explicitly adopt the cash-out-cash-in model as the underlying theory for the result oriented rules contained therein. The preamble to the proposed regulations, Partial Withdrawal of Notice of Proposed Rulemaking Notice of Proposed Rulemaking, and Notice of Public Hearing, Partnership Equity for Services, REG–105346–03, 70 F.R. 29675 (May 23, 2005), explains the proposed rules as follows:

> There is a dispute among commentators as to whether a partnership should recognize gain or loss on the transfer of a compensatory partnership interest. Some commentators believe that, on the transfer of such an interest, the partnership should be treated as satisfying its compensation obligation with a fractional interest in each asset of the partnership. Under this deemed sale of assets theory, the partnership would recognize gain or loss equal to the excess of the fair market value of each partial asset deemed transferred to the service provider over the partnership's adjusted basis in that partial asset. Other commentators believe that a partnership should not recognize gain or loss on the transfer of a compensatory partnership interest. They argue, among other things, that the transfer of such an interest is not properly treated as a realization event for the partnership because no property owned by the partnership has changed hands. They also argue that taxing a partnership on the transfer of such an interest would result in inappropriate gain acceleration, would be difficult to administer, and would cause economically similar transactions to be taxed differently.

> Generally, when appreciated property is used to pay an obligation, gain on the property is recognized. * * * However, the Treasury Department and the IRS believe that partnerships should not be required to recognize gain on the transfer of a compensatory partnership interest. Such a rule is more consistent with the policies underlying section 721—to defer recognition of gain and loss when persons join together to conduct a business— than would be a rule requiring the partnership to recognize gain on the transfer of these types of interests. Therefore, the proposed regulations [Prop. Regs. §§ 1.83–6(b) and 1.721–1(b)(2)] provide that partnerships are not taxed on the transfer or substantial vesting of a compensatory partnership interest. Under section 1.704–1(b)(4)(i) (reverse section 704(c) principles), the historic partners generally will be required to recognize any income or loss

attributable to the partnership's assets as those assets are sold, depreciated, or amortized.

The rule providing for nonrecognition of gain or loss does not apply to the transfer or substantial vesting of an interest in an eligible entity, as defined in section 301.7701–3(a) of the Procedure and Administration Regulations, that becomes a partnership under section 301.7701–3(f)(2) as a result of the transfer or substantial vesting of the interest. See McDougal v. Commissioner, 62 T.C. 720 (1974) (holding that the service recipient recognized gain on the transfer of a one-half interest in appreciated property to the service provider, immediately prior to the contribution by the service recipient and the service provider of their respective interests in the property to a newly formed partnership).

As explained in the above excerpt from the preamble, while Prop. Regs. §§ 1.83–6(b) (2005) and 1.721–1(b)(2) (2005) would provide that a partnership does not recognize any gain or loss upon the transfer of a partnership interest to a new partner in exchange for services to the partnership, the proposed regulations preserve the recognition result in *McDougal* if the transfer of property in exchange for services creates a partnership out of a relationship that previously was not classified as a partnership. What difference is there between the two situations that justifies different treatment? In both cases, one party or parties transfers an interest in property to a party in exchange for services. As held in *McDougal* and noted in the preamble to the proposed regulations, an exchange of an interest in property for services traditionally has been treated as a realization event.

As a practical matter, upon admission of a partner it generally is necessary to revalue the partnership's property and adjust the partners' capital accounts to reflect the revaluation. Treas. Reg. § 1.704–1(b)(2)(iv)(*f*) specifically allows the partnership to revalue its property and adjust the existing partners' capital accounts in connection with the grant of an interest in the partnership (other than a *de minimis* interest) in consideration of services to the partnership by an existing partner acting in a partner capacity or by a new partner acting in a partner capacity or in anticipation of being a partner. Thus, for capital account purposes, the exchange of an interest in partnership capital is reflected as a realization event for the partnership and a transfer of partnership capital from the continuing partners to the service partner. Under the proposed regulations, the revalued capital account interest of the compensated partner, as reflected in capital accounts, measures the amount of income to be recognized by the service partner. That same amount is allowed as a deduction to the partnership, or capitalized, as is appropriate. The major revision of the proposed regulations is to treat the exchange of an interest in partnership property for services as a nonrecognition event and to defer recognition of gain or loss to disposition of partnership property.

Contrary to assertions in the preamble to the proposed regulations, the broader pattern of Subchapter K as a whole, which significantly incorporates the aggregate theory of partnership taxation, suggests that the *McDougal* model is a more appropriate principle for determining the tax consequences to the other partners than the legal fiction employed in the cash-out-cash-in model. The position stated in the preamble that a transfer of interests in partnership assets is not a realization event is directly contrary to the result in *McDougal*, which upon careful reading is not really distinguishable on the grounds asserted in the preamble. The pervasive accepted doctrine, reflected in the cases cited in the *McDougal* opinion, is that the transfer of any interest in property in exchange for services results in recognition of gain or loss with respect to the transferred property, absent a nonrecognition rule. The only nonstatutory exception to this principle is found in § 1032 with respect to the issuance of corporate stock in exchange for services.

Section 1032, which provides for nonrecognition to a corporation upon receipt of property in exchange for stock, is somewhat analogous to § 721, although not entirely so. The regulations under § 1032, Treas. Reg. § 1.1032–1(a), apply this nonrecognition rule to the issuance of shares for services, but that regulatory provision is merely an extension of the rule in the regulations predating the enactment of § 1032, which provided that the issuance of shares by a corporation did not "give rise to taxable gain or deductible loss" unless the corporation was "deal[ing] in its own shares as it might in the shares of another corporation," i.e., buying and selling on the market for speculative profit. See Treas. Regs. 118, Sec. 29.22(a)–15 (1952). In Hercules Powder Co. v. United States, 180 F.Supp. 363 (Ct. Cl. 1960), the court interpreted this language in Treas. Regs. 118, Sec. 29.22(a)–15 (1952):

> [T]he words "gives rise to neither taxable gain nor deductible loss" in the regulation concerning the original issue of shares did not create an exemption of income from taxation. That could not be accomplished by regulation. That language must mean that such an issue does not give rise to income, within the meaning of section [61].

Thus, the apparent "extension" of § 1032 to stock issued for services in Treas. Reg. § 1.1031–1(a) is illusory. The issuance of corporate shares in exchange for services does not give rise to gross income wholly apart from § 1032.

Furthermore, unlike situations involving the issuance of corporate shares, where the corporation's tax consequences are determined under § 1032 and the shareholder's tax consequences normally are determined under § 351, in the case of the admission of a partner to a partnership, the tax consequences to both the partner and the partnership normally are determined under § 721. While asymmetrical treatment of the corporation and the service-provider partner is possible in the corporate situation, because different Code sections provide the nonrecognition rules for the corporation and the shareholder, respectively, § 721 cannot be interpreted asymmetrically. The transaction is either a nonrecognition transaction under § 721 for both the partner and the partnership or it is a recognition transaction for both the partnership and the partner. It cannot be a nonrecognition transaction for one and a recognition transaction for the other. And since there has been no prerequisite exchange of property, the admission of a partner with a capital interest in exchange for services cannot be a nonrecognition transaction for the partnership.

The tax policy problem is one of tax arbitrage. The proposed regulations, in effect, allow a partnership to purchase services in exchange for an interest in appreciated property without recognition of gain while obtaining a deduction (or capitalized amount, which might be depreciable or amortizable) without the concomitant recognition of gain—exactly the result rejected in *McDougal*, and a result clearly unobtainable outside of subchapter K. There is no policy reason or statutory support for allowing such a result through the use of subchapter K. The tax policy objections to the nonrecognition allowed by the proposed regulations could be avoided by limiting the partnership's deduction (or capitalized amount) to a pro rata portion of the partnership's aggregate basis for its assets. For example, if a service-provider partner is admitted to partnership that has assets with an aggregate basis of $20 and a fair market value of $200, and is given a capital account of $50, the partnership should be allowed a deduction (or capitalized amount) of only $5 ($20 × $50/$200). This approach eliminates the tax arbitrage, while avoiding current recognition. While at first blush it looks to be more administrable, the administrability advantage exists only if the partnership does not revalue the partnership's property and adjust the partners' capital accounts to reflect the revaluation pursuant to Treas. Reg. § 1.704–1(b)(2)(iv)(*f*). Thus, it might not be significantly more administrable. Nevertheless, even this solution would appear to constitute an attempt to amend the Code by regulation.

1.2. *Application of* McDougal *Principles to Exchange of Partnership Capital Interest for Services*

As noted above, if the principles of *McDougal* are applied to an existing partnership that admits a partner in exchange for services, the partnership recognizes gain or loss on the admission of the service partner. The partnership is taxed as if it transferred an undivided portion of each of its assets to the service partner as compensation, with gain and loss being recognized on the constructive transfer. This gain should be allocated to the other partners. As a corollary, the partnership constructively receives the property back from the service partner and takes a fair market basis in the recontributed undivided portion of each asset.

The following examples illustrate the application of the *McDougal* principle in a variety of contexts. All of the examples involve the admission of I in exchange for services to the GH Partnership, which holds a single asset, Blackacre. Note that even after the proposed regulations are adopted, if the transactions described in the examples transpired between two co-owners of property—G and H—who were not yet partners, and I performed the assumed services for G and H, with the result that the transfer of an undivided one-third interest in Blackacre gave rise to the GHI Partnership, the regulations would not provide G and H with nonrecognition and under *McDougal*, their gain would be recognized.

1.2.1 *Example of Admission of Service Partner in Exchange for Services Where Partnership is Entitled to a Deduction*

Assume that in exchange for services I is admitted to the GH Partnership, in which G and H previously were equal partners, as a full one third partner, obtaining a present vested capital interest. The partnership owns a single capital asset, Blackacre, having a fair market value of $180,000 and a basis of $60,000. G and H each have a basis in their partnership interest of $30,000. If in connection with I becoming a partner, the GH Partnership adjusts the book value of its assets and partners' capital accounts to fair market value, as permitted (and for practical purposes as required) by Treas.Reg. § 1.704–1(b)(2)(iv)(*f*), immediately before I is admitted as a partner, the GH Partnership balance sheet is as follows:

	Assets			Debts and Partners' Capital Accounts		
	Book	Tax Basis			Book	Tax Basis
Blackacre	$180,000	$60,000	G		$ 90,000	$30,000
			H		$ 90,000	$30,000
	$180,000	$60,000			$180,000	$60,000

If I receives a one third capital interest, G and H each reduce their capital accounts from $90,000 to $60,000, and I will receive a capital account of $60,000. As a result of receiving a capital account worth $60,000, I recognizes $60,000 of ordinary income and I's basis for his partnership interest is $60,000. As indicated by *McDougal,* however, the treatment of G and H, the original partners, and the determination of the partnership's basis in Blackacre, is a bit more complex. To tax all parties properly, including I, the entire transaction can be recast as follows.

1. The GH Partnership constructively transfers an undivided one third of Blackacre to I in exchange for services. On this transfer, the GH Partnership recognizes a gain of $40,000 (the $60,000 amount realized in the form of services, equal to 1/3 of the $180,000 fair market value of the property, minus 1/3 of the $60,000 basis in the property). See Treas. Reg. § 1.83–6(b). G and H must each recognize a proportionate share of this gain. Pursuant to § 705, G and H each increase the basis in their partnership interests by $20,000 as a result of the gain. Assuming that the payment to I is for a deductible expense, G and H also account for their pro rata share of this expense deduction and each decrease the basis in their partnership interests by $30,000 as a result of the partnership's $60,000 deduction. This results in a net decrease in the basis of G's and H's partnership interests of $10,000. At this interim point, the balance sheet of the partnership may be conceptualized as follows:

	Assets			Debts and Partners' Capital Accounts	
	Book	Tax Basis		Book	Tax Basis
2/3 Blackacre	$120,000	$40,000	G	$ 60,000	$20,000
			H	$ 60,000	$20,000
	$120,000	$40,000		$120,000	$40,000

2. Because I recognizes income of $60,000 on this hypothetical transfer of a one-third interest in Blackacre, I takes a basis in the one-third interest in Blackacre equal to that amount. When I constructively recontributes the one-third of Blackacre to the partnership, under § 721, I recognizes no gain. Under § 722, I's basis in his partnership interest is $60,000, his basis in the one-third interest in Blackacre, and under § 723 the GHI partnership takes a basis of $60,000 in this one third interest in Blackacre, which is added to the $40,000 basis in the other two-thirds of Blackacre, for a total basis of $100,000. After the transaction is completed, the GHI Partnership's balance sheet would be as follows:

	Assets			Debts and Partners' Capital Accounts	
	Book	Tax Basis		Book	Tax Basis
Blackacre	$180,000	$100,000	G	$ 60,000	$ 20,000
			H	$ 60,000	$ 20,000
			I	$ 60,000	$ 60,000
	$180,000	$100,000		$180,000	$100,000

1.2.2. *Example of Admission of Service Partner in Exchange for Services Where Partnership Must Capitalize Compensation for Services*

Assume alternatively that the payment for the services performed by I in the preceding example is not deductible to the partnership, but instead is a capital expense incurred to improve Blackacre. If this is true, from an economic perspective the total value of the improvements presumably is $90,000; I is contributing the services that produce two-thirds of the improvements, worth $60,000, for a one-third interest in unimproved Blackacre, worth $60,000, and is performing the services that create the remaining one-third of the improvement on his own account. The results of the transaction are as follows:

1. The GH Partnership constructively transfers an undivided one-third of Blackacre to I in exchange for services that produce a two-thirds interest in an improvement to Blackacre with a total value of $90,000, the two-thirds interest being worth $60,000. Again the GH Partnership recognizes a gain of $40,000, and pursuant to § 705, G and H each increase the basis in their partnership interests by $20,000 as a result of the gain recognition. In this case, however, there is no deduction. Instead the GH partnership capitalizes the $60,000 paid to I. At this interim point, the balance sheet of the partnership may be conceptualized as follows:

	Assets			Debts and Partners' Capital Accounts	
	Book	Tax Basis		Book	Tax Basis
2/3 Blackacre	$120,000	$ 40,000	G	$ 90,000	$ 50,000
2/3 Improvement	$ 60,000	$ 60,000	H	$ 90,000	$ 50,000
	$180,000	$100,000		$180,000	$100,000

2. Once again, I recognizes income of $60,000 and takes a basis in the one-third interest in Blackacre equal to that amount. When I constructively recontributes the one-third of Blackacre to the partnership, along with the remaining one-third interest in the improvements created by I's services, I's basis in his partnership interest under § 722 again is $60,000, I's basis in the one-third interest in Blackacre. The GHI partnership again takes a basis of $60,000 in this one third-interest in Blackacre under § 723, which is added to the $40,000 basis in the other two-thirds of Blackacre, for a total basis to the partnership of $100,000. Since I had no basis in the one-third interest in the improvements produced by his services, I does not increase his basis in his partnership interest with respect to this contribution and the partnership receives no basis in this portion of the improvements. After the transaction is completed, the GHI Partnership's balance sheet would be as follows.

	Assets			Debts and Partners' Capital Accounts	
	Book	Tax Basis		Book	Tax Basis
Blackacre	$180,000	$100,000	G	$ 90,000	$ 50,000
Improvements	$ 90,000	$ 60,000	H	$ 90,000	$ 50,000
			I	$ 90,000	$ 60,000
	$270,000	$160,000		$270,000	$160,000

1.2.3. *Example of Admission of Service Partner in Exchange for Services Where Partnership is Entitled to a Deduction and Holds Mortgaged Property*

Assume that in exchange for services I is admitted to the GH Partnership under the same circumstances as in the first example above involving the GHI partnership, except that Blackacre is subject to a mortgage of $30,000. Immediately before I is admitted as a partner, the GH Partnership balance sheet is as follows:

	Assets			Debts and Partners' Capital Accounts	
	Book	Tax Basis		Book	Tax Basis
Blackacre	$180,000	$60,000	Mortgage	$ 30,000	
			G	$ 75,000	$30,000
			H	$ 75,000	$30,000
	$180,000	$60,000		$180,000	$60,000

When the transaction is recast under the principles applied in the previous examples, the results are as follows.

1.   The transfer of an undivided one-third interest in Blackacre to I, subject to the mortgage, in exchange for I's services results in recognition of income to I of $50,000, the net fair market value of the encumbered one-third interest. (This is the same amount as results from viewing each of G and H as transferring to I one-third of each of their respective capital accounts.) When the GH Partnership constructively transfers the undivided one-third of Blackacre to I, the partnership recognizes a gain of $40,000, and pursuant to § 705, G and H each increase the basis in their partnership interests by $20,000 as a result of the gain. Since the payment to I is for a deductible expense, G and H also each decrease the basis in their partnership interests by $25,000 as a result of the partnership's $50,000 deduction. In addition, I assumes $10,000 of the mortgage attributable to the undivided one-third interest in Blackacre he has received, which reduces G's and H's liability for the mortgage by $5,000 each. Thus, G and H each decrease their basis by $5,000 as a result of a deemed distribution under § 752. This results in a net decrease in the basis of G's and H's partnership interests of $10,000. At this interim point, the balance sheet of the partnership may be conceptualized as follows:

	Assets			Debts and Partners' Capital Accounts	
	Book	Tax Basis		Book	Tax Basis
2/3 Blackacre	$120,000	$40,000	Mortgage	$ 20,000	
			G	$ 50,000	$20,000
			H	$ 50,000	$20,000
	$120,000	$40,000		$120,000	$40,000

2.   Because I recognizes income of $50,000 on this hypothetical transfer of a one-third interest in Blackacre, plus assumes a $10,000 mortgage lien on Blackacre, I takes a basis in the one-third interest in Blackacre equal to $60,000. When I constructively recontributes the one-third of Blackacre to the partnership, pursuant to § 721 I recognizes no gain. I's basis in his partnership interest is again $60,000, but the actual computation involves both § 722 and § 752, as follows:

(a)	basis of contributed property	$60,000
(b)	less liability relief (1/3 of mortgage	10,000)
(c)	plus share of partnership liabilities (1/3 × $30,000)	10,000
	Total basis in partnership interest	$60,000

Under § 723 the GHI partnership again takes a basis of $60,000 in this one-third interest in Blackacre, which is added to the $40,000 basis in the other two-thirds of Blackacre, for a total basis of $100,000. The bases of G and H in their partnership interests are unaffected by the recontribution of the encumbered one-third interest in Blackacre because both before and after contribution they each had a share of partnership debts equal to

$10,000. (Before the contribution the share was ½ × $20,000; after the contribution the share was 1/3 × $30,000.) After the transaction is completed, the GHI Partnership's balance sheet would be as follows.

	Assets			Debts and Partners' Capital Accounts	
	Book	Tax Basis		Book	Tax Basis
Blackacre	$180,000	$100,000	Mortgage	$ 30,000	
			G	$ 50,000	$ 20,000
			H	$ 50,000	$ 20,000
			I	$ 50,000	$ 60,000
	$180,000	$100,000		$180,000	$100,000

CHAPTER 3

TAXATION OF PARTNERSHIP TAXABLE INCOME TO THE PARTNERS

SECTION 1. PASS-THRU OF PARTNERSHIP INCOME AND LOSS

INTERNAL REVENUE CODE: Sections 61(a)(13); 701; 702; 703; 704(a), (b); 705; 706(a), (b); 6031.

REGULATIONS: Sections 1.702–1; 1.703–1; 1.706–1(a), (b), (d).

Subchapter K follows a conduit or pass-through approach to taxing partnership operations. Section 701 provides that a partnership is not taxable as an entity, but that the partners individually are liable for income taxes in their separate capacities. The starting point for determining the individual partner's tax liability, however, treats the partnership as a separate entity. Section 703(a) provides for the computation of partnership taxable income in the same manner as individuals, subject to certain exceptions.

After partnership taxable income is determined under § 703, in computing his individual taxable income each partner takes into account his "distributive share" of each of the separately stated items in § 702(a) and the residual taxable income or loss of the partnership, the so-called "bottom line" amount described in § 702(a)(8). Pursuant to § 704(a), a partner's distributive share is determined with reference to the partnership agreement, except as otherwise required by § 704(b), (c), or (e). Hence, the partners may provide in the agreement for a 50–50 sharing of profits and losses, a 75–25 sharing, etc. Partners may also designate different sharing ratios for profits and losses, e.g., A and B share profits 60 percent to A and 40 percent to B, but share losses 40 percent to A and 60 percent to B. Determination of a partner's distributive share is discussed in Chapter 4.

The conduit principle is the bedrock rule of Subchapter K. All partnership income must be taxed currently to the partners without regard to whether or not that income is distributed. This rule presents difficult problems in complex arrangements involving deferred distributions by the partnership to the partners, particularly where the partners' rights to future distributions of current income may be contingent. In analyzing such arrangements, it is helpful to keep in mind two other principles of partnership taxation. First, pursuant to § 705, a partner's basis in her partnership interest is increased by her share of partnership income; likewise a partner's basis in her partnership interest is decreased by his share of partnership losses and the amount of any distributions from the partnership. Second, if upon liquidation of a partner's interest solely for cash the partner receives an amount less than her basis in her partnership interest, the partner recognizes a deductible loss. Careful application of the principles governing maintenance of capital accounts, discussed at page 120, coupled with the application of these rules reveals that if a partner is taxed currently on undistributed partnership income and the partner never receives that income by way of a distribution, a loss deduction will be allowed at some time in the future. Consider how these principles relate to the holding in the following case.

United States v. Basye

Supreme Court of the United States, 1973.
410 U.S. 441.

■ MR. JUSTICE POWELL delivered the opinion of the Court.

* * *

I

Respondents, each of whom is a physician, are partners in a limited partnership known as Permanente Medical Group, which was organized in California in 1949. Associated with the partnership are over 200 partner physicians, as well as numerous nonpartner physicians and other employees. In 1959, Permanente entered into an agreement with Kaiser Foundation Health Plan, Inc., a nonprofit corporation providing prepaid medical care and hospital services to its dues-paying members.

Pursuant to the terms of the agreement, Permanente agreed to supply medical services for the 390,000 member-families, or about 900,000 individuals, in Kaiser's Northern California Region which covers primarily the San Francisco Bay area. In exchange for those services, Kaiser agreed to pay the partnership a "base compensation" composed of two elements. First, Kaiser undertook to pay directly to the partnership a sum each month computed on the basis of the total number of members enrolled in the health program. That number was multiplied by a stated fee, which originally was set at a little over $2.60. The second item of compensation—and the one that has occasioned the present dispute—called for the creation of a program, funded entirely by Kaiser, to pay retirement benefits to Permanente's partner and non-partner physicians.

The pertinent compensation provision of the agreement did not itself establish the details of the retirement program; it simply obligated Kaiser to make contributions to such a program in the event that the parties might thereafter agree to adopt one. As might be expected, a separate trust agreement establishing the contemplated plan soon was executed by Permanente, Kaiser, and the Bank of America Trust and Savings Association, acting as trustee. Under this agreement Kaiser agreed to make payments to the trust at a predetermined rate, initially pegged at 12 cents per health plan member per month. Additionally, Kaiser made a flat payment of

$200,000 to start the fund and agreed that its pro rata payment obligation would be retroactive to the date of the signing of the medical service agreement.

The beneficiaries of the trust were all partner and non-partner physicians who had completed at least two years of continuous service with the partnership and who elected to participate. The trust maintained a separate tentative account for each beneficiary. As periodic payments were received from Kaiser, the funds were allocated among these accounts pursuant to a complicated formula designed to take into consideration on a relative basis each participant's compensation level, length of service, and age. No physician was eligible to receive the amounts in his tentative account prior to retirement, and retirement established entitlement only if the participant had rendered at least 15 years of continuous service or 10 years of continuous service and had attained age 65. Prior to such time, however, the trust agreement explicitly provided that no interest in any tentative account was to be regarded as having vested in any particular beneficiary. The agreement also provided for the forfeiture of any physician's interest and its redistribution among the remaining participants if he were to terminate his relationship with Permanente prior to retirement.[4] A similar forfeiture and redistribution also would occur if, after retirement, a physician were to render professional services for any hospital or health plan other than one operated by Kaiser. The trust agreement further stipulated that a retired physician's right to receive benefits would cease if he were to refuse any reasonable request to render consultative services to any Kaiser-operated health plan.

The agreement provided that the plan would continue irrespective either of changes in the partnership's personnel or of alterations in its organizational structure. The plan would survive any reorganization of the partnership so long as at least 50% of the plan's participants remained associated with the reorganized entity. In the event of dissolution or of a nonqualifying reorganization, all of the amounts in the trust were to be divided among the participants entitled thereto in amounts governed by each participant's tentative account. Under no circumstances, however, could payments from Kaiser to the trust be recouped by Kaiser: once compensation was paid into the trust it was thereafter committed exclusively to the benefit of Permanente's participating physicians.

Upon the retirement of any partner or eligible non-partner physician, if he had satisfied each of the requirements for participation, the amount that had accumulated in his tentative account over the years would be applied to the purchase of a retirement income contract. While the program thus provided obvious benefits to Permanente's physicians, it also served Kaiser's interests. By providing attractive deferred benefits for Permanente's staff of professionals, the retirement plan was designed to "create

---

4. If, however, termination were occasioned by death or permanent disability, the trust agreement provided for receipt of such amounts as had accumulated in that physician's tentative account. Additionally, if, after his termination for reasons of disability prior to retirement, a physician should reassociate with some affiliated medical group his rights as a participant would not be forfeited.

an incentive" for physicians to remain with Permanente and thus "insure" that Kaiser would have a "stable and reliable group of physicians."

During the years from the plan's inception until its discontinuance in 1963, Kaiser paid a total of more than $2,000,000 into the trust. Permanente, however, did not report these payments as income in its partnership returns. Nor did the individual partners include these payments in the computations of their distributive shares of the partnership's taxable income. The Commissioner assessed deficiencies against each partner-respondent for his distributive share of the amount paid by Kaiser. Respondents, after paying the assessments under protest, filed these consolidated suits for refund.

The Commissioner premised his assessment on the conclusion that Kaiser's payments to the trust constituted a form of compensation to the partnership for the services it rendered and therefore was income to the partnership. And, notwithstanding the deflection of those payments to the retirement trust and their current unavailability to the partners, the partners were still taxable on their distributive shares of that compensation. Both the District Court and the Court of Appeals disagreed. They held that the payments to the fund were not income to the partnership because it did not receive them and never had a "right to receive" them. * * * They reasoned that the partnership, as an entity, should be disregarded and that each partner should be treated simply as a potential beneficiary of his tentative share of the retirement fund.[6] Viewed in this light, no presently taxable income could be attributed to these cash basis[7] taxpayers because of the contingent and forfeitable nature of the fund allocations. * * *

We hold that the courts below erred and that respondents were properly taxable on the partnership's retirement fund income. This conclusion rests on two familiar principles of income taxation, first, that income is taxed to the party who earns it and that liability may not be avoided through an anticipatory assignment of that income, and, second, that partners are taxable on their distributive or proportionate shares of current partnership income irrespective of whether that income is actually distributed to them. * * *

II

Section 703 of the Internal Revenue Code of 1954, insofar as pertinent here, prescribes that "[t]he taxable income of a partnership shall be

---

6. The Court of Appeals purported not to decide, as the District Court had, whether the partnership should be viewed as an "entity" or as a "conduit." 450 F.2d 109, 113 n. 5, and 115. Yet, its analysis indicates that it found it proper to disregard the partnership as a separate entity. After explaining its view that Permanente never had a right to receive the payments, the Court of Appeals stated: "When the transaction is viewed in this light, the partnership becomes a mere *agent* contracting on behalf of its members for payments to the trust for their ultimate benefit, rather than a *principal* which itself realizes taxable income." Id., at 115 (emphasis supplied).

7. Each respondent reported his income for the years in question on the cash basis. The partnership reported its taxable receipts under the accrual method.

computed in the same manner as in the case of an individual." 26 U.S.C. § 703(a). Thus, while the partnership itself pays no taxes, 26 U.S.C. § 701, it must report the income it generates and such income must be calculated in largely the same manner as an individual computes his personal income. For this purpose, then, the partnership is regarded as an independently recognizable entity apart from the aggregate of its partners. Once its income is ascertained and reported, its existence may be disregarded since each partner must pay a tax on a portion of the total income as if the partnership were merely an agent or conduit through which the income passed.[8]

In determining any partner's income, it is first necessary to compute the gross income of the partnership. One of the major sources of gross income, as defined in § 61(a)(1) of the Code, is "[c]ompensation for services, including fees, commissions, and similar items." 26 U.S.C. § 61(a)(1). There can be no question that Kaiser's payments to the retirement trust were compensation for services rendered by the partnership under the medical service agreement. These payments constituted an integral part of the employment arrangement. The agreement itself called for two forms of "base compensation" to be paid in exchange for services rendered—direct per-member, per-month payments to the partnership and other, similarly computed, payments to the trust. * * * Payments to the trust, much like the direct payments to the partnership, were not forfeitable by the partnership or recoverable by Kaiser upon the happening of any contingency.

Yet the courts below, focusing on the fact that the retirement fund payments were never actually received by the partnership but were contributed directly to the trust, found that the payments were not includable as income in the partnership's returns. The view of tax accountability upon which this conclusion rests is incompatible with a foundational rule, which this Court has described as "the first principle of income taxation: that income must be taxed to him who earns it." Commissioner v. Culbertson, 337 U.S. 733, 739–740 (1949). The entity earning the income—whether a partnership or an individual taxpayer—cannot avoid taxation by entering into a contractual arrangement whereby that income is diverted to some other person or entity. Such arrangements, known to the tax law as "anticipatory assignments of income," have frequently been held ineffective as means of avoiding tax liability. The seminal precedent, written over 40 years ago, is Mr. Justice Holmes' opinion for a unanimous Court in

---

8. There has been a great deal of discussion in the briefs and in the lower court opinions with respect to whether a partnership is to be viewed as an "entity" or as a "conduit." We find ourselves in agreement with the Solicitor General's remark during oral argument when he suggested that "[i]t seems odd that we should still be discussing such things in 1972." Tr. of Oral Arg. 14. The legislative history indicates, and the commentators agree, that partnerships are entities for purposes of calculating and filing informational returns but that they are conduits through which the taxpaying obligation passes to the individual partners in accord with their distributive shares. See, e.g., H.R.Rep. No. 1337, 83d Cong., 2d Sess., 65–66 (1954); S.Rep. No. 1622, 83d Cong., 2d Sess., 89–90 (1954) * * *.

Lucas v. Earl, 281 U.S. 111 (1930). There the taxpayer entered into a contract with his wife whereby she became entitled to one-half of any income he might earn in the future. On the belief that a taxpayer was accountable only for income actually received by him, the husband thereafter reported only half of his income. The Court, unwilling to accept that a reasonable construction of the tax laws permitted such easy deflection of income tax liability, held that the taxpayer was responsible for the entire amount of his income.

* * *

The principle of *Lucas v. Earl,* that he who earns income may not avoid taxation through anticipatory arrangements no matter how clever or subtle, has been repeatedly invoked by this Court and stands today as a cornerstone of our graduated income tax system. * * * And, of course, that principle applies with equal force in assessing partnership income.

Permanente's agreement with Kaiser, whereby a portion of the partnership compensation was deflected to the retirement fund, is certainly within the ambit of *Lucas v. Earl.* The partnership earned the income and, as a result of arm's-length bargaining with Kaiser, was responsible for its diversion into the trust fund. The Court of Appeals found the *Lucas* principle inapplicable because Permanente "never had the right itself to receive the payments made into the trust as current income." 450 F.2d, at 114. In support of this assertion, the court relied on language in the agreed statement of facts stipulating that "[t]he payments * * * were paid solely to fund the retirement plan, and were not otherwise available to [Permanente] * * *." Ibid. Emphasizing that the fund was created to serve Kaiser's interest in a stable source of qualified, experienced physicians, the court found that Permanente could not have received that income except in the form in which it was received. * * * We think it clear, however, that the tax laws permit no such easy road to tax avoidance or deferment. Despite the novelty and ingenuity of this arrangement, Permanente's "base compensation" in the form of payments to a retirement fund was income to the partnership and should have been reported as such.

III

Since the retirement fund payments should have been reported as income to the partnership, along with other income received from Kaiser, the individual partners should have included their shares of that income in their individual returns. 26 U.S.C. §§ 61(a)(13), 702, 704. For it is axiomatic that each partner must pay taxes on his distributive share of the partnership's income without regard to whether that amount is actually distributed to him. *Heiner v. Mellon,* 304 U.S. 271 (1938), decided under a predecessor to the current partnership provisions of the Code, articulates the salient proposition. After concluding that "distributive" share means the "proportionate" share as determined by the partnership agreement, id., at 280, the Court stated:

"The tax is thus imposed upon the partner's proportionate share of the net income of the partnership, and the fact that it may not be currently distributable, whether by agreement of the parties or by operation of law, is not material." Id., at 281.

Few principles of partnership taxation are more firmly established than that no matter the reason for nondistribution each partner must pay taxes on his distributive share. * * *

The courts below reasoned to the contrary, holding that the partners here were not properly taxable on the amounts contributed to the retirement fund. This view, apparently, was based on the assumption that each partner's distributive share prior to retirement was too contingent and unascertainable to constitute presently recognizable income. It is true that no partner knew with certainty exactly how much he would ultimately receive or whether he would in fact be entitled to receive anything. But the existence of conditions upon the actual receipt by a partner of income fully earned by the partnership is irrelevant in determining the amount of tax due from him. The fact that the courts below placed such emphasis on this factor suggests the basic misapprehension under which they labored in this case. Rather than being viewed as responsible contributors to the partnership's total income, respondent-partners were seen only as contingent beneficiaries of the trust. In some measure, this misplaced focus on the considerations of uncertainty and forfeitability may be a consequence of the erroneous manner in which the Commissioner originally assessed the partners' deficiencies. The Commissioner divided Kaiser's trust fund payments into two categories: (1) payments earmarked for the tentative accounts of *nonpartner* physicians; and (2) those allotted to *partner* physicians. The payments to the trust for the former category of nonpartner physicians were correctly counted as income to the partners in accord with the distributive-share formula as established in the partnership agreement.[16] The latter payments to the tentative accounts of the individual partners, however, were improperly allocated to each partner pursuant to the complex formula in the retirement plan itself, just as if that agreement operated as an amendment to the partnership agreement.

The Solicitor General, alluding to this miscomputation during oral argument, suggested that this error "may be what threw the court below off the track." It should be clear that the contingent and unascertainable nature of each partner's share under the retirement trust is irrelevant to the computation of his distributive share. The partnership had received as income a definite sum which was not subject to diminution or forfeiture. Only its ultimate disposition among the employees and partners remained uncertain. For purposes of income tax computation it made no difference that some partners might have elected not to participate in the retirement program or that, for any number of reasons, they might not ultimately receive any of the trust's benefits. Indeed, as the Government suggests, the

---

16. These amounts would be divided equally among the partners pursuant to the partnership agreement's stipulation that all income above each partner's drawing account "shall be distributed equally."

result would be quite the same if the "potential beneficiaries included no partners at all, but were children, relatives, or other objects of the partnership's largesse."[18] The sole operative consideration is that the income had been received by the partnership, not what disposition might have been effected once the funds were received.

IV

In summary, we find this case controlled by familiar and long-settled principles of income and partnership taxation. There being no doubt about the character of the payments as compensation, or about their actual receipt, the partnership was obligated to report them as income presently received. Likewise, each partner was responsible for his distributive share of that income. We, therefore, reverse the judgments and remand the case with directions that judgments be entered for the United States.

ILLUSTRATIVE MATERIAL

1. PARTNERSHIP TAXABLE INCOME AND SEPARATELY STATED ITEMS

Basye demonstrates the relationship between the determination of partnership taxable income and the treatment of the partnership itself as a mere conduit for purposes of imposing tax liability. While partnership taxable income is computed at the entity level, each partner is then currently taxed on his distributive share of that taxable income, even if it has not been distributed to him. This rule is so important to the operation of Subchapter K that it applies, as in *Basye,* even where the partnership agreement or a contractual agreement prevents the current distribution of income.

Partnership taxable income is computed following the same rules that govern the computation of the taxable income of any individual engaged in business, with a few specific statutory modifications. Section 703(a)(2) disallows deductions for personal exemptions, charitable contributions, net operating losses, foreign taxes, depletion on oil and gas wells, and the special deductions allowed to individuals under §§ 211–219. In addition, the standard deduction provided for individuals by § 63(b) is disallowed for partnerships. I.R.C. § 63(c)(6)(D). Because capital gains and losses are separately stated and flow through to the individual partners, who may carry over unused capital losses, Treas. Reg. § 1.703–1(a)(2)(viii) adds to the list of disallowed deductions the capital loss carryover deduction under § 1212. In addition, §§ 702(a) and 703(a)(1) require certain items entering

---

18. Brief for United States 21. For this reason, the cases relied on by the Court of Appeals, 450 F.2d, at 113, which have held that payments made into deferred compensation programs having contingent and forfeitable features are not taxable until received, are inapposite. Schaefer v. Bowers, 50 F.2d 689 (C.A.2 1931); Perkins v. Commissioner, 8 T.C. 1051 (1947); Robertson v. Commissioner, 6 T.C. 1060 (1946). Indeed, the Government notes, possibly as a consequence of these cases, that the Commissioner has not sought to tax the nonpartner physicians on their contingent accounts under the retirement plan. Brief for United States 21.

into the computation of an individual's income tax liability to be segregated and separately stated on the partnership's return. These items require separate consideration to determine their character as capital gain or loss or ordinary income or loss at the partner's level or the extent to which they are includable in or excludable or deductible from the partner's gross income. See also Treas. Regs. §§ 1.703–1(a), 1.702–1(a)(1)–(8). The separately stated items include capital gains and losses, § 1231 gains and losses, charitable contributions, dividends received (if there is a corporate partner), and foreign taxes. I.R.C. § 702(a)(1)–(6). Treas. Reg. § 1.702–1(a)(8)(i) and (ii) adds to the statutory list bad debt recoveries, wagering gains and losses, expenses for the production of nonbusiness income, medical expenses, dependents' care, alimony, taxes and interest paid to housing cooperatives, oil and gas intangible drilling and development costs, solid mineral exploration expenditures, gains and losses recognized under § 751(b) by a partnership possessing substantially appreciated inventory or unrealized receivables upon a disproportionate distribution, and any items of income, gain, loss deduction or credit subject to a specific allocation under the partnership agreement which differs from the general profit and loss ratio.

Because under Treas. Reg. § 1.702–2 each partner separately computes his individual net operating loss deduction by taking into account his distributive share of partnership items, any income or deduction item that requires special treatment in computing the partners' § 172 NOL deduction must be separately stated, even if not specifically identified in the regulations. Thus, the limitations on the deduction of passive losses under § 469, the disallowance of deductions for personal interest under § 163(h), and the limitation on the deduction of investment interest under § 163(d), require that investment interest paid or received be separately stated in many cases. See Rev. Rul. 84–131, 1984–2 C.B. 37 (requiring that interest paid be separately stated by a partnership which has any partner subject to the investment interest deduction limitations of § 163(d)); Rev. Rul. 86–138, 1986–2 C.B. 84 (extending the same rule to lower tier partnerships if any partner in an upper tier partnership is subject to § 163(d)).

Because § 108(d)(6) requires that the insolvency exception to discharge of indebtedness income be applied at the individual partner level rather than at the partnership level, partnership discharge of indebtedness income is a separately stated item under § 702(a). Rev. Rul. 92–97, 1992–2 C.B. 124. In Rev.Proc. 92–92, 1992–2 C.B. 505, the Service announced that it will not challenge the treatment by an insolvent or bankrupt partnership of a discharge of a purchase money indebtedness as an adjustment to purchase price under § 108(e)(5), rather than as separately stated cancellation of indebtedness income, if the discharge otherwise would have qualified as a purchase price adjustment, as long as all partners report the treatment consistently. In effect this permits an insolvent partnership to elect whether to treat the discharge as a purchase price reduction or to pass through discharge of indebtedness income that could be excluded only by insolvent partners.

Partnership business income (excluding separately stated items), which in general is the amount described in § 702(a)(8), is computed by including all of the income and deductions attributable to each separate business of the partnership. Because of the passive loss limitations of § 469, however, it may be necessary for a partnership to state separately the net income or loss from each separate business "activity" that it conducts; and this segregation will always be required of limited partnerships. Furthermore, when this segregation is required, it also is necessary to attribute separately to each such "activity" any partnership items that are separately stated as required by § 702(a)(1)–(7).

A partnership "loss" within the meaning of § 702(a)(8) is any excess of deductions over gross income, as distinguished from a loss within the meaning of § 165, which is a transactionally based concept. In Garcia v. Commissioner, 96 T.C. 792 (1991), the Commissioner attempted to apply § 165 to limit a general partner's deduction of his distributive share of the partnership's bottom line loss because the taxpayer-partner had filed suit against other partners demanding the return of his original capital investment. The Commissioner asserted that the taxpayer had not sustained a loss because the taxpayer had the prospect of recovery. In rejecting the Commissioner's argument, the court distinguished operational losses required to be taken into account by the partner under § 702(a) from a loss of capital investment cognizable under § 165, which is subject to limitation based on the prospect of recovery of the loss.

2.   CHARACTER OF ITEMS AND ACTIVITIES

2.1.   *Determination Based on Partnership Activities*

As previously indicated, § 702(a)(1)–(7) and the regulations thereunder adopt a conduit approach which requires the partners to report separately their distributive shares of any partnership item of income, credit or deduction receiving specialized treatment under the Code. These items must be separately stated on the partnership return. I.R.C. § 703(a)(1). Section 702(b) amplifies this conduit concept with respect to the segregated items by treating the partners as if "such item were realized directly from the source from which realized by the partnership, or incurred in the same manner as incurred by the partnership." Section 702(b) has been interpreted to require that the determination of the character of an income or deduction item be made by reference to its characterization at the partnership level. Treas. Reg. § 1.702–1(b); Podell v. Commissioner, 55 T.C. 429 (1970) (real property was not a capital asset in the hands of the partnership and hence the partner's share of income on the disposition of the asset was ordinary); Barham v. United States, 301 F.Supp. 43 (M.D.Ga.1969), aff'd per curiam, 429 F.2d 40 (5th Cir.1970) (same); Rev. Rul. 68–79, 1968–1 C.B. 310 (where an asset had a holding period of over six months in the hands of the partnership, the individual partner could treat the gain on disposition of the asset as long-term gain even though he had been a member of the partnership for less than six months). Consistent application of this approach would ignore the activities of the individual partner, as

where, for example, the partnership sells investment real estate and one of the partners in his individual capacity is a dealer in that type of property. Rev. Rul. 67–188, 1967–1 C.B. 216, held that a loss on real property determined to be § 1231 property at the partnership level retained that character in the hands of the individual partner, who was a real estate dealer; the ruling, however, did not deal expressly with the effect of the taxpayer's individual activity on the nature of the loss.

As illustrated by *Madison Gas & Electric,* page 6, whether a business has commenced or is in the startup period also is determined at the partnership level. The resolution of this issue affects whether expenses may be deducted currently or must be capitalized and amortized over sixty months under § 195.

Whether the partnership business is engaged in for profit is likewise determined at the partnership level. Brannen v. Commissioner, 722 F.2d 695 (11th Cir.1984). Where a limited partnership is involved, the relevant intent is that of the general partner. Deegan v. Commissioner, 787 F.2d 825 (2d Cir.1986). This inquiry is important in applying § 183, dealing with so-called "hobby losses" and in determining whether losses incurred by tax shelter partnerships will be disallowed. Unless there is a profit motive, the losses are allowed only to the extent of income from the activity. The absence of a joint profit motive, without which a partnership generally will not be found to exist, does not otherwise affect partnership treatment in these cases, a result which is somewhat difficult to square with the definitional test.

2.2. *Determination Based on Contributing Partner's Activities*

Section 724 provides special rules under which certain property contributed to a partnership by a partner retains the character that it had in the partner's hands. Unrealized receivables, such as cash method accounts receivable, retain their ordinary income character. I.R.C. § 724(a). Inventory, however, retains an ordinary income taint for only five years if the partnership holds the property as a capital asset or as § 1231 property (depreciable or real property held for use in the taxpayer's trade or business). I.R.C. § 724(b). After five years the character of gain or loss on the property will be determined with reference to the purpose for which the partnership holds the property at that time. Similarly, capital assets that have depreciated in value at the time of their contribution retain their capital character for five years after the date of the contribution, but only to the extent of the built-in loss at the time of the contribution. I.R.C. § 724(c). If the loss is greater because the property further depreciates while held by the partnership, the character of the excess loss is determined with reference to the purpose for which the partnership held the property. Suppose, for example, that a partner contributes land held as a capital asset, with a basis of $100 and a fair market value of $70, to a partnership that holds the land for sale to customers in the ordinary course of business. Four years later the partnership sells the land for $60. The $40 loss is treated as a $30 capital loss and a $10 ordinary loss. Under § 704(c), the $30 capital loss must be allocated to the partner who contributed the property. The purpose of these rules is to prevent the conversion of ordinary income into capital gain, thereby obtaining a rate preference, or capital loss into ordinary loss, thereby avoiding the capital loss limitation rules of § 1211 through the contribution of the property to a partnership.

3.   BASIS OF A PARTNER'S INTEREST

3.1.   *General*

In *Basye* the partnership income taxed to the physician partners is reflected as an upward adjustment to each partner's basis in his partnership interest under § 705(a). This adjustment to basis, coupled with the rule of § 731 that a partner does not recognize any gain on a partnership distribution unless the amount of money distributed exceeds the basis of the partnership interest, is the heart of the mechanism that assures that partners pay one level of tax on partnership profits. As income is earned by the partnership, the partner pays taxes on the income and adjusts his basis upward. When the previously taxed income is distributed, the partner owes no taxes and reduces his basis. Assuming that there have been no other events affecting the partner's basis, the basis after the distribution is identical to what it was before the income was earned. In the absence of a distribution, the partner will recover basis on sale or liquidation of the partner's interest in the partnership.

Section 705(a) prescribes a number of adjustments that must be taken into account in determining the basis of a partner's interest in a partnership. The partner starts with his basis determined under § 722 for contributions to the partnership; the basis is then increased by the partner's distributive share of the partnership profits, tax exempt receipts, and the excess of percentage depletion deductions over the adjusted basis of depletable property; and it is decreased by the partner's distributive share of losses, nondeductible expenditures not properly chargeable to a capital account, and distributions to the partner. See Treas. Reg. § 1.705–1(a)(2) and (3). However, a partner's basis is never reduced below zero. If the adjustment which would otherwise reduce basis below zero is a distribution, § 731 directs that the partner recognize gain.

While § 705(a)(1)(B) refers to "income * * * exempt from tax," Treas. Reg. § 1.705–1(a)(2)(ii) properly refers more broadly to "tax-exempt receipts." Suppose the partnership realizes gain on a transaction which it is not required to recognize because of the operation of a section like 1031 (deferral of gain and loss on like-kind exchanges), 1033 (deferral of gain on replacement of involuntarily converted property), etc. If the income item is merely deferred, rather than being completely tax-exempt, i.e. § 103 interest, there should not be an upward adjustment of partnership basis. Rev. Rul. 96–11, 1996–1 C.B. 140, describes the standard for determining whether a basis adjustment is appropriate: "In determining whether a transaction results in exempt income within the meaning of § 705(a)(1)(B), or a nondeductible, noncapital expenditure within the meaning of § 705(a)(2)(B), the proper inquiry is whether the transaction has a permanent effect on the partnership's basis in its assets, without a corresponding current or future effect on its taxable income."[1] If basis were increased when the unrecognized gain was realized, a "double crediting" of the accrued gain would be produced, i.e., once on the exchange and again on disposition of the property received in the exchange.

Similar principles apply with respect to losses and nondeductible expenditures not properly chargeable to a capital account (e.g., a fine that is nondeductible under § 162(f)). Deferred losses do not result in a basis reduction, but disallowed deductions and losses do result in a basis reduction. See Rev. Rul. 96–10, 1996–1 C.B. 138. In both cases the principle is that the partners' basis in their partnership interests should be reduced by the amount by which the partnership's basis in its assets was reduced. Thus, Rev. Rul. 96–11, supra, held that when a partnership makes a charitable contribution of appreciated property, the partners reduce their bases in their partnership interests only by their shares of the partnership's basis for the contributed property, even though each partner deducts her share of the fair market value of the contributed property. This treatment preserves the intended benefit of providing a deduction for the fair market value of the property without requiring the recognition of gain with respect to the appreciation. If the partners were required to reduce their bases in their partnership interests by the fair market value of the contributed property, then as a result of the basis reduction the gain attributable to the appreciation of the contributed property would be recognized upon a subsequent sale of the partnership interests.

Basis reduction is required whether deductions are disallowed at the partnership or individual partner level. See Rev. Rul. 89–7, 1989–1 C.B. 178 (a partner must reduce basis in his partnership interest by the full amount of § 179 expenditures deducted by the partnership even though the partner could not fully deduct his distributive share of such expenditures because of the application of the § 179(b)(1) limitation at the individual partner level).

3.2. *Alternative Basis Rules*

When a partnership is liquidated or a partnership interest sold, § 705(a) read literally would require a partner to go back to the beginning and laboriously determine her basis by adjusting each year for the distributive share of each item of the partnership and for each distribution to her. The same computation would be necessary to determine whether a distributive share of loss exceeds basis. The partnership records may or may not make this possible. Moreover, in a simple partnership, these computations are not really necessary. If the partners' profit and loss ratios are the same as their capital ratios, if their contributions were in cash or in properties whose basis and value were the same, if any current distributions were

---

1. Similarly, under § 265, which disallows deductions for expenses allocable to tax-exempt income, it has been held that nonrecognized gain is not income "wholly exempt" from tax and hence no disallowance of deduction is required. See, e.g., Hawaiian Trust Co. Ltd. v. United States, 291 F.2d 761 (9th Cir.1961); Commissioner v. McDonald, 320 F.2d 109 (5th Cir.1963).

likewise in cash or in such property and were pro rata, and if there have been no retirements or sales of a partner's interest (many partnerships meet these conditions) then a partner's basis may be obtained by a simple formula. Her basis will be her pro rata share of the total adjusted basis of the partnership's assets. In effect, all the adjustments of § 705(a) would in the end yield this result. Hence, § 705(b) authorizes Regulations permitting the use of this simple formula. It also authorizes variations of this formula taking account of adjustments necessary to reflect any significant discrepancies arising as a result of contributed property, transfers or distributions. See Treas. Reg. § 1.705–1(b).

4. ELECTIONS AND LIMITATIONS

Section 703(b) provides that, in general, elections under the Code are to be made by the partnership, except that the partners individually make separate elections in three cases: (1) elections to reduce the basis of depreciable property instead of other tax attributes when discharge of indebtedness income is not recognized under § 108(b)(5), relating generally to insolvent taxpayers, or § 108(c)(3), relating to cancellation of qualified real property indebtedness; (2) elections under § 617 with respect to mine exploration costs, and (3) elections with respect to the foreign tax credit under § 901. The partnership elects its taxable year and accounting method (including its inventory method), Treas. Reg. § 1.703–1(b)(1), as well as subsidiary elections with respect to MACRS deductions under § 168, the deduction of intangible drilling and development costs under § 263(c), see Rev. Rul. 68–139, 1968–1 C.B. 311, and election out of installment reporting under § 453(b).

In Demirjian v. Commissioner, 457 F.2d 1 (3d Cir.1972), a partnership realized a gain on the involuntary conversion of real property. The partners individually replaced the converted partnership property with property similar or related in service or use and attempted to elect nonrecognition of gain under § 1033. The court held that the gain was required to be recognized. Section 703(b) requires that the election under § 1033 be made by the partnership, and to be effective, the partnership, not the partners, must acquire the replacement property. See also McManus v. Commissioner, 583 F.2d 443 (9th Cir.1978) (same).

While Subchapter K is silent as to whether the limitations imposed by the Code on the amount of an item to be taken into account are to be imposed at the partner or partnership level, Treas. Reg. § 1.702–1(a)(8)(iii) applies the limitations in general at the partner level. Thus, the $3,000 limit on deducting capital losses against ordinary income, the percentage limitations on charitable contributions under § 170, the limitation on the deduction of investment interest under § 163(d), the $25,000 ceiling on the deduction against nonpassive income of losses from active participation real estate activities under § 469(i), and the limitation on percentage depletion of oil and gas under § 613A are applied at the partner level. Section 469, restricting the ability to deduct passive activity losses, also is applied at the individual partner level. Section 179(d)(8) applies the dollar value ceiling on expensing of depreciable property at *both* the partnership and individual partner level. In Hayden v. Commissioner, 204 F.3d 772 (7th Cir. 2000), the court upheld the validity of Treas. Reg. § 1.179–2(c)(2), which limits the amount of the partnership's § 179 deduction passed through to partners to the taxable income of the partnership. This result is dictated by §§ 179(b)(3)(A) and 179(d)(8) themselves.

5.   PARTNERSHIP TAXABLE YEAR

A partnership has its own taxable year under § 706(b)(1). Section 706(a) provides that a partner includes her distributive share of partnership items in the partner's taxable year in which or with which the partnership year ends. If the partnership's freedom to choose its taxable year were unfettered, this rule would permit significant tax deferral. Individual partners, who almost invariably use a calendar year, could cause the partnership to elect a fiscal year ending on January 31. Thus, all of the income of the partnership from February through December would not be reportable by the partners until the next calendar year. To prevent this type of avoidance, § 706(b) restricts the partnership's choice of its taxable year.

In general, a partnership must adopt the same taxable year as any one or more of its partners that have an aggregate interest in partnership profits and capital of more than fifty percent. Because most individuals use the calendar year, any partnership in which a majority of the partners are individuals usually will use a calendar year. If there is neither a more than fifty percent partner nor a majority group with the same year, the partnership must adopt the same taxable year as *all* of the "principal partners," who are the partners with a five percent or more interest in profits or capital.[2]

If neither the majority interest rule nor the principal partner rule can be used to determine a taxable year, Treas. Reg. § 1.706–1 requires the partnership to adopt the taxable year that results in the least aggregate deferral of reporting income by the partners. The aggregate deferral for a year is the sum of the products derived by multiplying the number of months of partnership income that is deferred into a later taxable year of each partner by that partner's interest in partnership income. Treas. Reg. § 1.706–1(b)(3)(i). The partnership must adopt the taxable year that produces the lowest sum when compared to other partnership taxable years. For example, if the ABC partnership has three equal partners A, with a January 31st fiscal year, B, with a July 31st fiscal year, and C, with a calendar year, the partnership must adopt a calendar year under Treas.

---

2. When determining a partnership's permitted year, Treas. Reg. § 1.706–1(b)(6) generally disregards any foreign partners who are not subject to U.S. taxation on a net basis (i.e., foreign partners who are not allocated any effectively connected income or, if claiming treaty benefits, that do not have a permanent establishment). This rule does not apply if as a result the partnership year would be determined with reference to domestic partners no one of which holds at least a 10 percent interest and which in the aggregate hold less than 20 percent of the partnership interests.

Reg. § 1.706–1 because the year ending on December 31 is the year of least aggregate deferral.

Year End	Interest in Partnership Profits	1/31 Year Months of Deferral	Interest X Deferral	7/31 Year Months of Deferral	Interest X Deferral	12/31 Year Months of Deferral	Interest X Deferral
A 1/31	33.3%	0	0	6	2.00	1	0.33
B 7/31	33.3%	6	2.00	0	0	7	2.33
C 12/31	33.3%	11	3.66	5	1.67	0	0
Sum			5.66		3.67		2.66

The methodology for computing least aggregate deferral is illustrated in Temp. Reg. § 1.706-1(b)(3).

Under the rules of § 706(b), a partnership may be compelled to change its taxable year if new partners are admitted or, in some cases, if existing partners' percentage interests change. For example, suppose that in the case of the ABC partnership described in the preceding paragraph on February 1, 2006, C sells his interest to A, who becomes a two-thirds partner. Under § 706(b)(1)(B)(i) the partnership must adopt a January 31st fiscal year. Section 706(b)(4)(B) provides, however, that once the partnership's taxable year has been changed under the "majority interest" rule, a subsequent change will not be required during the first two years following the initial change. Thus, continuing the above example, if on February 1, 2007, D and E, each having a July 31st fiscal year, were admitted to the ABC partnership as one-fifth partners, the partnership would not be required to change to a July 31st fiscal year (the year of B, D and E, who together hold three-fifths of the partnership interests), until after the fiscal year ending on January 31, 2009.

These strictures on the adoption of fiscal years by partnerships are relaxed by § 706(b)(1)(C), which allows a partnership to adopt a different taxable year with the permission of the Internal Revenue Service if the partnership can establish a business purpose for the fiscal year. The statute specifically provides that "deferral of income to partners shall not be treated as a business purpose." Rev.Proc. 87–32, 1987–2 C.B. 396, modified by Rev.Proc. 92–85, 1992–2 C.B. 490, and Rev.Proc. 93–28, 1993–2 C.B. 344, set forth procedures for Internal Revenue Service approval under § 704(b)(1)(C) of a different taxable year that coincides with the partnership's "natural business year." A partnership's natural business year is any twelve month period in the last two months of which the partnership realizes twenty-five percent of its gross receipts (under the method of accounting used to prepare its tax returns) for three consecutive years. If the partnership has more than one natural business year, it may only adopt the one in which the highest percentage of gross receipts are received in the last two months. Rev. Rul. 87–57, 1987–2 C.B. 117, explains the factors to be considered and deals with eight fact patterns in which the partnership does not have a natural business year under Rev.Proc. 87–32 or desires a taxable year different from its natural business year. Under the facts and circumstances test of Rev. Rul. 87–57, a business purpose for a particular year is not established merely by the use of a particular year for regulatory, financial accounting, or administrative purposes. If the desired taxable year creates deferral or distortion, which according to the ruling always occurs if the requested year differs from the taxable year of the partners, the partnership "must demonstrate compelling reasons for the requested tax year."

To prevent backdoor avoidance of the rules restricting the choice of the partnership's taxable year, § 706(b)(2) prohibits a principal partner from changing to a taxable year different from the partnership unless the partner can establish a business purpose for the change.

The rigid rules of § 706, limiting flexibility in choosing the partnership's taxable year, are ameliorated by § 444. This provision allows a partnership to elect a taxable year other than that required by § 706, provided that the selected year does not end more than three months before the end of the required year, even if there is no business purpose for the selected year. Thus, for example, if a partnership is required to use the calendar year because its partners use the calendar year and it either has no natural business year or no business purpose for a different year, it nevertheless may elect to adopt a fiscal year ending in September, October, or November.

If an election is made under § 444, the partnership must make a payment computed under § 7519 to compensate the Treasury for the deferral of taxes. This is a nondeductible entity level payment which is not credited against the partners' individual tax liabilities. (This payment in effect converts the interest free loan generated by any tax deferral resulting from the use of a fiscal year into an interest bearing loan.) The payment may, however, be refunded in a future year in which the use of a fiscal year does not effect deferral of taxes. See Semmes, Bowen & Semmes v. United States, 30 Fed.Cl. 134 (1993), aff'd by order, 34 F.3d 1080 9 Fed. Cir. (1994) (no interest accrues on § 7519 deposit between date of payment and date of refund). Sections 444 and 7519 do not apply to a partnership which qualifies for a fiscal year under Rev.Proc. 87–32 or Rev. Rul. 87–57.

The effect of termination of a partnership, the sale of a partnership interest, and the death or retirement of a partner on the partnership's and the partners' taxable years are considered later under those topics.

6.   SPECIAL RULES FOR ELECTING LARGE PARTNERSHIPS

Partnerships with more than 100 partners may elect to compute taxable income and state items to partners under §§ 771–777, as "electing large partnerships." Section 772 permits netting of several partnership items that normally would be passed through to the partners as separately stated items, rather than separately stating the items as otherwise required by § 702(a). Electing large partnerships are defined in § 775. The election does not apply to service partnerships, nor are service partners counted as partners for purposes of identifying a large partnership. I.R.C. § 775(b).

Similar to the rules of § 703, § 773(a)(1) and (b) provides for the computation of the taxable income of an electing large partnership in the same manner as an individual except that certain enumerated items must be separately stated and the partnership is not allowed deductions for personal exemptions, net operating losses, and additional itemized deductions for individuals. Unlike a normal partnership, which is denied a charitable contribution deduction by § 703(a)(2), an electing large partnership is allowed deductions for charitable contributions in computing taxable income, but the deduction is limited to ten percent of the partnership's taxable income, as modified in § 170(b)(2). I.R.C. § 773(b)(2). Also, under § 773(b)(3), miscellaneous itemized deductions, such as investment expenses, are deductible by an electing large partnership in computing adjusted gross income without regard to the two percent limitation of § 67, but at the price of disallowance of 70 percent of the miscellaneous itemized deductions.

The principal advantage for electing large partnerships is the ability provided by § 772 to net certain items such as passive activity income and expense and capital gains and losses for purposes of reporting to partners. Thus, under § 772(a)(1), an electing large partnership must separately state its *net* taxable income or loss from all passive loss limitation activities combined. For this purpose, passive loss limitation activities include any activity that involves the active conduct of a trade or business and any rental activities. I.R.C. § 772(d)(1). Section 772(c)(2) requires that each partner treat this net income or loss as being derived from a single passive activity. The at-risk and passive activity loss limitations of §§ 465 and 469 are then applied at the partner level. I.R.C. § 772(a)(3)(B). However, with respect to the interests of a general partner, the passive activity loss limitation will be applied separately to determine whether the income or loss of the general partner is passive activity income or loss. I.R.C. § 772(f). Net taxable income or loss from other activities is to be treated by the partners as investment (portfolio) income or loss. I.R.C. § 772(c)(3).

Section 772(a) also provides special treatment for some specific items. Tax exempt interest is separately stated. Net alternative minimum tax adjustments and preferences are combined at the partnership level and separately stated. Alternative minimum tax adjustments and preferences are separately computed for passive loss limitation activities and other activities. I.R.C. § 772(a)(5). Section 773(c) addresses partnership discharge of indebtedness income by excluding discharge of debt from partnership taxable income and from any of the items required to be separately stated under § 772(a). Instead, discharge of indebtedness income is separately stated to the partners who must individually account for the income under the provisions of § 108.

The election under §§ 771 though 777 is in fact only narrowly available. Relatively few partnerships have more than 100 partners. Many of the partnerships with more than 100 partners are engaged in the practice of law or accounting. Such service partnerships are effectively excluded from "electing large partnership" status by § 775(b)(2). More broadly, § 775(b) generally results in the election being available only to partnerships with more than 100 partners who do not perform substantial services in connection with the partnership's business. This largely confines the rules to large limited partnerships and to general partnerships in the oil and gas industry, although in the future there may come to exist a number of limited liability companies to which the rules could apply. On the other side, the ambit of the electing large partnership rules is hemmed-in by § 7704, discussed at page 31, which classifies as a corporation for tax purposes any partnership that is publicly traded.

7. PARTNERSHIP TAX RETURNS AND AUDIT PROCEDURES

7.1. *General*

As previously noted, § 6031 requires that a partnership return be filed. Section 6698 imposes additional penalties, over and above the general failure to file penalty of § 7203, on any partnership that fails to file a *complete* partnership tax return. Individual partners are liable for the penalty to the extent of their liability for partnership debts generally.

Sections 6221 through 6231 establish a procedure under which audits of partnerships, other than certain small partnerships, are conducted at the partnership level instead of by auditing the partners individually. Small partnerships excluded from these rules are partnerships that have ten or fewer partners each of which is a resident individual, a deceased partner's estate, or a C corporation. Section 6222 requires a partner to report partnership items on her own return consistently with the treatment on the partnership return, unless the partner has received incorrect information from the partnership or the partner identifies the inconsistent treatment on her return. Any partnership item reported by a partner consistently with the partnership return can be adjusted only in a partnership audit proceeding. I.R.C. § 6225.

Unless the partnership has more than 100 partners, all partners must be notified by the Internal Revenue Service of the commencement of a partnership audit, are entitled to participate in the proceedings, and must be given notice of the final partnership administrative adjustment resulting from the proceeding. If the partnership has more than 100 partners, generally only partners with a profits interest of at least one percent are entitled to notice from the IRS and to participate in the audit. Partnerships must designate a "tax matters partner," who is responsible for notifying other partners of the audit and the final partnership administrative adjustment and keeping all of the partners informed of the administrative and judicial proceedings with respect to the audit. I.R.C. §§ 6223; 6224(a). See Chef's Choice Produce, Ltd. v. Commissioner, 95 T.C. 388 (1990)(partnership audit procedures applied even though partnership has been dissolved between filing of return and audit; Tax Court can designate tax matters partner selected by IRS).

The Internal Revenue Service must offer to settle with all partners on consistent terms, and the tax matters partner generally may settle on behalf of non-notice partners. I.R.C. § 6224(c). The final partnership administrative adjustment is binding on all partners, subject to judicial review. The tax matters partner has ninety days after the notice of the final partnership administrative adjustment to seek judicial review. If the tax matters partner does not act within sixty days, any other partner may seek judicial review within 150 days of the date of the final partnership administrative adjustment. Special rules are provided in § 6226 to govern jurisdiction.

Similarly, § 6227 provides special rules governing requests for refunds, termed "administrative adjustment requests," with respect to partnership items. Section 6228 controls judicial review of the denial of such requests. As with audits, the tax matters partner generally may act on behalf of the partnership.

These rules do not apply to partnerships with ten or fewer partners as long as none of the partners is a pass-through entity. A partnership not subject to these procedures may elect to be governed by the partnership audit rules; the election can be revoked only with the consent of the Commissioner. I.R.C. § 6231(a)(1)(B).

Under § 6231(g) the Commissioner is entitled to reasonably rely on the partnership return to determine whether the partnership audit rules are applicable. However, if the Internal Revenue Service issues a statutory notice of deficiency to a partner without complying with the partnership audit procedures in a case to which they apply, the notice of deficiency is not valid with respect to the partnership items. See Maxwell v. Commissioner, 87 T.C. 783 (1986) (portion of Tax Court petition relating to partnership items dismissed for lack of jurisdiction, and IRS barred from assessing a deficiency based on the partnership items prior to the termination of the partnership audit proceedings); Stieha v. Commissioner, 89 T.C. 784 (1987) (Tax Court petition dismissed for lack of jurisdiction). Clovis I v. Commissioner, 88 T.C. 980 (1987), held that mere notice of a *proposed* final partnership administrative adjustment, analogous to the "30 day letter" that normally precedes a statutory notice of deficiency, is not a final partnership administrative adjustment; a Tax Court petition based on the proposed final partnership administrative adjustment is premature and will be dismissed for lack of jurisdiction. See also GAF Corp. v. Commissioner, 114 T.C. 519 (2000), which followed *Maxwell* to hold that the Tax Court lacks subject matter jurisdiction to consider a deficiency notice issued to a partner prior to completion of partnership level proceedings. The deficiency notice, based on items affected by the partnership proceeding, was invalid. Determination of items at the partner level must wait until resolution of the partnership proceeding.

Conversely, if a partnership is subject to the partnership audit procedure, a partner may not contest partnership items in an individual proceeding.[3] Treas. Reg. § 301.6221–1(a). If a partnership item adjusted in a partnership level proceeding affects a nonpartnership item, e.g., net § 1231 gains versus losses or capital loss limitations, computational adjustments to the individual partners' returns are made and any additional tax is assessed without an additional deficiency notice. I.R.C. § 6230(a)(1). However, normal individual deficiency procedures apply to "affected items" that require factual determination at the individual partner level. I.R.C. § 6230(a)(2). See Roberts v. Commissioner, 94 T.C. 853 (1990) (partner's "at-risk" amount under § 465, which was limited by a "side agreement," was not a partnership item); Crowell v. Commissioner, 102 T.C. 683 (1994) (partner may not raise in his individual "affected items" proceeding defenses that properly should have been raised in the partnership level proceeding).

7.2. *Electing Large Partnerships*

Partnership level audit rules for electing large partnerships under §§ 771 et seq., page 92, are provided in §§ 6240–6255. Partners in electing large partnerships are required by § 6241(a) to report all partnership items consistently with the partnership return. If a partner reports an item inconsistently, it will be treated as a mathematical or clerical error and any additional tax may be assessed against that partner without following the deficiency procedures. I.R.C. § 6241(b).

Electing large partnerships also are subject to the unified audit rules of §§ 6221 through 6234. Thus, the tax treatment of partnership items is determined at the partnership level, in a single proceeding to resolve the issue with respect to all partners, rather than at the individual partner level.[4] Section 6242, however, provides special rules for applying the unified audit procedures to electing large partnerships. Unlike in the case of normal partnerships, adjustments generally flow through to the partners for the year in which the adjustment occurs. I.R.C. § 6242(a). Current partners' shares of the partnership's current year's items of income, gain, loss, deduction, or credit are adjusted to reflect partnership adjustments made in that year with respect to an earlier year. Except in the case of changes to partners' distributive shares, see I.R.C. § 6241(c)(2)(A), adjustments generally do not affect the returns of any partners for prior years. I.R.C. § 6241(c)(1). Instead of passing an adjustment through to its partners, a partnership may elect to pay an "imputed underpayment" of tax.

---

3. Under § 6230(a)(3) a spouse of a partner may assert in an individual proceeding that the innocent spouse rules of § 6013(e) apply to the assessment. The Commissioner must abate the assessment against the spouse whose claim of innocent spouse relief (but not the partnership item) must be determined under the regular deficiency procedures.

4. An electing large partnership must designate a person (who need not be a partner) to act on its behalf in the proceedings.

I.R.C. § 6255(b). Individual partners have no right to participate in the audit process but are bound by the representative's actions and the decision in the proceeding. Only the partnership, and not partners individually, can petition for a readjustment of partnership items. Furthermore, only the partnership, and not partners individually, can petition the Tax Court for a determination of partnership items. I.R.C. § 6252.

I.R.C. § 6242(a)(2). The amount of imputed underpayment generally is calculated by netting the adjustments to the income and loss items of the partnership and multiplying that amount by the highest tax rate in effect for the year. I.R.C. § 6242(b)(4). If a partnership ceases to exist before a partnership adjustment takes effect, § 6255(d) requires the former partners to take the adjustment into account as provided in the regulations.

Although the partners of an electing large partnership generally are liable for any deficiency, the partnership, rather than the partners individually, generally is liable for any interest and penalties that result from a partnership adjustment. I.R.C. § 6242(b)(1). Interest, computed on the "imputed underpayment" amount determined under § 6242(b)(4), runs from the year with respect to which the adjustment was made, even though the adjusted items themselves flow through for the current year. I.R.C. § 6242(b)(2). No deductions are allowed for any payments of interest or penalties. I.R.C. § 6242(e).

SECTION 2.   LIMITATION ON PARTNERS' DEDUCTIONS OF PARTNERSHIP LOSSES

INTERNAL REVENUE CODE: Sections 704(d); 752.

REGULATIONS: Section 1.704–1(d).

Section 704(d) limits the deductibility of a partner's distributive share of a partnership loss to the partner's basis for her partnership interest. This limitation is related to the reduction of a partner's basis in her partnership interest by an amount equal to the partner's share of partnership losses and separately stated deductions pursuant to § 705; since the partner cannot reduce the basis of her partnership interest below zero, the pass through of deductions that otherwise would reduce the partner's basis for her partnership interest below zero is disallowed. Any disallowed deductions are held in suspense, to be allowed when a basis exists, as by additional contributions, a future share of partnership earnings left in the partnership, or the incurring of a partnership liability. See Treas. Reg. § 1.704–1(d). Thus, suppose A contributes $100,000 cash and B contributes $50,000 cash, but they agree to share profits and losses equally because B will devote her full time to the partnership's business but A will work only part time in the partnership's business. The partnership spends $125,000 on deductible research costs. A can deduct $62,500, but B can deduct only $50,000 currently. B may deduct an additional $12,500 when she obtains sufficient basis. Suppose the partnership realizes a loss in 2006 but an individual partner wishes to postpone the recognition of the loss until 2007. Can the partner withdraw her partnership capital at year end, hold the loss in the suspense account, and then recognize it in 2007 upon a recontribution of the capital to the partnership, an action which would thereby reestablish her basis? Rev. Rul. 66–94 addresses this issue.

Revenue Ruling 66–94

1966–1 C.B. 166.

Advice has been requested as to the manner in which a partner should compute the basis of his partnership interest under section 705(a) of the Internal Revenue Code of 1954 for purposes of determining the extent to which his distributive share of partnership losses will be allowed as a deduction, and the extent to which gain will be realized by a partner upon the distribution of cash to him by the partnership.

During the taxable year, A, a member of the partnership, contributed $50x$ dollars to the partnership as his initial capital contribution, and received $30x$ dollars as a cash distribution from the partnership. A's distributive share of partnership losses at the end of its taxable year was $60x$ dollars.

Section 705(a) of the Code provides, in part, that the adjusted basis of a partner's interest in a partnership shall be the basis of such interest determined under section 722 of the Code (relating to contributions to a partnership)—(1) increased by the sum of his distributive share for the taxable year and prior taxable years of taxable income of the partnership, tax exempt income of the partnership, and the excess of depletion deductions over the basis of depletable property, and (2) decreased, but not below zero, by distributions by the partnership as provided in section 733 and by the sum of his distributive share of partnership losses and nondeductible partnership expenditures not chargeable to capital account.

Section 1.704–1(d)(1) of the Income Tax Regulations provides, in part, that a partner's distributive share of partnership loss will be allowed only to the extent of the adjusted basis (before reduction by current year's losses) of such partner's interest in the partnership at the end of the partnership taxable year in which such loss occurred.

Section 1.704–1(d)(2) of the regulations provides, in part, that in computing the adjusted basis of a partner's interest for the purpose of ascertaining the extent to which a partner's distributive share of partnership loss shall be allowed as a deduction for the taxable year, the basis shall first be increased under section 705(a)(1) of the Code and decreased under section 705(a)(2) of the Code, except for losses of the taxable year and losses previously disallowed.

Section 1.731–1(a) of the regulations provides, in part, that where money is distributed by a partnership to a partner, no gain or loss shall be recognized to the partner except to the extent that the amount of money distributed exceeds the adjusted basis of the partner's interest in the partnership immediately before the distribution. For purposes of sections 731 and 705 of the Code, advances or drawings of money or property against a partner's distributive share of income shall be treated as current distributions made on the last day of the partnership taxable year with respect to such partner.

Based on the foregoing, it is concluded that:

(1) In computing A's adjusted basis for his interest in the partnership under section 705(a) of the Code, A's original basis, which is determined under section 722 relating to contributions to the partnership, should be decreased by first deducting distributions made to A by the partnership and thereafter, by deducting his distributive share of partnership losses. However, A's basis for his interest in the partnership may not be reduced below zero. Thus:

A's contribution to the partnership....................	50x dollars
Deduct cash distributions made to A by the partnership	$-$30x dollars
	20x dollars
Deduct A's distributive share of losses (60 $\times$ dollars) but only to the extent that A's basis is not reduced below zero	$-$20x dollars
A's basis for his interest in the partnership under section 705 of the Code	$-$0

(2) In order to determine the extent to which A's distributive share of partnership losses will be allowed as a deduction, A's basis for his interest in the partnership computed in accordance with section 705(a) of the Code, should be determined without taking into account his distributive share of partnership losses for the taxable year. Thus:

A's contribution to the partnership....................	50x dollars
Deduct cash distribution made to A by the partnership	$-$30x dollars
	20x dollars
A's distributive share of partnership losses for the taxable year are not taken into account.................	$-$0
A's basis for determining the amount of his allowable partnership losses	20x dollars

(3) In order to determine the extent to which gain will be realized by A upon the distribution of cash to him by the partnership, A's basis for his interest in the partnership computed in accordance with section 705(a) of the Code, should be determined without taking into account cash distributions made to him by the partnership during its current taxable year. Thus:

A's contribution to the partnership	50 x dollars
Cash distributions made by the partnership to A during the taxable year are not taken into account	$-$0
	50 x dollars
Deduct A's distributive share of partnership losses to the extent allowed by section 704(d) of the Code. (See examples (1) and (2).)	$-$20 x dollars
A's basis for determining the amount of gain he realized upon the distribution of cash to him by the partnership.......................................	30 x dollars

A may deduct his distributive share of the partnership loss to the extent of 20 *x* dollars (see example 2) and he realizes no gain from the cash distribution of 30 *x* dollars because his basis for determining the amount of gain upon such distribution is 30 *x* dollars (example 3).

ILLUSTRATIVE MATERIAL

1.   TRANSFER OF AN INTEREST WITH SUSPENDED LOSSES

Sennett v. Commissioner, 752 F.2d 428 (9th Cir.1985), upheld the portion of Treas. Reg. § 1.704–1(d) requiring that a partner continue to be a partner to take advantage of the carryover of disallowed losses. In that case the taxpayer's share of partnership losses for 1968, his last year as a partner when his basis was zero, was $109,061. At the close of 1968 he sold his partnership interest back to the partnership in consideration of the partnership's promise to pay him $250,000 in the future, and he agreed to repay the partnership his share of the 1968 losses. In 1969, the partnership's obligation to Sennett was modified to call for a $240,000 payment, and the transaction was completed by the partnership setting off the $109,061 due from Sennett against the $240,000 and paying him only $130,939. Sennett claimed the suspended $109,061 loss in 1969 as an ordinary deduction and reported $240,000 of long term capital gain. Sennett treated the set off as increasing his basis from zero to $109,061, which enabled him to claim the loss. He reduced his basis to zero and acknowledged the set off amount as included in his amount realized resulting in the $240,000 of long-term capital gain. The Commissioner, however, treated Sennett simply as having received $130,939 in exchange for a partnership interest with a basis of zero. The court held that since Sennett was no longer a partner in 1969 he could not have any basis in a partnership interest. Thus, no carryover of the ordinary loss deduction was allowed. Instead the repayment was an offset to the amount realized by Sennett on the sale of the partnership interest.

2.   RELATIONSHIP OF SECTION 704(d) TO CHANGES IN SHARES OF PARTNERSHIP INDEBTEDNESS

Suppose that the CD partnership, an equal partnership in which C and D have identical capital accounts, realizes a $5,000 loss in 1996, and D, whose distributive share of that loss is $2,500 (50%), has a zero basis. If the partnership were to borrow $5,000, under § 752(a), D would be treated as contributing $2,500 in cash and his basis would be increased by that amount. As a result, § 704(d) would not limit D's loss deduction. See Treas. Reg. § 1.704–1(d)(4), Ex. (2). Will year-end borrowing for the purpose of increasing basis to permit the deduction of losses be recognized? In Corum v. United States, 268 F.Supp. 109 (W.D.Ky.1967), a road building partnership borrowed funds on December 28th and repaid the loan on the following January 15th. The business purpose for the loan was to improve the liquidity on the partnership's year-end balance sheet, which was used by governmental authorities to determine the financial capability of the contractors bidding on jobs. The taxpayer was permitted to include his share of the indebtedness in basis for purposes of applying § 704(d) and thereby allowed to deduct his entire distributive share of the partnership's loss for the year.

If a new partner is admitted during a year in which a partnership with debts incurs a loss and, as a result, existing partners are treated under § 752(b) as receiving a cash distribution that reduces basis, when should the partners' basis be determined for purposes of applying § 704(d)? Suppose that G is admitted to the EF partnership on December 30. Before G's admission E and F each had a basis in his partnership interest of $160 and the partnership had debts of $300. During the current year prior to December 31, the EF partnership incurred a loss of $300, all of which will be allocated to E and F under § 706(d), discussed at page 173. As a result of G's admission on December 31, before taking into account the loss, E and F each have a basis of $110 ($160 minus the $50 of debt of which each was relieved on C's admission) and a distributive share of the loss of $150. If they can use their December 30 basis the entire loss is deductible by them. Richardson v. Commissioner, 693 F.2d 1189 (5th Cir.1982), held that the end of year basis was controlling for applying § 704(d). Hence, E and F may each deduct only $110 of the loss. G cannot deduct any of the loss by virtue of § 706(d).

3.   OTHER LIMITATION ON PARTNERS' LOSS DEDUCTIONS

Even if a loss is not limited by § 704(d), deductions may be restricted by § 465, the at-risk rules, or § 469, dealing with passive losses. Both of these provisions are particularly applicable to limited partners, but may also affect general partners. Sections 465 and 469 are discussed in Chapter 7.

CHAPTER 4

DETERMINING PARTNERS' DISTRIBUTIVE SHARES

INTERNAL REVENUE CODE: Sections 702; 704(a)–(e); 761(c).

REGULATIONS: Sections 1.702–1; 1.704–1(a); 1.761–1(c).

Section 702(a) requires each partner to take into account his distributive share of each separately stated item and the residual taxable income or loss entering into the partnership's taxable income. Section 704(a) provides that a partner's distributive share is determined by the partnership agreement, except as otherwise provided in Subchapter K. The partnership agreement is broadly defined as the original agreement plus any modifications agreed to by all the partners or adopted in any other manner provided by the partnership agreement. The modifications may be oral or written and may be made with respect to a particular taxable year subsequent to the close of that year but before the due date for filing the partnership return. Local law governs any matter on which the agreement is silent. I.R.C. § 761(c); Treas. Reg. § 1.761–1(c).

The latitude provided by Subchapter K, allowing partners to allocate items of income, expense, or loss as they choose, is one of the unique aspects of Subchapter K. Thus, if two partners agree to split partnership net profits or losses in a 75–25 ratio, their distributive shares of each item in § 702(a) will be in that ratio. See Treas. Reg. § 1.704–1(b)(1)(vii). If they agree that profits are to be split 50–50, but net operating losses are to be split 75–25, the profit sharing ratio would determine distributive shares in a profitable year, and the loss sharing ratio would control in an unprofitable year. This freedom to allocate distributive shares of partnership items is not unlimited, however. Allocations in the partnership agreement must satisfy the requirement of § 704(b)(2) that the allocations have "substantial economic effect." Although the regulations implementing the substantial economic effects test are lengthy and complicated, the test basically requires that allocations of items for tax purposes reflect the economic effect of the allocation to the partners in terms of money. The economic effect of an allocation is demonstrated with properly maintained capital accounts that reflect the amount available to a partner on liquidation of the partnership.[1] In a nutshell, if allocations of tax items in a partnership agreement are consistent with the economic allocation of income and expense or loss, allocations by the partners will be respected.

---

1. The concept that partnership capital accounts, which detail the economic relations between partners by maintaining an accounting of each partner's interest in the partnership that is available to the partner on liquidation of the partnership, was introduced in Chapter 2, Section 1.

If the partnership agreement does not provide for partners' distributive shares or if the allocation to a partner under the agreement of income, gain, loss, deduction, or credit does not have "substantial economic effect," § 704(b) requires that the partner's distributive share be determined "in accordance with the partner's interest in the partnership determined by taking into account all facts and circumstances." As under the substantial economic effect test, application of the facts and circumstances test involves identifying the economic arrangement between the partners. A special rule is provided in § 704(c), which allocates items of income, gain, loss and deduction attributable to property contributed to the partnership to take into account differences between fair market value and basis at the time of the contribution.

As discussed in Chapter 2, Section 2, and considered in greater detail in Chapter 5, under §§ 722 and 752(a) a partner's share of partnership liabilities in included in the partner's basis for the partnership interest. Allocation of items involving partnership debt complicates the application of the substantial economic effect test. Again, the focus of the regulations is to provide for allocation of items funded by partnership debt to the partner who is economically affected by the item, generally meaning the partner or partners who are ultimately liable for the debt in the case of recourse debt. In the case of nonrecourse debt, debt for which no partner is liable, allocations of items funded by the debt can have no economic effect. As a consequence, regulations provide special rules to identify partners' shares of deductions attributable to nonrecourse debt.

Section 706(d) provides that if there is a change in a partner's interest in the partnership during the year, each partner's distributive share of income, gain, loss and deduction shall be determined by a method prescribed by regulations which takes into account the varying interests of the partners during the taxable year. See Treas. Reg. § 1.706–1(c)(4). In addition, § 706(d)(2) requires that certain deductions be allocated over the year to which they are attributable, thus preventing a newly admitted partner from sharing in any deduction which had economically accrued prior to admission. This rule applies to interest, taxes, and payments for services or for the use of property, and the Internal Revenue Service has the authority to issue Regulations expanding the items covered.

Finally, § 704(e) provides special rules governing allocation of items with respect to certain family partnerships.

SECTION 1.   HISTORICAL BACKGROUND

Prior to its amendment by the Tax Reform Act of 1976, § 704(b) provided that special allocations would not be recognized if the "principal purpose" of the allocation was tax avoidance. The Regulations under that version of § 704(b), discussed in Orrisch v. Commissioner, which follows, were issued prior to the 1976 statutory changes, but focused on whether or not the attempted special allocation had "substantial economic effect."

Orrisch v. Commissioner*

Tax Court of the United States, 1970.
55 T.C. 395.

■ FEATHERSTON, JUDGE. Respondent determined deficiencies in petitioners' income tax for 1966 and 1967 in the respective amounts of $2,814.19 and $3,018.11. The only issue for decision is whether an amendment to a partnership agreement allocating to petitioners the entire amount of the depreciation deduction allowable on two buildings owned by the partnership was made for the principal purpose of avoidance of tax within the meaning of section 704(b).

Findings of Fact

* * *

In May of 1963, Domonick J. and Elaine J. Crisafi (hereinafter the Crisafis) and petitioners [Stanley C. and Gerta E. Orrisch] formed a partnership to purchase and operate two apartment houses, one located at 1255 Taylor Street, San Francisco, and the other at 600 Ansel Road, Burlingame, Calif. The cost of the Taylor Street property was $229,011.08, and of the Ansel Road property was $155,974.90. The purchase of each property was financed principally by a secured loan. Petitioners and the Crisafis initially contributed to the partnership cash in the amounts of $26,500 and $12,500, respectively. During 1964 and 1965 petitioners and the Crisafis each contributed additional cash in the amounts of $8,800. Under the partnership agreement, which was not in writing, they agreed to share equally the profits and losses from the venture.

During each of the years 1963, 1964, and 1965, the partnership suffered losses, attributable in part to the acceleration of depreciation—the deduction was computed on the basis of 150 percent of straightline depreciation. The amounts of the depreciation deductions, the reported loss for each of the 3 years as reflected in the partnership returns, and the amounts of each partner's share of the losses are as follows:

Year	Depreciation deducted	Total loss	Each partner's share of the losses—50 percent of the total loss
1963	$ 9,886.20	$ 9,716.14	$4,858.07
1964	21,051.95	17,812.33	[1] 8,906.17
1965	19,894.24	18,952.59	[1] 9,476.30

[1] The amounts of the losses allocated to the Crisafis for 1964 and 1965 were actually $8,906.16 and $9,476.29.

Petitioners and the Crisafis respectively reported in their individual income tax returns for these years the partnership losses allocated to them.

* The Tax Court decision was affirmed per curiam, 31 A.F.T.R.2d 1069 (9th Cir. 1973).

Petitioners enjoyed substantial amounts of income from several sources, the principal one being a nautical equipment sales and repair business. In their joint income tax returns for 1963, 1964, and 1965, petitioners reported taxable income in the respective amounts of $10,462.70, $5,898.85, and $50,832, together with taxes thereon in the amounts of $2,320.30, $1,059.80, and $12,834.

The Crisafis were also engaged in other business endeavors, principally an insurance brokerage business. They owned other real property, however, from which they realized losses, attributable largely to substantial depreciation deductions. In their joint income tax returns for 1963, 1964, and 1965, they reported no net taxable income.

Early in 1966, petitioners and the Crisafis orally agreed that, for 1966 and subsequent years, the entire amount of the partnership's depreciation deductions would be specially allocated to petitioners, and that the gain or loss from the partnership's business, computed without regard to any deduction for depreciation, would be divided equally. They further agreed that, in the event the partnership property was sold at a gain, the specially allocated depreciation would be "charged back" to petitioner's capital account and petitioners would pay the tax on the gain attributable thereto.

The operating results of the partnership for 1966 and 1967 as reflected in the partnership returns were as follows:

Year	Depreciation deducted	Loss (including depreciation)	Gain (or loss) without regard to depreciation
1966	$18,412.00	$19,396.00	($984.00)
1967	17,180.75	16,560.78	619.97

The partnership returns for these years show that, taking into account the special arrangement as to depreciation, losses in the amounts of $18,904 and $16,870.76 were allocated to petitioners for 1966 and 1967, respectively, and petitioners claimed these amounts as deductions in their joint income tax returns for those years. The partnership returns reported distributions to the Crisafis in the form of a $492 loss for 1966 and a $309.98 gain for 1967. The Crisafis' joint income tax returns reflected that they had no net taxable income for either 1966 or 1967.

The net capital contributions, allocations of profits, losses and depreciation, and ending balances of the capital accounts, of the Orrisch–Crisafi partnership from May 1963 through December 31, 1967, were as follows:

	Petitioners'	*Crisafis'*
Excess of capital contributions over withdrawals during 1963	$26,655.55	$12,655.54
Allocation of 1963 loss	(4,858.07)	(4,858.07)
Balance 12/31/63	21,797.48	7,797.47
Excess of capital contributions over withdrawals during 1964	4,537.50	3,537.50

	Petitioners'	Crisafis'
Allocation of 1964 loss	(8,906.17)	(8,906.16)
Balance 12/31/64	17,428.81	2,428.81
Excess of capital contributions over withdrawals during 1965	4,337.50	5,337.50
Allocation of 1965 loss	(9,476.30)	(9,476.29)
Balance 12/31/65	12,290.01	(1,709.98)
Excess of capital contributions over withdrawals during 1966	2,610.00	6,018.00
Allocation of 1966 loss before depreciation	(492.00)	(492.00)
Allocation of depreciation	(18,412.00)	0
Balance 12/31/66	(4,003.99)	3,816.02
Excess of withdrawals over capital contributions during 1967	(4,312.36)	(3,720.35)
Allocation of 1967 profit before depreciation	309.99	309.98
Allocation of depreciation	(17,180.75)	0
Balance 12/31/67	(25,187.11)	405.65

* * *

In the notice of deficiency, respondent determined that the special allocation of the depreciation deduction provided by the amendment to the partnership agreement "was made with the principal purpose of avoidance of income taxes" and should, therefore, be disregarded. Partnership losses for 1966 and 1967, adjusted to reflect a correction of the amount of depreciation allowable, were allocated equally between the partners.

Ultimate Finding of Fact

The principal purpose of the special allocation to petitioners of all of the deductions for depreciation taken by the Orrisch–Crisafi partnership for 1966 and 1967 was the avoidance of income tax.

Opinion

The only issue presented for decision is whether tax effect can be given the agreement between petitioners and the Crisafis that, beginning with 1966, all the partnership's depreciation deductions were to be allocated to petitioners for their use in computing their individual income tax liabilities. In our view, the answer must be in the negative, and the amounts of each of the partners' deductions for the depreciation of partnership property must be determined in accordance with the ratio used generally in computing their distributive shares of the partnership's profits and losses.

Among the important innovations of the 1954 Code are limited provisions for flexibility in arrangements for the sharing of income, losses, and deductions arising from business activities conducted through partnerships. The authority for special allocations of such items appears in section 704(a), which provides that a partner's share of any item of income, gain, loss, deduction, or credit shall be determined by the partnership agreement. That rule is coupled with a limitation in section 704(b), however, which states that a special allocation of an item will be disregarded if its "principal purpose" is the avoidance or evasion of Federal income tax. See

Smith v. Commissioner, 331 F.2d 298 (C.A.7, 1964), affirming a Memorandum Opinion of this Court; Jean V. Kresser, 54 T.C. 1621 (1970). In case a special allocation is disregarded, the partner's share of the item is to be determined in accordance with the ratio by which the partners divide the general profits or losses of the partnership. Sec. 1.704–1(b)(2), Income Tax Regs.

The report of the Senate Committee on Finance accompanying the bill finally enacted as the 1954 Code (S.Rept. No. 1622, to accompany H.R. 8300 (Pub.L. No. 591), 83d Cong., 2d Sess., p. 379 (1954)) explained the tax-avoidance restriction prescribed by section 704(b) as follows:

> Subsection (b) * * * provides that if the principal purpose of any provision in the partnership agreement dealing with a partner's distributive share of a particular item is to avoid or evade the Federal income tax, the partner's distributive share of that item shall be redetermined in accordance with his distributive share of partnership income or loss described in section 702(a)(9) [i.e., the ratio used by the partners for dividing general profits or losses].
> * * *
>
> Where, however, a provision in a partnership agreement for a special allocation of certain items has substantial economic effect and is not merely a device for reducing the taxes of certain partners without actually affecting their shares of partnership income, then such a provision will be recognized for tax purposes.
> * * *

This reference to "substantial economic effect" did not appear in the House Ways and Means Committee report (H.Rept. No. 1337, to accompany H.R. 8300 (Pub.L. No. 591), 83d Cong., 2d Sess., p. A223 (1954)) discussing section 704(b), and was apparently added in the Senate Finance Committee to allay fears that special allocations of income or deductions would be denied effect in every case where the allocation resulted in a reduction in the income tax liabilities of one or more of the partners. The statement is an affirmation that special allocations are ordinarily to be recognized if they have business validity apart from their tax consequences. * * *

In resolving the question whether the principal purpose of a provision in a partnership agreement is the avoidance or evasion of Federal income tax, all the facts and circumstances in relation to the provision must be taken into account. Section 1.704–1(b)(2), Income Tax Regs., lists the following as relevant circumstances to be considered:

> Whether the partnership or a partner individually has a business purpose for the allocation; whether the allocation has "substantial economic effect", that is, whether the allocation may actually affect the dollar amount of the partners' shares of the total partnership income or loss independently of tax consequences; whether related items of income, gain, loss, deduction, or credit from the same source are subject to the same allocation; whether the allocation was made without recognition of normal business

factors and only after the amount of the specially allocated item could reasonably be estimated; the duration of the allocation; and the overall tax consequences of the allocation. * * *

Applying these standards, we do not think the special allocation of depreciation in the present case can be given effect.

The evidence is persuasive that the special allocation of depreciation was adopted for a tax-avoidance rather than a business purpose. Depreciation was the only item which was adjusted by the parties; both the income from the buildings and the expenses incurred in their operation, maintenance, and repair were allocated to the partners equally. Since the deduction for depreciation does not vary from year to year with the fortunes of the business, the parties obviously knew what the tax effect of the special allocation would be at the time they adopted it. Furthermore, as shown by our findings, petitioners had large amounts of income which would be offset by the additional deduction for depreciation; the Crisafis, in contrast, had no taxable income from which to subtract the partnership depreciation deductions, and due to depreciation deductions which they were obtaining with respect to other housing projects, could expect to have no taxable income in the near future. On the other hand, the insulation of the Crisafis from at least part of a potential capital gains tax was an obvious tax advantage. The inference is unmistakably clear that the agreement did not reflect normal business considerations but was designed primarily to minimize the overall tax liabilities of the partners.

Petitioners urge that the special allocation of the depreciation deduction was adopted in order to equalize the capital accounts of the partners, correcting a disparity ($14,000) in the amounts initially contributed to the partnership by them ($26,500) and the Crisafis ($12,500). But the evidence does not support this contention. Under the special allocation agreement, petitioners were to be entitled, in computing their individual income tax liabilities, to deduct the full amount of the depreciation realized on the partnership property. For 1966, as an example, petitioners were allocated a sum ($18,904) equal to the depreciation on the partnership property ($18,412) plus one-half of the net loss computed without regard to depreciation ($492). The other one-half of the net loss was, of course, allocated to the Crisafis. Petitioners' allocation ($18,904) was then applied to reduce their capital account. The depreciation specially allocated to petitioners ($18,412) in 1966 alone exceeded the amount of the disparity in the contributions. Indeed, at the end of 1967, petitioners' capital account showed a deficit of $25,187.11 compared with a positive balance of $405.65 in the Crisafis' account. By the time the partnership's properties are fully depreciated, the amount of the reduction in petitioners' capital account will approximate the remaining basis for the buildings as of the end of 1967. The Crisafis' capital account will be adjusted only for contributions, withdrawals, gain or loss, without regard to depreciation, and similar adjustments for these factors will also be made in petitioners' capital account. Thus, rather than correcting an imbalance in the capital accounts of the partners, the special allocation of depreciation will create a vastly greater imbalance than existed at the end of 1966. In the light of these facts, we find it incredible that equalization of the capital accounts was the objective of the special allocation.[5]

Petitioners rely primarily on the argument that the allocation has "substantial economic effect" in that it is reflected in the capital accounts of the partners. Referring to the material quoted above from the report of the Senate Committee on Finance, they contend that this alone is sufficient to show that the special allocation served a business rather than a tax-avoidance purpose.

According to the regulations, an allocation has economic effect if it "may actually affect the dollar amount of the partners' shares of the total partnership income or loss independently of tax consequences."[6] The agreement in this case provided not only for the allocation of depreciation to petitioners but also for gain on the sale of the partnership property to be "charged back" to them. The charge back would cause the gain, for tax purposes, to be allocated on the books entirely to petitioners to the extent of the special allocation of depreciation, and their capital account would be correspondingly increased. The remainder of the gain, if any, would be shared equally by the partners. If the gain on the sale were to equal or exceed the depreciation specially allocated to petitioners, the increase in their capital account caused by the charge back would exactly equal the depreciation deductions previously allowed to them and the proceeds of the sale of the property would be divided equally. In such circumstances, the only effect of the allocation would be a trade of tax consequences, i.e., the Crisafis would relinquish a current depreciation deduction in exchange for exoneration from all or part of the capital gains tax when the property is sold, and petitioners would enjoy a larger current depreciation deduction but would assume a larger ultimate capital gains tax liability. Quite clearly, if the property is sold at a gain, the special allocation will affect only the tax liabilities of the partners and will have no other economic effect.

To find any economic effect of the special allocation agreement aside from its tax consequences, we must, therefore, look to see who is to bear

---

5. We recognize that petitioners had more money invested in the partnership than the Crisafis and that it is reasonable for the partners to endeavor to equalize their investments, since each one was to share equally in the profits and losses of the enterprise. However, we do not think that sec. 704(a) permits the partners' prospective tax benefits to be used as the medium for equalizing their investments, and it is apparent that the economic burden of the depreciation (which is reflected by the allowance for depreciation) was not intended to be the medium used.

This case is to be distinguished from situations where one partner contributed property and the other cash. In such cases sec. 704(c) may allow a special allocation of income and expenses in order to reflect the tax consequences inherent in the original contributions.

6. This language of sec. 1.704–1(b)(2), Income Tax Regs., listing "substantial economic effect" as one of the factors to be considered in determining the principal purpose of a special allocation, is somewhat similar to the material quoted in the text from S.Rept. No. 1622, to accompany H.R. 8300 (Pub.L. No. 591), 83d Cong., 2d Sess., p. 379 (1954). But the latter is broader. It is an explanation of the "principal purpose" test of sec. 704(b), and contemplates that a special allocation will be given effect only if it has business validity apart from its tax consequences. * * *

the economic burden of the depreciation if the buildings should be sold for a sum less than their original cost. There is not one syllable of evidence bearing directly on this crucial point. We have noted, however, that when the buildings are fully depreciated, petitioners' capital account will have a deficit, or there will be a disparity in the capital accounts, approximately equal to the undepreciated basis of the buildings as of the beginning of 1966.[7] Under normal accounting procedures, if the building were sold at a gain less than the amount of such disparity petitioners would either be required to contribute to the partnership a sum equal to the remaining deficit in their capital account after the gain on the sale had been added back or would be entitled to receive a proportionately smaller share of the partnership assets on liquidation. Based on the record as a whole, we do not think the partners ever agreed to such an arrangement. On dissolution, we think the partners contemplated an equal division of the partnership assets which would be adjusted only for disparities in cash contributions or withdrawals.[8] Certainly there is no evidence to show otherwise. That being true, the special allocation does not "actually affect the dollar amount of the partners' share of the total partnership income or loss independently of tax consequences" within the meaning of the regulation referred to above.
* * *

In the light of all the evidence we have found as an ultimate fact that the "principal purpose" of the special allocation agreement was tax avoidance within the meaning of section 701(b). Accordingly, the deduction for depreciation for 1966 and 1967 must be allocated between the parties in the same manner as other deductions.

Decision will be entered for the respondent.

ILLUSTRATIVE MATERIAL

1.   GAIN CHARGEBACK PROVISIONS

A gain chargeback is a provision in a partnership agreement providing that if depreciable property is sold at a gain, the partner who received a special allocation of depreciation with respect to the property will be specially allocated the gain, up to the amount of depreciation deductions previously allocated to him. Any remaining gain will be allocated according to the general profit sharing ratio. The operation of a gain chargeback provision can be illustrated by a simple example.

Suppose A and B each contribute $100,000 to the AB Partnership, which buys depreciable property for $200,000. A and B are equal partners except the partnership agreement specially allocates all depreciation to B. The partnership breaks even, apart from depreciation of $20,000 per year.

---

7. This assumes, of course, that all partnership withdrawals and capital contributions will be equal.

8. We note that, in the course of Orrisch's testimony, petitioners' counsel made a distinction between entries in the taxpayers' capital accounts which reflect actual cash transactions and those relating to the special allocation which are "paper entries relating to depreciation."

If at the beginning of the second year, when the property had a basis and book value of $180,000, the property were sold for $200,000, the entire $20,000 gain would be allocated to B. Likewise, if the property sold for $195,000, the entire $15,000 gain would be allocated to B. On the other hand, if the property sold for $210,000, B would be allocated $25,000 of gain and C would be allocated $5,000. These allocations of gain would be reflected in the partners' capital accounts so that in this last case each partner's capital account immediately prior to liquidation would be $105,000. Accordingly, the net proceeds of the sale would be divided equally since the liquidating distributions would be in accordance with positive capital account balances. Thus, while B initially bore the economic loss of the depreciation (which is assumed to have occurred in fact), that loss was made up by the subsequent allocation of a corresponding amount of income to B.

2.   ANALYSIS OF ORRISCH

The gain chargeback was not the flaw in the Orrish/Crisafi partnership agreement. The partnership maintained capital accounts. Nonetheless, as the court noted, the partners contemplated an equal division of partnership assets, adjusted only for disparities in cash contributions and withdrawals. As the court's rendition of the partnership capital accounts illustrates, with the special allocation of depreciation the partners' capital accounts did not reflect this 50–50 division of partnership assets. Indeed, Orrisch's capital accounts for the years ending in 1966 and 1967 showed deficits. If the partners intended a 50–50 division of assets, the capital account allocations of depreciation had no economic effect.

The court found that if the property was sold at a gain—presumably meaning a gain over its original cost, not gain computed with reference to adjusted basis—the effect of the special allocation of depreciation coupled with the gain chargeback would be that Orrisch would realize increased deductions in early years at the price of greater capital gains on the sale of the property and the Crisafis would realize greater income in early years and lesser capital gain on the sale of the property, but over the life of the partnership, neither Orrisch's or the Crisafis' aggregate income would be affected. The effect of the gain chargeback can be illustrated by a simplified example based on *Orrisch*.

Suppose O and C form a partnership by contributing $100 each and buy a depreciable asset for $200. The asset produces no gain or loss apart from depreciation (i.e., gross rental income equals cash flow deductible expenses), and the asset is depreciated by the straight line method over five years ($40 per year). The partnership's opening balance sheet would be as follows:

Assets				Partners' Capital Accounts		
	Book	Tax Basis			Book	Tax Basis
Asset	$200	$200	C		$100	$100
			O		$100	$100
	$200	$200			$200	$200

If all items were allocated equally, after two years the partnership balance sheet would be as follows:

	Assets			Partners' Capital Accounts	
		Tax			Tax
	Book	Basis		Book	Basis
Asset	$200	$200	C	$ 60	$ 60
	(80)	(80)	O	$ 60	$ 60
	$120	$120		$120	$120

If on the first day of year 3 the asset were sold for $210 and the $90 gain shared equally, as was the depreciation, the balance sheet would be as follows:

	Assets			Partners' Capital Accounts	
		Tax			Tax
	Book	Basis		Book	Basis
Cash	$210	$210	C	$105	$105
			O	$105	$105
	$210	$210		$210	$210

If, however, the partnership agreement specially allocated all of the depreciation to O with a gain chargeback to O of an amount equal to prior depreciation deductions, and all other items were allocated equally, after two years the balance sheet would be as follows:

	Assets			Partners' Capital Accounts	
		Tax			Tax
	Book	Basis		Book	Basis
Asset	$200	$200	C	$100	$100
	(80)	(80)	O	$ 20	$ 20
	120	120		$120	$120

If the property were sold for $210 on the first day of year 3, the gain chargeback would allocate the first $80 of gain to O, an amount equal to O's depreciation deductions, and the remaining $10 of gain would be allocated $5 to each of C and O. The balance sheet would be as follows:

	Assets			Partners' Capital Accounts	
		Tax			Tax
	Book	Basis		Book	Basis
Cash	$210	$210	C	$105	$105
			O	$105	$105
	$210	$210		$210	$210

Dividing the sales proceeds fifty-fifty, as was agreed upon in *Orrisch*, would match the balances in the partner's capital accounts.

Consider now the results of a special allocation of depreciation to O, coupled with a gain chargeback, if the asset were sold for only $180 on the first day of year 3. In this case, the gain would be only $60, all of which would be allocated to O. The partnership balance sheet would be as follows:

	Assets			Partners' Capital Accounts		
	Book	Tax Basis			Book	Tax Basis
Cash	$180	$180	C		$100	$100
			O		$ 80	$ 80
	$180	$180			$180	$180

In this case an equal division of the sales proceeds, $90, to each of C and O, as was agreed upon in *Orrisch*, does not match the partner's capital accounts. Thus, the allocation of depreciation deductions to O did not reflect economic reality. Over the life of the partnership, the asset actually declined in value by $20. If O really bore the risk of depreciation, O should receive $20 less than C upon liquidation. This analysis indicates that the provision in *Orrisch* for liquidation by a formula that was independent of the allocation of depreciation deductions was the fatal flaw.

3.   1976 REVISION OF SECTION 704(b)

Current section 704(b) was enacted in 1976 to codify the substantial economic effect test of the Regulations applied in *Orrisch*. The following excerpt from S. Rep. No. 94–938, 94th Cong., 2d Sess. 100 (1976), explains the change as follows:

Explanation of provisions

The committee amendment provides generally that an allocation of overall income or loss (described under section [702(a)(8)]), or of any item of income, gain, loss, deduction, or credit (described under section [702(a)(1)–(7)]), shall be controlled by the partnership agreement if the partner receiving the allocation can demonstrate that it has "substantial economic effect", i.e., whether the allocation may actually affect the dollar amount of the partners' shares of the total partnership income or loss independently of tax consequences. (Regs. Sec. 1.704–1(b)(2)). * * * If an allocation made by the partnership is set aside, a partner's share of the income, gain, loss, deduction or credit (or item thereof) will be determined in accordance with his interest in the partnership taking into account all facts and circumstances. * * * Among the relevant factors to be taken into account are the interests of the respective partners in profits and losses (if different from that of taxable income or loss), cash flow; and their rights to distributions of capital upon liquidation. * * *

SECTION 2.   THE SECTION 704(b) REGULATIONS

INTERNAL REVENUE CODE: Section 704(b).

Section 704(a) and (b) provide partners with considerable flexibility in structuring partnership agreements, going so far as to permit the partners, within certain limitations, to agree to individual shares of taxable profits and losses for a particular year that differ from the agreed upon shares of cash flow distributions for the year. Thus, the provisions of the partnership agreement dealing with allocations of items of income, gain, loss and credits may range from a simple percentage division of all items on the same basis to complex arrangements with separate allocations of profit and loss, cash flow, distributions from refinancing, liquidation distributions, etc., in different periods and at different levels of income. For example, the partnership agreement of the AB Partnership may provide that profits and losses are shared 50–50 but that current cash flow is distributed 60 percent to A and 40 percent to B. Alternatively (or additionally), the partnership agreement might provide that profits (or gross income) is to be allocated 50–50, but that losses (or deductions) are to be allocated 60 percent to A and 40 percent to B. The key to allowing such flexibility, of course, is to require an eventual reconciliation in which total taxable income or loss allocated to each partner over the life of the partnership equals the economic gain or loss realized by each partner over that same period. This reconciliation of tax allocations, book profit and loss allocations, and cash flow distributions is the heart of § 704(b), which requires that allocations of the items in the partnership agreement for tax purposes have "substantial economic effect." If the attempted tax allocations in the partnership agreement do not meet the substantial economic effect test, the partner's share of the item in question will be determined in accordance with the partner's overall interest in the partnership, including a consideration of items which are not specially allocated.

The organizing theme of the § 704(b) regulations is that an allocation "must be consistent with the underlying economic arrangement of the partners" in order to have "substantial economic effect." Treas. Reg. § 1.704–1(b). "This means that in the event there is an economic benefit or economic burden that corresponds to an allocation, the partner to whom the allocation is made must receive such economic benefit or bear such economic burden." Treas. Reg. § 1.704–1(b)(2)(ii). In general, the regulations apply the capital account analysis in *Orrisch,* but prescribe detailed rules that must be followed in making the capital account analysis if a partnership allocation is to be recognized, particularly where nonrecourse debt is involved. By requiring that tax allocations be reflected in the changes to each partner's capital account, the regulations assure that the tax consequences to each partner accurately reflect the economic gain or loss realized by the partners.

Treas. Reg. § 1.704–2(b)(1) provides that allocations attributable to nonrecourse debt never can have economic effect and always must be allocated among the partners in accordance with their interests in the partnership. However, Treas. Reg. § 1.704–2 provides a "safe harbor" under which allocations attributable to nonrecourse debt will be deemed to be made in accordance with the partners' interests in the partnership.

Although § 704(b) frequently is said to deal with *special* allocations, the regulations test *all* allocations for substantial economic effect, including straightforward identical fractional allocations of every item. However, as long as each partner for both tax and book accounting purposes is entitled to a fractional share of each and every item that does not vary from item to item for the partner, and the allocations are in the same proportion as the partners' contributions to the partnership, the allocation always will have substantial economic effect under the tests of the regulations, even though the partners' fractional shares may differ. But if any partner is entitled to a share of any item that differs from his share of any other item, including his liability for partnership debts and contributions to capital, then a detailed analysis under the regulations is required, regardless of whether the specially allocated item is identified by its tax characteristics or its financial characteristics.

Given the detailed nature of the § 704(b) regulations, it is important to keep in mind that the tax rules do not determine the economic deal between the partners. Rather, the rules are intended to insure that the tax results follow the economics, i.e., the partners cannot set up one reality for economic purposes and then try to construct a different reality solely for tax purposes. Nevertheless, since the rules in the § 704(b) regulations are designed to keep track of each partner's share of the economic profits and losses of the partnership, as a practical matter, most carefully prepared partnership agreements should closely follow the rules of the regulations.

As discussed in *Orrisch*, even though the pre–1976 version of § 704(b) provided that special allocations would not be recognized if the "principal purpose" of the allocation was tax avoidance, the regulations under pre–1976 § 704(b), nevertheless focused on whether or not an attempted special allocation had substantial economic effect. When the substantial economic effect test was specifically incorporated in the statute and the reference to tax avoidance purpose was dropped, the accompanying committee reports indicated that there was no intention to change the previously existing law as to what constitutes the requisite economic effect. S.Rep. No. 94–938, 94th Cong., 2d Sess. 100 (1976). Since the promulgation of regulations under current § 704(b), however, the emphasis has been almost exclusively on the detailed tests in the regulations. Although the Committee Report also left some room for the argument that a (presumably nontax) business purpose for a special allocation has some significance, the statutory stress is clearly on the substantial economic effect of the allocation, and the regulations provide no leeway for respecting an allocation that has a purported business purpose but does not meet the substantial economic effect test. Thus the presence of a colorable "business purpose" should not protect an allocation that does not have the necessary economic effect.

A. ALLOCATIONS OF ITEMS UNRELATED TO NONRECOURSE DEBT

REGULATIONS: Sections 1.704–1(b)(1)(i), (iii), (iv), and (vi); –1(b)(2)(i)–(ii), (iv)(a)–(i); –1(b)(3); –1(b)(5), Ex. (1) and (15).

Under the regulations, there are three methods by which an allocation generally can satisfy § 704(b): (1) the allocation has "substantial economic effect" under Treas. Reg. § 1.704–1(b)(2); (2) taking into account all of the facts and circumstances, the allocation is in accordance with the partners' interests in the partnership under Treas. Reg. § 1.704–1(b)(3); or (3) the allocation is deemed under Treas. Reg. § 1.704–1(b)(4) to be in accordance with the partners' interests in the partnership under a special rule. The application of the facts and circumstances test of Treas. Reg. § 1.704–1(b)(3) is not clearly delineated and, in order to be respected, partnership allocation provisions are generally written to meet one of the other tests.

Whether an allocation has "substantial economic effect" is determined under a two part analysis. First, Treas. Reg. § 1.704–1(b)(2)(ii) requires that the allocation have "economic effect." As noted above, this means that the partner receiving the allocation of the tax item must also bear the economic benefit or burden that corresponds to the allocation. Under the regulations, an allocation has economic effect only if three conditions are satisfied: (1) the allocation is reflected by an appropriate increase or decrease in the partner's capital account; (2) liquidation proceeds are, throughout the term of the partnership, to be distributed in accordance with the partners' positive capital account balances; and (3) any partner with a deficit capital account following the distribution of liquidation proceeds is required to restore the amount of that deficit to the partnership for distribution to partners with positive account balances or payment to partnership creditors. A partner's obligation to restore a negative capital account need not be unlimited; an allocation that creates or increases a negative capital account balance will be respected to the extent that the deficit does not exceed the amount that the partner is obligated to restore. The determination whether an allocation has economic effect is made annually. Treas. Reg. § 1.704–1(b)(2)(i). Thus, an allocation may be respected one year, but not the next, or may be respected only in part under Treas. Reg. § 1.704–1(b)(2)(ii)(*e*).

Second, the "economic effect" of the allocation must be "substantial." Treas. Reg. § 1.704–1(b)(2)(iii)(*a*). This requirement means that the economic effect of the allocation must have a reasonable possibility of affecting the dollar amounts to be received by the partners independent of the tax consequences of the allocation. Allocations that are transitory, e.g., offsetting allocations over a relatively brief period of years or that merely shift the character of items allocated among the partners are particularly suspect. However, any allocation that enhances the after-tax economic consequences to at least one partner, in present value terms, but which does not have a strong likelihood of diminishing the after-tax benefit to at least one other partner, in present value terms, will not be substantial.

(1) ECONOMIC EFFECT

Revenue Ruling 97–38

1997–2 C.B. 69.

ISSUE

If a partner is treated as having a limited deficit restoration obligation under § 1.704–1(b)(2)(ii)(c) of the Income Tax Regulations by reason of the partner's liability to the partnership's creditors, how is the amount of that obligation calculated?

FACTS

In year 1, GP and LP, general partner and limited partner, each contribute $100x to form limited partnership LPRS. In general, GP and LP share LPRS's income and loss 50 percent each. However, LPRS allocates to GP all depreciation deductions and gain from the sale of depreciable assets up to the amount of those deductions. LPRS maintains capital accounts according to the rules set forth in § 1.704–1(b)(2)(iv), and the partners agree to liquidate according to positive capital account balances under the rules of § 1.704–1(b)(2)(ii)(b)(2).

Under applicable state law, GP is liable to creditors for all partnership recourse liabilities, but LP has no personal liability. GP and LP do not agree to unconditional deficit restoration obligations as described in § 1.704–1(b)(2)(ii)(b)(3) (in general, a deficit restoration obligation requires a partner to restore any deficit capital account balance following the liquidation of the partner's interest in the partnership); GP is obligated to restore a deficit capital account only to the extent necessary to pay creditors. Thus, if LPRS were to liquidate after paying all creditors and LP had a positive capital account balance, GP would not be required to restore GP's deficit capital account to permit a liquidating distribution to LP. In addition, GP and LP agree to a qualified income offset, thus satisfying the requirements of the alternate test for economic effect of § 1.704–1(b)(2)(ii)(d). GP and LP also agree that no allocation will be made that causes or increases a deficit balance in any partner's capital account in excess of the partner's obligation to restore the deficit.

LPRS purchases depreciable property for $1,000x from an unrelated seller, paying $200x in cash and borrowing the $800x balance from an unrelated bank that is not the seller of the property. The note is recourse to LPRS. The principal of the loan is due in 6 years; interest is payable semi-annually at the applicable federal rate. GP bears the entire economic risk of loss for LPRS's recourse liability, and GP's basis in LPRS (outside basis) is increased by $800x. See § 1.752–2.

In each of years 1 through 5, the property generates $200x of depreciation. All other partnership deductions and losses exactly equal income, so that in each of years 1 through 5 LPRS has a net loss of $200x.

LAW AND ANALYSIS

Under § 704(b) of the Internal Revenue Code and the regulations thereunder, a partnership's allocations of income, gain, loss, deduction, or credit set forth in the partnership agreement are respected if they have substantial economic effect. If allocations under the partnership agreement would not have substantial economic effect, the partnership's allocations are determined according to the partners' interests in the partnership. The fundamental principles for establishing economic effect require an allocation to be consistent with the partners' underlying economic arrangement.

A partner allocated a share of income should enjoy any corresponding economic benefit, and a partner allocated a share of losses or deductions should bear any corresponding economic burden. See § 1.704–1(b)(2)(ii)(a).

To come within the safe harbor for establishing economic effect in § 1.704–1(b)(2)(ii), partners must agree to maintain capital accounts under the rules of § 1.704–1(b)(2)(iv), liquidate according to positive capital account balances, and agree to an unconditional deficit restoration obligation for any partner with a deficit in that partner's capital account, as described in § 1.704–1(b)(2)(ii)(b)(3). Alternatively, the partnership may satisfy the requirements of the alternate test for economic effect provided in § 1.704–1(b)(2)(ii)(d). LPRS's partnership agreement complies with the alternate test for economic effect.

The alternate test for economic effect requires the partners to agree to a qualified income offset in lieu of an unconditional deficit restoration obligation. If the partners so agree, allocations will have economic effect to the extent that they do not create a deficit capital account for any partner (in excess of any limited deficit restoration obligation of that partner) as of the end of the partnership taxable year to which the allocation relates. Section 1.704–1(b)(2)(ii)(d)(3) (flush language).

A partner is treated as having a limited deficit restoration obligation to the extent of: (1) the outstanding principal balance of any promissory note contributed to the partnership by the partner, and (2) the amount of any unconditional obligation of the partner (whether imposed by the partnership agreement or by state or local law) to make subsequent contributions to the partnership. Section 1.704–1(b)(2)(ii)(c).

LP has no obligation under the partnership agreement or state or local law to make additional contributions to the partnership and, therefore, has no deficit restoration obligation. Under applicable state law, GP may have to make additional contributions to the partnership to pay creditors. However, GP's obligation only arises to the extent that the amount of LPRS's liabilities exceeds the value of LPRS's assets available to satisfy the liabilities. Thus, the amount of GP's limited deficit restoration obligation each year is equal to the difference between the amount of the partnership's recourse liabilities at the end of the year and the value of the partnership's assets available to satisfy the liabilities at the end of the year.

To ensure consistency with the other requirements of the regulations under § 704(b), where a partner's obligation to make additional contributions to the partnership is dependent on the value of the partnership's assets, the partner's deficit restoration obligation must be computed by reference to the rules for determining the value of partnership property contained in the regulations under § 704(b). Consequently, in computing GP's limited deficit restoration obligation, the value of the partnership's assets is conclusively presumed to equal the book basis of those assets under the capital account maintenance rules of § 1.704–1(b)(2)(iv). See § 1.704–1(b)(2)(ii)(d) (value equals basis presumption applies for purposes of determining expected allocations and distributions under the alternate test for economic effect); § 1.704–1(b)(2)(iii) (value equals basis presumption applies for purposes of the substantiality test); § 1.704–1(b)(3)(iii) (value equals basis presumption applies for purposes of the partner's interest in the partnership test); § 1.704–2(d) (value equals basis presumption applies in computing partnership minimum gain).

The LPRS agreement allocates all depreciation deductions and gain on the sale of depreciable property to the extent of those deductions to GP. Because LPRS's partnership agreement satisfies the alternate test for economic effect, the allocations of depreciation deductions to GP will have economic effect to the extent that they do not create a deficit capital account for GP in excess of GP's obligation to restore the deficit balance. At the end of year 1, the basis of the depreciable property has been reduced to $800x. If LPRS liquidated at the beginning of year 2, selling its depreciable property for its basis of $800x, the proceeds would be used to repay the $800 principal on LPRS's recourse liability. All of LPRS's creditors would be satisfied and GP would have no obligation to contribute to pay them. Thus, at the end of year 1, GP has no obligation to restore a deficit in its capital account.

Because GP has no obligation to restore a deficit balance in its capital account at the end of year 1, an allocation that reduces GP's capital account below $0 is not permitted under the partnership agreement and would not satisfy the alternate test for economic effect. An allocation of $200x of depreciation deductions to GP would reduce GP's capital account to negative $100x. Because the allocation would result in a deficit capital account balance in excess of GP's obligation to restore, the allocation is not permitted under the partnership agreement, and would not satisfy the safe harbor under the alternate test for economic effect. Therefore, the deductions for year 1 must be allocated $100x each to GP and LP (which is in accordance with their interests in the partnership).

The allocation of depreciation of $200x to GP in year 2 has economic effect. Although the allocation reduces GP's capital account to negative $200x, while LP's capital account remains $0, the allocation to GP does not create a deficit capital account in excess of GP's limited deficit restoration obligation. If LPRS liquidated at the beginning of year 3, selling the depreciable property for its basis of $600x, the proceeds would be applied toward the $800x LPRS liability. Because GP is obligated to restore a deficit capital account to the extent necessary to pay creditors, GP would be required to contribute $200x to LPRS to satisfy the outstanding liability. Thus, at the end of year 2, GP has a deficit restoration obligation of $200x, and the allocation of depreciation to GP does not reduce GP's capital account below its obligation to restore a deficit capital account.

This analysis also applies to the allocation of $200x of depreciation to GP in years 3 through 5. At the beginning of year 6, when the property is fully depreciated, the $800x principal amount of the partnership liability is due. The partners' capital accounts at the beginning of year 6 will equal negative $800x and $0, respectively, for GP and LP. Because value is conclusive presumed to equal basis, the depreciable property would be worthless and could not be used to satisfy LPRS's $800x liability. As a result, GP is deemed to be required to contribute $800x to LPRS. A contribution by GP to satisfy this limited deficit restoration obligation would increase GP's capital account balance to $0.

HOLDING

When a partner is treated as having a limited deficit restoration obligation by reason of the partner's liability to the partnership's creditors, the amount of that obligation is the amount of money that the partner would be required to contribute to the partnership to satisfy partnership liabilities if all partnership property were sold for the amount of the partnership's book basis in the property.

ILLUSTRATIVE MATERIAL

1. PARTNERS' CAPITAL ACCOUNTS

Treas. Reg. § 1.704–1(b)(2)(iv) provides detailed rules regarding the maintenance of partners' capital accounts which must be followed throughout the life of the partnership for an allocation to have economic effect. In applying these rules, a partner who has more than one interest in the partnership is treated as having a single capital account that reflects all of the partner's interests, even if one interest is as a general partner and the other is as a limited partner, and without regard to the time or manner of acquisition of the interests. Treas. Reg. § 1.704–1(b)(2)(iv)(*b*).

A partner's capital account must be increased by the amount of any money contributed by the partner and by income (including tax exempt income) allocated to the partner; and it must be decreased by the amount of any money distributed to the partner and by the partner's share of losses, deductions, and expenditures that are neither deductible nor capitalized, e.g., fines and penalties subject to § 162(f) or interest subject to § 265(a)(2). When the amount of these items differs for partnership book accounting purposes from the amount of such items for tax purposes, for example, because a partner has contributed appreciated or depreciated property, special rules apply to allocate tax gain or loss and depreciation. If the disparity between book and tax amounts is attributable to contributed property, § 704(c), discussed at page 154, applies to allocations of tax gain, loss, and depreciation. See Treas. Regs. §§ 1.704–1(b)(1)(vi), 1.704–1(b)(2)(iv)(*d*)(*3*). If the disparity is attributable to a revaluation of partnership assets for book accounting purposes pursuant to Treas. Reg. § 1.704–1(b)(2)(iv)(*f*), then Treas. Reg. § 1.704–1(b)(4)(i) controls the allocation of tax items. In any situation in which book income or loss differs from taxable income or loss, partners' capital accounts always are adjusted by amounts computed for book accounting purposes, Treas. Reg. § 1.704–1(b)(2)(iv)(g), and tax items must be allocated among the partners in a manner that properly takes into account the difference between book value and basis.

In addition, a partner's capital account must be increased by the fair market value (not the basis) of any property contributed by the partner to the partnership. A partner's own promissory note contributed to the partnership is not taken into account, however, until the disposition of the note by the partnership or the partner pays the principal. Treas. Reg. § 1.704–1(b)(2)(iv)(*d*)(*2*). If property is distributed to a partner, the partner's capital account must be reduced by the fair market value of the property. Treas. Reg. § 1.704–1(b)(2)(iv)(*e*). If property that is contributed to the partnership or distributed by the partnership is subject to a debt, the effect of the debt must be taken into account. Treas. Reg. § 1.704–1(b)(2)(iv)(*c*). Thus, for example, if a parcel of real estate worth $100, but subject to a $60 mortgage, is distributed to a partner who assumes the mortgage debt (or who simply takes the property subject to the mortgage debt), the partner's capital account is reduced by only the $40 net fair market value of the distributed property (total fair market value minus the mortgage). This treatment is parallel to the treatment when encumbered property is contributed to a partnership; in that event only the net fair market value of the contributed property is added to the contributing partner's capital account.

Upon liquidation of the partnership, all capital accounts must be adjusted to reflect appreciation and depreciation of partnership property. In addition, partners' capital accounts may, but technically are not required to, be increased or decreased to reflect a revaluation of the partnership's property on the happening of certain events, such as the admission of a new partner (whether in exchange for a capital contribution or for services), the distribution of property, or the liquidation of a partner's interest. Treas. Reg. § 1.704–1(b)(2)(iv)(*f*). As a practical matter, however, all of the partnership's assets and the partners' capital accounts must be revalued upon the occurrence of any of these events; failure to do so generally would result in a new partner contributing cash to a partnership immediately acquiring an interest more valuable than the amount of her contribution—reflecting a share of the unrealized appreciation of the partnerships assets—a result that would be unacceptable to the continuing partners because the new partner's windfall would be at their expense. If the partnership elects to reflect current values in the capital accounts, the partnership must thereafter adjust capital accounts to reflect certain items, such as depreciation, as computed for revalued book purposes. Treas. Reg. § 1.704–1(b)(2)(iv)(*g*). In general, the partners' determination of the fair market value of property will be accepted if it results from arm's length negotiations in which the partners' have sufficiently adverse interests. Treas. Reg. § 1.704–1(b)(2)(iv)(*h*).

Capital accounts are maintained with reference to the fair market value of property contributed to the partnership and property distributed by the partnership, and are increased or reduced by income or gain and deductions or losses as measured for book accounting rather than tax accounting. Treas. Reg. § 1.704–1(b)(2)(iv)(*f*) and (*g*), and –1(b)(4). Thus, a partner's capital account is not the same as his basis in his partnership interest.

2. LIQUIDATION ACCORDING TO CAPITAL ACCOUNTS

As demonstrated by *Orrisch*, the requirements that the partnership agreement provide for liquidation according to capital accounts and that the partners be obligated to restore any deficit in their capital accounts upon liquidation often are the most difficult of the requirements of the economic effect test with which to comply while still meeting the business and economic objectives of the partners. In practice, however, taking partners through a capital account analysis under the regulations often reveals that the partners have not thoroughly considered the economics of their transaction all the way through to liquidation of the partnership. On the other hand, sometimes the parties understand the economic deal quite well and are trying to engage in the type of avoidance that the regulations are designed to forestall.

The requirement of restoration of negative capital accounts presents a serious problem for recognition of allocations in limited partnerships, particularly where deduction items are disproportionately allocated to limited partners. The essence of a limited partnership interest is that there is no obligation to restore a negative capital account balance. Similar problems arise with respect to limited liability companies that are taxed as partnerships. Treas. Reg. § 1.704–1(b)(3)(iii) provides some leeway in situations in which a partnership agreement satisfies the capital account maintenance rules except for the unlimited deficit restoration requirement, and all allocations meet the substantiality requirement. In such a case, allocations that do not cause or increase a deficit in the capital account of a partner who does not have a restoration requirement generally will be respected, but allocations of items that would cause or increase a deficit will be reallocated. For example, Elrod v. Commissioner, 87 T.C. 1046 (1986), involved a partnership agreement under which losses were charged to capital accounts and distributions in liquidation of the partnership would be in accordance with capital accounts, but the taxpayer-partner was not required to restore any deficit in his capital account. The loss allocation was recognized only to the extent that it did not create a capital account deficit; for years in which the taxpayer maintained a positive capital account, the allocation was recognized in full. Because *Elrod* involved years before publication of the § 704 regulations, the court applied the judicially developed capital account analysis rather than the regulations. See Treas. Reg. § 1.704–1(b)(1)(ii). Although the court stated that it was "unclear" whether the same result would be reached under the regulations, nothing in the stated facts of the opinion indicates that the regulations mandate a different result.

As illustrated by Rev.Rul. 97–38, page 116, an obligation to make future contributions will be treated as an obligation to restore a negative capital account balance to the extent of the required contribution, as long as the additional contribution is due no later than the close of the taxable year in which the partner's partnership interest is liquidated (or within 90 days of the close of the taxable year, if later). Treas. Reg. § 1.704–1(b)(2)(ii)(*c*)(*2*). In addition, if a partner contributes her own promissory note to the partnership, even though her capital account is not increased by the amount of the promissory note, she will be treated as having an obligation to restore a negative capital account to the extent of the principal amount of the promissory note. Treas. Reg. § 1.704–1(b)(2)(ii)(c)(1).

The operation of the basic rules is illustrated by the following example. Suppose A and B each contribute $15,000 to the AB Partnership, which then borrows $170,000 with full recourse and buys depreciable property for $200,000. A and B each have a capital account of $15,000 since partnership liabilities have no effect on partners' capital accounts. At this point, the partnership's balance sheet, for book accounting and tax purposes, respectively, is as follows:[2]

| | Assets | | | Liabilities and Partners' Capital Accounts | | |
	Book	Tax Basis			Book	Tax Basis
Property	$200,000	$200,000	Mortgage		$170,000	
			A		$ 15,000	$100,000
			B		$ 15,000	$100,000
	$200,000	$200,000			$200,000	$200,000

In the first year the partnership has no taxable income or loss except for a $20,000 depreciation deduction. If the full $20,000 depreciation deduction is specially allocated to B, the allocation will be recognized only if two conditions are met. First, B's capital account must be reduced by $20,000 to negative $5,000 (A's capital account will be unaffected and remain $15,000); the partnership balance sheet then would be as follows:

| | Assets | | | Liabilities and Partners' Capital Accounts | | |
	Book	Tax Basis			Book	Tax Basis
Property	$180,000	$180,000	Mortgage		$170,000	
			A		$ 15,000	$100,000
			B		($ 5,000)	$ 80,000
	$180,000	$180,000			$180,000	$180,000

Second, assuming that the building were sold for $180,000 at the beginning of the second year and the partnership liquidated, B must be required to contribute $5,000 to the partnership so that A will receive $15,000 on the liquidation.

If, however, the agreement of the partners was that B would not be required to restore any negative capital account, for example, because B was a limited partner, the special allocation will be only partly recognized.

---

2. The partners bases in their partnership interests depends on the ratio in which they share the risk on the debt if the property becomes worthless, see Treas. Reg. § 1.752–2. Computation of basis of partnership interests attributable to partnership indebtedness is discussed in Chapter 5.

See Treas. Reg. § 1.704–1(b)(2)(ii)(*e*), –1(b)(5), Ex. (15)(ii). The partners' interest in the portion of the allocation that does not have economic effect is determined by comparing how distributions (and contributions) would be made if the partnership sold its property for an amount equal to adjusted basis at the end of the prior year with the results of such a sale or liquidation at the end of the current year. Applying this methodology, only $15,000 of depreciation could be specially allocated to B, because A would bear the economic risk of the remaining $5,000 of depreciation. The balance sheet at the end of year 1 would be as follows:

	Assets			Liabilities and Partners' Capital Accounts	
	Book	Tax Basis		Book	Tax Basis
Property	$180,000	$180,000	Mortgage	$170,000	
			A	$ 10,000	$180,000
			B	$ 0	$ 0 [3]
	$180,000	$180,000		$180,000	$180,000

In this case, however, since the first year's special allocation reduced B's capital account to zero and A's capital account to $10,000, in year 2 the first $10,000 of depreciation must be allocated to A, thereby reducing A's capital account to zero. Furthermore, because B is not required to restore a negative capital account, A bears the entire risk of loss. Thus, the remaining $10,000 of depreciation cannot be allocated equally; it must be allocated entirely to A, who as the general partner is required to restore a negative capital account, e.g., to repay the loan if the partnership was unprofitable. The partnership's balance sheet at the end of year 2 would be as follows:

	Assets			Liabilities and Partners' Capital Accounts	
	Book	Tax Basis		Book	Tax Basis
Property	$160,000	$160,000	Mortgage	$170,000	
			A	($ 10,000)	$160,000
			B	$ 0	$ 0
	$160,000	$160,000		$160,000	$160,000

Now suppose that B has an obligation to restore a negative capital account, but that the obligation is limited to $20,000. In this case, depreciation deductions could be allocated to B until B's capital account balance is negative $20,000. All of the depreciation in the first year could be allocated to B; in year 2, only the first $15,000 of depreciation deduction could be allocated to B, and the remaining $5,000 of depreciation would have to be allocated to A. The partnership's balance sheet at the end of year 2 would be as follows:

3. B's basis is zero, because as a limited partner, B bears no risk of loss with respect to recourse liabilities of the partnership and thus under Treas. Reg. § 1.752–2, B is not allocated any portion of the partnership's debt to be treated as deemed contribution to the partnership under § 752(a).

Assets			Liabilities and Partners' Capital Accounts		
Property	Book	Tax Basis		Book	Tax Basis
Property	$160,000	$160,000	Mortgage	$170,000	
			A	$ 10,000	$160,000
			B	($ 20,000)	$ 0
	$160,000	$160,000		$160,000	$160,000

Finally, if the agreement of the parties is that notwithstanding the capital account balances (or if the partnership did not maintain capital accounts) the net proceeds from the sale of the building would be divided equally, then the special allocation of depreciation would fail entirely. In this case, A and B share the economic risk equally. and the depreciation must be allocated equally from the outset. See Treas. Reg. § 1.704–1(b)(3).

3. ALTERNATIVE TEST

Treas. Reg. § 1.704–1(b)(2)(ii)(d) provides a special rule for recognizing allocations that do not create or increase a capital account deficit when the partner does not have an unlimited obligation to restore the negative capital account upon liquidation. This provision is essential to allocate deductions to limited partners, is crucial to allocations in any limited liability company, and it may be relevant in general partnerships. To qualify under this provision, the partnership must maintain the required capital accounts and liquidate according to capital account balances. Under the alternative test, a limited partner (or a general partner without an unlimited obligation to restore a negative capital account) cannot be allocated items of deduction or loss that would create a deficit capital account or increase a deficit in the partner's capital account in excess of any limited amount that the partner is obligated to restore. To prevent manipulations by the partnership, when determining whether an allocation creates a deficit capital account balance under this test, reasonably anticipated distributions to be made in future years that will not be offset by future income allocations must be taken into account. In addition, the partnership agreement must provide for a "qualified income offset." This required provision must allocate to any partner who has a negative capital account as a result of an *unexpected* distribution sufficient income or gain to eliminate the deficit as soon as possible. The required income allocation must be made as soon as the partnership has gross income, even though in that year the partnership may have deductions that result in the partnership realizing no taxable income.

The alternative test in Treas. Reg. § 1.704–1(b)(2)(ii)(d) often is applied when the partnership agreement requires partners to restore negative capital accounts only to the extent necessary to pay partnership creditors, but not to make distributions to partners with positive capital accounts. Assume for example that C and D form an equal partnership to which C and D each contribute $30,000, the CD Partnership borrows $120,000, and it purchases depreciable property for $180,000. The property is depreciated over six years under the straightline method, and the partnership's gross income equals cash flow deduction items; thus the partnership's bottom line loss is $30,000 per year. C and D agree that D is obligated to restore a negative capital account only to the extent necessary to pay creditors (C is unconditionally obligated to restore a negative capital account), the agreement has a qualified income offset provision, and all items are allocated equally. The CD Partnership's initial balance sheet is as follows:

	Assets			Liabilities and Partners' Capital Accounts	
	Book	Tax Basis		Book	Tax Basis
Property	$180,000	$180,000	Debt	$120,000	
			C	$ 30,000	$ 90,000
			D	$ 30,000	$ 90,000
	$180,000	$180,000		$180,000	$180,000

In each of the first two years, D may be allocated his $15,000 share of the partnership's loss. At the end of two years, the partnership's balance sheet is as follows:

	Assets			Liabilities and Partners' Capital Accounts	
	Book	Tax Basis		Book	Tax Basis
Property	$120,000	$120,000	Debt	$120,000	
			C	$ 0	$ 60,000
			D	$ 0	$ 60,000
	$120,000	$120,000		$120,000	$120,000

In year 3 the partnership again loses $30,000, attributable to the depreciation deduction. Because C's capital account is not positive, D may be allocated his share of the depreciation deductions. Both C and D will have capital accounts of negative $15,000 at the end of year three, but in this case, D will be obligated to restore the negative capital account to repay the debt, since (assuming that the asset actually did lose value commensurate with depreciation) the partnership holds an asset worth $90,000 and owes a debt of $120,000.

If, however, D were a limited partner, with no obligation to restore a negative capital account, no portion of the loss in year 3 could be allocated to D. The entire loss would be allocated to C, who bears the risk of loss. In this case the partnership balance sheet would be as follows at the end of year 3.

	Assets			Liabilities and Partners' Capital Accounts		
		Tax				Tax
	Book	Basis			Book	Basis
Property	$90,000	$90,000		Debt	$120,000	
				C	($ 30,000)	$90,000
				D	0	0
	$90,000	$90,000			$ 90,000	$90,000

The existence of a negative capital account for D and the operation of the qualified income offset can be illustrated by a cash distribution by the CD partnership. Assume that in year 4 the CD partnership, which again loses $30,000 (all attributable to the depreciation deduction) borrows $20,000 and distributes $10,000 to each of C and D. Again, the entire $30,000 loss is allocated to C; but each partner's capital account also is reduced by the $10,000 distribution, and D now has a negative capital account.[4] The balance sheet at the end of year 4 is as follows:

	Assets			Liabilities and Partners' Capital Accounts		
		Tax				Tax
	Book	Basis			Book	Basis
Property	$60,000	$60,000		Debt	$140,000	
				C	($ 70,000)	$60,000
				D	($ 10,000)	0
	$60,000	$60,000			$ 60,000	$60,000

Now assume that in year 5 the CD partnership again loses $30,000. Because D has a negative capital account due to a distribution, if the partnership has gross income, D must be allocated the first $10,000 of gross income while any remaining gross income and all of the deductions are allocated to C. For example, if the $30,000 loss consisted of gross income of $11,000, § 162 deductible expenses of $11,000, and the $30,000 depreciation deduction, D would be allocated gross income of $10,000, while C would be allocated a loss of $40,000. D's $10,000 of income would consist of a pro rata share (i.e., 10/11th) of each item of gross income. Thus, the partnership's balance sheet at the end of year 5 would be as follows:

	Assets			Liabilities and Partners' Capital Accounts		
		Tax				Tax
	Book	Basis			Book	Basis
Property	$30,000	$30,000		Debt	$140,000	
				C	($110,000)	$20,000
				D	0	$10,000
	$30,000	$30,000			$ 30,000	$30,000

4. Pursuant to § 731, D recognized gain of $10,000 on the distribution because D had a zero basis prior to the distribution.

Rev.Rul. 92–97, 1992–2 C.B. 124, provides another example of the operation of a qualified income offset provision. That ruling dealt with the allocation of discharge of indebtedness income where the partners shared losses in a different ratio than they shared profits. A and B shared profits equally, but agreed that A would bear 10 percent of the losses while B would bear 90 percent of the losses. A contributed $10 and B contributed $90, and the partnership borrowed $900 with recourse. Accordingly, under Treas. Reg. § 1.752–2, A bore $90 of the economic risk of loss associated with the recourse loan and B bore $810 of the risk. In Situation 1 of the Ruling, the partnership maintained capital accounts but because the partners were obligated to restore negative capital accounts only to the extent necessary to pay creditors, the partnership met the alternative test for economic effect under Treas. Reg. § 1.704–1(b)(2)(ii)(*d*). At the time the debt was canceled, both partners had negative capital accounts, and their capital accounts both would have remained negative after being increased for discharge of indebtedness income allocated equally, $450 to each, as provided in the partnership agreement. The cancellation of the debt eliminated the partners' obligations to restore their negative capital accounts. Thus, A neither could enjoy any economic benefit from an allocation of discharge of indebtedness income in excess of $90 nor suffer any economic detriment from an allocation of discharge of indebtedness income of less than $90. Similarly, B neither could enjoy any economic benefit from an allocation of discharge of indebtedness income in excess of $810 nor suffer any economic detriment from an allocation of discharge of indebtedness income of less than $810. Accordingly, the equal allocation of discharge of indebtedness income did not have economic effect. Instead the income must have been allocated $90 to A and $810 to B, which was the same ratio as the decrease in their shares of partnership liability resulting from the cancellation of the debt. Situation 2 of the ruling was identical to Situation 1 except that A and B had an unlimited deficit capital account restoration obligation as provided in Treas. Reg. § 1.704–1(b)(2)(ii)(*b*)(*3*). In this situation the equal allocation of the discharge of indebtedness income had economic effect because the income allocation could result in one partner's negative capital account restoration obligation being invoked to satisfy the other partner's positive capital account balance.

For additional examples, see Treas. Reg. § 1.704–1(b)(5), Ex. (1)(iii)–(x), (15), (16)(ii).

4. ECONOMIC EFFECT EQUIVALENCE

Treas. Reg. § 1.704–1(b)(2)(ii)(*i*) provides that an allocation that does not have economic effect under the rules prescribed in Treas. Reg. § 1.704–1(b)(2)(ii) will be deemed to have economic effect if, as of the end of each partnership year, a liquidation of the partnership at that time or at the end of any future year would produce the same economic results to the partners as would occur if the requirements of Treas. Reg. § 1.704–1(b)(2)(ii)(*i*) had been satisfied, regardless of economic performance of the partnership. This provision assures the recognition of any allocation that allocates a consistent fraction of all items to each partner, as long as the partners are fully liable for partnership debts and the partners' capital contributions were in the same ratios as their shares of profits and losses. See Treas. Reg. § 1.704–1(b)(5), Ex. (4)(ii). Thus, for example, if A contributes $40, B contributes $35, and C contributes $25 to form the ABC Partnership, and the partners' respective shares of all items of income and loss are A, 40 percent, B, 35 percent, and C, 25 percent, allocations in those ratios will be respected even if the partnership does not maintain capital accounts. If, however, one of the partner's initial capital contribution differed from the profit and loss sharing ratio, for example, if A had contributed only $38, then the safe harbor would not apply.

5.   FACTS AND CIRCUMSTANCES ALLOCATIONS

Treas. Reg. § 1.704–1(b)(3) provides rules governing the determination of a partner's interest in a partnership that must be used if the partnership agreement does not allocate partners' distributive shares or if the allocation in the agreement does not have substantial economic effect. Under the regulation, all of the facts and circumstances are to be taken into account. The regulation states that except for allocations of deductions attributable to nonrecourse debt, the allocation with respect to any particular item of partnership income, gain, deduction, loss, or credit does not necessarily have to correspond to any other partnership item. The starting point, however, is the presumption that all partners share every item on a per capita basis. Additional factors that may overcome the presumption include the partners' relative capital contributions, their interests in economic profits or losses (in contrast to tax profits and losses), their interests in cash flow, and the relative rights of the partners upon liquidation. No specific guidance regarding the application of these factors is provided, but Treas. Reg. § 1.704–1(b)(5), Ex. (1)(i) and (ii), (4)(i), (5)(i) and (ii), (6), (7), and (8) illustrate reallocation of items according to the partners' interests in a partnership. In PNRC Limited Partnership v. Commissioner, T.C. Memo. 1993–335, the Tax Court held that the allocation of losses in the partnership agreement did not have substantial economic effect because the limited partner was not required to restore a negative capital account. Taking into account the specific facts, losses were allocated in proportion to capital contributions, which was most consistent with the partners' interests in the partnership.

In Estate of Ballantyne v. Commissioner, 341 F.3d 802 (8th Cir. 2003), the deceased taxpayer and his brother had operated a partnership for many years. The partnership conducted an oil and gas business, which was managed by the decedent, and a farming business, which was managed by the decedent's brother. The brothers had reported as equal partners, even though the decedent consistently withdrew the profits from the oil and gas business and decedent's brother consistently withdrew the profits from the farming business. After the decedent's death, the estate took the position that all of the income from the farming activity—the more profitable activity—was reportable as the decedent's brother's distributive share. Because the partnership was an oral partnership and the partnership did not maintain capital accounts, any allocation failed the substantial economic effect test, and the partners' interests in the partnership were determined under the facts and circumstances test of Treas. Reg. § 1.704–1(b)(3). Based on the evidence, the estate could not overcome the presumption that the partners were equal partners. There was no record of capital contributions; the amount of profits of each activity varied from year to year, as did withdrawals. The partners' economic interests and interests in cash flow could not be determined because the partnership books and records were inadequate. However, the "facts"—mostly the witnesses' "beliefs" that the brothers were 50/50 partners—indicated that they were to share liquidating distributions equally. That factor, combined with the brothers long-time consistent reporting as equal partners and the absence of any evidence that the brothers' reporting position involved tax avoidance, was sufficient to convince the court that they were equal partners.

6. ALLOCATIONS TO SERVICE PARTNERS WITH FORFEITABLE INTERESTS

As discussed at page 58, proposed regulations under §§ 83 and 721 deal with the transfer of a partnership interest in exchange for services. When a transferred partnership interest is subject to a substantial risk of forfeiture, unless an election is made under section 83(b), the holder of the partnership interest is not treated as a partner until the interest becomes substantially vested. See Treas. Reg. § 1.83–1(a)(1). If a section 83(b) election is made with respect to such an interest, the service provider will be treated as a partner, even though the interest remains forfeitable. These rules raise special problems regarding the tax treatment of allocations of items of gain or loss to a partner during the period in which the partner's interest remains forfeitable. If the partner who receives a forfeitable partnership interest in exchange for services does not make a § 83(b) election with respect to that interest, the partner cannot be allocated any portion of partnership income or loss, and any distributions made to the service provider with respect to the partnership interest are treated as additional compensation and not partnership distributions. But if a service partner who receives a substantially nonvested partnership interest makes a valid § 83(b) election, the service provider is treated as a partner with respect to such an interest, and the partnership must allocate partnership items to the service provider as if the partnership interest were substantially vested. See Notice 2005–43, 2005–24 I.R.B. 1221.

Further complications arise if a service provider who has received a forfeitable compensatory partnership interest makes a § 83(b) election, is allocated items of partnership income and loss, and subsequently forfeits the partnership interest. Prop. Reg. § 1.704–1(b)(4)(xii) (2005) would address these issues. The operation of the proposed regulations is described in the preamble to Partial Withdrawal of Notice of Proposed Rulemaking Notice of Proposed Rulemaking, and Notice of Public Hearing, Partnership Equity for Services, REG–105346–03, 70 F.R. 29675 (May 23, 2005), as follows:

If an election under section 83(b) has been made with respect to a substantially nonvested interest, the holder of the nonvested interest may be allocated partnership items that may later be forfeited. For this reason, allocations of partnership items while the interest is substantially nonvested cannot have economic effect. Under the proposed regulations, such allocations will be treated as being in accordance with the partners' interests in the partnership if: (a) the partnership agreement requires that the partnership make forfeiture allocations if the interest for which the section 83(b) election is made is later forfeited; and (b) all material allocations and capital account adjustments under the partnership agreement not pertaining to substantially nonvested partnership interests for which a section 83(b) election has been made are recognized under section 704(b). This safe harbor does not apply if, at the time of the section 83(b) election, there is a plan that a substantially nonvested interest will be forfeited. All of the facts and circumstances (including the tax status of the holder of the substantially nonvested interest) will be considered in determining whether there is a plan that the interest will be forfeited. In such a case, the partners' distributive shares of partnership items shall be determined in accordance with the partners' interests in the partnership under [Treas. Reg. §] 1.704–1(b)(3).

Generally, forfeiture allocations are allocations to the service provider of partnership gross income and gain or gross deduction and loss (to the extent such items are available) that offset prior distributions and allocations of partnership items with respect to the forfeited partnership interest. These rules are designed to ensure that any partnership income (or loss) that was allocated to the service provider prior to the forfeiture is offset by allocations on the forfeiture of the interest. Also, to carry out the prohibition under section 83(b)(1) on deductions with respect to amounts included in income under section 83(b), these rules generally cause a forfeiting partner to be allocated partnership income to offset any distributions to the partner that reduced the partner's basis in the partnership below the amount included in income under section 83(b).

Forfeiture allocations may be made out of the partnership's items for the entire taxable year. In determining the gross income of the partnership in the taxable year of the forfeiture, the rules of [Treas. Reg. §] 1.83–6(c) apply. As a result, the partnership generally will have gross income in the taxable year of the forfeiture equal to the amount of the allowable deduction to the service recipient partnership upon the transfer of the interest as a result of the making of the section 83(b) election, regardless of the fair market value of the partnership's assets at the time of forfeiture.

In certain circumstances, the partnership will not have enough income and gain to fully offset prior allocations of loss to the forfeiting service provider. The proposed revenue procedure includes a rule that requires the recapture of losses taken by the service provider prior to the forfeiture of the interest to the extent that those losses are not recaptured through forfeiture allocations of income and gain to the service provider. This rule does not provide the other partners in the partnership with the opportunity to increase their shares of partnership loss (or reduce their shares of partnership income) for the year of the forfeiture by the amount of loss that was previously allocated to the forfeiting service provider.

In other circumstances, the partnership will not have enough deductions and loss to fully offset prior allocations of income to the forfeiting service provider. It appears that, in such a case, section 83(b)(1) may prohibit the service provider from claiming a loss with respect to partnership income that was previously allocated to the service provider. However, a forfeiting partner is entitled to a loss for any basis in a partnership that is attributable to contributions of money or property to the partnership (including amounts paid for the interest) remaining after the forfeiture allocations have been made. See [Treas. Reg. §] 1.83–2(a).

(2) SUBSTANTIALITY

REGULATIONS: Section 1.704–1(b)(2)(iii); –1(b)(5), Ex. (2)–(6), (10).

The substantial economic effect test has two parts. To be respected, an allocation must have economic effect (or its alternative) and the allocation must be "substantial." To be considered substantial the economic effect of the allocation must have a reasonable possibility of affecting the dollar amounts to be received by the partners independent of the tax consequences of the allocation. Treas. Reg. § 1.704–1(b)(2)(iii)(a). An allocation is not substantial if, as a result of the allocation, the after-tax economic consequences to at least one partner may, in present value terms, be enhanced, and there is a strong likelihood that the after-tax consequences of no partner will, in present value terms, be diminished. Determining whether an allocation that has economic effect also is "substantial" often requires an examination of factors extrinsic to the partnership, such as the individual partners' income tax brackets.

Revenue Ruling 99–43

1999–2 C.B. 506.

ISSUE

Do partnership allocations lack substantiality under § 1.704–1(b)(2)(iii) of the Income Tax Regulations when the partners amend the partnership agreement to create offsetting special allocations of particular items after the events giving rise to the items have occurred?

FACTS

A and B, both individuals, formed a general partnership, PRS. A and B each contributed $1,000 and also agreed that each would be allocated a 50–percent share of all partnership items. The partnership agreement provides that, upon the contribution of additional capital by either partner, PRS must revalue the partnership's property and adjust the partners' capital accounts under § 1.704–1(b)(2)(iv)(f).

PRS borrowed $8,000 from a bank and used the borrowed and contributed funds to purchase nondepreciable property for $10,000. The loan was nonrecourse to A and B and was secured only by the property. No principal payments were due for 6 years, and interest was payable semi-annually at a market rate.

After one year, the fair market value of the property fell from $10,000 to $6,000, but the principal amount of the loan remained $8,000. As part of a workout arrangement among the bank, PRS, A, and B, the bank reduced the principal amount of the loan by $2,000, and A contributed an additional $500 to PRS. A's capital account was credited with the $500, which PRS used to pay currently deductible expenses incurred in connection with the workout. All $500 of the currently deductible workout expenses were allocated to A. B made no additional contribution of capital. At the time of the workout, B was insolvent within the meaning of § 108(a) of the Internal Revenue Code. A and B agreed that, after the workout, A would have a 60–percent interest and B would have a 40–percent interest in the profits and losses of PRS.

As a result of the property's decline in value and the workout, PRS had two items to allocate between A and B. First, the agreement to cancel $2,000 of the loan resulted in $2,000 of cancellation of indebtedness income (COD income). Second, A's contribution of $500 to PRS was an event that required PRS, under the partnership agreement, to revalue partnership property and adjust A's and B's capital accounts. Because of the decline in value of the property, the revaluation resulted in a $4,000 economic loss that must be allocated between A's and B's capital accounts.

Under the terms of the original partnership agreement, PRS would have allocated these items equally between A and B. A and B, however, amend the partnership agreement (in a timely manner) to make two special allocations. First, PRS specially allocates the entire $2,000 of COD income to B, an insolvent partner. Second, PRS specially allocates the book loss from the revaluation $1,000 to A and $3,000 to B.

While A receives a $1,000 allocation of book loss and B receives a $3,000 allocation of book loss, neither of these allocations results in a tax loss to either partner. Rather, the allocations result only in adjustments to A's and B's capital accounts. Thus, the cumulative effect of the special allocations is to reduce each partner's capital account to zero immediately following the allocations despite the fact that B is allocated $2,000 of income for tax purposes.

LAW

Section 61(a)(12) provides that gross income includes income from the discharge of indebtedness.

Rev. Rul. 91–31, 1991–1 C.B. 19, holds that a taxpayer realizes COD income when a creditor (who was not the seller of the underlying property) reduces the principal amount of an under-secured nonrecourse debt.

Under § 704(b) and the regulations there under, allocations of a partnership's items of income, gain, loss, deduction, or credit provided for in the partnership agreement will be respected if the allocations have substantial economic effect. Allocations that fail to have substantial economic effect will be reallocated according to the partners' interests in the partnership (as defined in § 1.704–1(b)(3)).

Section 1.704–1(b)(2)(iv)(f) provides that a partnership may, upon the occurrence of certain events (including the contribution of money to the partnership by a new or existing partner), increase or decrease the partners' capital accounts to reflect a revaluation of the partnership property.

Section 1.704–1(b)(2)(iv)(g) provides that, to the extent a partnership's property is reflected on the books of the partnership at a book value that differs from the adjusted tax basis, the substantial economic effect requirements apply to the allocations of book items. Section 704(c) and § 1.704–1(b)(4)(i) govern the partners' distributive shares of tax items.

Section 1.704–1(b)(2)(i) provides that the determination of whether an allocation of income, gain, loss, or deduction (or item thereof) to a partner has substantial economic effect involves a two-part analysis that is made at the end of the partnership year to which the allocation relates. In order for an allocation to have substantial economic effect, the allocation must have both economic effect (within the meaning of § 1.704–1(b)(2)(ii)) and be substantial (within the meaning of § 1.704–1(b)(2)(iii)).

Section 1.704–1(b)(2)(iii)(a) provides that the economic effect of an allocation (or allocations) is substantial if there is a reasonable possibility that the allocation (or allocations) will substantially affect the dollar amounts to be received by the partners from the partnership independent of the tax consequences. However, the economic effect of an allocation is not substantial if, at the time the allocation becomes part of the partnership agreement, (1) the after-tax economic consequences of at least one partner may, in present value terms, be enhanced compared to the consequences if the allocation (or allocations) were not contained in the partnership agreement, and (2) there is a strong likelihood that the after-tax economic consequences of no partner will, in present value terms, be substantially diminished compared to the consequences if the allocation (or allocations) were not contained in the partnership agreement. In determining the after-tax economic benefit or detriment to a partner, tax consequences that result from the interaction of the allocation with the partner's tax attributes that are unrelated to the partnership will be taken into account.

Section 1.704–1(b)(2)(iii)(b) provides that the economic effect of an allocation (or allocations) in a partnership taxable year is not substantial if the allocations result in shifting tax consequences. Shifting tax consequences result when, at the time the allocation (or allocations) becomes part of the partnership agreement, there is a strong likelihood that (1) the net increases and decreases that will be recorded in the partners' respective capital accounts for the taxable year will not differ substantially from the net increases and decreases that would be recorded in the partners' respective capital accounts for the year if the allocations were not contained in the partnership agreement, and (2) the total tax liability of the partners (for their respective tax years in which the allocations will be taken into account) will be less than if the allocations were not contained in the partnership agreement.

Section 1.704–1(b)(2)(iii)(c) provides that the economic effect of an allocation (or allocations) in a partnership taxable year is not substantial if the allocations are transitory. Allocations are considered transitory if a partnership agreement provides for the possibility that one or more allocations (the "original allocation(s)") will be largely offset by other allocations (the "offsetting allocation(s)"), and, at the time the allocations become part of the partnership agreement, there is a strong likelihood that (1) the net increases and decreases that will be recorded in the partners' capital accounts for the taxable years to which the allocations relate will not differ substantially from the net increases and decreases that would be recorded in such partners' respective capital accounts for such years if the original and offsetting allocation(s) were not contained in the partnership agreement, and (2) the total tax liability of the partners (for their respective tax years in which the allocations will be taken into account) will be less than if the allocations were not contained in the partnership agreement.

Section 761(c) provides that a partnership agreement includes any modifications made prior to, or at, the time prescribed for filing a partnership return (not including extensions) which are agreed to by all partners, or which are adopted in such other manner as may be provided by the partnership agreement.

ANALYSIS

PRS is free to allocate partnership items between A and B in accordance with the provisions of the partnership agreement if the allocations have substantial economic effect under § 1.704–1(b)(2). To the extent that the minimum gain chargeback rules do not apply,* COD income may be

---

* [Ed: Under certain circumstances, the COD income would be allocated between the partners in accordance with their shares of partnership minimum gain, discussed in Section 2.B. of this chapter, page 148, because the cancellation of the nonrecourse debt would result in a decrease in partnership minimum gain. See § 1.704–2(d). However, in this situation, there is no minimum gain because the principal amount of the debt never exceeded the property's book value. Therefore, the minimum gain charge-back reallocated in accordance with the rules under § 1.704–1(b)(2). This is true notwithstanding that the COD income arises in connection with the cancellation of a nonrecourse debt.

The economic effect of an allocation is not substantial if, at the time that the allocation becomes part of the partnership agreement, the allocation fails each of two tests. The allocation fails the first test if the after-tax consequences of at least one partner may, in present value terms, be enhanced compared to the consequences if the allocation (or allocations) were not contained in the partnership agreement. The allocation fails the second test if there is a strong likelihood that the after-tax economic consequences of no partner will, in present value terms, be substantially diminished compared to such consequences if the allocation (or allocations) were not contained in the partnership agreement.

A and B amended the PRS partnership agreement to provide for an allocation of the entire $2,000 of the COD income to B. B, an insolvent taxpayer, is eligible to exclude the income under § 108, so it is unlikely that the $2,000 of COD income would increase B's immediate tax liability. Without the special allocation, A, who is not insolvent or otherwise entitled to exclude the COD income under § 108, would pay tax immediately on the $1,000 of COD income allocated under the general ratio for sharing income. A and B also amended the PRS partnership agreement to provide for the special allocation of the book loss resulting from the revaluation. Because the two special allocations offset each other, B will not realize any economic benefit from the $2,000 income allocation, even if the property subsequently appreciates in value.

The economics of PRS are unaffected by the paired special allocations. After the capital accounts of A and B are adjusted to reflect the special allocations, A and B each have a capital account of zero, Economically, the situation of both partners is identical to what it would have been had the special allocations not occurred. In addition, a strong likelihood exists that the total tax liability of A and B will be less than if PRS had allocated 50 percent of the $2,000 of COD income and 50 percent of the $4,000 book loss to each partner. Therefore, the special allocations of COD income and book loss are shifting allocations under § 1.704–1(b)(2)(iii)(b) and lack substantiality. (Alternatively, the allocations could be transitory allocations under § 1.704–1(b)(2)(iii)(c) if the allocations occur during different partnership taxable years).

This conclusion is not altered by the "value equals basis" rule that applies in determining the substantiality of an allocation. See § 1.704–1(b)(2)(iii)(c)(2). Under that rule, the adjusted tax basis (or, if different, the book value) of partnership property will be presumed to be the fair market value of the property. This presumption is appropriate in most cases because, under § 1.704–1(b)(2)(iv), property generally will be reflected on

quirement does not govern the manner in which the COD income is allocated between A and B, and PRS's special allocation of COD income must satisfy the substantial economic effect standard. See Rev. Rul. 92–97, 1992–2 C.B. 124.]

the books of the partnership at its fair market value when acquired. Thus, an allocation of gain or loss from the disposition of the property will reflect subsequent changes in the value of the property that generally cannot be predicted.

The substantiality of an allocation, however, is analyzed "at the time the allocation becomes part of the partnership agreement," not the time at which the allocation is first effective. See § 1.704–1(b)(2)(iii)(a). In the situation described above, the provisions of the PRS partnership agreement governing the allocation of gain or loss from the disposition of property are changed at a time that is after the property has been revalued on the books of the partnership, but are effective for a period that begins prior to the revaluation. See § 1.704–1(b)(2)(iv)(f).

Under these facts, the presumption that value equals basis does not apply to validate the allocations. Instead, PRS's allocations of gain or loss must be closely scrutinized in determining the appropriate tax consequences. Cf. § 1.704–1(b)(4)(vi). In this situation, the special allocations of the $2,000 of COD income and $4,000 of book loss will not be respected and, instead, must be allocated in accordance with the A's and B's interests in the partnership under § 1.704–1(b)(3).

Close scrutiny also would be required if the changes were made at a time when the events giving rise to the allocations had not yet occurred but were likely to occur or if, under the original allocation provisions of a partnership agreement, there was a strong likelihood that a disproportionate amount of COD income earned in the future would be allocated to any partner who is insolvent at the time of the allocation and would be offset by an increased allocation of loss or a reduced allocation of income to such partner or partners.

HOLDING

Partnership special allocations lack substantiality when the partners amend the partnership agreement to specially allocate COD income and book items from a related revaluation after the events creating such items have occurred if the overall economic effect of the special allocations on the partners' capital accounts does not differ substantially from the economic effect of the original allocations in the partnership agreement.

ILLUSTRATIVE MATERIAL

1. GENERAL PRINCIPLES

The operation of Treas. Reg. § 1.704–1(b)(2)(iii)(a) to invalidate an allocation that has "economic effect" but is not "substantial" is illustrated by the following facts. I and J contribute equal amounts to become partners in an investment partnership. The partnership distributes currently all income credited to the partners' capital accounts. I expects consistently to be subject to tax at the 15 percent bracket, and J expects consistently to be subject to tax at the 28 percent bracket. There is a strong likelihood that over the next several years the IJ Partnership will realize $500 of tax-exempt interest and $500 of taxable interest and dividends on its investments. If all items were allocated equally between I and J, which would be consistent with their capital interests, each would have $250 of tax-exempt income and $250 of taxable income. As a result, I would realize $462.50 of after-tax income, and J would realize only $430 of after-tax income.

	I		J	
	Before–Tax	After–Tax	Before–Tax	After–Tax
Taxable	$250	$212.50	$250	$180
Tax–Exempt	$250	$250	$250	$250
	$500	$462.50	$500	$430

If, however, the tax-exempt interest were allocated 42 percent to I and 58 percent to J, and the taxable income was allocated 60 percent to I and 40 percent to J, and each partner's capital account were increased according to those percentages, I would realize $210 of tax-exempt income and $300 of taxable income, and J would realize $290 of tax-exempt income and $200 of taxable income. On an after-tax basis, however, I would realize a total of $465 and J would realize a total of $434.

	I		J	
	Before–Tax	After–Tax	Before–Tax	After–Tax
Taxable	$300	$255	$200	$144
Tax–Exempt	$210	$210	$290	$290
	$510	$465	$490	$434

Each of the partners would have more after-tax income as a result of the allocation than if the allocation had been consistent with capital interests. Therefore, even though it has economic effect, the allocation is not "substantial," and it will not be respected for tax purposes. Because under the allocation, I's capital account is credited with $510 and J's capital account is credited with $490, all items will be allocated 51 percent to I and 49 percent to J in accordance with Treas. Reg. § 1.701–1(b)(3). See Treas. Reg. § 1.704–1(b)(5), Ex. (5). The result is as follows:

	I		J	
	Before–Tax	After–Tax	Before–Tax	After–Tax
Taxable	$255	$216.75	$245	$176.40
Tax–Exempt	$255	$255	$245	$245
	$510	$471.75	$490	$421.40

As a result of attempting to reduce taxes through a special allocation that is not substantial, J is left worse off than she would have been if all items had been allocated equally, while I is better-off at J's expense.

2. SHIFTING ALLOCATIONS

Treas. Reg. § 1.704–1(b)(2)(iii)(*b*) elaborates the general rule by providing that an allocation that merely shifts tax consequences within a given year and does not affect the economic consequences to the partners will not be substantial. This special rule addresses allocations that when viewed together with other allocations result in a net increase or decrease in the partners' capital accounts that does not differ from what would have resulted without the special allocations, but which have the effect of reducing the partners' total tax liability. Assume, for example that C and D are equal partners. In the year in question, the CD partnership realizes a $10,000 capital loss and an operating loss of $10,000. In that same taxable year C individually realizes capital gains of $10,000 and D individually realizes no capital gains. If both items were allocated equally between the partners, C and D each would decrease her capital account by $10,000. C would be able to personally deduct $5,000 of the operating loss and $5,000 of the capital loss. D would be able to deduct $5,000 of the operating loss, but due to § 1211(b) only $3,000 of the capital loss. If the partners amended the partnership agreement to allocate the entire capital loss to C and the entire operating loss to D, C and D each would still decrease her capital account by $10,000. Thus such an allocation has economic effect. However, the net decreases in the partners' capital accounts do not differ substantially from the net decreases that would have occurred without the allocation. Due to the ability of C to deduct currently all of the capital losses, the total tax liability of the partners' will be less than it would be without the allocation. Thus, the allocation does not have "substantial" effect. The allocation will not be respected, and each item will be allocated in proportion to the net decreases in the partners' capital accounts—in this case, equally.

If, on the other hand, at the time the partnership agreement was amended to provide for the above described allocation there was not a strong likelihood that the partnership would have substantially equal amounts of capital losses and operating losses, then the allocation would have substantial economic effect. Avoiding the shifting allocation rule is difficult, however. The regulations provide that if at the end of the year for which a special shifting allocation is in effect the changes in partners capital accounts during the year do not differ substantially from the changes that would have occurred if the special allocation had not been in effect, a presumption arises that there was a strong likelihood that the proscribed effect would occur. See Treas. Reg. § 1.704–1(b)(5), Ex. (6), (7), and (10).

3.   TRANSITORY ALLOCATIONS

3.1.   *In General*

Treas. Reg. § 1.704–1(b)(2)(iii)(*c*) provides another special application of the substantiality rule by treating transitory allocations as insubstantial. An allocation is transitory if: (1) the allocation may be offset by another allocation; (2) at the time the allocations are included in the partnership agreement there is a strong likelihood that the net increases and decreases in the partners' respective capital accounts will not differ substantially from what they would have been absent the initial special allocation and the offsetting allocation; and (3) the total tax liability of the partners will be less than it would have been if the allocations were not in the partnership agreement. If, however, there is a strong likelihood that the offsetting allocations will not be made within five years of the initial allocation, the allocations are presumed to be substantial. As in the case of shifting allocations, occurrence of the proscribed result raises the presumption that it would occur.

The transitory allocation rule applies, for example, in the following circumstances. Assume that the EFGH Partnership owns and operates a rental property which can be predicted to produce net income of $12,000 per year for each of the next four years. Each partner has a one-quarter capital interest. E has a $9,000 net operating loss carryover under § 172 from an unrelated business that is about to expire. The partnership agreement is amended to allocate to E three-quarters of the partnership net income for the last year in which E can use his net operating loss carryover, with the other one-quarter being divided equally among F, G, and H, and to allocate one-twelfth of the net income of the partnership to E and the remaining eleven-twelfths equally among F, G, and H for each of the next three years. As a result, E is allocated an additional $6,000 of net income in the first year, while each of the other partners is allocated $2,000 less net income than they otherwise would have been allocated. Over the next three years, E is allocated a total of $6,000 less than he would otherwise have been allocated, and each of the other partners is allocated a total of $2,000 more.

Without Special Allocation

	Year 1	Year 2	Year 3	Year 4	Total
E	$3,000	$3,000	$3,000	$3,000	$12,000
F	$3,000	$3,000	$3,000	$3,000	$12,000
G	$3,000	$3,000	$3,000	$3,000	$12,000
H	$3,000	$3,000	$3,000	$3,000	$12,000

With Special Allocation

	Year 1	Year 2	Year 3	Year 4	Total
E	$9,000	$1,000	$1,000	$1,000	$12,000
F	$1,000	$3,667	$3,667	$3,666	$12,000
G	$1,000	$3,667	$3,667	$3,666	$12,000
H	$1,000	$3,667	$3,667	$3,666	$12,000

On these facts, there was at the time the allocations were made a strong likelihood that over the four year span each partner would be allocated $12,000 of net income. The allocation to E of more of the income in the first year was cancelled out by the allocation to him of less of the income in any of the next three years. Thus the allocation is transitory and, since it reduced the partners' taxes over the four year span by allowing E to use his net operating loss carryover, it will not be respected. The net income of the partnership will be allocated equally in each of the four years. See Treas. Reg. § 1.704–1(b)(5), Ex. (8).

3.2. *Gain Chargebacks*

An important factor in applying the transitory allocation rule is the presumption in Treas. Reg. § 1.704–1(b)(2)(iii)(c)(2) that the actual fair market value of property decreases by tax depreciation. In some cases this rule is necessary to prevent a special allocation of depreciation coupled with a gain chargeback on the disposition of property from giving rise to a transitory allocation. (For an illustration, of a gain chargeback see page 111.) As a result of this assumption, any gain that may be realized on the sale of depreciable property is not taken into account in determining whether there was a strong likelihood that an allocation of gain offsetting the depreciation deductions would occur within five years.

Because liquidating distributions must be made in accordance with positive capital account balances, economic considerations of the partners dictate that gain chargebacks be part and parcel of provisions in partnership agreements specially allocating depreciation deductions. As the *Orrisch* opinion points out, if the property is sold for at least its original cost, the special allocation of deductions and the corresponding "chargeback" of gain only affect tax liabilities and do not affect the proceeds received by each partner. The cash proceeds are distributed as if no special allocation had been made. The regulations, however, take the position that this does not mean that there is no substantial economic effect to the allocations if there is a strong likelihood that the offsetting allocations will not be made within five years. The theory underlying this rule appears to be that an allocation which has effect for such a time interval interposes sufficient risk that the partnership will suffer an actual loss that cannot be eliminated by offsetting a future special allocation, such as a gain chargeback. Furthermore, due to the conclusive presumption in Treas. Reg. § 1.704–1(b)(2)(iii)(c)(2) that the fair market value of the property decreased by tax depreciation, even if a sale of the property within five years at a price equal to its original cost is a virtual certainty, the allocation of depreciation coupled with the gain chargeback is not transitory, since there is no strong likelihood of the gain occurring.

3.3. *Recapture Gain*

An allocation of recapture gain on disposition of property, usually § 1245 depreciation recapture, cannot have substantial economic effect because classifying gain as recapture merely changes the tax characterization of the gain from § 1231 gain to ordinary income. Furthermore, if recapture gain were allocated in the same manner as total gain, a partner might be allocated recapture gain that exceeded the partner's share of prior depreciation attributable to the property while another partner would be allocated recapture gain less than that partner's share of prior depreciation attributable to the property. Because recapture gain is intended to offset the earlier depreciation deductions, recapture should be allocated to the partner who received those depreciation deductions. Treas. Reg. § 1.1245–1(e)(2) addresses this issue by providing that a partner's share of recapture gain equals the lesser of (1) the partner's share of total gain arising from the disposition of the property, or (2) the partner's share of depreciation or amortization from the property. Any recapture gain that is not allocated under the general rule is allocated among those partners whose shares of total gain on the disposition of the property exceed their shares of depreciation or amortization with respect to the property. If after applying these rules, the aggregate amount of recapture income allocated to the partners exceeds the partnership's recapture income, the partnership's recapture income is allocated among the partners in proportion to their shares of prior depreciation (subject to the gain ceiling rule). Treas. Reg. § 1.1245–1(e)(2)(ii)(C)(4). These rules are intended to insure, to the extent possible, that on the disposition of property each partner will recognize recapture income equal to the depreciation or amortization deductions previously allocated to that partner with respect to the property. A mismatch nevertheless may occur if, for example, the gain allocated to a partner on the sale of a property is less than the depreciation previously allocated to that partner. The regulations provide special rules for determining a partner's share of depreciation or amortization from contributed property subject to § 704(c). See page 154.

(3) "BUSINESS PURPOSE" AND "TAX AVOIDANCE" WITH RESPECT TO PARTICULAR ALLOCATIONS

Judicial interpretation of the pre–1976 version of § 704(b), which disallowed allocations if the principal purpose was tax avoidance or evasion, focused primarily on the substantial economic effect test, but sometimes the partners' tax avoidance motives were considered as well. See Goldfine v. Commissioner, 80 T.C. 843 (1983). The statutory stress of current § 704(b), however, is on an objective economic effect test for determining the validity of partnership allocations. Estate of Carberry v. Commissioner, 933 F.2d 1124 (2d Cir.1991), specifically rejected the taxpayer's argument that a business purpose could validate an allocation of loss to a partner when the loss did not have substantial economic effect. Even if there is an alleged business purpose for an allocation, the validity of the allocation for tax purposes turns on whether it has substantial economic effect. See also Young v. Commissioner, 923 F.2d 719 (9th Cir.1991). But the Senate Finance Committee Report states that the intent of the 1976 version of § 704(b) is "to prevent the use of special allocations for tax avoidance purposes while allowing their use for bona fide business purposes." Arguably, this language leaves room to consider the partners' purpose for the allocation. Nevertheless the Committee Report should not be read to stand for the proposition that an allocation that has substantial economic effect under the regulations will be invalidated if it has a tax avoidance purpose. Any allocation that meets the mechanical tests of the regulations must reflect the true economic gain or loss realized by the partners. No alternative allocation will more accurately reflect the economic results. The very purpose of the regulations is to determine whether an alternative allocation provision involves tax avoidance.

In Gershkowitz v. Commissioner, 88 T.C. 984 (1987), the Tax Court applied the judicial capital account analysis for substantial economic effect for a year prior to the effective date of the regulations, but its reasoning illustrated the close relationship of that analysis to the tests of the regulations. In that case the partnership agreement was amended in December 1977 to provide that for all transactions on or after January 1, 1977, net profits from capital transactions would first be allocated among the partners to eliminate any deficits in their capital accounts, and thereafter 95 percent of profits would be allocated to the limited partners and 5 percent would be allocated to the general partner. Prior to the amendment the partnership agreement provided that all gains and losses were to be allocated 95 percent to the limited partners and 5 percent to the general partner, until all limited partners had received distributions equal to their capital contributions, and thereafter among all partners relative to their capital contributions. At the time the partnership agreement was amended, the partnership was insolvent, had ceased to conduct business, and was in the process of liquidation. During 1977 the partnership realized discharge of indebtedness income under § 61(a)(12) and gain from the transfer of property subject to nonrecourse mortgages in excess of adjusted basis. All of the partners had negative capital account balances. The Commissioner asserted that the allocations lacked substantial economic effect because their sole purpose was to limit the tax liability of the partners. The taxpayer asserted that the allocations should be recognized because they were designed to leave each partner with a capital account of zero, which accurately reflected the economic status of the partnership at the time of liquidation. After first noting that "the purpose underlying the 1976 amendments to § 704(b) was to permit partnerships to use special allocations for bona fide business purposes, but not for tax avoidance purposes," the Tax Court concluded that the effect of the special allocation was to defeat the requirement in Treas. Reg. § 1.704–1(b)(2)(ii)(b)(2) that liquidating distributions be made in accordance with capital accounts. Accordingly, without any more detailed explanation of its reasoning, it invalidated the allocations.

Close examination of the facts in *Gershkowitz* reveals that the result was correct based on the particular facts of the case without resort to the tax-avoidance purpose for the allocation. Superficially, it appears that since all of the partnership's income from the year in question was from discharge of indebtedness and gain from the transfer of mortgaged property, the partnership was, in effect, applying the "gain chargeback" concept of Treas. Reg. § 1.704–2(f) to bring all partners' capital accounts to zero. But because gain was allocated under the amended agreement using a formula which did not correlate the gain allocated to a particular partner with the deductions previously allocated to that partner, this was not a true gain chargeback. Since *Gershkowitz* involved nonrecourse debt, which could not have had any *real* economic effect, the allocation could be treated as having economic effect only if it matched the gain realized by each partner with prior deductions allocated to that partner. The effect of the amended allocation, however, was to defeat that matching.

Nonetheless, the Commissioner's argument in *Gershkowitz* that the allocation should be disregarded because it had a tax avoidance purpose and the court's recitation that the purpose of the 1976 amendment to § 704(b) was to permit partnerships to use special allocations for bona fide business purposes, but not for tax avoidance purposes, raises the question of whether an allocation that meets the mechanical tests of the regulations may be invalidated if it has a tax avoidance purpose. In TIFD III–E Inc. v. United States, 342 F.Supp.2d 94 (D.Conn. 2004), the District Court concluded that satisfaction of the mechanical rules of the regulations under § 704(b) transcends both an intent to avoid tax and the avoidance of significant tax through agreed upon partnership allocations. That case (commonly referred to as the *Castle Harbour* case) involved a tax shelter partnership in which 2 percent of both operating and taxable income was allocated to GECC, a United States partner, and 98 percent of both book and taxable income was allocated to partners who were Dutch banks, foreign partners who were not liable for United States taxes and thus were indifferent to the U.S. tax consequences of their participation in the partnership. The partnership had very large book depreciation deductions and no tax depreciation. As a result, most of the partnership's taxable operating income, which was substantially in excess of book taxable income, was allocated to the tax-indifferent foreign partners, even though a large portion of the cash receipts reflected in that income was devoted to repaying the principal of loans secured by property that GECC had contributed to the partnership. The overall partnership transaction saved GECC approximately $62 million in income taxes, and the court found that "it appears likely that one of GECC's principal motivations in entering into this transaction—though certainly not its only motivation—was to avoid that substantial tax burden." The court understood the effects of the allocations and concluded that "by allocating 98% of the income from fully tax-depreciated aircraft to the Dutch Banks, GECC avoided an enormous tax burden, while shifting very little book income. Put another way, by allocating income less depreciation to tax-neutral parties, GECC was able to 're-depreciate' the assets for tax purposes. The tax-neutrals absorbed the tax consequences of all the income allocated to them, but actually received only the income in excess of book depreciation." Nevertheless, the court upheld the allocations:

> The tax benefits of the * * * transaction were the result of the allocation of large amounts of book income to a tax-neutral entity, offset by a large depreciation expense, with a corresponding allocation of a large amount of taxable income, but no corresponding allocation of depreciation deductions. This resulted in an enormous tax savings, but the simple allocation of a large percentage of income violates no rule. The government does not—and cannot—dispute that partners may allocate their partnership's income as they choose. Neither does the government dispute that the taxable income allocated to the Dutch Banks could not be offset by the allocation of non-existent depreciation deductions to the banks.

And * * * the bare allocation of a large interest in income does not violate the overall tax effect rule.

The *Castle Harbour* case has generated significant commentary suggesting that the court erred in its determination that the allocations had substantial economic effect. See, e.g., Karen C. Burke, Castle Harbour: Economic Effect and the Overall–Tax–Effect Test, 107 Tax Notes 1163 (May 30, 2005). Although the allocations might have had economic effect under Treas. Reg. § 1.704–1(b)(2)(ii), the allocations were not substantial under Treas. Reg. § 1.704–1(b)(2)(iii). The factual analysis is quite complex. Because the income stream was completely predictable and under the partnership agreement the end result was that the Dutch banks merely recouped their investment plus a guaranteed 8.5 percent return, the allocations were not substantial under Treas. Reg.§ 1.704–1(b)(2)(iii)(*a*). As a result of the allocations, when compared to an allocation of book income that simply reflected the amounts actually to be ultimately distributed to the partners under the agreement, the after-tax economic consequences of the other partners were enhanced, and there was a strong likelihood that the after-tax consequences to the Dutch banks would not be diminished.

B.   ALLOCATIONS ATTRIBUTABLE TO NONRECOURSE DEBT

REGULATIONS: Section 1.704–2 (omitting (i), (k) and (m)).

It is common for real estate transactions and other acquisitions to be financed with nonrecourse mortgage debt or other nonrecourse secured debt. Allocations of deductions, e.g. depreciation, attributable to nonrecourse debt present special problems. Treas. Reg. § 1.704–2(b)(1) provides that an allocation of such deductions never can have economic effect because only the creditor bears the burden of economic loss. Accordingly, losses and deductions attributable to nonrecourse debt, which are termed "nonrecourse deductions," must be allocated in accordance with the partners' interests in the partnership. Since allocation of losses under Treas. Reg. § 1.704–1(b)(3), which determines a partner's interest in the partnership if an allocation in the agreement does not have economic effect, turns on risk of loss, it would appear that no partner could be allocated any deductions attributable to nonrecourse debt. Pursuant to Treas. Reg. § 1.704–2, however, allocations will be deemed to be made in accordance with the partners' interest in the partnership, and thus given effect, if certain requirements are met.

The rules governing allocations of nonrecourse deductions come into play only after previous allocations of losses and deductions have eliminated the partnership's equity in property subject to nonrecourse debt. See Treas. Reg. § 1.704–2(f)(7), Ex. 2. In addition, deductions attributable to recourse debt are stacked before deductions attributable to nonrecourse debt. Assume, for example, that E and F form a limited partnership in which E is the general partner and F is the limited partner. As equal partners, E and F each contribute $10, the partnership borrows $20 with recourse, borrows $60 nonrecourse, and purchases a depreciable asset for $100. Each year the partnership realizes neither a profit nor a loss apart from depreciation deductions. The opening balance sheet of the EF Partnership is as follows:

	Assets			Liabilities and Partners' Capital Accounts		
		Tax				Tax
	Book	Basis			Book	Basis
Property	$100	$100	Recourse Debt	$ 20	
			Nonrecourse Debt	$ 60	
			E	$ 10	$ 60
			F	$ 10	$ 40
	$100	$100			$100	$100

The first $40 of depreciation deductions are attributable to E's and F's capital contributions representing an equity investment in the property and the recourse debt. Thus, Treas. Reg. § 1.704–2 does not apply until the basis of the depreciable asset has been reduced to $60. The first $40 of depreciation deductions, which result in reduction of the partnership's basis for the asset to $60, must be allocated under the substantial economic effect test of Treas. Reg. § 1.704–1(b). Deductions attributable to the recourse debt must be allocated to E, as the general partner, since only E bears the economic risk for repayment of that debt.

A partnership can have nonrecourse deductions generated by a property subject to nonrecourse debt even though the partners still have positive capital accounts attributable to an equity investment in another property. See Treas. Reg. § 1.704–2(f)(7), Ex. 2. Assume, for example, that G and H form the GH Partnership to which they each contribute $50. The GH Partnership purchases undeveloped land, with $80 of the money that G and H contributed. Contemporaneously, the GH Partnership borrows $180 from a third-party lender on a nonrecourse basis and purchases a depreciable asset for $200. Assume further that the basis of the depreciable asset is recovered over 5 years on the straight-line method. The initial balance sheet of the partnership is as follows:

	Assets			Liabilities and Partners' Capital Accounts		
		Tax				Tax
	Book	Basis			Book	Basis
Land	$ 80	$ 80	Debt	$180	
Depreciable			G	$ 50	$140
Asset	$200	$200	H	$ 50	$140
	$280	$280			$280	$280

After one year, the book value and tax basis of the depreciable asset both have been reduced to $160 as a result of $40 of depreciation in the first year. Assuming that the partnership had neither net income nor loss part from the depreciation $40 deduction, the balance sheet of the partnership after the first year is as follows:

	Assets				Liabilities and Partners' Capital Accounts	
	Book	Tax Basis			Book	Tax Basis
Land	$ 80	$ 80	Debt		$180	
Depreciable			G		$ 30	$120
Asset	$160	$160	H		$ 30	$120
	$240	$240			$240	$240

Because the amount of the nonrecourse debt encumbering the depreciable asset is $180, and its book value/tax basis is only $140, the partnership has $20 of minimum gain with respect to the asset after year 1, and $20 of the $40 of depreciation in the first year was a nonrecourse deduction.

The requirements of Treas. Reg. § 1.704–2 are based on the fact that under the principles of Commissioner v. Tufts, 461 U.S. 300 (1983), now codified in § 7701(g), on the disposition of the property the partnership always will recognize gain equal to the depreciation deductions attributable to nonrecourse debt. The object of these rules is to allocate the gain on the disposition to the partners who enjoyed the benefit of the earlier depreciation deductions. This result is achieved through the interaction of four provisions that must be included in the partnership agreement.

First, Treas. Reg. § 1.704–2(e)(1) requires that capital accounts be maintained under the rules of Treas. Reg. § 1.704–1(b)(4) as required by Treas. Reg. § 1.704–1(b)(2)(ii)(*b*)(*1*), and liquidating distributions must be made in accordance with positive capital account balances under the rules of Treas. Reg. § 1.704–1(b)(2)(ii)(*b*)(*2*). In addition, the partnership agreement is required either (1) to provide a deficit make-up obligation with respect to partners with negative capital account balances or (2) to contain a "qualified income offset." See Treas. Reg. § 1.704–1(b)(2)(ii)(*b*)(3) and (*d*)(3). Thus, where, as is usually the case in a partnership with nonrecourse deductions, one or more of the partners do not have a deficit make-up obligation, the partnership agreement is required to satisfy the alternative test for economic effect under Treas. Reg. § 1.704–1(b)(2)(ii)(*d*). For purposes of the alternative test, a partner's share of minimum gain is treated as an obligation to restore a negative capital account in that amount. Treas. Reg. § 1.704–2(g)(1). Thus, nonrecourse deductions may be allocated to a partner even though they result in a partner having a negative capital account without violating the requirements of the alternative economic effect test.

Second, beginning in the first year of the partnership in which the partnership has deductions attributable to nonrecourse indebtedness, and for all partnership years thereafter, the partnership agreement must provide for allocations of nonrecourse deductions among the partners in a manner that is reasonably consistent with allocations that have substantial economic effect of some other significant partnership item attributable to the property securing the nonrecourse liability (other than minimum gain realized by the partnership). Although the regulations do not specify a list of "significant partnership items," Treas. Reg. § 1.704–2(m), Ex. 1(ii) indicates that gross operating income and cash flow deductions qualify, as do gain or loss on a sale of the property. If the partners' shares of operating income and gain or loss on a sale of the property differ, either ratio, or any ratio in between the two, will meet the "reasonably consistent" requirement.

Third, beginning with the year in which nonrecourse deductions are first claimed or the proceeds of a nonrecourse borrowing are first distributed, the partnership agreement must provide for a "minimum gain chargeback," described below.

Fourth, all other material partnership allocations and capital account adjustments must be recognized under Treas. Reg. § 1.704–1(b). This final requirement means that allocations of net income or of losses attributable to partners' capital accounts must have substantial economic effect.

ILLUSTRATIVE MATERIAL

1. NONRECOURSE DEDUCTIONS

The special rules of Treas.Reg. § 1.704–2 apply only to the allocation of "nonrecourse deductions." The amount of nonrecourse deductions of a partnership equals the increase, if any, in the amount of partnership "minimum gain" during the year. "Minimum gain" is the sum of the amounts, computed separately with respect to each item of partnership property, that would be realized if in a taxable transaction the partnership disposed of the property in full satisfaction of the nonrecourse liability secured by it. Treas. Reg. § 1.704–2(d). Thus a partnership cannot have minimum gain as long as the basis of property secured by a nonrecourse mortgage equals or exceeds the amount of the mortgage debt. For example, assume that the CD partnership purchased an apartment building for $100, paying $20 of the purchase price with partnership capital and $80 with the proceeds of a nonrecourse mortgage. At a time when the adjusted basis of the property is $60 and the balance due on the mortgage is $75, the minimum gain is $15 since that is the amount of gain that would be recognized if the partnership were to deed the property to the mortgagee in satisfaction of the debt. If a property is properly carried on the books of the partnership at a book value that differs from its tax basis, the book value basis is used to compute minimum gain. See Treas. Reg. § 1.704–2(d)(3). Nonrecourse deductions are treated as consisting first of cost recovery or depreciation deductions attributable to properties giving rise to the increase in "minimum gain," and then of a pro rata share of other partnership deductions. Treas. Reg. § 1.704–2(c).

2. "MINIMUM GAIN CHARGEBACK"

2.1. *In General*

A partnership agreement contains a "minimum gain chargeback" only if it provides that if there is a net decrease in partnership minimum gain during a partnership year, each partner must be allocated income or gain in proportion to the greater of the deficit in the partner's capital account (excluding a deficit the partner must restore) or the partner's share of the decrease in minimum gain. Treas. Reg. § 1.704–2(b)(2) and (f). Minimum gain obviously is reduced when it is realized through the sale or other disposition of the mortgaged property, for example foreclosure of the mortgage. More often, however, minimum gain is reduced and the charge-back triggered as a mortgage loan is amortized. The chargeback also can be triggered by other events, e.g., by a capital contribution by one partner which is invested to increase the basis of partnership assets or by one partner guaranteeing all or part of a previously nonrecourse debt. A minimum gain chargeback must be allocated before any other allocation of any partnership items for the year is made under § 704(b). The regulations provide rules for determining a partner's share of minimum gain, as well as certain exceptions to the general rules and specific rules to cover a variety of particular transactions. Treas. Reg. § 1.704–2(g). The purpose of the minimum gain chargeback rule is to assure that an offsetting amount of gain is allocated to the partners who received the economic benefit that gave rise to partnership minimum gain. That benefit could have been in the form of either nonrecourse deductions or distributions of proceeds from nonrecourse refinancing of partnership property. Treas. Reg. § 1.704–2(b)(2).

The minimum gain chargeback concept is derived from the more general gain chargeback principle discussed in *Orrisch,* page 104, and in connection with Treas. Reg. § 1.704–1(b) at page 141. Minimum gain chargebacks under Treas. Reg. § 1.704–2, however, differ significantly from ordinary gain chargebacks. First, special allocations of deductions attribut- able to partners' contributions and recourse debt may or may not be subject to a gain chargeback provision, as the partners choose, but all allocations attributable to nonrecourse debt must be subject to a minimum gain chargeback. Second, an ordinary gain chargeback may relate to what- ever portion of prior deductions the partners want, while a minimum gain chargeback must apply to all prior deductions attributable to nonrecourse debt.

2.2. *Waiver of Minimum Gain Chargeback Requirement*

Treas. Reg. § 1.704–2(f)(4) provides that a partnership may request that the Internal Revenue Service waive application of the requirement that a decrease in partnership minimum gain triggers a minimum gain chargeback if application of the minimum gain chargeback would distort the economic relationship among the partners (because of the effect of the chargeback on capital accounts), and it is expected that the partnership will not have sufficient other income to correct the distortion. A waiver of the gain chargeback may be appropriate where there has been additional capital contributed to the partnership to pay down nonrecourse debts or if before the partnership realizes a decrease in partnership minimum gain the partnership has allocated income to a partner to offset prior nonrecourse deductions allocated to that partner. Treas. Reg. § 1.704–2(f)(7), Ex. 1 illustrates a situation in which such a waiver may be appropriate.

3. EXAMPLES

3.1. *Depreciation Deductions and Gain on Sale*

Operation of the basic rules governing allocations of nonrecourse deductions is illustrated in the following example. Suppose that C and D respectively contribute $20,000 and $80,000 to the CD Partnership, which then borrows $900,000 from an unrelated lender on a nonrecourse promissory note secured by depreciable property for which the partnership pays $1,000,000. Also suppose that no principal payments are due on the note for the first five years and that $50,000 of depreciation is allowable on the property each year. The partnership agreement requires that capital accounts be maintained in accordance with the regulations, that liquidation be in accordance with capital accounts, and that C, but not D (who is a limited partner), is required to restore a negative capital account. Because the partnership has $100,000 of equity in the property, the first two years' depreciation deductions (assuming that the partnership does not have any income or loss from other items) are not nonrecourse deductions. At the end of two years the basis of the property will be $900,000 and the mortgage lien will be the same amount; there is no "minimum gain." Accordingly, D may be allocated up to $80,000 of the first two year's depreciation, and C must be allocated at least $20,000 of depreciation. (C may be allocated more than $20,000 of depreciation, and D may be allocated correspondingly less depreciation.)

At the end of year 2, the CD Partnership's balance sheet is as follows:

	Assets			Liabilities and Partners' Capital Accounts	
	Book	Tax Basis		Book	Tax Basis
Property	$900,000	$900,000	Debt	$900,000	
			C	0	$180,000
			D	0	$720,000
	$900,000	$900,000		$900,000	$900,000

In the third year, the depreciation deduction reduces the property's basis to $850,000, and $50,000 of minimum gain arises since, if the partnership transferred the property subject to the mortgage (and for no additional consideration), it would recognize this amount of gain. See Treas. Reg. § 1.704–2(m), Ex. 1(i). Neither partner bears the economic risk of loss with respect to this deduction, and no allocation of the deduction can have substantial economic effect. Nevertheless, an allocation will be deemed to have substantial economic effect, and thereby be respected, if the partnership agreement contains a minimum gain chargeback provision. The deduction could be allocated between C and D in any proportion that is reasonably consistent with some other significant allocation that has substantial economic effect, as long as a corresponding amount of minimum gain is allocated to each partner.

A special allocation of depreciation alone, with all other items being allocated according to a different consistent fraction, will not be recognized.[5] Thus, for example, if C and D agreed to share all income, gain, cash flow deductions, and distributions, 60 percent to C and 40 percent to D, the only permissible allocation of depreciation attributable to nonrecourse debt (as well as accrued interest if the partnership was an accrual method taxpayer) would be 60 percent to C and 40 percent to D. However, partnership agreements often provide for different allocations of items at different times. For example, the agreement may provide that all items of income and deduction and all distributions will be allocated 80 percent to D and 20 percent to C until D has received distributions of $100,000, and thereafter all items and distributions will be allocated fifty-fifty (a so-called "flip-flop"). In this case depreciation may be allocated either equally or 80 percent to D and 20 percent to C, or anywhere in the range between those two allocations. In any case, C and D must be allocated the proper amount of minimum gain chargeback. Note that an allocation of minimum gain chargeback alone is not another significant item with substantial economic effect.

Assume, then that the agreement validly allocates the depreciation 80 percent to D and 20 percent to C. At the end of the third year, D has a deficit in his capital account of $40,000, and C has a deficit of $10,000. The balance sheet of the partnership is as follows:

	Assets			Liabilities and Partners' Capital Accounts		
	Book	Tax Basis			Book	Tax Basis
Property	$850,000	$850,000	Debt		$900,000	
			C		($ 10,000)	$170,000
			D		($ 40,000)	$680,000
	$850,000	$850,000			$850,000	$850,000

If the property were deeded to the lender in lieu of foreclosure of the mortgage on the first day of year four, the partnership would recognize a gain of $50,000—the "minimum gain" —which would be allocated $40,000 to D and $10,000 to C, thereby restoring their respective capital accounts to a zero balance.

3.2. *Depreciation Deductions and Loan Principal Amortization*

A minimum gain chargeback must occur not only when the property is sold, but anytime that there is a decrease in partnership minimum gain. Thus, loan principal amortization requires that income be allocated to the partners in the same ratio as the special allocation of depreciation. For example, suppose that the CD Partnership did not sell the property at the beginning of year four, but continued to hold the property and paid $100,000 of principal on the first day of year six. At that time the basis of

---

5. The requirement that allocations of deductions be consistent with allocations of some other item that has substantial economic effect is unique to allocations of deductions attributable to nonrecourse debt. No such requirement attaches to allocations attributable to recourse debt.

the property would be $750,000. Reduction of the loan principal from $900,000 to $800,000 reduces partnership minimum gain from 150,000 to $50,000, and assuming that the partnership has at least $100,000 of taxable income in year six, that amount must be allocated among C and D in the same ratio that nonrecourse depreciation deductions previously had been allocated. Thus if in years three through five, D had been allocated $120,000 of depreciation and C had been allocated $30,000 of depreciation, D must be allocated $80,000 of the income, and C must be allocated $20,000. Note that the depreciation allocated in the first two years, which had actual substantial economic effect, is not considered in allocating income pursuant to the minimum gain chargeback.

Despite the fact that nonrecourse depreciation deductions never can have substantial economic effect because they cannot affect the actual dollar amounts received by any partner, the regulations allow them to be allocated among the partners as long as the corresponding income items are allocated in the same manner. Through the minimum gain chargeback provision, the regulations assure that allocations of nonrecourse depreciation ultimately will be entirely offset by future income allocations. This system is justifiable because otherwise there would be no way to allocate nonrecourse deductions to *any* partner, even though the deductions must be taken into account in computing partnership taxable income. The requirement that allocations of nonrecourse deductions be reasonably consistent with allocations having substantial economic effect of some other significant partnership item attributable to the secured property is designed to prevent abusive special allocations designed to specially allocate deductions (but not income) to one or more partners when the minimum gain which will eventually offset those deductions is not expected to be realized until many years in the future.

4. PARTNERSHIP NONRECOURSE DEBT FOR WHICH A PARTNER BEARS THE RISK OF LOSS

Special rules govern the allocation of deductions attributable to debt that is nonrecourse as to the partnership but for which a partner bears the economic risk of loss (e.g., a partnership nonrecourse debt that is guaranteed by a partner without any right of indemnification). Treas. Reg. § 1.704–2(i) requires that all deductions attributable to such debt be allocated to the partner (or partners) who bear the risk of loss.

5. JUDICIAL INTERPRETATION OF NONRECOURSE DEBT DEDUCTION REGULATIONS

In Vecchio v. Commissioner, 103 T.C. 170 (1994), the allocations provided in the partnership agreement did not have economic effect because upon liquidation of the partnership, liquidating distributions were not required to be made according to positive capital account balances and partners were not obligated to restore negative capital account balances. The partnership maintained capital accounts that accurately reflected losses and had a gain chargeback provision similar to the one in *Orrisch*, but the partnership agreement provided for a liquidation preference equal to the original capital contribution of $766,100 by one partner coupled with a pro rata distribution of any remaining partnership property among all other partners relative to their capital interests. Depreciation deductions totaling $2,017,998 were disproportionately allocated to the one partner who had the liquidation preference, resulting in a negative capital account balance of $1,251,898. The other partners had positive capital account balances. Upon the sale of the partnership's building, which effected its dissolution, the partnership attempted to allocate only $1,251,898 of its recognized gain of $1,986,913 to the partner with the negative capital account of $1,251,898 and to allocate the remaining gain among the partners according to the partnership's general profit sharing provisions. The court held, however, that because the entire recognized gain ($1,986,-913) was less than the sum of the depreciation deductions subject to the gain chargeback and the liquidation preference ($2,017,998), in order to reflect the partners' interest in the partnership under Treas. Reg. § 1.704–1(b)(3)(i), the entire gain was required to be allocated to the partner holding the liquidation preference. The result in this case is correct because only with the allocation of the entire gain to that partner would his positive capital account balance have supported a distribution to him equal to his original capital contribution.

In Interhotel Co. Ltd. v. Commissioner, T.C. Memo. 2001–151, on remand from 221 F.3d 1348 (9th Cir. 2000), rev'g, T.C. Memo. 1997–44, the Tax Court applied the minimum gain chargeback rules to determine whether special allocations were consistent with the partners' interest in a partnership under the hypothetical comparative liquidation test of Treas. Reg. § 1.704–1(b)(3)(iii). The Interhotel partnership owned interests in two second tier partnerships that held hotel properties subject to nonrecourse debt and which were depreciated below the amount of the debt, thereby creating minimum gain. The Interhotel partnership agreement provided for liquidation according to positive capital account balances, but neither required the restoration of negative capital accounts nor provided a qualified income offset as required by Treas. Reg. § 1.704–1(b)(2)(ii)(d). The general partner's partnership interest nominally was 85 percent and the limited partner's interest nominally was 15 percent, but as a result of special allocations, the partnership income was allocated 1 percent to the general partner and 99 percent to the limited partner, while losses were allocated 85 percent to the general partner and 15 percent to the limited partner. As of June 20, 1991, the general partner's capital account was negative $5,920,614, and the limited partner's capital account was positive $14,879,392. In a complex transaction effective on June 21, 1991, the original limited partner's partnership interest was transferred to a new limited partner, who succeeded to the limited partner's positive capital account. In connection with the transfer of the limited partnership interest, the partnership agreement was amended to allocate all partnership income to any partner with a negative capital account, i.e., to the general partner, and after negative capital accounts had been eliminated in proportion to the partners' pro rata interests (85 percent to the general partner and 15 percent to the new limited partner). Pursuant to this amendment, all of the partnership's income for the remainder of 1991 was allocated to the general partner. The Commissioner asserted that the special allocation of 100 percent of the income to the general partner was not valid and that 99 percent of the partnership income—the share of partnership income that reflected the partnership interest of the limited partner's predecessor—was allocable to the limited partner. Because the partnership agreement, as amended, lacked economic effect under the basic test, the alternate economic effect test of Treas. Reg. § 1.704–1(b)(2)(ii)(d), or the economic effect equivalence test of Treas. Reg. § 1.704–1(b)(2)(ii)(*i*), the partners' interests in the partnership were determined under the comparative liquidation test of Treas. Reg. § 1.704–1(b)(3)(iii). That test was applied by comparing the liquidation proceeds available to the partners on a hypothetical liquidation of the partnership at the end of 1990, and again at the end of the 1991 tax year. The Commissioner conceded that liquidation of the Interhotel partnership would trigger recognition of its share of the built-in minimum gain of the two second-tier partnerships in which it held interests. Recognition of the minimum gain chargeback would increase the general partner's capital account and thereby eliminate the general partner's capital account deficit. As a consequence, allocation of the partnership income to the general partner was reflected in an increased positive capital account that would be distributable to the general partner in the hypothetical liquidation contemplated under Treas. Reg. § 1.704–1(b)(3)(iii). Allocation of all of the partnership income to the general partner therefore was consistent with the partners' interests in the partnership, even though it technically lacked economic effect.

Section 3. Allocations With Respect to Contributed Property

Internal Revenue Code: Section 704(c)(1).

Regulations: Section 1.704–3 (omitting (e)(3)); 1.197–2(g)(4).

Section 704(c) requires that allocations of income, deductions or losses attributable to contributed property take into account the difference between the fair market value and basis of the property at the time of contribution. The purpose of this provision is to ensure that pre-contribution gains and losses are not shifted from the contributing partner to other partners. For example, assume that A and B form a partnership in which they will share profits and losses equally. A contributes property with a basis of $400 and a value of $1,000, and B contributes $1,000 cash. As between the partners each has contributed property of equal value and each has a capital account of $1,000. But from a tax standpoint, the low basis of A's property presents problems. Since gain or loss is not recognized on the formation of the partnership, § 723 provides that this basis carries over to the partnership. Hence, if the property is later sold the partnership will have a tax gain of $600, but has no gain for book purposes. The general principles of the § 704(b) regulations do not apply to the tax allocation of the first $600 of gain because those provisions require tax gain to be allocated in the same manner as book gain, and here there is no book gain.

The entire gain accrued while A held the property prior to formation of the partnership. Thus, the entire gain ought to be taxed to A, with B being allocated none of the gain because no gain was allocated to B's capital account. A, on the other hand, received an opening capital account of $1,000, which included the unrealized appreciation. This problem is solved by § 704(c), which requires the first $600 of gain in this case to be taxed to A. If the property were to be sold for $1,200, the first $600 of gain is allocated by § 704(c) to A, and the remaining $200 of gain, which represents book gain to the partnership, is allocated equally between A and B in accord with their distributive shares under the partnership agreement.

Similar problems arise if the property is not sold but is held by the partnership as depreciable property. The depreciation on the partnership books will differ from that allowable for tax purposes because, among other things, the depreciable cost will be $1,000 for book purposes, but the depreciable basis for tax purposes will be only $400. Again the § 704(b) regulations are largely displaced by § 704(c) and the regulations thereunder.

Section 704(c)(1)(C) provides that built-in losses are personal to the partner who contributed the loss property. If the contributing partner ceases to be a partner before the loss is realized, no partner may realize a loss on the sale of the property. As far as the remaining partners are concerned, the basis of the property is treated as being equal to its fair market value at the time of the contribution. This provision is intended to prevent the transfer of built-in tax losses from one partner (a low tax bracket person, a tax exempt entity, or a foreign person) to another partner. Although the statute is silent on the point, if the property is depreciable (or amortizable) in the hands of the partnership that fair-market-value-at-date-of-contribution basis presumably must be adjusted for prior depreciation (or amortization) claimed by the partnership.

A disparity between a partner's capital account and the partner's share of basis can exist when a partner is admitted with a cash contribution to an on-going partnership that has property with a difference between fair market value and basis. In this situation, built-in gains and losses in the partnership might be attributed to the new partner. Section 704(c) does not apply in this context. Although Congress was aware of the situation in 1986 when § 704(c) was made mandatory rather than elective, Congress was content to rely on a regulatory solution. General Explanation of the Tax Reform Act of 1984, Staff of the Joint Committee on Taxation, 215 (1984). Treas. Reg. §§ 1.704–3(a)(6)(i) and 1.704–1(b)(4)(i) require the application of § 704(c) principles when a partnership revalues partnership assets under Treas. Reg. § 1.704–1(b)(2)(iv)(f). This issue is discussed in this section at page 169.

ILLUSTRATIVE MATERIAL

1. ALLOCATION OF GAIN AND LOSS

Reconsider the example above, in which A and B form an equal partnership to which A contributes property with a basis of $400 and a value of $1,000 and B contributes $1,000 cash. If the AB Partnership sells the contributed property for $1,000, under § 704(c)(1)(A), the $600 gain recognized by the partnership must be allocated entirely to A, even though that gain is not added to A's capital account. This rule does not conflict with the requirement of § 704(b) that an allocation have substantial economic effect to be recognized because the pre-contribution appreciation is already reflected in capital accounts under Treas. Reg. § 1.704–1(b)(2)(iv)(*d*). See Treas. Reg. § 1.704–1(b)(1)(vi), which subordinates the § 704(b) regulations to § 704(c). Likewise, where the AB partnership sold the property for $1,200, realizing an $800 gain for tax purposes § 704(c) requires that $600 of gain be allocated to A, while the balance of the $200 gain is allocated under § 704(a), subject to the substantial economic effect rules of § 704(b). Since A and B are equal partners, $100 of the remaining gain is allocated to each of A and B. Thus A is allocated $700 of gain and B $100. For book purposes, however, the partnership realized a gain of only $200, which is allocated equally between A and B. That these tax results correspond with economic reality is easily illustrated by comparing the partnership's balance sheet, at both book account and tax basis amounts, before and after the sale of the asset. Before the sale, the AB partnership's balance sheet is as follows:

Assets			Partners' Capital Accounts		
		Tax			Tax
	Book	Basis		Book	Basis
Cash	$1,000	$1,000	A	$1,000	$ 400
Asset	$1,000	$ 400	B	$1,000	$1,000
	$2,000	$1,400		$2,000	$1,400

As a result of the sale of the asset, all disparities between book and tax basis amounts have been eliminated. The partnership's balance sheet is as follows:

Assets			Partners' Capital Accounts		
		Tax			Tax
	Book	Basis		Book	Basis
Cash	$2,200	$2,200	A	$1,100	$1,100
			B	$1,100	$1,100
	$2,200	$2,200		$2,200	$2,200

Suppose now that the AB partnership sold the property for only $800. For tax purposes, the gain recognized is $400, but for partnership book purposes, there is a $200 loss. Theoretically, A should be allocated $600 of gain attributable to the pre-contribution gain that was realized but not recognized upon formation of the partnership, and A and B should each be allocated $100 of loss realized since the partnership was formed. For many years, however, the regulations under § 704(c), prior to its amendment in 1984, provided an inviolate "ceiling rule," under which only the amount of gain recognized by the partnership, in this case $400, could be allocated among the partners. Thus, the closest that the partners could get to an appropriate allocation was to allocate the entire $400 gain to A. (Ultimately, of course, B might recognize the $100 loss upon sale of his partnership interest, which would have a basis $100 higher than it would have had if B had been allowed a current $100 loss.) Congress intended the 1984 amendments to § 704(c) to remedy this distortion. Treas. Reg. § 1.704–3(a)–(d) provides three optional allocation methods to avoid the distortions caused by the ceiling rule. The operative premise of the regulations is that the partner who contributed the appreciated or depreciated property and the partnership should be allowed to use any reasonable consistently applied method that allocates to the contributing partner the tax burdens and benefits of any pre-contribution gain or loss. Accordingly, the regulations specifically permit making allocations under § 704(c) by using either the (1) "traditional method" including the "ceiling rule", (2) the "traditional method" with "curative allocations," or (3) "remedial allocations." The method to be used for each partnership asset subject to § 704(c) should be specified in the partnership agreement.

1.1.   *Traditional Method with the Ceiling Rule*

Under the "traditional method" with the "ceiling rule" provided in Treas. Reg. § 1.704–3(b), upon the disposition of contributed property the partnership must allocate to the contributing partner the built-in gain or loss inherent in the property at the time it was contributed to the partnership. Thus, in the AB Partnership example, A would be allocated $400 of tax gain and B would be allocated no gain for tax purposes. This option cannot result in the allocation of a net gain of $500 to A and a loss of $100 to B. It does not avoid the distortions.

1.2.   *Traditional Method with Curative Allocations*

Under Treas. Reg. § 1.704–3(c), a partnership may eliminate the distortions caused by the ceiling rule by using reasonable curative allocations of other partnership tax items of income, gain, loss, or deduction. These allocations "cure" disparities caused by the ceiling rule by equalizing the overall allocations of economic and tax items to noncontributing partners. Assume, for example, that in the year the property contributed by A was sold for $800, the AB Partnership also realized gross income of $400 and deductions of $400, thus breaking-even apart from the gain on the property. Under the traditional method with curative allocations, A could be allocated net taxable income of $500 and B could be allocated a net taxable loss of $100 by allocating these items as follows:

	A	B
Gain from Property	$400	$ 0
Other Gross Income	$200	$200
Deductions	($100)	($300)
	$500	($100)

Curative allocations involve only tax items and differ from economic allocations of the same items. For book accounting purposes, A and B would have allocated the items as follows:

	A	B
Loss from Property	($100)	($100)
Other Gross Income	$200	$200
Deductions	($200)	($200)
	($100)	($100)

Because the tax allocations of the deductions did not follow the book allocations to capital accounts, apart from Treas. Reg. § 1.704–3(c), curative allocations generally would not be valid under Treas. Reg. § 1.704–1(b).

A curative allocation is reasonable only if it is made using items of the same character as the tax items affected by the ceiling rule and only to the extent it offsets the effect of the ceiling rule. Treas. Reg. § 1.704–3(c)(3). Thus, if the gain from the sale of the property was capital gain and the deductions were ordinary deductions for business expenses, interest, and depreciation, making a curative allocation would not have been allowed. Only capital losses could have been allocated to B. Curative allocations, however, are flexible. If the gain on the sale of the property contributed by A was capital gain and the other gross income also was capital gain, B could have been allocated a disproportionately low share of the other capital gain, as follows:

	A	B
Gain from Property	$400	$ 0
Other Capital Gain	$300	$100
Deductions	($200)	($200)
	$500	($100)

1.3. *Remedial Allocations*

The final method of ameliorating the ceiling rule is the remedial allocation method provided in Treas. Reg. § 1.704–3(d). This is the most flexible method available to partnerships for dealing with the ceiling rule because remedial allocations are tax allocations of *notional* gain or income *created by the partnership* that are *offset* by tax allocations of *notional* deduction or loss that are *created by the partnership*. Remedial allocations under Treas. Reg. § 1.704–3(d) are the only permissible method of creating notional tax items. Treas. Reg. § 1.704–3(d)(5)(i). Unlike curative allocations, which allocate recognized partnership income and deduction items differently for tax purposes than for book purposes, remedial allocations may be created for tax purposes even though the partnership has no corresponding book items of income or deduction. Remedial allocations must result in each partner recognizing total partnership income, gains, deductions, or loss for the year equal to the partner's share of book gain or loss. These allocations are in addition to the allocations under the traditional method described in Treas. Reg. § 1.704–3(b). Thus, if the ceiling rule results in a tax allocation to a noncontributing partner different than the corresponding book allocation, the partnership makes a remedial allocation of notional income, gain, deduction, or loss (without affecting allocations of actual partnership income, gain, deduction, or loss) to the noncontributing partner equal to the amount of the difference caused by the ceiling limitation and a simultaneous offsetting allocation of income, gain, deduction, or loss to the contributing partner. Unlike the curative allocation approach under Treas. Reg. § 1.704–3(c), a remedial allocation has no effect on the allocation among the partners of actual partnership items of income, gain, deduction, or loss.

Consider the AB Partnership discussed in the preceding examples, which recognized a $400 tax gain and a $200 book loss on the sale of property contributed by A. Even if the partnership had no other items of income or deduction for the year, it could make remedial allocations to give each partner aggregate tax items equal to her book items. B would be allocated a $100 loss, and A would be allocated an additional $100 gain, as follows:

	A		B	
	Tax	Book	Tax	Book
Gain (Loss) from Property	$400	($100)	$ 0	($100)
Remedial Allocation	$100	n.a.	($100)	n.a.
	$500	($100)	($100)	($100)

B's remedial deduction and A's corresponding remedial income item must be of the same character as the income item from the property that was sold. Treas. Reg. § 1.704–3(d)(3). If the property is a capital asset, the remedial allocations must be capital gain and loss; if the property is an ordinary income asset, the remedial allocations must be ordinary gain and loss. If, as is often likely, the property is a § 1231 asset, the remedial allocations must be § 1231 gain and loss, even though in some cases a character mismatch may occur after taking into account each partners other items of § 1231 gain and loss. Finally, for purposes of applying the passive activity loss rules of § 469, discussed at page 258, the offsetting item is deemed to arise from the partnership activity in which the contributed property is used.

Even though remedial allocations involve purely notional tax items, remedial allocations of income, gain, deduction, and loss are taken into account in adjusting partners' bases in their partnership interests under § 705 in the same manner as distributive shares of partnership taxable income. Treas. Reg. § 1.704–3(d)(4)(ii). Remedial allocations, however, do not affect either partnership taxable income under § 703 or the partnership's adjusted basis in any of its property. Treas. Reg. § 1.704–3(d)(4)(i).

1.4. *Comparison*

When the current effects of the traditional approach with the ceiling rule, on the one hand, and the curative and remedial allocation methods, on the other hand, are balanced with the results upon liquidation, the overall amount of gain or loss recognized by each partner will be identical. Under the traditional method, when the ceiling rule applies, the partner contributing low basis property recognizes less current gain, while the other partner is not entitled to a loss on the sale. However, because of the effect of basis adjustments under § 705, the contributing partner recognizes a pro tanto greater gain (or smaller loss) on final liquidation, while the other partner has a smaller gain (or greater loss). Under the curative and remedial allocation methods, the partner who contributed the low basis-high value asset in effect includes the full amount of pre-contribution appreciation when the asset is sold. Consequently, on liquidation she does not have any remaining pre-contribution gain to account for with respect to the asset. Conversely, as a result of either curative and remedial allocation, the other partner has recognized less net taxable income during the life of the partnership than she would have realized under the traditional method with the ceiling rule and therefor realizes a relatively larger gain (or smaller loss) on liquidation of the partnership. There are two other differences. First, the character of the gain or loss may be transmuted from ordinary to capital under the traditional approach, while curative and remedial allocations require matching of character. Second, if the partners receive property other than cash in liquidation, recognition of gain or loss may be further postponed. See § 731(a), discussed at page 338.

2. DEPRECIABLE PROPERTY

2.1. *In General*

Section 704(c) requires that allocations of depreciation and of gain or loss on depreciable property also reflect the difference between the contributing partner's basis in the property and the book value of the property included in the contributing partner's capital account. Section 704(c) principles work to assure that depreciation deductions allocated to the partners for tax purposes reflect the economic deductions allocated to the partners' capital accounts. For example, suppose that C and D form a partnership to which C contributes $1,000 cash and D contributes depreciable property with a basis of $600 and a fair market value of $1,000. Each partner has a fifty percent interest in partnership capital and profits. Assume, for simplicity, that under § 168 the property has a ten-year cost recovery period with five years remaining, and its cost is recoverable using the straight line method. (Tax depreciation and book depreciation generally must be computed using the same methods in order to maintain capital accounts in the required manner, see Treas. Reg. § 1.704–1(b)(2)(iv)(*g*)(3).) Under the traditional method, book depreciation is computed using the property's remaining tax cost recovery period for the entire book value. See Treas. Reg. § 1.704–3(b)(2), Ex. (2). Tax depreciation would be $120 per year and book depreciation would be $200 per year. In effect, C purchased a one-half interest in the asset for $500. Since the property has a five year life, using the straight line method, C, who contributed the cash, should be entitled to $100 of depreciation per year. The additional $20 of tax depreciation is allocated to D. This approach to allocating depreciation deductions between the partners, which is the traditional method in Treas. Reg. § 1.704–3(b), gives C, the partner contributing cash to the partnership, the tax benefits of acquiring by purchase an interest in the property contributed by D, while preserving for D the nonrecognition treatment accorded by § 721. Under Treas. Reg. § 1.704–3(b)(1), for tax purposes depreciation deductions are first allocated to noncontributing partners up to their share of the book deductions. Any remaining tax deductions may be allocated by any method consistent with Treas. Reg. § 1.704–1(b). Generally the remaining deductions are allocated to the contributing partner. The result of this rule is to reduce the disparity, if any, between each partners' book capital account and tax basis in her partnership interest each year over the cost recovery period of the contributed depreciable asset; at the end of the cost recovery period, the disparity has been eliminated.

Assume that the CD partnership breaks even, for both tax and book purposes, apart from depreciation. The partners' capital accounts, at both book and tax basis, change over the years, as follows:

	C		D	
	Book	Tax	Book	Tax
Initial Capital Account	$1,000	$1,000	$1,000	$600
Year 1 depreciation	($ 100)	($ 100)	($ 100)	($ 20)
End of Year 1 Capital Account	$ 900	$ 900	$ 900	$580
Year 2 depreciation	($ 100)	($ 100)	($ 100)	($ 20)
End of Year 2 Capital Account	$ 800	$ 800	$ 800	$560
Year 3 depreciation	($ 100)	($ 100)	($ 100)	($ 20)
End of Year 3 Capital Account	$ 700	$ 700	$ 700	$540
Year 4 depreciation	($ 100)	($ 100)	($ 100)	($ 20)
End of Year 4 Capital Account	$ 600	$ 600	$ 600	$520
Year 5 depreciation	($ 100)	($ 100)	($ 100)	($ 20)
End of Year 5 Capital Account	$ 500	$ 500	$ 500	$500

Section 704(c) applies to the allocation of depreciation deductions not only when one partner contributes cash and the other property, but also when both contribute property. Assume that E and F form a partnership in which each partner has a fifty percent interest in partnership profits and capital. E contributes depreciable machinery with a fair market value of $1,000 and a basis of $750. The machinery has a remaining cost recovery period of five years and is depreciated under the straight line method. F contributes depreciable equipment with a fair market value of $1,000 and a basis of $1,500. The equipment has a remaining cost recovery period of ten years and is depreciated using the straight line method. In each of the first five years, $200 of book depreciation on the machinery is allocated equally to E and F, and the tax depreciation of $150 is allocated $50 to E and $100 to F. The book depreciation of $100 on the equipment is allocated equally to E and F, and the tax depreciation of $150 is allocated $50 to E and $100 to F.

Cross-Allocations of § 704(c) Depreciation

Asset	Book	Basis	E Book	E Tax	F Book	F Tax
Machinery (contributed by E) 5 years	$1,000	$ 750				
Machinery Depreciation	$ 200	$ 150	$100	$ 50	$100	$100
Equipment (Contributed by F) 10 years	$1,500	$1,000				
Equipment Depreciation	$ 150	$ 100	$ 50	$ 50	$ 50	$100
			$150	$100	$150	$200

2.2. *Sales of Depreciable Property*

Section 704(c) further applies to allocate gains and losses on the sale of depreciable property that was contributed to a partnership with a difference between fair market value and basis and that was subject to further depreciation deductions by the partnership. Section 704(c) principles operate to match book gains and losses allocated to the non-contributing partner with tax gains and losses. Suppose that the CD Partnership in the earlier example held the property (contributed by D with a book value of $1,000 and a tax basis of $600) for two years and claimed $240 of tax depreciation deductions, which reduced the tax basis of the property to $360, and $400 of book depreciation, which reduced the book basis to $600. On the first day of year 3, the partnership sold the property for $900, recognizing a $540 gain for tax purposes and a $300 gain for book purposes. How should this gain be allocated between C and D?

	Amount Realized/ Sales Price	Basis/ Book Value	Gain/ Profit
Tax	$900	$360	$540
Book	$900	$600	$300

Treas. Reg. § 1.704–3(b)(2), Ex. 1(iii) indicates that taxable gain equal to book gain is allocated to each partner according to the partnership agreement, subject to the § 704(b) regulations. Taxable gain in excess of book gain is allocated to the contributing partner. Thus, the $240 of tax gain ($540) in excess of book gain ($300) is allocated to D; the remaining tax gain is allocated equally, $150 to each partner. D recognizes total gain of $390 and C recognizes total gain of $150. Each partner's capital account should be increased by $150. The capital accounts of C and D thus are $950 each and their respective bases in their partnership interests are also $950.[6]

6. The partnership has $1,900 in cash to satisfy the partners' capital accounts in the event of liquidation.

	C		D	
	Tax	Book	Tax	Book
Initial Capital Account	$1,000	$1,000	$600	$1,000
Years 1–2 Depreciation	($ 200)	($ 200)	($ 40)	($ 200)
Gain on Sale of Asset	$ 150	$ 150	$390	$ 150
Capital Accounts After Sale	$ 950	$ 950	$950	$ 950

Under this allocation method, the amount of potential tax gain allocated to the contributing partner decreases each year as the difference between tax basis and book value of the asset gradually decreases. Note, however, that whenever there is a loss for book purposes but a gain for tax purposes, the entire gain is allocated to the contributing partner. Once property is fully depreciated, all of the gain on a sale is allocated under the § 704(b) regulations.

Once property has been fully depreciated, significant income shifting can occur as a result of the intersection of the rule that book and tax depreciation are computed under the same method—with the cost recovery period of contributed property for both book and tax purposes being the remaining § 168 cost recovery period (or § 167 useful life or § 197 amortization period, if applicable)—and the rule that the gain on property is allocated pursuant to § 704(b), rather than § 704(c). Suppose that G and H form the GH partnership to which G contributes $1,000 in cash and H contributes a depreciable asset with a basis of $100 and a fair market value of $1,000. If the property were sold immediately after it was contributed, G would recognize all $900 of built-in gain. Assume further than the depreciable asset is 15–year property with one year of cost recovery remaining. Book depreciation would be $1,000 and tax depreciation would be $100. If the asset were sold for $1,000 on the first day of year 2, after both book value and tax basis had been reduced to zero, pursuant to the regulations, the $1,000 gain would be allocated $500 to G and $500 to H.

For purposes of allocating § 1245 recapture gain among the partners on the sale of depreciable or amortizable property, Treas. Reg. § 1.1245–1(e)(2)(ii)(C) provides special rules for determining a partner's share of depreciation or amortization with respect to property subject to § 704(c). In addition to his distributive share of prior depreciation, the contributing partner's share of depreciation includes depreciation allowed prior to the contribution. The regulation also provides that curative and remedial allocations reduce the contributing partner's share of depreciation (but not below zero) and increase the noncontributing partners' shares of depreciation.

2.3.   *The Ceiling Limitation*

The ceiling rule also presents problems with respect to the allocation of depreciation under § 704(c)(1)(A). Suppose J and K form the JK Partnership as equal partners. J contributes depreciable property with an adjusted basis of $2,000 and a fair market value of $10,000, and K contributes $10,000 in cash. The property is depreciated using the straight-line method with a 10–year cost recovery period, with five years remaining at the time of the transfer to the partnership. Tax depreciation is $400 per year. Book depreciation (except under the remedial allocation method) is $2,000. K's share of book depreciation, however, is $1,000. K would like her share of tax depreciation to mirror the amount of book depreciation she is allocated. Again, the partners may choose to apply one of the three § 704(c) allocation methods—(1) the "traditional method" including the ceiling rule, (2) the "traditional method" with curative allocations, or (3) the "remedial allocation" method.

2.3.1. Traditional Method

Under the traditional method, depreciation deductions are subject to the ceiling rule, limiting total deductions allocated to the partners to the partnership's deductions. Treas. Reg. § 1.704–3(b). Applying this method to the JK Partnership, tax depreciation of $400 is allocated to K. K's share of book depreciation is $1,000, which is $600 more than K's share of tax depreciation under the traditional rule. Under the traditional method the book and tax depreciation for each partner would be as follows:

	J		K	
Year	Book	Tax	Book	Tax
1	($1,000)	0	($1,000)	($ 400)
2	($1,000)	0	($1,000)	($ 400)
3	($1,000)	0	($1,000)	($ 400)
4	($1,000)	0	($1,000)	($ 400)
5	($1,000)	0	($1,000)	($ 400)
Total	($5,000)	$0	($5,000)	($2,000)

If the partnership also realized an income item of $2,000 in each year, the allocations would be as follows:

		J		K	
Year		Book	Tax	Book	Tax
1	Depreciation	($1,000)	0	($1,000)	($ 400)
	Income	$1,000	$1,000	$1,000	$1,000
2	Depreciation	($1,000)	0	($1,000)	($ 400)
	Income	$1,000	$1,000	$1,000	$1,000
3	Depreciation	($1,000)	0	($1,000)	($ 400)
	Income	$1,000	$1,000	$1,000	$1,000
4	Depreciation	($1,000)	0	($1,000)	($ 400)
	Income	$1,000	$1,000	$1,000	$1,000
5	Depreciation	($1,000)	0	($1,000)	($ 400)
	Income	$1,000	$1,000	$1,000	$1,000
Total		0	$5,000	0	$3,000

When the ceiling rule applies, under the traditional rule noncontributing partners will be allocated tax deductions in an amount less than their share of book deductions, resulting in a shifting of taxable income. For this reason, in some cases the general anti-abuse rule may apply to limit the use of the traditional method. See Treas. Reg. § 1.704–3(b)(2), Ex. (2)(ii). The anti-abuse rule might apply in the above example, for instance, if K was a tax-exempt entity and J was subject to tax.

2.3.2. Curative Allocations

To apply the curative allocation method provided in Treas. Reg. § 1.704–3(c), the partnership must have either income that can be allocated to J for tax purposes disproportionately to J's book allocation or other deductions that can be allocated to K for tax purposes disproportionately to K's book allocation. Under the traditional method, as described above, J and K each would be allocated $1,000 of the income item each year for both book and tax purposes. Under a curative allocation, however, while both J and K would be allocated $1,000 of income for book purposes, J would be allocated $1,600 and K would be allocated only $400 for tax purposes. The effect on J and K would be as follows:

		J		K	
Year		Book	Tax	Book	Tax
1	Depreciation	($1,000)	0	($1,000)	($400)
	Income	$1,000	$1,600	$1,000	$400
2	Depreciation	($1,000)	0	($1,000)	($400)
	Income	$1,000	$1,600	$1,000	$400
3	Depreciation	($1,000)	0	($1,000)	($400)
	Income	$1,000	$1,600	$1,000	$400
4	Depreciation	($1,000)	0	($1,000)	($400)
	Income	$1,000	$1,600	$1,000	$400
5	Depreciation	($1,000)	0	($1,000)	($400)
	Income	$1,000	$1,600	$1,000	$400
Total		0	$8,000	0	0

A curative allocation is reasonable only if it is made using items of the same character as the tax items affected by the ceiling rule and only to the extent it offsets the effect of the ceiling rule. Treas. Reg. § 1.704–3(c)(3). Thus, if the ceiling rule limits an allocation of depreciation to a tax-exempt partner, a curative allocation of dividend income away from the other partners and to the tax-exempt partner would not be valid, but a curative allocation of depreciation deductions from other property would be valid. For other examples of curative allocations, see Treas. Reg. § 1.704–3(c)(4).

2.3.3. *Remedial Allocations*

Application of the remedial allocation method by the JK Partnership is somewhat more complex. To start with, special rules apply to determine the partners' shares of book items to determine whether tax allocations differ from book allocations. The general rules of Treas. Reg. § 1.704–1(b)(2)(iv)(*g*)(3), which provide for computing book depreciation using the applicable tax depreciation method over the portion of the cost recovery period remaining at the time the property was contributed to the partnership, do not apply. Instead, book depreciation is calculated differently, under a two step process prescribed in Treas. Reg. § 1.704–3(d)(2). First, an amount of the book value of the asset equal to its tax basis is recovered for book purposes over the remaining tax cost recovery period of the contributed asset. In the JK Partnership example, this amount is $400 ($2,000 tax basis divided by 5–year remaining recovery period). Second, the excess of book value over tax basis is recovered for book purposes over the cost recovery period, using the applicable cost recovery method, for new property of the same type if purchased by the partnership. In the JK

Partnership, this amount is $800 ($8,000 excess of book value over tax basis, divided by the new ten year recovery period). Book depreciation for year 1 is $1,200 ($400 plus $800). K's share of book depreciation is $600, which is $200 more than K's share of tax depreciation under the traditional rule. Accordingly, the partnership would create a remedial allocation of an additional $200 of depreciation to K offset by an allocation of $200 of income to J. The same allocations would be made in each of years 2 through 4. In years 5 through 10, tax depreciation would be zero. K's share of book depreciation would be $400 [($8,000/10) × 50%]. Accordingly, the partnership would create a remedial allocation of an additional $400 of depreciation to K offset by an allocation $400 of income to J.

As a result of the remedial allocation, over the ten year period that the remedial allocations were in effect, the allocations of the $2,000 annual gross income, $400 tax depreciation, and remedial items would be as follows:

Year		J Book	J Tax	K Book	K Tax
1	Depreciation	($ 600)	0	($ 600)	($ 600)
	Income	$1,000	$1,200	$1,000	$1,000
2	Depreciation	($ 600)	0	($ 600)	($ 600)
	Income	$1,000	$1,200	$1,000	$1,000
3	Depreciation	($ 600)	0	($ 600)	($ 600)
	Income	$1,000	$1,200	$1,000	$1,000
4	Depreciation	($ 600)	0	($ 600)	($ 600)
	Income	$1,000	$1,200	$1,000	$1,000
5	Depreciation	($ 600)	0	($ 600)	($ 600)
	Income	$1,000	$1,200	$1,000	$1,000
6	Depreciation	($ 400)	0	($ 400)	($ 400)
	Income	$1,000	$1,400	$1,000	$1,000
7	Depreciation	($ 400)	0	($ 400)	($ 400)
	Income	$1,000	$1,400	$1,000	$1,000
8	Depreciation	($ 400)	0	($ 400)	($ 400)
	Income	$1,000	$1,400	$1,000	$1,000
9	Depreciation	($ 400)	0	($ 400)	($ 400)
	Income	$1,000	$1,400	$1,000	$1,000
10	Depreciation	($ 400)	0	($ 400)	($ 400)
	Income	$1,000	$1,400	$1,000	$1,000
Total		$5,000	$13,000	$5,000	$5,000

According to the regulations, J's income must be "the same type of income that the contributing property produces." Treas. Reg. § 1.704–3(d)(3). Although this arguably may include either the type of income recognized on a sale, e.g., § 1231 or § 1245 gain, or the type of income realized from operations, e.g., rent or gross receipts from sales, the regulations specify that if the ceiling rule limited item is depreciation, the offsetting item to the contributing partner is ordinary income.

2.3.4. *Comparison*

A comparison of the total amounts of income or loss realized by the partners in the preceding examples involving the JK partnership reveals that the aggregate income or loss realized by the partners does not differ under the three allocation methods: the traditional method with the ceiling rule, the curative allocation method, and the remedial allocation method. What differs is the amount of income or loss recognized by different partners in different years. One partner's timing advantage is another partner's timing disadvantage. Comparing these alternative allocations reveals that the curative allocation is most beneficial to K, allowing K to receive the additional $3,000 of depreciation deductions more rapidly than either of the other methods, while the traditional method is the least beneficial to K because K must recognize taxable income in excess of book income. Conversely, the traditional method is the most beneficial to J, allowing J to avoid any additional taxable income, while the curative allocation method is the least beneficial to J because it requires recognition of additional taxable income earlier than under the remedial method.

Apart from the tax arbitrage issue that arises because the partners are in different tax rate brackets, including the situation in which one of the partners is a tax exempt entity, the Treasury, however, is merely a stakeholder. At any given discount rate, the net present value of the aggregate net income or loss of the partners over the cost recovery period of the asset is identical. This is the reason that partners are given the flexibility to choose among the different methods. Because of the tax arbitrage potential, however, the regulations, provide an anti-abuse rule. An allocation method, or combination of methods if multiple assets are involved, is not reasonable if the allocations are made with a view to shifting tax consequences of built-in gain or built-in loss among the partners in a manner that substantially reduces the present value of the partners' tax liabilities. Treas. Reg. § 1.704–3(a)(10).

3. DE MINIMIS EXCEPTION

To avoid complexity where the disparity between the book value and basis of contributed property is small, Treas. Reg. § 1.704–3(e)(1) permits a partnership to disregard § 704(c) entirely if the aggregate fair market value of all properties contributed by a partner does not differ from their aggregate adjusted bases by more than 15 percent of basis *and* the total disparity for all properties contributed by the partner during the year does not exceed $20,000. For this purpose built-in gains and losses are both treated as positive numbers. Thus, for example, if A contributes Blackacre, with a basis of $1,000 and a fair market value of $19,000, and B contributes Whiteacre, with a basis of $5,000 and a fair market value of $4,000, the de minimis rule applies because the aggregate disparity between basis and book value is $19,000 (($19,000 − $1,000) + ($5,000 − 4,000)). But if Whiteacre were worth only $2,000, the disparity between basis and book value would be $21,000 (($19,000 − $1,000) + ($5,000 − 2,000)), and the de minimis rule would not apply. Alternatively, the partnership may elect to allocate gain or loss upon disposition, but not depreciation, under § 704(c).

4.   APPLICATION OF SECTION 704(c) TO MULTIPLE PARTNERSHIP ASSETS

Generally, § 704(c) is applied property-by-property; aggregation is not allowed in making allocations under § 704(c). However, Treas. Reg. § 1.704–3(e)(2) permits aggregation of three classes of property (other than real property): (1) depreciable property included in the same general asset account of the contributing partner; (2) zero basis property; and (3) inventory.

A partnership may use different allocation methods with respect to different items of § 704(c) property, but may not use more than one method with respect to the same item of property. The selected allocation method must be consistently applied to any item of property. In addition, the overall combination of methods must be reasonable under the facts and circumstances. For example, it may be unreasonable to use one method with respect to appreciated property and a different method with respect to depreciated property. Furthermore, it is not reasonable to use an allocation method that creates tax allocations of income, deduction, gain, or loss independent of allocations affecting book capital accounts. Nor is it reasonable to use any method that increases or decreases the basis of property from its basis otherwise properly determined. Treas. Reg. § 1.704–3(a)(1) and (2). Finally, no allocation method is reasonable if the property contribution and tax allocations have been made with a view to reducing substantially the partners' aggregate overall tax liability. Treas. Reg. § 1.704–3(a)(10).

5.   ALLOCATION OF BUILT–IN LOSSES

Section 704(c)(1)(C) requires that built-in losses be allocated only to the partner who contributed the loss property. If the contributing partner ceases to be a partner before the loss is realized, as far as the remaining partners are concerned the basis of the property is treated as being equal to its fair market value at the time of the contribution, and the built-in loss is eliminated. There is no time limit on the application of § 704(c)(1)(C). Assume, for example, that A, B, and C formed the ABC Partnership with A and B each contributing cash of $1,000 and C contributing property with a a fair market value of $1,000 and a basis of $7,000. The $6,000 built-in loss with respect to the property contributed by C can be allocated only to C. Assume further that eight years later C withdraws from the partnership, in which A and B continue as equal partners, and the next year the AB partnership sells the property contributed by C for any price between $1,000 and $7,000. The partnership does not recognize any loss. If, alternatively, the partnership sold the property for $700, as far as A and B are concerned the property has a $1,000 basis, the partnership would recognize a $300 loss, and A and B each would be allocated a $150 loss. Note that § 704(c)(1)(C) creates an asymmetrical basis rule. If the property were sold for more than $7,000, the partnership's gain always would be computed with respect to the $7,000 § 723 transferred basis.

Section 704(c)(1)(C) operates similarly if instead of C withdrawing from the partnership, which was continued by A and B, C sold the partnership interest to D. In the case of a transferred partnership interest, the transferee partner does not "step into the shoes" of the transferor with respect to the § 704(c) built-in loss. The built-in loss is again eliminated.

6. CONTRIBUTIONS TO PARTNERSHIP POSSESSING APPRECIATED OR DEPRECIATED PROPERTY

The same problem as is dealt with by § 704(c) arises when a new partner contributes cash to enter an existing partnership that holds appreciated or depreciated property. Suppose that G contributes $150 cash to the EF Partnership, which owns property having a fair market value of $300 and a basis of $180, to become a one-third partner. Immediately before the contribution, the EF partnership revalues its assets and partners' capital accounts, as provided in Treas. Reg. § 1.704–1(b)(2)(iv)(*f*). The partnership's balance sheet is as follows:

	Assets			Partners' Capital Accounts		
		Tax				Tax
	Book	Basis			Book	Basis
Asset	$180	$180		E	$ 90	$ 90
				F	$ 90	$ 90
	$180	$180			$180	$180

After the asset and partners' capital accounts are revalued and G is admitted, the partnership's balance sheet is as follows:

	Assets			Partners' Capital Accounts		
	Book	Basis			Book	Basis
Cash	$150	$150		E	$150	$ 90
Asset	$300	$180		F	$150	$ 90
				G	$150	$150
	$450	$330			$450	$330

As a result of the revaluation, a disparity between book value and basis arises that is analogous to the disparity created by contributions of appreciated property, with E and F being analogous to a partner who has contributed appreciated property. Accordingly, E and F should be taxable on that built-in gain. G has in effect paid $100 for a one-third interest in the property and should not recognize any gain if it were sold for $300. All of the first $120 of gain should be recognized by E and F; any gain in excess of $120 should be allocated among the partners according to the principles of § 704(b). Thus, if the property were sold for $390, E and F each should be allocated $90 of gain and G should be allocated $30 of gain. Conversely, if the property were sold for $270, E and F each should recognize a gain of $50, and G should recognize a loss of $10.

Section 704(c) does not expressly apply to this situation, but Treas. Regs. §§ 1.704–1(b)(2)(iv)(*f*), 1.704–3(a)(6)(i), and 1.704–1(b)(4)(i) require the application of § 704(c) principles in allocating tax items whenever the partnership property is revalued and existing partnership capital accounts are adjusted in connection with the admission of a new partner. See Treas. Reg. § 1.704–1(b)(5), Ex. (14)(i)–(ii). Thus, if the asset were sold for $390, E and F each would be allocated $90 of gain and G would be allocated $30 of gain. Likewise, because the rules governing alternative allocation methods in Treas. Reg. § 1.704–3 are applicable in the case of tax/book disparities due to revaluations, if the property were sold for $270, the ceiling rule could be avoided and G could recognize a loss of $10 while E and F each recognized a $50 gain. (See also Treas. Reg. § 1.704–1(b)(5), Ex. (18), applying § 704(c) principles to book/tax depreciation disparities due to revaluations.) The same results may be achieved by special allocations without increasing E's and F's capital accounts at the time of G's admission. Treas. Reg. § 1.704–1(b)(5), Ex. (14)(iv). If neither of these alternatives is utilized by the partnership, the result will be that G will be allocated gain of $40 when the property is sold for $300 and his capital account will be increased by the same amount, even though based on the economics of the transaction his share of both should have been zero. In this circumstance, Treas. Reg. § 1.704–1(b)(1)(iii) authorizes the recharacterization of the transaction under other provisions of the Code. For example, the amount allocated to G may constitute compensation.

Suppose that C contributes money to the existing AB partnership in exchange for a partnership interest and the partnership revalues its assets under Treas. Reg. § 1.704–1(b)(2)(iv)(*f*). Among the partnership's assets is purchased goodwill, a § 197 intangible that was amortizable by the AB partnership. Rev. Rul. 2004–49, 2004–1 C.B. 939, held that the § 197 anti-churning rules do not apply and that consistent with Treas. Reg. § 1.197–2(h)(12)(vii)(A), the ABC Partnership may make reverse § 704(c) allocations (including curative and remedial allocations) of amortization to take into account the built-in gain or loss from the revaluation of the intangible. Thus, C could be allocated notional § 197 amortization deductions while A and B were allocated notional ordinary income or, alternatively, the partnership could allocate other deduction items to C (or income items to A and B) for tax purposes differently than they were allocated for book purposes. But if the goodwill were self created goodwill, it would not have been amortizable by the AB partnership. In that case, the ruling held that the anti–churning rules apply and that the ABC Partnership, consistent with Treas. Reg. § 1.197–2(h)(12)(vii)(B), could make remedial, but not traditional or curative, allocations of amortization to take into account the built-in gain or loss from the revaluation of the intangible, provided that C is not related to A or B. Thus, C could be allocated notional § 197 amortization deductions while A and B were allocated notional ordinary income.

7.   DISTRIBUTIONS OF SECTION 704(c) PROPERTY

Section 704(c)(1)(B) requires the contributing partner to recognize gain or loss upon the distribution of property by the partnership to another partner within seven years of the date the property was contributed to the partnership. This provision is discussed at page 395.

SECTION 4.   ALLOCATIONS RELATING TO NONCOMPENSATORY PARTNERSHIP OPTIONS

Prop. Reg. § 1.721–2 (2003), would provide that upon the exercise of a noncompensatory partnership option, the option holder would be treated as contributing property to the partnership in exchange for the partnership interest; the contributed property would be the original premium paid by the option holder to the partnership, the exercise price, and the option privilege. Section 721 would apply even if the option holder received a partnership interest with a value greater or less than the sum of the option premium and exercise price, i.e., a capital shift resulted from the exercise. To deal with the fact that the option holder generally receives a partnership interest with a value that is greater or less than the sum of the option premium and exercise price, i.e., there is a capital shift, the Treasury Department has proposed amending the regulations under § 704 to allocate a disproportionate share of gross income, without a corresponding allocation of book income, to any partner who has benefited from such a capital shift.

Under Prop. Reg. § 1.704–1(b)(2)(iv)(*d*)(4) (2003), the option holder's initial capital account equals the consideration paid to the partnership for the option plus the fair market value of any property (other than the option itself) contributed to the partnership upon exercise. To meet the substantial economic effect test of Treas. Reg. § 1.704–1(b), Prop. Regs. §§ 1.704–1(b)(2)(iv)(*h*)(2) (2003) and 1.704–1(b)(2)(iv)(*s*) (2003) require the partnership to revalue its property following the exercise of the option, and to allocate the unrealized income, gain, loss, and deductions from the revaluation, first, to the option holder to reflect the holder's right to partnership capital, and then, to the historic partners. To the extent that unrealized appreciation or depreciation in the partnership's assets has been allocated to the option holder's capital account, under § 704(c) principles the holder will recognize correlative allocations of any income or loss attributable to that appreciation or depreciation as the underlying assets are sold, depreciated, or amortized.

Suppose the AB Partnership, in which A is a one–third partner and B is a two-thirds partner, had the following assets and partners' capital accounts:

Assets				Partners' Capital Accounts		
	Book	Tax Basis			Book	Tax Basis
Blackacre	$300	$300		A	$400	$400
Whiteacre	$900	$900		B	$800	$800

In consideration of $100, C is granted an option to acquire a one-quarter partnership interest within two years in exchange for a contribution of $400 at the time C exercises the option. (Upon exercise of the option, A's interest is reduced to one-quarter and B's interest is reduced to one-half.) When C exercises the option, the fair market value of Blackacre is $500 and the fair market value of Whiteacre is $1,500. After revaluation of the partnerships assets and partners' capital accounts as required by Prop. Regs. §§ 1.704–2(b)(2)(iv)(h)(2) (2003) and 1.704–2(b)(2)(iv)(s) (2003), and taking into account C's contributions, the ABC Partnership's balance sheet is as follows:

	Assets			Partners' Capital Accounts		
	Book	Tax Basis			Book	Tax Basis
Cash	$ 500	$ 500	A		$ 625	$ 400
Blackacre	$ 500	$ 300	B		$1,250	$ 800
Whiteacre	$1,500	$ 900	C		$ 625	$ 500
	$2,500	$1,700			$2,500	$1,700

There has been a reallocation of $125 of capital from A and B to C, as required by Prop. Reg. § 1.704–2(b)(2)(iv)(s)(3) (2003). Pursuant to Prop. Reg. § 1.704–2(b)(2)(iv)(x) (2003), the first $125 of gross income thereafter realized by the ABC Partnership, whether upon the sale of Blackacre, Whiteacre, from rental receipts or from any other source, must be allocated to C. For example, if Blackacre were sold for $500, reflecting no book gain, the tax gain of $200 would be allocated $125 to C, $25 to A and $50 to B. If the partnership had inadequate gross income to eliminate C's book / tax disparity, the partnership would be required to allocate tax deductions differently than book deductions by allocating to A and B tax deductions the correlative book deductions for which were allocated to C. For example, if Blackacre were to be sold for $180 and the $320 book loss allocated $80 to each of A and C and $160 to B, none of the $120 tax loss—being less than the prior $125 capital shift from A and B to C—would be allocated to C; the tax loss would be allocated $40 to A and $80 to B.

If after all of the unrealized appreciation or depreciation in the partnership's assets has been allocated to the option holder and the option holder's capital account still does not equal the amount of partnership capital to which the option holder is entitled, then the partnership must adjust the capital accounts of the historic partners by the amounts necessary to provide the option holder with a capital account equal to the holder's rights to partnership capital under the agreement. Starting with the year the option is exercised, the partnership must make corrective allocations of tax items—that differ from the partnership's allocations of book items—of gross income or loss to the partners to reflect any shift in the partners' capital accounts occurring as a result of the exercise of an option.

ILLUSTRATIVE MATERIAL

1. REVALUATIONS OF PARTNERS' CAPITAL ACCOUNTS

The proposed regulations would amend Treas. Reg. § 1.704–1(b)(2)(iv)(f)(2) to provide rules for revaluing the partners' capital accounts while an option is outstanding. Under the proposed amendments, in revaluing partnership property under Treas. Reg. § 1.704–1(b)(2)(iv)(f), the aggregate value of partnership property would be reduced by the amount by which the value of the option exceeds its price or is increased by the amount by which the price of the option exceeds its value.

2.   RECHARACTERIZATION OF OPTION HOLDER AS A PARTNER

An option holder will be recharacterized as a partner if (1) under a facts and circumstances test, the option holder's rights are substantially similar to the rights afforded to a partner and (2) as of the date that the noncompensatory option is issued, transferred, or modified, there is a strong likelihood that the failure to treat the option holder as a partner would result in a substantial reduction in the present value of the partners' and the option holder's aggregate tax liabilities. Prop. Reg. § 1.761–3 (2003). If an option is reasonably certain to be exercised, the first half of this test is generally met. If the option holder is treated as a partner under the proposed regulations, then the holder's distributive share of the partnership's income, gain, loss, deduction, or credit must be determined in accordance with such partner's interest in the partnership under Treas. Reg. § 1.704–1(b)(3). For this purpose, the option holder's share of partnership items should reflect the lesser amount of capital investment if appropriate; the option holder's distributive share of partnership losses and deductions may be limited by §§ 704(b) and (d) to the amount paid for the option.

SECTION 5.   ALLOCATIONS WHERE INTERESTS VARY DURING THE YEAR

INTERNAL REVENUE CODE: Section 706(c)(2)(B), (d).

REGULATIONS: Section 1.706–1(c)(2), (4).

Section 706(c)(1) provides that a partnership's taxable year does not close on admission of a new partner, the liquidation of a partner's interest, or the sale of a partnership interest.[7] This rule, coupled with the ability of partnerships to provide for special allocations of tax items, raises the question whether an allocation to a partner of items attributable to a portion of a taxable year during which he was not a partner will be respected. This problem most frequently arises on the admission of a new partner, either by contribution or by purchase of a partnership interest from a partner, but it may also arise when an existing partner increases his interest through contribution or purchase.

Suppose, for example, that a calendar year cash method partnership has incurred a loss of $100,000 prior to December 1, and on that date admits a new partner to whom all of the loss is specially allocated. Prior to

---

7. Section 706(c)(2)(A) provides that the taxable year of the partnership closes with respect to a partner who retires or sells or exchanges his *entire* partnership interest.

the Tax Reform Act of 1976, there was some judicial support for giving effect to retroactive allocations, see Smith v. Commissioner, 331 F.2d 298 (7th Cir.1964), although the Tax Court disapproved such allocations. Moore v. Commissioner, 70 T.C. 1024 (1978). The 1976 Act expressly prohibited such retroactive allocations. In 1984, § 706 was amended again to tighten further the restrictions on retroactive allocations and give the Commissioner broad authority to promulgate regulations governing the allocation of items to take into account the varying interests of the partners in the partnership during the taxable year.

Section 706(d)(1) requires that if there is any change in a partner's interest in the partnership during the year, each partner's distributive share of any partnership item of income, gain, loss, deduction or credit must be determined using a method prescribed by the regulations that takes into account the varying interests of the partners in the partnership during the year. Although this section does not on its face require that in the absence of regulations partners' distributive shares be determined so as to take into account the partner's varying interests during the year, and the regulations have not yet been amended to reflect the 1976 amendments, Congress intended that § 706(d)(1) be treated as directly imposing this requirement. The language of § 706(d)(1) is substantially similar to that of the 1976 version of § 706(c)(2)(B), which directly imposed a similar requirement. The 1984 changes were intended to extend the application of the pre–1984 rules to situations in which they arguably did not apply, not to narrow the application of the rule. The old rules were expressly triggered by sales and exchanges of partnership interests and the admission of a new partner, but the statutory language applied only to the old partners; extension of the rules to new partners was by necessary implication. Under current § 706(d)(1), however, the distributive share of "each partner" must be determined taking into account the varying interests of the partners if there is a change in "any partner's interest." See H.Rep. No. 98–432, 98th Cong., 2d Sess. 1213 (1984).

ILLUSTRATIVE MATERIAL

1. INTERIM CLOSING OF THE BOOKS VERSUS PRORATION

1.1. *General*

Treas. Reg. § 1.706–1(c)(2) prescribes two methods for taking into account the partners' varying interests during the year when a partner sells his entire interest or retires. These regulations were issued under the pre–1976 version of § 706 and do not specifically address the method to be used on admission of a new partner by contribution or on a disposition of less than all of a partner's interest. However, the legislative history of pre–1984 § 706(c)(2)(B), the 1976 statutory predecessor to § 706(d)(1), indicates that the same methods are to be used, S.Rep. No. 94–938, 94th Cong., 2d Sess. 97–98 (1976), and judicial application of pre–1984 § 706(c)(2)(B) employed these methods. See Richardson v. Commissioner, 76 T.C. 512 (1981), aff'd, 693 F.2d 1189 (5th Cir.1982).

Under these regulations, the interim closing of the books method is mandatory, unless the partners agree to use the proration method when a partner retires or sells his entire interest in the partnership. Presumably, the election is now available whenever § 706(d)(1) applies. Under the proration method, the partnership's items for the entire year are prorated over the days in the taxable year and are allocated among the partners based on their respective percentage interests on each day. To avoid undue complexity, in 1976 Congress authorized the Internal Revenue Service to promulgate regulations under which changes in partnership interests would be accounted for using a semimonthly convention, but no regulations to this effect have been published yet.

1.2. *Proration Method*

Rev.Rul. 77–310, 1977–2 C.B. 217, illustrates the computation of allocations under the proration method as follows. Assume that A, B, and C each have both a profits and a capital interest in the ABC partnership of 90 percent, 5 percent, and 5 percent, respectively. The ABC partnership uses the calendar year. On December 1, B and C contribute additional cash and the partnership agreement is amended to reduce A's profits and capital interest to 30 percent and increase the interest of each of B and C to 35 percent. During the year the partnership sustained a loss from business operations of $1,200. The partners must compute their distributive shares as follows:

Partner	Profit/Loss Percentages	Months Held	Computations	Distributive Shares of Loss
A	90	11	$.90 \times {}^{11}\!/_{12} \times 1200 =$	$ 990
	30	1	$.30 \times {}^{1}\!/_{12} \times 1200 =$	30
B	5	11	$.05 \times {}^{11}\!/_{12} \times 1200 =$	55
	35	1	$.35 \times {}^{1}\!/_{12} \times 1200 =$	35
C	5	11	$.05 \times {}^{11}\!/_{12} \times 1200 =$	55
	35	1	$.35 \times {}^{1}\!/_{12} \times 1200 =$	35
				$1,200

IR–84–129 (Dec. 13, 1984), allows a partnership to use a semimonthly convention when using the proration method. Under this convention partners entering the partnership during the first fifteen days of the month are treated as entering on the first day of the month and partners entering the partnership thereafter are treated as entering on the first day of the next month.

1.3. *Interim Closing of the Books*

Under the interim closing of the books method, the partnership would determine the exact amount of the operating loss incurred from January 1 through November 30, using its normal method of accounting, except as described below, and that loss would be allocated 90 percent to A and 5 percent to each of B and C. The actual loss incurred in December would be allocated 30 percent to A and 35 percent to each of B and C. Thus, if $1,000 of the loss was incurred before December 1 and $200 was incurred during December, the loss would be allocated among the partners as follows:

Partner	Profit/Loss Percentages	Loss Incurred During Months Held	Distributive Shares of Loss
A	90	$1,000	$ 900
	30	200	60
B	5	1,000	50
	35	200	70
C	5	1,000	50
	35	200	70
			$1,200

The interim closing of the books is the more accurate method for apportioning income between the period before a change in the partners' interests and the period after the change. The proration method, however, is more convenient. In deciding whether to agree to use the proration method, each partner must consider the effect of its inaccuracies on his tax liability for the year. When a partnership interest is disposed of in its entirety, the selling partner must bear in mind that if the proration method is used, events occurring after the sale can significantly and unexpectedly affect his tax liability for the year of the sale.

Where the Internal Revenue Service asserts a deficiency under § 706(d) it may apply either the proration or closing of the books method. Johnsen v. Commissioner, 84 T.C. 344 (1985), rev'd on other grounds, 794 F.2d 1157 (6th Cir.1986). If the Service applies the proration method, the taxpayer may prove at trial that the interim closing of the books method is more reasonable. See Sartin v. United States, 5 Cl.Ct. 172 (1984); Richardson v. Commissioner, 76 T.C. 512 (1981) aff'd, 693 F.2d 1189 (5th Cir. 1982). However, if the taxpayer elects to use the interim closing of the books method, the taxpayer must establish the date on which each item was earned, received, accrued, or paid. Sartin v. United States, supra; Moore v. Commissioner, 70 T.C. 1024 (1978).

1.4. *Allocable Cash Method Items*

1.4.1. *General*

When the interim closing of the books method is used by a cash method partnership, certain items are not taken into account on the date of payment. Section 706(d)(2) requires the proration over the taxable year by cash method partnerships of deductions for interest, taxes, rents, and other items which may be specified in the Regulations. This provision reflects the fact that these items may accrue over extended periods either before or after payment, and taking them into account on the date of payment may result in a significant misstatement of the partners' taxable incomes. Thus, for example, if the ABC partnership in the preceding example had operated without any gain or loss except for a $1,200 rent payment attributable to the entire year made in arrears on December 31, the interim closing of the books method would result in the same allocation as results under the proration method since $100 of the rent must be attributed to each month. If the rental payment were attributable to only the last six months of the year, however, then $200 of rent would be allocated to each of the last six months of the year. As a result, A's distributive share of the loss would be $960 ((.9 × ⅚ × $1,200) + (.3 × ⅙ × $1,200)), and B's and C's shares would be $120 ((.05 × ⅚ × $1,200) + (.35 × ⅙ × $1,200)).

In addition to the items specified in § 706(d)(2), cash method partnerships are required to apportion depreciation ratably over the year, rather than attributing it entirely to the last day of the year. See Hawkins v. Commissioner, 713 F.2d 347 (8th Cir.1983).

Accrual method partnerships are required to prorate deductions for interest, rent, taxes, depreciation, and similar items over the year without any specific statutory directive. See Williams v. United States, 680 F.2d 382 (5th Cir.1982).

1.4.2.   *Items Attributable to Prior or Future Years*

Suppose that the $1,200 rent paid in December by the ABC partnership in the preceding example was attributable to the year preceding the year in which it was paid and in which there was a change in partnership interests. Since the ABC partnership uses the cash method, the payment must be taken into account in the year in which it was paid, but for purposes of determining the partners' distributive shares, § 706(d)(2)(C) requires that the payment be treated as paid on the first day of the taxable year. Section 706(d)(2)(D) then provides that it is allocated among the partners according to their interests in the prior year to which the payment was attributable. Thus, A's distributive share of the loss would be $1,080 (.9 × $1,200) and B's and C's shares would be $60 (.05 × $1,200). If any person who was a partner in the prior year is no longer a partner in the year in which the item is paid, the distributive share of the item attributable to that partner is not deductible by the partnership. It must be capitalized and allocated to the basis of partnership assets under the rules of § 755. (Section 755 is discussed at page 299.)

Similarly, if in a year in which there is a change in partnership interests, a cash method partnership makes a deductible payment of an item attributable to a future year, the item is attributed to the last day of the year. Assume that the ABC partnership in the preceding examples had neither a profit nor a loss for the taxable year of the change except for a $1,200 payment on July 1 of local real property taxes for the year beginning July 1. The $600 attributable to the current year is allocated ratably over the last six months of the year, and the remaining $600 is attributed to the last day of the year. Accordingly, A's distributive share of the loss is $660 (($600 × ⅚ × .9) + ($600 × ⅙ × .3) + ($600 × .30)), and B's and C's shares each are $270 (($600 × ⅚ × .05) + ($600 × ⅙ × .35) + ($600 × .35)).

2.   RELATIONSHIP OF SECTION 706(d) TO SECTION 704(b)

Suppose that C is admitted to the AB partnership on December 30 as a one-third partner with A and B, and the partnership agreement specially allocates all of the depreciation on the partnership's property for the year to C. The ABC partnership maintains capital accounts as required by the

§ 704(b) regulations, charges the depreciation to C's capital account, will liquidate according to the partners' capital accounts, and C is required to restore any deficit in his capital account upon liquidation. The allocation has substantial economic effect. Will it be recognized? Ogden v. Commissioner, 84 T.C. 871 (1985), aff'd per curiam, 788 F.2d 252 (5th Cir.1986), held that § 704(b)(2) does not override the requirements of § 706(d). A retroactive allocation is ineffective even if it has substantial economic effect. See also Treas. Reg. § 1.704–1(b)(1)(iii), providing that § 704(b)(2) does not override § 706(d).

Snell v. United States, 680 F.2d 545 (8th Cir.1982), rejected the taxpayer's argument that § 706(d) applies only when the partnership agreement does not expressly provide for allocation of an item for the year. However, § 706(d) does not apply to retroactive reallocations of items among existing partners where the reallocation is not attributable to a capital contribution that results in the reduction of the interest of one or more partners. Lipke v. Commissioner, 81 T.C. 689 (1983). Treas. Reg. § 1.761–1(c) permits amendments to a partnership agreement made after the close of the taxable year, but on or before the due date for the partnership's return, to be given retroactive effect. In such a case, however, the reallocation must have substantial economic effect under § 704(b)(2). Thus, for example, if the DEF law partnership, in which each partner had a one third interest in profits and capital, amended its partnership agreement on April 14, 2007, effective January 1, 2006, to give D a one half interest in partnership profits and E and F each a one-quarter interest, for the purpose of more accurately reflecting the relationship of their services to firm profits for the year, the amended allocation would be effective.

3. RELATIONSHIP OF SECTION 706(d) TO GENERAL ASSIGNMENT OF INCOME DOCTRINE

In Cottle v. Commissioner, 89 T.C. 467 (1987), the taxpayer held a 1 percent limited partnership interest and a 25 percent general partnership interest in a partnership organized to acquire an apartment building and convert it to condominiums. Almost all of the effort required to effect the conversion and sale of the units occurred prior to October 21, 1977, but none of the sales of units had been closed. On that day, the taxpayer transferred his 25 percent general partnership interest to his wholly-owned corporation in a transaction subject to § 351. On November 15, 1977 the partnership closed the sale of most of the condominium units. Applying the interim closing of the books method, the taxpayer reported no income for the year attributable to the general partnership interest which he held until October 21. The Commissioner asserted that the taxpayer and not the corporation was taxable on all of the partnership income attributable to the units sold on November 15 because "due to the assignment of income doctrine, the interim closing of the books was not a reasonable method of determining who should report the income in question." Neither the taxpayer nor the Commissioner urged use of the proration method. Because the taxpayer retained his 1 percent limited partnership interest, the statutory predecessor of § 706(d) rather than § 706(c)(2)(A) applied. Nevertheless, relying on the legislative history of the statutory predecessor of § 706(d), the court allowed the taxpayer to apply Treas. Reg. § 1.706–1(c)(2), mandating the closing of the books method. The court reasoned that Subchapter K dictates that the timing of the includability of income (and of deductions) is determined at the partnership level under the method of accounting used by the partnership. Because there were contingencies attached to the closing of the sales by the partnership, the court concluded that the income was not earned by the partnership until November 15. Thus, as of October 21, when the partnership closed its books, it had no income and, accordingly, there was no partnership income to be allocated to the taxpayer at that time. The court then turned to the applicability of more general assignment of income principles, which it described as follows:

> Respondent argues that the principles of Commissioner v. Court Holding Co., 324 U.S. 331 (1945), as applied in Murry v. Commissioner, T.C. Memo. 1984–670, should govern the instant case to cause petitioners rather than DRC to be taxable on the profits from the condominium sales.

> In *Murry,* the taxpayer owned an apartment complex that was to be converted to a condominium, and the units therein would subsequently be sold. The taxpayer's wholly-owned corporation was to undertake the development of the property as a condominium. Because of certain financial difficulties, the taxpayer had to sell the apartment complex to the lender. However, in order to accommodate the taxpayer's tax considerations, the lender agreed to buy the property from the taxpayer's corporation. The taxpayer thus agreed to make a capital contribution of the property to the corporation, if the corporation agreed to sell the property immediately thereafter to the lenders.

> We held in *Murry* that the taxpayer and not the corporation was taxable on the sale of the property to the lender. In so holding, we applied the *Court Holding* doctrine which provides that "a sale by one person cannot be transformed for tax purposes into a sale by another by using the latter as a conduit through which to pass title." Commissioner v. Court Holding Co., 324 U.S. at 334.

> We agree with petitioners that *Murry* is not relevant to this case. Associates in the instant case was the owner and developer of the property. It converted the property to condominium units, sold the units therein, and reported the profits from these sales on its partnership return. There is no question in this case, as was present in *Murry,* as to who earned the income. No conduit was used by Associates to sell the condominium units. The parties agree that Associates earned the income; the only question in the instant case is how that income is to be allocated among the partners. And that question is resolved solely by application of section 706(c)(2)(B), which governs the allocation of partnership items when there are transfers of partial partnership interests

during the tax year. The rules thereunder are specifically designed to avoid assignments of income and retroactive allocation of losses between transferor and transferee partners. Moore v. Commissioner, 70 T.C. at 1032–1033. We think they adequately resolve the question in the instant case, and that their use is specifically mandated by Richardson v. Commissioner, 76 T.C. at 526–527.

We hold for petitioners on this issue.

What would have been the result in the *Cottle* case if the partners had agreed to use the proration method?

4.   TIERED PARTNERSHIPS

Prior to the enactment of § 706(d)(3) in 1984, it arguably was possible to sidestep the prohibition on retroactive allocations through the use of tiered partnerships. Assume for example that the UT partnership held a 90 percent interest in the LT partnership, and both partnerships used the calendar year. LT had a $10,000 loss for the year. UT's share of that loss was $9,000. On December 30, A contributed cash to UT in exchange for an eighty percent interest, and UT used the interim closing of the books method to apply § 706(d). Arguably, UT's $9,000 loss from LT was incurred on December 31, the last day of LT's taxable year, and A's distributive share of the loss would be $7,200. Section 706(d)(3) prevents this avoidance technique by, in effect, ignoring UT, the upper tier partnership, for allocation purposes and flowing through to the partners of UT in accordance with their effective interests in LT on the close of each day UT's distributive share of each LT item. Thus, in the example, if UT's entire $9,000 loss from LT was attributable to depreciation, since A was a partner for two days of LT's taxable year within UT's taxable year, A's share would be $39 (80% × (2/365 × $9,000)). These principles apply whether the upper tier partnership uses the cash or the accrual method. In addition, the rules governing allocable cash method items must be applied in allocating lower tier partnership items to the partners of the upper tier partnership by the flow through method. Section 706(d)(3) generally adopts the position of the Internal Revenue Service set forth in Rev.Rul. 77–311, 1977–2 C.B. 218.

SECTION 6.   FAMILY PARTNERSHIPS

INTERNAL REVENUE CODE: Section 704(e).

REGULATIONS: Section 1.704–1(e).

Allocations of partnership items in partnerships in which the partners are family members present additional problems that are not present when the partnership allocations are bargained at arms' length. In so-called family partnerships, allocations may reflect an attempt to shift income for tax purposes in a manner inconsistent with the principles of Lucas v. Earl, 281 U.S. 111 (1930), and Helvering v. Horst, 311 U.S. 112 (1940). The principal problems involved partnerships where one (or more) partner's capital interest was derived by gift from a family member partner and partnerships in which personal services were important but one or more partners did not provide any significant services.

The landmark case dealing with family partnerships is Commissioner v. Culbertson, 337 U.S. 733 (1949). That case involved a ranching partnership composed of a father and four sons, two of whom were minors. The sons had received their interests partly by gift from the father and partly by contribution of funds loaned to them by the father, which were repaid from the proceeds of partnership operations. The Court articulated the relevant test as follows:

> The Tax Court read our decisions in Commissioner v. Tower, (327 U.S. 280), and Lusthaus v. Commissioner, (327 U.S. 293), as setting out two essential tests of partnership for income-tax purposes: that each partner contribute to the partnership either vital services or capital originating with him. Its decision was based upon a finding that none of respondent's sons had satisfied those requirements during the tax years in question. * * *

> The question is not whether the services or capital contributed by a partner are of sufficient importance to meet some objective standard supposedly established by the *Tower* case, but whether, considering all the facts the agreement, the conduct of the parties in execution of its provisions, their statements, the testimony of disinterested persons, the relationship of the parties, their respective abilities and capital contribution, the actual control of income and the purposes for which it is used, and any other facts throwing light on their true intent-the parties in good faith and acting with a business purpose intended to join together in the present conduct of the enterprise. There is nothing new or particularly difficult about such a test. Triers of fact are constantly called upon to determine the intent with which a person acted. * * *

> Unquestionably a court's determination that the services contributed by a partner are not "vital" and that he has not participated in "management and control of the business" or contributed "original capital" has the effect of placing a heavy burden on the taxpayer to show the bona fide intent of the parties to join together as partners. But such a determination is not conclusive, * * *.

Two years after the *Culbertson* decision, Congress enacted the predecessor of § 704(e). This section provides that a donee of a partnership interest is to be treated as the owner of the interest unless the facts and circumstances attending the gift, including the conduct of partnership affairs before and after the transfer, indicate that the purported gift was a sham or that the donor retained so many incidents of control that he would be treated as the owner of the interest under Helvering v. Clifford, 309 U.S. 331 (1940). Powers retained by the donor in his capacity as managing partner, however, do not generally indicate lack of true ownership in the transferee. Retained powers are closely scrutinized, and a power exercisable for the benefit of the donee partner (such as a power exercisable as a custodian under the Uniform Gifts to Minors Act) is distinguishable from a power vested in the transferor for his own benefit.

Because § 704(e) recognizes the donee of a partnership interest as the true owner of the interest, it incorporates express rules to prevent the deflection to the donee of partnership income in excess of the share properly attributable to his capital interest. Partnership allocations under § 704(a) that do not take into account a proper allowance for services rendered to the partnership are not respected. Similarly, if the partnership agreement provides for partnership allocations disproportionate to the partners' capital interests, § 704(e) reallocates partnership income in proportion to partnership capital. See S.Rep. No. 82–81, 82d Cong., 1st Sess. (1951).

The incentive to engage in the income-shifting activities to which § 704(e) was directed was greatly reduced by relative flattening of the progressive tax rates in 1980s and the enactment in 1986 of the so-called "kiddie tax" in § 1(g) where children under age fourteen are involved.

ILLUSTRATIVE MATERIAL

1. RELATIONSHIP OF SECTION 704(e) AND *CULBERTSON*

Section 704(e) applies only when a partnership interest is acquired by gift or in a transfer between family members, see § 704(e)(2), (3), *and* capital is a material income producing factor in the partnership. See Treas. Reg. § 1.704–1(e)(4) for the application of § 704(e) to purchased partnership interests. Carriage Square, Inc. v. Commissioner, 69 T.C. 119 (1977), held that capital was not a material income producing factor and § 704(e) did not apply where the partners contributed only de minimis capital and the balance of the partnership's income producing capital was borrowed on the strength of corporate general partner's credit.

If the partnership is a service partnership, the *Culbertson* test is still determinative as to whether the partnership will be recognized. See Poggetto v. United States, 306 F.2d 76 (9th Cir.1962); Payton v. United States, 425 F.2d 1324 (5th Cir.1970). In such cases a putative partnership in which one family member fails to perform services generally will fail the *Culbertson* test. Id.

2. APPLICATION OF SECTION 704(e) WHERE PARTNERS PERFORM SERVICES

Even where capital is a material income producing factor and § 704(e) applies, due regard must be given to the performance of services by the partners in allocating partnership income. Section 704(e)(2) provides that distributive shares that do not make an "allowance of reasonable compensation for services rendered to the partnership by the donor" will not be respected. Treas. Reg. § 1.704–1(e)(3) extends the reasonable allowance for services concept to take services performed by the donee into account in determining the donor's distributive share. See Woodbury v. Commissioner,

49 T.C. 180 (1967), in which an allowance was made for the services of both the donor and donee partners.

3.   RESTRICTIONS ON DONEE'S CONTROL

Treas. Reg. § 1.704–1(e)(2) sets forth a number of factors to be taken into account in determining whether the donee actually has acquired ownership of a partnership interest. More stringent standards are applied when a partnership interest is held by a trustee or a minor child, and when the donated interest is a limited partnership interest. See Virgil v. Commissioner, T.C.Memo. 1983–757 (failure to appoint trustees or guardians for minor children who were donee partners resulted in taxation of their distributive share to donor parent).

Cirelli v. Commissioner, 82 T.C. 335 (1984), involved a partnership in which five children (four of whom were minors) were equal partners in an equipment leasing partnership. The children contributed no capital and performed no services. The partnership leased property only to a corporation controlled by the children's father, and financed its purchases through loans from the father or rental receipts. The father in fact had total control over the partnership's affairs. Even though § 704(e) was not directly applicable, the Tax Court applied the factors enumerated in Treas. Reg. § 1.704–1(e)(2) to determine that the purported partnership was a sham.

CHAPTER 5

ALLOCATION OF PARTNERSHIP LIABILITIES

INTERNAL REVENUE CODE: Sections 704(d); 705; 733; 752.

Section 752(a) provides that any increase in a partner's share of partnership liabilities is treated as a cash contribution. As a cash contribution, an increase in a partner's share of partnership liabilities increases the partner's outside basis under § 722. A partner's outside basis is crucial to the conduit theory of partnership taxation because that basis is the ceiling on the amount of partnership losses that can be passed through to the partner's individual return. See § 704(d), discussed at page 97. Conversely, if a partner's share of partnership liabilities decreases or the partner's individual liabilities decrease as a result of assumption of those liabilities by the partnership, the amount by which such liabilities is decreased is treated by § 752(b) as a partnership distribution of cash. This deemed cash distribution reduces the partner's basis in his partnership interest pursuant to § 705(a)(2) and § 733. Gain is recognized to the extent that the deemed distribution exceeds outside basis. I.R.C. § 731(a)(1).

The Code contains no rules for determining a partner's share of partnership liabilities. The guiding principles are found in Treas. Regs. §§ 1.752–1 through 1.752–5. These rules are intended to treat as a partner's share of the partnership liabilities only that portion of those liabilities for which the partner bears the ultimate economic risk of loss. In very general terms, debts for which no partner bears a risk of loss, nonrecourse debts, are allocated to the partners in accord with their share of gain attributable to encumbered property, or their share of partnership profit.

Section 752 and the regulations thereunder apply whenever the partnership borrows money or repays a loan. For example, if A and B form a general partnership to which each contributes $20,000 and in which they are equal partners, and the AB general partnership then borrows $100,000, A and B each increase their basis in the partnership by $50,000. If $20,000 of the loan subsequently is repaid, A and B each reduce their basis in the partnership by $10,000; and if either or both has a basis of less than $10,000 at that time, the partner recognizes gain: the reduction of liabilities treated as a cash distribution in excess of basis requires recognition of gain under § 731(a). Because § 752 is Subchapter K's way of incorporating the principles that generally govern the treatment of liabilities in computing basis and amount realized with respect to purchases and sales of property, including Crane v. Commissioner, 331 U.S. 1 (1947), and its progeny (dealing with nonrecourse debt), § 752(c) applies these rules to liabilities attached to property that are not assumed when the property is transferred subject to the liabilities. Whether the liability is recourse or nonrecourse makes a difference under § 752. For example, if a partner transfers property to a partnership subject to a recourse liability that is not assumed by the partnership and for which the contributing partner remains personally liable, the liability remains a recourse liability of the contributing partner. The liability of the contributing partner is not changed; no other partners treat the liability as a cash contribution that increases basis, and the contributing partner does not reduce her basis in the partnership interest. See Treas. Reg. § 1.752–1(g), Ex. (1).

Furthermore, different rules apply to transfers of encumbered property between partners and the partnership, whether by contribution or distribution, and transfers by the partnership to third parties. When the transfer is between the partnership and partners, § 752(c) provides that liabilities to which the property is taken subject, but that are not assumed, are taken into account under § 752(a) and (b) only to the extent of the fair market value of the property; but if the property is sold by the partnership, pursuant to § 752(d), liabilities in excess of the fair market value are taken into account as well. See Commissioner v. Tufts, 461 U.S. 300 (1983).

Allocations of partnership liabilities are closely related to allocations of partnership income and loss. As is explained in the following material, if a partnership agreement specially allocates deductions to a particular partner, the provisions of Treas. Reg. § 1.752–2, governing the allocation of partnership recourse debt, generally result in a year-by-year reallocation of partnership debt away from the partners who do not receive the deductions and to the partner who received the special allocation of the deductions. As a result, the partner receiving the special allocation will increase her basis by the amount of her increased share of partnership indebtedness. This basis increase will prevent § 704(d) from coming into play to defer her deductions. (Concomitantly, the other partners will receive deemed distributions that reduce their bases.) Likewise, Treas. Reg. § 1.752–3, which governs the allocation of nonrecourse debt, coordinates allocations of nonrecourse debt with allocations of nonrecourse deductions under Treas. Reg. § 1.704–2, with the result that a partner to whom nonrecourse deductions are allocated will be allocated sufficient debt to prevent § 704(d) from affecting him.

SECTION 1.   ALLOCATION OF RECOURSE LIABILITIES

REGULATIONS: Sections 1.752–1, –2(a)–(d), (f)–(h), –4(b), (d).

A "recourse liability" is any liability "to the extent * * * that any partner or related person bears the economic risk of loss for that liability." Treas. Reg. § 1.752–1(a)(1). A partner's share of any recourse liability is the portion of the economic risk of loss for the liability borne by the partner or a person related to that partner. Treas. Reg. § 1.752–2(a).

For purposes of § 752, the term "liability", as defined in Treas. Reg. § 1.752–1(a)(4), is limited to debts that: (1) create or increase basis (including cash balances); (2) give rise to a deduction (e.g., accrual method accounts payable); or (3) give rise to a nondeductible expenditure not chargeable to a capital account (under § 263 or § 263A). Cash method accounts payable are not liabilities for purposes of § 752 and do not increase the partners' bases in their partnership interests. See Rev. Rul. 88–77, 1988–2 C.B. 128, which holds that cash method accounts payable, which are not deductible until paid and do not give rise to basis in any asset, should not be treated as liabilities for purposes of § 752 and should not increase the partners' bases in their partnership interests. Treas. Reg. § 1.752–2 provides detailed rules for determining the extent to which a partner bears the economic risk of loss associated with partnership liabilities. Generally speaking, a partner's share of partnership recourse liabilities is the amount of the partnership's liabilities for which the partner bears the ultimate burden of payment if the partnership is unable to make the payment. This ultimate burden is determined by taking into account the net effect of: (1) partners' obligations to restore negative capital accounts; (2) partner's obligations to pay notes to the partnership executed by them; (3) partners' obligations to creditors under guarantee agreements; (4) partners' obligations to other partners under any agreement; (5) partners' rights to contribution or indemnification under the partnership agreement or any other agreement; and (6) rights of contribution or indemnification arising by operation of law (e.g., subrogation rights of a guarantor). Contingent obligations, however, are ignored if it appears unlikely that they will be satisfied. See Treas. Reg. § 1.752–2(b)(3)–(6).

ILLUSTRATIVE MATERIAL

1. DEFINITION OF RECOURSE LIABILITY

Treas. Reg. § 1.752–1(a)(1) defines a "recourse liability" as any liability to the extent any partner or related person bears the risk of loss for the liability. Thus, a nonrecourse mortgage loan to the partnership that is guaranteed by a partner is a recourse liability. Treas. Reg. § 1.752–2(f), Ex. (5). If only a portion of the nonrecourse liability has been guaranteed, then the obligation is bifurcated and the guaranteed amount is treated as a recourse obligation while the remaining portion is treated as a nonrecourse liability. Treas. Regs. §§ 1.752–1(i); 1.752–2(f), Ex. (5). A nonrecourse loan to a partnership by a partner or a person related to a partner (as determined under Treas. Reg. § 1.752–4(b)) also is treated as a recourse liability, the economic risk of which is borne by the creditor-partner or partner related to the lender. Treas. Reg. § 1.752–2(c)(1). Treas. Reg. § 1.752–2(d)(1) excepts from the partner-lender rules certain loans by partners having a partnership interest of ten percent or less; in such a case the debt is allocated under the nonrecourse liability allocation rules of Treas. Reg. § 1.752–3.

Under applicable state law, members of a limited liability company are not personally liable for payment of any of the LLC's debts. Thus, LLC members are analogous to corporate shareholders. Accordingly, the recourse debts owed by an LLC that is taxed as a partnership are not recourse debts as defined by Treas. Reg. § 1.752–1(a)(1) because no member (partner) bears any risk of loss. Such debt is a nonrecourse debt that is allocated under Treas. Reg. § 1.752–3, discussed at page 197. If, however, a member of an LLC personally guarantees a debt of the LLC, the debt becomes a recourse debt, subject to the allocation rules of Treas. Reg. § 1.752–2 because the guaranteeing partner bears the risk of loss associated with the debt. Likewise, if a member transfers property to an LLC subject to a debt for which the contributing member continues to bear personal liability, the debt remains a recourse liability to the contributing member.

2. ECONOMIC RISK OF LOSS

2.1. *In General*

Economic risk of loss, which is the linchpin for determining whether a debt is recourse or nonrecourse and for allocating recourse debts among partners, is defined in Treas. Reg. § 1.752–2(b). A partner bears the economic risk of loss with respect to a partnership liability (even if the liability is nonrecourse as to the partnership) if upon a hypothetical liquidation of the partnership in which all of its assets are treated as worthless, the partner (or a related person) "would be obligated to make a payment to any person (or a contribution to the partnership) * * * and the partner or related person would not be entitled to reimbursement from another partner [or person related to that partner]." This means, in general, that a partner is economically at risk if following the liquidation of a partnership with no assets, and after the exercise of all rights to obtain reimbursement from others, the partner is responsible for payment of the debt. An obligation for which a partner is not entitled to reimbursement generally will exist to the extent that a partner would have a negative capital account as a result of the constructive liquidation and the partner is obligated to restore that negative capital account. An unreimbursable payment obligation also may exist if a partner guarantees a loan that is nonrecourse as to the partnership. But if a partner guarantees a loan that is recourse as to the partnership, payment of the loan by the guaranteeing partner would give rise to right of subrogation under state law. Thus the partner would have a right to reimbursement of a portion of the debt from the other partners and does not bear the risk of loss as to that portion of the debt. See Treas. Reg. § 1.752–2(f), Ex. (3).

A partner bears the economic risk of loss with respect to a debt that is nonrecourse to the partnership if the partner or a related party (as defined in Treas. Reg. § 1.752–4(b)) is the creditor with respect to the nonrecourse liability. Treas. Reg. § 1.752–2(c)(1). Related persons for this purpose are identified in Treas. Reg. § 1.752–4(b) through cross references to § 267(b) and § 707(b), with certain modifications. Thus, for example, the risk on a nonrecourse loan to a partnership from a corporation in which a partner owns more than fifty percent of the stock is treated as borne entirely by the shareholder-partner.

Although under Treas. Reg. §§ 1.752–1(a)(1) and 1.752–2(c)(2) a liability is recourse if a partner or a related party bears the risk of loss, an exception to this related party provision in Treas. Reg. § 1.752–4(b)(2)(iii) provides that persons owning directly or indirectly interests in the same partnership are not treated as related. In IPO II v. Commissioner, 122 T.C. 295 (2004), an individual was a partner with X Corporation, which he wholly owned, in a partnership that borrowed money to purchase an airplane. The loan was guaranteed by the individual, but not by X Corporation. In addition, the loan was guaranteed by Y Corporation, 70 percent of the stock of which was owned by the individual partner. The parties claimed that X Corporation was at-risk for the partnership debt because X Corporation was related to Y Corporation that had guaranteed the debt by virtue of the individual's common ownership of both corporations. The Tax Court held that the relationship between X Corporation and Y Corporation was severed by Treas. Reg. § 1.752–4(b)(2)(iii) because the relationship was traced through the individual who was a partner in the partnership. Thus, none of the liability was allocated to X Corporation.

2.2.   *Constructive Liquidation of Partnership*

Treas. Reg. § 1.752–2(b) prescribes the rules governing constructive liquidation analysis for determining partners' economic risk of loss. The following events are considered to happen in the constructive liquidation: (1) all of the partnership's assets (other than property contributed to the partnership solely for the purpose of securing a partnership obligation) become worthless; (2) all of the partnership's liabilities become due and payable in full; (3) the partnership transfers any property contributed to the partnership solely for the purpose of securing a partnership obligation to the creditor in partial or full satisfaction of the debt; (4) the partnership disposes of all its remaining assets for no consideration, except that property subject to nonrecourse mortgage liens is treated as transferred to the creditor in satisfaction of the debt; and (5) the partnership allocates all items of income, gain, deduction or loss among the partners as provided in the partnership agreement.

In making the required adjustments to the partners' capital accounts, gain is recognized by the partnership to the extent that any property is encumbered by a nonrecourse mortgage in excess of the basis, and loss is recognized to the extent of all remaining basis of the partnership's assets. However, if § 704(c) or Treas. Reg. § 1.704–1(b)(4)(i), governing allocations after capital accounts properly have been revalued (discussed at page 154), applies, gain is computed with reference to the excess of nonrecourse mortgages over the book value of the encumbered asset, and loss is computed with respect to the remaining book value of the partnership's assets. The partnership assets that are treated as worthless in the hypothetical liquidation presumably do not include any obligations of partners (or related persons) to make contributions or payments to the partnership. Such obligations are presumed to be satisfied regardless of the obligor's actual net worth or the likelihood of actual performance, unless the facts and circumstances indicate a plan to avoid the obligation. Treas. Reg. § 1.752–2(b)(6).

Operating on the assumption that the partnership is unable to pay its creditors, the constructive liquidation analysis will provide the final capital account balances, both positive and negative, of all partners, prior to any contributions required to wind up the partnership. Partners with a capital account of zero or more generally are not obligated to make any contribution to the partnership. Thus, they will not be allocated any share of partnership recourse liabilities unless they have an independent obligation to make a payment to a creditor or another party, including a partner. Partners having negative capital accounts will have an economic risk of loss and generally will be allocated an amount of partnership recourse liabilities equal to the negative capital account, unless they are entitled to reimbursement from a partner or other person. In addition, the constructive liquidation triggers deemed satisfaction of all obligations to make payments to creditors and reimbursements to other partners and persons related to other partners. The net result of the constructive settlement of capital accounts and these other payments equals each partner's economic risk of loss.

2.3. *Obligation to Make a Payment*

Treas. Reg. § 1.752–2(b)(5) provides that a partner's economic risk of loss equals the amount the partner would be required to pay another person or to contribute to the partnership in a constructive liquidation minus reimbursements that the partner is entitled to receive from other partners or persons as a result of making such payments or contributions. Treas. Reg. § 1.752–2(b)(6) deems all partners and related persons capable of making a reimbursement. Thus, the *right* to reimbursement controls without regard to the actual financial condition of the obligor or the likelihood that the obligor actually will reimburse the partner. Contingent obligations, however, are not taken into account if it is unlikely that the obligation ever will be discharged. Treas. Reg. § 1.752–2(b)(4).

Payments which a partner would be obligated to make and which are taken into account in determining economic risk of loss include all statutory and contractual obligations relating to partnership liabilities. In addition to any obligation to restore a negative capital account imposed by the partnership agreement or state law, contractual obligations outside the partnership agreement must be taken into account in determining each partner's economic risk of loss. Treas. Reg. § 1.752–2(b)(3). Examples of such contractual obligations include a partner's individual guarantees to creditors of partnership indebtedness, payments to reimburse another partner for paying more than his share of partnership debts (whether by contract or under state law), or payments pursuant to an agreement by one partner to indemnify another partner against loss. If a partner guarantees a partnership obligation, but is subrogated to the creditor's rights against the partnership if he pays the obligation, the right of reimbursement under the subrogation rights offsets the obligation on the guarantee. See Treas. Reg. § 1.752–2(f), Ex. (3) and Ex. (4).

In recent years an increasing number of partnership interests have been held through limited liability companies (LLCs) that are treated as disregarded entities under Treas. Reg. § 301.7701–1 through Treas. Reg. § 301.7701–3. In such a case, even though the limited liability company has an obligation to restore a negative capital account, the owner of the limited liability company, who is treated as the partner, has no such obligation under state partnership law. Because only the LLC's assets will be available to satisfy its payment obligations as a partner, the owner should be treated as bearing the economic risk of loss for a partnership liability as a result of those payment obligations only to the extent of the net value of the disregarded entity's assets. This result can be reached through a careful reading and application of the current regulations, but Prop. Reg. § 1.752–2(k) (2004) would clarify this treatment by providing that in determining the extent to which a partner bears the economic risk of loss for a partnership liability under Treas. Reg. § 1.752–2, payment obligations of a disregarded entity are taken into account only to the extent of the net value of the disregarded entity's assets (including the disregarded entity's enforceable rights to contributions from its owner, but excluding the disregarded entity's interest in the partnership and the fair market value of property pledged to secure a partnership liability, minus the disregarded entity's liabilities), except to the extent the owner of the disregarded entity is otherwise required to make a payment with respect to the disregarded entity's obligation.

If an obligation to make a payment, whether by contribution to the partnership or to another partner or a creditor of the partnership, is not required to be satisfied by the end of the taxable year in which the partner's partnership interest is liquidated (if there were to be such a liquidation) or, if later, 90 days after such liquidation, then the obligation will be taken into account only at its discounted present value. Treas. Reg. § 1.752–2(g). If the obligation bears interest at the applicable Federal rate (determined under § 1274(d)(1)), its value is its face value. Otherwise, the imputed principal amount is determined under § 1274(b). The regulations do not explain how to reallocate the portion of the partnership indebtedness that would have been allocated to a particular partner absent this time-value-of-money consideration but which is not allocated to that partner because of this rule. If other partners are the obligees, presumably any such portion of the indebtedness would be allocated among the other partners, but if a creditor is the obligee, allocation among the other partners would not correspond with risk of loss. Perhaps in such a case the "unallocated" recourse debt becomes nonrecourse debt for purposes of the § 752 regulations.

Treas. Reg. § 1.752–2(g)(3) provides that the transfer of a partner's promissory note is not a satisfaction of the partner's obligation unless the note is readily tradable on an established securities market. Since the context of the operation of this rule is the hypothetical liquidation of the partnership, the rule appears to be directed to situations in which either the partnership agreement or another contractual provision permits a partner to satisfy an obligation by delivery of a promissory note. Actual transfer to the partnership of a partner's promissory note prior to the liquidation should be treated as an obligation to make an additional contribution to the partnership, at the time and on the conditions specified in the promissory note, and should be taken into account as such. Treas. Reg. § 1.704–1. Applied literally, Treas. Reg. § 1.752–2(g)(3) would require reallocation of economic risk of loss from the partner who is entitled to satisfy an obligation by delivery of a note to the holder of the note. If the holder would be another partner, then that partner would bear the risk of loss; if the holder would be a creditor, that portion of the debt presumably would be classified as a nonrecourse debt allocable under Treas. Reg. § 1.752–3. However, because this rule is contained in the provisions governing "time-value-of-money considerations," its intended effect may be merely to require that promissory notes used to satisfy obligations bear interest at the applicable Federal rate where it has been agreed in advance that an obligation may be satisfied with a note.

Treas. Reg. § 1.752–2(h) provides rules for determining who bears the economic risk of loss where a partner directly or indirectly pledges individual property to secure a partnership debt. Where a partner makes an accommodation pledge of his individual property to secure a partnership debt, without guaranteeing the debt itself, the partner pledging the property bears an economic risk of loss for an amount of the partnership liability equal to the fair market value of the property (but not more than the partnership debt), determined at the time the property is pledged. Treas. Reg. § 1.752–2(h)(1) and (3). Thus, continued revaluation of pledged property is not required. A partner who contributes property to a partnership solely for the purpose of securing a partnership liability bears the economic risk of loss for the partnership liability, subject to the same valuation rules applicable to direct pledges of individual property to secure partnership indebtedness. Treas. Reg. § 1.752–2(h)(2) and (3). Although the regulations do not expressly so provide, economic risk of loss based on a pledge of property under Treas. Reg. § 1.752–2(h) presumably is subject to being offset by any right of the pledging partner to indemnification from other partners.

3. EXAMPLES

Partners' shares of recourse liabilities do not always correspond to the partners' shares of losses. A partners' risk of loss is determined largely by analyzing the amounts which the partners would be required to contribute to the partnership upon a hypothetical liquidation in which the partnership's assets are deemed to be worthless, and the required contribution generally is determined with reference to negative balances in partners' capital accounts. Suppose, for example, that C and D each contribute $500 in cash to form the CD partnership, in which profits and losses are to be divided 40% to C and 60% to D. The partnership then borrows $9,000 from an unrelated lender and purchases an asset for $10,000. Initially C and D each had a $500 capital account (following the requirements of Treas. Reg. § 1.704–1(b)(2)(iv), discussed at page 120). The CD Partnership's opening balance sheet, without the partners' bases in their partnership interests, would be as follows:

	Assets			Indebtedness and Partners' Capital Accounts		
		Tax				Tax
	Book	Basis			Book	Basis
Property	$10,000	$10,000	Debt		$ 9,000	
			C		$ 500	?
			D		$ 500	?
	$10,000	$10,000			$10,000	?

If the building were to become worthless, under the partnership agreement and the § 704(b) regulations, $4,000 of the $10,000 loss would be allocated to C, reducing C's capital account to negative $3,500, and $6000 of the loss would be allocated to D, reducing D's capital account to negative $5,500. The partnership's balance sheet would be as follows:

	Assets			Indebtedness and Partners' Capital Accounts		
		Tax				Tax
	Book	Basis			Book	Basis
Property	$ 0	$ 0	Debt		$9,000	
			C		($3,500)	$ 0
			D		($5,500)	$ 0
	$ 0	$ 0			$ 0	$ 0

Thus only $3,500 of the $9,000 partnership indebtedness is allocated to C as a deemed contribution under § 752(a), and $5,500 is allocated to D as a deemed contribution. See Treas. Reg. § 1.752–2(f), Ex. (2). C's basis for her partnership interest immediately after the debt is incurred would be $4,000 ($500 contribution + $3,500 debt share); D's basis in his partnership interest immediately after the debt is incurred would be $6,000 ($500 contribution + $5,500 debt share).

	Assets			Indebtedness and Partners' Capital Accounts		
		Tax				Tax
	Book	Basis			Book	Basis
Property	$10,000	$10,000	Debt		$ 9,000	
			C		$ 500	$ 4,000
			D		$ 500	$ 6,000
	$10,000	$10,000			$10,000	$10,000

Note that the effect of allocating the CD Partnership's indebtedness in this manner is to assure that D has sufficient basis to deduct D's disproportionate share of partnership losses without running afoul of the § 704(d) limitation.

Partners will be allocated shares of partnership indebtedness disproportionately to their loss sharing ratios if partners share profits and losses disproportionately to their capital contributions. Assume, for example, that E and F form a partnership in which they share profits and losses equally, but E contributes $4,000 and F contributes $5,000. The partnership borrows $10,000. The EF Partnership's opening balance sheet, without the partners' bases for their partnership interests, would be as follows:

Assets			Indebtedness and Partners' Capital Accounts		
	Book	Tax Basis		Book	Tax Basis
Property	$19,000	$19,000	Debt	$10,000	
			E	$ 4,000	?
			F	$ 5,000	?
	$19,000	$19,000		$19,000	?

If the partnership lost $19,000 and allocated the loss $9,500 to each partner, E's capital account would be reduced from $4,000 to negative $5,500; F's capital account would be reduced from $5,000 to negative $4,500. The partnership's balance sheet (without the partners' bases for their partnership interests) would be as follows:

Assets			Indebtedness and Partners' Capital Accounts		
	Book	Tax Basis		Book	Tax Basis
Property	$ 0	$ 0	Debt	$10,000	
			E	($ 5,500)	?
			F	($ 4,500)	?
	$ 0	$ 0		$ 0	?

Thus, $5,500 of the debt would be allocated to E, resulting in E having a basis for her partnership interest immediately after the debt is incurred of $9,500 ($4,000 contribution + $5,500 debt share) and F having a basis in his partnership interest immediately after the debt is incurred of $9,500 ($5,000 contribution + $4,500 debt share). E and F have the same basis in their partnership interests, even though their contributions were different, because they bear the risk of loss on the debt differently. As result of each of them having equal partnership interest bases, since E and F share losses equally, neither will run afoul of the § 704(d) limitation of losses to basis rule.

The principles explained in the preceding paragraphs are the key to an important interrelationship between the § 704(d) limitation on losses, special allocations under Treas. Reg. § 1.704–1(b) of deductions attributable to recourse debt, and § 752(a) and (b). The rules for allocation of partnership recourse indebtedness under Treas. Reg. § 1.752–2 assure that a partner who has an unlimited obligation to restore a negative capital account always will have sufficient basis in his partnership interest to be able to deduct currently any special allocation to him of partnership deduction items that are attributable to the debt. Assume, for example, that the GH Partnership is formed by G and H, each of whom contributes $15,000. The partnership borrows $120,000 and purchases an asset, the cost of which is recoverable over ten years under the straightline method. G and H will share all items equally, except depreciation, all of which is allocable to H. Initially, G and H bear the risk of loss on the debt equally and the GH Partnership's opening balance sheet is as follows:

	Assets			Indebtedness and Partner's Capital Accounts		
	Book	Tax Basis			Book	Tax Basis
Property	$150,000	$150,000		Debt	$120,000	
				G	$ 15,000	$ 75,000
				H	$ 15,000	$ 75,000
	$150,000	$150,000			$150,000	$150,000

Each year for the first five years, the partnership breaks even, apart from depreciation deductions, thus losing $15,000 per year, all of which is allocated to H. As a result of being allocated $75,000 of partnership losses over those five years, H's capital account is reduced to negative $60,000, but H's basis for his partnership interest has not been reduced to zero. At the end of five years, the partnership's balance sheet, apart from partners' bases in their partnership interests, is as follows:

	Assets			Indebtedness and Partners' Capital Accounts		
	Book	Tax Basis			Book	Tax Basis
Property	$75,000	$75,000		Debt	$120,000	
				G	$ 15,000	?
				H	($ 60,000)	?
	$75,000	$75,000			$ 75,000	?

Applying Treas. Reg. § 1.752–2, if all of the partnership assets were worthless, and the $75,000 loss deduction were allocated equally between G and H, G's capital account would be reduced to negative $22,500, and H's capital account would be reduced to negative $97,500. Thus, at the end of six years, G's share of the debt is $22,500 and H's share is $97,500. H's basis at that time is thus $37,500, computed as follows:

	Cash Contribution	$15,000
+	Original share of debt	$60,000
−	Deductions in years 1–5	($75,000)
+	Increase in debt share ($97,500 − $60,000)	$37,500
		$37,500

Because the basis of H's partnership interest has been increased by an amount equal to H's increased share of the partnership's indebtedness,[1] the partnership can continue to allocate all depreciation to H without running afoul of § 704(d). Indeed, continued allocations of depreciation to H during years 6–9 will result in a further shift of the risk of loss on the debt from G to H, thus allowing H to deduct the depreciation for the nine years without running afoul of § 704(d). After nine years, however, H will have exhausted her basis. At the end of eight years, the partnership's balance sheet, apart from partners' bases in their partnership interests, is as follows:

Assets			Indebtedness and Partners' Capital Accounts		
		Tax			Tax
	Book	Basis		Book	Basis
Property	$30,000	$30,000	Debt	$120,000	
			G	$ 15,000	?
			H	($105,000)	?
	$30,000	$30,000		$ 30,000	?

Applying the hypothetical liquidation principle after eight years, if a $30,000 loss from the worthlessness of the property were split equally, G would have a capital account of zero, and H would have a capital account of negative $120,000. H bears the full risk of loss on the debt because only H would have a negative capital account. Thus, at the end of eight years H has a remaining basis in her partnership interest of $15,000, computed as follows:

	Cash Contribution	$ 15,000
+	Original share of debt	$ 60,000
−	Deductions in years 1–8	($120,000)
+	Increase in debt share ($120,000 − $60,000)	$ 60,000
		$ 15,000

Accordingly, H has sufficient basis to support deducting $15,000 of partnership losses in year 9. After nine years, however, H will have exhausted her basis and continuing to allocate the depreciation deduction to H will result in neither partner being able to claim a current deduction. Deductions will be deferred until H, the partner to whom they have been allocated, acquires additional basis in a future year.

In contrast to the above examples, when each partner's capital account is proportionate to the partner's share of partnership profits and losses

---

1. Although the example computes the increase in H's share of partnership indebtedness by comparing the end of year 6 and the beginning of the partnership, technically under § 705(a) each change should be taken into account separately and all of the changes cumulated. See Treas. Reg. § 1.752–4(d).

(which also are the same), as a rule of thumb each partner's share of partnership recourse liabilities generally can be determined by multiplying the total liabilities by the partner's profit and loss share percentage. This is a corollary of the shortcut alternative basis rule in § 705(b). However, where any partner's profit sharing ratio differs from his loss sharing ratio, or either ratio differs from the partners' capital contributions ratio, the constructive liquidation analysis must be applied.

4. CONTINGENT LIABILITIES

Treas. Reg. § 1.752–7 deals with the assumption by a partnership of a partner's fixed or contingent obligation to make a payment that is not one of the three types of liabilities defined in Treas. Reg. § 1.752–1(a)(4)(i) as a liability for purposes of § 752.[2] Accrual method liabilities the deduction for which is deferred under the economic performance rules of § 453(h), such as future environmental remediation expenses, are not a "liability" under this definition. If the partnership satisfies the liability while the originally obligated partner remains in the partnership, the deduction with respect to the built-in loss associated with the § 1.752–7 liability is allocated to the originally obligated partner, thereby reducing that partner's outside basis. Alternatively, if one of three events occurs that separate the originally obligated partner from the liability, then the partner's outside basis is reduced immediately before the occurrence of the event. The events are: (1) a disposition (or partial disposition) of the partnership interest by the partner, (2) a liquidation of the partner's partnership interest, and (3) the assumption (or partial assumption) of the liability by another partner. The basis reduction generally is the lesser of (1) the excess of the partner's basis in the partnership interest over the adjusted value of the interest, or (2) the remaining built-in loss associated with the liability. (In the event of a partial disposition, the reduction is pro rated.) Thereafter, to the extent of the remaining built-in loss associated with the liability, the partnership (or the assuming partner) is not entitled to any deduction or capital expense upon satisfaction (or economic performance) of the liability, but if the partnership notifies the partner, the partner is entitled to a loss or deduction. If another partner assumed the liability, the partnership must immediately reduce the basis of its assets by the built-in loss, and upon satisfaction, the assuming partner must make certain basis adjustments to his partnership interest. There are exceptions for (1) the transfer of the trade or business with which the liability is associated (not merely the particular assets with which the liability is associated) to the partnership, and (2) *de minimis* transactions (liabilities less that 10 percent of the partnership's assets or $1,000,000).[3]

2. Under Treas. Reg. § 1.752–1(a)(4)(i), an obligation is a liability for purpose of § 752 to the extent that incurring the obligation: (1) creates or increases the basis of any of the obligor's assets (including cash); (2) gives rise to an immediate deduction; or (3) gives rise to an expense that is not de- ductible in computing taxable income and is not properly chargeable to capital.

3. These regulations are intended to defeat an abusive tax shelter scheme referred to as "Son of Boss" undertaken through a partnership that attempted to generate tax deductions on disposition of a partnership in-

SECTION 2.   ALLOCATION OF NONRECOURSE DEBT

REGULATIONS: Sections 1.752–1, –3.

1.   *In General*

Allocations of partnership nonrecourse debt are based on an entirely different set of principles than are allocations of recourse debt.[4] The rules governing allocation of nonrecourse debt are based on the premise that none of the partners suffers an actual risk of individual loss from nonrecourse debt. The debt will be repaid, if at all, only out of partnership profits. For example, assume a limited partnership composed of a general partner and two limited partners who share profits equally acquires property subject to a nonrecourse mortgage of $15,000. Each partner increases his basis in his partnership interest by $5,000. As the loan is repaid out of partnership profits, each partner increases his basis by the amount of profits, see § 705(a), and decreases his basis by the reduction in partnership liabilities. Thus, when the loan is fully repaid, each partner's basis is unchanged. However, if the mortgage were with recourse to the partnership, thus making the general partner but not the limited partners liable on the mortgage, the general partner would be treated as solely responsible for the mortgage and would be entitled to the full basis adjustment. This result is justified by the fact that the debt, if not satisfied out of partnership profits, ultimately is the responsibility of the general partner.

Partnership indebtedness is considered to be nonrecourse debt only to the extent that no partner (nor any person related to a partner under Treas. Reg. § 1.752–4(b)) bears the economic risk of loss for the liability. Treas. Reg. § 1.752–1(a)(2). Thus a debt which is nonrecourse to the partnership, but which is guaranteed by a partner, is subject to the rules governing partners' shares of recourse debt rather than those applicable to nonrecourse debt. See Treas. Reg. § 1.752–2(f), Ex. (5). Under Treas. Reg. § 1.752–3(a), a partner's share of partnership nonrecourse liabilities is the sum of three amounts: (1) an amount of partnership nonrecourse debt equal to the partner's share of "minimum gain" under Treas. Reg. § 1.704–2(g)(1); (2) an amount equal to the gain that would be recognized to the partner under § 704(c), dealing with contributions of appreciated

---

terest that were not reflected in an economic loss.

4. Occasionally, limited partners seek to disavow the form of partnership borrowing structures as recourse financing in an attempt to come within the special rules governing allocation of nonrecourse debt. In Kingbay v. Commissioner, 46 T.C. 147 (1966), limited partners were not allowed to include liabilities in the basis for their partnership interests where the general partner was liable on the mortgage obligation. The taxpayers argued that the corporate general partner should be disregarded since it was a corporation with capital of only $1,000 and was wholly owned by one of the partners. But the court held the taxpayers were bound by the form of the transaction; they could not argue that in substance no partner was personally liable on the mortgage obligation, thereby increasing their bases.

property (or under Treas. Reg. § 1.704–1(b)(2)(ii)(*f*) or (b)(4)(i) using § 704(c) principles when partnership capital accounts have been revalued), if all of the partnership's property subject to nonrecourse mortgages were disposed of in satisfaction of the mortgages and for no additional consideration; and (3) a portion of the remaining partnership nonrecourse indebtedness equal to the partner's share of partnership profits. Under these principles, limited partners are allocated a share of partnership nonrecourse liabilities. These rules also are applicable to allocate among the members of a limited liability company all of its indebtedness except any debts that have been guaranteed by a member of the LLC. The debts of the LLC that have been guaranteed by one or more members are recourse debts that must be allocated under Treas. Reg. § 1.752–2.

Computation of the first two components of the allocation under Treas. Reg. § 1.752–3 is complex. But in any case in which each partner's share of each item of income, gain, deduction, loss, and credit is a uniform fraction (or percentage), which may differ from partner to partner, as long as the partnership has no § 704(c) gain or loss and capital accounts never have been revalued, each partner's share of partnership nonrecourse debt will be equal to the total partnership nonrecourse debt multiplied by his fractional profits interest, and from a practical perspective it is unnecessary to apply the first and second components of the allocation formula.

2.   *Allocation According to Profit Shares*

In most cases, the third component of a partner's share of nonrecourse indebtedness, based on the partner's share of profits, actually is the starting point for allocating nonrecourse liabilities among the partners. This ordering occurs because the first component, partnership minimum gain, does not exist until the partnership has been in operation at least one taxable year; and the second component, based on § 704(c) allocations or reverse § 704(c) allocations, does not come into play unless a partner contributes appreciated property subject to a nonrecourse mortgage or the partnership has revalued capital accounts after it has been in existence for some period of time. Thus, it is logical to examine the third component first, even though it technically applies only to debt that has not been allocated under either of the first two components of the allocation formula.

Allocation of the partnership's residual nonrecourse debt under Treas. Reg. § 1.752–3(a)(3) generally is dependent upon determining the partners' respective profit shares. That determination may present a problem if the partners' interests in various types of profits differ. This problem may be avoided by specifying in the partnership agreement the partners' respective shares in partnership profits for purposes of allocating residual partnership nonrecourse debt, as is permitted by Treas. Reg. § 1.752–3(a)(3). The specified shares will be respected as long as they are reasonably consistent with some other significant item of partnership income or gain which has substantial economic effect under the § 704(b) regulations. Alternatively, Treas. Reg. § 1.752–3(a)(3) permits the partnership agreement to specify that excess nonrecourse indebtedness will be allocated with respect to the proportion in which partners reasonably can be expected to be allocated nonrecourse deductions. It is important, for example, that the partnership agreement take advantage of this latter provision to specify the residual ratio for purposes of allocating nonrecourse debt where depreciation deductions based on nonrecourse debt are not allocated according to profit shares. Otherwise, as the partnership claims depreciation deductions which increase minimum gain, the share of partnership debt allocated to the partners receiving the special allocation will increase. The other partners will have a corresponding decrease in partnership debt which will give rise to a deemed distribution under § 752(b) and may cause gain recognition.

3. Allocation According to Minimum Gain

The first component of a partner's share of nonrecourse indebtedness, "minimum gain," is the partner's distributive share of gain which would be recognized by the partnership if the partnership's property subject to nonrecourse mortgages were disposed of in satisfaction of the mortgages and for no additional consideration. The purpose of providing that nonrecourse indebtedness is first allocated among the partners relative to their shares of minimum gain under the § 704(b) regulations is to assure that each partner has sufficient basis to be able to claim his share of deductions based on nonrecourse debt without running afoul of the § 704(d) limitation, discussed at page 97. This debt allocation rule also assures that partners will not recognize gain if the proceeds of a nonrecourse second mortgage loan are distributed, because Treas. Reg. § 1.704–2(g)(1)(i) provides that a partner's share of minimum gain is increased by any such distribution.

The operation and interaction of the first and third components of the formula for allocating nonrecourse indebtedness, and the relationship of these rules to the rules of Treas. Reg. § 1.704–2, governing allocations of deductions attributable to nonrecourse debt, can be illustrated by the following example. Suppose that C and D respectively contribute $20,000 and $80,000 to the CD Partnership, which then borrows $900,000 from an unrelated lender on a nonrecourse promissory note secured by depreciable property for which the partnership pays $1,000,000. Also suppose that no principal payments are due on the note for ten years and that $50,000 of depreciation is allowable on the property each year. The partnership agreement complies with Treas. Reg. § 1.704–2 and provides that all items of income and deduction and all distributions will be allocated 20 percent to C and 80 percent to D. Assuming that the partnership agreement did not have any provisions specially allocating the nonrecourse debt between C and D, the debt would be allocated according to their 20/80 profit sharing ratio, and C would be allocated $180,000 and D would be allocated $720,000. The CD Partnership's opening balance sheet would be as follows:

	Assets			Indebtedness and Partners' Capital Accounts		
	Book	Tax Basis			Book	Tax Basis
Property	$1,000,000	$1,000,000	Debt		$ 900,000	
			C		$ 20,000	$ 200,000
			D		$ 80,000	$ 800,000
	$1,000,000	$1,000,000			$1,000,000	$1,000,000

Because the partnership has $100,000 of equity in the property, the first two years' depreciation deductions (assuming that the partnership does not have any net income or loss from other items) are not nonrecourse deductions and do not give rise to any minimum gain. Thus, allocations of the depreciation deductions must satisfy the substantial economic effect test, or one of its alternatives, under Treas. Reg. § 1.704–1(b)(2). That generally occurs only by allocating the loss against the partners' positive capital account balances. Thus, in each of the first two years, C's distributive share is a $10,000 loss and D's distributive share is a $40,000 loss. At the end of year 2, the CD Partnership's balance sheet is as follows:

	Assets			Indebtedness and Partner's Capital Accounts		
	Book	Tax Basis			Book	Tax Basis
Property	$900,000	$900,000	Debt		$900,000	
			C		0	$180,000
			D		0	$720,000
	$900,000	$900,000			$900,000	$900,000

Each partner's basis in his partnership interest at this point is entirely attributable to that partners' share of the partnership's nonrecourse indebtedness, allocated under the third component of the formula in Treas. Reg. § 1.752–3(a)(3).[5]

The $50,000 of depreciation in year 3 will give rise to $50,000 of minimum gain, since the basis of the property will be reduced to $850,000 and the mortgage principal will remain at $900,000. Thus the first $50,000 of the debt will be allocated between C and D under the first component of the formula in Treas. Reg. § 1.752–3(a)(1), and the remaining $850,000 will be allocated according to the third component of the formula in Treas. Reg. § 1.752–3(a)(3). At the end of three years the partnership's balance sheet would be as follows:

5. The allocation of the indebtedness would be the same if C had contributed $40,000 to the partnership and D had contributed $160,000, and the partnership had used $100,000 as an equity investment in the property and retained $100,000 of cash. The allocation of depreciation to the extent of the $100,000 of equity in the property must satisfy the substantial economic effect test, although the allocation could be made to either partner to the extent of the partner's positive capital account balance. Thereafter, depreciation deductions attributable to the property would create nonrecourse deductions, allocable to the partners to the extent of their respective shares of minimum gain, then profit shares.

	Assets			Indebtedness and Partners' Capital Accounts		
		Tax				Tax
	Book	Basis			Book	Basis
Property	$850,000	$850,000	Debt		$900,000	
			C		($ 10,000)	$170,000
			D		($ 40,000)	$680,000
	$850,000	$850,000			$850,000	$850,000

C's share of minimum gain is $10,000; D's share of minimum gain is $40,000. Thus, the first $50,000 of the nonrecourse debt is allocated between C and D in those amounts: $10,000 to C and $40,000 to D. The remaining $850,000 of nonrecourse debt is allocated with the partners' 20/80 ratio for sharing profits, $170,000 to C and $680,000 to D. Thus C's total share of the debt is $180,000 and D's total share of the debt is $720,000. Since the minimum gain is allocated between C and D in the same ratio as the residual profit shares (20/80) the total debt continues to be allocated in that ratio.

Now assume that instead of all items being allocated 20 percent to C and 80 percent to D during the life of the partnership, the partnership agreement provided for a 20/80 split only for the first three years, and that starting in year 4 profits from the sale of the asset and depreciation would be allocated 40 percent to C and 60 percent to D, although all other items would continue to be split in the 20/80 ratio. In year 4, C would be allocated $20,000 of depreciation and D would be allocated $30,000 of depreciation; C's distributive share would be a $20,000 loss and D's distributive share would be a $30,000 loss. Under Treas. Reg. § 1.704–2, the partnership's minimum gain of $100,000 at the end of year 4 would be allocable $30,000 to C and $70,000 to D. At the end of year 4, the partnership's balance sheet would be as follows:

	Assets			Indebtedness and Partners' Capital Accounts		
		Tax				Tax
	Book	Basis			Book	Basis
Property	$800,000	$800,000	Debt		$900,000	
			C		($ 30,000)	$160,000
			D		($ 70,000)	$640,000
	$800,000	$800,000			$800,000	$800,000

The first component of the formula, based on minimum gain, allocates $30,000 of the debt to C and $70,000 to D. Absent a special allocation agreement, as permitted by Treas. Reg. § 1.752–3(a)(3), the third component, based on profit shares, allocates $160,000 to C ($800,000 × 20%) and $640,000 to D ($800,000 × 80%). C's total share of the debt is now $190,000 ($10,000 more than at the end of year 3) and D's total share of the debt is now $710,000 ($10,000 less than at the end of year 3). As a result, C is treated as contributing $10,000 to the partnership, thereby increasing C's basis by $10,000, and D is treated as receiving a $10,000 distribution, thereby reducing D's basis by a like amount. (C and D also reduced their bases by $20,000 and $30,000, respectively, as a result of their shares of depreciation deductions.)

This shifting of allocations and the concomitant deemed contribution and distribution could be avoided by specifying, as permitted by Treas. Reg. § 1.704–3(a)(3), the partners' respective shares of partnership nonrecourse debt. In this case, however, such an agreement probably would not be desirable. The change of the ratios in which the partner's shared the debt was caused by the allocation of debt first according to the partner's shares of minimum gain, and the purpose of that allocation is to assure that C will have sufficient basis to claim his share of the partnership's depreciation deductions without running afoul of the § 704(d) limitation.

4. *Allocation Based on Section 704(c) Gain*

The second component of the nonrecourse debt allocation formula, as provided in Treas. Reg. § 1.752–3(a)(2), allocates to each partner an amount of partnership nonrecourse debt equal to the gain that would be recognized to the partner under § 704(c), dealing with contributions of appreciated property, if all of the partnership's property subject to nonrecourse mortgages were transferred in satisfaction of the mortgages and for no additional consideration. This allocation is necessary because under Treas. Reg. § 1.704–2(d)(3) partnership minimum gain exists only to the extent that the nonrecourse mortgage exceeds the book value of the encumbered property. Furthermore, this allocation prevents immediate recognition of gain to a partner upon contribution to the partnership of property encumbered by a nonrecourse mortgage because any deemed distribution under § 752(b) will not exceed the contributing partner's basis for her partnership interest.

Assume that D, E and F form an equal general partnership. D contributes property with a fair market value of $9,000 and a basis of $6,000, subject to a nonrecourse mortgage of $7,500. E and F each contribute $1,500 in cash. Because partnership minimum gain is computed with reference to book value, Treas. Reg. § 1.704–2(d)(3), the partnership has no minimum gain (book value of the property is $9,000 and the mortgage is only $7,500). Thus, none of the debt is allocated under the first component. Under § 704(c), $1,500 of gain ($7,500 amount realized, the mortgage, minus $6,000 basis) would be allocated to D if the property were transferred to the lender in satisfaction of the mortgage. Accordingly, the first $1,500 of the nonrecourse debt would be allocated to D. The remaining $6,000 of the debt initially would be allocated equally among the partners under the third component because they share profits equally. See Rev. Rul. 95–41, 1995–1 C.B. 132. Thus, a total of $3,500 of the indebtedness is allocated to D, and $2,000 is allocated to each of E and F. D's basis for his partnership interest is $2,000 (the $6,000 basis of the contributed property minus the net relief from indebtedness of $4,000), and E and F each have a basis of $3,500 (the $1,500 contribution plus $2,000 share of indebtedness). Immediately after formation, the DEF Partnership's balance sheet would be as follows:

	Assets			Indebtedness and Partners' Capital Accounts		
		Tax				Tax
	Book	Basis			Book	Basis
Cash	$ 3,000	$ 3,000		Debt	$ 7,500	
Property	$ 9,000	$ 6,000		D	$ 1,500	$ 2,000
				E	$ 1,500	$ 3,500
				F	$ 1,500	$ 3,500
	$12,000	$ 9,000			$12,000	$ 9,000

Now assume that in its first year the partnership breaks even, apart from tax depreciation of $3,000 attributable to the property. Also assume that book depreciation is $4,500 and that under § 704(c) and Treas. Reg. § 1.704–3, the partnership chose to allocate the depreciation under the traditional method with the ceiling rule. Each partner would be allocated $1,500 of book depreciation; D would be allocated no tax depreciation, and E and F each would be allocated $1,500 of tax depreciation. The partners' bases in their partnership interests also must be adjusted to account for the impact of nonrecourse depreciation deductions on the partners' share of the partnership debt. The partners' shares of the nonrecourse debt at the end of the first year depends on how the gain would be allocated among them if the property hypothetically were conveyed to the lender in lieu of foreclosure. In such an event, the partnership would recognize a taxable gain of $4,500 and a book gain of $3,000. First, pursuant to § 704(c) and Treas. Reg. § 1.704–3, D would be allocated $1,500 of the $4,500 of taxable gain (the excess of tax gain over book gain). Second, because under Treas. Reg. § 1.704–2(d)(3) partnership minimum gain is computed with reference to the excess of the nonrecourse debt over book value, the amount of the partnership's minimum gain is $3,000. That gain would be allocated between E and F in the ratio they claimed the nonrecourse depreciation deductions—$1,500 to each of E and F. Thus, under the first component of the formula in Treas. Reg. § 1.752–3, $1,500 of the nonrecourse debt is allocated to each of E and F; under the second component of the formula, $1,500 is allocated to D; and under the third component of the formula, the remaining $3,000 of the debt is allocated equally among the partners, $1,000 to each. D's total share of the indebtedness is $2,500, and the total share of each of E and F is $2,500. As a result of the shifting shares of partnership indebtedness, E and F each is deemed to have contributed $500 to the partnership, while D is deemed to have received a distribution of $1,000, thereby requiring appropriate basis adjustments for all three partners. At the end of year, the partnership balance sheet would be as follows:

	Assets			Indebtedness and Partners' Capital Accounts		
		Tax				Tax
	Book	Basis			Book	Basis
Cash	$3,000	$3,000		Debt	$7,500	
Property	$4,500	$3,000		D	$ 0	$1,000
				E	$ 0	$2,500
				F	$ 0	$2,500
	$7,500	$6,000			$7,500	$6,000

Treas. Reg. § 1.752–3(a)(3) also allows the partners to allocate a portion of the liabilities in excess of the liabilities allocated under the first two components of the formula on the basis of the amount of § 704(c) gain that exceeds § 704(c) gain allocated under the second component, which is limited to the excess of the nonrecourse debt over basis. Thus, in the above example, at the time of contribution § 1.752–3(a)(3) would allow an allocation to D of $3,000 of the nonrecourse debt consisting of $1,500 of the debt allocated under Treas. Reg. § 1.752–3(a)(2) (the excess of the $7,500 mortgage over $6,000 basis) and the remaining $1,500 of § 704(c) gain attributable to the property ($9,000 fair market value less the $6,000 basis and less the first $1,500 allocated under § 1.752–3(a)(2)). The remaining $4,500 of the nonrecourse debt would be allocated equally between D, E, and F, based on their profit share, $1,500 each. D's share of the debt is $4,500. D's basis is reduced by $3,000, the reduction of D's share of liabilities from $7,500 to $4,500. E's and F's share of the debt is $1,500 each and their bases are increased by $1,500. The partnership balance sheet is as follows:

	Assets			Indebtedness and Partners' Capital Accounts		
	Book	Tax Basis			Book	Tax Basis
Cash	$ 3,000	$3,000		Debt	$ 7,500	
Property	$ 9,000	$6,000		D	$ 1,500	$3,000
				E	$ 1,500	$3,000
				F	$ 1,500	$3,000
	$12,000	$9,000			$12,000	$9,000

5. Allocation Based on "Reverse Section 704(c) Gain"

When partnership capital accounts are revalued in connection with the admission of a partner or upon a distribution, the revaluation creates book/tax disparities similar to the disparities that trigger allocations under section 704(c). See the discussion at page 169. Thus, in addition to § 704(c) gain, Treas. Reg. § 1.752–3(a)(2) allocates to each partner an amount of partnership nonrecourse debt equal to the gain that would be allocated to the partner if all of the partnership's property subject to nonrecourse mortgages were transferred in satisfaction of the mortgages and for no additional consideration under Treas. Reg. § 1.704–1(b)(2)(ii)(f) or (b)(4)(i), which apply § 704(c) principles when partnership capital accounts have been revalued. This allocation also is required by the definitional limitation of partnership minimum gain to the excess of the mortgage over the book value of the encumbered property. When capital accounts are revalued, book value may exceed the basis of the property and gain attributable to the excess of book value over basis is allocated under Treas. Reg. § 1.704–1(b)(2)(ii)(f) or (b)(4)(i). In this context, when a new partner is admitted, the regulations allocate nonrecourse debt to the preexisting partners disproportionately to post-admission profit sharing ratios. This allocation reduces the amount of the deemed distribution to the original partners under § 752(b) arising from shifting a portion of the nonrecourse debt to the new partner, and the consequent possibility that gain will be recognized to the original partners under § 731. This rule is very important in workout situations for financially troubled real estate partnerships where the original partners' interests are reduced from 100 percent to a much lower percentage, for example to 20 percent, without the recognition of any gain.

Assume that I is admitted to the GH Partnership, which owns a single property, with a basis of $90,000 and a fair market value of $120,000, encumbered by a nonrecourse mortgage of $108,000. Immediately before revaluing the partnership's assets and G's and H's capital accounts in connection with the admission of I, the GH Partnership's balance sheet is follows:

Assets				Indebtedness and Partners' Capital Accounts		
			Tax			Tax
	Book	Basis			Book	Basis
Property	$90,000	$90,000		Debt	$108,000	
				G	($ 9,000)	$45,000
				H	($ 9,000)	$45,000
	$90,000	$90,000			$ 90,000	$90,000

At this point, G's and H's share of minimum gain under Treas. Reg. § 1.704–2 is $9,000 each. Each of their shares of the partnership's debt is $54,000.

I contributes $12,000 to become a one-half partner, and G and H each become one-quarter partners. After the partnership's assets and the partners' capital accounts are revalued in connection with I's admission, the GHI Partnership balance sheet is as follows:

Assets				Indebtedness and Partners' Capital Accounts		
			Tax			Tax
	Book	Basis			Book	Basis
Cash	$ 12,000	$ 12,000		Debt	$108,000	
Property	$120,000	$ 90,000		G	$ 6,000	$ 22,500
				H	$ 6,000	$ 22,500
				I	$ 12,000	$ 57,000
	$132,000	$102,000			$132,000	$102,000

Because partnership minimum gain under Treas. Reg. § 1.704–2(d)(3) is computed with reference to the excess of the mortgage ($108,000) over book value of the property ($120,000), there is no partnership minimum gain.[6] Thus, none of the nonrecourse mortgage debt is allocated among the partners under the first component of the formula in Treas. Reg. § 1.752–3(a). If the property were deeded to the mortgagee in lieu of foreclosure,

---

6. The reduction of partnership minimum gain attributable to the revaluation does not trigger a minimum gain chargeback.   See Treas. Reg. § 1.704–2(d)(4)(ii), (m), Ex. (3)(ii).

under Treas. Reg. § 1.704–2(d)(4)(i), G and H each would be allocated $9,000 of the $18,000 tax gain recognized on the disposition. Thus, pursuant to Treas. Reg. § 1.752–3(a)(2), G and H each are allocated $9,000 of the nonrecourse debt. The remaining $90,000 of the nonrecourse debt is allocated among G, H, and I under the residual rule of Treas. Reg. § 1.752–3(a)(3). As a fifty percent partner, I will be allocated $45,000. G and H as one-quarter partners each will be allocated $22,500 of the debt under the residual rule, thereby decreasing each of their shares to $31,500.

As result of their shares of partnership indebtedness being reduced from $54,000 to $31,500, G and E each receive a constructive distribution of $22,500 and reduce their bases from $45,000 to $22,500. I includes his $45,000 increase in partnership indebtedness in his basis for a total basis of $57,000 ($12,000 cash contribution + $45,000 debt share).

ILLUSTRATIVE MATERIAL

1. LIABILITIES THAT ARE PART RECOURSE AND PART NONRECOURSE

Treas. Reg. § 1.752–1(i) provides that if one or more partners bear an economic risk of loss for only part of a partnership liability, the liability will be treated as a recourse liability to the extent that any partner bears an economic risk of loss and the excess will be treated as a nonrecourse liability. This rule applies, for example, when one or more partners personally guarantee part, but less than all, of a partnership nonrecourse debt. See Treas. Reg. § 1.752–2(f), Ex. (5). Suppose, for example, that the ABC limited partnership borrows $1,000 on a nonrecourse basis and A, the sole general partner guarantees $800 of the debt. The regulations treat $800 of the indebtedness as a recourse loan for which A bears the economic risk of loss. This result follows because if A pays the debt pursuant to the guarantee, A's subrogation rights are limited to the rights of a nonrecourse lender and, under the regulations, the property secured by the loan is deemed to be worthless for purposes of determining which partners bear the economic risk of loss. Under this test, only A would bear the risk of loss of the $800. Thus, only $200 of the debt would be allocated among the partners according to their profit sharing ratios. The results would be similar if B, a limited partner guaranteed the debt: $800 of the debt would be treated as a recourse debt allocated to B. See Abramson v. Commissioner, 86 T.C. 360 (1986) (under prior regulations, limited partners who personally guaranteed a pro rata part of partnership nonrecourse debt were allowed to increase their respective bases in their partnership interests under § 752(a) by the amount of debt which they had guaranteed). Treas. Reg. § 1.752–2(c)(2) similarly bifurcates the partnership liability where a partner sells property to the partnership for a nonrecourse obligation that wraps around a primary nonrecourse mortgage. The excess of the debt from the partnership to the partner is a recourse debt, the economic risk of loss of which is borne by the selling partner; the underlying debt is a nonrecourse debt. See Treas. Reg. § 1.752–2(f), Ex. (6).

2. ALLOCATION OF A SINGLE LIABILITY AMONG MULTIPLE PROPERTIES

2.1.   *Generally*

Treas. Reg. § 1.752–3(b) permits a partnership that holds multiple properties subject to a single liability to allocate the liability among the properties using any reasonable method. When a partnership holds multiple properties subject to a single nonrecourse liability the amount of § 704(c) minimum gain or reverse § 704(c) minimum gain cannot be readily determined under the rules of Treas. Reg. § 1.752–3(a)(2). This problem typically occurs when a partnership that holds several properties subject to individual mortgages refinances the individual liabilities with a single nonrecourse mortgage. In order to apply Treas. Reg. § 1.752–3(a)(2), the partnership must determine the amount of the liability that encumbers each asset in order to determine the § 704(c) minimum gain attributable to each asset. A method is not reasonable under Treas. Reg. § 1.752–3(b) if it allocates to any property an amount that exceeds the fair market value of the property. Thus, for example, the liability may be allocated to the properties based on the relative fair market value of each property. The portion of the nonrecourse liability allocated to each item of partnership property is then treated as a separate liability under Treas. Reg. § 1.752–3(a)(2). Once a liability is allocated among the properties, a partnership may not change the method for allocating the liability. If, however, one of the properties ceases to be subject to the liability, the portion of the liability originally allocated to that property must be reallocated to the properties still subject to the liability.

2.2.   *Allocation of Limited Liability Company Debts*

Because no member of an LLC bears the risk of loss with respect to an LLC's recourse debts, for purposes of § 752 the debts owed by an LLC are not recourse debts as defined by Treas. Reg. § 1.752–1(a)(1). Except to the extent a member (partner) guarantees any such debt, the debt is a nonrecourse debt that is allocated under Treas. Reg. § 1.752–3. (If, however, a member of an LLC personally guarantees a debt of the LLC, the debt becomes a recourse debt, subject to the allocation rules of Treas. Reg. § 1.752–2 because the guaranteeing partner bears the risk of loss associated with the debt.) This rule applies even with respect to the LLC's unsecured debts. Furthermore, for purposes of allocating the debts among the members, under Treas. Reg. § 1.752–3, all of the LLC's property can be viewed as cross-collateralizing all of the LLC's debts that are recourse as to the LLC but nonrecourse as to the members. (If a debt is nonrecourse to the LLC under applicable debtor/creditor law, it is not cross-collateralized by all LC property, but it is secured only by the property specifically mortgaged or pledged.) Thus, the rules of Treas. Reg. § 1.752–3(b) should be applicable to virtually every LLC that has more than one asset and any debt that is recourse as to the LLC. There is, however, no specific guidance regarding the method for allocating the LLC's debts among the members beyond the general principles described in the preceding materials.

3.   BASIS IN TIERED PARTNERSHIP

Suppose that A contributes $25 to the AB limited partnership in exchange for an interest as a 20 percent limited partner. The AB limited partnership in turn contributes $100 to become a one-third limited partner in the ABC limited partnership, which acquires a building subject to a nonrecourse liability of $1,200. In the year in question, the ABC limited partnership incurs a loss of $600, of which $200 is allocable to the AB limited partnership. In addition, the AB limited partnership loses an additional $50. A's distributive share of the $250 loss of the AB limited partnership is $50. Rev. Rul. 77–309, 1977–2 C.B. 216, held that the AB limited partnership is entitled to include one-third ($400) of the nonrecourse liability of the ABC partnership in its basis for its interest in that partnership, and that A is, in turn, entitled to include 20 percent of that amount ($80) in his basis for his interest in the AB limited partnership. Thus, A's basis for his interest is $105 and A can deduct the entire amount of the loss. This approach now is incorporated in Treas. Reg. § 1.752–4(a).

CHAPTER 6

TRANSACTIONS BETWEEN PARTNERS AND THE PARTNERSHIP

SECTION 1. TRANSACTIONS INVOLVING SERVICES, RENTS, AND LOANS

INTERNAL REVENUE CODE: Sections 707(a)(1), (a)(2)(A), (c); 267(a)(2), (e)(1)–(4).

REGULATIONS: Sections 1.707–1(a), (c); 1.267(a)–2T(c).

Section 707 requires entity rather than aggregate treatment for various types of transactions between a partner and the partnership. Generally speaking, § 707 imposes on transactions within its ambit the same tax consequences that would occur if the partner had dealt with a person other than a partner in such a transaction, subject to certain safeguards commonly imposed by the Code to prevent tax avoidance in transactions between related parties. Section 707(a), the most broadly applicable subsection of § 707, typically applies to transactions such as (1) a lease of property between a partner and the partnership, regardless of which is the lessor and which is the tenant, (2) a loan from a partner to the partnership of from the partnership to a partner, (3) fees for services rendered to a partner by the partnership or fees for services rendered by a partner to the partnership *if in the provision of the services the partner is not acting as a partner*, e.g., a lawyer who is a partner in a real estate investment partnership receives a fee from the partnership for services in connection with performing a title search on property purchased by the partnership, and (4) sales of property by a partner to the partnership or by the partnership to a partner. Section 707(b) is designed to limit tax avoidance possibilities in cases of sales of property between partners and the partnership by limiting loss deductions in certain cases and requiring ordinary income treatment rather than capital gain treatment on the sale between a partner and the partnership in certain cases where capital gain treatment otherwise would be available. (The application of § 707 to sales of property between a partner and the partnership is discussed in Section 2.) Finally, § 707(c) requires the recognition of gross income by a partner who receives a payment form the partnership in exchange for services or the use of capital if the partner's right to receive the payment is not dependent on partnership income. The partnership receives a correlative deduction for the payment, provided that the payment would have been deductible if made to a person who is not a partner, i.e., the payment is not a capital expenditure or a noncapital expenditure for which a deduction is expressly disallowed (for example, lobbying expenses under § 162(e)). Section 707(c) is most frequently applied when a partnership pays a "salary" to a partner or makes interest-like payments to a partner as a preferred return on a capital contribution that is not a loan.

Once a transaction between a partner and the partnership has been properly categorized, the tax treatment under a particular subsection of § 707 is relatively clear. The most difficult legal issues in applying § 707 are, first, to distinguish payments from a partnership to a partner subject to either § 707(a) or § 707(c) from allocations and distributions of partnership income, and, second, to distinguish payments from a partnership to a partner subject to § 707(a) from payments subject to § 707(c). The latter distinction is necessary because the timing of the income and deduction item attributable to payments subject to § 707(a) are governed by normal tax accounting rules, but the timing of the income and deduction item attributable to payments subject to § 707(c) are governed by the timing rule of § 706(a), discussed at page 90.

Revenue Ruling 81–301

1981–2 C.B. 144.

Is an allocation based on a percentage of gross income paid to an advisor general partner subject to section 707(a) of the Internal Revenue Code, under the circumstances described below?

FACTS

ABC is a partnership formed in accordance with the Uniform Limited Partnership Act of a state and is registered with the Securities and Exchange Commission as an open-end diversified management company pursuant to the Investment Company Act of 1940, as amended. Under the partnership agreement, *ABC*'s assets must consist only of municipal bonds, certain readily-marketable temporary investments, and cash. The agreement provides for two classes of general partners: (1) "director general partners" (directors) who are individuals and (2) one "adviser general partner" (adviser) that is a corporate investment adviser registered as such in accordance with the Investment Advisers Act of 1940, 15 U.S.C.A., section 80b–5 (1971).

Under the partnership agreement, the directors are compensated and have complete and exclusive control over the management, conduct, and operation of *ABC*'s activities. The directors are authorized to appoint agents and employees to perform duties on behalf of *ABC* and these agents may be, but need not be, general partners. Under the partnership agreement, the adviser has no rights, powers, or authority as a general partner, except that, subject to the supervision of the directors, the adviser is authorized to manage the investment and reinvestment of *ABC*'s assets. The adviser is responsible for payment of any expenses incurred in the performance of its investment advisory duties, including those for office space and facilities, equipment, and any of its personnel used to service and administer *ABC*'s investments. The adviser is not personally liable to the other partners for any losses incurred in the investment and reinvestment of *ABC*'s assets.

The nature of the adviser's services are substantially the same as those it renders as an independent contractor or agent for persons other than *ABC* and, under the agreement, the adviser is not precluded from engaging in such transactions with others.

Each general partner, including the adviser general partner, is required to contribute sufficient cash to *ABC* to acquire at least a one percent interest in the partnership. The agreement requires an allocation of 10 percent of *ABC*'s daily gross income to the adviser. After reduction by the compensation allocable to the directors and the adviser, *ABC*'s items of income, gain, loss, deduction, and credit are divided according to the percentage interests held by each partner.

The adviser's right to 10 percent of *ABC*'s daily gross income for managing *ABC*'s investment must be approved at least annually by a majority vote of the directors or a majority vote of all the partnership interests. Furthermore, the directors may remove the adviser as investment manager at any time on 60 days written notice to the adviser. The adviser can terminate its investment manager status by giving 60 days written notice to the directors. The agreement provides that the adviser will no longer be a general partner after removal or withdrawal as investment manager, but will continue to participate as a limited partner in the income, gains, losses, deductions, and credits attributable to the percentage interest that it holds.

LAW AND ANALYSIS

Section 61(a)(1) of the Code provides that, except as otherwise provided by law, gross income means all income from whatever source derived, including compensation for services, including fees, commissions, and similar items.

Section 702(a) of the Code provides that in determining the income tax of a partner each partner must take into account separately such partner's distributive share of the partnership's items of income, gain, loss, deduction, or credit.

Section 707(a) of the Code provides that if a partner engages in a transaction with a partnership other than as a member of such partnership, the transaction shall, except as otherwise provided in section 707, be considered as occurring between the partnership and one who is not a partner.

Section 1.707–1(a) of the Income Tax Regulations provides that a partner who engages in a transaction with a partnership other than in the capacity as a partner shall be treated as if not a member of the partnership with respect to such transaction. Such transactions include the rendering of services by the partner to the partnership. In all cases, the substance of the transaction will govern rather than its form.

Section 707(c) of the Code provides that to the extent determined without regard to the income of the partnership, payments to a partner for services shall be considered as made to one who is not a member of the partnership, but only for purposes of section 61(a) and, subject to section 263, for purposes of section 162(a).

Although the adviser is identified in the agreement as an "adviser general partner," the adviser provides similar services to others as part of its regular trade or business, and its management of the investment and reinvestment of *ABC*'s assets is supervised by the directors. Also it can be relieved of its duties and right to compensation at any time (with 60 days notice) by a majority vote of the directors. Further, the adviser pays its own expenses and is not personally liable to the other partners for any losses incurred in the investment and reinvestment of *ABC*'s assets. The services performed by the adviser are, in substance, not performed in the capacity of a general partner, but are performed in the capacity of a person who is not a partner.

The 10 percent daily gross income allocation paid to the adviser is paid to the adviser in its capacity other than as a partner. Therefore, the gross income allocation is not a part of the adviser's distributive share of partnership income under section 702(a) of the Code or a guaranteed payment under section 707(c).

HOLDING

The 10 percent daily gross income allocation paid to the adviser is subject to section 707(a) of the Code and taxable to the adviser under section 61 as compensation for services rendered. The amount paid is deductible by the partnership under section 162, subject to the provisions of section 265.

* * *

ILLUSTRATIVE MATERIAL

1. THE ENTITY APPROACH TO PARTNER SERVICES TO A PARTNERSHIP

Section 707(a) treats a partner performing services in a non-partner capacity as separate from the partnership, which is treated as an entity separate from its partners. The alternative is to recognize the partnership as an aggregate of its members, which would affect both the timing and character of items of income and deduction related to partner services. Suppose that A, who is a lawyer and who is also a partner in the AB Partnership, in the course of her law practice, performs services for the AB Partnership and receives a fee of $300. Under the entity approach, A recognizes $300 of compensation income and, assuming that the payment of the fee is deductible by the AB Partnership, a $150 deduction flows through to A from the partnership. Because of the deduction, A reduces her basis in her interest in the AB Partnership by $150. As a result of the transaction A's recognizes net taxable income of $150 in the current year and, because of the basis reduction, will recognize an additional $150 of capital gain (or $150 less capital loss) in a future year upon sale or liquidation of her partnership interest. As for B, a $150 deduction flows through to B from the partnership, and B reduces his basis in his interest in the AB Partnership by $150. As a result of the transaction, B receives a $150 deduction in the current year and will recognize an additional $150 of capital gain (or $150 less capital loss) in a future year upon sale or liquidation of his partnership interest. In this particular fact pattern, the results would not differ under an aggregate approach. Under an aggregate approach, A would recognize only $150 of current compensation income— representing A's share of the $300 payment—and the other $150 would be treated as a distribution, reducing A's basis in he partnership interest. A also would have a $150 deduction representing A's share of the partnership's $300 deduction for the expenditure. Again, as a result of the transaction, A's recognizes net taxable income of $150 in the current year and an additional $150 of capital gain (or $150 less capital loss) in a future year upon sale of her interest or liquidation of her partnership interest.

If, however, the payment was a nondeductible capital expenditure by the partnership, the results would differ under the entity and aggregate approaches. Under the entity approach, the only tax consequence in the current year is that A recognizes $300 of compensation income. No deduction flows through to either A or B. Under an aggregate approach, A would recognize only $150 of current compensation income—representing A's share of the $300 payment—and the other $150 would be treated as a distribution, reducing A's basis in her partnership interest. Under this approach, as a result of the transaction, A recognizes net taxable income of $150 in the current year and an additional $150 of capital gain (or $150 less capital loss) in a future year upon sale of her interest or liquidation of her partnership interest (unless the asset to which A's services related was depreciable or amortizable). When A is compensated by the partnership for services that must be capitalized, the aggregate approach results in deferral and, possibly, conversion, relative to the entity approach.

The aggregate and entity approaches produce even clearer differences when the partnership performs services for a partner in exchange for a payment. For example, suppose C, an equal partner in the CD Partnership, which is engaged in the stock brokerage business, pays the partnership a $200 commission for stock purchased for his individual account. Under the entity approach of § 707(a), the partnership has $200 of income and C and D are each taxed on their $100 share of the $200 partnership income. C would add $200 to the basis of the purchased stock, and recover C's $100 distributive share of partnership income as a tax-free distribution or as a loss at a later date, often on liquidation of the partnership.[1] Under the

---

1. Several cases decided before enactment of § 707(a) adopted this approach. See Wegener v. Commissioner, 119 F.2d 49 (5th Cir.1941) (partner received income from drilling wells for partnership); Shirley v. O'Malley, 91 F.Supp. 98 (D.Neb.1950) (partnership deducted rent on assets leased from partner).

aggregate theory, C would not be taxed on any part of the $200 partnership income; $100 of the income is properly allocated to D and the other $100 is attributable to services C has performed for himself. Instead, C will be regarded as having contributed $100 to the partnership, and he will add the $100 paid to D to the cost basis of his stock. D will be taxed on $100.[2] C will recognize an additional $100 of income on a future distribution or on liquidation of the partnership as capital gain, thereby deferring the recognition and re-characterizing the income relative to the entity approach.

Some of the same problems that arise in transactions governed by § 707(a) arise when a partner is entitled to a "salary" or "guaranteed payment" from the partnership that is unrelated to partnership net income. Suppose E and F decide to form the EF Partnership but, as a condition of participating in the venture, E insists on being paid a salary of $5,000 a year whether or not the partnership makes a profit. The partnership has no income for the year, and E is paid $5,000. Under the aggregate approach, as applied in situations arising prior to 1954, assuming each partner's capital account is reduced by $2,500, E would be taxed on $2,500 income as a payment from F (that would not affect the basis of his partnership interest) and would treat the remaining $2,500 as a distribution, reducing the basis in his partnership interest by that amount; F would have a $2,500 loss. Synthesizing early case law, in G.C.M. 6582, VIII–2 C.B. 200 (1929), the Internal Revenue Service ruled that partners work for themselves and as a matter of law could not be employees of the partnership. Whatever was received by a partner in the form of a salary was treated in substance as a withdrawal from the partnership of anticipated profits, and if at the end of the partnership's taxable year, the total amounts so withdrawn by the partners exceeded profits, the excess would be considered as withdrawals from capital. I.T. 2503, VIII–2 C.B. 145 (1929), and Commissioner v. Banfield, 122 F.2d 1017 (9th Cir.1941), adopted this approach as to "interest" paid on the capital contribution of a partner.

Under the entity approach of § 707(c), payments to partners in the form of salary or guaranteed payments, that is payments that are computed without regard to partnership profits or loss, are treated for purposes of § 61 as gross income to the partner and are deducted by the partnership under § 162 or capitalized under § 263 as appropriate. Thus, under the entity approach, E has $5,000 compensation income, the partnership has a $5,000 deduction, and E and F each have a partnership distributive share of a $2,500 loss, leaving E with a net income of $2,500. While this usually leaves the same dollar result as under the aggregate approach, the tax results may differ where the partnership has special income items. Thus, assume that the partnership had $5,000 of capital gain. Under the aggregate approach, E presumably would merely have a distributive share of $5,000 capital gain. Under the entity approach of § 707(c), C has $5,000

2. Benjamin v. Hoey, 139 F.2d 945 (2d Cir.1944), adopted this approach. In Heggestad v. Commissioner, 91 T.C. 778 (1988), the Tax Court held that § 707(a) expressly overrules any precedential value of Benjamin v. Hoey.

compensation, E and F each have a distributive share of $2,500 of the capital gain and a distributive share of $2,500 of the partnership $5,000 ordinary loss. See Treas. Reg. § 1.707–1(c), Ex. (4). There also is a difference if the payment to E is for services of a nature that require capitalization. In this case, E will have $5,000 of income and the nondeductible partnership expenditure will be added to the basis of partnership property.

In most cases, the effect of a payment to a partner by the partnership is identical under both § 707(a) and § 707(c). The most important difference between § 707(a) payments to a partner and § 707(c) payments to a partner is that § 707(a) payments to a cash method partner are taken into account by both the partnership and the partner in the year paid, while § 707(c) payments always are taken into account by both the partnership and the partner in the year to which the item relates under the partnership's method of accounting. Thus, in some cases it is crucial to determine whether a payment is governed by § 707(a) or § 707(c).

Unlike § 707(a)(1), which applies both to payments to a partner by a partnership for services rendered to the partnership and payments by a partner to the partnership for services rendered by the partnership (as well as to rental payments and interest on loans whether paid by a partner to the partnership or by the partnership to the partner), § 707(c) applies only to payments from the partnership to the partner.

The distinction between § 707 payments in general and a special allocation of partnership income to a partner who has rendered services to the partnership is particularly important when a payment to a partner is for an item that must be capitalized by the partnership if § 707 applies. To distinguish § 707 payments from special allocations of distributive shares requires careful analysis of the economic bargain between the partners. Once again, Subchapter K provides significant flexibility. Generally speaking, partners are free to choose whether to compensate a partner through an increased distributive share of partnership income, subject to the rules of § 704(b), or through guaranteed payments, subject to the rules of § 707(c). The economic bargain is different in each case, however, and to obtain the particular tax consequences may require an economic arrangement that differs from that which is acceptable to all of the partners. A special allocation to compensate a partner for services requires an allocation of partnership income to that partner's capital account, which may be coupled with a distribution to that partner. A § 707(a) transaction or a guaranteed payment, in contrast, has only an indirect effect on partners' capital accounts, and it is no different than any other partnership expenditure. The differing results of characterizing a payment as a § 707 payment versus an increased distributive share can produce abusive transactions that are designed to avoid § 707 in cases in which the entity approach results in capitalization of payments that are made to a partner. To prevent abuse, § 707(a)(2)(A) requires that certain transactions purporting to be special allocations of a partner's distributive share of partnership income be recharacterized as § 707(a) transactions.

2. WHEN DOES A PARTNER PROVIDE SERVICES UNRELATED TO HIS CAPACITY AS A PARTNER

The instances where § 707 payments have a different impact than payments received as a partner's distributive share have lead to litigation over the distinction between the two concepts. In Pratt v. Commissioner, 64 T.C. 203 (1975), aff'd, 550 F.2d 1023 (5th Cir. 1977), cash method general partners of limited partnerships received 5 percent of the gross profits of the partnership in exchange for the performance of management services with respect to partnership properties. The accrual method partnerships deducted fees in the year the obligation to make the payments accrued, but the cash method partners accounted for the fees in the later year in which the fees were paid and received (the case pre-dated the application of § 267 to these facts). The Tax Court refused to treat the management fees as § 707(a) payments stating that, "Petitioners in this case were to receive the management fees for performing services within the normal scope of their duties as general partners and pursuant to the partnership agreement. There is no indication that any one of the petitioners was engaged in a transaction with the partnership other than in his capacity of a partner." The court thus held that the fees were not deductible to the partnership. As a consequence the fees did not reduce the partners' distributive share of partnership income includible in the partners' income in the year that the obligation to pay the fees accrued.

The court in Pratt also indicated that it did not need to decide whether a continuing payment to a partner for services could ever be treated as a § 707(a) payment. This comment in Pratt raised a question whether § 707(a) might not have been intended to apply to continuing payments to a partner. In affirming the Tax Court, the Court of Appeals stressed the fact that "in order for the partnership to deal with one of its partners as an 'outsider' the transaction dealt with must be something outside the scope of the partnership." 550 F.2d at 1026. However, Rev. Rul. 81–301 appears to reject this theory, since the services rendered in Rev. Rul. 81–301 were ongoing services just as were the services in Pratt. Where § 707(a) is not confined to isolated transactions as suggested in Pratt, it is difficult to find a workable distinction between a § 707(a) payment and a § 707(c) payment. Perhaps a key factor is the extent to which the partner provides similar services to other customers, a fact highlighted by Rev. Rul. 81–301 in holding that § 707(a) rather than § 707(c) applied. (The Pratt opinion does not discuss the extent to which the taxpayer provided management services other than to the two partnerships involved in the case.) But see Zahler v. Commissioner, T.C. Memo. 1981–112, rev'd on other grounds, 684 F.2d 356 (6th Cir.1982), holding that commissions paid to a partner in a securities brokerage firm, which paid sales commissions to partner and non-partner sales personnel alike, were not subject to § 707(a).

On the other hand, payments from a partner to a partnership for services provided to the partner in her individual capacity clearly should be subject to § 707(a) even though the payments are of a continuing nature. Rev. Rul. 72–504, 1972–2 C.B. 90, allowed a partner whose individual business paid rent to a partnership of which he was a member to deduct the full amount of the rent paid.

3.   IDENTIFYING GUARANTEED PAYMENTS SUBJECT TO SECTION 707(c)

3.1.   *"Salary" Versus "Draw"*

Section 707(c) most often is applied to amounts received by a partner as "salary" as opposed to "draw." Often the issue arises when a partner receives payments from the partnership in a year in which the partnership has an operating loss. If § 707(c) is not applicable, the payments are distributions, which are charged against the basis of the partner's interest and are taxable only after basis has been reduced to zero. In Falconer v. Commissioner, 40 T.C. 1011 (1963), payments to a partner referred to in the partnership agreement as "salary" were classified as § 707(c) payments in a situation in which the partnership had been operating at a loss when the payments were made. The taxpayer unsuccessfully argued that the amounts were advances that he was obligated to repay to the other partners. Clark v. Commissioner, T.C. Memo. 1982–401, reached the same result on similar facts. At a time when the taxpayer-partner had a negative capital account, the partnership made payments to him by, first, increasing his capital account by an amount that was unrelated to partnership profits and, second, distributing to him an identical amount, which reduced his capital account and left it at its original negative balance.

In Grubb v. Commissioner, T.C. Memo. 1990–425, the taxpayer agreed to perform sales services for a partnership, and the partnership paid him fixed payments of $1,600 per month. Although the checks from the partnership to the taxpayer referred to the payments as "draw," after the taxpayer withdrew as a partner he continued to perform sales services and to receive $1,600 per month. On these facts, the court concluded that the payments were compensation for services. The court rejected the taxpayer's argument that the partnership's failure to deduct the payments precluded treating them as guaranteed payments: "Includability at the partner level and deductibility at the partnership level of guaranteed payments are two different questions. * * * Accordingly, the fact that a partnership improperly characterizes guaranteed payments or fails to take such payments into account on its information return does not negate the fact that the guaranteed payments were incurred and became fixed at the partnership level, nor does it exonerate the partner receiving such payments from including the payments in gross income."

3.2.   *Payments Based on Partnership Gross Income Versus Partnership Net Income*

The Tax Court in Pratt v. Commissioner, supra, also rejected the taxpayers' argument that the payments were § 707(c) payments. The court held that the management fees, based on a fixed percentage of "gross rentals" represented a payment based on "income" which was thereby not to be treated as a § 707(c) payment. Even though the holding of the Tax

Court in *Pratt* adopted the Commissioner's argument, the Internal Revenue Service specifically rejected this aspect of *Pratt* in Rev. Rul. 81–300, 1981–2 C.B. 143. That ruling involved payments to the general partners of a limited partnership formed to operate a shopping center. In addition to a specified percentage interest in the partnership's bottom line profit or loss, each general partner was entitled to five percent of the gross rentals received by the partnership in consideration of providing managerial services. The Ruling held that the payments of 5 percent of gross rents were § 707(c) payments:

> Although a fixed amount is the most obvious form of guaranteed payment, there are situations in which compensation for services is determined by reference to an item of gross income. For example, it is not unusual to compensate a manager of real property by reference to the gross rental income that the property produces. Such compensation arrangements do not give the provider of the service a share in the profits of the enterprise, but are designed to accurately measure the value of the services that are provided.

> Thus, [in] view of the legislative history and the purpose underlying section 707 of the Code, the term "guaranteed payment" should not be limited to fixed amounts. A payment for services determined by reference to an item of gross income will be a guaranteed payment if, on the basis of all of the facts and circumstances, the payment is compensation rather than a share of partnership profits. Relevant facts would include the reasonableness of the payment for the services provided and whether the method used to determine the amount of the payment would have been used to compensate an unrelated party for the services.

> It is the position of the Internal Revenue Service that in *Pratt* the management fees were guaranteed payments under section 707(c) of the Code. On the facts presented, the payments were not disguised distributions of partnership net income, but were compensation for services payable without regard to partnership income.

3.3. *Distinguishing Section 707(c) Payments From Section 707(a) Payments*

The legislative history of § 707(a)(2)(A), discussed at page 225, a provision that has nothing to do with the fact pattern in Rev. Rul. 81–300, supra, endorses the conclusion in Rev. Rul. 81–300 that compensation measured by a percentage of gross income may be a § 707 payment, but gratuitously states that by virtue of § 707(a)(2)(A), the transaction in the Ruling should be governed by § 707(a) rather than § 707(c). S.Rep. No. 98–169, 98th Cong., 2d Sess. 230 (1984). There is no express explanation of either the rationale for this conclusion or the reasons why the writers of the legislative history believe the statement to have any precedential value. If the Service and the courts follow the suggestion in the legislative history of § 707(a)(2)(A) that the payments in Rev. Rul. 81–300 are subject to

§ 707(a) rather than § 707(c), the precise scope of § 707(c) vis-a-vis § 707(a) is unclear.

There never has been a clear demarcation of the line between a partner acting in the capacity of a partner and a partner acting in a capacity other than as a partner. Treas. Reg. § 1.707–1(a) provides that "the substance of the transaction will govern rather than its form," but fails to give any guidance as to what aspects of the "substance" are relevant. Prior to the 1984 Act, the inquiry focused on the nature of the services provided. Payments for occasional services always have been considered § 707(a) payments. Payments for ongoing services, however, generally were considered to be subject § 707(c) unless, as in Rev. Rul. 81–301, the partner provided similar services to customers and/or was subject to removal as a general partner. By all standards previously applied, the general partners in Rev. Rul. 81–300 appear to have been acting in their capacity as partners. But the direction in the Senate Finance Committee Report accompanying the 1984 Act that the payment in Rev. Rul. 81–300 is a § 707(a) payment has blurred the distinction and there is scant post–1984 interpretative authority. In one private letter ruling the Service has adhered to its position in Rev. Rul. 81–300 and declined to follow the suggestion in the Senate Finance Committee Report. Tech. Adv. Mem. 8642003 (June 30, 1986).

4. CAN SECTION 707 PAYMENTS BE EXCLUDABLE FRINGE BENEFITS?

In Armstrong v. Phinney, 394 F.2d 661 (5th Cir.1968), the court held that the entity approach adopted in § 707(a) was also applicable for purposes of the § 119 exclusion for meals and lodging provided to employees. Thus it would be possible as a matter of law for a partner to qualify as an employee entitled to the exclusion; the case was remanded for findings of fact concerning the partner's employee status. Wilson v. United States, 376 F.2d 280 (Ct.Cl.1967), consistent with prior law, reached the opposite conclusion on the ground that "[a] partnership is not a legal entity separate and apart from the partners, and, accordingly, a partnership cannot be regarded as the employer of a partner for the purposes of section 119," with no discussion of § 707. In Armstrong v. Phinney, the court applied § 707(a), rather than § 707(c), even though the partner in question was providing services as a ranch manager for a ranch owned by the partnership. Under the reasoning of *Pratt*, § 707(c) should have been the relevant statutory provision. Does section § 707(c) help resolve the § 119 issue? Rev. Rul. 91–26, 1991–1 C.B. 184, held that accident and health insurance premiums paid by a partnership for the benefit of partners performing services for the partnership were to be treated as § 707(c) guaranteed payments, includable in the partners' income and deductible by the partnership. The partners were not allowed to exclude the premiums under § 106, but were allowed to claim deductions for the premiums to the extent allowed under § 162(*l*). See also Rev. Rul. 69–184, 1969–1 C.B. 256, holding that members of a partnership are not employees of the partnership for employment tax (FICA) purposes.

Various provisions in the § 132 regulations treat partners who perform services for the partnership as employees for purposes of the exclusion of miscellaneous fringe benefits under § 132. See e.g., Treas. Reg. § 1.132–1(b)(1) (partners are treated as employees for purposes of excluding no additional cost fringe benefits and qualified employee discounts); Treas. Reg. § 1.132–1(b)(2)(ii) (partners are treated as employees for purposes of excluding working condition fringe benefits).

Jenkins v. Commissioner, 102 T.C. 550 (1994), suggested that a § 707(c) payment to a partner retiring due to disability might be excludable under § 104(a)(3), but did not resolve the issue; the court merely held that it had jurisdiction to decide whether § 104(a)(3) excluded the payment.

5. PROPER YEAR FOR INCLUSION AND DEDUCTION OF SECTION 707 PAYMENTS

5.1. *Section 707(a) Payments For Services Other Than As a Partner*

The proper year for inclusion and deduction of payments subject to § 707(a) is determined under normal tax accounting principles and depends on whether the partner in question and the partnership, respectively, use the cash or the accrual method of accounting. Difficulties arise only where a payment from an accrual method partnership to a cash method partner is deferred beyond the close of the year in which the services are performed. Suppose that the ABC Partnership is a calendar year, accrual method partnership engaged in the real estate business. B, a lawyer, performs legal services for the partnership in November of year 1 and sends the partnership a bill for $200. The partnership pays B the $200 in January of year 2. Section 267(a)(2), which controls the timing of deductions for amounts paid to related taxpayers, defers the payor's deduction until the year in which the item is properly includable by the payee. Section 267(e)(1) treats a partnership and each partner as related for purposes of applying § 267(a)(2), regardless of the percentage interest which the partner has in the partnership. Thus the ABC partnership may not deduct the amount until year 2. See Temp. Reg. § 1.267(a)–2T(c), Q & A.1. In addition, § 267(e)(3) invokes attribution rules. Thus, the partnership's deduction also would be deferred if in the above example the services were performed by B's child or spouse and payment was similarly delayed. The attribution rules also result in deferral of deductions for amounts due to a cash method partnership from a related accrual method partnership. See Temp. Reg. § 1.267(a)–2T(c), Q & A.3.

5.2. *Section 707(c) Guaranteed Payments*

Section 707(c) applies the entity approach only with respect to § 61, requiring inclusion of the payment as ordinary income, and § 162, permitting a deduction, subject to the capitalization requirement. For all other purposes, a guaranteed payment is considered to be part of the partner's distributive share of ordinary income and is thus taken into account in the year that the item is accounted for by the partnership. See Treas. Reg.

§ 1.707–1(c). The guaranteed payment is not considered an interest in profits under §§ 706(b)(3), 707(b), and 708(b). See Treas. Reg. § 1.707–1(c).

Suppose A, who is entitled to a guaranteed payment is on a calendar year and the ABC Partnership is on a fiscal year ending July 31. Under § 706(a) a partner reports his distributive share of partnership income as part of his own income for the year with or within which the partnership year ends. Treas. Regs. §§ 1.706–1(a)(1) and 1.707–1(c) require guaranteed payments to be similarly reported, i.e., to be included in the partner's year with or within which the partnership year of the payment ends. Thus, if a guaranteed payment is due to A in August 2006, A would not include the payment in 2006 when it was received, but rather in 2007 along with the rest of his distributive share for the year ended July 31, 2007.

Treatment of § 707(c) payments as part of the partner's distributive share for purposes of timing of inclusion is a two-edged sword. In Gaines v. Commissioner, T.C.Memo. 1982–731, a cash method partner was entitled to guaranteed payments for management services provided to a real estate partnership, but the amounts due were not paid. The partnership, which used the accrual method, claimed deductions for the unpaid guaranteed payments. The Commissioner did not challenge the partnership's deductions, except to the extent the guaranteed payments should have been capitalized, but required the cash-method partner to include the accrued unpaid guaranteed payments. This inclusion was upheld by the Tax Court:

> The statutory language of section 707(c) addresses only the character of the guaranteed payments and not the timing. Respondent's regulation under section 707(c), section 1.707–1(c), Income Tax Regs., addresses the timing question, as follows:
>
> > Payments made by a partnership to a partner for services or for the use of capital are considered as made to a person who is not a partner, to the extent such payments are determined without regard to the income of the partnership. However, a partner must include such payments as ordinary income for his taxable year within or with which ends the partnership taxable year in which the partnership deducted such payments as paid or accrued under its method of accounting. See section 706(a) and paragraph (a) of § 1.706–1.

As the regulation makes clear, the statutory authority for the timing of the inclusion of these guaranteed payments is section 706(a), which provides:

> In computing the taxable income of a partner for a taxable year, the inclusions required by section 702 and section 707(c) with respect to a partnership shall be based on the income, gain, loss, deduction, or credit of the partnership for any taxable year of the partnership ending within or with the taxable year of the partner.

The separate reference of § 707(c) guaranteed payments in the timing provisions of § 706(a) was explained by the Senate Report as simply—

> to make clear that payments made to a partner for services or for the use of capital are includible in his income at the same time as his distributive share of partnership income for the partnership year when the payments are made or accrued * * *. (S.Rept. No. 1622, to accompany H.R. 8300 (Pub.L. No. 591), 83d Cong., 2d Sess. 385 (1954)).

In Cagle v. Commissioner, 63 T.C. 86 (1974), affd. 539 F.2d 409 (5th Cir.1976), we held that includability and deductibility of guaranteed payments are two separate questions, and specifically that guaranteed payments are not automatically deductible simply by reason of their being included in the recipient's income. In *Cagle,* we stated * * *:

> We think that all Congress meant was that guaranteed payments should be included in the recipient partner's income in the partnership taxable year ending with or within which the partner's taxable year ends and in which the tax accounting treatment of the transaction is determined at the partnership level. S.Rept. No. 1622, supra at pp. 94, 385, 387.

We believe our statement in *Cagle* is an accurate description of the Congressional intent. We have found nothing in the statutory language, regulations, or legislative history to indicate that includability in the recipient partner's income was intended to be dependent upon deductibility at the partnership level.

> Petitioners seem to argue that there is a patent unfairness in taxing them on nonexistent income, namely income that they have neither received nor benefited from (e.g. through a tax deduction at the partnership level). Their argument has a superficial appeal to it, but on closer analysis must fail. Except for certain very limited purposes, guaranteed payments are treated as part of the partner's distributive share of partnership income and loss. Sec. 1.707–1(c), Income Tax Regs. For timing purposes guaranteed payments are treated the same as distributive income and loss. Sec. 706(a); sec. 1.706–1(a) and sec. 1.707–1(c), Income Tax Regs. A partner's distributive share of partnership income is includable in his taxable income for any partnership year ending within or with the partner's taxable year. Sec. 706(a). As is the case with a partner's ordinary distributive share of partnership income and loss, any unfairness in taxing a partner on guaranteed payments that he neither receives nor benefits from results from the conduit theory of partnerships, and is a consequence of the taxpayer's choice to do the business in the partnership form. We find no justification in the statute, regulations, or legislative history to permit these petitioners to recognize their income pro rata as deductions are allowed to the partnership. * * *

Sicard v. Commissioner, T.C.Memo. 1996–173, reached a similar result, holding that unpaid guaranteed payments were includable by the cash method partner to whom they were due in the year in which the partnership accrued the amounts into its cost of goods sold, rather than in the later year in which the payments were actually received.

If a guaranteed payment is not paid, but as is required is included in income by the partner, the question of whether the claim is a separate asset with a separate "tax cost" basis arises. There is no definitive answer to this question, but a footnote in *Gaines* suggests that the inclusion of a § 707(c) guaranteed payment increases the partner's basis for his partnership interest and the subsequent payment is governed by § 731.

6.   PAYMENTS FOR CAPITAL EXPENDITURES

6.1.   *Capitalization of Section 707 Payments*

Payments by a partnership to a partner governed by § 707(a) are not automatically deductible. If the payment is a capital expenditure, the partnership must capitalize it. Even though there is no deduction, the payee partner nevertheless realizes gross income by reason of the payment. See Rev. Rul. 75–214, 1975–1 C.B. 185, holding that payments by a limited partnership to the general partner as compensation for organizing the partnership were subject to § 707 and were required to be capitalized by the partnership pursuant to § 263. (Under current law, the same result is reached under § 709, discussed at page 43.)

Guaranteed payments subject to § 707(c) likewise are subject to the usually applicable requirements of § 263 and cannot be deducted simply because the expenditures take the form of guaranteed payments. I.R.C. § 707(c). Cagle v. Commissioner, 539 F.2d 409 (5th Cir.1976), reached the same result under a prior version of § 707(c) that did not expressly subject guaranteed payments to § 263. The capitalization rule was applied to guaranteed payments in consideration of services in organizing a partnership and syndicating interests in Tolwinsky v. Commissioner, 86 T.C. 1009 (1986). Rev. Rul. 80–234, 1980–2 C.B. 203, treated a fee paid to a partner for finding acceptable loan applicants as a guaranteed payment. The partner was required currently to include the payment in income, but the partnership was required to capitalize it as a cost of the loan amortizable over the life of the loan.

6.2.   *Effect of Section 707: Comparison to Special Allocations*

Assume that A and B each contributed $30,000 to form a partnership that purchased land for $55,000. The partnership balance sheet is as follows:

Assets				Capital Accounts		
	Book	Tax Basis			Book	Tax Basis
Cash	$ 5,000	$ 5,000	A		$30,000	$30,000
Land	$55,000	$55,000	B		$30,000	$30,000
	$60,000	$60,000			$60,000	$60,000

Special Allocation:

Assume the partnership earns $7,000 in 2006. A and B agree to allocate $5,000 plus 50% of the balance as A's distributive share and 50% of the income in excess of $5,000 as B's share, and to distribute $5,000 to A. This allocation reflects A's performance of services for the partnership that created a new capital asset worth $5,000. Treating this arrangement as an allocation and distribution, A would have income of $6,000 in 2006 and B would have income of $1,000. Assuming that A and B did not want to change their residual sharing arrangement, the partnership balance sheet at the end of 2006 would be as follows:

	Assets			Capital Accounts	
	Book	Tax Basis		Book	Tax Basis
Cash	$ 7,000	$ 7,000	A	$31,000	$31,000
Land	55,000	55,000	B	31,000	31,000
New Asset	$ 0	0			
	$62,000	$62,000		$62,000	$62,000

Assuming that this arrangement is respected, the AB Partnership has avoided the capitalization requirement of § 263; concomitantly, the new asset has a basis of zero. If the partnership sold its assets and liquidated in 2007, each of A and B would include $2,500 as distributive share of partnership income and would have no gain on the liquidation of the partnership. They would recognize income as follows:

	A	B
2006	$6,000	$1,000
2007	2,500	2,500
	$8,500	$3,500

Section 707:

If the allocation and distribution to A is a § 707(a) payment, A has $5,000 of compensation income as an individual in 2006 and, because the expense is a nondeductible capital expense, the AB partnership has $7,000 of income in 2006, which is taxed equally to the partners. The AB Partnership's balance sheet at the end of 2006 is as follows:

	Assets			Capital Accounts	
	Book	Tax Basis		Book	Tax Basis
Cash	$ 7,000	$ 7,000	A	$33,500	$33,500
Land	55,000	55,000	B	33,500	33,500
New Asset	5,000	5,000			
	$67,000	$67,000		$67,000	$67,000

When the assets are sold in 2007, no gain or loss is realized and neither A nor B realizes gain or loss on the liquidation. Thus the income recognized by A and B over the life of the partnership is as follows:

	A	B
2006	$8,500	$3,500
2007	0	0
	$8,500	$3,500

Comparison:

As is easily seen, § 707 affects neither the total amount of income realized nor the individual to whom that income is taxed. Rather, § 707(c) affects the timing of the income recognized by A, the partner who performed the services and, quite possibly, the character of the income recognized by both partners. If the asset created by A's services was a capital asset (or a § 1231 asset) rather than an ordinary income asset, e.g., inventory, the special allocation would have resulted in both A and B recognizing $2,500 of capital gain in 2007, while A recognized $6,000 of ordinary income in 2006 and B recognized $1,000 of ordinary income in 2006. As a result of the application of § 707, neither partner recognizes any capital gain in this example; all of the income is ordinary income.

7. GUARANTEED MINIMUM PAYMENTS

Suppose that A and B are partners in the AB Partnership, in which A is a 25 percent partner, but that the partnership agreement provides that A is entitled to receive not less than $100 per year. If the partnership's income for the year is $400 or more, no portion of A's distributive share is a guaranteed payment. Treas. Reg. § 1.707–1(c), Ex. (2). This is true even if the partnership agreement provides that A's minimum is to be treated as an expense item in computing partnership profits. Rev. Rul. 66–95, 1966–1 C.B. 169. If, however, partnership profits were only $200, under the approach in Treas. Reg. § 1.707–1(c), Ex. (2), $50 (25% of $200) would be A's distributive share, and $50 would be a guaranteed payment. Suppose further that the partnership's taxable income, apart from A's guaranteed payment, consists of $120 of ordinary income and $80 of capital gains. In this case the $50 guaranteed payment would be deducted from the $120 of ordinary income, leaving $70 of ordinary income and $80 of capital gains to be apportioned between A and B in the ratio that they share partnership profits for the year after deducting the guaranteed payment. Reflecting the partners' economic interests in the partnership, this sharing ratio is one-third to A and two-thirds to B. A's share is $50/$150 and B's share is $100/$150. Thus, in addition to $50 of ordinary income from the guaranteed payment, A has $23.33 of ordinary income and $26.67 of capital gain; B has $46.67 of ordinary income and $53.33 of capital gain. See Rev. Rul. 69–180, 1969–1 C.B. 183.

8. DISGUISED TRANSACTIONS BETWEEN PARTNERS AND THE PARTNERSHIP

Suppose A, who is a one–third partner in the ABC partnership, performs services for the partnership related to the acquisition of a new building. If A is paid a fixed sum for performing these services under either

§ 707(a) or § 707(c), the partnership will be required to capitalize the payment and A will be required currently to include the payment in income. On the other hand, if the partnership makes a special income allocation to A, which is subsequently distributed, B's and C's distributive shares will be reduced proportionately, in effect allowing the capital expenditure for A's services to be deducted by B and C. Section 707(a)(2)(A) authorizes regulations, which have not been issued, treating as a § 707(a)(1) transaction the performance of services for the contribution of property to the partnership by a partner coupled with a related allocation *and* distribution to the partner if, when viewed together, the two events are more properly characterized as a transaction occurring between the partnership and a partner acting in his capacity other than as a partner.

The Senate Finance Committee Report indicates that § 707(a)(2)(A) may apply both to one-time transactions and to continuing arrangements which use allocations and distributions in lieu of direct payments. The provision specifically is intended to apply to partnership organization and syndication fees which must be capitalized pursuant to § 709. Furthermore, the regulations may recharacterize a purported partner as not being a partner. The Committee Report lists the following six factors as relevant in determining whether a partner is receiving a putative allocation and distribution in his capacity as a partner: (1) whether the amount of the payment is subject to appreciable risk; (2) whether the partnership status of the recipient is transitory; (3) whether the allocation and distribution are close in time to the performance of services for, or the transfer of property to, the partnership; (4) whether considering all of the facts and circumstances it appears that the recipient became a partner primarily to obtain for himself or the partnership benefits which would not have been available if he had rendered services to the partnership in a third party capacity; (5) whether the value of the recipient's interest in general and in continuing partnership profits is small relative to the allocation in question; and (6) whether the requirements for maintaining capital accounts under § 704(b) makes it unlikely that income allocations are disguised payments for capital because it is economically unfeasible. Transitory special allocations are particularly suspect when coupled with the existence of another factor. Furthermore, the mere fact that the amount of an allocation is contingent does not insulate it under § 707(a)(2)(A). Contingent allocations generally will be recharacterized as fees, however, only where the partner in question normally performs, has previously performed or is capable of performing similar services for third parties. S.Rep. No. 98–169, 98th Cong., 2d Sess. 226–229 (1984).

The Senate Finance Committee Report gives the following example of the anticipated application of § 707(a)(2)(A):

> A commercial office building constructed by a partnership is projected to generate gross income of at least $100,000 per year indefinitely. Its architect, whose normal fee for such services is $40,000, contributes cash for a 25–percent interest in the partnership and receives both a 25–percent distributive share of net

income for the life of the partnership, and an allocation of $20,000 of partnership gross income for the first two years of partnership operations after leaseup. The partnership is expected to have sufficient cash available to distribute $20,000 to the architect in each of the first two years, and the agreement requires such a distribution. The purported gross income allocation and partnership distribution should be treated as a fee under sec. 707(a), rather than as a distributive share. Factors which contribute to this conclusion are (1) the special allocation to the architect is fixed in amount and there is a substantial probability that the partnership will have sufficient gross income and cash to satisfy the allocation/distribution; (2) the value of his interest in general and continuing partnership profits is relatively small in relation to the allocation in question; (3) the distribution relating to the allocation is fairly close in time to the rendering of the services; and (4) it is not unreasonable to conclude from all the facts and circumstances that the architect became a partner primarily for tax motivated reasons. If, on the other hand, the agreement allocates to the architect 20 percent of gross income for the first two years following construction of the building a question arises as to how likely it is that the architect will receive substantially more or less than his imputed fee of $40,000. If the building is pre-leased to a high credit tenant under a lease requiring the lessee to pay $100,000 per year of rent, or if there is low vacancy rate in the area for comparable space, it is likely that the architect will receive approximately $20,000 per year for the first two years of operations. Therefore, he assumes limited risk as to the amount or payment of the allocation and, as a consequence, the allocation/distribution should be treated as a disguised fee. If, on the other hand, the project is a "spec building," and the architect assumes significant entrepreneurial risk that the partnership will be unable to lease the building, the special allocation might (even though a gross income allocation), depending on all the facts and circumstances, properly be treated as a distributive share and partnership distribution.

Nonetheless, until regulations are promulgated, this technique appears to remain available.

9.   LOANS AND GUARANTEED PAYMENTS FOR THE USE OF CAPITAL

9.1.   *General*

Section 707(c) expressly contemplates guaranteed payments by the partnership for the use of a partner's capital. Guaranteed payments for the use of capital that are subject to § 707(c) are distinguishable from interest on a loan, which is subject to § 707(a), in that § 707(c) governs payments in the nature of a return paid with respect to contributed capital, even if determined under an interest-like computation, while § 707(a) governs interest payments on a bona fide loan. See Treas. Reg. § 1.707–1(a). In Pratt v. Commissioner, page 216, the Tax Court applied § 707(c) to tax a partner on accrued but unpaid interest on a loan from the partner to the partnership, 64 T.C. 203, 212–214, but on appeal the Commissioner conceded that because the transaction was a true loan, § 707(a) controlled, and the cash method partner was not taxable until he received the interest payment. 550 F.2d 1023 (5th Cir.1977). A bona fide loan from a partner to the partnership exists only if there is an unconditional obligation to pay a sum certain at a determinable date. Rev. Rul. 73–301, 1973–2 C.B. 215. In contrast, a contribution credited to a partner's capital account, repayable only as a distribution from partnership capital under the terms of the partnership agreement, is not a loan even though it may bear "interest." Thus, strict adherence to the requirements for maintaining partners' capital accounts pursuant to Treas. Reg. § 1.704–1(b)(2)(iv) can be a determining factor in distinguishing true loans from contributions to capital bearing guaranteed payments.

Guaranteed payments for the use of partnership capital are used by partnerships which, for example, desire generally to allocate profits to reflect services provided to the partnership, while providing a proper allowance for disproportionate capital contributions. Assume, for example, that D, E, and F desire to form a partnership in which both capital and services will be a material income producing factor. D, E, and F intend to be "equal" partners, but the partnership requires $300,000 of capital, and E and F each can contribute only $50,000. The solution is for D to contribute $200,000, while E and F each contribute $50,000, and to provide in the partnership agreement that D will receive an annual guaranteed payment equal to a specified percentage of the amount by which his capital contribution exceeds that of the other partners. Thus, the partnership agreement may provide that D is to receive a guaranteed payment of $15,000 (10% × $150,000) after which the profits of the partnership are to be split equally. Under this arrangement, D's capital account remains at $200,000 after receiving the payments, and E and F have not been taxed on the income used to make the guaranteed payments.

A more flexible formula can be devised to take into account the possibility that the partners desire ultimately to equalize their capital contributions. Thus the partnership agreement might provide that any partner who has contributed more than any other partner is entitled to an annual guaranteed payment equal to a stated percentage, e.g., 10 percent, of the partner's excess contribution. As the partnership earns profits, E and F may leave a portion of their distributive shares in the partnership, thereby increasing their capital accounts, while D withdraws not only his share of profits, but also a portion of his original capital contribution. Thus, if at the end of a future year the respective capital account balances of the partners are D, $120,000, E, $100,000, and F, $80,000, D would be entitled to a guaranteed payment of $4,000 (10% × ($120,000–$80,000)) and E would be entitled to a guaranteed payment of $2,000 (10% × ($100, 000 − $80,000)). When all partners' capital accounts were equalized, any guaranteed payments would cease. Under this arrangement, E and F must pay tax on amounts they do not currently receive so that all of the partners eventually will have equal capital accounts. The choice between which of the two methods is adopted depends on many factors, only some of which are tax considerations.

9.2. *Characterization of Guaranteed Payments for the Use of Capital*

Guaranteed payments for the use of capital raise characterization questions analogous to some of the characterization questions relating to guaranteed payments for services. In general, guaranteed payments for the use of capital are ordinary income, see Treas. Reg. § 1.707–1(c), but whether they are interest is not clear. Characterization of guaranteed payments for the use of capital as interest may be relevant to both the recipient partner and to the partnership. Section 707(c) payments for capital are treated by the partner as interest in applying the passive activity loss rules of § 469. Treas. Reg. § 1.469–2(e)(2)(ii)(A). Characterization as interest also is relevant for purposes of applying other rules, such as the investment interest limitation of § 163(d), but there is no direct precedential authority on this point. However, as far as the recipient is concerned, in private letter rulings the Internal Revenue Service has characterized such payments with reference to the character of the partnership's ordinary income from which they were made. See, e.g., Private Letter Ruling 8728033. From the partnership's perspective, determining whether the deduction is to be treated as an ordinary and necessary business expense under § 162 or as an interest expense under § 163 may be relevant in applying the uniform capitalization rules of § 263A. As far as characterization from the perspective of the partnership is concerned, however, § 707(c) expressly refers to § 162. This raises the possibility that such payments may be characterized differently from the perspective of the recipient and the partnership, since characterization of a deduction as a § 162 deduction is not helpful in characterizing the nature of the receipt.

10.   OTHER ASPECTS OF GUARANTEED PAYMENTS

Section 707(c) applies the entity approach only with respect to § 61 and § 162. For all other purposes guaranteed payments are considered part of the partner's distributive share of ordinary income. Thus, a guaranteed payment is not considered an interest in profits under § 706(b)(3), 707(b), and 708(b). Treas. Reg. § 1.707–1(c).

A guaranteed payment is not covered by the deferred compensation rules of § 404(a) and (b) or the withholding rules. Treas. Reg. § 1.707–1(c). However, Miller v. Commissioner, 52 T.C. 752 (1969), held that guaranteed payments received by a partner for services performed abroad were excludable under former § 911 as income earned abroad and not, as urged by the Commissioner, simply a distributive share of partnership income. Carey v. United States, 427 F.2d 763 (Ct.Cl.1970), reached the same result. Compare also Armstrong v. Phinney, page 219.

SECTION 2. SALES OF PROPERTY

INTERNAL REVENUE CODE: Sections 707(a)(1), (a)(2)(B), (b); 1239(a)–(c); 267(a)(1), (e)(1)–(3).

REGULATIONS: Sections 1.707–1(b); 1.707–3(a)–(d); 1.707–4(a)(1)–(3); 1.707–5(a)(1), (5), (6), (7)(i); 1.267(b)–1(b); 1.267(a)–2T(c).

Problems similar to those that arise when a partner purchases services from the partnership in an individual capacity or provides services to a partnership of which he is a member for a stated salary also arise when a partner sells an asset to the partnership or buys an asset from the partnership. As with transactions in which a partner deals with a partnership as a stranger with respect to the provision of services, § 707(a)(1) applies the entity theory to tax sales of property by a partner to a partnership or by the partnership to a partner. The basic rule of § 707(a)(1) is supplemented by § 707(a)(2)(B), which recharacterizes certain allocations and distributions related to the transfer of property by a partner to the partnership as a transaction subject to § 707(a)(1). Section 707(b) disallows loss deductions on sales between a partner and a partnership in which the partner owns more than fifty percent of either the profits or capital interests (or between two partnerships in which the same partners own more than fifty percent of the profits or capital interests). In addition, gain on a sale of property other than a capital asset (i.e., § 1231 property) between a partner and a related, i.e., more than fifty percent owned, partnership is recharacterized as ordinary income.

For example, suppose that C, a fifty percent partner in the CD Partnership, who has a basis for her partnership interest of $75, sells the partnership property with a $100 basis and a fair market value of $200. Under the aggregate theory, she has sold a one-half interest to her partner, so she has a $50 gain, and continues to own a one-half interest which would be considered as a contribution to the partnership, increasing her basis by $50 to $125. C also is regarded as receiving a distribution of $100 from the partnership, reducing the basis of her partnership interest to $25. The partnership's basis in the property is $150 ($100 cost basis for the purchased portion + $50 transferred basis for the contributed portion). If the partnership sells the property for $200, it has a gain of $50, which is allocable to C under § 704(c), increasing her basis to $75. If the partnership then liquidates with C receiving $100, C will be taxed on $25 so that she is ultimately taxed on a total of $125. Under the entity approach, C would have been taxed on a $100 gain when she sold the property to the partnership, nothing when the partnership sold the property for $200, and another $25 gain upon receipt of $100 on liquidation of the partnership. Since these three events can be widely separated in time, the aggregate theory provides significant opportunity for deferral that is not available under the entity theory. In addition, since the partnership may hold property for a different purpose than did the contributing partner, the character of the gain also can be affected.

ILLUSTRATIVE MATERIAL

1. LIMITATIONS ON LOSS RECOGNITION

1.1. *Scope of Limitations*

Section 707(b)(1)(A) disallows any loss on a sale or exchange between a person and a partnership in which the person owns, directly or indirectly, more than 50 percent of either a capital or a profits interest. Section 707(b)(1)(B) applies the same rule to sales or exchanges between two partnerships in which the same persons own more than 50 percent of either a capital or a profits interest.

Davis v. Commissioner, 866 F.2d 852 (6th Cir.1989), illustrates two aspects of the breadth of § 707(b)(1)(B). A bank foreclosed on real property held by a limited partnership and one month later the bank sold the property to another partnership in which the profits and capital interests were 100 percent owned directly or indirectly by the same persons as the first partnership, but in different percentages. First, the court held that § 707(b)(1)(B) applied to the sale even though it was indirect. Second, and more importantly, in applying § 707(b)(1)(B) to deny the first partnership a loss on the foreclosure, the court did not analyze the percentage ownership of each partner in each partnership, even though it appears from the stated facts that the partner in question did not have more than a 50 percent interest in each partnership. For § 707(b)(1)(B) to apply, however, it is not necessary that the *commonly owned interests* of each partner in each partnership total more than 50 percent. Thus, § 707(b)(1)(B) applies to deny the loss if the AB partnership in which A holds a 99 percent interest and B holds a 1 percent interest sells property at a loss to the BA partnership in which B owns a 99 percent interest and A holds a 1 percent interest.

The American Law Institute recommended in 1984 that § 707(b)(1)(B) be applied to disallow losses on sales between related partnerships only if the same persons owned more than 50 percent of either the profits or capital interests in each partnership, taking into account only the common holdings in each partnership. A partner's common holding is his percentage ownership in the partnership in which he has a smaller interest. American Law Institute, Federal Income Tax Project, Subchapter K (1984). Assume, for example, that the profits and capital interests in the ABCDE Partnership are held as follows: A, 5 percent, B, 10 percent, C, 15 percent, D, 20 percent, and E, 50 percent; and the profits and capital interests in the EDCBA Partnership are held as follows: E, 5 percent, D, 10 percent, C, 15 percent, B, 20 percent, and A, 50 percent. The common holdings in the two partnerships are as follows: A, 5 percent, B, 10 percent, C, 15 percent, D, 10 percent, and E, 5 percent. The aggregate common holdings are 45 percent, and therefore, the partnerships would not be under common control. The ALI proposal appears to better implement the policy of disallowing losses in situations in which there has not been a significant change in beneficial interest, while allowing losses where there is some relationship between the buyer and seller but there has been a significant change in beneficial interest. Nonetheless, the proposal has languished for decades.

Section 707(b)(3) applies the constructive ownership rules of § 267(c)(1), (2), (4), and (5) to determine who is a partner when applying § 707(b)(1)(A). Thus a loss on a sale between a partnership and a person who does not actually own any interest in the partnership may be disallowed. For example, if G holds a 51 percent interest in both profits and capital of the GH partnership and the partnership sells property with a basis of $1000 to I, who is G's spouse for $500, the loss will be disallowed under § 707(b)(1) because I constructively owns more than a 50 percent interest in the partnership. However, if G holds only a 50 percent or less interest in the GH partnership, then § 707(b) does not apply; but the general rule of § 267 still applies to disallow a portion of the loss based on the related partner's percentage interest in the partnership. See Treas. Reg. § 1.267(b)–1(b). For example, if G was a 40 percent partner, 40 percent of the loss would be disallowed. When a portion of the loss is disallowed under § 267 on the sale of property by a partnership to a related person, the disallowed loss should be allocated to the partner related to the purchaser. See Casel v. Commissioner, 79 T.C. 424 (1982).

1.2. *Effect of Loss Disallowance on Partners' Bases in Partnership Interests*

If § 707(b)(1) applies to disallow a loss on the sale of partnership property, pursuant to § 705(a)(2) all of the partners nevertheless must reduce the basis of their partnership interests by their distributive shares of the disallowed loss. The basis adjustment applies to all partners, not only the partners directly related to the purchaser. Rev. Rul. 96–10, 1996–1 C.B. 138. Since the partnership's aggregate basis for its assets has been decreased by the amount of the loss, the partners likewise must decrease the basis of their partnership interests by a like amount. This adjustment is necessary in order to prevent the partners from indirectly recognizing the disallowed loss (or reducing gain) upon a subsequent sale of their partnership interests.

Conversely, if § 707(b)(1) applied to disallow a loss on the sale of partnership property by one partnership to a related partnership, and upon the sale of the property by the second partnership § 267(d) applies to limit the amount of gain recognized, the partners of the second partnership nevertheless increase the basis of their partnership interests pursuant to § 705(a)(1) by their distributive shares of the full amount of the gain realized, not only the gain recognized. Rev. Rul. 96–10, supra. Because the nonrecognition accorded by § 267(d) is permanent, this adjustment is necessary to preserve the intended benefit of § 267(d) in cases in which § 707(b)(1) applies.

Suppose, for example, the ABCD partnership, in which A, B, C, and D are equal partners, sold land with a basis of $100 and a fair market value of

$60, to the BCDE Partnership, in which B, C, D, and E are equal partners. Subsequently, the BCDE partnership sells the land to an unrelated party for $116. Section 707(b)(1) disallows the $40 loss realized by the ABCD partnership, but each partner must reduce her basis in her partnership interest by $10. Upon the sale of the property by the BCDE Partnership, a $56 gain is realized, but pursuant to § 267(d), $40 of that gain is not recognized; only $16 of gain is recognized and each partner reports only a $4 gain. Nevertheless, each partner is entitled to increase the basis of her partnership interest by $14.

2. RECHARACTERIZATION OF CAPITAL GAIN AS ORDINARY INCOME

If gain is recognized on a sale or exchange between a person and a more than 50 percent controlled partnership, § 707(b)(2) requires that the gain be treated as ordinary gain if the property is *not a capital asset* in the hands of the *transferee*. One object of § 707(b)(2) is § 1231 property. In this respect § 707(b)(2) overlaps § 1239, which requires ordinary gain treatment for property sold between a person and a more than fifty percent controlled partnership if the property is depreciable in the hands of the purchaser. Both provisions are designed to prevent the transferee from claiming deductible depreciation on a stepped-up basis when the seller is taxed at the preferential capital gains rate. On this rationale, § 707(b)(2) is over-inclusive to the extent that it applies to land, apart from improvements, which will be held for use in the transferee's trade or business. The 1984 ALI Subchapter K project recommended excepting land from the rules of § 707(b)(2). Like the other 1984 ALI Subchapter K proposals, this one too has languished.

Section 707(b)(2), but not § 1239, also applies to sales of property that will be inventory in the hands of the purchaser. Thus, for example, if a partnership that holds unimproved real property as a capital asset sells that property to a controlling partner who will hold the land for sale to customers in the ordinary course of business, the gain recognized by the partnership is ordinary, not capital gain.

The same attribution rules that are used to apply § 707(b)(1) are used to apply § 707(b)(2). See Rev. Rul. 67–105, 1967–1 C.B. 167, for the application of the attribution rules. Section 1239 also invokes the attribution rules of § 267(c).

In addition, § 453(g) denies installment sale treatment on any sale between a partner and a partnership in which the partner owns, directly or indirectly, more than 50 percent of either a capital or a profits interest, unless the transferor establishes that the transaction did not have tax avoidance as one of its principal purposes. Section 453(g) does not apply, however, to sales between related partnerships. There is little administrative or judicial guidance as to what establishes the absence or presence of a tax avoidance purpose in this context. Guenther v. Commissioner, T.C. Memo. 1995–280, suggests that any increase in the amount of depreciation deductions otherwise available as a result of a sale to a related buyer is a factor in determining whether the transfer was motivated by tax avoidance.

3.   DISGUISED SALES AND EXCHANGES OF PROPERTY

3.1.   *Background*

In Otey v. Commissioner, 70 T.C. 312 (1978), aff'd per curiam, 634 F.2d 1046 (6th Cir.1980), the taxpayer and another individual formed a partnership to construct housing on property owned by the taxpayer. Under the partnership agreement the taxpayer contributed the property to the partnership with an agreed value of $65,000 and an FHA-insured construction loan was taken out in an amount greater than that needed for the construction. The taxpayer then withdrew $65,000 of the excess mortgage proceeds from the partnership. The Commissioner argued that the taxpayer in effect sold his property to the partnership and recognized gain under § 707(a). The Tax Court, however, held that §§ 721 and 731 controlled with the result that the money distribution merely reduced the taxpayer's basis in his partnership interest: "Were there no partnership at all, a taxpayer could borrow funds on the security of appreciated property and apply them to his personal use without triggering gain. Had the distributed funds come directly from the other partner, [the Commissioner's] case would be stronger. While it may be argued that the funds have come indirectly from [the partner] because his credit facilitated the loan, the fact is that the loan was a partnership loan on which the partnership was primarily liable, and both partners were jointly and separately liable for the full loan if the partnership defaulted. We do not view the factual pattern here as constituting a disguised sale of the land to [the other partner] or the partnership." Similar results were reached in slightly different contexts in Communications Satellite Corp. v. United States, 625 F.2d 997 (Ct.Cl.1980), and Jupiter Corp. v. United States, 2 Cl.Ct. 58 (1983), where the Service unsuccessfully attempted to recharacterize distributions to old partners in connection with contributions by new partners as sales of partnership interests.

3.2.   *The Legislative Response*

Congress disagreed with the courts' conclusions that the transactions in *Otey, Communications Satellite Corp.*, and *Jupiter Corp.* did not resemble sales, and in 1984 enacted § 707(a)(2)(A) and (B), which authorize the Treasury to promulgate regulations treating as a sale subject to § 707(a) any transaction in which there is a direct or indirect distribution of money or property to a partner related to his direct or indirect transfer of money or property to the partnership. The Senate Finance Committee Report indicates that the regulations should apply this rule only to attempts to disguise sales and not to "nonabusive transactions that reflect the various economic contributions of the partners." S.Rep. No. 98–169, 98th Cong., 2d Sess. 230 (1984). It gives the following example of circumstances in which the rule may be applied:

For example, when a partner contributes appreciated property to a partnership and receives a distribution of money or property within a reasonable period before or after such contribution, that is approximately equal in value to the portion of contributed property that is in effect given up to the other partner(s) the transaction will be subject to this provision. However, the distribution would not be so subject if there is a corresponding partnership allocation of income or gain, but that arrangement may instead be subject to the new provision [§ 707(a)(2)(A)] relating to partnership payments for property or services * * *. The disguised sale provision also will apply to the extent (1) the transferor partner receives the proceeds of a loan related to the property to the extent responsibility for the repayment of the loan rests, directly or indirectly, with the partnership (or its assets) or the other partners, or (2) the partner has received a loan related to the property in anticipation of the transaction and responsibility for repayment of the loan is transferred, directly or indirectly, to the partnership (or its assets) or the other partners.

Although the rule applies to sales of property to the partnership, the committee does not intend to prohibit a partner from receiving a partnership interest in return for contributing property which entitles him to priorities or preferences as to distributions, but is not in substance a disguised sale. Similarly, the committee generally does not intend this provision to adversely affect distributions that create deficit capital accounts (maintained in a manner consistent with Treasury regulations under § 704(b)) for which the distributee is liable, regardless of the timing of the distribution, unless such deficit capital account is improperly understated or not expected to be made up until such a distant point in the future that its present value is small. However, if this deficit creating distribution is coupled with an allocation of income or gain, the distribution/allocation arrangement may be subject to [§ 707(a)(2)(A)] relating to partnership payments for services or property. Similarly, the contribution of encumbered property to a partnership would not suggest a disguised sale to the extent responsibility for the debt is not shifted, directly or indirectly, to the partnership (or its assets) or to the noncontributing partners. The committee anticipates that the Treasury regulations will treat transactions to which the provision applies as a sale of property or partnership interests among the partners or as a partial sale and partial contribution of the property to the partnership, with attendant tax consequences, depending upon the underlying economic substance of the transaction. These regulations may provide for a period, such as three years, during which contributions by and distributions to the same or another partner normally will be presumed related.

Section 707(a)(2)(B) also may recharacterize a contribution by one partner coupled by a distribution to another partner as a transaction between the two partners acting in capacities other than as a partner. This provision may apply if one partner transfers property to the partnership while another transfers cash, followed by the distribution of cash to the partner who contributed property and property to the partner who contributed cash, or in situations such as those presented in *Communications Satellite Corp.* and *Jupiter Corp.,* supra.

To some extent, § 707(a)(2)(B) is redundant. Treas. Reg. § 1.731–1(c)(3) long has provided that a contribution to a partnership followed "within a short period" by a distribution of other property to the contributing partner or a distribution of the contributed property to another partner may be treated as a taxable exchange. This regulation, which the courts failed to apply, would have been adequate to treat as taxable sales or exchanges the contributions and distributions in *Otey*, *Communications Satellite Corp.*, and *Jupiter Corp.* Thus, § 707(a)(2)(B) and the detailed regulations promulgated under its authority have been necessitated by the failure of the courts to look through form to determine the true substance of the transactions in those cases.

3.3.   *Section 707(a)(2) Regulations*

3.3.1.   *General*

Treas. Regs. §§ 1.707–3 through –9 implement § 707(a)(2)(B) and so much of § 707(a)(2)(A) as applies to disguised sales. The general theory of these regulations is that when a partner transfers property to a partnership in a nominal contribution and receives property or money nominally as a distribution, the two transfers should be viewed as related and recharacterized as components of a disguised sale only to the extent that their combined effect allows the transferring partner to withdraw all or a part of his or her equity in the transferred property. If a partner contributes property to a partnership in exchange for a genuine entrepreneurial interest in partnership capital, any subsequent distributions that liquidate that capital interest will not be treated as related to the contribution. But if the partner's equity in the contributed property is not converted, in substance as well as form, into a genuine interest in partnership capital subject to the entrepreneurial risks of partnership operations, distributions that represent a withdrawal of the partner's equity in the transferred property will be recharacterized as part of a disguised sale of the property under § 707(a)(2). See Notice of Proposed Rulemaking, PS–163–84, 1991–1 C.B. 952.

To implement this approach, Treas. Reg. § 1.707–3(b)(1) provides that the disguised sale rule of § 707(a)(2) applies only if, based on all the facts and circumstances, the transfer of money or other consideration would not have been made but for the transfer of the property and, in cases in which the transfers are not made simultaneously, the subsequent transfer is not dependent on the entrepreneurial risks of partnership operations. Treas. Reg. § 1.707–3(b)(2) sets forth a list of various facts and circumstances to aid in determining whether the transfers are a disguised sale. In addition, Treas. Reg. § 1.707–3(c) provides a rebuttable presumption that transfers within a two year period constitute a disguised sale, unless one of the exceptions under Treas. Reg. § 1.707–4, applicable to guaranteed payments for capital, reasonable preferred returns or operating cash flow distributions, applies. Treas. Regs. §§ 1.707–3(c)(2) and 1.707–8 require disclosure to the Internal Revenue Service of reciprocal transfers by a partner to the partnership and by the partnership to the partner within the presumptive two year period that the parties do not treat as a sale. (Prop. Regs. §§ 1.707–5(a)(8) (2004) and 1.707–8 (2004) would increase the period for disclosure of transactions possibly subject to § 707(a)(2)(B) from two years to five years.) Conversely, transfers more than two years apart are presumed not to be components of a disguised sale. Treas. Reg. § 1.707–3(d). For examples of nonsimultaneous transfers, see Treas. Reg. § 1.707–3(f), Ex. (2)–(8).

Distributions of money to a partner during a taxable year that do not exceed the partner's interest in net operating cash flow are presumed not to be part of a sale unless the facts and circumstances clearly establish otherwise. Treas. Reg. § 1.707–4(b). A partner's interest in a net operating cash flow distribution generally is the lesser of the partner's percentage interest in overall partnership profits for the year and the partner's percentage interest in overall partnership profits for the life of the partnership. Treas. Reg. § 1.707–4(b)(2). In addition, Treas. Reg. § 1.707–4(d) treats payments by a partnership to reimburse partners for capital expenditures and costs incurred in anticipation of the formation of a partnership as distributions under § 731, rather than as part of a disguised sale under § 707(a)(2)(B). This exception applies only to expenditures incurred within one year of the transfer of property by the partner to the partnership, and the reimbursed capital expenditures may not exceed 20 percent of the fair market value of the property.

Any transfer of property to a partnership that is treated as part of a disguised sale is not reflected in the transferring partner's capital account. If the consideration treated as transferred to a partner pursuant to a sale is less than the fair market value of the property transferred to the partnership, the transfer will be treated as a sale in part and a capital contribution in part, and the transferring partner must prorate her basis in the property between the portion of the property sold and the portion of the property contributed. Suppose, for example, that individuals A, B, and C each contribute $1,000,000 in cash to the ABCD Partnership in exchange for one-quarter partnership interests, while individual D transfers Blackacre to the ABCD Partnership in exchange for a one-quarter interest in the partnership. At the time of the transfer, the fair market value of Blackacre is $4,000,000 and its adjusted basis to D is $1,200,000. Contemporaneously, the ABCD Partnership transfers $3,000,000 in cash to D. Because the cash received by D is less than the fair market value of Blackacre, D is considered to have sold a portion of Blackacre with a value of $3,000,000 to the partnership in exchange for cash; because Blackacre is worth $4,000,000, D is treated as selling an undivided three-quarter interest in Blackacre for $3,000,000. Accordingly, D recognizes $2,100,000 of gain ($3,000,000 amount realized less $900,000 adjusted tax basis ($1,200,000 multiplied by $3,000,000/$4,000,000)). D has contributed to the partnership, in D's capacity as a partner, an undivided one-quarter of the property, with a fair market value of $1,000,000 and an adjusted tax basis of $300,000. See Treas. Reg. § 1.707–3(f), Ex. (1).

If a transfer to a partner that is part of a disguised sale occurs subsequent to the partner's transfer of property to the partnership, the partner will be treated as receiving a partnership obligation as consideration for the property on the date the partnership acquired ownership of the property. If § 453 is otherwise applicable, the partner will be permitted to report gain on the sale under the installment sale rules, but otherwise gain (or loss) will be recognized in the year of the transfer to the partnership. Treas. Reg. § 1.707–3(a)(2).

If the parties structure a disguised sale as a contribution to a partnership, they may not subsequently assert either that the transferor was not a partner or that no partnership existed in order to avoid the application of § 707(a)(2). If no partnership actually exists, the transaction will be considered a sale between the purported partners rather than a sale to a partnership. Treas. Reg. § 1.707–3(a)(3).

3.3.2. *Assumption of Liabilities*

The legislative history of § 707(a)(2) indicates that a transfer of property by a partner to a partnership should be treated as a disguised sale if the transferor-partner incurs debt in anticipation of the transfer and the partnership assumes or takes the property subject to the debt. See H.R.Rep. No. 98–432, 98th Cong., 2d Sess. 1221 (1984). However, "there will be no disguised sale under [§ 707(a)(2)] to the extent the contributing partner, in substance, retains liability for repayment of the borrowed amounts (i.e., to the extent the other partners have no direct or indirect risk of loss with respect to such amounts) since, in effect, the partner has simply borrowed through the partnership." H.R.Rep. No. 861, 98th Cong., 2d Sess. 862 (1984) (Conf.Rep.). Treas. Reg. § 1.707–5 implements this policy by providing that the assumption of (or taking the property subject to) any liabilities, other than *"qualified liabilities,"* by the partnership is treated as a withdrawal of the partner's equity in the transferred property to the extent responsibility for those liabilities is shifted to the other partners. "Qualified liabilities" include all debt incurred more than two years before the transfer, which is never treated as debt incurred in anticipation of the transfer. Treas. Reg. § 1.707–5(a)(6)(i)(A). Purchase money debt, debt to finance improvement of the transferred property, and trade payables related to the transferred property, even if incurred within two years of the transfer, are qualified debt and never are treated as debt incurred in anticipation of the transfer. Treas. Reg. § 1.707–5(a)(6)(i)(C) and (D). All other debt incurred within two years of the transfer is presumed to have been incurred in anticipation of the transfer and therefore as consideration for a sale of the property to the extent responsibility for the debt is shifted to other partners. Treas. Reg. § 1.707–5(a)(7).

Assumption by the partnership of liabilities that are not "qualified liabilities" is treated as consideration for the transferred property to the extent the amount of the liabilities exceeds the transferring partner's share of the liabilities after the transfer. Treas. Reg. § 1.707–5(a)(1). The assumption of a "qualified liability," however, is treated as part of a sale only to the extent the partner is otherwise treated as having sold a portion of the property. See Treas. Reg. § 1.707–5(a)(5). To the extent the assumption of (or taking subject to) a liability is not treated as part of a sale, the consequences of a shift of the liability are determined under § 752.

For purposes of § 707(a)(2) a partner's share of a recourse liability is the partner's share of the liability under § 752. Treas. Reg. § 1.707–5(a)(2)(i). However, Treas. Reg. § 1.707–5(a)(2)(ii) provides special rules for determining a partner's share of nonrecourse liabilities for purposes of § 707(a)(2). A partner's share of nonrecourse liabilities is determined by multiplying the liability by the partner's percentage interest in partnership profits used generally to determine the partner's share of nonrecourse liability under Treas. Reg. § 1.752–3(a)(3). This formula ignores the allocation of nonrecourse liabilities based on minimum gain and § 704(c) gain. Treas. Reg. § 1.707–5(a)(2)(ii) does not use the rules under Treas. Reg. § 1.752–3 to determine a partner's share of nonrecourse liabilities because to do so would cause the transferring partner's share of a nonrecourse liability to reflect the full amount of built-in gain under § 704(c). If the debt allocation rules of Treas. Reg. § 1.752–3 were used to determine the consideration received by the transferor, the extent to which a disguised sale of the property results from the encumbrance would vary inversely with the gain inherent in the contributed property. The Internal Revenue Service considered such a result to be inappropriate. See Notice of Proposed Rulemaking, PS–163–84, 1991–1 C.B. 951, 955.

Reduction of a partner's share of a liability subsequent to a transfer may be considered to be part of a disguised sale if the reduction was anticipated when the partner transferred the property to the partnership and if the reduction was part of a plan one of the principal purposes of which was minimizing the extent to which the assumption of the liability would be treated as part of a sale. Treas. Reg. § 1.707–5(a)(3).

The application of Treas. Reg. § 1.707–5 to the transfer of property encumbered by a recourse debt is illustrated by the following example, based on Treas. Reg. § 1.707–5(f), Ex. (2). Suppose that individuals C and D form the CD Partnership. C contributes $200,000 for a one-third interest. In exchange for a two-thirds partnership interest, D transfers to the partnership Whiteacre, which has a fair market value of $1,000,000 and is encumbered by a $600,000 mortgage. The partnership assumes the $600,000 liability, which D incurred immediately before transferring Whiteacre to the partnership; D used the proceeds for purposes unrelated to Whiteacre. Under Treas. Reg. § 1.752–2, immediately after the partnership's assumption of the liability encumbering Whiteacre, D's share of that liability is $400,000. Because the liability is not a qualified liability, the partnership's assumption of $200,000 of the liability (the excess of the liability assumed by the partnership ($600,000) over D's share of the liability immediately after the assumption ($400,000)) is treated as consideration to D in connection with D's sale of an undivided portion of Whiteacre to the partnership. Since the consideration of $200,000 equals one-fifth of the value of Whiteacre, D is treated as selling an undivided one-fifth of Whiteacre to the CD Partnership and as contributing to the CD Partnership an undivided four-fifths of Whiteacre, having a fair market value of $800,000 and subject to a $400,000 debt. If D's basis for Whiteacre were $250,000, then D's gain recognized on the sale would be $150,000; the $200,000 of debt relief is D's amount realized and D's basis for the undivided one-fifth is $50,000 ($\frac{1}{5}$ × $250,000). D contributed the other four-fifths of Whiteacre, having a basis of $200,000.

For an example of the treatment under § 707(a)(2)(B) of a transfer of property subject to a nonrecourse mortgage that is not a qualified debt, see Treas. Reg. § 1.707–5(f), Ex. (1).

3.3.3. *Guaranteed Payments and Preferred Returns*

A guaranteed payment for capital is not subject to the entrepreneurial risks of partnership operations and, if received with respect to a contribution of property other than cash, would be treated as part of a sale if the payment were tested under the general rules of Treas. Reg. § 1.707–3. Because, however, guaranteed payments for capital are in substance payments for the use of property, Treas. Reg. § 1.707–4(a)(1) provides that "reasonable" guaranteed payments for capital contributions are not treated as amounts paid in exchange for property. The partnership's characterization of a purported guaranteed payment for capital does not determine whether a transfer actually is a guaranteed payment as opposed to a payment to complete a sale. Whether a transfer is part of a sale or a guaranteed payment for capital is determined by examining whether the transfer is designed to liquidate all or part of the partner's interest in property transferred to the partnership or, on the other hand, is designed to provide the partner with a return on an investment in the partnership. Treas. Reg. § 1.707–4(a)(1).

Treas. Reg. § 1.707–4(a)(1)(ii) provides that a payment characterized by the parties as a guaranteed payment will be presumed to be a guaranteed payment for capital if the amount of the guaranteed payment is "reasonable," under standards set forth in Treas. Reg. § 1.707–4(a)(3). A purported guaranteed payment for capital that is not reasonable in amount is presumed not to be a guaranteed payment. Treas. Reg. § 1.707–4(a)(1)(iii). Either presumption can be rebutted by facts and circumstances which clearly establish the contrary. If a purported guaranteed payment for capital is not respected, the payment is treated as any other distribution and, if made within two years of a transfer of property to the partnership, will be presumed to be in exchange for the property. The regulations do not address the question of whether a guaranteed payment for services is subject to recharacterization as a transfer in consideration of property.

Treas. Reg. § 1.707–4(a) provides that a distribution of money characterized by the parties as a preferred return is presumed not to be part of a sale if the amount is reasonable under Treas. Reg. § 1.707–4(a)(3)(ii) unless the facts and circumstances clearly establish that the transfer is part of a sale.

3.3.4.   *Outbound Transactions Involving a Disguised Sale of Property by a Partnership to a Partner*

Treas. Reg. § 1.707–6 provides rules governing disguised sales by a partnership to a partner that are subject to § 707(a)(2)(B). These rules are similar to those provided in Treas. Regs. §§ 1.707–3 and 1.707–5 for disguised sales by a partner to a partnership. For example, if the partnership places a mortgage on property and then distributes the property to a partner in partial or full liquidation of her partnership interest, the transaction will be recharacterized as in part a sale of the property from the partnership to the partner in her individual capacity, and in part a distribution. As a result the partnership will recognize gain or loss, and the partner's basis in the property will be determined in part under § 1012 (purchase price basis) and in part under § 732. This result follows from the theory of § 707(a)(2)(B) because, under the principles of § 752, the distributee partner's obligation for a share of the debt has been shifted to the other partners.

CHAPTER 7

SPECIAL LIMITATIONS ON LOSS DEDUCTIONS AT THE PARTNER LEVEL

SECTION 1. TAX SHELTER LOSSES

The combination of the principle of Crane v. Commissioner, 331 U.S. 1 (1947), and its progeny, allowing the taxpayer to include nonrecourse debt in basis and § 752, which adjusts a partner's basis in a partnership interest to reflect partnership indebtedness, whether recourse or nonrecourse, formed the backbone of the tax shelter phenomenon that reached its zenith in the 1970's and early 1980's. Tax shelter investments provided a significant portion of the investor's return in the form of tax benefits that not only offset any tax liability that might arise from the investment but also "sheltered" other income, usually from the investor's regular business or professional activities. Investors purchased interests in tax shelter investments, usually in the form of an interest in a limited partnership, and received an after-tax return on the purchase price even though the investment was not profitable before taxes.

Virtually all tax shelters had three common elements: deferral, conversion, and leverage. Deferral is obtained by accelerating deductions, that is claiming deductions in excess of economic costs in the early years of an investment so that income is concentrated in the later years. These accelerated deductions result in taxable income being less than economic income in the years the deductions are claimed. In later years the investment produces taxable income in excess of economic income. The earlier deductions are offset, but in the interim the taxpayer has received what was in effect an interest free loan from the government equal to the amount of the taxes on the deferred income. The value of the deferral increases as the span of time between the year deductions are claimed and the year of disposition of the investment increases.

The second element of many tax shelters was conversion of ordinary income to capital gains. Conversion is achieved when the taxpayer claims a deduction against ordinary income, but the income that later offsets the deduction is taxed at a lower rate, usually due to the capital gains preference. In some cases conversion was eliminated or limited by "recapture" rules, requiring a portion of the later income realized on a sale of the investment to be recharacterized as ordinary income, but the recapture rules never have been comprehensive.

Leverage, the use of borrowed money to purchase the tax shelter investment, magnifies the effect of the first two elements of the tax-shelter, as well as providing the normal economic benefit of financial leverage. Whenever an investor uses borrowed money to finance an investment that has a yield rate greater than the interest rate on the loan, the investor receives a before tax rate of return from invested equity greater than would have been received if the entire investment had been equity financed. In addition, because taxpayers are allowed deductions for expenditures paid with borrowed funds, the tax shelter benefits of the investment also are increased.[1]

One or more of the basic elements of a tax shelter could be used by tax shelter promoters in a wide-variety of activities—real estate, oil and gas, drilling, equipment leasing, master recordings, films and video productions, animal breeding and feeding, mining operations, farm crops, vineyards and many more. Initially, the IRS attacked these tax shelter operations by using generalized statutory or judicially developed approaches. In some cases, the courts applied § 183 to deny deductions, even though that section had been enacted originally to distinguish personal from profits seeking activities. Compare, e.g., Karr v. Commissioner, 924 F.2d 1018 (11th Cir.1991) and Smith v. Commissioner, 937 F.2d 1089 (6th Cir.1991). In other cases, the courts disallowed deductions associated with tax shelter investments on the basis that the transactions were "shams" or "lacked economic substance." See e.g., Rose v. Commissioner, 868 F.2d 851 (6th Cir.1989). In still other cases, the courts would allow deductions for any actual cash investment but would disallow those related to non-economical debt. See, e.g., Brannen v. Commissioner, 722 F.2d 695 (11th Cir.1984).

While there were a number of weapons at the disposal of the Internal Revenue Service, the result of litigation in any given case was always unpredictable and taxpayers prevailed in tax shelter litigation in a significant number of cases. As a result, in 1976 and again in 1986, Congress responded with statutory provisions designed to limit tax shelter deductions (which, of course, it had encouraged in the first place by enacting or continuing the preferential tax provisions on which the shelters were built). The initial provision, § 465, was rather limited in scope, and even though its applicability has been expanded a number times since 1976, it continues to limit only deductions attributable to nonrecourse debt or some other financing arrangement under which the taxpayer-investor is not "at risk." Even then, most commercially financed real estate investment partnerships are beyond its ambit. The second provision, the limitation on "passive activity" loss deductions in § 469, is far more draconian and applies to virtually all limited partners, "silent" general partners, and members of limited liability companies taxed as partnerships who are not managers of the limited liability company.

Both of these provisions are applied at the partner level, after the partners' distributive shares have been determined and the § 704(d) limita-

---

1. For more detailed discussion, see McDaniel, McMahon, Simmons, and Abreu, Federal Income Taxation, 5th ed., 1273–77 (Foundation Press 2004).

tion of partnership losses to the individual partner's basis for the partnership interest has been applied. Nevertheless, the terms of the partnership agreement and related collateral agreements often are crucial in determining whether one or both of § 465 and § 469 apply to a particular partner.

SECTION 2.   THE AT RISK RULES OF SECTION 465

INTERNAL REVENUE CODE: Sections 465(a)(1) and (2), (b), (d), (e).

PROPOSED REGULATIONS: Sections 1.465–6(b), –24(a)(2).

Senate Finance Committee Report, Tax Reform Act of 1976

S.Rep. No. 94–938, 94th Cong., 2D. Sess. 47–51 (1976).

To prevent a situation where the taxpayer may deduct a loss in excess of his economic investment in certain types of activities, [§ 465(a)] provides that the amount of any loss (otherwise allowable for the year under present law) which may be deducted in connection with one of these activities, cannot exceed the aggregate amount with respect to which the taxpayer is at risk in each such activity at the close of the taxable year. * * *

The at risk limitation is to apply on the basis of the facts existing at the end of each taxable year.

In applying the at risk limitation, the amount of any loss which is allowable in a particular year reduces the taxpayer's at risk investment (but not below zero) as of the end of that year and in all succeeding taxable years with respect to that activity. Thus, if a taxpayer has a loss in excess of his at risk amount, the loss disallowed will not be allowed in a subsequent year unless the taxpayer increases his at risk amount.

Losses which are suspended under this provision with respect to a taxpayer because they are greater than the taxpayer's investment which is "at risk" are to be treated as a deduction with respect to the activity in the following year. Consequently, if a taxpayer's amount at risk increases in later years, he will be able to obtain the benefit of previously suspended losses to the extent that such increases in his amount at risk exceed his losses in later years.

The at risk limitation also applies regardless of the method of accounting used by the taxpayer and regardless of the kind of deductible expenses which contributed to the loss.

The at risk limitation is only intended to limit the extent to which certain losses in connection with the covered activities may be deducted in the year claimed by the taxpayer. The rules of this provision do not apply for other purposes, such as the determination of basis. * * *

For purposes of this provision, a taxpayer is generally to be considered "at risk" with respect to an activity to the extent of his cash and the adjusted basis of other property contributed to the activity, as well as any amounts borrowed for use in the activity with respect to which the taxpayer has personal liability for payment from his personal assets. (Also, * * * a taxpayer is at risk to the extent of his net fair market value of personal assets which secure nonrecourse borrowings.)

A taxpayer is not to be considered at risk with respect to the proceeds from his share of any nonrecourse loan used to finance the activity or the acquisition of property used in the activity. In addition, if the taxpayer borrows money to contribute to the activity and the lender's recourse is either the taxpayer's interest in the activity or property used in the activity, the amount of the proceeds of the borrowing are to be considered amounts financed on a nonrecourse basis and do not increase the taxpayer's amount at risk.

Also, under these rules, a taxpayer's capital is not "at risk" in the business, even as to the equity capital which he has contributed to the extent he is protected against economic loss of all or part of such capital by reason of an agreement or arrangement for compensation or reimbursement to him of any loss which he may suffer. Under this concept, an investor is not "at risk" if he arranges to receive * * * compensation for an economic loss after the loss is sustained, or if he is entitled to reimbursement for part or all of any loss by reason of a binding agreement between himself and another person.

* * *

A taxpayer's at risk amount is generally to include amounts borrowed for use in the activity which is secured by property other than property used in the activity. For example, if the taxpayer uses personally-owned real estate to secure nonrecourse indebtedness, the proceeds from which are used in an equipment leasing activity, the proceeds may be considered part of the taxpayer's at risk amount. In such a case, the portion of the proceeds which increases the taxpayer's at risk amount is to be limited by the fair market value of the property used as collateral (determined as of the date the property is pledged as security), less any prior (or superior) claims to which the collateral is subject.

* * *

The rules treating a taxpayer as being "at risk" with respect to the net value of pledged property also do not apply to nonrecourse loans if the lender has an interest, other than as a creditor, in the activity or if the lender is related to the taxpayer (within the meaning of section 267(b)). * * *

Pritchett v. Commissioner

United States Court of Appeals, Ninth Circuit, 1987.
827 F.2d 644.

■ SKOPIL, CIRCUIT JUDGE:

We must decide in this case whether taxpayers, limited partners in five similar partnerships engaged in oil and gas drilling operations, were "at risk" pursuant to 26 U.S.C. § 465 on certain recourse notes and thus entitled to deduct distributive shares of non-cash partnership losses. The Tax Court in a reviewed, split decision held that each taxpayer was at risk only to the extent of actual cash contribution. Pritchett v. Commissioner, 85 T.C. 580 (1985). We reject the Tax Court's rationale in holding that taxpayers were not at risk on the recourse debt. We remand to allow the Tax Court to consider the Commissioner's alternative theory that taxpayers were not at risk because the creditor had an impermissible role in the activity at issue. See 26 U.S.C. § 465(b)(3).

FACTS AND PROCEEDINGS BELOW

Taxpayers are each members in similar limited partnerships formed to conduct oil and gas operations. All five partnerships entered into agreements with Fairfield Drilling Corporation ("Fairfield") whereby Fairfield agreed to drill, develop, and exploit any productive wells. Fairfield provided all necessary equipment and expertise. Pursuant to a "turnkey" agreement, each partnership paid cash and executed a recourse note to Fairfield. Each note was non-interest-bearing and matured in fifteen years. Each was secured by virtually all of the maker-partnership's assets. The principal for each note was to be paid from net income available to each partnership if the drilling operations proved successful. Only the general partners were personally liable under the notes. Nevertheless, each partnership agreement provided that if the notes were not paid off at maturity, the limited partners would be personally obligated to make additional capital contributions to cover the deficiency when called upon to do so by the general partners.

Each partnership elected to use accrual accounting and to deduct intangible drilling costs as an expense. The partnership agreements provided that all losses were to be allocated among limited partners in proportion to their respective capital contributions. Because there was no income in the tax year in question, each limited partner deducted from taxable income a distributive share of partnership loss. The Commissioner disallowed that portion of the deduction based on the note.

The Tax Court affirmed by a 9–7 vote the Commissioner's action. The majority held that under the partnership agreements the limited partners had no personal liability on the notes for the tax year in question and therefore they were at risk under section 465 only for the actual cash contribution made to the partnerships. *Pritchett*, 85 T.C. at 590. Any potential liability was "merely a contingency" since in the first year of the partnership it was not known whether income would be sufficient to pay off the note or even whether the general partners would in fact exercise their discretion to make a cash call on an unpaid balance fifteen years later. Id. at 588.

Seven judges dissented in three separate opinions. One judge reasoned that for federal tax purposes, "both general and limited partners are personally liable for a pro rata portion of the partnership's recourse obligation to Fairfield." Id. at 594 (Whitaker, J., dissenting). Another found nothing in the agreements to indicate the general partners had unilateral discretion to waive the cash call. Id. at 599 (Cohen, J., dissenting). A majority of the dissenting judges apparently believed, however, that the Commissioner's actions might be affirmed on the alternative ground that section 465(b)(3)(A) provides that amounts borrowed are not at risk if the money is borrowed from someone with an interest in the activity at issue. E.g., id. at 593 (Whitaker, J., dissenting)("majority may have inadvertently reached the right result, although for the wrong reasons"). The majority notes this alternative ground but expressly does not adopt it. Id. at 590.

These timely appeals followed.

DISCUSSION

In 1976 Congress added section 465 to the Internal Revenue Code to combat abuse of tax shelters caused by nonrecourse financing. * * * Section 465 forbids a taxpayer from taking a loss in excess of amounts at risk in the investment.

The limited partners argue that the notes create at risk debt because each limited partner is personally liable. The contract provisions provide that if the notes are not paid off by the successful drilling operations, "the General Partners will by written notice call for additional capital contributions in an amount sufficient to pay the outstanding balance" and that "[e]ach Limited Partner shall be obligated to pay in cash to the Partnership" the amount called. (Emphasis added). It is clear, however, as the majority opinion notes, that the limited partners are not directly and personally liable to Fairfield. *Pritchett*, 85 T.C. at 587–88. Even assuming a third party beneficiary right, Fairfield had no recourse against the limited partners until the end of the note's fifteen year term.

Whether the Tax Court's decision is correct hinges on its characterization of taxpayers' obligation as indirect and secondary. In a decision rendered shortly after *Pritchett*, the Tax Court sought to distinguish between direct and indirect liability. Abramson v. Commissioner, 86 T.C. 360, 375–76 (1986). In that reviewed decision, the Tax Court, by a 15–1 vote, held that limited partners' pro rata shares of partnership debt that was to be repaid in whole or in part out of partnership revenues was at risk. Id. The limited partners had a direct contractual liability to a third party seller of goods. *Abramson* distinguished *Pritchett* by noting:

> In Pritchett the limited partners were not directly liable to the lender on the partnership obligation. Rather, the general partner was personally liable to the lender on the recourse obligation, and the limited partners were, if anything, potential indemnitors of the general partner. The limited partners were not obligated on any debt for purposes of section 465 until the general partner called for contributions to the partnership. Consequently, in *Pritchett*, the limited partners had not borrowed any amount within the meaning of section 465(b)(2). In this case, to the contrary, each partner

is personally and directly liable for a pro rata part of the amount owed to the seller * * *. Because each partner's liability for the partnership debt (in the words of the statute, for the "amounts borrowed") ran directly to the seller and each partner's liability was personal, each partner is at risk for his proportionate share of amount owed to the seller.

Id. at 376.

We agree that Congress intended to condition section 465's exclusion of deductions in part on whether the liability for borrowing is primary or secondary. The statute expressly requires that the taxpayer be "personally liable for the repayment." 26 U.S.C. § 465(b)(2)(A). In debate on the Deficit Reduction Act of 1984, a House Report explained that section 465 limits an at-risk loss to, *inter alia*, "amounts borrowed for use in the activity with respect to which the taxpayer has *personal* liability." H.R.Rep. No. 98–432, Part II, 98th Cong., 2d Sess. 1506, reprinted in 1984 U.S.Code Cong. & Admin.News 697, 1146 (emphasis added). If the limited partnership agreements here create only contingent liability, we will affirm the Tax Court's decision to disallow taxpayers' deductions.

We conclude, however, that the liability of the limited partners was unavoidable and hence not contingent. In Melvin v. Commissioner, 88 T.C. 63 (1987), the Tax Court appeared to answer the question posed here by concluding that

> the fact that the partnership or other partners remain in the "chain of liability" should not detract from the at-risk amount of the parties who do have the ultimate liability. The critical inquiry should be who is the obligor of last resort, and in determining who has the ultimate economic responsibility for the loan, the substance of the transaction controls.

Melvin, 88 T.C. at 75 (citing Raphan v. United States, 759 F.2d 879, 885 (Fed.Cir.1985)). Applying that standard we have no reservation in concluding that taxpayers, by virtue of their contractual obligations, have ultimate responsibility for the debt. See Bennion v. Commissioner, 88 T.C. 684, 695 (1987) (applying the *Melvin* standard to taxpayer's "Guarantee Agreement" to determine that taxpayer was ultimately liable on a debt obligation even though the obligation flowed through others). Furthermore, we are not dissuaded by the Tax Court's reasoning that the debt is contingent because the general partners may elect to not make the cash calls. The contracts made the call mandatory and "economic reality" dictates that the partners would do so. See Durkin v. Commissioner, 87 T.C. 1329, 1379 (1986) (concluding that economic reality assured that promissory notes of limited partners to the partnership would be enforced).

The Tax Court also reasoned that the debt was contingent since it was not known in the tax year in question whether sufficient partnership revenues would satisfy the notes prior to or on maturity. We find the Tax Court's reasoning on this point faulty. If the notes required balloon payments upon maturity, the limited partners' obligation to contribute additional funds would be "certain." The acceleration of payments should not be a factor in the taxation analysis. In *Abramson*, like this case, early payment was tied to the success of the operation. No mention was made in *Abramson* that the debt was contingent. Furthermore, the fact that the obligation may not become due for several years in the future is of no significance to the allocation of a pro rata share of the taxpayers' debt in the tax year in question. See Taube v. Commissioner, 88 T.C. 464, 487 (1987) (debt due years in future is nevertheless genuine indebtedness fully includable in basis) * * *.

The Commissioner argued below and on appeal that taxpayers' deductions are alternatively barred by section 465(b)(3). That subsection provides that "amounts borrowed shall not be considered to be at risk with respect to an activity if such amounts are borrowed from any person who * * * has an interest (other than an interest as a creditor) in such activity." 26 U.S.C. § 465(b)(3)(A). The legislative history suggests that "*any type of financial interest* in the activity (other than as a creditor) would constitute a prohibited 'other interest' under section 465." *Bennion*, 88 T.C. at 696 (citing to Staff of Joint Committee on Taxation, General Explanation of Tax Reform Act of 1976 at 39, 1976–3 C.B. (Vol. 2) 51) (emphasis in original). Furthermore, proposed Treasury regulations provide that a lender will be deemed to have a prohibited interest if it has either a capital interest or an interest in the net profits of the activity. See id. (citing Sec. 1.465–8(b), Proposed Income Tax Regs., 44 Fed.Reg. 32239 (June 5, 1979)).

The agreements here provided that Fairfield would receive twenty percent of the gross sales of oil and gas, payable if the partnerships achieved certain profit levels. Judge Simpson concluded that these arrangements gave Fairfield a "substantial interest" in the partnership. *Pritchett*, 85 T.C. at 592 (Simpson, J., concurring). Judge Cohen stated that she shared Judge Simpson's impression that Fairfield appears to be a person having an interest in the activity, but that "[t]his should be explored further by the finder of facts." Id. at 599 (Cohen J., dissenting). We agree with Judge Cohen's suggestion that this possibility should be explored further. Although we may affirm a correct decision on any basis supported by the record, remand is appropriate when a lower court's "application of an incorrect legal standard leaves * * * an inadequate factual record on which to affirm." United States v. Washington, 641 F.2d 1368, 1371 (9th Cir.1981), cert. denied, 454 U.S. 1143 (1982).[*]

* * *

ILLUSTRATIVE MATERIAL

1. COVERED ACTIVITIES

Section 465 applies to any activity conducted as a business or for profit by individuals (including trusts and estates), whether as a proprietor, a

---

* On remand, in Pritchett v. Commissioner, T.C. Memo. 1989–21, aff'd by order, 944 F.2d 908 (9th Cir.1991), the Tax Court held that a mineral royalty interest is not a prohibited interest, but that a mineral net profits interest is a prohibited interest.

partner, or as a shareholder in an S corporation. I.R.C. § 465(c). See Peters v. Commissioner, 77 T.C. 1158 (1981). Prior to 1987, § 465 did not apply to the activity of holding real estate, but this exception was repealed in the Tax Reform Act of 1986. However, because many real estate activities are financed through nonrecourse borrowing that meets the definition of "qualified nonrecourse financing" in § 465(b)(6), discussed below, most real estate investments continue to be effectively excepted.

Identifying the scope of each activity conducted by the taxpayer is an important issue in applying the at risk rules. Section 465(c)(2) specifically provides that certain activities will be treated as separate, but most business activities are subject to the vague aggregation rules of § 465(c)(3)(B). Suppose that a limited partnership operates a hotel and a shopping center located on the same tract of land. Is it engaged in one activity or two activities? No regulations governing this issue have been promulgated. Compare Temp. Reg. § 1.465–1T (permitting partnerships and S corporations to aggregate, by type, activities described in § 465(c)(2)(A)(i), and (iii)–(v) during 1984); Ann. 87–26, 1987–15 I.R.B. 39 (extending application of Temp. Reg. § 1.465–1T to certain later taxable years).

2. AT RISK AMOUNT

2.1. *General*

2.1.1. *Contributions and Recourse Borrowing*

Section 465(b) prescribes the rules for determining the amount that a taxpayer has at risk. The taxpayer is at risk for the amount of any money contributed to the activity (e.g., the partnership) and for the basis of any contributed property. Generally, amounts borrowed with respect to the property are at risk to the extent that the taxpayer is personally liable for payment of the debt or has pledged property, other than property used in the activity, to secure the debt. Amounts borrowed from any person with an interest in the activity are not at risk. I.R.C. § 465(b)(3). Thus, if Partner A borrows $50,000 from Partner B, with full recourse, to invest in the ABC Partnership, A is not at risk for the $50,000. Presumably, this result rests on the view that B is the one at risk. But if A has adequate resources to stand behind the liability, as long as the debtor-creditor relationship is not a sham, it is difficult to see how the situation presents the problem to which § 465 is addressed. On the other hand, the bright line rule in § 453(b)(3) eliminates the need to make this inquiry in every case of inter-investor borrowing.

The statutory exclusion of amounts borrowed from lenders with an interest in the activity or from related parties from a taxpayer's "at-risk" amount automatically applies only to activities listed in § 465(c)(1). All other activities, which are subject to § 465 by virtue of § 465(c)(3), are subject to § 465(b)(3) only as provided in regulations. I.R.C. § 465(c)(3)(D). Treas. Regs. §§ 1.465–8 and 1.465–20 extend to all activities the rule that amounts borrowed from another party with an interest in the activity (other than a creditor) are not at risk, even if the borrowing is with full recourse. This rule does not apply, however, to amounts that are qualified nonrecourse borrowing under § 465(b)(6), or that would have been qualified nonrecourse borrowing if the debt had been nonrecourse.

Suppose that A, B, and C each contribute $10,000 to the ABC Partnership. Thereafter, A loans the partnership $180,000, with full recourse, and the partnership purchases depreciable real property for $210,000. Under § 707(a), discussed at page 209, A's loan generally is treated as if it were made by a person other than a partner. In addition, Treas. Reg. § 1.752–2, discussed in Chapter 5, treats the liability as a recourse liability of the partnership allocable among the partners according to their economic risk of loss. Under those regulations, A, B and C each would be entitled to increase their bases in their partnership interests by $60,000 from $10,000 to $70,000, on account of the borrowing. Prop.Reg. § 1.465–7(a) (1979) provides that when a partner lends money to a partnership, the lending partner's at risk amount is increased only by the lending partner's share of the resulting partnership liability under the § 752 regulations. Thus, A is at risk for $70,000, the sum of his contribution of $10,000 plus his $60,000 share of the debt. B and C, however, each are at risk only with respect to their $10,000 contribution, even though they each have a basis of $70,000 in their partnership interests. Their at risk amounts will increase as the loan is repaid out of partnership earnings.

Application of § 465(b)(3) in complex arrangements raises numerous interpretative issues regarding exactly what is a prohibited interest and the identity of the true lender. Waddell v. Commissioner, 86 T.C. 848 (1986), held that a creditor had a prohibited interest because payments on the note were contingent on profits. In contrast, Bennion v. Commissioner, 88 T.C. 684 (1987), held that § 465(b)(3) did not apply where a partner was liable to all creditors in a chain and the ultimate lender, who had no interest in the activity, could proceed directly against the taxpayer upon default, even though intermediate creditors had an interest in the activity. In many cases the question is whether a lender who also has another contractual relationship with the partnership has a prohibited interest through the other contract. See also Brady v. Commissioner, T.C. Memo. 1990–626, holding that a right to rental payments computed with respect to gross receipts was not a prohibited interest.

2.1.2. *Adjustments for Partnership Income and Distributions*

A partner's at risk amount is increased by his distributive share of partnership income items and is decreased by distributions to him and his distributive share of partnership deductions. See Prop.Reg. § 1.465–22 (1979); Lansburgh v. Commissioner, 92 T.C. 448 (1989). When a partnership earns net income that is applied to make principal payments on a nonrecourse loan, a partner's at risk amount increases by the partner's share of the income. Thus, depreciation deductions grounded on nonrecourse debt may be claimed to the extent of loan principal amortization. Generally there will be no net increase in the partner's at risk amount unless loan principal amortization payments exceed depreciation deductions for the year. To the extent that loan principal payments are out of partnership capital, however, a partner's at risk amount is unaffected. See generally Prop. Reg. § 1.465–25 (1979); Cooper v. Commissioner, 88 T.C. 84 (1987).

2.2. *Qualified Nonrecourse Financing*

A partner is not at risk with respect to nonrecourse partnership indebtedness, unless the debt is "qualified nonrecourse financing" as defined in § 465(b)(6). This term generally includes only nonrecourse borrowing related to the holding of real property, which is borrowed from an unrelated party (other than the seller of the mortgaged property or the promoter of the partnership) who is regularly engaged in the lending business. Borrowing from related parties regularly engaged in the lending business qualifies only if the terms are commercially reasonable and on substantially the same terms as loans from unrelated persons. In addition, borrowing guaranteed by the federal, state or local government qualifies. Section 465(b)(6) emphasizes the point that the primary abuse at which § 465 is directed is overvaluation in seller financed transactions in which the seller is reporting gain under § 453. In the case of third party lending in real estate transactions, the potential for abuse through artificially inflating basis is not present. Nevertheless, § 465 does apply to third party nonrecourse financing of activities other than real estate, although third party nonrecourse financing of such activities never was as common as it was with respect to real estate.

2.3. *Partner's Guarantee of Partnership Debt*

Generally, a partner's guarantee of a nonrecourse loan made to the partnership avoids the application of § 465. In addition, the entire loan is allocated to the guarantor partner to determine his basis in his partnership interest under Treas. Reg. § 1.752–2(f), Ex. (5). As illustrated in *Pritchett*, guarantees by limited partners of a portion of a loan to a partnership is a method of limiting each limited partner's liability to the partnership's creditors to the partner's pro rata share of the specific debt while rendering the partner at risk as to that amount.

Partners' guarantees do not always work to avoid § 465, however. In Peters v. Commissioner, 89 T.C. 423 (1987), the taxpayer, along with other limited partners, guaranteed a portion of the partnership's nonrecourse indebtedness. Each partner's guarantee extended only to an amount equal to the aggregate deductions that the partner expected to claim. Relying on Brand v. Commissioner, 81 T.C. 821 (1983), the court concluded that Congress did not intend that a guarantor entitled to reimbursement from the primary obligor would be personally liable under § 465(b)(2)(A). Accordingly, because under the applicable state law the guarantor partners were entitled to reimbursement from the partnership if they made good the partnership debt, they were not at risk under § 465(b)(4).[3] The court

---

3. Likewise, if a partner who guarantees a partnership debt is entitled to indemnification or contribution from the partnership or another partner, the guaranteeing partner does not bear the risk of loss with respect to the portion of that debt and concomitantly receives no basis increase. See Treas. Reg. § 1.752–2(f), Ex. (3).

distinguished its earlier opinion in *Abramson*, discussed in *Pritchett*, on the ground that under the agreements in *Abramson* "the limited partners were primarily and ultimately liable because neither the partnership nor its general assets (other than the motion picture film in question) was subject to the nonrecourse obligation. Thus, there was no primary obligor against whom the taxpayers would have had a right of subrogation." In contrast, in *Peters* the court concluded that the partnership was the only primary obligor, as evidenced by the manner in which the amounts of the guarantees were computed; the guarantees "having in effect been voluntarily given, were at most lagniappe as far as [the lender] was concerned."

Is the difference between *Peters* and *Pritchett* merely form? Suppose that the partners were called upon to make good on their guarantees. The *Peters* court acknowledged that in such an event it would be unlikely that the partnership would have any assets with which to reimburse the guarantor-partners. Nevertheless, it concluded that since the taxpayers chose the use of guarantees "as their means of making an end run around the rules of § 465," they could not selectively ignore their legal rights as guarantors. The opinion in *Peters* indicates that the court was influenced by the blatancy of the method of computing the guaranteed amounts.

In part, the court in *Pritchett* based its holding on the Tax Court's decision in Melvin v. Commissioner, 88 T.C. 63 (1987), aff'd. 894 F.2d 1072 (9th Cir.1990). In *Melvin*, a limited partner contributed his own $70,000 recourse promissory note to a limited partnership to reflect his obligation to make future capital contributions. The partnership borrowed over $3,000,000 from an unrelated lender on a nonrecourse basis, pledging partnership property, including the taxpayer's promissory note, to secure the loan. The taxpayer stipulated that the mere contribution of the note did not increase his at risk amount under § 465(b)(1), and the Tax Court approved the stipulation, noting that the contributed promissory note reflected neither a cash contribution nor a borrowing under § 465(b)(1). Nonetheless, the Tax Court held that the taxpayer was at risk with respect to the $70,000 promissory note even though primary responsibility for repayment of the nonrecourse note fell to the partnership: "The relevant question is who, if anyone, will ultimately be obligated to pay the partnership's recourse obligations if the partnership is unable to do so. It is not relevant that the partnership may be able to do so. The scenario that controls is the worst-case scenario, not the best case. Furthermore, the fact that the partnership or other partners remain in the 'chain of liability' should not detract from the at-risk amount of the parties who do have the ultimate liability. The critical inquiry should be who is the obligor of last resort, and in determining who has the ultimate economic responsibility for the loan, the substance of the transaction controls." 88 T.C. at 75. The court also held, however, that under substantive partnership law, each partner had a right to reimbursement from the other partners for any portion of the partnership debt satisfied from the partner's recourse promissory note in excess of the partner's individual share of partnership liabilities. This right of reimbursement protected the taxpayer from any loss in excess of the taxpayer's pro rata share of partnership debt, and thus constituted a stop loss arrangement under § 465(b)(4). As a consequence, the taxpayer was at risk only to the extent of his $21,000 share of the total partnership debt.

Despite the taxpayer's stipulation in *Melvin*, given the holding in *Pritchett*, it is not clear why the contribution of a partner's promissory note should not increase the partner's at risk amount. Even if the contributed promissory note is not pledged, the contributing partner does not appear be in a significantly different economic position from the taxpayer in *Pritchett*, who was obligated under the partnership agreement to make additional contributions to pay partnership debts. Perhaps the crucial distinction is one of form in that the contributed promissory note is "property," but its basis to the contributing partner is zero. Hence, the limitation of a partner's at risk amount to the basis of contributed property in § 465(b)(1)(A) applies. In any event, whether the partner guarantees a partnership nonrecourse debt or contributes a promissory note, the partner's at risk amount might not be increased if there is no realistic possibility that the partner may be called upon to make a payment on the guarantee or promissory note. See Callahan v. Commissioner, 98 T.C. 276 (1992), in which a limited partner who had the right under the partnership agreement to decline to comply with a cash call by the general partner was held to be at risk only for his capital contributions.

2.4. *Loss Limiting Arrangements*

In American Principals Leasing Corp. v. United States, 904 F.2d 477 (9th Cir.1990), the Ninth Circuit took the application of § 465(b)(4) a step further than *Peters* and *Melvin*, and rejected the "worst case scenario approach" in favor of a test based on whether the taxpayer had a realistic possibility of being called upon to satisfy the indebtedness. The taxpayers in *American Principals Leasing Corp.* were limited partners in June Properties, a partnership engaged in computer equipment leasing. June Properties acquired an interest in computer equipment in a series of sale and leaseback transactions. Southwestern Bell Telephone Company originally acquired the equipment from IBM for approximately $2.6 million. Southwestern sold the equipment to an entity called Finalco for an amount equal to Southwestern's purchase price. Finalco borrowed the purchase price from a third party lender. Finalco leased the equipment back to Southwestern for a lease payment that was equivalent to Finalco's debt obligations. The indebtedness was secured by Finalco's lease to Southwestern. Finalco sold the equipment, subject to the lease and security agreement, to Softpro for $4.8 million consisting of $20,000 of cash and two recourse notes for the difference. Softpro sold the equipment to June Properties for $4.8 million consisting of $20,000 cash and recourse notes back to Softpro. June properties leased the equipment to Finalco for rental payments equal to its payment obligation to Softpro. Thus, Finalco's lease payments to June Properties, June Properties' debt obligations on the Softpro note, and Softpro's debt payments to Finalco, were identical. In addition, no party had sufficient resources to make its payments without receiving the payments due it. The parties satisfied the three equal obligations each month by offsetting bookkeeping entries. No cash ever changed hands. The taxpayers were personally liable for $120,000 of June Properties recourse debt and claimed that this amount was at risk. Although the taxpayers were ultimately liable for their share of the partnership's recourse obligation, the court held that they were not at risk under section 465(b)(4):

> We believe that although the * * * analysis of whether a taxpayer would legally be responsible for his debt in a worst-case scenario is proper to determine whether under subsection 465(b)(2) a taxpayer is personally liable for amounts he has borrowed for use in an activity, Pritchett v. Commissioner, 827 F.2d 644, 647 (9th Cir.1987) (quoting Melvin v. Commissioner, 88 T.C. 63, 75 (1987), affirmed, 894 F.2d 1072 (9th Cir.1990)), such analysis is improper to determine whether the taxpayer has engaged in a loss-limiting arrangement prohibited by subsection 465(b)(4). * * * [S]ubsection 465(b)(4)'s use of the term 'arrangement'—rather than 'agreement'—indicates that a binding contract is not necessary for this subsection to be applicable. See Melvin at 1075–76, (holding that subsection 465(b)(4) countenances loss protection resulting from California's tort right of contribution among partners); id. at 1074–75 (noting that S.Rep. No. 938's list of examples of 465(b)(4) arrangements, which includes only binding contractual agreements, 'does not constitute an exhaustive list of such arrangements' ''); Capek, 86 T.C. at 50–53.

> Rather, the purpose of subsection 465(b)(4) is to suspend at risk treatment where a transaction is structured-by whatever method-to remove any realistic possibility that the taxpayer will suffer an economic loss if the transaction turns out to be unprofitable. See Melvin, at 1074. A theoretical possibility that the taxpayer will suffer economic loss is insufficient to avoid the applicability of this subsection. We must be guided by economic reality. See id. at 1075; Pritchett, 827 F.2d at 647. If at some future date the unexpected occurs and the taxpayer does suffer a loss, or a realistic possibility develops that the taxpayer will suffer a loss, the taxpayer will at that time become at risk and be able to take the deductions for previous years that were suspended under this subsection. I.R.C. § 465(a)(2).

Young v. Commissioner, 926 F.2d 1083 (11th Cir.1991), reached a similar result. Investors in a sale and leaseback transaction with a circular flow of funds effected through bookkeeping entries gave an intermediary a partially recourse note. The investor-partners were not personally liable because the intermediary had purchased the leased equipment on a wholly nonrecourse basis, and "the stated recourse liabilities of the taxpayers were not realistically subject to collection after a discharge of the nonrecourse note." Likewise, in Levien v. Commissioner, 103 T.C. 120 (1994), the Tax Court declined to apply the "worst case scenario" test.

However, in Emershaw v. Commissioner, 949 F.2d 841 (6th Cir.1991), the court reached a contrary result on facts similar to those in *American Principals Leasing Corp.* and *Young.* The court in *Emershaw* held that a circular sale and leaseback was not in itself a loss limiting arrangement, because "[a] loss limiting arrangement within the meaning of § 465(b)(4) is *a collateral agreement* protecting a taxpayer from loss *after the losses have occurred,* either by excusing him from his obligation to make good on losses or by compensating him for losses he has sustained." (849, emphasis in original). In Martuccio v. Commissioner, 30 F.3d 743 (6th Cir.1994), the Sixth Circuit expressly rejected American Principals Leasing Corp. and Young and continued to adhere to a "worst case scenario" test.

3.   EFFECT OF AT RISK LIMITATION

3.1.   *Deferral of Deductions*

In general, the effect of § 465 is to defer deductions attributable to nonrecourse debt until the debt is repaid. In computing allowable deductions for the year, however, the taxpayer is permitted to treat deductions as being wholly attributable to his at risk amount-his equity investment or share of recourse debt-until the at risk amount has been exhausted. Thereafter, deductions in excess of current increases in the partner's at risk amount are suspended until the taxpayer increases his at risk amount. A partner's at risk amount can be increased by an additional contribution. Most often, however, partners' at risk amounts are increased when mortgage principal amortization payments in a particular year exceed the depreciation deductions on the property for that year. Upon the sale or other taxable disposition of the activity, deductions that have been deferred under § 465 will be allowable to the extent the sales proceeds are used to repay the debt, thereby increasing the taxpayer's at risk amount. Likewise, if the property is transferred subject to the nonrecourse debt, the partner's at risk amount is increased by his distributive share of the gain from the property, thereby allowing suspended deductions to offset some or all of the gain.

Section 465 operates independently of the rules governing a partner's basis in his partnership interest. Even though a partner has sufficient basis to avoid the application of § 704(d), discussed at page 97, deduction of his distributive share of partnership losses will be postponed if his at risk amount is insufficient. Nevertheless, his basis in his partnership interest is reduced by the full amount of his distributive share of partnership losses. Assume, for example, that A contributes $5,000 cash to acquire a one third interest in profits and capital of the ABC general partnership. The partnership then borrows $285,000 on a nonrecourse basis to drill an oil well. A's basis in his partnership interest, applying the rules of § 752, is $100,000 ($5,000 + ($\frac{1}{3}$ × $285,000)). His at risk amount, however, is only $5,000. Thus, if for the current year A's distributive share of partnership items is a $100,000 loss from drilling a dry hole, he may deduct currently only $5,000 of the loss; § 465 defers the remaining $95,000 deduction. But under § 705, A must reduce the basis of his partnership interest by the full $100,000 loss. Thus, A's basis for his partnership interest is zero. If the oil property is abandoned to the mortgagee the following year, A's distributive share of partnership income will be $95,000, but he will be entitled to claim the $95,000 deduction previously suspended by § 465. The basis of A's partnership interest is unaffected by the allowance of the deduction in the later year under § 465. Basis is increased by his $100,000 share of partnership income, and is reduced by a like amount due to the cancellation of the partnership debt, leaving A with a basis of zero.

3.2. *Recapture of Amounts Previously At Risk*

Section 465(e) requires recapture of previous deductions following a reduction in the taxpayer's amount at risk below the amount previously deducted by the taxpayer. Section 465(e) provides that if the taxpayer's amount at risk in an activity is reduced below zero, the taxpayer will recognize gross income to the extent that zero exceeds the amount at risk. For example, if A purchases an investment in an activity for $10,000 cash plus a recourse note for $90,000, then claims $20,000 of deductions from the activity, A's total amount at risk, reduced by the deductions, is $80,000. See I.R.C. § 465(b)(5). If the note is then converted to a nonrecourse note, A's amount at risk becomes a negative $10,000 ($10,000 cash investment minus $20,000 of deductions). A's at risk amount exceeds zero by $10,000 requiring A to recognize $10,000 of income. Thus A recaptures $10,000 of deductions as gross income. The amount recaptured into income is treated as a suspended deduction from the activity available in a later year when the taxpayer's amount at risk increases. The amount subject to recapture in any taxable year is limited to the total amount of losses from the activity claimed by the taxpayer in prior years reduced by amounts recaptured in prior years. I.R.C. § 465(e)(2).

4. APPLICATION TO LIMITED LIABILITY COMPANIES

The limitations imposed by § 465 are of particular importance to members of a limited liability company (LLC) taxed as a partnership. The members are taxed as partners, and thus pursuant to § 752 increase their bases in their interests in the LLC by their respective shares of the LLC's indebtedness, whether the indebtedness is recourse or nonrecourse to the LLC. For purposes of § 465, however, no member of the LLC is at risk with respect to any portion of the LLC's indebtedness except to the extent that the member has guaranteed the indebtedness without a right of indemnification or contribution.

Assume, for example, that A, B, and C form the ABC LLC, and each contributes $10. The ABC LLC then borrows $330 with full recourse to the entity and pays $360 to purchase depreciable property with a ten year cost recovery period, using straight line depreciation. The ABC LLC breaks even apart from depreciation, the year one depreciation (ignoring conventions) is $36, and no principal payments are made. Each member's distributive share of the loss is $12. A, B and C each have a $120 basis in their interest in the LLC but are at risk for only $10. Thus, only $10 of the $12 loss is currently deductible by each member of the LLC. The remaining $2 of each member's share of the loss is deferred. A, B, and C will not be able to deduct losses in any subsequent years until their at risk amounts increase through either additional contributions or the retention of earnings by the LLC.

Section 3.   The Passive Activity Loss Rules of Section 469

Internal Revenue Code: Sections 469(a), (b), (c)(1)–(4), (7)(A)–(C), (d)(1), (e)(1), (g), (h)(1) and (2), (i)(1)–(3), (6).

Regulations: Section 1.469–4.

Temporary Regulations: Sections 1.469–2T(d)(6)(ii)(A), –5T(a), (b)(2), (c), (e), (f)(2).

Senate Finance Committee Report, Tax Reform Act of 1986

S.Rep. No. 99–313, 99th Cong., 2d Sess. 713–718 (1986).

[Pre–1987] Law

In general, no limitations are placed on the ability of a taxpayer to use deductions from a particular activity to offset income from other activities. Similarly, most tax credits may be used to offset tax attributable to income from any of the taxpayer's activities.

* * *

In the absence of more broadly applicable limitations on the use of deductions and credits from one activity to reduce tax liability attributable to other activities, taxpayers with substantial sources of positive income are able to eliminate or sharply reduce tax liability by using deductions and credits from other activities, frequently by investing in tax shelters. Tax shelters commonly offer the opportunity to reduce or avoid tax liability with respect to salary or other positive income, by making available deductions and credits, possibly exceeding real economic costs or losses currently borne by the taxpayer, in excess or in advance of income from the shelters.

Reasons for Change

* * * Extensive [tax] shelter activity contributes to public concerns that the tax system is unfair, and to the belief that tax is paid only by the naive and the unsophisticated. This, in turn, not only undermines compliance, but encourages further expansion of the tax shelter market, in many cases diverting investment capital from productive activities to those principally or exclusively serving tax avoidance goals.

The committee believes that the most important sources of support for the Federal income tax system are the average citizens who simply report their income (typically consisting predominantly of items such as salaries, wages, pensions, interest, and dividends) and pay tax under the general rules. To the extent that these citizens feel that they are bearing a disproportionate burden with regard to the costs of government because of their unwillingness or inability to engage in tax-oriented investment activity, the tax system itself is threatened.

* * *

The question of how to prevent harmful and excessive tax sheltering is not a simple one. One way to address the problem would be to eliminate substantially all tax preferences in the Internal Revenue Code. For two reasons, however, the committee believes that this course is inappropriate.

First, while the bill reduces or eliminates some tax preference items that the committee believes do not provide social or economic benefits commensurate with their cost, there are many preferences that the committee believes are socially or economically beneficial. This is especially true when such preferences are used primarily to advance the purposes upon which Congress relied in enacting them, rather than to avoid taxation of income from sources unrelated to the preferred activity.

Second, it would be extremely difficult, perhaps impossible, to design a tax system that measures income perfectly. For example, the statutory allowance for depreciation, even under the normative system used under the bill for alternative minimum tax purposes, reflects broad industry averages, as opposed to providing precise item-by-item measurements. Accordingly, taxpayers with assets that depreciate less rapidly than the average, or that appreciate over time (as may be the case with certain real estate), may engage in tax sheltering even under the minimum tax, unless Congress directly addresses the tax shelter problem.

* * *

The question of what constitutes a tax shelter that should be subject to limitations is closely related to the question of who Congress intends to benefit when it enacts tax preferences. For example, in providing preferential depreciation for real estate or favorable accounting rules for farming, it was not Congress's primary intent to permit outside investors to avoid tax liability with respect to their salaries by investing in limited partnership syndications. Rather, Congress intends to benefit and provide incentives to taxpayers active in the businesses to which the preferences were directed.

* * *

The availability of tax benefits to shelter positive sources of income also has harmed the economy generally, by providing a non-economic return on capital for certain investments. This has encouraged a flow of capital away from activities that may provide a higher pre-tax economic return, thus retarding the growth of the sectors of the economy with the greatest potential for expansion.

The committee believes that, in order for tax preferences to function as intended, their benefit must be directed primarily to taxpayers with a substantial and bona fide involvement in the activities to which the preferences relate. The committee also believes that it is appropriate to encourage nonparticipating investors to invest in particular activities, by permitting the use of preferences to reduce the rate of tax on income from those activities; however, such investors should not be permitted to use tax benefits to shelter unrelated income.

There are several reasons why it is appropriate to examine the materiality of a taxpayer's participation in an activity in determining the extent to which such taxpayer should be permitted to use tax benefits from the activity. A taxpayer who materially participates in an activity is more likely than a passive investor to approach the activity with a significant nontax economic profit motive, and to form a sound judgment as to whether the activity has genuine economic significance and value.

A material participation standard identifies an important distinction between different types of taxpayer activities. In general, the more passive investor is seeking a return on capital invested, including returns in the form of reductions in the taxes owed on unrelated income, rather than an ongoing source of livelihood. A material participation standard reduces the importance, for such investors, of the tax-reduction features of an investment, and thus increases the importance of the economic features in an investor's decision about where to invest his funds.

Moreover, the committee believes that restricting the use of losses from business activities in which the taxpayer does not materially participate against other sources of positive income (such as salary and portfolio income) addresses a fundamental aspect of the tax shelter problem. As discussed above, instances in which the tax system applies simple rules at the expense of economic accuracy encourage the structuring of transactions to take advantage of the situations in which such rules give rise to undermeasurement or deferral of income. Such transactions commonly are marketed to investors who do not intend to participate in the transactions, as devices for sheltering unrelated sources of positive income (e.g., salary and portfolio income). Accordingly, by creating a bar against the use of losses from business activities in which the taxpayer does not materially participate to offset positive income sources such as salary and portfolio income, the committee believes that it is possible significantly to reduce the tax shelter problem.

Further, in the case of a nonparticipating investor in a business activity, the committee believes that it is appropriate to treat losses of the activity as not realized by the investor prior to disposition of his interest in the activity. The effort to measure, on an annual basis, real economic losses from passive activities gives rise to distortions, particularly due to the nontaxation of unrealized appreciation and the mismatching of tax deductions and related economic income that may occur, especially where debt financing is used heavily. Only when a taxpayer disposes of his interest in an activity is it possible to determine whether a loss was sustained over the entire time that he held the interest.

The distinction that the committee believes should be drawn between activities on the basis of material participation bears no relationship to the question of whether, and to what extent, the taxpayer is at risk with respect to the activities.[6] In general, the fact that a taxpayer has placed a particular amount at risk in an activity does not establish, prior to a disposition of the taxpayer's interest, that the amount invested, or any amount, has as yet been lost. The fact that a taxpayer is potentially liable with respect to future expenses or losses of the activity likewise has no bearing on the question whether any amount has as yet been lost, or otherwise is an appropriate current deduction or credit.

At-risk standards, although important in determining the maximum amount that is subject to being lost, are not a sufficient basis for determining whether or when net losses from an activity should be deductible against other sources of income, or for determining whether an ultimate economic loss has been realized. Congress' goal of making tax preferences available principally to active participants in substantial businesses, rather than to investors seeking to shelter unrelated income, can best be accomplished by examining material participation, as opposed to the financial stake provided by an investor to purchase tax shelter benefits.

In certain situations, however, the committee believes that financial risk or other factors, rather than material participation, should be the relevant standard. A situation in which financial risk is relevant relates to the oil and gas industry, which at present is suffering severe hardship due to the worldwide collapse of oil prices. The committee believes that relief for this industry requires that tax benefits be provided to attract outside investors. Moreover, the committee believes that such relief should be provided only with respect to investors who are willing to accept an unlimited and unprotected financial risk proportionate to their ownership interests in the oil and gas activities. Granting tax shelter benefits to investors in oil and gas activities who did not accept unlimited risk, proportionate to their ownership investments in the activities, would permit the benefit of this special exception to be diverted unduly to the investors, while providing less benefit to oil and gas activities and threatening the integrity of the entire rule limiting the use of nonparticipatory business losses.

A further area in which the material participation standard is not wholly adequate is that of rental activities. Such activities predominantly involve the production of income from capital. * * *

Rental activities generally require less ongoing management activity, in proportion to capital invested, than business activities involving the

---

6. The at-risk rules of present law, while important and useful in preventing overvaluation of assets, and in preventing the transfer of tax benefits to taxpayers with no real equity in an activity, do not address the adverse consequences arising specifically from such transfers to nonparticipating investors.

production or sale of goods and services. Thus, for example, an individual who is employed full-time as a professional could more easily provide all necessary management in his spare time with respect to a rental activity than he could with respect to another type of business activity involving the same capital investment. The extensive use of rental activities for tax shelter purposes under present law, combined with the reduced level of personal involvement necessary to conduct such activities, make clear that the effectiveness of the basic passive loss provision could be seriously compromised if material participation were sufficient to avoid the limitations in the case of rental activities.

A limited measure of relief, however, is believed appropriate in the case of certain moderate-income investors in rental real estate, who otherwise might experience cash flow difficulties with respect to investments that in many cases are designed to provide financial security, rather than to shelter a substantial amount of other income.

Further, additional considerations apply in the case of limited partnerships. In order to maintain limited liability status, a limited partner generally is precluded from materially participating in the business activity of the partnership; in virtually all respects, a limited partner more closely resembles a shareholder in a C corporation than an active business entrepreneur. Moreover, limited partnerships commonly are used as vehicles for marketing tax benefits to investors seeking to shelter unrelated income. In light of the widespread use of limited partnership interests in syndicating tax shelters, the committee believes that losses from limited partnership interests should not be permitted, prior to a taxable disposition, to offset positive income sources such as salary.

* * *

ILLUSTRATIVE MATERIAL

1. GENERAL

Section 469 applies to individual partners, not directly to the partnership. Section 469 does not apply to a partner that is a C corporation, however, unless the corporation is "closely held." I.R.C. § 469(a)(2)(B). The rules of § 469 may disallow a partner's deduction of his distributive share of a partnership loss, even though the loss is allowable under both § 704(d) and § 465. For rules governing the coordination of § 469 with § 704(d) and § 465, see Temp. Reg. § 1.469–2T(d)(6). When § 469 disallows a partner's distributive share of a partnership loss the partner's basis in his partnership interest should be reduced by the full distributive share of partnership losses notwithstanding that § 469 defers the deduction. See S.Rep. No. 993–13, 99th Cong., 2d Sess. 723, n. 9 (1986).

2. TREATMENT OF PASSIVE ACTIVITY LOSSES

Mechanically, § 469(a) disallows any "passive activity loss." A passive activity loss is defined in § 469(d)(1) as the aggregate losses from all passive activities for the year in excess of the aggregate income from such activities for the year. In this context, the term losses means the amount by which all otherwise allowable deductions exceed gross income; and income means the amount by which gross income exceeds deductions. Thus, if Passive Activity A generates $1,000 of income and $1,200 of deductions, and Passive Activity B generates $500 of deductions and $600 of gross income, the taxpayer has a $100 passive activity loss for the year which will be disallowed. Temp. Reg. § 1.469–1T(f) provides rules for allocating the disallowed loss among the various passive activities that contributed to it, and then allocating the loss attributable to each activity among the component deductions. The disallowed loss carries over to the next year, where it enters the computation again; and this carry-over continues until the loss is allowed or permanently disallowed. I.R.C. § 469(b). Thus, § 469, like § 465, generally operates to defer, not totally disallow, deductions attributable to passive activities. Furthermore, it allows a full current deduction for passive activity losses to the extent the taxpayer has current passive activity income from other sources.

3.   DEFINITION OF PASSIVE ACTIVITY

3.1.   *"Passive Activity"*

A "passive activity" generally is any trade or business activity in which the taxpayer does not "materially participate." I.R.C. § 469(c)(1). However, all rental activities are deemed to be passive activities regardless of the level of the taxpayer's participation. I.R.C. § 469(c)(2). For the definition of rental activity, see Temp. Reg. § 1.469–1T(e)(3). Section 469(h) defines material participation as regular, continuous, and substantial involvement in the operations of the activity. In addition, § 469(h)(2) specifically provides that except as provided in regulations, "no interest in a limited partnership as a limited partner shall be treated as an interest with respect to which a taxpayer materially participates." The temporary regulations generally test for material participation by counting the number of hours devoted to the activity each year by the taxpayer and permit limited partners to be treated as materially participating under certain circumstances. Temp. Reg. § 1.469–5T(a). In applying these rules each partner's individual participation must be tested separately.

3.2.   *"Material Participation"*

Under Temp. Reg. § 1.469–5T(a), a taxpayer materially participates in an activity if any of the following tests are met: (1) the taxpayer devotes more than 500 hours to the activity in the year; (2) the taxpayer is the only individual who participates in the activity; (3) the taxpayer participates in the activity for more than 100 hours during the year and his participation is not less than that of any other individual; (4) the activity is a trade or business, the taxpayer participates in the activity for more than 100 hours (but not more than 500 hours) during the year, and the taxpayer's total participation in all such trade or business activities during the year exceeds 500 hours; (5) the taxpayer materially participated in the activity for five of the preceding ten taxable years; (6) the activity is a personal service activity in which the taxpayer materially participated for any three preceding years; or (7) based on all the facts and circumstances, the taxpayer participates in the activity on a regular, continuous, and substantial basis. Work not customarily performed by the owner of a business is not taken into account if one of the principal purposes of performing such work is to meet the material participation requirement. Unless an individual also participates in the day-to-day management or operations of the business, work performed in the capacity of an investor is not counted. Temp. Reg. § 1.469–5T(f)(2). A taxpayer who participates in an activity for 100 hours or less during the year cannot qualify as materially participating under the facts and circumstances test. Temp. Reg. § 1.469–5T(b)(2)(iii). Management services are taken into account in determining material participation only to a limited extent in applying the facts and circumstances test. Temp. Reg. § 1.469–5T(b)(2)(ii).

3.3. *"Significant Participation Activities"*

If the taxpayer's gross income from certain passive activities that are "significant participation activities" exceeds the deductions from all significant participation activities for the taxable year, then a portion of the net income from significant participation activities is treated as active income. Temp. Reg. § 1.469–2T(f)(2). The temporary regulations define as a "significant participation activity" any activity in which the taxpayer participates for more than 100 hours during the year, but in which he does not materially participate.

3.4. *Application to Partners and LLC Members*

It is clear from these rules that a general partner does not qualify as materially participating merely because of his status as a general partner. The level of participation in each activity in which the partnership is engaged must be tested separately. A partner may be active as to some partnership activities and passive as to others.

Section 469(h)(2) generally requires that a limited partner be treated as not materially participating in any partnership activity. The definition of a limited partner in Treas. Reg. § 1.469–5T(e)(3)(B) as a partner whose liability is limited to a fixed amount (including the partner's capital contribution) includes a member of an LLC. Temp. Reg. § 1.469–5T(e) provides two exceptions to § 469(h)(2). First, a limited partner materially participates in a partnership activity if any one of tests (1), (5), or (6) for material participation described above are met. Second, a limited partnership interest held by a general partner is not treated as a limited partnership interest in applying § 469; whether the partner materially participates is determined for both interests together under the above described tests. This final rule may appear to contradict the statutory language of § 469(h)(2), but is within the Treasury's regulatory authority under that provision.

3.5. *Special Rule for Oil and Gas Working Interests*

Section 469(c)(3) provides that any working interest in an oil or gas property is treated as not being a passive activity if the taxpayer holds the interest in a form that does not limit liability, even though the taxpayer does not materially participate. Thus, a general partnership interest qualifies as active, but a limited partnership interest does not. If any losses from a property are treated as active under this rule, all income from the property in future years must be treated as active income. I.R.C. § 469(c)(3)(B); see Temp. Reg. § 1.469–2T(c)(6).

4. APPLICATION ON ACTIVITY–BY–ACTIVITY BASIS

4.1. *General*

Whether a partner's distributive share of any partnership item is treated as active or passive is determined by whether the taxpayer materially participated in the particular activity that gave rise to the item during the partnership's taxable year. Temp. Reg. § 1.469–2T(e)(1). The Code does not provide guidance for determining the scope of an activity, but such a determination is crucial in applying § 469. The Committee Reports indicate that a single activity consists of those "undertakings [that] consist of an integrated and interrelated economic unit, conducted in coordination with or reliance upon each other, and constituting an appropriate unit for the measurement of gain or loss." S.Rep. No. 99–313, 99th Cong., 2d Sess. 739 (1986). Thus, it is clear that a single partnership may be engaged in more than one activity. It is also clear that two related partnerships may be engaged together in a single activity. Under this standard, a partner may materially participate with respect to one partnership activity, but not with respect to a different partnership activity during the same year. In such a case, the partner's distributive share of partnership items attributable to the activity in which he did not materially participate would be passive income or loss.

4.2. *Scope of "Activity"*

Treas. Reg. § 1.469–4 adopts a facts and circumstances approach to identifying separate business activities. Two or more business activities are treated as a single activity "if the activities constitute an appropriate economic unit for the measurement of gain or loss for purposes of section 469." Treas. Reg. § 1.469–4(c)(1). In making this determination, five evidentiary factors are given the greatest weight: (1) similarities and differences in the type of business, (2) the extent of common control, (3) the extent of common ownership, (4) geographical location, and (5) business interdependency, such as the extent to which the activities purchase or sell goods between themselves, involve products or services that are normally provided together, have the same customers, have the same employees, or share a single set of books and records. Treas. Reg. § 1.469–4(c)(2).

A taxpayer may use any reasonable method of applying the relevant facts and circumstances in grouping activities, subject to a consistency requirement. Treas. Reg. § 1.469–4(c)(1). Once a taxpayer has grouped activities, they may not be regrouped unless the original grouping was inappropriate. Furthermore, the taxpayer subsequently must regroup the activities if warranted by a material change in facts and circumstances. Treas. Reg. § 1.469–4(e)(2). Finally, a taxpayer generally may elect to treat the disposition of a substantial part of an activity as a complete disposition of a separate activity, thus allowing suspended losses to be used in that year. Treas. Reg. § 1.469–4(g). The taxpayer's grouping generally is binding on the Service. It may group activities differently than the taxpayer only if the taxpayer's grouping fails to reflect appropriate economic units and one of the primary purposes of the taxpayer's grouping was to circumvent § 469. Treas. Reg. § 1.469–4(f).

Taxpayers have significant flexibility under these regulations. For example, if a taxpayer owns a video arcade and a restaurant at a shopping mall in Sacramento and a video arcade and a restaurant in San Francisco, depending on other relevant facts and circumstances, it may be reasonable to (1) group the video arcades and restaurants into a single activity, (2) group the Sacramento video arcade and restaurant into a single activity and the San Francisco video arcade and restaurant into a different activity; or (3) treat each video arcade and restaurant as a separate activity. See Treas. Reg. § 1.469–4(c)(3), Ex. (1).

A rental activity (as defined in Temp. Reg. § 1.469–1T(e)(3)) may not be grouped with a nonrental activity unless one of the activities is insubstantial relative to the other. Treas. Reg. § 1.469–4(d). Thus, for example, if the taxpayer owned a six-story office building, occupying three floors to conduct a business and leasing out three floors to tenants, the rental business is a separate activity from the other business. Real property rental activities and personal property rental activities never may be grouped, unless the personal property is provided in connection with the real property, for example, the rental of furnished apartments. Treas. Reg. § 1.469–4(d)(2).

Application of these rules to a taxpayer who is a partner can be a bit more complex. First, the partnership must group its activities under the general rules, and the individual partners must group their interests in activities conducted directly or through different partnerships. A partner may not treat activities that have been grouped by the partnership as separate activities. Treas. Reg. § 1.469–4(d)(5). Special rules further limit grouping by limited partners of activities conducted through different limited partnerships. Treas. Reg. § 1.469–4(d)(3).

5. SPECIAL RULE FOR RENTAL REAL ESTATE ACTIVITIES OF PERSONS IN REAL PROPERTY BUSINESS

Section 469(c)(7) relaxes the passive activity loss rules for taxpayers who provide more than one-half of their work effort during the year in one or more real estate businesses if (1) the taxpayer materially participates within the meaning of § 469(h), and (2) the taxpayer works more than 750 hours in such activities. If these tests are met, the taxpayer's real estate rental activities are not automatically treated as passive activities under

§ 469(c)(2). Instead each activity is evaluated using the material participation rules of § 469(h)(2). Any rental activity in which the taxpayer materially participates under that test is not subject to § 469; any losses from that activity are fully deductible against the taxpayer's income from other sources. Material participation in a rental real estate activity is determined separately with respect to each interest unless the taxpayer elects to aggregate all real estate activities.

This relief provision was intended primarily to benefit real estate developers, allowing them to offset income from development activities with losses from rental operations, but because real estate activities are broadly defined, its application is wider. For example, a real estate broker who is the managing general partner of a limited partnership holding an apartment building for rental may be able to deduct losses from the partnership against commission income from a brokerage business or investment income completely unrelated to real estate activities. Furthermore, if married taxpayers file joint returns and one spouse meets the test for being engaged in a real estate business, losses from that spouse's material participation rental real estate activities may be deducted against all income on the joint return, including the other spouse's income. Rental activity losses of the spouse not in the real estate business, however, remain subject to § 469 and may not be deducted other than as passive activity losses.

6.   "ACTIVE PARTICIPATION" RENTAL REAL ESTATE ACTIVITIES

For individuals and some decedent's estates, § 469(i) relaxes the restrictions on deducting losses from passive activities with respect to losses from rental real estate activities in which the taxpayer "actively participates." Section 469(i)(6) defines "active participation." Under this provision, no partner with less than a 10 percent interest (by value) in the activity (as distinguished from the partnership) may be considered as actively participating. However, no limited partner, regardless of the extent of his interest, can be treated as actively participating. If the active participation standard is met, a taxpayer may deduct against income that is not passive income up to $25,000 of rental real estate losses. These losses must first be offset against any passive income, however, and the $25,000 ceiling is reduced by one half of the amount by which the taxpayer's adjusted gross income (without taking such losses into account) exceeds $100,000. Thus a partner who fails the material participation standard, but who meets the active participation standard may be able to deduct currently all or a part of his distributive share of partnership losses attributable to rental real estate activities. This provision, however, is directed primarily to individuals who live in one part of a multi-unit residence and rent out the remaining units.

7.   PORTFOLIO INCOME

Even if a partner does not materially participate in the activities of a partnership, her distributive share of portfolio income items (defined generally as all income other than income derived in the ordinary course of a trade or business) received by the partnership is not passive income. Temp.

Reg. § 1.469–2T(c)(3). Thus, for example, interest on a reserve maintained in connection with a partnership activity with respect to which a partner is passive is not passive activity income for the partner. See Temp. Reg. § 1.469–2T(c)(3)(iv), Ex. (2).

Income from publicly traded limited partnerships that escape classification as associations under § 7704, discussed at page 31, largely resembles portfolio income, such as dividends. To prevent the sheltering of such income by losses from tax shelter limited partnerships, § 469(k) requires that the passive loss rules be applied separately to income and losses from each publicly traded limited partnership. Thus, if a taxpayer has net income from a publicly traded limited partnership and net losses from another limited partnership, whether or not publicly traded, the loss cannot be deducted against the income. In addition, § 469(*l*)(3) authorizes the Treasury to promulgate regulations "requiring net income or gain from a limited partnership or other passive activity to be treated as not from a passive activity."

8.   EFFECT OF DISPOSITION OF ACTIVITY

Because § 469 is intended to disallow only "artificial" losses, § 469(g) allows the taxpayer to deduct previously disallowed losses attributable to any activity in the year in which he makes a fully taxable disposition of his entire interest in the activity. Deduction of suspended losses on disposition of an activity is appropriate because artificial losses that were previously suspended will be offset by an equal amount of artificial (phantom) gain on the taxable disposition so that only real losses will remain to offset other income.

Generally, a sale or taxable exchange to an unrelated taxpayer of all of the assets used in the activity is required in order to satisfy the requirements of § 469(g). Abandonment, which is a taxable event, also qualifies. The sale by a partner of all of her interest in a partnership will permit the partner to deduct suspended losses attributable to all partnership activities in which she did not materially participate. If the partnership was engaged in two or more activities in which the partner did not materially participate and the partnership sells all of the assets used in one activity, the suspended losses attributable to that activity may be claimed by the partner, but suspended losses attributable to other activities of the partnership remain in suspense. It is important to bear in mind that if the partner sells her entire interest in the partnership, she should be allowed to deduct all suspended losses notwithstanding that she has no remaining basis. This result is required because a partner's outside basis should be reduced by her full distributive share of partnership losses notwithstanding that § 469 may operate to defer the deduction.

If a partner disposes of less than her entire interest in the partnership (or a partnership disposes of less than its entire interest in a passive activity), disposes of her interest in a nontaxable transaction, or sells the interest to a related party (as defined in either § 267(b) or § 707(b)), any previously disallowed losses continue to be suspended and will be allowed in a future year in which the taxpayer realizes passive activity income from other sources or upon the completion of the disposition. If the initial disposition was a nontaxable transaction, any remaining suspended losses will be allowed upon the fully taxable sale of the property received in the tax-free exchange.

Gain or loss on the sale or other taxable disposition of a partnership interest is characterized as passive or active by looking through the partnership entity to its activities. Temp. Reg. § 1.469–2T(e)(3). However, the gain or loss realized on the sale of the entire partnership interest is a ceiling on the look-through computation. A sale at a gain may be treated as composed of both passive gain and active gain; a sale at a loss may include both passive loss and active loss; but a sale at no gain, for example, will not be treated as composed of equal amounts of active gain and passive loss (or passive gain and active loss). See Temp. Reg. § 1.469–2T(e)(3)(vii) Ex. (1). For the sale of a partnership interest, see Chapter 8.

The deferred deductions are allowable, in order, to the extent of: (1) income from the passive activity, including gain (if any) recognized on the disposition; (2) net income or gain for the year from all other passive activities; (3) other income or gain, including salaries, dividends, etc. If any of the deductions otherwise allowable upon the disposition of the activity are capital losses, either from the disposition or as suspended deductions allowed upon the disposition, § 1211 may limit the amount of the deductions currently allowed. If a disposition is an installment sale and gain recognition is deferred under § 453, suspended losses are allowed in each year payments are received in proportion to the portion of the total gain reportable in each year.

9. PAYMENTS TO PARTNERS

Payments received by a partner in a transaction subject to § 707(a) are never treated as passive activity income with respect to the partnership activity. Temp. Reg. § 1.469–2T(e)(2)(i). Payments to a partner subject to § 707(c) are treated as compensation or interest in applying the passive loss rules. Treas. Reg. § 1.469–2(e)(2)(ii). For discussion of § 707(a) and (c), see Chapter 6.

Under the authority of § 469(*l*)(2), and following the direction of the legislative history of § 469, Treas. Reg. § 1.469–7 provides that interest income and expense on a loan from a member of a passthrough entity to the entity (or from the entity to a member) will be treated as passive activity income and expense with respect to the lender. As a consequence, the member's share of the "self-charged" interest, which would otherwise be treated as portfolio income, can be offset with the member's share of the entity's passive activity interest expense, or vice versa. For a tax year after the proposal, but before the finalization of Treas. Reg. § 1.469–7, Hillman v. Commissioner, 250 F.3d 228 (4th Cir. 2001), held that, in the absence of regulations, a real estate management fee paid by a partnership to a Subchapter S corporation (which is a pass-through entity that operates similarly to a partnership) that was wholly owned by a partner was not subject to the same rule. When the proposed regulations were finalized after the *Hillman* decision was handed down, the Treasury Department declined to expand the proposed regulations to provide relief for taxpayers in Hillman's position, because in 1993 Congress provided relief for real estate professionals in § 469(c)(7), discussed supra at page 266. See T.D. 9013, Limitations on Passive Activity Losses and Credits—Treatment of Self–Charged Items of Income and Expense, 67 F.R. 54087 (Aug. 21, 2002). Taxpayers who are not real estate professionals who perform services for a partnership in which they are not material participants remain subject to the rule of *Hillman* that the income is active while the deduction is passive.

Rev. Rul. 95–5, 1995–1 C.B. 100, held that gain recognized under § 731 as a result of a current distribution of cash in excess of the partner's basis in her partnership interest is treated as gain from the sale of a partnership interest under Temp. Reg. § 1.469–2T(e)(3). Thus, if with respect to the partner receiving the distribution the partnership conducts both passive activities and other activities, the gain will be bifurcated into passive activity gain and nonpassive activity gain.

Payments to a retired partner or a deceased partner's successor in interest which are subject to § 736(b) are treated as passive income only if they would have been characterized as passive income if received at the time the liquidation of the partner's interest commenced. Treas. Reg. § 1.469–2(e)(2)(iii)(A). Payments subject to § 736(a) which are attributable to unrealized receivables (as defined in § 751(c)) and goodwill are treated as passive activity income only if the activity to which they are attributable was a passive activity of the partner for the partnership taxable year in which payments commenced. Treas. Reg. § 1.469–2(e)(2)(iii)(B). Section 736 payments are discussed at page 349.

CHAPTER 8

SALES OF PARTNERSHIP INTERESTS BY PARTNERS

SECTION 1. THE SELLER'S SIDE OF THE TRANSACTION

A. GENERAL PRINCIPLES

INTERNAL REVENUE CODE: Sections 1(h)(6)(B), (7)(A), (11); 706(c); 708(a)–(b)(1); 741; 752(d); 1031(a)(2)(D).

REGULATIONS: Sections 1.1(h)–1(a), (b)(1)–(3), (c); 1.704–1(b)(2)(iv)(*l*); 1.741–1; 1.752–1(h); 1.1223–3.

Generally, under the entity approach of § 741, the sale or exchange of a partnership interest results in capital gain or loss to the selling partner. In this case, the partnership interest is treated as a unitary asset in its own right, like corporate stock, independent of the assets owned by the partnership, with a resulting capital gain or loss. However, in certain circumstances § 751(a) overrides § 741 to impose a modified aggregate approach, under which a partner is treated as having sold his share of certain types of partnership assets that produce ordinary income.

As long as a partnership does not own any "unrealized receivables" or "inventory," the presence of which invokes § 751, which requires bifurcation of the sale of a partnership interest into an ordinary income component and a capital gain or loss component, the primary issues in sales of partnership interests involve the determination of the amount of the selling partner's basis properly taken into account in computing gain or loss and properly taking into account the effect of partnership indebtedness as respects both the selling partner's basis and amount realized. Finally, when a partnership interest is sold part-way through the partnership's taxable year, the selling partner's taxable income and basis of her partnership interest must be computed to account for the short year.

Revenue Ruling 84–53

1984–1 C.B. 159.

ISSUE.

What are the tax consequences of the sale of a partnership interest in the situations described below?

FACTS.

Situation 1. In 1978, Y was formed as a limited partnership under the Uniform Limited Partnership Act of State N for the purpose of investing and trading in stocks and securities. Y has a calendar taxable year. A contributed $50x to Y in exchange for a general partner interest, entitling A to a 50 percent interest in all partnership distributions and in partnership income, gain, loss, and deduction. B contributed $50x to Y in exchange for a limited partner interest, entitling B to a 50 percent interest in all partnership distributions and in partnership income, gain, loss, and deduction.

On January 1, 1980, when the stock and securities of Y had decreased in value from $100x to $64x, B sold to A one-half of B's limited partner interest for $16x, which interest A holds as a limited partner.

On January 1, 1982, when the stock and securities of Y has risen in value from $64x (its 1980 value) to $120x, A sold to C one-half of A's general partner interest for $30x. Immediately prior to the sale, A's entire partnership interest had a fair market value of $90x and the transferred portion of the interest had a fair market value of $30x. Since formation, the partnership has made cash distributions in an amount equal to its total income (including tax-exempt income). Assume that all partnership allocations (in all situations) are valid, and that A, B, and C are unrelated parties.

Situation 2. The facts are the same as in *Situation 1* except that, in 1981, Y borrowed $80x recourse which was invested in securities that became worthless on December 31, 1981. Furthermore, immediately prior to A's sale to C, A's entire partnership interest had a fair market value of $30x and the transferred portion of A's interest had a fair market value of $10x.

Situation 3. The facts are the same as in *Situation 2* except that, on January 1, 1982, A sold A's entire limited partner interest to C for its fair market value of $10x (rather than one-half of A's general partner interest).

Situation 4. The facts are the same as in Situation 1 except that, in 1981, Y borrowed $96x recourse which is invested in securities that become worthless on December 31, 1981. Furthermore, immediately prior to A's sale to C, A's entire partnership interest had a fair market value of $18x and the transferred portion of A's interest had a fair market value of $6x.

LAW AND ANALYSIS.

Section 705 of the Internal Revenue Code provides rules for determining the adjusted basis of a partner's interest in a partnership.

Section 722 of the Code provides that the basis of an interest in a partnership acquired by a contribution of property equals the transferor partner's adjusted basis in the contributed property.

Section 752(a) of the Code provides that any increase in a partner's share of the partnership's liabilities is considered to be a contribution of money by the partner to the partnership.

Section 752(b) of the Code provides that any decrease in a partner's share of a partnership's liabilities is considered to be a distribution of money by the partnership to the partner.

Section 1.752–[2 and 3] of the Income Tax Regulations provides rules for determining a partner's share of partnership liabilities with respect to both limited partnerships and general partnerships.

Section 752(d) of the Code provides that in the case of a sale or exchange of an interest in a partnership, liabilities shall be treated in the same manner as liabilities in connection with the sale or exchange of property not associated with partnerships.

Section 1.1001–2 of the regulations provides that the amount realized from a sale or other disposition of property includes the amount of liabilities from which the transferor is discharged as a result of the sale or disposition.

Section 1.61–6(a) of the regulations provides that when a part of a larger property is sold, the basis of the entire property shall be equitably apportioned among the several parts for purposes of determining gain or loss on the part sold.

Consistent with the provisions of Subchapter K of the Code, a partner has a single basis in a partnership interest, even if such partner is both a general partner and a limited partner of the same partnership. See Rev. Rul. 84–52, [1984–1 C.B. 157]. Thus, for example, in applying the limitations of section 704(d) of the Code, losses allocated with respect to a partner's limited partner interest will be allowed so long as they do not exceed the partner's basis in the entire partnership interest.

Under section 1.61–6(a) of the regulations, when a partner makes a taxable disposition of a portion of an interest in a partnership, the basis of the transferred portion of the interest generally equals an amount which bears the same relation to the partner's basis in the partner's entire interest as the fair market value of the transferred portion of the interest bears to the fair market value of the entire interest. However, if such partnership has liabilities, special adjustments must be made to take into account the effect of those liabilities on the basis of the partner's interest.

In cases where the partner's share of all partnership liabilities does not exceed the adjusted basis of such partner's entire interest (including basis attributable to liabilities), the transferor partner shall first exclude from the adjusted basis of such partner's entire interest an amount equal to such partner's share of all partnership liabilities, as determined under section 1.752–[2 and 3] of the regulations. A part of the remaining adjusted basis (if any) shall be allocated to the transferred portion of the interest according to the ratio of the fair market value of the transferred portion of the interest to the fair market value of the entire interest. The sum of the amount so allocated plus the amount of the partner's share of liabilities that is considered discharged on the disposition of the transferred portion of the interest (under section 752(d) of the Code and section 1.1001–2 of the regulations) equals the adjusted basis of the transferred portion of the interest.

On the other hand, if the partner's share of all partnership liabilities exceeds the adjusted basis of such partner's entire interest (including basis attributable to liabilities), the adjusted basis of the transferred portion of the interest equals an amount that bears the same relation to the partner's adjusted basis in the entire interest as the partner's share of liabilities that is considered discharged on the disposition of the transferred portion of the interest bears to the partner's share of all partnership liabilities, as determined under section 1.752–[2 and 3].

HOLDINGS.

Situation 1. Prior to the sale of one-half of B's limited partner interest to A, the adjusted basis of B's entire partnership interest was $50x. Because the fair market value of the transferred portion of B's interest ($16x) is one-half of the fair market value of B's entire partnership interest ($32x), $25x (1/2 of $50x) of adjusted basis must be allocated to the interest transferred by B. B sustained a $9 loss ($16x-$25x) on the sale of A. The adjusted basis of the remainder of B's partnership interest is $25x.

Prior to the sale of one-half of A's general partner interest to C, the adjusted basis of A's entire partnership interest was $66x. Because the fair market value of the transferred portion of A's interest ($30x) is one-third of the fair market value of A's entire partnership interest ($90x), $22x (1/3 of $66x) of the adjusted basis must be allocated to the portion of the interest transferred by A. A realizes an $8x gain ($30x-$22x) on the sale of C. The basis of the remainder of A's partnership interest is $44x. The results would be the same to A if A, instead, sold to C the limited partner interest acquired earlier from B.

Situation 2. The tax consequences of B's sale of one-half of B's limited partner interest to A are identical to those described in *Situation 1.*

In 1981, A's basis in A's entire partnership interest was increase[d] from $66x to $146x as a result of the $80x recourse borrowing (which increases only the basis of A, the sole general partner, under * * * sections 752(a) and 722 of the Code) and was decreased to $86x as a result of the $60x loss allocated to A that year when the securities became worthless. Thus, prior to the sale of one-half of A's general partner interest to C, the adjusted basis of A's entire partnership interest was $86x. To take into account the effect of the liability sharing rules of [the section 752 regulations] on A's adjusted basis, $80x (A's share of all partnership liabilities) is subtracted from $86x, leaving $6x. Because the fair market value of the transferred portion of A's interest ($10x) is one-third of the fair market value of the entire interest ($30x), $2x (1/3 of $6x) of the remaining adjusted basis must be allocated to the transferred portion of A's general partner interest. The sum of that amount ($2x) plus the amount of partnership liabilities from which A is discharged on the disposition of the transferred portion of A's general partner interest ($40), or $42x, equals the adjusted basis of the transferred portion of the interest. A realizes an $8x gain ($10x + $40x – $42x) on the sale to C. The basis of the remainder of A's partnership interest is $44x ($86x – $42).

Situation 3. The tax consequences of B's sale of one-half of B's limited partner interest to A are identical to those described in *Situation 1.*

As in *Situation 2*, prior to the sale of A's limited partner interest to C, the adjusted basis of A's entire partnership interest was $86x. To take into account the effect of the liability sharing rules of section 1.752–[2 and 3] of the regulations on A's adjusted basis, $80x (A's share of all partnership liabilities) is subtracted from $86x, leaving $6x. Because the fair market value of the transferred portion of A's limited partner interest ($10x) is one-third of the fair market value of A's entire interest ($30x), $2x (1/3 of $6x) of the remaining adjusted basis must be allocated to the transferred limited partner interest. The sum of that amount ($2x) plus the amount of partnership liabilities from which A is discharged on the disposition of the transferred limited partner interest ($0x), or $2x, equals the adjusted basis of the transferred portion of the interest. A realizes an $8x gain ($10x − $2x) on the sale to C. The basis of the remainder of A's partnership interest is $84x ($86x − $2x).

Situation 4. The tax consequences of B's sale of one-half of B's limited partner interest to A are identical to those described in *Situation 1*.

In 1981, A's basis in A's entire partnership interest was increased from $66x to $162x as a result of the $96x recourse borrowing and was decreased to $90x as a result of the $72x loss allocated to A that year when the securities became worthless. Thus, prior to the sale of one-half of A's general partner interest to C, the adjusted basis of A's entire partnership interest was $90x. In this situation, A's share of all partnership liabilities ($96x) exceeds the adjusted basis of A's entire interest ($90x). Thus, the adjusted basis of the transferred portion of A's general partner interest equals $45x, the amount which bears the same relation to A's adjusted basis in the entire interest ($90x) as the amount of partnership liabilities from which A is discharged on the disposition of the transferred portion of the general partner interest ($48x) bears to A's share of all partnership liabilities ($96x). A realizes a $9x gain ($48x + $6x – $45x) on the sale of C. The basis of the remainder of A's partnership interest is $45x ($90x – $45x).

ILLUSTRATIVE MATERIAL

1. TREATMENT OF PARTNERSHIP LIABILITIES

As explained in Rev.Rul. 84–53, § 752(d) requires the selling partner to include his share of partnership liabilities, determined under Treas. Regs. §§ 1.752–2 and 1.752–3, in the amount realized on the sale or exchange of a partnership interest. This treatment corresponds to the inclusion of the partner's share of partnership liabilities in the basis of his partnership interest and incorporates the general tax treatment of the transfer of liabilities on a sale or exchange of property into Subchapter K. Furthermore, in Commissioner v. Tufts, 461 U.S. 300 (1983), the Supreme Court held that § 752(d) applied to include in amount realized nonrecourse liabilities in excess of the fair market value of the mortgaged property.

In Slavin v. Commissioner, T.C. Memo. 1989–221, the taxpayer assigned his 50 percent partnership interest to the other partner for no cash consideration and was discharged by the partnership's creditors from liability on partnership mortgage indebtedness. The taxpayer argued that the transaction gave rise to discharge of indebtedness income under § 61(a)(12), which was excludable under § 108 because he was insolvent. The court found a sale because the debt was not extinguished, it was assumed by the other partner.

2.   TREATMENT OF PARTNERSHIP INCOME FOR PORTION OF YEAR PRIOR TO SALE OF INTEREST

2.1. *General Principles*

Under § 708(b)(1)(B), if 50 percent or more of the partnership interests in capital and profits are sold within a 12–month period, the partnership is considered as terminated.[1] See page 390. As a result, under § 706(c)(1), the taxable year of the partnership closes and each partner, whether or not she is a partner who has sold her interest, must include her distributive share of the partnership's income. If less than 50 percent of the interests are sold, the partnership's taxable year does not close as a general matter. (The sale to the other partner of a partnership interest in a two-person partnership, however, terminates the partnership and immediately ends the partnership's taxable year, even if the selling partner owned less than a 50 percent interest. Rev. Rul. 55–68, 1955–1 C.B. 372.) Nevertheless, under § 706(c)(2)(A), the partnership's taxable year does close as to the partner who sells her interest. As a result she must include in her income her distributive share of the partnership profits of the year up to that point, and is thus prevented from obtaining capital gain treatment respecting that share through a sale of her partnership interest. This income is characterized as ordinary or capital under § 702(b). Under Treas. Reg. § 1.705–1(a)(1), when computing gain or loss realized on the sale of the partnership interest, the selling partner adjusts her basis in her partnership interest as of the date of the sale to reflect her distributive share of partnership income (or loss) so taken into account.

If the partner does not sell her entire partnership interest, her partnership year does not close under § 706(c)(2)(A). See I.R.C. § 706(c)(2)(B). Instead, § 706(d)(1) applies, requiring that her distributive share for the year be determined by taking into account her varying interests. See Chapter 4, Section 5. In the case of the sale of a partial interest, only a proportional part of the taxpayer's basis for her entire interest in the partnership, computed as in Rev. Rul. 84–53 is taken into account.

2.2. *Modifications of Partners' Distributive Shares In Connection With the Sale of a Partnership Interest*

In Smith v. Commissioner, 331 F.2d 298 (7th Cir.1964), one partner purchased the partnership interest of the other partner and, as part of the negotiations over the purchase price, the partners modified the partnership agreement to allocate all of the income of the partnership for the fiscal year

---

1. The partnership termination rule of § 708(b)(1)(B) does not apply, however, to   "electing large partnerships," discussed at page 92. See I.R.C. § 774(c).

of the sale to the purchasing partner. It was not clear at the time of the modification whether the partnership would have a profit or a loss for the period in question. The court held that the modification was valid under § 704(b) and taxed the purchasing partner on the entire partnership income for the year. The court never considered the rules of § 706(d), which at that time were incorporated in § 706(c)(2), and which clearly were applicable to the facts. Such an agreement should not be recognized. Ogden v. Commissioner, 84 T.C. 871 (1985), aff'd per curiam, 788 F.2d 252 (5th Cir.1986), held that the predecessor of § 706(d)(1) (which was a prior versions of § 706(c)(2)) disallowed retroactive allocations to a new partner, even though the allocation is otherwise valid under § 704(b). Similarly, Lipke v. Commissioner, 81 T.C. 689 (1983), held that § 706(d)(1) (at that time § 706(c)(2)(B)) disallowed retroactive allocations to continuing partners whose interests were increased as a result of making additional capital contributions late in the year. However, *Lipke* allowed retroactive allocations to continuing partners who did not make any additional capital contributions. There is no readily apparent policy reason for permitting retroactive allocations to partners who do not make an additional capital contribution when retroactive allocations to partners who do make an additional capital contribution are statutorily invalid.

3.   DISPOSITIONS OTHER THAN SALES

3.1.   *Abandonment of a Partnership Interest*

In Citron v. Commissioner, 97 T.C. 200 (1991), the taxpayer was a limited partner in a partnership organized to produce a movie. At a time when the partnership had no net assets (other than the partially completed movie) and no liabilities, the general partner called for additional contributions to complete the movie. The taxpayer, along with the other limited partners, decided not to advance further funds to the partnership, and the limited partners voted to cease operations; the limited partners disavowed their interest in the movie negative, which the general partner thereafter attempted to develop into an X-rated movie. The Tax Court allowed the taxpayer-limited partner a loss deduction under § 165 for the abandonment of a partnership interest, finding sufficient manifestation of the taxpayer's intent to abandon the partnership interest from the taxpayer's affirmative refusal to contribute additional funds and the vote of the limited partners to dissolve the partnership and abandon their interest in the negative. Ordinary loss treatment was allowed because there was no sale or exchange. The absence of liabilities precluded a deemed distribution under § 752(b) and exchange treatment under § 731(a). Rev.Rul. 93–80, 1993–2 C.B. 239, reaches the same result where the partnership has no liabilities, but treats the transaction as a liquidating distribution resulting in capital gain or loss if the partnership has liabilities from which the "abandoning" partner is discharged. Echols v. Commissioner, 935 F.2d 703 (5th Cir.1991), reh. denied, 950 F.2d 209 (1991), rev'g, 93 T.C. 553 (1989), allowed a § 165(a) loss deduction for the abandonment of a partnership interest by a partner who "walked away" from the partnership, even though the partnership had not abandoned its assets and the partnership property was subject to a mortgage which was not foreclosed upon by the mortgagee until the following year. Under the principles that govern liquidating distributions from partnerships, discussed at page 338, *Echols* appears to have been wrongly decided.

3.2. *Gifts*

In Madorin v. Commissioner, 84 T.C. 667 (1985), the taxpayer established a grantor trust of which he was treated as the owner under § 674 because of certain retained powers. The trust acquired a partnership interest and during the period that the partnership reported losses, the taxpayer properly included the trust's distributive share of those losses in his return. When the partnership began to show income, the taxpayer renounced his retained powers, thereby completing the transfer. At that time the trust's share of partnership liabilities exceeded its basis in the partnership interest and the partnership had unrealized receivables. The termination of the grantor trust status was treated as a part gift-part sale transaction, applying Treas. Reg. § 1.1001–2(c), Ex. (5), and the gain was characterized as ordinary gain under § 751. See also Rev.Rul. 75–194, 1975–1 C.B. 80 (applying part gift-part sale analysis to charitable contribution of partnership interest where partner's share of debt exceeded basis).

3.3. *Exchanges of Partnership Interests*

Section 1031(a)(2)(D) specifically excludes partnership interests from the categories of property which may be exchanged without recognition of gain or loss.

4. SALE VERSUS LIQUIDATION

While § 741 generally allows capital gain treatment to the selling partner on the sale of a partnership interest, amounts paid in liquidation of a partnership interest may result in ordinary income under § 736. Thus, the characterization of the transaction as a "sale" or as a "liquidation" is of crucial importance. See Chapter 9, Section 4.

The sale to the other partner of a partnership interest in a two-person partnership terminates the partnership. When a partnership liquidates in this manner, Treas. Reg. § 1.741–1(b) provides that the transferor partner is treated as selling his partnership interest, not an undivided share of the partnership assets, even though McCauslen v. Commissioner, 45 T.C. 588 (1966), held that in such a case the purchaser is treated as having acquired by direct purchase the portion of partnership assets attributable to the acquired partnership interest.

5. HOLDING PERIOD OF PARTNERSHIP INTEREST

Treas. Reg. § 1.1223–3 deals with the holding period of a partnership interest acquired in separate transactions at different times. Although under Rev. Rul. 84–53, page 271, a partner has a single basis in a partnership interest, if components of that interest were acquired at different times the components of the partnership interest nevertheless can have different holding periods under § 1223. Thus, upon the sale of all or a portion of the partnership interest, it might be necessary to apportion the unitary basis between the part of the transaction that results in short-term capital gain, if any, and the part that results in long-term capital gain, if any. Under the regulations, any capital gain or loss resulting from the sale of a partnership interest is allocated between long-term and short-term capital gain or loss in the same proportion that the holding period of the interest in the partnership is allocated between the portion of the interest held for more than one year and the portion of the interest held for one year or less. The portion of a partnership interest to which a holding period relates is a percentage that equals: (1) the fair market value of the portion of the partnership interest received in the transaction to which the holding period relates (2) divided by the fair market value of the entire partnership interest, (determined immediately after that transaction). Assume, for example, that in 2004 *B* purchased a 1/4 interest in a partnership for $1,000, and in January of 2006, B purchased an additional 1/4 interest for $5,000. Immediately after the second purchase, B holds a 1/2 interest with a fair market value of $10,000 and a basis of $6,000. If B then sells the entire 1/2 partnership interest in July 2006 for $14,000, B will recognize an $8,000 gain ($14,000 − [$1,000 + $5,000]). Under the regulations, one-half of this gain, $4,000, will be short-term capital gain and the other one-half will be long-term capital gain, even though economically B realized a $6,000 gain on the 1/4 interest purchased in 2004 and only a $2,000 gain on the 1/4 interest purchased and sold in 2006.

Under the regulations, a split holding period also can result when a partner's interest in the partnership is increased as a result of cash contributions. But if a partner both makes cash contributions and receives cash distributions within one year prior to the date of sale of the partnership interest, only the net amount of cash contributions are taken into account in determining the portion of the partnership interest with respect to which the partner has a short-term holding period. Treas. Reg. § 1.1223–3(b)(2). In addition, deemed cash contributions and distributions under § 752(a) and (b) are not taken into account at all in determining whether a partner has a split holding period. Treas. Reg. § 1.1223–3(b)(3).

A selling partner may use the actual holding period of the portion of a partnership interest sold if the partnership is a "publicly traded partnership" (see, page 31), the partnership interest is divided into identifiable units with ascertainable holding periods, and the selling partner can identify the portion of the interest transferred. The Service has cautioned taxpayers that it may apply judicial doctrines, e.g., substance over form or step transaction, or Treas. Reg. § 1.701–2, see, page 33, to attack abusive transactions designed to shift gain from the portion of a partnership interest with a short-term holding period to the portion with a long-term holding period. See Notice of Proposed Rulemaking, Capital Gains, Partnership, Subchapter S, and Trust Provisions, REG–106527–98, 1999–2 C.B. 304.

B.   CAPITAL GAIN VERSUS ORDINARY INCOME: SECTION 751

INTERNAL REVENUE CODE: Sections 1(h)(7)(A); 751.

REGULATIONS: Section 1.751–1(a), (c), (d), (g), Ex. (1).

Section 741, premised on the entity treatment of a partnership, as a general rule treats a partnership interest as a capital asset per se, so that its sale results in capital gain or loss. Due to the preferential rate for capital gains, however, this approach presents tax avoidance possibilities. When a sole proprietor sells his business, § 1060 requires that each asset be classified separately as to capital gain or loss and ordinary gain or loss; the business is not regarded as a unitary capital asset.[2] The treatment of a partnership interest as a unitary capital asset would avoid the comminution rule of § 1060, even though some of the partnership assets are ordinary assets, such as inventory or cash method accounts receivable. Accordingly, § 751(a) is designed to limit the tax avoidance possibilities of the general rule of § 741.

Where a partnership has "unrealized receivables" or inventory, a sale or taxable exchange by a partner of his interest in the partnership is treated, as respects these items, on an aggregate approach. The partner is regarded as having sold pro tanto his interest in each of those ordinary assets.[3] Under Treas. Reg. § 1.751–1(a)(2) the gain is determined as if the partnership had sold those assets and distributed to the partner his distributive share of the ordinary income. The items selected, unrealized receivables and inventory, represent the significant ordinary income items held by a business or personal service partnership. Section 741 continues to control the character of the gain or loss recognized with respect to the portion of the partner's basis and the amount realized on the sale of the partnership interest that are not allocable to unrealized receivables and inventory. This bifurcated approach may create ordinary income and a related capital loss, even in instances where a partnership interest is sold at no gain or an overall net loss.

Ledoux v. Commissioner

Tax Court of the United States, 1981.
77 T.C. 293.[*]

■ STERRETT, JUDGE:

Pari-mutuel wagering at greyhound dogracing tracks was legalized in the State of Florida in 1935. Prior to July 1955, the Sanford–Orlando

2. Prior to the enactment of § 1060, this result was dictated by Williams v. McGowan, 152 F.2d 570 (2d Cir.1945).

3. Section 751(a) does not apply if a partnership interest is disposed of by gift even though the partnership holds unrealized receivables. In Rev.Rul. 60–352, 1960–2 C.B. 208, a partner made a charitable contribution of an interest in a partnership holding § 453 installment obligations. The partner was required to recognize the gain attributable to his share of the partnership's installment obligations. If a § 453 installment obligation is viewed as not substantially different than any other unrealized receivable, this Ruling is not consistent with the mechanics of § 741 and § 751(a). It is however, consistent with the policy of § 453B, and presumably reflects the view that § 453B applies aggregate theory to override §§ 741 and 751.

* Aff'd per curiam, 695 F.2d 1320 (11th Cir.1983).

Kennel Club, Inc. (hereinafter referred to as the corporation), held a greyhound racing permit issued by the Florida State Racing Commission to operate a racetrack in Seminole County, Fla. The corporation owned certain land in Seminole County, Fla., and improvements thereon including a grandstand, kennels, track, and other facilities and equipment necessary to operate a racetrack and to handle pari-mutuel pools. * * *

Due to problems in managing the dog track, the Sanford–Orlando Kennel Club copartnership entered into a written agreement (dog track agreement) on July 9, 1955, with Jerry Collins, an experienced operator of dogracing tracks, and his son, Jack Collins. Pursuant to the dog track agreement, the Collinses acquired the right "to manage and operate the Greyhound Racing Track, owned by the Sanford–Orlando Kennel Club, Inc.," for a period of 20 years commencing on October 1, 1955. In return, the Collinses agreed to pay to the copartnership the first $200,000 of net annual profit from track operations. * * *

On October 1, 1955, petitioner John W. Ledoux, his father-in-law, Jerry Collins, and his brother-in-law, Jack Collins, entered into a partnership agreement creating a partnership (hereinafter the Collins–Ledoux partnership or partnership) for the stated purpose of "carrying on of the business of managing and operating a greyhound dog racing plant in Seminole County, Florida." * * *

* * *

During the period from October 1, 1955, to September 30, 1972, the Collins–Ledoux partnership operated the greyhound racetrack pursuant to and in accordance with the July 9, 1955, agreement, as amended. Petitioner John W. Ledoux was a manager of the operations of the racetrack for the Collins–Ledoux partnership. Petitioner received compensation for his services in the form of salary, which was charged as an expense of the track operation. Along with his salary, petitioner received a share of the net profits of the Collins–Ledoux partnership. Petitioner's duties included, among other things, the directing of promotional, advertising, and development activities on behalf of the Collins–Ledoux partnership.

* * *

The partnership's actions with respect to operation and management of the dog track were eminently successful. During the period from 1955 to 1972, the gross income from track operations increased from $3.6 million to $23.6 million, and the net income to the Collins–Ledoux partnership increased from $72,000 to over $550,000. The increases in gross and net income were attributable to the work of the partnership, including petitioner, and to the general economic growth in the Central Florida area. Accordingly, the fair value of the right to operate the greyhound racetrack in Seminole County, Fla., pursuant to the racing permit held by the corporation and pursuant to the dog track agreement, increased significantly during the period from 1955 to 1972.

* * *

After the 1972 racing season two of the partners, Jerry Collins and Jack Collins, decided to purchase petitioner's 25–percent partnership interest. They agreed to allow Ledoux to propose a fair selling price for his interest. Ledoux set a price based on a price-earnings multiple of 5 times his share of the partnership's 1972 earnings. This resulted in a total value for his 25–percent interest of $800,000. There was no valuation or appraisal of specific assets at the time, and the sales price included his interest in all of the assets of the partnership.

At the request of Jerry Collins, petitioner drafted a "Memorandum Agreement," which reflected the arm's-length agreement of the parties. The memorandum was submitted to Jerry Collins and his attorney, and after slight revision, was executed by the parties to the sale on July 19, 1972. It stated, in part, that the "Seller agrees to sell his complete interest in the partnership of Collins, Collins, and Ledoux and to give up all rights, benefits, and obligations of the various agreements involved." It also stated that "In the determination of the purchase price set forth in this agreement, the parties acknowledge no consideration has been given to any item of goodwill."

* * *

At the closing, there was no discussion about values of, or allocation to, any specific assets. In fact, no part of the sales price was allocated to any specific partnership asset. At the time of the sale, the partnership assets consisted of an escrow deposit; certain prepaid expenses; a stock investment in Sanford–Seminole Development Co.; investment in land, buildings, and equipment; improvements on the corporation's property used in connection with the operation of the dog track; and rights arising out of the dog track agreement. * * *

On his 1972 Federal income tax return, petitioner properly elected to report the gain from the sale of his partnership interest under the installment method as prescribed in section 453. * * * In each of those years, he characterized the reported gain, calculated pursuant to the installment sales method, as capital gain.

* * *

Respondent, in his notice of deficiency, did not disagree with petitioner's calculation of the total gain. However, he determined that $575,392.50 of the gain was related to petitioner's interest in the dog track agreement and should be subject to ordinary income treatment pursuant to section 751.

OPINION

The sole issue presented is whether a portion of the amount received by petitioner on the sale of his 25–percent partnership interest is taxable as ordinary income and not as capital gain. More specifically, we must decide whether any portion of the sales price is attributable to "unrealized receivables" of the partnership.

Generally, gain or loss on the sale or exchange of a partnership interest is treated as capital gain or loss. Sec. 741. Prior to 1954, a partner could escape ordinary income tax treatment on his portion of the partnership's unrealized receivables by selling or exchanging his interest in the partnership and treating the gain or loss therefrom as capital gain or loss. To curb such abuses, section 751 was enacted to deal with the problem of the so-called "collapsible partnership." See S. Rept. 1622, 83d Cong., 2d Sess. 98 (1954). Section 751 provides, in part, as follows:

SEC. 751. UNREALIZED RECEIVABLES AND INVENTORY ITEMS.

(a) Sale or Exchange of Interest in Partnership.—The amount of any money, or the fair market value of any property, received by a transferor partner in exchange for all or a part of his interest in the partnership attributable to—

(1) unrealized receivables of the partnership * * *

* * *

(c) Unrealized Receivables.—For purposes of this subchapter, the term "unrealized receivables" includes, to the extent not previously includible in income under the method of accounting used by the partnership, any rights (contractual or otherwise) to payment for—

* * *

(2) services rendered, or to be rendered. * * *

Petitioner contends that the dog track agreement gave the Collins–Ledoux partnership the right to manage and operate the dog track. According to petitioner, the agreement did not give the partnership any contractual rights to receive future payments and did not impose any obligation on the partnership to perform services. Rather, the agreement merely gave the partnership the right to occupy and use all of the corporation's properties (including the racetrack facilities and the racing permit) in operating its dog track business; if the partnership exercised such right, it would be obligated to make annual payments to the corporation based upon specified percentages of the annual mutuel handle. Thus, because the dog track agreement was in the nature of a leasehold agreement rather than an employment contract, it did not create the type of "unrealized receivables" referred to in section 751.

Respondent, on the other hand, contends that the partnership operated the racetrack for the corporation and was paid a portion of the profits for its efforts. As such, the agreement was in the nature of a management employment contract. When petitioner sold his partnership interest to the Collinses in 1972, the main right that he sold was a contract right to receive income in the future for yet-to-be-rendered personal services. This, respondent asserts, is supported by the fact that petitioner determined the sales price for his partnership interest by capitalizing his 1972 annual income (approximately $160,000) by a factor of 5. Therefore, respondent contends that the portion of the gain realized by petitioner that is attributable to the management contract should be characterized as an amount received for unrealized receivables of the partnership. Consequently, such gain should be characterized as ordinary income under section 751.

The legislative history is not wholly clear with respect to the types of assets that Congress intended to place under the umbrella of "unrealized receivables." The House report states:

> The term "unrealized receivables or fees" is used to apply to any rights to income which have not been included in gross income under the method of accounting employed by the partnership. The provision is applicable mainly to cash basis partnerships which have acquired a contractual or other legal right to income for goods or services. * * * [H. Rept. 1337, 83d Cong., 2d Sess. 71 (1954).]

Essentially the same language appears in the report of the Senate committee. S. Rept. 1622, 83d Cong., 2d Sess. 98 (1954). In addition, the regulations elaborate on the meaning of "unrealized receivables" as used in section 751. Section 1.751–1(c), Income Tax Regs., provides:

> Sec. 1.751–1(c) Unrealized receivables. (1) The term "unrealized receivables", * * * means any rights (contractual or otherwise) to payment for—
>
> (i) Goods delivered or to be delivered (to the extent that such payment would be treated as received for property other than a capital asset), or
>
> (ii) Services rendered or to be rendered, to the extent that income arising from such rights to payment was not previously includible in income under the method of accounting employed by the partnership. Such rights must have arisen under contracts or agreements in existence at the time of sale or distribution, although the partnership may not be able to enforce payment until a later time. For example, the term includes trade accounts receivable of a cash method taxpayer, and rights to payment for work or goods begun but incomplete at the time of the sale or distribution.
>
>   * * *
>
> (3) In determining the amount of the sale price attributable to such unrealized receivables, or their value in a distribution treated as a sale or exchange, any arm's length agreement between the buyer and the seller, or between the partnership and the distributee partner, will generally establish the amount or value. In the absence of such an agreement, full account shall be taken not only of the estimated cost of completing performance of the contract or agreement, but also of the time between the sale or distribution and the time of payment.

The language of the legislative history and the regulations indicates that the term "unrealized receivables" includes any contractual or other right to payment for goods delivered or to be delivered or services rendered or to be rendered. Therefore, an analysis of the nature of the rights under the dog track agreement, in the context of the aforementioned legal framework, becomes appropriate. A number of cases have dealt with the meaning of "unrealized receivables" and thereby have helped to define the scope of the term. Courts that have considered the term "unrealized receivables" generally have said that it should be given a broad interpretation. * * * For instance, in *Logan v. Commissioner*, 51 T.C. 482, 486 (1968), we held that a partnership's right in quantum meruit to payment for work in progress constituted an unrealized receivable even though there was no express agreement between the partnership and its clients requiring payment.[5]

In *Roth v. Commissioner*, 321 F.2d 607 (9th Cir.1963), affg. 38 T.C. 171 (1962), the Ninth Circuit dealt with the sale of an interest in a partnership which produced a movie and then gave a 10–year distribution right to Paramount Pictures Corp. in return for a percentage of the gross receipts. The selling partner claimed that his right to a portion of the payments expected under the partnership's contract with Paramount did not constitute an unrealized receivable. The court rejected this view, however, reasoning that Congress "meant to exclude from capital gains treatment any receipts which would have been treated as ordinary income to the partner if no transfer of the partnership interest had occurred." 321 F.2d at 611. Therefore, the partnership's right to payments under the distribution contract was in the nature of an unrealized receivable.

A third example of the broad interpretation given to the term "unrealized receivable" is *United States v. Eidson*, 310 F.2d 111 (5th Cir.1962), revg. an unreported opinion (W.D. Tex. 1961). The court there considered the nature of a management contract which was similar to the one at issue in the instant case. The case arose in the context of a sale by a partnership of all of its rights to operate and manage a mutual insurance company. The selling partnership received $170,000 for the rights it held under the management contract, and the Government asserted that the total amount should be treated as ordinary income. The Court of Appeals agreed with the Government's view on the ground that what was being assigned was not a capital asset whose value had accrued over a period of years; rather, the

---

5. In Hale v. Commissioner, T.C. Memo. 1965–274, we went a step further in dealing with the definition of "unrealized receivable." In that case, we dealt with the situation where a withdrawing partner received real property and a promissory note in exchange for his interest in the partnership assets. One such asset was the right to share in future profits of a real estate development company, which right was conditioned upon the partnership's promise to render future services. We held that the right to future income constituted an unrealized receivable because it was based on the obligation to render future services. The fact that the partnership's development rights had not yet become fixed did not affect the status of the development rights as an unrealized receivable, and did not bar the partner's interest therein from being considered an ordinary income asset.

right to operate the company and receive profits therefrom during the remaining life of the contract was the real subject of the assignment. 310 F.2d at 116. The Fifth Circuit found the Supreme Court's holding in *Commissioner v. P. G. Lake, Inc.*, 356 U.S. 260 (1958), to be conclusive:

> The substance of what was assigned was the right to receive future income. The substance of what was received was the present value of income which the recipient would otherwise obtain in the future. In short, consideration was paid for the right to receive future income, not for an increase in the value of the income-producing property. [356 U.S. at 266, cited in 310 F.2d at 115.]

In *United States v. Woolsey*, 326 F.2d 287 (5th Cir.1963), revg. 208 F. Supp. 325 (S.D.Tex.1962), the Fifth Circuit again faced a situation similar to the one that we face herein. The Fifth Circuit considered whether proceeds received by taxpayers on the sale of their partnership interests were to be treated as ordinary income or capital gain. There, the court was faced with the sale of interests in a partnership which held, as one of its assets, a 25–year contract to manage a mutual insurance company. As in the instant case, the contract gave the partners the right to render services for the term of the contract and to earn ordinary income in the future. In holding that the partnership's management contract constituted an unrealized receivable, the court stated:

> When we look at the underlying right assigned in this case, we cannot escape the conclusion that so much of the consideration which relates to the right to earn ordinary income in the future under the "management contract," taxable to the assignee as ordinary income, is likewise taxable to the assignor as ordinary income although such income must be earned. Section 751 has defined "unrealized receivables" to include any rights, contractual or otherwise, to ordinary income from "services rendered, *or to be rendered*," (emphasis added) to the extent that the same were not previously includable in income by the partnership, with the result that capital gains rates cannot be applied to the rights to income under the facts of this case, which would constitute ordinary income had the same been received in due course by the partnership. * * * It is our conclusion that such portion of the consideration received by the taxpayers in this case as properly should be allocated to the present value of their right to earn ordinary income in the future under the "management contract" is subject to taxation as ordinary income. * * * [326 F.2d at 291.]

Petitioner attempts to distinguish *United States v. Woolsey, supra,* and *United States v. Eidson, supra,* from the instant case by arguing that those cases involved a sale or termination of contracts to manage mutual insurance companies in Texas and that the management contracts therein were in the nature of employment agreements. After closely scrutinizing the facts in those cases, we conclude that petitioner's position has no merit. The fact that the *Woolsey* case involved sale of 100 percent of the partnership interests, as opposed to a sale of only a 25–percent partnership interest herein, is of no consequence. In addition, the fact that *Eidson* involved the surrender of the partnership's contract right to manage the insurance company, as opposed to the continued partnership operation in the instant case, also is not a material factual distinction.

The dog track agreement at issue in the instant case is similar to the management contract considered by the Fifth Circuit in *Woolsey*. Each gives the respective partnership the right to operate a business for a period of years and to earn ordinary income in return for payments of specified amounts to the corporation that holds the State charter. Therefore, based on our analysis of the statutory language, the legislative history, and the regulations and relevant case law, we are compelled to find that the dog track agreement gave the petitioner an interest that amounted to an "unrealized receivable" within the meaning of section 751(c).

Petitioner further contends that the dog track agreement does not represent an unrealized receivable because it does not require or obligate the partnership to perform personal services in the future. The agreement only gives, the argument continues, the Collins–Ledoux partnership the right to engage in a business.

We find this argument to be unpersuasive. The words of section 751(c), providing that the term "unrealized receivable" includes the right to payment for "services rendered, or to be rendered," do not preclude that section's application to a situation where, as here, the performance of services is not required by the agreement. As the Fifth Circuit said in *United States v. Eidson, supra*:

> The fact that * * * income would not be received by the [partnership] unless they performed the services which the contract required of them, that is, actively managed the affairs of the insurance company in a manner that would produce a profit after all of the necessary expenditures, does not, it seems clear, affect the nature of this payment. It affects only the amount. That is, the fact that the taxpayers would have to spend their time and energies in performing services for which the compensation would be received merely affects the price at which they would be willing to assign or transfer the contract. * * * [310 F.2d at 115.]

Consequently, a portion of the consideration received by Ledoux on the sale of his partnership interest is subject to taxation as ordinary income.

Having established that the dog track agreement qualifies as an unrealized receivable, we next consider whether all or only part of petitioner's gain in excess of the amount attributable to his share of tangible partnership assets should be treated as ordinary income. Petitioner argues that this excess gain was attributable to goodwill or the value of a going concern.

With respect to goodwill, we note that petitioner's attorney drafted, and petitioner signed, the agreement for sale of partnership interest, dated October 17, 1972, which contains the following statement in paragraph 7:

7. In the determination of the purchase price set forth in this agreement, the parties acknowledge no consideration has been given to any item of goodwill.

The meaning of the words "no consideration" is not entirely free from doubt. They could mean that no thought was given to an allocation of any of the sales price to goodwill, or they could indicate that the parties agreed that no part of the purchase price was allocated to goodwill. The testimony of the attorney who prepared the document indicates, however, that he did consider the implications of the sale of goodwill and even did research on the subject. He testified that he believed, albeit incorrectly, that, if goodwill were part of the purchase price, his client would not be entitled to capital gains treatment.

Petitioner attempts to justify this misstatement of the tax implications of an allocation to goodwill not by asserting mistake, but by pointing out that his attorney "is not a tax lawyer but is primarily involved with commercial law and real estate." We find as a fact that petitioner agreed at arm's length with the purchasers of his partnership interest that no part of the purchase price should be attributable to goodwill. The Tax Court long has adhered to the view that, absent "strong proof," a taxpayer cannot challenge an express allocation in an arm's-length sales contract to which he had agreed. See, e.g., *Major v. Commissioner*, 76 T.C. 239, 249 (1981), appeal pending (7th Cir., July 7, 1981); *Lucas v. Commissioner*, 58 T.C. 1022, 1032 (1972). In *Spector v. Commissioner*, 641 F.2d 376 (5th Cir.1981), revg. 71 T.C. 1017 (1979), the Fifth Circuit, to which an appeal in this case will lie, appeared to step away from its prior adherence to the "strong proof" standard and move toward the stricter standard enunciated in *Commissioner v. Danielson*, 378 F.2d 771, 775 (3d Cir.1967), remanding 44 T.C. 549 (1965), cert. denied 389 U.S. 858 (1967). However, in this case, we need not measure the length of the step since we hold that petitioner has failed to introduce sufficient evidence to satisfy even the more lenient "strong proof" standard.

We next turn to petitioner's contention that part or all of the purchase price received in excess of the value of tangible assets is attributable to value of a going concern. In *VGS Corp. v. Commissioner*, 68 T.C. 563 (1977), we stated that—

> Going-concern value is, in essence, the additional element of value which attaches to property by reason of its existence as an integral part of a going concern. * * * [The] ability of a business to continue to function and generate income without interruption as a consequence of the change in ownership, is a vital part of the value of a going concern. * * * [68 T.C. at 591–592; citations omitted.]

However, in the instant case, the ability of the dogracing track to continue to function after the sale of Ledoux's partnership interest was due to the remaining partners' retention of rights to operate under the dog track agreement. Without such agreement, there would have been no continuing right to operate a business and no right to continue to earn income. Thus, the amount paid in excess of the value of Ledoux's share of the tangible assets was not for the intangible value of the business as a going concern but rather for Ledoux's rights under the dog track agreement.

Finally, we turn to petitioner's claim that a determination of the value of rights arising from the dog track agreement has never been made and no evidence of the value of such rights was submitted in this case. We note that the $800,000 purchase price was proposed by petitioner and was accepted by Jack Collins and Jerry Collins in an arm's length agreement of sale evidenced in the memorandum of agreement of July 19, 1972, and the agreement for sale of partnership interest of October 17, 1972. In addition, the October 17, 1972, sales agreement, written by petitioner's attorney, provided in paragraph 1 that the "Seller [Ledoux] sells to buyer [Jerry Collins and Jack Collins] all of his interest in [the partnership] * * * including but not limited to, *the seller's right to income* and to acquire the capital stock of The Sanford–Orlando Kennel Club, Inc." (Emphasis added.) Section 1.751–1(c)(3), Income Tax Regs., provides that an arm's-length agreement between the buyer and the seller generally will establish the value attributable to unrealized receivables.

Based on the provision in the agreement that no part of the consideration was attributable to goodwill, it is clear to us that the parties were aware that they could, if they so desired, have provided that no part of the consideration was attributable to the dog track agreement. No such provision was made.[8] Furthermore, the agreement clearly stated that one of the assets purchased was Ledoux's rights to future income. Considering that petitioner calculated the purchase price by capitalizing future earnings expected under the dog track agreement, we conclude that the portion of Ledoux's gain in excess of the amount attributable to tangible assets was attributable to an unrealized receivable as reflected by the dog track agreement.

Decision will be entered for the respondent.

ILLUSTRATIVE MATERIAL

1. DEFINITION OF SECTION 751 "HOT" ASSETS

1.1. *Unrealized Receivables*

1.1.1. *Future Income and Going Concern Value*

Unrealized receivables are broadly defined in § 751(c) to include any rights to payment for goods delivered or to be delivered or for services rendered or to be rendered, to the extent not previously includible in income. Cash method accounts receivable are the most easily recognized unrealized receivable. In contrast, accrual method accounts receivable, having been included in income when they arose, are not "unrealized." The Tax Court's opinion in *Ledoux,* makes it clear that more items than just

---

8. We do not mean to imply that an opposite holding would automatically pertain if a provision had been made with respect to the dog track agreement.

cash method accounts receivable give rise to ordinary income under § 751(a). Thus, Logan v. Commissioner, 51 T.C. 482 (1968), which is discussed in *Ledoux,* held, in connection with the sale of a partnership interest in a law firm, that unbilled fees for work in progress constituted unrealized receivables. The taxpayer argued that the partnership had no express contractual rights against the clients and that claims in quantum meruit were not covered by § 751(c). The court held to the contrary, finding a Congressional intent for a broad interpretation of § 751(c), and stressing the fact that the partner, if he had remained in the partnership, would have realized ordinary income on the collection of the fees.

As result of the broad definition ascribed to "unrealized receivable" in *Ledoux* and similar cases, § 751(a) can be applied to virtually any partnership holding valuable contracts to provide personal services. There is a fine line, however, between contractual rights, which may be classified as an unrealized receivable invoking § 751(a), and goodwill and going concern value, which is the present value of the ability of a business to earn income in the future. Miller v. United States, 181 Ct.Cl. 331 (1967), held that a partnership had no unrealized receivables because it merely had the expectancy of continuing to represent a client which generated most of its income. The contract with the client was on a day-to-day basis and cancelable at any time. See also Phillips v. Commissioner, 40 T.C. 157 (1963), and Baxter v. Commissioner, 433 F.2d 757 (9th Cir.1970), both finding no § 751 property where the contracts were cancelable at will or with a short notice period. Aliber v. Commissioner, T.C. Memo. 1987–10, held that accounts receivable representing rights to reimbursement for real estate taxes paid by the partnership on behalf of owners of condominium properties managed by the partnership were not unrealized receivables.

1.1.2. *Recapture Gain*

As defined in § 751(c), "unrealized receivables" also include gain that would have been treated as ordinary income under the various recapture rules (e.g., § 1245(a)) on the sale of an asset by the partnership. For purposes of § 751, the amount of potential recapture income is treated as an unrealized receivable with a basis of zero. Treas. Reg. § 1.751–1(c)(4), (5). Inclusion of recapture income in the definition of unrealized receivables is significant because it results in the potential applicability of § 751(a) to every sale of partnership interest in a partnership holding depreciable personalty, such as machinery, equipment, and amortizable § 197 intangible assets, even though the partnership uses the accrual method of reporting and thus has no unrealized accounts receivable.

1.2. *Inventory*

Section 751(a)(2) requires the selling partner to recognize gain from the disposition of the partner's share of inventory as ordinary income. Under § 751(d)(2), "inventory" includes, in addition to stock in trade, all non-capital assets except depreciable property and land governed by § 1231. In determining whether property is to be classified as inventory, the activities of the selling partner are taken into account. For a series of cases dealing with different partners in the same partnership and reaching different results on the § 751 question as to the status of real property held by the partnership, see Morse v. United States, 371 F.2d 474 (Ct.Cl.1967) (capital asset); Estate of Freeland v. Commissioner, 393 F.2d 573 (9th Cir.1968) (inventory); Ginsburg v. United States, 396 F.2d 983 (Ct.Cl. 1968)(capital asset).[4]

2.   COMPUTATIONS UNDER SECTION 751(a)

2.1.   *In General*

Treas. Reg. § 1.751–1(a)(2) provides that the amount of the § 751(a) gain taxed as ordinary income is the net amount of ordinary income that would have been reflected in the partner's distributive share if the partnership had sold all of its items of § 751 property at fair market value for cash (and assumption of liabilities) immediately before the partner sold the partnership interest. This calculation includes the effect of any remedial allocations to the selling partner under Treas. Reg. § 1.704–3(d), discussed at page 165. After calculating the § 751(a) gain, the selling partner's gain or loss on the sale of the partnership interest, recognized as capital gain or loss under § 741, is the difference between the partner's overall gain or loss on disposition of the partnership interest and the amount treated as ordinary gain under § 751(a).

For example, assume that A sells her one-third interest in the ABC partnership for $100 and that her basis in that interest is $75. ABC owns inventory having a value of $210 and a basis of $150, and a capital asset having a value of $90 and a basis of $75. If the partnership were to have sold the inventory, A would be allocated $20 of the $60 ordinary income recognized by the partnership. Thus, under § 751(a), A recognizes $20 of ordinary income on the sale of her partnership interest. A's remaining $5 of gain on the sale of her partnership interest is taxed as capital gain under § 741. This result is illustrated as follows:

Asset Class	Amount Realized	Basis	Gain
Total Transaction	$100	$75	$25
Section 751			$20
Section 741			$ 5

Alternatively, if A had sold her interest for only $90, she again would recognize $20 of ordinary income under § 751(a) attributable to the inventory, but this time the difference between her overall realized gain of $15, and the amount treated as ordinary income under § 751(a), produces a $5 capital loss under § 741.

---

4. Treas. Reg. § 1.751–1(d)(2)(ii) includes within the definition of inventory all accounts receivable, including those of both cash and accrual method taxpayers. Inventory does not include other "unrealized receivables," as defined in § 751(c), such as depreciation recapture. The gain attributable to accounts receivable included in inventory is not taxed twice. Rather, including these items in inventory affects the calculation to determine whether the inventory is substantially appreciated. The distinction is important under § 751(b) which applies to distributions, discussed at page 330.

Asset Class	Amount Realized	Basis	Gain
Total Transaction	$90	$75	$15
Section 751			$20
Section 741			($ 5)

This calculation of ordinary gain is satisfactory where the seller's basis for his partnership interest is equivalent to his pro rata share of partnership basis. But where the seller's basis differs, for example, as the result of his previous purchase of his partnership interest, the allocated gain attributable to § 751 assets may be higher than the selling partner's actual portion of gain based on the selling partner's cost allocable to the § 751 assets unless the partnership has elected to adjust basis pursuant to an election under § 754 (discussed at page 296), or the sale is made within two years after his original purchase. (A transferee partner selling or receiving a distribution within two years of his purchase may elect to treat the partnership basis of the assets as though an inside basis adjustment reflecting the purchase price of the partnership interest had been made. I.R.C. § 732(d).) For example, suppose that the partnership assets consist of inventory with a zero basis but worth $100,000, and that partner A's basis for his one-fourth partnership interest is $25,000 because of his previous purchase of the interest at that price. If A sells his interest for $25,000, he will recognize $25,000 ordinary income and $25,000 capital loss in the absence of an inside basis adjustment. This result can be avoided, however, if a § 743(b) or § 732(d) election to adjust basis is in effect, in which case he would have a $25,000 basis for his interest in the inventory and no gain or loss would be recognized as a result of the sale. Basis adjustments are discussed at page 296.

2.2. *Loss Situations*

Section 751(a) applies to require recognition of ordinary income even though the partnership interest is not sold at an overall gain. For example, assume that C, with a basis for his interest of $75, sells his one-half interest in CD Partnership for $65. The partnership owns inventory having a basis of $50 and a value of $100 and a § 1231 asset with a basis of $100 and a value of $30. Although C has realized an overall loss of $10, C must fragment that overall loss into $25 of ordinary income and $35 of capital loss. Treas. Reg. § 1.751–1(a)(2).

Asset Class	Amount Realized	Basis	Gain
Total Transaction	$65	$75	($10)
Section 751			$25
Section 741			($35)

In addition, § 751(a) allows recognition of a selling partner's share of ordinary loss attributable to the partner's interest in depreciated inventory. The language of § 751(a) applies to inventory whether or not it is appreciated.[5] Thus, assume that D, with a basis for her partnership interest of $75, sells for $100 her one-half interest in DE Partnership, which owns inventory having a basis of $100 and a value of $80 and a § 1231 asset with a basis of $50 and a value of $120. D has recognized an overall gain of $25, but D can fragment that overall gain into $10 of ordinary loss, reflecting D's allocable share of the loss on a hypothetical sale of the § 751 asset, and $35 of capital gain on her remaining partnership interest.

Asset Class	Amount Realized	Basis	Gain
Total Transaction	$100	$75	$25
Section 751			($10)
Section 741			$35

The legislative history states that the effect of the 1997 amendment to § 751(a) is to eliminate the requirement that inventory be substantially appreciated in order to give rise to ordinary income. See H. Rep. No. 148, 105th Cong, 1st Sess. 148 (1997); S. Rep. No. 33, 105th Cong., 1st Sess. 193 (1997). Nothing in the statute, however, so limits its application.

3. INSTALLMENT SALES OF PARTNERSHIP INTERESTS

Gain realized on the sale of a partnership interest sold for deferred payments may be reported on the installment method under § 453. See Rev.Rul. 76–483, 1976–2 C.B. 131. Section 453 is not difficult to apply as long as a partnership does not hold any property that could not be sold on the installment method if the property were owned and sold directly by the partner. On the other hand, if the partnership holds property that may not be sold on the installment method under § 453 (such as inventory, see § 453(b)(2)(A)), the analysis is more complex, and the existing statutory pattern is unclear.

Denying installment reporting entirely if the partnership holds any assets ineligible for installment treatment is inconsistent with the basic entity theory of § 741 as modified by § 751(a). On the other hand, allowing installment reporting on the full gain in such cases may circumvent the restrictions of § 453. Section 453 itself provides a partial answer in § 453(i)(2). That provision treats as recapture income under § 453(i) any ordinary income realized on the sale of a partnership interest under § 751 that is attributable to depreciation recapture under § 1245 or § 1250. Thus, any gain on the sale of a partnership interest characterized as ordinary income under § 751(a) and (c) because it represents the selling

---

5. Prior to 1997 § 751(a) applied only to unrealized receivables, which generally have zero basis, and " 'substantially appreciated inventory' ", which refers to inventory with a fair market value in excess of 120 percent of basis. See I.R.C. § 751(b)(3)(A), discussed at page 336. Thus, before 1997, the aggregate approach under § 751(a) applied only on the gain side; where the inventory was depreciated, a capital loss resulted. After 1997, by its terms, § 751 allows recognition of loss on inventory that is depreciated. The different treatment under prior law apparently was the result of a desire not to further complicate the matter, even though the "one-way door" aspect of the rule was somewhat unfair.

partner's share of depreciation recapture on the partnership's assets is not eligible for installment reporting. On the one hand, this statutory structure might be read to imply that absent a specific statutory directive, the entity approach is to be applied in the case of installment sales of partnership interests, and only depreciation recapture will be denied installment reporting. On the other hand, § 453(i)(2) was a minor technical correction to the depreciation rules, inserted in Conference Committee. See H.R.Rep. No. 99–841, 99th Cong., 2d Sess. II–845 (1986). The relative obscurity of this amendment supports an argument that it does not preclude a more comprehensive melding of the policies of §§ 453, 741 and 751. Rev.Rul. 89–108, 1989–2 C.B. 100, held that installment reporting is not available for the gain on the sale of a partnership interest to the extent that the gain is attributed to substantially appreciated inventory and taxed as ordinary income under § 751. Although the ruling is silent as to the treatment of § 741 gain that is attributable to partnership inventory that is not substantially appreciated, after the 1997 amendment to § 751(a) requiring ordinary income treatment for all gain recognized on disposition of the selling partner's interest in inventory, the holding of the ruling would seem to encompass all gain attributable to inventory. The facts of the ruling indicate that the partnership held no unrealized receivables and thus provides no guidance on that issue.

A compromise solution, which would be consistent with the basic structure of the sections involved, but which is without any clear statutory basis, would be to require current recognition of the entire portion of the gain attributable to partnership property ineligible for installment method reporting.

4. DETERMINATION OF APPLICABLE CAPITAL GAINS TAX RATE

Upon the sale of depreciable real property, any § 1231 gain that is taxed as capital gain that is attributable to prior depreciation deductions claimed with respect to the property is termed "unrecaptured section 1250 gain" by § 1(h)(7), and pursuant to § 1(h)(1)(D) is taxed a maximum rate of 25 percent, not the more favorable 15 percent rate otherwise available for gains on § 1231 assets held for more than one year. When a partnership holds depreciable real property, § 1(h)(7)(A) requires that a portion of the amount of long-term capital gain recognized on the sale of an interest in the partnership be characterized as "unrecaptured § 1250 gain," subject to tax at the 25 percent maximum rate, rather than the normal 15 percent maximum rate. Treas. Reg. § 1.1(h)–1(b)(3) provides that upon the sale of a partnership interest held for more than one year, the amount of the gain that would have been ordinary income under § 751(a) if the partnership's unrecaptured § 1250 gain had been ordinary income is treated as unrecaptured § 1250 gain by the selling partner. Thus, the amount of the overall gain that is unrecaptured § 1250 gain equals the amount that would have been the partner's share of unrecaptured § 1250 gain if the partnership had sold all of its § 1250 property in a taxable transaction immediately before the transfer of the partnership interest. If the partner recognizes less than all of the gain upon the sale of the interest, a proportionate part of the gain is treated as unrecaptured § 1250 gain.

Section 1(h)(6)(B) provides that any gain from the sale of an interest in a partnership that has been held for more than one year and which is attributable to unrealized appreciation in the value of collectibles held by the partnership is treated as gain from the sale or exchange of a collectible, taxable at rates up to 28 percent rather than taxable at a maximum rate of 15 percent. Rules similar to those of § 751(a) are used to determine the amount of the gain on the sale of a partnership interest that is attributable to collectibles held by the partnership. Treas. Reg. § 1.1(h)–1(b)(2) provides that the amount of collectibles gain equals the collectibles gain that would have been allocated to the selling partner with respect to the portion of the transferred interest if the partnership had sold all of its collectibles in a taxable transaction immediately before the transfer of the interest. If the partner recognizes less than all of the gain upon the sale of the interest, a proportionate part of the gain is treated as collectibles gain.

5. TIERED PARTNERSHIPS

Section 751(f) prevents the use tiered partnerships to avoid § 751 by holding business assets in a lower tier partnership. When a partner in an upper-tier partnership sells his interest, 751(f) requires looking through the upper tier partnership to the assets of the lower tier partnership to apply § 751. Thus the partner selling an interest in an upper-tier partnership must recognize the partner's distributive share of gain attributable to assets held by a lower tier partnership. Prior to the 1984 enactment of § 754(f), Madorin v. Commissioner, 84 T.C. 667 (1985), reached this result without the benefit of statutory authority.

6. CORPORATE DISTRIBUTIONS

Section 761(e) treats any distribution of a partnership interest by a corporation or a trust as an exchange for purposes of § 708 (relating to termination of a partnership) and § 743 (relating to optional basis adjustments). Section 761(e) also authorizes the Treasury Department to promulgate regulations treating such a distribution as an exchange for purposes of § 751 but, as of yet, no such regulations have been promulgated. In the absence of regulations, the application of § 751 to a corporate dividend distribution of an interest in a partnership with unrealized receivables and/or inventory depends on whether the fair market value of the distributed interest exceeds basis. If the distribution is a dividend and the fair market value of the partnership interest exceeds its basis to the corporation § 751 applies because § 311 treats the distribution as a sale or exchange of the property by the corporation. But if the distribution is not in liquidation of the corporation and the fair market value of the partnership interest is less than its basis, § 311 does not treat the distribution as a sale or exchange, and § 751 presumably does not apply even though the partnership holds unrealized receivables or substantially appreciated inventory. Section 336 treats all corporate distributions in liquidation of a corporation as a sale or exchange, so § 751 applies to these distributions.

In Holiday Village Shopping Center v. United States, 773 F.2d 276 (Fed.Cir.1985), a corporation liquidated and distributed its interest in a limited partnership that held property subject to depreciation recapture. On the facts, § 751 did not apply. The court disregarded the partnership and treated the distribution as a distribution of property directly by the corporation, reflecting an aggregate approach which cannot be reconciled with the entity approach governing dispositions of partnership interests where § 751 does not apply.

Section 2. The Purchaser's Side of the Transaction: Basis Aspects

Internal Revenue Code: Sections 732(d); 742; 743; 752(a); 754; 755; 761(e).

Regulations: Sections 1.197–2(h)(12)(iv)(A); 1.704–1(b)(2)(iv)(*l*); 1.732–1(d); 1.742–1; 1.743–1(a)–(e), (j)(1)–(3), (4)(i)(A) and (B), (ii)(A) and (B); 1.754–1; 1.755–1(a) and (b).

Section 742 provides that a person buying an interest in a partnership has a basis for her partnership interest equal to its cost. "Cost" in this context includes not only the amount paid to the selling partner, but, as a result of § 752(d), the purchasing partner's share of partnership liabilities, determined under Treas. Regs. §§ 1.752–2 and 1.752–3. The purchasing partner's concern, however, is not limited to the basis of the partnership interest. The purchasing partner's share of basis in partnership assets is important to determine the amount of gain or loss recognized by the purchasing partner on a subsequent sale of the assets or the amount of depreciation allowable to the purchasing partner with respect to the assets. As a general matter, § 743(a) provides that the basis of partnership assets is not adjusted as a result of a sale or exchange of a partnership interest. However, on an elective basis, § 743(b) provides for adjustments to the basis of partnership assets to reflect the price paid by the purchasing partner. Once again, Subchapter K adopts a dual approach, with the general rule under § 743(a) being the entity approach, but aggregate treatment being permitted under § 743(b) at the election of the partnership.

For example, suppose the ABC partnership has inventory worth $1,500 with a basis of $600, and other assets worth $3,000 with a basis of $3,000. A sells his one-third interest to D for $1,500. The partnership now sells the inventory for $1,500. The partnership would have a $900 profit and B, C and D would each be taxed on ordinary income of $300. But economically D has not realized any profit, since she in effect paid $500, the fair market value, for her share of the inventory. The entity approach of § 743(a) would require D to recognize her $300 distributive share of the partnership's ordinary gain. Sections 743(b) and 755 avoid this result by allowing the partnership to elect under § 754 to apply an aggregate approach that provides D with a special upward adjustment in the basis of the partnership inventory to reflect D's $500 cost. Although the adjustment applies to "partnership property," the adjustment is applied only with respect to the transferee partner; it does not affect the "inside" basis of the other partners. Thus, the upward adjustment in the basis of partnership inventory to $500 reduces only D's share of the partnership gain. In broad terms, the purpose of § 743(b) is to put the partner who purchases a partnership interest in the same tax position she would have occupied if she had purchased a proportionate share of the assets directly.

Section 743(b) can be a two way street. If a purchasing partner's proportionate share of the basis in the partnership assets is greater than the amount paid for the partnership interest, a § 754 election would require a downward adjustment in the basis of partnership property under § 743(b). Furthermore, as amended in 2004, § 743 requires adjustments under § 743(b) to the basis of the partnership's assets whenever the aggregate basis of the partnership's assets exceeds the aggregate fair market value of the partnership's assets by more than $250,000, even if the adjustment with respect to the purchasing partner will not exceed $250,000. Section 743(b) basis adjustments remain elective in all other cases.

The desirability of a § 754 election from the point of view of the incoming partner is generally a function of whether the partnership assets have appreciated or declined in value. Since the election, once made, generally is irrevocable and applies to a number of different situations, it is difficult to generalize as to when it is appropriate for a particular partnership. A § 754 election that was made because it was advantageous at the time may come home to haunt the partnership in the future by resulting in a reduction of basis for partnership assets. In addition, some partnerships that experience frequent changes in partner personnel might find the aggregate approach which the election provides too bothersome a complication. On the other hand, from the point of view of an incoming partner, it may be important that he have a commitment from the partnership to make the requisite election or else the basis adjustment which he may desire will not be available. Even if the partnership does not make a § 754 election, § 732(d) provides a special basis rule akin to § 743(b) with respect to partnership assets distributed in kind to a buying partner within two years from the date of purchase, see page 328.

ILLUSTRATIVE MATERIAL

1. COMPUTATION OF BASIS ADJUSTMENTS UNDER SECTION 743(b)

1.1. *General*

Sections 743(b) and 755 allow the partnership to adjust the basis of the partnership assets upon the transfer of a partnership interest by sale or upon the death of a partner.[6] This basis adjustment is solely for the benefit

---

6. In Mushro v. Commissioner, 50 T.C. 43 (1968) (Nonacq.), the receipt of insurance proceeds by the deceased partner's wife was treated as payment by the ramaining part-of the transferee. Treas. Regs. §§ 1.743–1 and 1.755–1(a) and (b) provide detailed rules for computing the amount of the aggregate § 743(b) basis adjustment and allocating the adjustment among the partnership's assets.[7] The goal of the regulations is to provide a transferee partner with a fair market value basis in the partnership's assets for purposes of computing that partner's distributive share of future partnership items.

The amount of the aggregate § 743(b) adjustment is the difference between the transferee's basis in his partnership interest and the transferee's "proportionate share of the adjusted basis of the partnership property." Under Treas. Reg. § 1.743–1, the transferee partner's share of the adjusted basis of the partnership property (inside basis) equals the sum of (1) the transferee partner's interest as a partner in the partnership's "previously taxed capital," plus (2) the transferee partner's share of partnership liabilities. The starting point for determining the transferee partner's share of the partnership's previously taxed capital is a hypothetical transaction in which the partnership is assumed to have sold all of its assets for cash (plus assumption of liabilities) equal to the fair market value of the assets immediately after the transfer of the partnership interest, but without taking into account any existing § 743(b) adjustments. The transferee partner's share of the partnership's previously taxed capital is then equal to (1) the amount of cash that the transferee partner would have received on liquidation of the partnership immediately following the hypothetical sale of the partnership's assets, increased by (2) the amount of tax loss that would have been allocated to the transferee from the hypothetical transaction, and decreased by (3) the amount of tax gain that would have been allocated to the transferee from the hypothetical transaction.

For example, suppose that the ABC Partnership has two assets, Blackacre and Whiteacre (both of which are § 1231 assets). Blackacre has a fair market value of $3,000 and a basis of $1,800; Whiteacre has a value of $5,400 and a basis of $3,600. A sells his one-third interest to D for $2,800 and the partnership makes a § 754 election. Before the adjustment, D's share of the partnership's previously taxed capital is $1,800, computed as follows. If the BCD Partnership sold Blackacre and Whiteacre for their fair market values, it would receive $8,400 of cash and, upon an immediate liquidation of the partnership, $2,800 of cash would be distributed to D. The partnership also would recognize gain of $3,000: $1,200 on Blackacre and $1,800 on Whiteacre. One third of this gain, $1,000, would be allocated to D. D's interest in previously taxed capital is equal to the amount of cash D would receive in the hypothetical liquidation, $2,800, minus D's share of hypothetical gain, $1,000, which equals $1,800. Thus, D's special § 743(b) basis adjustment is $1,000—the excess of D's $2,800 basis in the partnership interest over D's $1,800 interest in previously taxed capital.

ners for the deceased partner's partnership interest and hence a § 743 basis adjustment was allowed.

7. See generally, McMahon, Optional Partnership Inside Basis Adjustments, 52 Tax Lawyer 35 (1998).

Under the regulations, as long as the partnership has neither previously made any special allocations nor holds any property to which § 704(c) applies, if the purchaser pays a price for the partnership interest at least equal to the proportionate fair market value of the partnership's assets, the purchasing partner's share of inside basis will equal the aggregate inside basis of the partnership's assets multiplied by the partner's percentage interest (as is the case in the example above). See Treas. Reg. § 1.743–1(g)(5), Ex. There are situations, however, where application of § 704(c) or prior differential allocations of partnership items will eliminate this proportional relationship. In determining a partner's "previously taxed capital," the hypothetical allocations of gain and loss are necessary to account for any § 704(c) items of income, deduction, gain or loss that would have been allocated to the transferee partner as a result of stepping into the shoes of the transferor partner, as well as any remedial allocations to the transferor partner. Prior special allocations to the selling partner under § 704(b) also are taken into account because the buyer succeeds to his seller's capital account pursuant to Treas. Reg. § 1.704–1(b)(2)(iv)(*l*).

The following example illustrates the application of § 743(b) where § 704(c) allocations are required. Assume that E contributed nondepreciable property with a fair market value of $100 and an adjusted basis of $10 and F contributed $100 of cash to the EF partnership, in which each of them received a fifty percent interest. E's share of the partnership's basis in the partnership property is $10, and F's share is $100. When the contributed property has appreciated in value to $120, E sells her interest to G for $110. G's § 743(b) basis adjustment is $100. G's share of inside basis is the $110 that would be distributable to G following a hypothetical sale of the partnership's assets for cash, decreased by the sum of the $90 of § 704(c) gain and the $10 of § 704(b) gain that would have been allocated to G's interest. The $100 adjustment is the difference between G's $110 outside basis and her $10 share of inside basis.

For further examples of the application of these rules, see Treas. Reg. § 1.743–1(d)(3).

1.2. *Allocation Among Partnership Assets*

1.2.1. *General Principles*

After the aggregate amount of the partner's basis adjustment is determined under § 743(b), the basis adjustment is allocated among the various assets of the partnership, including goodwill, by the rules of § 755. First, the adjustment is divided into two portions: (1) a portion attributable to § 1231(b) assets and capital assets ("capital gain property") and (2) a portion attributable to other types of property ("ordinary income property"). In general, the amount of the aggregate adjustment allocated to the ordinary income property is the amount of gain or loss that would have been allocated to the purchasing partner on the hypothetical sale by the partnership of the ordinary income property. The amount of the adjustment allocated to the capital gain property is the net § 743(b) adjustment minus the adjustment to the ordinary income property. Treas. Reg. § 1.755–1(b).

Section 1231 properties with § 1245 recapture are treated as two separate assets. Treas. Reg. § 1.755–1. The portion of any gain that is § 1245 recapture is treated as a zero basis ordinary income property. Thus, any adjustment attributable to gain that would be § 1245 recapture is assigned to the ordinary income category. The remaining value of § 1231 property, to which all of the original basis is attributed, is treated as a capital asset. Most often all of the excess of the fair market value of equipment over its adjusted basis represents § 1245 recapture and the adjustment in the basis of the asset will be part of the ordinary income class. To the extent a partnership holds amortizable section 197 intangibles, however, there is a greater likelihood that the asset may be appreciated beyond its recomputed basis and thus its basis will be adjusted in two steps—in part as a constituent of the ordinary income group and in part as a constituent of the capital asset group.

If the assets of the partnership constitute a trade or business, a portion of the basis adjustment usually will have to be allocated to partnership goodwill and other § 197 intangibles, (e.g., customer lists, licenses, franchises, trademarks, trade names, advantageous contracts, etc.). In applying the apportionment rules of Treas. Reg. § 1.755–1, the fair market value of the partnership's § 197 intangibles, including goodwill and going concern value, must be determined using the residual method required by § 1060 for applicable asset acquisitions. Pursuant to Treas. Reg. § 1.755–1(a)(5), § 197 intangibles are valued by applying the following procedure. First, the partnership determines the value of all of its assets other than § 197 intangibles. Second, the partnership determines the "partnership gross value." Generally speaking, "partnership gross value" is the amount that, if assigned to all partnership property, would result in a liquidating distribution to the transferee partner equal to that partner's basis (reduced by the amount, if any, of the partner's basis that is attributable to partnership liabilities) in the transferred partnership interest immediately following the acquisition. For most § 743(b) basis adjustments, the benchmark for determining the gross partnership value is the amount paid for a transferred partnership interest. Third, the partnership determines the value of its § 197 intangibles under the residual method, i.e., the value of § 197 intangibles equals the partnership gross value minus the value of partnership assets other than § 197 intangibles. If the aggregate value of partnership property other than § 197 intangibles is equal to or greater than the partnership gross value, all § 197 intangibles are treated as having zero value. If there is any value assigned to the § 197 intangibles, that value is allocated among § 197 intangibles other than goodwill and going concern value before any value is assigned to goodwill and going concern value. In allocating values and basis to § 197 intangibles, value is assigned first to those § 197 intangibles (other than goodwill and going concern value) that would produce § 751(c) flush language unrealized receivables, i.e., those that have been previously amortized or depreciated, to the extent of their basis and the unrealized receivable amount; then among all § 197 intangibles (other than goodwill and going concern value) relative to fair market value. In simpler terms, if a partner pays more for a partnership interest than the fair market value of all of the tangible and intangible assets other than goodwill, the excess of the purchase price over the fair market value of the assets other than goodwill must be allocated to goodwill.

The operation of the basic rules of § 755 is illustrated in the following example. Suppose that the ABC Partnership has three assets: a capital asset having a fair market value of $3,000 and a basis of $1,800; a depreciable § 1231 asset (not subject to § 1245 recapture because it is real estate) having a value of $5,400 and a basis of $3,600; and inventory having a value of $3,000 and an adjusted basis of $1,500. A sells her one-third interest to D for $3,800 and the partnership makes a § 754 election. Under the rules of Treas. Reg. § 1.743–1, D's share of the partnership's basis in its assets is $2,300, and his § 743(b) special basis adjustment is $1,500 ($3,800 − $2,300). If no § 743(b) adjustment were made and the ordinary income asset was sold by the partnership, D's share of the gain would be $500. Thus, under Treas. Reg. § 1.755–1(b)(2), $500 of the overall adjustment is allocated to the ordinary income asset. The remaining $1,000 of the adjustment is allocated to the capital asset class (the capital and the § 1231 asset). The $1,000 adjustment allocated to a particular class of assets is allocated among the assets in the class under Treas. Reg. § 1.755–1(b)(3) according to a formula that generally results in allocating to each asset within the class an adjustment equal to the amount of gain or loss that would be allocated to the transferee partner, D, upon a sale of the assets. Thus, a $400 positive adjustment is allocated to the capital asset and a $600 positive adjustment is allocated to the § 1231 asset. These basis adjustments are added to D's proportionate share of the partnership's basis in its assets solely for purposes of computing D's distributive share of partnership gain, loss and depreciation. D's special basis in the partnership assets is illustrated in the following computation.

Asset	D's share of Partnership Basis Before Adjustment	+ Adjustment	=	D's Special § 743(b) Basis
Capital Asset	$ 600	$400		$1,000
§ 1231 Asset	$1,200	$600		$1,800
Inventory	$ 500	$500		$1,000

As far as B and C are concerned, however, the basis of the partnership property remains unchanged.[8]

Even though on its face § 755 allocates either a positive or negative § 743(b) adjustment between the class of assets consisting of capital assets

---

8. In Rev. Rul. 79–92, 1979–1 C.B. 180, a § 754 election was in effect, and as a result under § 743(b) one partner had a higher basis in partnership assets than the other partners. The Ruling held that if the partner-ship sold the assets for deferred payments and the partner with the higher basis realized a loss while the other partners realized a gain, the other partners could report the gain on the installment method under § 453.

and § 1231 assets and the class consisting of all other assets, the regulations provide that one class of property may be allocated a negative adjustment while the other class of property is allocated a positive adjustment, with the two opposite signed adjustments netting out to an amount equal to the overall § 743(b) adjustment. See Treas. Reg. § 1.755–1(b)(2)(ii), Ex. (1).

Assume for example, that the EF Partnership, in which E and F are equal partners (and to which each contributed an equal amount of cash), held the following assets.

Asset Class	Basis	F.M.V.
Capital Gain Assets		
§ 1231 Asset	$3,000	$6,000
Ordinary Income Assets		
Inventory	$4,000	$3,000
	$7,000	$9,000

G purchases E's interest for $4,500. G's § 743(b) basis adjustment is $1,000 ($4,500 – $3,500). If no § 743(b) adjustment were made, on sale of the partnership's assets G would be allocated a $1,500 gain on the sale of the § 1231 asset ([$6,000 – $3,000] ÷ 2) and a $500 loss on the sale of inventory ([$3,000 – $4,000] ÷ 2). If a § 754 election is in effect, a negative adjustment of $500 is allocated to the class of ordinary income assets and a positive adjustment of $1,500 ($1,000 – ($500)) is allocated to the class of capital gain assets. Since there is only one asset in each class in this example, no question arises regarding allocation of the class adjustment among assets within each class.

Basis adjustments also are allowed when, as a result of offsetting appreciation and depreciation in value, the net § 743(b) adjustment is zero. Assume for example, that the AB Partnership, in which A and B are equal partners (and to which each contributed an equal amount of cash), held the following assets.

Asset Class	Basis	F.M.V.
Capital Gain Assets		
§ 1231 Asset	$3,000	$6,000
Ordinary Income Assets		
Inventory	$6,000	$3,000
	$9,000	$9,000

If C buys A's fifty percent partnership interest for $4,500, the net § 743(b) basis adjustment is zero. Nevertheless, if a § 754 election is in effect, C is allocated a positive basis adjustment of $1,500 with respect to the § 1231 asset, increasing C's special basis from $1,500 to $3,000. Simultaneously, C is allocated a negative basis adjustment of $1,500 with respect to the inventory asset, decreasing C's special basis from $3,000 to $1,500. See Treas. Reg. § 1.755–1(b)(2)(ii), Ex. (2).

1.2.2. *Situations Involving Section 704(c) Allocations*

Now consider the situation in which the purchasing partner acquires a partnership interest from a selling partner to whom a § 704(c) allocation would have been made with respect to one partnership asset, while a continuing partner would receive a § 704(c) allocation with respect to a different asset. Assume that the JK Partnership, in which J and K are equal partners, was formed by J's contribution of Blackacre, a capital asset that had a fair market value of $4,000 and a basis of $1,000 at the time of the contribution, and K's contribution of Whiteacre, a § 1231 asset that had a fair market value of $4,000 and a basis of $5,000 at the time of the contribution. L purchased J's partnership interest for $5,500 when the partnership held the following assets.

Asset Class	Basis	F.M.V.
Capital Gain Assets		
Blackacre	$ 1,000	$ 8,000
Whiteacre	$ 5,000	$ 3,000

If no § 743 adjustment were made, on sale of the partnership's assets, after taking into account allocations that would have been required by § 704(c), L would be allocated a $5,000 gain on the sale of Blackacre ($3,000 of § 704(c) gain + [($8,000 − $4,000) ÷ 2]), and a $500 loss on the sale of Whiteacre. K would be allocated a $1,000 built-in loss on the sale of Whiteacre. K and L would share the remaining $1,000 of loss equally. L's § 743(b) basis adjustment is thus $4,500. A positive basis adjustment of $5,000 is allocated to Blackacre, giving L a special basis in Blackacre of $6,000, and a negative basis adjustment of $500 is allocated to Whiteacre, giving L a special basis in Whiteacre of $1,500. (As a result of § 704(c), K is effectively allocated $3,000 of basis in Whiteacre, while L is allocated the remaining basis.)

Asset	L's share of Partnership Basis Before Adjustment	+ Adjustment =	L's Special § 743(b) Basis
Blackacre	$1,000	$5,000	$6,000
Whiteacre	$2,000	($ 500)	$1,500

Upon the subsequent sale by the partnership of Blackacre for $8,000, L will recognize no gain, while K will recognize a gain of $2,000. Upon the subsequent sale of Whiteacre for $3,000, L will recognize no loss, while K will recognize a $1,500 loss. See Treas. Reg. § 1.755–1(b)(2)(ii), Ex. (1). When § 704(c) allocations are involved, the purchasing partner's special basis will not be proportionate to the fair market value of the assets; the purchasing partner's basis will be higher than proportionate fair market value if an allocation of § 704(c) gain would have been made to the purchasing partner absent a § 743(b) adjustment and it will be lower than proportionate fair market value if an allocation of § 704(c) loss must be allocated to other partners.

1.2.3. *Technical Aspects of the Apportionment Formula: Allocation to Specific Assets*

In general, the allocation of § 743(b) adjustments between the classes of ordinary income and capital asset properties and among assets within a class of properties depends on the gain or loss that would be allocated to the purchasing partner on a hypothetical sale of the assets for fair market value at the time of the purchase. The general rule for apportioning the § 743(b) basis adjustment between ordinary income assets and capital gain assets is subject to one significant limitation. Treas. Reg. § 1.755–1(b)(2)(i)(B) provides that a negative adjustment to capital gain property may not exceed the partnership's basis in its capital gain property. If a decrease in basis allocated to capital gain property exceeds the partnership's basis in that property, the excess negative adjustment is applied to reduce the basis of ordinary income property. This situation will arise if the purchasing partner acquires the purchased interest for an amount that is less than the selling partner's share of the partnership's inside basis. The regulations do not provide an example of the application of this rule.

The formula provided in Treas. Reg. § 1.755–1(b)(3) for the allocation of § 743(b) adjustments to specific assets within a class of property is multi-faceted and varies for ordinary income and capital gains assets in order to account for the limitation on the adjustment to the basis of capital assets under Treas. Reg. § 1.755–1(b)(2)(i)(B). The basis adjustment to each ordinary income asset equals:

> (1) the amount of income, gain, or loss (including remedial allocations under Treas. Reg. § 1.704–3(d)) that would be allocated to the purchasing partner on the hypothetical sale of the item, minus

> (2) any reduction of basis adjustment to ordinary income property required under Treas. Reg. § 1.755–1(b)(2)(i)(B) because the partnership did not have enough basis in capital gain property to reduce, multiplied by a fraction, the numerator of which is the fair market value of the asset whose basis is being adjusted and the denominator of which is the total fair market value of all of the partnership's ordinary income assets.

This formula applies the general rule for allocating adjustments by the purchasing partner's share of gain or loss on a hypothetical sale plus an apportionment of any decrease required by the limitation on allocations to capital gain property based on relative fair market values. In algebraic form, the formula for the basis adjustment to a particular ordinary income asset is as follows:

$$\text{Hypothetical gain or loss allocable to the purchasing partner on sale of the asset} - \left\{ \left(\text{Negative Adjustment to capital assets} - \text{Basis of Capital Assets} \right) \times \frac{\text{FMV of Asset}}{\text{FMV of all ordinary income assets}} \right\}$$

The basis adjustment to each capital gain asset equals:

> (1) the amount of income, gain, or loss (including remedial allocations under Treas. Reg. § 1.704–3(d)) that would be allocated to the purchasing partner on the hypothetical sale of the asset, minus

(2) the total amount of gain or loss (including remedial allocations) that would be allocated to the purchasing partner on the hypothetical sale of all capital gain assets minus the positive adjustments to all capital gain assets or plus the negative basis adjustments to all capital gain assets, multiplied by a fraction, the numerator of which is the fair market value of the item of property to the partnership and the denominator of which is the total fair market value of all of the partnership's items of capital gain property.

The amount subtracted under part (2) of this formula will be zero unless the limitation of Treas. Reg. § 1.755–1(b)(2)(i)(B) applies to restrict the amount allocated to capital gains property. Thus, this part of the formula allocates the purchasing partner's share of gain or loss that would be recognized on hypothetical sale of capital gain assets, then reduces the allocation by the reduction of Treas. Reg. § 1.755–1(b)(2)(i)(B) apportioned to each asset by fair market value. In algebraic form, the formula for the basis adjustment to a particular capital asset is as follows:

$$
\begin{array}{l}
\text{Hypothetical} \\
\text{gain or loss} \\
\text{allocable to} \\
\text{the purchasing} \\
\text{partner on sale} \\
\text{of the asset}
\end{array}
-
\left\{
\left[
\begin{array}{l}
\text{Total} \\
\text{hypothetical} \\
\text{gain from} \\
\text{all capital} \\
\text{assets}
\end{array}
-
\begin{array}{l}
\text{Total basis} \\
\text{adjustment} \\
\text{to} \\
\text{capital} \\
\text{assets}
\end{array}
\right]
\times
\frac{\text{FMV of Asset}}{\begin{array}{l}\text{FMV of all}\\\text{capital assets}\end{array}}
\right\}
$$

If the buying partner would have been allocated gain with respect to an asset (including gain attributable to a § 704(c) allocation that would have been made to the selling partner had she remained a partner), the asset's basis is increased by that amount. If the buying partner would have been allocated loss with respect to an asset (including loss attributable to a § 704(c) allocation that would have been made to the selling partner had she remained a partner), the asset's basis is decreased by that amount. If some assets in a class have appreciated in value while other assets within the class have depreciated in value, the appreciated assets must be allocated a positive basis adjustment and the depreciated assets must be allocated a negative basis adjustment.

Assume, for example, that the AB Partnership, in which A and B are equal partners (and to which each contributed an equal amount of cash), held the following assets.

Asset Class	Basis	F.M.V.
Capital Gain Assets		
Capital Asset	$ 2,000	$ 8,000
§ 1231 Asset	$ 6,000	$ 4,000
Ordinary Income Assets		
Inventory	$ 3,000	$ 2,000
Unrealized Receivable	$ 0	$ 4,000
	$11,000	$18,000

C purchases A's interest for $9,000. If no § 743 adjustment were made, on a sale of the partnership's assets C would be allocated a $3,000 gain on the sale of the capital asset ([$8,000 – $2,000] ÷ 2), a $1,000 loss on the sale of the § 1231 asset ([$4,000 – $6,000] ÷ 2), a $500 loss on the sale of inventory ([$3,000 – $4,000] ÷ 2), and a $2,000 gain on the sale of the unrealized receivable ([$4,000 – $0] ÷ 2). These items result in net gain of $3,500, which is C's total § 743(b) adjustment. The net gain allocated to C on the hypothetical sale of the ordinary income assets is $1,500, the net of the $2,000 gain on the sale of the unrealized receivables and the $500 loss on the sale of the inventory allocable to C's interest. Thus, a net adjustment of $1,500 is allocated to the ordinary income assets. The adjustment allocated to the capital gain assets is $2,000, the $3,500 total adjustment minus the $1,500 adjustment allocated to the ordinary income items. Within the ordinary income asset class, the $1,500 net adjustment is allocated by making a $500 negative adjustment to the basis of the inventory, an amount equal to the loss that would have been allocated to C if the inventory had been sold without a § 743(b) adjustment. C's special basis in the inventory is $1,000. A positive adjustment of $2,000 is allocated to the basis of the unrealized receivables, reflecting the gain that would have been allocated to C if the unrealized receivables had been sold without a § 743(b) basis adjustment. C's special basis in the unrealized receivables is $2,000. Within the capital gain class of assets, the $2,000 net adjustment is allocated by making a positive adjustment of $3,000 to the basis of the capital asset, which is an amount equal to the gain that would have been allocated to C if the capital asset had been sold without a § 743(b) basis adjustment. C's special basis in the capital asset is $4,000. A negative adjustment of $1,000 is allocated to the basis of the § 1231 asset, reflecting the loss that would have been allocated to C if the § 1231 asset had been sold without a § 743(b) basis adjustment. C's special basis in the § 1231 asset is $2,000.

Asset	C's share of Partnership Basis Before Adjustment	+ Adjustment =	C's Special § 743(b) Basis
Capital Gains Property			
Capital Asset	$1,000	$3,000	$4,000
§ 1231 Asset	$3,000	($1,000)	$2,000
Ordinary Income Property			
Inventory	$1,500	($500)	$1,000
Unrealized Receivables	0	$2,000	$2,000

In this example, C, a fifty percent partner, ends up with a special basis in each asset equal to fifty percent of its fair market value on the date C purchased the partnership interest. As long as a partnership interest is purchased for an amount that equals the proportionate fair market value of its assets, including goodwill, this is the result that generally occurs under the regulations. See Treas. Reg. § 1.755–1(b)(3)(iv), Ex. (1).

If, however, a partnership interest is purchased for an amount that is less than the proportionate fair market value of its assets, the provisions of Treas. Reg. § 1.755–1(b)(3)(ii)(B) apply and the capital gain assets will be allocated a basis increase that is insufficient to increase the purchasing partner's special basis in those assets to proportionate fair market value. See Treas. Reg. § 1.755–1(b)(3)(iv), Ex. (2).

1.3. Application of Special Basis Adjustment

1.3.1. Sales and Exchanges of Partnership Property

Although Treas. Reg. § 1.743–1(j)(1) describes the § 743(b) basis adjustment as an increase or decrease to "the basis of partnership property," Treas. Reg. § 1.743–1(j) provides for the treatment of the § 743(b) basis adjustment as an adjustment to the transferee partner's distributive share of partnership gain or loss computed without regard to the basis adjustment. See Treas. Reg. § 1.743–1(j)(3)(ii), Ex's. (1)–(3). Converting the basis adjustment to an adjustment of the purchasing partner's distributive share avoids cumbersome computations that would be required by allocating different bases to each partner.

For example, suppose that the BC Partnership in the immediately preceding example sells the capital asset for $9,000. Under Treas. Reg. § 1.743–1(j) C's gain with respect to the capital asset is computed as one-half of the partnership's gain of $7,000 using the partnership's common basis of $2,000, i.e., $3,500, minus C's special basis adjustment of $3,000, for a gain of $500.

Because the basis of partnership property is adjusted only with respect to the transferee partner, the computations of partnership income and loss would be more complicated if the basis adjustment actually were made directly to the partnership's basis for the property. C has a special basis for his one-half interest in the capital asset of $4,000 consisting of C's $3,000 basis adjustment plus one-half of the partnership's initial $2,000 basis. The partnership's total basis is $5,000 ($1,000 + $4,000). Although the partnership's gain is $4,000 ($9,000 – [$4,000 + $1,000]), C's distributive share of the gain is only $500. If the partnership's basis was changed by treating the partnership as having a $5,000 basis, C's distributive share of the gain would be computed by adding his $3,000 basis adjustment to one-half of the $2,000 basis the partnership had before the adjustment ($1,000), resulting in a $4,000 basis that would offset C's one-half share of the amount realized ([$9,000/2] – $4,000), while B's share would be $3,500 ([$9,000/2] – [$1,000]).

1.3.2. Depreciation Deductions With Respect to Property Subject to Section 743(b) Basis Adjustment

Treas. Reg. § 1.743–1(j)(4) provides detailed rules regarding the effect of § 743(b) basis adjustments on depreciation and amortization deductions with respect to property subject to the basis adjustment. If the basis of a partnership's depreciable property is increased, the increased portion of the basis generally must be depreciated as if it were newly-purchased property placed in service on the date the transfer of the partnership interest occurred. The partnership's original basis in the property continues to be depreciated as if there had been no basis increase. This treatment is consistent with the treatment under § 168(i)(7) of increases to basis resulting from the transfers to partnerships subject to § 721.

Assume, for example, that the EF Partnership held two § 1231 assets, Blackacre and Whiteacre, both of which are residential rental buildings on leased land. The basis and fair market values of the properties are as follows:

Asset	Basis	F.M.V.
Blackacre	$18,000	$46,000
Whiteacre	$10,000	$10,000

Blackacre has 12 years remaining in its cost recovery period. (For simplicity, assume a 28 year cost recovery period and ignore the mid-month convention.) G purchases E's partnership interest for $26,000. G's special basis in Blackacre is $23,000. Of that special basis, $9,000 is recovered through annual depreciation deductions of $750 for the remaining 12 years of Blackacre's original class life, and $14,000 is recovered through annual depreciation deductions of $500 over a new 28 year class life. Thus, G is entitled to annual depreciation deductions with respect to Blackacre of $1,250 ($750 + $500) for 12 years, followed by annual depreciation deductions of $500 for another 16 years.

If, however, the partnership has remedial allocations in effect under Treas. Reg. § 1.704–3(d) (discussed at page 158) that affect an item of property for which a § 743(b) basis adjustment has been made with respect to the § 704(c) gain to which the remedial allocation relates, then the additional basis attributable to the basis adjustment with respect to § 704(c) is depreciated over the property's remaining cost recovery period. Treas. Reg. § 1.743–1(j)(4)(i). Any remaining basis increase in the § 704(c) property is depreciated over a new recovery period. The purpose of these bifurcated rules is to attempt to provide a purchasing partner with identical depreciation deductions regardless of whether the purchasing partner purchases an interest from the partner who contributed the § 704(c) property or from a noncontributing partner.

If § 743(b) requires a basis decrease, the decrease in basis must be taken into account over the remaining cost recovery period of the property, beginning with the recovery period in which the basis is decreased. Treas. Reg. § 1.743–1(j)(4)(ii). In general, a negative basis adjustment results in a proportional reduction of the transferee partner's distributive share of depreciation deductions attributable to the property with respect to which the negative basis adjustment is required. Treas. Reg. § 1.743–1(j)(4)(ii)(A) and (B). If the negative basis adjustment attributable to any particular year exceeds the transferee partner's distributive share of depreciation attributable to the property to which the adjustment relates, the negative adjustment is applied to reduce the transferee partner's share of depreciation attributable to other partnership property. If the adjustment does not absorb the entire adjustment attributable to the year, then the distributee partner must recognize ordinary income. Treas. Reg. § 1.743–1(j)(4)(ii)(C), Ex. (3), illustrates the application of the recognition of ordinary income rule, but hypothesizes rather than explains how the circumstances for applying this rule can arise.

Because the basis adjustment under § 743(b) applies only to the transferee partner, the basis adjustment does not affect the common basis of partnership property and thus does not affect the tax consequences of the other partners.

1.4. *Application to Partners in Electing Large Partnerships*

An electing large partnership (discussed at page 92) may elect to adjust the basis of partnership assets with respect to a purchasing partner under § 743(b). The computation of an electing large partnership's taxable income is made without regard to the § 743(b) adjustment and the partner's distributive share is appropriately adjusted to take the § 743(b) adjustment into account. I.R.C. § 774(a).

2.   ELECTION PROCEDURES

Pursuant to § 754, a § 743(b) election is made by the partnership—not the incoming partner. The regulations require the election to be made on the partnership return "for the taxable year during which the distribution or transfer occurs." Treas. Reg. § 1.754–1(b)(1). Jones v. United States, 553 F.2d 667 (Ct.Cl.1977), upheld the validity of the regulations in a situation in which an election was filed in 1969 with respect to a transfer which had taken place in 1967 on the death of a partner. If such an election is made it applies not only upon all subsequent sales and purchases of partnership interests, but also to require basis adjustments under § 734, attributable to distributions of partnership property (see page 355).

3.   MANDATORY NEGATIVE SECTION 743(b) BASIS ADJUSTMENTS

As noted previously, as amended in 2004, § 743 requires a negative § 743(b) adjustment to the basis of the partnership's assets whenever the aggregate basis of the partnership's assets exceeds the aggregate fair market value of the partnership's assets by more than $250,000. This mandatory basis adjustment is required even if the adjustment with respect to the purchasing partner will not exceed $250,000. The purpose of the 2004 amendment is to prevent the duplication of losses in a manner that allows a partner to recognize for tax purposes a loss that was not realized economically. See Notice 2005–32, 2005–16 I.R.B. 895, for procedural details and examples of the application of the rule.

A special rule for certain "electing investment partnerships" permits the partnership to avoid making the basis adjustment, but limits the transferee partner's distributive share of any losses with respect to partnership property to the amount that exceeds the loss recognized on the sale of the partnership interest by the transferor partner from whom the partnership interest was purchased. I.R.C. § 743(e). The definition of a qualifying "electing investment partnership" in § 743(e)(6) is very restrictive and narrowly limits the application of the special rule. The election is made at the partnership level. See Notice 2005–32, 2005–16 I.R.B. 895. Section 743 (f) provides an additional exception for a very narrow category of "securitization partnerships."

4. EFFECT ON PARTNER'S CAPITAL ACCOUNT

A § 743(b) basis adjustment does not affect the amount of partnership book gain or loss that will be allocated to the purchasing partner's capital account upon the sale of property with respect to which such an adjustment is in effect. Treas. Reg. § 1.704–1(b)(2)(iv)(m)(2). Thus, for example, if the BCD Partnership in 1.1.1, at page 301, sold the capital asset for $4,200, the partnership's book gain would be $2,400 ($4,200 sale price – $1,800 book value). D's share of book gain added to her capital account would be $800 (1/3 × $2,400), even though as a result of the basis adjustment, D's taxable gain was only $400 ((1/3 × $800) – $400).

5. PURCHASER OF ALL INTERESTS IN A PARTNERSHIP

McCauslen v. Commissioner, 45 T.C. 588 (1966), held that when one partner in a two person partnership purchases the other partner's entire interest, the purchaser is treated as having acquired by direct purchase the portion of partnership assets attributable to the acquired partnership interest (even though Treas. Reg. § 1.741–1(b) provides that the selling partner is treated as selling his partnership interest). Thus, in such a case the purchasing partner obtains a fair market value basis in the newly acquired portion of the former partnership's assets without resort to §§ 754 and 734(b). This same rule would apply whenever all of the interests in a partnership are purchased by one purchaser in an integrated transaction.

6. APPLICATION TO TIERED PARTNERSHIPS

Suppose that A purchases from B for $50 a one-fourth partnership interest in UTP Partnership which owns inventory having a basis of $40 and a fair market value of $80 and a one-third interest in LTP Partnership, having a basis of $80 and a fair market value of $120. LTP's sole asset is a capital asset having a basis of $330 and a fair market value of $360. UTP's basis in LTP is less than its pro rata basis in LTP's assets because UTP purchased its interest in LTP at a time when LTP did not have a § 754 election in effect. Assuming that B's pro rata share of UTP's basis in its assets is $30, if UTP has a § 754 election in effect, B is entitled to a § 743(b) basis adjustment of $20, of which $10 is attributable to UTP's interest in LTP.

Rev.Rul. 87–115, 1987–2 C.B. 163, held that a § 743(b) adjustment to the basis of LTP's asset is available if LTP also has a § 754 election in effect. In that case the sale of A's interest in UTP to B is treated as a deemed sale of an interest in LTP. If LTP does not have a § 754 election in effect, no basis adjustment is allowed. Similarly, if LTP has a § 754 election in effect, but UTP does not, no basis adjustment is allowed.

If a § 743(b) adjustment is available to LTP, it is determined as follows. The deemed price paid by B for an indirect interest in LTP is $30 (¼ of UTP's $80 basis in LTP plus B's $10 special adjustment). B's share of the adjusted basis of LTP's asset is $27.50 (¼ of $110). Thus, B's § 743(b) adjustment in the basis of LTP's asset is only $2.50. What happened to the remaining $7.50 of B's § 743(b) adjustment to UTP's basis in LTP? What would be B's basis adjustment in LTP's basis for its asset if UTP's basis in LTP had been $110, an amount equal to one third of its pro rata basis of LTP's assets?

CHAPTER 9

PARTNERSHIP DISTRIBUTIONS

SECTION 1. CURRENT DISTRIBUTIONS

A. CASH DISTRIBUTIONS AND REDUCTION OF LIABILITIES

INTERNAL REVENUE CODE: Sections 731; 733; 741; 752(b); 761(d).

REGULATIONS: Sections 1.731–1(a)(1) and (3), (b); 1.733–1; 1.761–1(d).

Under the conduit approach to the taxation of partnership income adopted by Subchapter K, a partner is taxed currently on his share of the partnership income whether the income is distributed or not. Income taxed to a partner is added to the partner's basis in his partnership interest, which thereafter permits a distribution of the income without further tax. I.R.C. § 705(a)(1). The circle is closed by § 731(a)(1), which provides that distributions of cash do not result in gain to the partner except to the extent that distributed cash exceeds the partner's adjusted basis for her partnership interest. Section § 752(b) treats a reduction in a partner's share of partnership liabilities as a cash distribution. Thus, under §§ 731(a)(1) and 733, a reduction of liabilities also reduces the distributee partner's basis and results in recognized gain if the reduction in liability exceeds the partner's basis in the partnership interest.

Distributions of property likewise, in general, do not result in gain to the partner, even if the fair market value of the distributed property exceeds the partner's basis for the partnership interest. Instead, under § 732(a)(1), the partnership's basis in the distributed property is transferred from the partnership to the partner. The transferred basis is limited by § 732(a)(2) to the partner's basis in the partnership interest. These rules are subject to several limitations and qualifications. Section 751(b), for example, creates a constructive taxable exchange whenever a partner receives a current distribution that alters the partners' respective interests in unrealized receivables or substantially appreciated inventory. Additional rules, discussed in Section 2, apply in the case of a distribution in liquidation of a partner's interest in the partnership.

Revenue Ruling 81–242

1981–2 C.B. 147.

ISSUE

May gain be recognized to each partner when mortgaged property owned by a partnership is involuntarily converted even though the partnership elects to defer the recognition of gain under section 1033 of the Internal Revenue Code?

FACTS

P is a general partnership of five individuals. In 1969, P purchased a building for commercial use. Through depreciation and other adjustments and distributions, the bases of the partners' interests had been reduced below their share of liabilities.

In 1980, City Y, through appropriate proceedings, acquired by condemnation the building owned by P for 20x dollars. At the time of the condemnation, the mortgage debt owed by P was 15x dollars, and P's basis in the property was 10x dollars. The award made by City Y was used to pay off the mortgage debt.

P elected to replace the building within the meaning of section 1033(a)(2) of the Code and within the time prescribed by section 1033(a)(2)(B).

LAW AND ANALYSIS

Section 1033(a)(2) of the Code provides that if property is involuntarily converted into money by condemnation, then any gain shall be recognized. However, section 1033(a)(2)(A) provides that if replacement property is purchased (under circumstances that comply with the pertinent provisions of section 1033), then, at the election of the taxpayer, gain shall be recognized only to the extent that the amount realized on the conversion exceeds the cost of the replacement property.

Section 703(b) of the Code provides that any election affecting the computation of taxable income derived from a partnership must be made by the partnership.

Furthermore, Rev.Rul. 66–191, 1966–2 C.B. 300, holds that the election under section 1033 of the Code not to recognize gain from an involuntary conversion can be made only by the partnership and not by the partners individually.

Section 731(a)(1) of the Code provides that when there is a distribution by a partnership to a partner, gain shall not be recognized to that partner, except to the extent that any money distributed exceeds the adjusted basis of that partner's interest in the partnership immediately before the distribution.

Section 752(b) of the Code provides that any decrease in a partner's share of the liabilities of a partnership, or any decrease in a partner's individual liabilities by reason of the assumption by the partnership of the individual liabilities, shall be considered as a distribution of money to the partner by the partnership.

In this case, P realized 10x dollars of gain from the condemnation of its building. Because P elected to replace the condemned building within the meaning of section 1033(a)(2) of the Code and within the time prescribed by section 1033(a)(2)(B), P is not required to recognize the 10x dollars gain realized from the condemned building.

The award by City Y was used to pay off the 15x dollars of liability on the condemned building, resulting in a decrease in each partner's share of the liability of P. Under section 752(b) of the Code, the decrease is treated as a distribution of money to each partner. Thus, under section 731(a)(1), gain is recognized to each partner to the extent that the deemed distribution to each partner exceeds the adjusted basis of each partner's interest in P immediately before the distribution.

The transaction described above is distinguishable from that considered in Rev.Rul. 79–205, 1979–2 C.B. 255. In that ruling, a partnership made non-liquidating distributions of property to its two equal partners. Because the properties in question were subject to liabilities, the distributions resulted in a decrease in the liabilities of the partnership (a deemed distribution to each partner under section 752(b)), and an increase in each partner's individual liabilities (a deemed contribution by each partner under section 752(a)). The ruling concludes that the distributions were part of a single transaction and that the properties were treated as having been distributed simultaneously to the two partners. Thus, the resulting liability adjustments were treated as having occurred simultaneously.

In this case, the condemnation of the building and the subsequent reinvestment of the proceeds were separate transactions that did not occur simultaneously. When P subsequently acquired replacement property that was subject to a liability, each partner's share of the liability of P increased. Because this increase resulted from a separate transaction, it may not be netted against the decrease in liability on the prior condemnation of the original property. Therefore, the full amount of the decrease in liability was a deemed distribution of money to the partners.

HOLDING

Under section 1033 of the Code, the 10x dollars of gain from the condemnation of P's building is not recognized in 1980. However, under section 731(a)(1), gain is recognized to each partner to the extent that partner's proportionate share of the deemed distribution of the 15x dollars of liability exceeds the adjusted basis of that partner's interest in P immediately before the distribution.

ILLUSTRATIVE MATERIAL

1. CURRENT DISTRIBUTIONS OF CASH

1.1. *Treatment of Distributee Partner*

Current distributions of cash reduce the basis of the partner's interest under § 733 and § 705(a)(2), but otherwise have no tax effect unless the amount of the distribution exceeds the partner's basis in the partnership interest. Since a partner's basis is adjusted upwards under § 705(a)(1) for the partner's distributive share of partnership income that has been taxed to the partner, the distribution of money representing the previously taxed income of necessity gives rise to a downward adjustment. The two adjustments cancel out, leaving the partner's basis the same as it was before the partnership earned and distributed its income. In this simple case, the basis adjustments merely eliminate any possibility of recognition of gain on the distribution of previously taxed partnership income. Cash distributions also are tax-free to the extent of the distributee partner's basis that is attributable to contributions to the partnership (or to the partner's share of liabilities), representing a return of partnership capital.

Section 731(a)(1) provides for recognition of gain to the extent that a cash distribution exceeds the partner's basis in her partnership interest, since otherwise the excess cash would go untaxed. The gain recognized under § 731 is treated as gain on the sale of a partnership interest and hence, under § 741, is capital gain, unless the partnership has unrealized receivables or substantially appreciated inventory so that § 751(b) applies.

A partner's distributive share of income and hence the basis increase on account of that share is not computed until the end of the year. As a consequence, interim distributions of earnings during the taxable year might exceed a partner's basis at the time of the distribution. Treas. Reg. § 1.731–1(a)(1)(ii) treats advances or drawings against a partner's distributive share of income as made on the last day of the partnership year for the purposes of § 731 and § 705. Thus, any basis increase attributable to a partner's distributive share of partnership income for the year is available to offset the distribution.

Section 731(a)(2) prohibits recognition of loss on a current distribution. Because the partner's interest has not been liquidated, there has not been a closed and completed transaction—the prerequisite for a loss deduction—and the partner's remaining basis can attach to his remaining partnership interest.

1.2. *Treatment of Other Partners*

When a current distribution of cash results in recognition of gain, the bases of the other partners in their partnership interests do not change, even though the distribution has reduced the partnership's aggregate basis for its assets. In effect, some of the basis of their partnership interests, represented by the amount by which the cash distributed by the partnership exceeded the distributee partner's proportionate share of the partnership's basis for its assets, has been used to acquire an increased interest in the remaining partnership assets. As a general rule, § 734(a) provides that the bases of the remaining partnership property is not affected by the distribution. However, if the partnership has made an election under § 754, then the bases of the partnership assets will be adjusted upwards under § 734(b) by the amount of gain recognized under § 731(a). This adjustment, in effect, reflects the transfer of the basis from the distributed cash to the remaining assets. A current distribution of cash can only effect an increase in bases of partnership assets; it cannot cause a decrease. Section 734(b) is discussed in more detail at page 355.

1.3. *Definition of a Current Distribution*

Subchapter K distinguishes between distributions "in liquidation of the partner's interest" and distributions to a partner "other than in liquidation of the partner's interest." The term "liquidation" has reference to the entire interest of the partner and hence applies to the complete dissolution of a partnership or one of a series of distributions in complete termination of a partner's interest. Treas. Reg. § 1.761–1(d). Any other distribution to a partner falls within the second category, that of distributions other than in liquidation. This latter category is referred to as current distributions. Current distributions include the distribution of a partner's distributive share of profits, distributions from a partner's capital account that reduce the amount which the partner is entitled to receive upon the dissolution of the partnership but which do not otherwise affect the partner's interest in future partnership profits, and distributions in partial liquidations, which reduce a partner's interest but do not end that interest (as where a partner having a 10 percent interest in capital becomes one with a 5 percent interest). Treas. Reg. § 1.761–1(d).

In applying § 731, all of a partner's interests in a partnership are considered to be a unitary interest, the bases of general and limited partnership interests are combined into a unitary basis. Thus, for example, Chase v. Commissioner, 92 T.C. 874 (1989), held that a loss could not be recognized by a partner who received a cash distribution of $929,582 in liquidation of an 11.72 percent limited partnership interest having an adjusted basis of $1,710,344, because the taxpayer continued to hold a general partnership interest. The excess of the basis of the limited partnership over the amount of the distribution is included in the partner's basis in his general partnership interest.

2. REDUCTION OF PARTNERSHIP LIABILITY AS A CASH DISTRIBUTION: SECTION 752(b)

As illustrated by Rev. Rul. 81–242, § 752(b) treats a decrease in the partner's share of partnership liabilities as a distribution of money to the partner by the partnership, thus bringing into play the rules of § 731. A reduction in liabilities reduces the partner's basis pro tanto and will result in the recognition of gain if the constructive distribution exceeds the partner's basis in his partnership interest. Section 752(b) is a corollary of § 752(a), which treats any increase in a partner's share of partnership liabilities as a contribution of money by the partner to the partnership, thereby increasing his basis in the partnership interest.

Partnership liabilities can be reduced not only by repayment, but by the transfer (or distribution) of encumbered property, the abandonment of encumbered property, or by discharge through compromise. A partner's share of partnership liabilities also will be reduced upon the admission of a new partner to the partnership who assumes liability for a proportionate share of partnership liabilities, thereby resulting in a constructive distribution under § 752(b) to the original partners that may require recognition of gain under § 731(a). See Rev.Rul. 84–102, 1984–2 C.B. 119. As discussed at page 44, when a partner contributes encumbered property to a partnership, the partner generally is treated as receiving a current distribution to the extent that the liability attached to the property is allocated to other partners. If that portion of the liability exceeds the contributing partner's basis in his partnership interest, the contributing partner recognizes gain under § 731(a), and the partner's basis in the partnership interest is reduced to zero. See Rev.Rul. 84–15, 1984–1 C.B. 158.

Rev.Rul. 94–4, 1994–1 C.B. 195, held that a deemed distribution of money pursuant to § 752(b) is treated as an advance or draw under Treas. Reg. § 1.731–1(a)(1)(ii). Thus the constructive distribution, like distributions in the nature of a draw, is not taken into account until after the increase in the partner's basis in the partnership interest (under § 705) attributable to the partner's distributive share of partnership income.

This timing issue was addressed in Rev. Rul. 2003–56, 2003–1 C.B. 985, in the context of a § 1031 like-kind exchange of encumbered property by a partnership that occurred over two taxable years. In situation 1 of the ruling, a partnership in year one transferred property subject to a liability of $100x in a like-kind exchange for property received in year two subject to a liability of $60x. Under Treas. Reg. § 1.1031(b)–1(c), the net decrease in liabilities in a like-kind exchange is treated as the receipt of cash boot thereby requiring recognition of gain to the extent of the boot. The Service ruled that this gain is recognized by the partnership in year one, even though the transaction is not closed until the receipt of property in year two.[1] The ruling also provides, without any statutory or regulatory authority, that the decrease in partnership liabilities in year one is netted with the increase in partnership liabilities in year two. Thus the decrease in partnership liabilities of $100 in year one is netted with the increase of liabilities in year two. The overall $40x decrease in partnership liabilities is taken into account by the partners under § 752(b) as a constructive distribution in year one. As a consequence, with respect to a partner whose outside basis prior to the transaction is less than the partner's share of the reduction of liabilities, the increase in partner's basis in year one under § 705(a)(1) because of the partnership gain recognized on the exchange permits the § 752(b) distribution without further recognition of gain. The second situation of Rev. Rul. 2003–56 addresses the situation where the liability attached to the transferred property is less than the liability attached to the property received in the exchange. Under Treas. Reg. § 1.1031(b)–1(c) the liabilities are netted and because there is a net increase in liabilities on the exchange, there is no boot and thus no gain is recognized by the partnership. The ruling also concludes that the net increase in partnership liabilities is taken into account under § 752(a) in year two when the exchange property subject to the higher liability is received. Thus the partners' basis increase under § 722 occurs in year two of the transaction.

3. PARTNERSHIP CANCELLATION OF INDEBTEDNESS INCOME UNDER SECTION 61(a)(12) AND RELATED CONSTRUCTIVE DISTRIBUTIONS

Under § 108(d)(6) cancellation of indebtedness income is computed at the partnership level and allocated among the partners, who may exclude

---

1. Arguably this conclusion is wrong. Since the receipt of consideration is deferred until year 2, there is no amount realized for the transferred property in year 1. The transaction is a deferred payment sale and, unless there is an election under § 453(b), recognition of the boot is deferred under § 453(a) and (f)(6) until there is a payment in year 2 in the form of the receipt of the exchange property.

the income if one of the exceptions of § 108 is applicable to the partner. Stackhouse v. United States, 441 F.2d 465 (5th Cir.1971), dealt with the effect of cancellation of a partnership's indebtedness for a year prior to the enactment of § 108(d)(6). In that case, a partnership liability to a third party was compromised for $97,000 less than its face amount. The court held that the reduction in partnership liabilities constituted a distribution to the partners under § 752(b) and the tax results were controlled solely by § 731(a). The court rejected the Government's argument that the $97,000 reduction in liabilities should be treated as cancellation of indebtedness income to the partners under § 61(a)(12). Section 108(d)(6) was added in 1980 to adopt the Commissioner's position in *Stackhouse* and require that the exceptions to recognition of discharge of indebtedness income provided in § 108 be applied at the individual partner level. Thus, under current law, the correct analysis in the *Stackhouse* situation would be that there was cancellation of indebtedness income at the partnership level with a corresponding increase in the basis of the taxpayer's partnership interest under § 705, followed by the constructive distribution under § 752(b) of a like amount, which resulted in gain to the extent that the deemed distribution exceeded the partner's basis for the partnership interest.

Rev.Rul. 92–97, 1992–2 C. B. 124, held that under Treas. Reg. § 1.731–1(a)(1)(ii) a deemed distribution to a partner resulting from the cancellation of a partnership debt that gave rise to cancellation of indebtedness income under § 61(a)(12) is treated as occurring after the increase in the partners' bases in their partnership interests resulting from the cancellation of indebtedness income. Thus, if the partners share income and loss in the same percentages as they share the discharged indebtedness, and no partner is insolvent, each partner will recognize a pro rata share of ordinary cancellation of indebtedness income and the basis adjustments exactly offset each other with no gain resulting under § 731. On the other hand, if a particular partner's share of partnership liabilities exceed the partner's distributive share of partnership income from the cancellation of the debt, the constructive distribution might exceed the partner's basis for his partnership interest, resulting in recognition of gain under § 731.

Pursuant to § 108(a)(1)(B), if a partner is insolvent, cancellation of indebtedness income at the partnership level is not included in gross income by the partner.

4.   DISTRIBUTIONS CONTROLLED BY SECTION 707

4.1.   *Payments for Partner Transactions*

Section 707(a)(2), as discussed at page 225, treats as § 707(a) payments certain distributions related to the performance of services for the partnership or the transfer of property to the partnership. When § 707(a)(2) applies, no part of the distribution is treated as a distribution under § 731. Section 707(a) payments received in exchange for services are ordinary income to the payee partner and are deductible by the partnership, subject to the general capitalization rules. If, as suggested in Gaines v. Commissioner, T.C. Memo. 1982–731, at page 221, the inclusion of a

§ 707(c) guaranteed payment increases the partner's basis for his partnership interest, then the distribution of a guaranteed payment is governed by § 731.

4.2. *Distribution Versus Loan*

A receipt of money or property by a partner under an obligation to repay such amount or return the property to a partnership is treated as a loan under § 707(a) rather than as a current distribution. A withdrawal will not be treated as a loan, however, unless there is a definite obligation to repay a sum certain at a determinable time. The fact that the distribution creates a deficit in the partner's capital account that must be restored on liquidation or will otherwise be taken into account in making liquidating distributions does not alone establish that the transaction is a loan. Rev.Rul. 73–301, 1973–2 C.B. 215. See Seay v. Commissioner, T.C. Memo. 1992–254 (cash withdrawal from partnership characterized as distribution subject to § 731 rather than a loan subject to § 707(a) because partner never made any attempt to repay and the partnership never made any demand or attempt to enforce repayment). Of course, if the distribution is treated as a loan and the obligation is later canceled, the obligor partner will be considered to have received a distribution of money or property at the time of the cancellation. Treas. Reg. § 1.731–1(c)(2). But where a partner's indebtedness to the partnership is satisfied by the partnership setting off the debt against a distribution otherwise due to the partner, there has been no forgiveness of indebtedness; the transaction is a constructive distribution. See Zager v. Commissioner, T.C. Memo. 1987–107.

B. PROPERTY DISTRIBUTIONS

INTERNAL REVENUE CODE: Sections 731 (a), (b) & (d); 732(a), (c)–(d); 733; 734; 735; 741; 752(a)–(c); 761(d).

REGULATIONS: Sections 1.731–1(a)(1); 1.732–1(a), (d)(1)(i)–(v) and (2)–(4), –2; 1.733–1; 1.734–1; 1.735–1; 1.752–1(e), (f); 1.761–1(d).

In general, on a distribution of property that is not in liquidation of a partner's interest in the partnership, the distributee partner recognizes no gain or loss under § 731(a)(1), and the partnership's basis in the distributed property is transferred to the partner under § 732(a)(1). The distributee partner reduces his basis in the partnership interest by the amount of the basis assigned to the distributed property. I.R.C. § 733(2).

If a current distribution of property is pro rata among all the partners, the distributee partners simply take a transferred basis in the distributed assets because each partner receives his own undivided share of the distributed assets. If a property distribution is not pro rata, however, in effect there is an exchange among the partners. Nevertheless, unless the distribution alters the partners' interests in substantially appreciated inventory or unrealized receivables, Subchapter K does not treat the distribution as an exchange. Instead, in the case of any distribution of property that is not in complete termination of a partner's interest, Subchapter K applies a simpler rule and merely transfers the basis of the partnership asset, as in a pro rata distribution. See Treas. Reg. § 1.732–1(a), Exs. (1) and (2). As in the case of pro rata distributions, the partner's basis in the partnership interest is reduced by the amount of the transferred basis of the distributed asset. I.R.C. § 733. In contrast, the § 704(b) regulations, which govern the maintenance of capital accounts, require that distributed property be revalued to fair market value and that the capital accounts of all partners be adjusted to reflect the gain or loss that would have been allocated to each partner if the property had been sold. The distributee partner's capital account is then reduced by the fair market value of the distributed property. See Treas. Reg. § 1.704–1(b)(2)(iv)(e).

Section 732(a)(2) provides that if the distributee partner's basis for his partnership interest (reduced by any cash received) is less than the basis of the asset in the partnership's hands, then the basis of the asset in the partner's hands is limited to the partner's basis in his partnership interest (reduced by any cash received), i.e. an "exchanged basis." This limitation eliminates the necessity of having to recognize a gain to the distributee partner on a distribution of property.

In the case of a distribution of several properties having an aggregate partnership basis greater than the distributee partner's basis for the partnership interest (less any cash received), the partner's exchanged basis is allocated among the properties according to a complex formula contained in § 732(c). The distributee partner's exchanged basis first is allocated to distributed inventory and unrealized receivables, as defined in § 751(c), to the extent of the partnership's basis in these assets. (Unrealized receivables, which includes depreciation and other recapture as a separate asset, generally have a zero basis.) If the distributee partner's outside basis is less than the partnership's basis in the distributed inventory and receivables, the basis reduction is allocated among depreciated inventory and receivables in proportion to the relative unrealized depreciation in each distributed asset (determined before any basis decrease). I.R.C. § 732(c)(3)(A). Once the unrealized depreciation in distributed inventory and receivables is eliminated, any further required reduction is allocated in proportion to the adjusted basis of the distributed inventory and receivables. I.R.C. § 732(c)(3)(B).

If the distributee partner's outside basis is sufficient to permit receipt of inventory and receivables with a transferred basis (or there are no distributed inventory and unrealized receivables), then any reduction in basis required by the limitation of § 732(a)(2) is allocated among other distributed property. Again, the reduction is allocated under § 732(c)(3) among depreciated assets in proportion to the unrealized depreciation of each distributed asset determined before any basis reduction. Once unrealized depreciation is eliminated, the basis reduction is allocated in proportion to the adjusted bases of distributed assets.

Under the allocation rules for current distributions of property, the same overall amount of gain is recognized whether the partners sell the property after the distribution or the partnership sells the property before the distribution. But these rules can result in a different allocation of that gain or loss among the partners. Suppose partners A and B each receive property worth $100, but A's property has a transferred basis of $50 while B's has a transferred basis of $150. Upon a later sale of the property by the partners A would realize a gain of $50 and B a loss of $50. But, because each partner's basis in his or her partnership interest is reduced by an amount equal to the transferred basis assigned to the distributed property, I.R.C. § 733, B will recognize $100 more gain than A on the sale of their partnership interests or upon the liquidation of the partnership following a cash sale of its assets. On the other hand, if the partnership had first sold the property and distributed $100 of cash to each partner, no net gain or loss would have resulted. The partners should be able to resolve any inequities resulting from the possible shifting of gains and losses by arm's-length negotiations, e.g., an arrangement to compensate the partner currently receiving disproportionately low basis property. Alternatively, the partners might find that a disproportionate allocation of the burdens is desirable, in that the low basis property might be currently distributed to a tax exempt partner, a low bracket taxpayer, or to one with compensating losses.

The degree of tax avoidance that can be achieved by distributing appreciated inventory or unrealized receivables to low basis partners is considerably reduced by § 751(b), discussed in Section C, page 330, which treats an exchange of an interest in unrealized receivables and substantially appreciated inventory as a taxable transaction.

ILLUSTRATIVE MATERIAL

1. BASIS OF DISTRIBUTED PROPERTY

Generally, in a current (non-liquidating) distribution of property, under § 732(a)(1) the partnership's basis in the distributed property is transferred to the distributee partner, with a corresponding reduction of the distributee's basis in her partnership interest pursuant to § 733(2). Section 732(a)(2) limits the basis of distributed assets to the distributee partner's basis in the partnership interest.

In the case of a distribution of multiple assets, when the distributee partner's basis in distributed assets is limited by § 732(a)(2), § 732(c) provides complex rules for allocating the limited basis among distributed assets. At the first level, § 732(c)(1)(A) requires allocation of basis to distributed unrealized receivables and inventory to the extent of the partnership's basis in these assets. If the distributee partner's outside basis is less than the partnership's basis in distributed unrealized receivables and inventory, the decrease in basis required by § 732(a) is allocated among the distributed receivables and inventory, first in proportion to the unrealized depreciation (if any) built-in to these assets. For this purpose, unrealized depreciation is determined by using the partnership's basis in the assets before reducing the basis of the properties because of the distributee's partner's lower aggregate basis. Any further reduction required by the § 732(a)(2) limitation is then allocated among distributed assets in proportion to the adjusted basis of the distributed assets, as reduced in the first step.

Assume, for example, that a partner with a $1,500 basis in her partnership interest received three parcels of real estate held as inventory: Blackacre, with a fair market value of $1,200 and a basis of $600, White-acre, with a fair market value of $200 and a basis of $500, and Greenacre, with a fair market value of $400 and a basis of $1,000. Absent the limitation of § 732(a)(2), the partner's transferred basis would be $600 in Blackacre, $500 in Whiteacre, and $1,000 in Greenacre. Because the aggregate basis of all three properties to the partnership was $2,100 and the partner is entitled to only a $1,500 aggregate basis for the three properties, the aggregate bases of the properties must be reduced by $600. The first step under § 732(c)(3)(A) is to reduce the basis of the depreciated properties, Whiteacre and Greenacre, in proportion to their built in depreciation. (The basis reduction under § 732(c)(3)(A), however, cannot result in a reduction of basis to less than fair market value.)

	FMV	Basis	Depreciation		Decrease	Partner's Basis
Blackacre	$1,200	$ 600				$ 600
Whiteacre	200	500	$300	(600) × (300/900) = $200	300
Greenacre	400	1,000	600	(600) × (600/900) = 400	600
Total		$2,100	$900		$600	$1,500

Since the total basis reduction of $600 was absorbed by Whiteacre and Greenacre, each of which still has a basis in excess of fair market value, the basis of Blackacre is not adjusted

If the required basis reduction exceeds the depreciation in value inherent in the distributed depreciated assets, a portion of the aggregate basis decrease cannot be allocated in proportion to relative depreciation under § 732(c)(3)(A). In that case, under § 732(c)(3)(B) the remaining portion of the decrease is allocated among all of the assets received in the distribution relative to their adjusted bases after the adjustments required by § 732(c)(3)(A). Assume that the partner in the above example had a basis in her partnership interest of only $900. Section 732(c) would allow the partner an aggregate basis in the distributed properties of only $900, requiring an aggregate basis reduction of $1,200. Under § 732(c)(3)(A) the basis of distributed property cannot be reduced to less than the unrealized depreciation built-in to the property. Thus, under § 732(c)(2)(A), the adjusted basis of distributed property cannot be reduced below fair market value. The first part of the $1,200 basis reduction is allocated as follows:

	FMV	Basis	Depreciation		Decrease	Partner's Basis
Blackacre	$1,200	$ 600				
Whiteacre	200	500	$300	(900) × (300/900) = $300	200
Greenacre	400	1,000	600	(900) × (600/900) = 600	400
Total		$2,100	$900		$900	

Because only $900 of the total required basis reduction of $1,200 was absorbed by Whiteacre and Greenacre under § 732(c)(3)(A), a further basis adjustment of $300 is required under § 732(c)(3)(B). This adjustment affects the basis of Blackacre as well as the bases of Whiteacre and Greenacre. In this final step, the negative adjustment of $300 is allocated among the properties relative to their adjusted bases to the partner after the application of § 732(c)(3)(A). Thus:

	Partner's Tentative Basis		Decrease	Partner's Basis
Blackacre	$ 600	(300) × (600/1200) = $150	$450
Whiteacre	200	(300) × (200/1200) = 50	150
Greenacre	400	(300) × (400/1200) = 100	300
Total	$1,200		$300	$900

If any basis remains after allocation among inventory and accounts receivable, the remaining basis is allocated among all other assets. Pursuant to § 732(c)(3), the basis of any other property with a fair market value that is less than its transferred basis to the partner before the limitation of § 735(a) is applied is reduced in proportion to the built-in depreciation in the same manner as applies to inventory and unrealized receivables. For example, if all of the properties in either of the preceding two examples had been § 1231 assets or capital assets (or any combination of capital assets or § 1231 assets), the calculations would have be the same.

If a partner receives both inventory (and/or unrealized receivables) and other property, and there is any basis remaining after allocating to the inventory and unrealized receivables a basis equal to their basis in the hands of the partnership, the basis decrease rules of § 732(c)(3) are applied solely with respect to the other property. Assume that in the immediately preceding example Blackacre was held as inventory and Whiteacre and Greenacre were held as capital assets. The transferred basis of Blackacre would be $600. As above, in the first part of the allocation, $900 of the basis decrease is allocated $300 to Whiteacre and $600 to Greenacre. In the second step the bases of Whiteacre and Greenacre are further reduced by the remaining $300 adjustment as follows:

	Partner's Tentative Basis		Decrease	Partner's Basis
Whiteacre	$200	(300) × (200/600) = $100	$100
Greenacre	400	(300) × (400/600) = 200	200
Total	$600		$300	$300

This allocation scheme serves two purposes. First, it is designed to prevent inventory and unrealized receivables from ever receiving a higher basis in the hands of the distributee than they had at the partnership level. Second, it is designed to prevent assets with a relatively low value from taking a higher basis in the partner's hands than assets with a relatively high value, but which had a lower basis in the partnership's hands. See H. Rep. No. 148, 105th Cong, 1st Sess. 148 (1997). The allocation formula clearly is not designed to allocate basis among distributed assets relative to their fair market value. See H. Rep. No. 148, 105th Cong, 1st Sess. 148 (1997).

2. ANCILLARY EFFECTS OF PROPERTY DISTRIBUTIONS THAT DO NOT ALTER INTERESTS IN SUBSTANTIALLY APPRECIATED INVENTORY OR UNREALIZED RECEIVABLES

2.1. *Character of Distributed Property*

If the distributed asset is an unrealized receivable, § 735 provides a perpetual carryover of its non-capital character. The character of partnership inventory, however, is retained for only five years. See Luckey v. Commissioner, 334 F.2d 719 (9th Cir.1964), and Sanford Homes, Inc. v. Commissioner, T.C. Memo. 1986–404, both, applying this rule to inventory sold within the five-year period. Section 735(c)(2) extends these characterization rules to substituted basis property received by the partner in a partially or wholly tax free exchange for the tainted distributed property. Finally, these carryovers of asset character apparently apply only to the distributee, and not to a donee of the distributee.

2.2. *Effect on Nondistributee Partners*

Where the distributee partner's basis in the distributed property is limited by § 732(a)(2), the remaining partners, by utilizing property with a basis higher than the distributee partner's basis, have in effect purchased part of his interest with that excess amount. Nevertheless, § 731(b) provides that the partnership, and hence the other partners, does not recognize gain or loss on the distribution of property. However, under §§ 754 and 734(b), the effect of this exchange may be reflected in the bases of the remaining partnership assets. Section 734(b) is discussed at page 355.

2.3. *Capital Accounts*

Capital account adjustments must be made as if the distribution were a recognition event, even though pursuant to § 731(a) and (b) no taxable gain is recognized by a partner on the distribution of property. Treas. Reg. § 1.704–1(b)(2)(iv)(e)(1) requires that the partnership capital accounts be adjusted to reflect the gain or loss that would have been recognized if the property had been sold for its fair market value instead of distributed. The capital account of each partner is adjusted to reflect each partner's distributive share of the partnership's book gain or loss. Then the capital account of the distributee partner is decreased by the fair market value of the distributed property.

Assume for example that the ABC Partnership has the following balance sheet:

	Assets			Partners' Capital Accounts		
		Tax				Tax
	Book	Basis			Book	Basis
Cash	$360	$360	A		$198	$198
Whiteacre	$ 75	$ 75	B		$198	$198
Blackacre	$ 60	$ 60	C		$198	$198
Greenacre	$ 99	$ 99				
	$594	$594			$594	$594

Whiteacre, Blackacre, and Greenacre all have a fair market value of $90. The partnership makes a distribution of Whiteacre to A, Blackacre to B, and Greenacre to C. Assume that the partnership does not revalue all its properties and capital accounts pursuant to Treas. Reg. § 1.704–1(b)(2)(iv)(f)(5)(ii) because the distribution is pro rata. Nevertheless, under Treas. Reg. § 1.704–1(b)(2)(iv)(e)(1) the partnership must adjust the partners' capital accounts as if Whiteacre, Blackacre, and Greenacre each were sold for $90, and then subtract $90 from each partner's capital account. The deemed sale for $90 results in gains of $15 with respect to Whiteacre and $30 with respect to Blackacre, and a loss of $9 with respect to Greenacre. The net deemed gain is $36. Accordingly, each partner's capital account is increased by $12 and decreased by $90. Each partner's basis for the partnership interest, however, is decreased by the partnership's basis for the particular property distributed. After the distribution, the ABC Partnership's balance sheet is as follows:

	Assets			Partners' Capital Accounts		
		Tax				Tax
	Book	Basis			Book	Basis
Cash	$360	$360	A		$120	$123
			B		$120	$138
			C		$120	$ 99
	$360	$360			$360	$360

Thus, upon the subsequent distribution of the $360 cash in liquidation of the partnership, A would recognize a loss of $3, B a loss of $18, and C a gain of $21. If each of A, B, and C sold the real property received in the prior distribution at its fair market value at the time of the distribution ($90), A would recognize a $15 gain on the sale of Whiteacre ($90 – $75), B a $30 gain on the sale of Blackacre ($90 – $60), and C a $9 loss on the sale of Greenacre ($90 – $99). The combined result of the transactions would be that each partner would recognize $12 of net gain. This is identical to the amount of gain that A, B, and C each would have recognized if the partnership had sold all of its properties and distributed the cash proceeds in a complete liquidation.

Some distributions are an appropriate occasion for revaluation of all of the partnership's properties and the partners' book accounts. Treas. Reg. § 1.704–1(b)(2)(iv)(f)(5)(ii) provides that such an adjustment may be made for a substantial non-tax business purpose in connection with a distribution of more than a de minimis amount of money or property. Whenever a current distribution is disproportionate and intended to reduce one or more partner's interest in future profits and losses, a complete revaluation under Treas. Reg. § 1.704–1(b)(2)(iv)(f)(5)(ii) will be necessary (although not required by the regulations) to achieve the economic objectives of the partners.

3.   DISTRIBUTIONS OF ENCUMBERED PROPERTY

Under the rules of § 752(a) and (b), a distribution of encumbered property gives rise to three simultaneous events: (1) a distribution of property; (2) a deemed distribution of cash; and (3) a deemed contribution of cash. The partner who received the encumbered property has received a property distribution. The other partners have received a deemed distribution of cash under § 752(b) because the debt encumbering the property no longer is a partnership debt and their shares of partnership indebtedness therefore have been reduced. Finally, the partner who received the encumbered property has made a deemed cash contribution to the partnership under § 752(a) because the amount of the encumbrance that she has assumed exceeds her share of the debt when it was a partnership indebtedness.

The tax results can differ dramatically depending on the order in which these events are deemed to occur. Normally, when cash and property are distributed simultaneously, the cash is deemed to have been distributed first and the property second. See Treas. Reg. § 1.732–1(a), Ex. (1). This ordering minimizes the potential for recognition of gain. Treatment of the deemed cash contribution and deemed cash distribution is also crucial. Treas. Reg. § 1.752–1(f) provides that only the net effect of liabilities is taken into account. Rev.Rul. 79–205, 1972–2 C.B. 255, applied this principle in the case of simultaneous distributions of encumbered property to different partners.

Suppose that the AB Partnership distributes to A property having an adjusted basis to the partnership of $2,000, which is subject to liabilities of $1,600. A's basis for his partnership interest prior to the distribution is $1,000. The partnership distributes to B property having an adjusted basis of $3,200, subject to liabilities of $2,800. B's adjusted basis for her partnership interest is $1,500. As a result of these distributions, each partner reduces his or her share of partnership liabilities by $2,200 (½ of $1,600 plus $2,800). A's individual liabilities treated as a contribution under § 752(a) are increased by $1,600. A is treated as receiving a net cash distribution of $600, which reduces A's basis in the partnership interest from $1,000 to $400: the property then takes a basis of $400; and A has a zero basis in the partnership interest. B's individual liabilities increase by $2,800. B is treated as having contributed $600 to the partnership. The basis adjustment attributable to this deemed contribution is treated as occurring before the property distribution, with the result that the basis for B's partnership interest is increased from $1,500 to $2,100. Then under

§ 732(a)(2) the distributed property takes a $2,100 basis, and B's basis in the partnership interest is reduced to zero.

When encumbered property is distributed, as with any distribution of property, the partnership's capital accounts are adjusted to recognize book gain or loss with respect to the distributed property. Under Treas. Reg. § 1.704–1(b)(2)(iv)(*e*)(*1*), each partner's capital account is then adjusted for the partner's distributive share of the book gain or loss. Under Treas. Reg. § 1.704–1(b)(2)(iv)(*b*)(*5*), the distributee partner's capital account is reduced by the fair market value of the property minus the encumbrance.

4.   DISTRIBUTIONS OF MARKETABLE SECURITIES

Section 731(c) generally treats distributions of marketable securities as cash distributions. The distributed securities are taken into account at their fair market value. While marketable securities obviously include stock and bonds traded on an established exchange or on the over the counter market, the definition in § 731(c)(2) encompasses other items as well, such as interests in precious metals. Section 731(c)(3) provides a number of exceptions to the rule treating distributions of actively traded securities as cash. The most important exceptions are for distributions of securities to the partner who contributed them, which restores the status quo ante, and distributions by certain investment partnerships that never have conducted an active business. If the distributed securities are inventory items or unrealized receivables, as defined in § 751(c) and (d), to the partnership, then the gain recognized will be ordinary income rather than capital gain. I.R.C. § 731(c)(6). See generally, Treas. Reg. § 1.731–2.

When § 731(c) applies, the distributee partner's basis in the securities equals the basis the securities would have had under § 732, generally the partnership's basis in the case of a current distribution, plus the amount of any gain recognized by the distributee partner on the distribution. I.R.C. § 731(c)(4). The adjustment is allocated among the securities relative to their appreciation before the distribution. The partner's basis in his partnership interest is reduced under § 733 only by the partnership's basis in the distributed securities, and adjustment to the basis of remaining partnership assets under § 734(b) is permitted. I.R.C. § 731(c)(5).

5.   DISTRIBUTIONS OF PROPERTY WHERE BASIS ADJUSTMENTS ARE IN EFFECT

If a § 754 basis adjustment election is in effect, any basis adjustments with respect to distributed property previously made under § 743(b) (upon a transfer of a partnership interest) or under § 734(b) (upon a partnership distribution) are taken into account in determining the partnership's basis for distributed assets. Treas. Reg. § 1.732–2. Assume, for example, that C acquired B's interest in the AB Partnership for $2,000 at a time when the partnership had a nondepreciable capital asset with a basis of $2,000 and value of $3,000 and depreciable property with a basis of $500 and a value of $1,000. If a § 754 election is in effect, under § 743(b) the basis of the capital asset is increased for C's benefit by $500 and the basis of the depreciable property is increased for C's benefit by $250. If the partnership later distributes the depreciable asset to C, the basis carried over to him will be $750. If the depreciable asset is distributed to A, however, A's basis in the asset will still be $500, and C's special basis adjustment of $250 will be shifted to the nondepreciable capital asset, so that C's basis adjustment with respect to that asset will become $750. Treas. Reg. § 1.732–2(b) and § 1.743–1(g)(2)(ii). This basis shift can only be made to property of the same class as the property having the special basis adjustment. As noted previously, page 299, § 755 divides property into two classes: capital assets and depreciable property in one class, and all other property in the other class. Hence, if the partnership had no other capital assets or depreciable property at the time of the distribution to A, C's $250 special basis adjustment would stay in abeyance until the partnership acquired property of the required character. Cf. Treas. Reg. § 1.755–1(c)(4). If no such property is ever acquired, the basis adjustment is permanently lost.

6. DISTRIBUTIONS OF PROPERTY TO TRANSFEREE PARTNER WHERE ELECTION TO ADJUST BASIS IS NOT IN EFFECT

If a distribution is made to a transferee partner within two years from the time he acquired his partnership interest and the partnership did not elect under § 754 to adjust the basis of partnership assets under § 743(b), § 732(d) allows the transferee to elect to treat the partnership basis for the distributed property as if the basis adjustment had been in effect. See Treas. Reg. § 1.732–1(d)(1)(iii).

Assume, for example, that the ABC Partnership owned three parcels of land, each of which had an adjusted basis of $5,000 and a fair market value of $55,000, and a depreciable asset with an adjusted basis of $30,000 and a value of $50,000. D purchased A's partnership interest for $105,000 and no § 754 election was in effect. A year later, when D's basis in his partnership interest was $100,000, the partnership distributed one parcel of land to each of the partners in a current distribution and D received land that had a basis to the partnership of $5,000. Absent a basis adjustment to the land, D would reduce the basis of the partnership interest from $100,000 to $95,000, and take a $5,000 basis in the land. However, under § 732(d), D can elect to increase the basis of the land by $50,000 to $55,000, and concomitantly as result of the distribution reduce the basis of the partnership interest by $55,000. However, because no § 754 election was in effect, and § 732(d) applies only to distributed property, D does not receive an inside basis adjustment with respect to the depreciable property.

The transferee-distributee is required to apply the special basis rule of § 732(d) in situations in which not applying it would result in a shift of basis to depreciable property if the transferee partner's interest were liquidated immediately after its acquisition. Treas. Reg. § 1.732–1(d)(4). This rule applies even if the distribution occurs more than two years after the partner acquired the partnership interest. However, application of § 732(d) is required only if the fair market value of the partnership property (other than money) at the time of the transfer exceeds 110 percent of its adjusted basis to the partnership. Treas. Reg. § 1.732–1(d)(4) was promulgated at a time when such a basis shift was frequently possible under the provisions of § 732(c). Under the current version of § 732(c), such a basis shift rarely, if ever, can occur.

7. DISTRIBUTIONS BY PARTNERSHIP HOLDING SECTION 704(c) PROPERTY

Section 704(c)(1)(A), discussed at page 154, requires the partnership to allocate gain or loss on the sale of contributed property to the contributing partner to the extent of the built-in gain or loss at the time of the contribution of the property. To prevent avoidance of such an allocation through the subsequent distribution of contributed property having a built-in gain or loss to a different partner, § 704(c)(1)(B) treats the distribution of such property within seven years of its contribution to the partnership as a recognition event to the contributing partner.

Section 704(c)(1)(B) does not apply if the contributing partner's interest in the partnership is completely liquidated before the contributed property is distributed to another partner. This situation is governed by § 737, which is designed to prevent avoidance of § 704(c)(1)(B). Sections 704(c)(1)(B) and 737 are discussed in detail in Section 6 of this Chapter.

8. DISTRIBUTIONS OF PARTNER'S INDEBTEDNESS

Rev.Rul. 93–7, 1993–1 C.B. 125, held that a partner receiving a distribution of the partner's own debt instrument recognizes capital gain to the extent that the fair market value of the debt instrument exceeds the partner's basis for its partnership interest and recognizes discharge of indebtedness income to the extent the adjusted issue price, which is the original issue price adjusted for accrued original issue discount and payments, exceeds the fair market value of the debt instrument. For example, suppose that X issues a debt instrument with a $100 issue price and redemption value. Subsequently, the debt instrument is purchased from the original holder by the XYZ Partnership for $100. X is a 50 percent partner in the XYZ partnership and is otherwise unrelated to Y and Z.[2] Still later, X's interest in the XYZ Partnership is liquidated by a distribution of the indebtedness. At the time of the distribution X's basis for its partnership interest was $25 and the fair market value of both X's partnership interest and the indebtedness was $90. Because the indebtedness is extinguished by the distribution, the mechanism by which § 731 and § 732 permit nonrecognition on distributions by preserving gain or loss through basis adjustments does not work. Current recognition of gain or loss is required. X would recognize capital gain of $65 ($90 − $25) and discharge of indebtedness income of $10. (Treas. Reg. § 1.731–1(c)(2) does not apply because that provision applies only to debt incurred directly from a partner to the partnership.) If, however, the partnership has made a § 754 election, for purposes of determining the partnership's basis adjustment under § 734(b),

---

2.   Since X is only a 50 percent partner, § 108(e)(3) does not apply to treat the acqui-   sition of X's indebtedness by the partnership as cancellation of indebtedness income.

the distribution will be treated as a property distribution. Accordingly, the XYZ partnership would be entitled to a basis adjustment of $75. See page 355.

C. DISTRIBUTIONS BY PARTNERSHIPS HOLDING UNREALIZED RECEIVABLES OR SUBSTANTIALLY APPRECIATED INVENTORY

INTERNAL REVENUE CODE: Section 751(b)–(d).

REGULATIONS: Section 1.751–1(b)–(e).

When a distribution of either cash or property changes a partner's interest in partnership unrealized receivables or "substantially appreciated inventory," Subchapter K abandons the nonrecognition rule of § 731 and treats the distribution in part as a taxable exchange between the distributee partner and the partnership. This taxable exchange treatment generally applies whenever a partnership has unrealized receivables or substantially appreciated inventory and makes a non-pro rata distribution to one or more partners, regardless of whether the distribution is of unrealized receivables or substantially appreciated inventory, on the one hand, or of other assets (including cash), on the other hand. Under § 751(b), if a partner reduces the partner's interest in unrealized receivables and/or substantially appreciated inventory, and increases an interest in other property, the partner is treated as exchanging an interest in the inventory and receivables for the other property in a taxable exchange. On the other side of the exchange, the partnership is treated as purchasing an increased interest in the unrealized receivables and inventory in exchange for the partner's increased interest in the other property. Similarly, if a partner increases an interest in unrealized receivables and/or substantially appreciated inventory, the partner is treated as selling an interest in other property in a taxable exchange for the inventory and receivables. The partnership is treated as selling the interest in unrealized receivables and inventory in exchange for an increased interest in the other property.

In general, unrealized receivables include payments to be received for goods and services. I.R.C. § 751(c), discussed at page 289. In addition, recapture of depreciation and other capital recovery deductions are treated as an unrealized receivable. Inventory is "substantially appreciated" if the fair market value of inventory held by the partnership exceeds 120 percent of the partnership's basis in inventory. I.R.C. § 751(b)(3)(A). For purposes of this calculation, inventory includes any item which if sold would produce ordinary income, including unrealized receivables. I.R.C. § 751(d).

Section 751(b) applies if the distribution of one class of property is "in exchange for" the partner's interest in the other class of property. Whether a non-pro rata distribution is to be considered "in exchange for" an interest in other property depends upon the effect of the distribution on the partners' interests in particular partnership assets. Assuming that partnership capital accounts generally are maintained in accordance with the principles of the § 704(b) regulations, any non-pro rata distribution that is charged to a partner's capital account (which is to say all non-pro rata distributions) will have the effect of a distribution in exchange for an interest in other partnership property. Furthermore, if different partners receive distributions of like amounts, but the distributions are disproportionate as to unrealized receivables and substantially appreciated inventory, § 751(b) will apply.

Section 751(b) generally is intended to prevent partners from allocating among themselves the character of the gain recognized from sales of partnership property. Without this provision a partnership would be free, for example, to distribute capital gain property to a partner who had capital losses to be offset, while the partnership recognized and allocated to the other partners an offsetting amount of ordinary income. Conversely, the partnership might distribute ordinary income property to a low tax bracket partner, while retaining capital gain property. Given this purpose, § 751(b) does not apply to a distribution of property that the distributee partner contributed to the partnership, presumably on the rationale that the status quo prior to the contribution is being restored. I.R.C. § 751(b)(2)(A).

ILLUSTRATIVE MATERIAL

1. GENERAL

1.1. *Example (1)*

The following example illustrates the operation of § 751(b). Suppose that C and D are equal partners in the CD Partnership, which owns a capital asset having a fair market value of $300 and a basis of $60 and inventory having a fair market value of $900 and a basis of $210. C's basis for her partnership interest is $135. Suppose further that the partnership distributes the capital asset to C to effect the reduction of her interest to that of a one-third partner. The inventory is "substantially appreciated" as defined in § 751(d); $900 is greater than $210 × 120%. Section 751(b) first treats C as having received a § 731 distribution of an undivided interest in a portion of the inventory (none of which was actually distributed). C is then treated as exchanging with the partnership in a taxable transaction the portion of the inventory deemed to have been distributed for an undivided portion of the capital asset (which actually was distributed) of equal value. The remaining portion of the capital asset (which actually was distributed) is received by C as a distribution subject to § 731. The general rules for determining gain or loss under §§ 731 and 741 and basis under § 732 are applied to the preliminary deemed distribution, and this hypothetical exchange is taxed under § 1001, using normal characterization rules, as modified by §§ 724 and 735. See, Treas. Reg. § 1.751–1(g), Exs. (2), (3), (4) and (5).

The hypothetical exchange that is at the heart of § 751(b) is best understood by constructing a table to determine the change in the distributee partner's interest in the partnership assets and the partnership's interest in the assets.[3] In the case of the CD Partnership, C's exchange would be as follows:

3. This analytical method was first advanced in W. McKee, W. Nelson & R. Whitmire, Federal Income Taxation of Partnerships and Partners (Warren, Gorham & Lamont 1977).

C's Exchange

Property	Value of Distributee's Post-distribution Interest as a Partner	+	Value of Distributed Property	−	Value of Distributee's Pre-distribution Inter est	=	Increase (Decrease) in Distributee's Interest
Section 751 Property							
Inventory	$300		$ 0		$450		($150)
Other Property							
Capital Asset	$ 0		$300		$150		$150

This table demonstrates that C has exchanged a $150 interest in inventory held by the partnership for an interest in other property (the capital asset) worth the same amount. To reflect this exchange, C is treated as having received $150 worth of the inventory in a § 731 distribution. Under § 732, C's basis for this inventory is $35, which equals the partnership's basis in the distributed portion of the inventory ($150/$900 × $210). C is then treated as having received $150 worth of the capital asset from the partnership in a taxable exchange for the inventory. C's amount realized on the exchange is $150, the fair market value of the capital asset received in exchange for the inventory. C subtracts the $35 basis in the inventory that is treated as distributed, and C recognizes ordinary gain of $115 on the exchange ($150 – $35).

On the other side of the exchange, the partnership is treated as having received the $150 worth of the inventory from C in exchange for $150 worth of the capital asset. The partnership's amount realized on this exchange is $150, the fair market value of the increased interest in inventory received from C. The partnership's basis in the exchanged interest in the capital asset is $30 representing the partnership's basis in portion of the capital asset transferred to C in the exchange ($150/$300 × $60). The partnership recognizes a $120 capital gain on the exchange of the capital asset ($150 – $30). The remaining $150 worth of the capital asset ($300 distributed less $150 treated as sold) is received by C in a § 731 distribution. C's basis in the distributed capital asset is $180, consisting of $150 for the portion acquired in the taxable exchange under § 751(b) plus $30 under § 732 for the portion received in the § 731 distribution. C's basis in the partnership interest is reduced from $135 to $70, reflecting the deemed distribution under § 751(b) of inventory with a basis of $35 and the distribution under § 731 of the capital asset with a basis of $30. The partnership's basis in the inventory is increased from $210 to $325 ($175 for the undistributed five-sixths, plus $150 purchase price for one-sixth).

Treas. Reg. § 1.751–1(b)(2)(ii) and (b)(3)(ii) allocates partnership gain recognized on a constructive § 751(b) exchange to the nondistributee partners, who are the partners whose interest in distributed property is reduced. The distributee partner recognizes gain only on her own side of the exchange. Thus, in the CD Partnership example, all of the partnership gain on the exchange of the capital asset would be allocated to D.

Section 751(b) also applies if the distributee partner receives more than her share of the receivables and inventory and hence less than her share of other property or money. In this case under § 751(b)(1)(A) the partnership is regarded as having sold its interest in the distributed receivables or inventory. The partnership will recognize ordinary income on that imputed sale, and the basis of its remaining assets will be adjusted to reflect the purchase of the distributee partner's share. Likewise, the distributee partner will recognize gain or loss on the imputed sale of other property to the partnership. This gain or loss will be characterized as ordinary or capital with respect to the character of the property.

1.2. *Example (2)*

Application of § 751(b) is more complex when, as is usually the case, the partnership has multiple assets in each class. Consider the EFG Partnership, the assets and partners' capital accounts of which are as follows:

	Assets			Partners' Capital Accounts	
	F.M.V.[4]	Basis		F.M.V.	Basis
Cash	$126,000	$126,000	E	$150,000	$102,000
Accounts	$ 63,000	$ 0	F	$150,000	$102,000
Receivable			G	$150,000	$102,000
Inventory	$ 90,000	$ 63,000			
Whiteacre	$ 90,000	$ 76,500			
Blackacre	$ 81,000	$ 40,500			
	$450,000	$306,000		$450,000	$306,000

To reduce E's partnership interest from one-third to one-ninth, the partnership distributes $112,500, in the form of Blackacre and $31,500 of cash, to E. Assuming that Whiteacre and Blackacre are capital assets, the constructive exchange under § 751(b) is computed as follows:

E's Exchange

Property	Value of Distributee's Post-distribution Interest as a Partner	+	Value of Distributed Property	−	Value of Distributee's Pre-distribution Interest	=	Increase (Decrease) in Distributee's Interest
Section 751 Property							
Acc'ts Rec.	$ 7,000		$ 0		$21,000		($14,000)
Inventory	$10,000		$ 0		$30,000		($20,000)
Total § 751 Property							($34,000)

4. It is assumed that in connection with this distribution, pursuant to Treas. Reg. § 1.704–1(b)(2)(iv)(*f*)(*5*), the partnership will revalue its assets and partners' capital accounts for book purposes so that book value equals fair market value immediately prior to the distribution.

Property	Value of Distributee's Post-distribution Interest as a Partner	+ Value of Distributed Property	− Value of Distributee's Pre-distribution Interest	= Increase (Decrease) in Distributee's Interest
Other Property				
Cash	$10,500	$31,500	$42,000	$ 0
Whiteacre	$10,000	$ 0	$30,000	($20,000)
Blackacre	$ 0	$81,000	$27,000	$54,000
Total Other Property				$34,000

Although the exchange table reveals that E has exchanged interests in the accounts receivable, inventory and Whiteacre for an interest in Blackacre, § 751(b) applies only to the exchange of interests in the inventory and accounts receivable for an interest in Blackacre. See Treas. Reg. § 1.751–1(g), Ex. (2). Thus, E is treated as engaging in a taxable exchange of $34,000 of accounts receivable and inventory for a $34,000 interest in Blackacre. E is treated as having received in a hypothetical distribution $14,000 of accounts receivable, in which he takes a zero basis, and $20,000 worth of inventory, in which he takes a $14,000 basis ($63,000 partnership basis × ($20,000/$90,000)). E then exchanges these assets to the partnership for an undivided interest in Blackacre worth $34,000. E's amount realized on this exchange is $14,000 worth of Blackacre for the accounts receivable and $20,000 of Blackacre for the inventory. E recognizes $14,000 of ordinary income attributable to the accounts receivable ($14,000 – 0) and $6,000 of ordinary income attributable to the inventory ($20,000 – $14,000).

The partnership's amount realized for the $34,000 interest in Blackacre transferred in the exchange is a $14,000 interest in accounts receivable and a $20,000 interest in inventory. The partnership allocates $17,000 of the basis of Blackacre ($40,500 × (34,000/81,000)) to this exchange and recognizes a gain of $17,000 on the sale or exchange of Blackacre, all of which is allocated to F and G.

Finally, E is treated as receiving the remaining $47,000 interest in Blackacre ($81,000 − $34,000) and the $31,500 of cash in a § 731 distribution. E's basis in Blackacre is $57,500, consisting of $34,000 for the portion acquired in the taxable exchange under § 751(b) and $23,500 under § 732 for the portion received in the § 731 distribution ($40,500 × $47,000/$81,000). E's basis in his partnership interest is reduced by $69,000 to $33,000, reflecting the deemed distribution under § 751(b) of inventory with a basis of $14,000, the distribution under § 731 of a portion of Blackacre with a basis of $23,500, and cash of $31,500. The partnership's basis in the inventory is increased from $63,000 to $69,000 ($49,000 for the undistributed seven-ninths, plus $20,000 purchase price for one-sixth) and its basis in the accounts receivable is increased to $14,000.

1.3. *Example (3)*

Assume that the partnership in Example (2) distributed to E the $63,000 of accounts receivable and $49,500 of cash. In that case the exchange table would be as follows:

E's Exchange

Property	Value of Distributee's Post-distribution Interest as a Partner	+	Value of Distributed Property	−	Value of Distributee's Pre-distribution Interest	=	Increase (Decrease) in Distributee's Interest
Section 751 Property							
Acc'ts Rec.	$ 0		$63,000		$21,000		$42,000
Inventory	$10,000		$ 0		$30,000		($20,000)
Total § 751 Property							$22,000
Other Property							
Cash	$ 8,500		$49,500		$42,000		$16,000
Whiteacre	$10,000		$ 0		$30,000		($20,000)
Blackacre	$ 9,000		$ 0		$27,000		($18,000)
Total Other Property							($22,000)

In this transaction, E has exchanged interests in inventory, Whiteacre, and Blackacre for interests in accounts receivable and cash. Section 751(b), however, is concerned only with the net exchange of interests in § 751 property for other property. Thus E has received $22,000 of accounts receivable in exchange for other property, i.e., Whiteacre and Blackacre. See Treas. Reg. § 1.751–1(g), Ex. (5). Identifying the precise exchange, however, is more difficult because the Regulations allow some flexibility in this case. Treas. Reg. § 1.751–1(g) Ex. (3) and Ex. (5) appear to sanction an agreement between the partners specifying the "other property" in which the distributee partner has relinquished an interest in situations in which he receives § 751 assets in the distribution. Thus, for example, the partners might agree that E surrendered an interest worth $22,000 in Whiteacre and surrendered no interest in Blackacre. Such an agreement would minimize the gain realized by E on the constructive exchange following the hypothetically distributed interest in other assets, i.e., Whiteacre, for an interest in the accounts receivable because Blackacre is more highly appreciated than Whiteacre. If E is treated as hypothetically receiving and exchanging an interest in Whiteacre worth $22,000, E recognizes only $3,300 of gain because a distribution of a 22/90ths undivided interest in Whiteacre would give E a basis of $18,700 in the exchanged property. Conversely, a distribution of a 22/81sts undivided interest in Blackacre would give E a basis of only $11,000 for the property surrendered in the constructive exchange, resulting in a gain to E of $11,000.

In the converse situation, i.e., the distributee relinquishes an interest in § 751 assets, as illustrated in Example (2), the Regulations are silent regarding the ability to designate the property in which the distributee partner surrendered his interest. Allowing such a designation, either of § 751 assets or of other assets, permits the partners to select assets for the exchange that will minimize the gain realized on the deemed exchange. To permit this with respect to the capital and § 1231 assets retained by the partnership is not inconsistent with the purpose of § 751 and, in light of the flexibility of the other provisions of Subchapter K, is defensible. But to permit such selection if the distributee partner surrenders his share of ordinary income assets is inconsistent with its purpose.

2. SECTION 751 PROPERTY: UNREALIZED RECEIVABLES AND SUBSTANTIALLY APPRECIATED INVENTORY

2.1. *Unrealized Receivables*

As the Tax Court held in Ledoux v. Commissioner, page 280, unrealized receivables as defined in § 751(c) include any rights to payment for goods and services. Section 751(c) also includes within the definition of unrealized receivables gain that would be treated as ordinary income under any of the various recapture rules such as § 1245. Under Treas.Reg. § 1.751–1(c)(4) and (5), the amount of potential recapture income of the distributing partnership is treated as an unrealized receivable with zero basis. The remaining value of such property is treated as a § 1231 asset with all of the partnership's basis in the asset. As a consequence, § 751(b) potentially is applicable to any distribution by a partnership holding depreciable personal property such as machinery, equipment, and amortizable § 197 intangibles.

2.2. *Substantially Appreciated Inventory*

Under § 751(d), in addition to stock in trade and property held for sale to customers, inventory includes any property that would on sale be treated as property that is not a capital asset or § 1231 property, e.g. any property that would produce ordinary gain on sale. See discussion at page 290. In addition, property that is not a capital or § 1231 asset in the hands of the distributee is included within the definition of inventory. I.R.C. § 751(d)(4).

Treas. Reg. § 1.751–1(d)(2)(ii) includes within the definition of inventory all accounts receivable, including those of both cash and accrual method taxpayers. However, inventory does not include other "unrealized receivables," as defined in § 751(c), such as depreciation recapture. The gain attributable to a change in a partner's interest in accounts receivable included in inventory is not taxed twice. Rather, including these items in inventory affects the determination whether the inventory is substantially appreciated.

A partnership owns inventory that has "appreciated substantially in value" if the fair market value of the inventory is more than 120 percent of its basis. I.R.C. § 751(b)(3)(A). Even though inventory had not actually appreciated economically it has been held to be appreciated inventory in a situation in which it had been treated as an expensed item and hence had a zero tax basis. Yourman v. United States, 277 F.Supp. 818 (S.D.Cal.1967).

The inclusion in inventory of accounts receivable of an accrual method partnership makes it more difficult to meet the 120 percent test for substantial appreciation. Assume, for example, that an accrual method partnership holds actual inventory, having a basis of $79 and a fair market value of $100, and accounts receivable having a basis and fair market value of $30. If the accounts receivable were not treated as inventory, the 120 percent appreciation test would be measured by the $79 basis and $100 fair market value benchmarks, and that test would be met ($100 > [120% × $79 = $94.80]). If the accounts receivable are included in inventory, however, the 120 percent test is not met because the $130 fair market value of the inventory does not exceed 120 percent of its $109 basis (120% × $109 = $130.80).

If a partnership's inventory has appreciated in value but not to an extent that results in classification as substantial appreciation under § 751(b)(3), then no part of a distribution that affects a partner's interest in inventory will be subject to exchange treatment under § 751(b). To prevent artificial manipulations of inventories designed to avoid § 751(a) by reducing the amount of appreciation in the partnership's inventory, § 751(b)(3)(B) excludes from the computation of substantial appreciation any inventory property if a principal purpose of the acquisition of the property was avoiding § 751(b). Section 751(b)(3)(B) presumably would apply, for example, if a partnership purchased accrual method accounts receivable at near face value, other than in the ordinary course of business, shortly before a distribution, so as to reduce inventory appreciation below 20 percent.

3.   INTERACTION OF SECTIONS 751(b) AND 752(b)

Section 751(b) can require recognition of gain in some unexpected situations due to the deemed distribution rule of § 752(b). Suppose that the HIJ partnership, of which H, I, and J are equal partners, has assets with a value of $175, of which $40 are unrealized receivables (having a basis of zero), and liabilities of $100. Suppose further, that K contributes $25 to the partnership to become a one-quarter partner. Because H, I, and J each have reduced their share of partnership liabilities from $33.33 to $25, each has a deemed distribution of $8.33. Furthermore, because each has reduced his interest in the partnership's unrealized receivables from $13.33 to $10, § 751(b) applies. H, I, and J are each treated as having received $3.33 of receivables in a distribution to which § 731(a) applies. Under § 732 each takes a zero basis in the receivables. Section 751(b) then treats them each as having sold the receivables to the partnership for $3.33, and each must recognize that amount of gain. The remaining $5 deemed distribution to each of H, I, and J is treated as a distribution of cash under § 731. K did not receive a constructive distribution, so § 751(b) does not apply to K. See Rev.Rul. 84–102, 1984–2 C.B. 119. The partnership now has a $10 basis for its unrealized receivables. Although § 743(b) does not apply to give K a $10 basis in his share of the unrealized receivables, if the partnership's assets and partners' capital accounts were revalued pursuant to Treas. Reg. § 1.704–1(b)(2)(iv)(f), reverse § 704(c) allocations of the remaining $30 of income subsequently realized with respect to the unrealized receivables would be required by Treas. Reg. § 1.704–3(a)(6)(i) and 1.704–1(b)(4)(i).

See page 169. Furthermore, if the partnership's assets were not revalued, Treas. Reg. § 1.704–1(b)(5), Ex. (14)(iv) indicates that a special allocation to H, I, and J of all of the income subsequently realized with respect to the receivables will be respected.

4. ANALYSIS

Section 751(b) is theoretically flawed because it measures disproportionality by the value of substantially appreciated inventory and accounts receivable rather than by the excess of value over basis. Thus, it fails to fulfill completely its stated purpose. In Examples (1) through (3), above, each partner's share of ordinary income before the distribution is $30,000. If, however, the partnership distributed $38,250 of accounts receivable and $74,250 of cash to E to reduce her interest to one-ninth, § 751(b) would be inapplicable because E will have no net change in her total interest in aggregate § 751 property-accounts receivable and inventory taken together. This result is illustrated in the following computation:

Property	Value of Distributee's Post-distribution Interest as a Partner	+ Value of Distributed Property	− Value of Distributee's Pre-distribution Interest	= Increase (Decrease) in Distributee's Interest
Section 751 Property				
Acc'ts Rec.	$ 2,750	$38,250	$21,000	$20,000
Inventory	$10,000	$ 0	$30,000	($20,000)
Total § 751 Property				0
Other Property				
Cash	$ 5,750	$74,250	$42,000	$38,000
Whiteacre	$10,000	$ 0	$30,000	($20,000)
Blackacre	$ 9,000	$ 0	$27,000	($18,000)
Total Other Property				0

Upon collection of the $63,000 of accounts receivable and sale of the inventory, E recognizes ordinary income of $41,000 attributable to the accounts receivable and $3,000 attributable to the inventory, for a total of $42,000, while F and G each recognize only $24,000 of ordinary income. These results are inconsistent with the objectives of § 751 because the partners have been able to choose among themselves which partners will disproportionately recognize ordinary income and capital gain without affecting the overall amount of gain recognized by each partner.

SECTION 2. DISTRIBUTIONS IN LIQUIDATION OF A PARTNER'S INTEREST

INTERNAL REVENUE CODE: Sections 706(c); 731(a), (b), & (d); 732(b)–(d); 736; 741; 751(b).

REGULATIONS: Sections § 1.704–1(b)(2)(iv)(e)(1), (b)(2)(iv)(f)(5)(ii); 1.708–1(b)(1); 1.736–1(a)(6).

On the complete liquidation of the interest of a retiring partner the application of § 736 may give rise to two different categories of distribution, each of which is treated differently. On the one hand, the partnership may distribute partnership assets, including cash, to compensate the retiring partner for the fair market value of the retiring partner's share of partnership assets. Section 736(b) treats payments for the retiring partner's interest in partnership assets as distributions to the partner subject to the distribution rules of §§ 731 and 751. The retiring partner also may receive distributions that represent a share of future partnership profits for some defined term, or some other form of premium payment in excess of the value of the retiring partner's share of partnership assets. Under § 736(a), payments to a retiring partner that are not payments for the partnership interest of the partner, and that vary on the basis of partnership income, are treated as a distributive share of partnership income, or, if not based on income, as a guaranteed payment under § 707(c). Payments classified as § 736(a) payments result in ordinary income to the retiring partner. In addition, § 736(a) payments either reduce the continuing partners' distributive shares of partnership income, or, as § 707(c) guaranteed payments to the retiring partner, are deductible by the partnership, thereby reducing the taxable income passed through to the continuing partners. Payments that are treated as distributions under § 736(b) do not reduce the income of continuing partners and, at best, may provide for basis adjustments if a § 754 election is in effect. Although the statutory language treats payments as distributive share under § 736(a), "except as provided in subsection (b)," in actuality § 736(b) is the general rule and § 736(a) is the exception. As a consequence of this matrix of rules, a retiring partner would prefer payments in liquidation of his interest to be classified as § 736(b) payments with basis recovery and capital gain treatment. The continuing partners would prefer classification of payments as § 736(a) payments that are taxable in full as ordinary income to the retiring partner, but which reduce the income of the continuing partners.

Two different sets of rules apply under § 736 for the purpose of distinguishing payments that fall under § 736(b) from § 736(a) payments, depending on whether or not capital is a material income producing factor for the partnership. Generally speaking, capital is not a material income producing factor for partnerships engaged in a business that provides services. Capital is a material income producing factor in other partnership businesses.

If capital is a material income producing factor for the partnership, payments to the withdrawing partner equal to the fair market value of retiring partner's interest (including the partner's interest in unrealized receivables and goodwill) will be treated under § 736(b) as distributions and §§ 731 and 732 are the generally applicable provisions. If the partnership holds unrealized receivables or substantially appreciated inventory, § 751(b) applies to require exchange treatment to the extent that the retiring partner's interest in § 751 assets is changed.[5] Distributions to the retiring partner in excess of the fair market value of his partnership interest are taxed as ordinary income under § 736(a). See I.R.C. § 736(b)(3). As long as the partnership has maintained capital accounts as required by § 704(b), and the capital accounts are booked-up to fair market value at the time of the liquidation distribution, any such excess payments will be in the nature of a retirement bonus, pension, or mutual insurance.

Section 736(a) is of much greater significance if capital is not a material income producing factor for the partnership, e.g., the partnership is in a service-oriented business, and the retiring partner is a general partner. See I.R.C. § 736(b)(3). In this case, § 736(b)(2) provides that payments to a retiring partner for the partner's share of the partnership's unrealized receivables and goodwill (unless provided for in the partnership agreement) are not distributions attributable to partnership property subject to § 736(b), and thus are subject to § 736(a). Distributions to a retiring general partner in a partnership in which capital is not a material income producing factor are treated under § 736(b) as liquidating distributions subject to the rules of §§ 731, 732, and 751(b) only to the extent they equal the fair market value of the partner's interest in partnership assets other than goodwill and unrealized receivables. Any amount distributed in excess of that value generally will be attributable to the retiring partner's interest in unrealized receivables or goodwill of the partnership or to a premium or retirement bonus. In the absence of a provision in the partnership agreement calling for a payment to the retiring partner for her interest in goodwill, all of such excess payments (except to the extent attributable to any basis in goodwill) are taxed under § 736(a) as ordinary income to the distributee. However, if the partnership agreement calls for the retiring partner to be paid for her share of partnership goodwill, then payments for goodwill are subject to § 736(b). As a consequence, the partners in a service partnership may designate whether some portion of a distribution to a retiring partner is subject to either § 736(a) or § 736(b) by providing in the partnership agreement for payment for the retiring partner's share of goodwill.

Treas. Reg. § 1.736–1(b)(1) and (2) provide that payments attributable to unrealized receivables are governed by § 736(b) to the extent of the retiring partner's basis in any unrealized receivables, generally basis resulting from any special basis adjustments under § 743(b). Otherwise, payments for a retiring partner's interest in unrealized receivables of a partnership in which capital is not a material income producing factor are governed by § 736(a), and not by § 751(b), even though they fall within the definition of § 751 assets.

Liquidating distributions to a *limited partner* in a partnership in which capital is not a material income producing factor are subject to the same set of rules that govern liquidating distributions to partners in partnerships in

---

5. As with current distributions, § 751(b) does not apply to a distribution of property that the distributee partner contrib-uted to the partnership. I.R.C. § 751(b)(2)(A).

which capital is a material income producing factor. I.R.C. § 736(b)(3). This situation will be encountered rarely. However, § 736(a) payments are more likely to be encountered in liquidations of a member's interest in a limited liability company in which capital is not an income producing factor.

ILLUSTRATIVE MATERIAL

1. EFFECT ON PARTNERS' CAPITAL ACCOUNTS

In the case of a distribution of any property other than money to the retiring partner, Treas. Reg. § 1.704–1(b)(2)(iv)(e)(1) requires that all partners capital accounts must be adjusted to reflect the gain or loss that would have been recognized if the distributed property had been sold for its fair market value instead of distributed. The retiring partner's capital account is then reduced by the fair market value of distributed property, which should reduce the retiring partner's capital account to zero as a result of a distribution in complete liquidation of that interest. Only the payments classified as § 736(b) payments, however, will apply to reduce the retiring partner's capital account. Alternatively, Treas. Reg. § 1.704–1(b)(2)(iv)(f)(5)(ii) provides that in connection with the liquidation of a partner's interest in the partnership all of the partnership's properties and the partners' book accounts may be adjusted to reflect fair market values if there is a substantial non-tax business purpose for doing so. This book-up often is advisable as the partnership must determine the fair market value of the retiring partner's interest in partnership property in any event in order to determine the amount distributable to the partner.

2. VALUATION OF PARTNERSHIP ASSETS

Determining the amount taxable as income under § 736(a) or treated as a distribution under § 736(b) requires a valuation of the distributee's interest in all the partnership's assets, including the work in progress (unrealized receivables) held by the partnership at the time of the distribution and, if the partnership agreement provides for payments with respect to goodwill, the partnership's goodwill. Treas. Reg. § 1.736–1(b)(1) states: "Generally, the valuation placed by the partners upon a partner's interest in partnership property in an arm's length agreement will be regarded as correct." Treas. Reg. § 1.736–1(b)(3) similarly allows the valuation placed on goodwill, whether the valuation is specific in amount or based on a formula, to be fixed for purposes of § 736(b) by an arm's length agreement among the partners. However, Treas. Reg. § 1.755–1(a)(2) and (5) provides that for purposes of determining the fair market value of all partnership property when allocating any § 734(b) basis adjustment available to the partnership as a result of a § 736(b) distribution (see page 355), the fair market value of all partnership property other than goodwill is to be determined taking into account all the facts and circumstances, and the fair market value of goodwill must be determined using the residual method. Whether the broad discretion under that temporary regulation to ignore arms' length agreements as to value will be extended to the operation of § 736 is unclear as a matter of statutory interpretation. It would be incongruous, however, to respect a bargained for allocation for purposes of § 736, but not for purposes of §§ 743 and 755.

3.   EFFECT OF RETIREMENT ON PARTNERSHIP TAXABLE YEAR

Where a retiring partner has no continuing interest in partnership profits, § 706(c) provides for the closing of the taxable year of the partnership as respects the distributee partner and the result is similar to the sale of his interest. If, on the other hand, a retiring partner is to receive continuing payments, the distributee is treated as a partner so long as the § 736(a) payments continue. Treas. Reg. § 1.736–1(a)(1)(ii) and (6).

The liquidation of a partner's interest does not usually close the taxable year of partnership with respect to the remaining partners. I.R.C. § 706(c)(1). However, a liquidation of an interest in a two-person partnership may result in a termination of the partnership under § 708(b)(1)(A) "because no part of any business * * * continues to be carried on * * * in a partnership." A termination would result in a closing of the partnership taxable year for all the partners. The regulations, however, provide that such a termination will not occur so long as payments are being made under § 736, since the recipient is deemed a continuing partner until those payments cease. Treas. Reg. §§ 1.736–1(a)(6); 1.708–1(b)(1)(i) and (ii).

A.   Section 736(b) Payments: Distributions

Internal Revenue Code: Sections 731(a), (b), & (d); 732(b)–(d); 734; 735; 736; 741; 751(b); 752(b).

Regulations: Sections 1.731–1; 1.732–1(b)–(c), –2; 1.736–1(b).

As a general rule, assuming that § 751(b) does not apply, liquidating distributions classified as § 736(b) payments do not result in the recognition of gain to the distributee partner unless there is a distribution of cash in excess of the partner's basis for the partnership interest. I.R.C. § 731(a)(1). Any property distributed generally will take an exchanged basis equal to the distributee's basis for the partnership interest less any cash received. I.R.C. § 732(b). The exchanged basis, i.e., partnership interest basis less cash received, is then allocated among the distributed assets according to the formula of § 732(c), discussed below. If cash received in a liquidating distribution exceeds the retiring partner's basis for the partnership interest and the partner recognizes a gain under § 731, any property received in the distribution will take a zero basis. Gain recognized under § 731 is treated as capital gain by § 741.

The general rules governing liquidating distributions to a partner are subject to certain modifications in situations in which inventory or unrealized receivables are distributed but §§ 736(a) and 751(b) are not applicable. This situation will occur, for example, if inventory and unrealized receivables, in the aggregate, are distributed in pro rata amounts to the partners in a complete liquidation, or if the partnership's inventory is not substantially appreciated. Section 732(c) generally requires a transfer to the distributee partner of the partnership's basis for such assets, and § 735 requires the same carryover of asset character as occurs on current distributions. See Wilmot Fleming Engineering Co. v. Commissioner, 65 T.C. 847 (1976), for an application of these rules. Thus, in the allocation of the partner's basis in the partnership interest (less cash received) among the various assets, that basis is first allocated to the inventory or unrealized receivables in an amount equal to the partnership's basis, with any remaining basis of the partner allocated to the remaining assets. If a partner's basis for his partnership interest (less any cash received) is less than the partnership's basis for distributed inventory or unrealized receivables, the partnership's transferred basis in these assets is decreased as provided in § 732(c)(3), first by allocating the decrease to depreciated inventory (or receivables with a basis in excess of value), and then among the inventory and receivables in proportion to adjusted basis. Any other distributed assets take a zero basis.

A retiring partner may recognize a loss if (1) a distribution consists solely of cash that is less than the distributee's basis for his partnership interest; or (2) the distributee partner receives only cash, unrealized receivables, and inventory, and the sum of the amount of the cash and the distributee partner's basis under § 732(a)(2) for the unrealized receivables and inventory—which cannot exceed the partnership's basis therefor—is less than the partner's basis for the partnership interest. I.R.C. § 731(a)(2). See Pinson v. Commissioner, T.C. Memo. 1990–234 (upon liquidation of a law partnership whose only assets were zero basis accounts receivable, partner was allowed capital loss deduction under § 731(a)(2) equal to the basis of his partnership interest). Any loss recognized under § 731(a) will be a capital loss under § 741. This recognized loss compensates for the loss of basis resulting from the exchanged basis rule and has no relation to whether any economic loss is sustained. For example, assume that A's basis in her partnership interest is $1,000 and that she received a liquidating distribution of $500 in cash and inventory having a zero basis to the partnership and a value of $1,000. Although A has realized a $500 gain, she will take the inventory at a zero basis and recognize a $500 capital loss.

If non-inventory assets are distributed, no loss will be recognized and the distributed assets will acquire the entire remaining basis of the partner in her partnership interest (the partner's basis less any cash and basis assigned to unrealized receivables and inventory). In extreme situations, assets with a very low value may receive a very high basis. For example, if partner A, above, in addition to receiving cash and the inventory item had received an additional non-inventory asset, A's basis for the asset would be $500. While no loss would be recognized on the distribution, if the asset were then sold for $50, A would recognize a $450 loss. The character of that loss would be determined with respect to the character of the distributed asset in the partner's hands.

As with current distributions, the effect of changes in the partners' shares of partnership liabilities must be taken into account. A distributee partner has a deemed cash distribution under § 752(b) equal in amount to his entire share of partnership liabilities prior to the liquidation of his interest. If a partnership is terminated and the partnership distributes encumbered property to the partners, the increases and decreases in each partner's share of partnership liabilities under §§ 752(a) and (b) are treated as occurring simultaneously. Thus, only the net decrease in liabilities is treated as a cash distribution; and if a partner assumes a greater amount of partnership liabilities than he is relieved of, the partner increases his basis in his partnership interest by the net increase prior to determining the basis of distributed property. Treas. Reg. § 1.752–1(f) and (g), Ex.1; Rev.Rul. 87–120, 1987–2 C.B. 161.

The deemed exchange rules of § 751(b), discussed at page 330, apply to liquidating distributions in which a partner receives either more or less than his pro rata share of partnership unrealized receivables and substantially appreciated inventory. As a result, most non-pro rata liquidating distributions are partially taxable at the time of the distribution. Indeed, most distributions to retiring partners in general are subject to § 751(b) because in most cases a retiring partner receives cash from the continuing partnership, which usually has some § 751 assets. If the distribution is non-pro rata and the retiring partner receives less than the partner's share of unrealized receivables and substantially appreciated inventory, and hence more of the partner's share of other property or cash, the retiring partner is treated under § 751(b)(1)(B), as having sold to the partnership in a transaction which produces ordinary income the partner's interest in the inventory and unrealized receivables retained by the partnership. The partnership will recognize gain or loss as respects the sale by it of the other property to the retiring partner and will make an adjustment in the basis of its remaining inventory and unrealized receivables reflecting its purchase from the retiring partner. These basis adjustments for the partnership occur even though no election had been made under § 754. The gain or loss recognized by the partnership will be characterized with reference to the character of the property in its hands.

Unrealized receivables and substantially appreciated inventory are defined in § 751(c) and (d) respectively. For discussion of the meaning of unrealized receivables and substantially appreciated inventory, see page 336. Remember that unrealized receivables include recapture income, which significantly expands the sweep of § 751(b). As a result, § 751(b) will apply in virtually all cases in which a partner withdraws from a partnership, including an accrual method partnership, that holds any depreciable property other than real property (which often is not subject to any recapture rule). However, because the § 751(b) exchange computation is based on aggregate substantially appreciated inventory and unrealized receivables, a distribution that is non-pro rata with respect to each category separately, but not with respect to the fair market value of both together, will not be subject to § 751(b). For example, if the ABC partnership held inventory with a basis of $120 and a value of $180 and unrealized receivables of $90 (e.g., an item of depreciable property subject to $90 of § 1245 depreciation recapture), a liquidating distribution of all of the unrealized receivables would not invoke § 751(b) because the distributee partner did not receive a disproportionate share of the partnership's § 751 assets. Similarly, a liquidating distribution of $90 of inventory would not bring § 751(b) into play. See Treas. Reg. § 1.751–1(b)(1)(ii).

ILLUSTRATIVE MATERIAL

1. EFFECT OF CONTINUING LIABILITY FOR PARTNERSHIP DEBTS

Under state law a general partner who has withdrawn from a partnership may remain liable to partnership creditors for debts incurred before his withdrawal. Generally, however, the continuing partners agree to indemnify the withdrawing partner if he is required to pay any debts other than those which he has agreed to pay. Barker v. Commissioner, T.C. Memo. 1983–643, involved a situation in which such an agreement between the partnership and the retiring partner was not entered into until a taxable year following the year in which the retiring partner withdrew from the partnership and received an actual liquidating distribution. The court held that the deemed distribution under § 752(b) attributable to the assumption by the continuing partners of the retiring partner's share of partnership indebtedness did not occur until the subsequent year in which the agreement became effective.

In Weiss v. Commissioner, 956 F.2d 242 (11th Cir.1992), a partner was expelled from a partnership. The partnership agreement did not contain an express provision in which the continuing partners agreed to indemnify the expelled partner for partnership liabilities, including partnership debts that had been guaranteed by the expelled partner. Nor did any creditor release the partner from liability. Following *Barker*, the court held that the expelled partner's share of partnership liabilities was not treated as a distribution in the year he was expelled from the partnership. The court concluded that whether or not the partner ultimately would be responsible for payment of the debts did not change the fact of his continuing liability to creditors during the year in question. Presumably, the expelled partner would realize subsequent distributions as the partnership's debts were paid, although this treatment gives rise to difficult administrative problems. The issue in *Weiss* arises because under substantive partnership law it is not entirely clear whether a withdrawing partner is entitled to be indemnified for partnership debts by the continuing partners in the absence of an express agreement to that effect.

2. LOSS DEDUCTIONS FOR ABANDONMENT OF A PARTNERSHIP INTEREST

In Neubecker v. Commissioner, 65 T.C. 577 (1975), the Tax Court held that no loss was currently recognized by a partner who received assets other than money, receivables, and inventory. The court rejected the taxpayer's argument that he was entitled to an ordinary loss under § 165 for the forfeiture or abandonment of his partnership interest. The court found that as an independent provision, § 731 precluded any recourse to the general loss provisions of § 165 as to a fact situation falling within the ambit of § 731. Compare Johnson v. Commissioner, 66 T.C. 897 (1976), which held that where the taxpayer received the proceeds of a life insurance policy on the life of his partner, he was not entitled to a loss deduction under § 731(a)(2) and § 741 on the liquidation of the partnership following the partner's death. The court rested its decision on the ground that under § 165(a) no deduction is allowed for a loss which is "compensated for by insurance or otherwise." Implicit in this reasoning is the premise that § 731 does not provide a statutory ground for claiming losses independently of § 165, but instead establishes further limitations on the availability of a loss deduction on the liquidation of a partnership interest. These two cases might be reconciled on the theory that a loss is allowable to a retiring partner with respect to his partnership interest only if the conditions of both § 165 and § 731 have been met; these two sections are not to be viewed as alternative grounds for establishing a loss.

Echols v. Commissioner, 935 F.2d 703 (5th Cir.1991), reh. denied, 950 F.2d 209 (5th Cir.1991), rev'g, 93 T.C. 553 (1989), allowed a § 165(a) abandonment loss deduction for a partner who "walked away" from a partnership interest, without considering the significance of existing partnership indebtedness. Alternatively, the court held that a "worthlessness" loss was allowable with respect to the partnership interest because the partnership's only asset was real estate encumbered by a nonrecourse mortgage in excess of the value of the real estate and the partnership had no sources of income.

Because the partnership's sole asset was encumbered by a nonrecourse mortgage, upon ceasing to be a partner by virtue of an abandonment the taxpayer-partner would have been relieved of a share of partnership debt, thereby receiving a constructive distribution under § 752(b). Thus, the transaction in *Echols* should have been treated as a sale or exchange of the partnership interest under §§ 731 and 741, with the resulting loss constituting a capital loss rather than an ordinary loss. In light of § 731, it is difficult to conceptualize how a partner can "abandon" a partnership interest. In O'Brien v. Commissioner, 77 T.C. 113 (1981), the taxpayer "abandoned" an interest in a joint venture that held real estate encumbered by nonrecourse mortgages and claimed an ordinary loss deduction. The court upheld the Commissioner's treatment of the transaction as a liquidating distribution, resulting in capital loss under §§ 731 and 741. Relying on § 752(c), the court rejected the taxpayer's argument that there was no constructive distribution under § 752(b).

The Service applies the analysis in *O'Brien*, not *Echols*. Rev.Rul. 93–80, 1993–2 C.B. 239, held that a loss from abandoning a partnership interest could qualify for ordinary loss treatment as long as the abandoning partner received neither an actual nor a constructive distribution. Receipt of even a de minimis distribution or any reduction of a share of partnership liabilities results in the entire loss being characterized as a capital loss. Furthermore, ordinary loss treatment will be allowed only if the abandonment is not in substance a sale or exchange.

3. ALLOCATION OF EXCHANGED BASIS AMONG DISTRIBUTED ASSETS

Section 732(b) provides the partner whose interest is liquidated with an exchanged basis in the property received equal to his basis in his partnership interest less any cash received. This exchanged basis is allocated among the distributed assets in a multi-step process prescribed in § 732(c). Generally speaking, each asset first is assigned a transferred basis equal to its basis in the hands of the partnership. The bases of the various assets are then adjusted either upwards or downwards, depending on whether the partner's exchanged basis exceeds the aggregate transferred basis or is less than the transferred basis. If the exchanged basis is less than the aggregate transferred basis, negative basis adjustments are made. If a negative basis adjustment is required, the adjustments are made in the same manner as are negative adjustments occasioned by a current distribution of property. See page 355. If the exchanged basis exceeds the aggregate transferred basis, positive basis adjustments are made. In no event, however, may inventory or unrealized receivables take a basis in the hands of the partner that is greater than their basis to the partnership. I.R.C. § 732(c)(1).

If the partner's basis for the partnership interest exceeds the partnership's basis for the property received in the liquidating distribution, the basis increase must be allocated among the assets. First, inventory and accounts receivable are allocated a basis equal to their bases in the hands of the partnership. If any basis remains after the allocation to inventory and accounts receivable, the remaining basis is allocated among all other assets. Each such asset is tentatively allocated a transferred basis in the partner's hands equal to the partnership's basis for the asset. I.R.C. § 732(c)(2)(A). Then the basis of any such property with a fair market value greater than its basis to the partnership is increased in proportion to the relative built-in appreciation. I.R.C. § 732(c)(2)(B). The basis increase in this step cannot increase an asset's basis above its fair market value. Any § 734(b) or § 743(b) basis adjustments previously made with respect to the retiring partner's basis for those assets are taken into account in determining the partnership basis for its assets in making the adjustment. Treas. Reg. § 1.732–2.

Assume, for example, that a partner with an $1,800 basis in her partnership interest received three parcels of real estate held as capital assets: Blackacre, with a fair market value of $1,400 and a basis of $600, Whiteacre, with a fair market value of $400 and a basis of $200, and Greenacre, with a fair market value of $200 and a basis of $400. The partner's transferred basis would be $600 in Blackacre, $200 in Whiteacre, and $400 in Greenacre. Because the aggregate basis of all three properties to the partnership was only $1,200 and the partner is entitled to an aggregate basis of $1,800 for the three properties, the bases must be increased by $600. The first step, under § 732(c)(2)(A) is to increase the bases of the appreciated properties, Blackacre and Whiteacre. Blackacre is appreciated by $800 and Whiteacre is appreciated by $200. Thus the partner increases the basis of Blackacre by $480, from $600 to $1,080, and increases the basis of Whiteacre by $120, from $200 to $320.

	FMV	Basis	Appreciation		Partner's Increase	Partner's Basis
Blackacre	$1,400	$ 600	$800	(600) × (800/1000) =	$480	$1,080
Whiteacre	400	200	200	(600) × (200/1000) =	120	320
Greenacre	200	400	(200)			400
Total		$1,200	$800		$600	$1,800

Since the basis increase allocated to each property did not exceed the amount of the appreciation in each property, the total basis increase of $600 was absorbed by Blackacre and Whiteacre. Greenacre takes a basis of $400.

If the required basis increase exceeds the appreciation inherent in the distributed appreciated assets, a portion of the aggregate basis increase cannot be allocated in proportion to relative appreciation. In such a case, the remaining portion of the increase is allocated among all of the properties (other than inventory and unrealized receivables) received in the distribution relative to their fair market values. I.R.C. § 732(c)(2)(B). Assume that in the preceding example the partner's basis in his partnership interest was $2,400. Because the aggregate basis of all three properties to the partnership was only $1,200 and the partner is entitled to an aggregate basis of $2,400 for the three properties, the bases must be increased by $1,200. The partner's transferred basis would have been $600 in Blackacre, $200 in Whiteacre, and $400 in Greenacre. If the total basis increase of $1,200 were allocated between Blackacre and Whiteacre relative to appreciation, the partner would increase the basis of Blackacre by $960 to $1,560 and the basis of Whiteacre by $240 to $440. However, since the basis increase allocated to each property under § 732(c)(2)(A) cannot exceed the amount of the appreciation in each property, the basis of Blackacre is increased to only $1,400 and the basis of Whiteacre is increased to only $400.

	FMV	Basis	Appreciation		Partner's Increase	Partner's Basis
Blackacre	$1,400	$ 600	$800	(1,200) × (800/1000) =	$960	$1,400
Whiteacre	400	200	200	(1,200) × (200/1000) =	240	400
Greenacre	200	400	(200)			
Total		$1,200	$800			

Because only $1,000 of the total basis increase of $1,200 was allocated under § 732(c)(2)(A), the remaining $200 of basis increase is allocated among all three properties, including Greenacre, which is depreciated, relative to fair market value pursuant to § 732(c)(2)(B). Thus:

	FMV		Partner's Increase	Partner's Basis
Blackacre	$1,400	(200) × (1400/2000) =	$140	$1,540
Whiteacre	400	(200) × (400/2000) =	40	440
Greenacre	200	(200) × (200/2000) =	20	420
Total	$2,000		$200	$2,400

The allocation formula under § 732 is not designed to reduce all disparities between fair market value and basis because it does not provide for simultaneous increases and decreases in basis if a partner receives some appreciated assets and some depreciated assets. Assume for example that a partner with a basis in her partnership interest of $1,000 receives a liquidating distribution of two capital assets, Blackacre, with a fair market value of $300 and a basis of $600, and Whiteacre, with a fair market value of $700 and a basis of $400. Because the partner's basis in the partnership interest equaled the partnership's basis in the distributed assets, there are no § 732(c) adjustments, and the partner takes a $600 basis in Blackacre and a $400 basis in Whiteacre.

4. SPECIAL ALLOCATION OF BASIS UNDER SECTION 732(d)

As discussed at page 328, § 732(d) applies a special basis allocation rule where the retiring partner obtained his interest by purchase, death, or other transfer within the prior two years and the partnership did not have a § 754 election in effect. If a § 754 election had been in effect, the purchase price for his partnership interest would be reflected in his share of the basis of the partnership's assets under § 743(b), and the allocation rule of § 732(c)(1) would be coordinated with his purchase cost. Treas. Reg. § 1.732–2. But if the partnership did not so elect (the election is made by the partnership, not the partner), then the partnership basis would not reflect the purchasing partner's cost and the allocation limitation under § 732(c)(1) for inventory and unrealized receivables might operate unfairly. Section 732(d) allows the retiring partner to elect a hypothetical adjustment to the basis of the assets to reflect the partner's original purchase price for the partnership interest and then applies the allocation rules of § 732(c) discussed above. Treas. Reg. § 1.732–1(d). Where the absence of an election would result in a shift of basis to depreciable property and at the time of the transfer the value of partnership property (other than money) exceeds 110 percent of its adjusted basis to the partnership, the regulations require that the distributed partnership's basis in its assets must be determined as though the § 732(d) election had been made by the distributee partner. See Treas. Reg. § 1.732–1(d)(4). However, under the basis allocation rules in § 732(c), it is difficult to hypothesize a situation to which Treas. Reg. § 1.732–1(d)(4) applies.

B.   Section 736(a) Payments

Internal Revenue Code: Sections 706(c), (d); 734; 736; 751(b); 761(b).

Regulations: Sections 1.706–1(c); 1.736–1(a); 1.761–1(d).

Distributions from a continuing partnership to a retiring partner that are not in exchange for the retiring partner's interest are governed by § 736(a) and are treated as ordinary income to the distributee. Distributions treated as § 736(a) payments to the retiring partner either are deductible by the partnership or reduce the continuing partners' distributive shares of partnership income. This is accomplished by treating payments for unrealized receivables as either a § 707(c) payment or as the retiring partner's distributive share of partnership income. Section 736(a) thus assures that a retiring partner is taxed on not less than the partner's share of unrealized receivables, usually cash method accounts receivable, if the partner is paid for them. For purposes of § 736(a), however, unrealized receivables do not include depreciation and other cost recovery allowance recapture income. Section 751(b) will apply to any distribution to a retiring partner attributable to the value of partnership property subject to depreciation recapture.

Since § 736(a) reduces the ordinary income realized by the continuing partners, the partnership generally may not adjust its basis for the distributee's share of the receivables which it retained, even if a § 754 election is in effect; § 734 adjustments are not allowable for amounts taxed to a distributee under § 736(a).

ILLUSTRATIVE MATERIAL

1. CLASSIFICATION OF GOODWILL BETWEEN SECTION 736(a) AND SECTION 736(b)

With respect to liquidating distributions to a general partner of a service partnership (capital is not a material income producing factor), payments for goodwill are classified as § 736(a) payments "except to the extent that the partnership agreement provides for a payment with respect to goodwill." However, Treas. Reg. § 1.736–1(b)(3) treats the retiring partner's proportionate share of the partnership's basis, if any, in the goodwill as § 736(b) property. If the partnership agreement specifically provides for payments to a retiring partner with respect to partnership goodwill (in excess of any basis), all payments for goodwill are classified as § 736(b) payments. I.R.C. § 736(b)(2)(B). In Smith v. Commissioner, 313 F.2d 16 (10th Cir.1962), the court required the retiring taxpayer to treat as an ordinary income payment a "premium" paid in excess of the book value of his interest in the partnership property on the date of withdrawal. The taxpayer argued that the premium was a payment for goodwill entitled to capital gain treatment, but the court held that the failure of the partnership agreement to refer expressly to payments for goodwill required the distribution to be treated under § 736(a): "Paragraph (2)(B) of subsection (b) exempts from ordinary income treatment payments made for goodwill only when the partnership agreement so provides specifically and does not permit an intent to compensate for goodwill to be drawn from the surrounding circumstances as the taxpayer here urges us to do."

In Commissioner v. Jackson Investment Co., 346 F.2d 187 (9th Cir. 1965), the original partnership agreement did not make any provision for payment for goodwill on liquidation of a partner's interest. Subsequently, one of the partners withdrew and the partners entered into an agreement referring to a $40,350 payment to the withdrawing partner as "a guaranteed payment or a payment for good will." The Tax Court held, 41 T.C. 675 (1964) (Nonacq.), that the subsequent agreement did not constitute a modification of the original partnership agreement; hence the payment was controlled by § 736(a)(2) and was deductible by the partnership. The Court of Appeals reversed, finding that the partners' subsequent agreement was a modification of the original partnership agreement. The language of the agreement was internally inconsistent since "payment for goodwill" and "guaranteed payment" in this context were mutually exclusive, but the court concluded that the parties intended the payments to be governed by § 736(b)(2)(B) and as such were not deductible by the partnership.

In the cases of liquidation distributions from a partnership in which capital is a material income producing factor, and in the case of all liquidation distributions to limited partners or to members of limited liability companies, payments for the value of the partner's share of goodwill and unrealized receivables always are treated as § 736(b) payments. I.R.C. § 736(b)(3).

2. ALLOCATION OF PAYMENTS BETWEEN SECTIONS 736(a) AND 736(b)

When distributions consist of both § 736(a) payments and § 736(b) payments, the portion of each payment subject to the respective rules must be determined. Specific rules for the allocation of payments between §§ 736(a) and 736(b) are provided by Treas. Reg. § 1.736–1(b)(5), which, however, allows the parties to provide for any other reasonable method of allocation. When the interest of a partner is liquidated, § 736 applies to determine the treatment of payments or property distribution received in liquidation of his interest, whether the distribution is a lump sum payment, single property distribution, or a series of payments representing a continuing interest in partnership income. See Smith v. Commissioner, 313 F.2d 16 (10th Cir.1962) (§ 736 applied to lump sum payment). When continuing payments are received, the application of § 736 is somewhat more complex than when a partner's interest is liquidated by a lump sum distribution.

If the total payments to be made are fixed in amount, each payment is pro rated between an amount governed by § 736(a) and an amount governed by § 736(b); the portion of each annual payment that the total agreed § 736(b) payments bear to the total payments to be received is taxed as a § 736(b) distribution. Any balance is treated as a § 736(a) income payment. Treas. Reg. § 1.736–1(b)(5)(i). As § 736(b) payments are received, the normal rules of § 731(a) apply. Gain is not recognized under § 731(a) until the total amount of § 736(b) cash payments exceeds the partner's basis for the partnership interest, but any gain realized with respect to the § 736(b) payments can be reported ratably as the § 736(b) payments are received if the recipient so elects. Treas. Reg. § 1.736–1(b)(6).

Assume, for example, that A retires from the ABC Partnership, in which A was a one-third partner, and A is entitled to distributions of $30,000 annually for five years. A's basis in the partnership interest is $76,000. The fair market value of the partnership's assets, other than unrealized receivables, is $300,000 and the amount of partnership's unrealized receivables is $150,000. The $150,000 aggregate distribution to A consists of $100,000 of § 736(b) payments ($300,000/3) and $50,000 of § 736(a) payments ($150,000/3). Of each $30,000 annual payment, $20,000 is a § 736(b) payment ($30,000 × $100,000/$150,000), and $10,000 is a § 736(a) payment ($30,000 × $50,000/$150,000). The annual $10,000 § 736(a) payment is included in gross income as ordinary income. The annual $20,000 § 736(b) payment is treated as a distribution subject to § 731. All of the $20,000 § 736(b) payments received in each of the first three years are excluded as a recovery of basis under § 731, leaving A with a $16,000 basis the partnership interest at the beginning of year 4. The $20,000 § 736(b) distribution in year 4 exceeds A's $16,000 basis by $4,000, resulting in a $4,000 long-term capital gain. All of the $20,000 § 736(b) payment received in year 5 is treated as long-term capital gain.

If the total amount to be received is not fixed, e.g., the retiring partner is merely to receive a certain percentage of the partnership income for a period of time, then the payments received are treated entirely as distributions subject to § 736(b) until they equal the fair market value of the retiring partner's interest in tangible personal property plus any amount called for in the partnership agreement for goodwill. Again, gain under § 731(a) is not realized until the retiring partner's basis has been recouped. Treas. Reg. § 1.736–1(b)(6). Only after all § 736(b) payments have been received does § 736(a) apply to tax the retiring partner on ordinary income. Treas. Reg. § 1.736–1(b)(5)(ii).

Assume, for example, that D retires from the DEF Partnership, in which D was a one-third partner, and a is entitled to annual distributions for five years equal to $20,000, plus 10 percent of the partnership's net income. D's basis in the partnership interest is $76,000. The fair market value of the partnership's assets, other than unrealized receivables, is $300,000 and that the amount of partnership's unrealized receivables is $150,000. Assume further that the partnership's net income in each of the next five years is $100,000, which results in total payments of $30,000 annually to D. D's share of § 736(b) property held by the partnership is $100,000 ($300,000/3). Thus, the first $100,000 received by D is subject to § 736(b). All of the $30,000 payment in each of the first three years, and $10,000 of the $30,000 payment in year 4 is governed by § 736(b) and § 731. The remaining $20,000 payment in year 4 and all of the $30,000 payment in year 5 is governed by § 736(a).

3.   TREATMENT OF RETIRING PARTNER

Section 736(a) payments that are dependent on partnership income are taxed to the retiring partner as a distributive share of partnership income and, are excludable by the remaining partners when they compute their distributive shares. In this case the character of income, determined at the partnership level, flows through to the distributee partner. Fixed payments that are determined without regard to partnership income are ordinary income taxed to the retiring partner as guaranteed payments under § 707(c) and are deductible by the partnership. Treas. Reg. § 1.736–1(a)(4).

If a partner receives both § 736(a) payments and § 736(b) payments treated as distributions, and § 751(b) does not apply, the general rules for liquidating distributions are applicable. The excess of § 736(b) cash payments over the partner's basis for the partnership interest is recognized as a capital gain. I.R.C. §§ 731(a), 741. If only cash is received and the total amount of § 736(b) payments is less than the retiring partner's basis in the partnership interest, a capital loss is recognized. But if the partnership holds substantially appreciated inventory or has unrealized receivables attributable to depreciation recapture, ordinary income might result under § 751(b). If the retiring partner receives only § 736(a) payments and he has a basis for his partnership interest, under § 731(a)(2) the partner would recognize a loss equal to that basis. The loss would be considered as loss from the sale of the partnership interest and, accordingly, would be a capital loss under § 741.

Holman v. Commissioner, 564 F.2d 283 (9th Cir.1977), held that the rules of § 736 apply even if the partner has been expelled from the partnership. The partner is still treated as a "retiring partner" for tax purposes despite the involuntary nature of his "retirement." See also Milliken v. Commissioner, 72 T.C. 256 (1979), aff'd by order, 612 F.2d 570 (1st Cir.1979). In Estate of Quirk v. Commissioner, 928 F.2d 751 (6th Cir.1991), the taxpayer withdrew from a partnership and received payments attributable to unrealized receivables. Because the taxpayer and the continuing partners were unable to agree on the value of his interest, however, the taxpayer brought an action in state court to resolve the valuation issue. In the tax litigation, the taxpayer argued that under state law, the partnership did not terminate until the valuation issue was resolved. Accordingly, the taxpayer further argued that § 736(a) could not apply to treat the distributions as ordinary income, even though they were attributable to his share of partnership unrealized receivables, because under Treas. Reg. § 1.761–1(d) the payments were not in liquidation of his partnership interest. Affirming the Tax Court's decision that § 736(a) was applicable, the Court of Appeals held that under *Holman* and *Milliken*, supra, for purposes of § 736 a partner ceases to be a partner "when that partner ceases to share in the ongoing business of the partnership, rather than in the last year of the liquidation of his interest."

4. TREATMENT OF REMAINING PARTNERS

4.1. *Payments Treated as Distributive Share or Guaranteed Payments*

If the payments to the retiring partner are classified under § 736(a) as a distributive share or guaranteed payment, the payments reduce the income of the remaining partners. The retiring partner's distributive share is taxed directly to him; the guaranteed payment is a deductible partnership expense. Treas. Reg. § 1.736–1(a)(4). If the partnership is terminated and the withdrawing partners assume the liability to continue the guaranteed payments owing to a former retired partner, those payments are deductible by them under § 162. Rev.Rul. 75–154, 1975–1 C.B. 186. Similarly, if the business of the partnership is subsequently incorporated and the corporation succeeds to the obligation to make § 736(a) payments to a retired partner, the payments are deductible by the corporation. Rev.Rul. 83–155, 1983–2 C.B. 38.

Section 736(a) payments treated as § 707(c) guaranteed payments in effect represent the purchase price to the partnership of the retiring partner's share of unrealized receivables and partnership goodwill, and thus seemingly should be capitalized as are other § 707(c) payments to acquire an asset. However, the legislative history of the 1976 amendments to § 707(c), expressly imposing the capitalization requirement, indicate that § 736(a) payments treated as § 707(c) payments are to be deductible in all events. See S.Rep. No. 94–938, 94th Cong., 1st Sess. 94, n. 7 (1976). The continued deductibility of these payments thus obviates the need for any optional basis increase under § 734(b).

4.2. *Payments Treated for Interest in Partnership Property*

If the payments to the retiring partner are classified under § 736(b) as in exchange for the retiring partner's interest in partnership property, then the remaining partners are taxable on the partnership income unreduced by the payments. To the extent that the payments are made out of partnership capital, these payments appropriately do not increase the continuing partners' bases in their partnership interests. But if the payments are made from partnership income, the partners' bases in their partnership interests are increased by their distributive shares of partnership income paid to the retiring partner. This result also is appropriate. The remaining partners, however, may desire that the cost of the additional interests purchased from the retiring partner be reflected directly in the bases of the partnership assets as well. While the standard rule in § 734(a) does not permit an adjustment to the bases of partnership property, § 734(b) does provide on an elective basis for adjusting the basis of partnership assets.

5. INTERACTION OF SECTION 751(b) AND SECTION 736(b)

Payments to the retiring partner of a service partnership for the partner's interest in unrealized receivables are treated as § 736(a) payments. For purposes of § 736(a) the term "unrealized receivables" is limited to contractual rights to receive payments for goods or services that have not yet been included in income under the taxpayer's method of accounting, most commonly, cash method accounts receivable. As a result, § 736(a) does not apply to potential recapture income that is defined as an unrealized receivable for purposes of § 751. Furthermore, §§ 732 and 736(a) do not assure that the distributee partner and the partnership are each taxed on a proportionate share of the ordinary income attributable to the partnership's inventory at the time of the distribution. Section 751(b), however, applies to tax the retiring partner from a service partnership on disposition of his interest in recapture income and substantially appreciated inventory. Since § 736(a) applies to unrealized receivables other than recapture items, payments for unrealized receivables treated as ordinary income under § 736(a) are not taken into account under the § 751(b) computation.

The interaction of § 736(a) and § 751(b) is illustrated as follows. Assume that the DEF partnership held inventory with a value of $180 and a basis of $120 and unrealized receivables—cash method accounts receivable—of $90. A liquidating distribution to D of $90 of inventory would not bring § 751 into play because D did not receive a disproportionate amount of § 751 assets. See Treas. Reg. § 1.751–1(b)(1)(ii). However, § 736(a) would result in D recognizing $30 of income at the time of the distribution. As a result, A would increase her basis for the inventory received in the distribution from $60 to $90.

A partnership that maintains inventories, however, almost always will use the accrual method of accounting. Also, a partnership that maintains inventories is not likely to be treated as a service partnership from which a distribution for a partner's interest in unrealized receivables is treated as a § 736(a) payment. I.R.C. § 736(b)(3). Thus, it is unlikely for both § 736(a) to apply to accounts receivable and § 751(b) to apply to substantially appreciated inventory. On the other hand, service business partnerships frequently have cash method accounts receivable, subject to § 736(a), and potential depreciation recapture income with respect to equipment, subject to § 751(b), so the interaction is important.

SECTION 3. BASIS ADJUSTMENTS TO REMAINING PARTNERSHIP ASSETS

INTERNAL REVENUE CODE: Sections 731(b); 734; 754; 755.

REGULATIONS: Sections 1.197–2(g)(3); 1.734–1, –2; 1.754–1; 1.755–1(a) and (c).

Section 734(a) provides as a general rule that the basis of remaining partnership assets is not affected by either a current or a liquidating distribution to a partner. (Of course, if § 751(b) applies to the distribution, the basis of the partnership's remaining assets that are involved in the deemed exchange will have been affected.) However, if a § 754 election is in effect, § 734(b) provides for adjustments to the bases of the partnership's remaining assets. Under § 734(b), the partnership's basis for its remaining assets is increased by any gain recognized to the distributee partner under § 731 and by any excess of partnership basis for distributed assets over their basis to the distributee. Conversely, the partnership' basis for its remaining assets is decreased by any loss recognized to the distributee and by any excess of the basis of distributed assets to the distributee over their basis to the partnership. While § 734(b) applies to all distributions, only the increases can apply in the case of a current distribution. A current distribution does not trigger any partnership basis reductions since loss cannot be recognized on a non-liquidating distribution and the distributee's basis in distributed assets cannot exceed that of the partnership. After the aggregate adjustment is computed, it must be spread among the partnership assets under the allocation rules of § 755.

As amended in 2004, § 734 requires adjustments under § 734(b) to the basis of the partnership's assets whenever an aggregate basis reduction in excess of $250,000 results even though no § 754 election has been made.[6] See Notice 2005–32, 2005–16 I.R.B. 895, for procedural details and examples of the application of the rule. The purpose of 2004 amendments is to prevent the duplication of losses in a manner that allows a partner to recognize for tax purposes a loss that was not realized economically. Section 734(b) basis adjustments remain elective if the aggregate reduction to the partnership's basis would not exceed $250,000 or if the adjustment would result in a basis increase.

ILLUSTRATIVE MATERIAL

1.   AGGREGATE THEORY AND THE APPLICATION OF § 734(b)

The general rule of § 734(a), which provides no partnership basis adjustment in the case of distributions, presents no problem to the other partners where a partner receives the partner's pro rata share of each and every partnership asset in the distribution. In that case the remaining partners simply own the remaining assets to the same extent as they did before. But where the distribution is not pro rata, there is in effect an exchange of properties between the distributee partner and the remaining partners. In a non-pro rata distribution, the remaining partners purchase the distributee's interest in the remaining assets with their interests in the distributed assets. In this case, the remaining partners realize any gain or loss in their share of the distributed assets because, by distributing the assets to the distributee partner, they acquire in exchange the distributee partner's prior share of the remaining partnership assets. This realized gain is reflected in capital account adjustments under Treas. Reg. § 1.704–1(b)(2)(iv)(e), which requires that the distributed property be revalued, that all partners' capital accounts be adjusted to reflect the gain or loss that would have been allocated to each partner if the property had been sold by the partnership, and the distributee partner's capital account be reduced by the fair market value of the distributed property. Section 731(b), however, prevents recognition of this gain or loss for tax purposes.

The § 734(b) adjustment is a device for incorporating the aggregate view of a non-pro rata distribution or a retirement as an exchange of interests between the distributee partner and the remaining partners without, however, requiring the immediate recognition of gain or loss that a fully taxable exchange would entail. The basis adjustment reflects the cost to the other partners of purchasing the distributee partner's interest in the remaining partnership assets. Thus, the partnership increases the basis of its remaining assets when a cash distribution results in gain

---

6. Section 734(e) provides an exception for certain "securitization partnerships" as   defined in § 743(f).

because the other partners have in effect paid cash for the distributee partner's share of undistributed assets. The cash distribution in excess of the distributee partner's share of basis (the partner's outside basis) represents a purchase of unrealized value in remaining partnership assets. The adjustments under § 734(b) also are intended to reflect any realized gain or loss to the partnership that goes unrecognized by virtue of § 731(b). This aspect of the basis adjustment is the reason that the partnership must decrease the basis of its remaining assets if the distributee partner takes a basis in the assets that is higher than the partnership's basis in those assets. In this case, the remaining partners have in effect exchanged an interest in low basis assets for high basis assets.

Example (1)

Assume that the ABC Partnership holds Blackacre with a value of $90 and a basis of $0; Whiteacre with a value and a basis of $90; and $90 of cash. Each partner has a $60 basis for his partnership interest. (Both Blackacre and Whiteacre are capital assets and § 751(b) is thus inapplicable.) Blackacre is distributed to partner A on his retirement. In connection with the distribution, the partnership revalued its assets and capital accounts pursuant to Treas. Reg. § 1.704–1(b)(2)(iv)(*f*). Immediately before the distribution, the ABC Partnership's balance sheet, with book accounts reflecting fair market value, is as follows:

Assets				Partners' Capital Accounts		
		Tax				Tax
	Book	Basis			Book	Basis
Cash	$ 90	$ 90		A	$ 90	$ 60
Whiteacre	$ 90	$ 90		B	$ 90	$ 60
Blackacre	$ 90	$ 0		C	$ 90	$ 60
	$270	$180			$270	$180

On the distribution of Blackacre to A, it's zero tax basis to the partnership is increased to $60—its exchanged basis in A's hands under § 732(b). Under § 734(b)(2)(B) the partnership's basis in its other property must be decreased by the excess of A's $60 basis in Blackacre over the partnership's former zero basis. When the partnership distributed Blackacre to A, the remaining partners, B and C, in effect exchanged their two-thirds interest in Blackacre, worth $60, with A for one-third of the $90 cash, or $30 each, and A's one-third interest in Whiteacre, worth $30 to each partner. Hence, $30 of the $60 value paid to A, in the form of an undivided two-thirds of Blackacre, is for A's interest in the cash and $30 is for A's interest in Whiteacre. Thus, the basis of Whiteacre to the AB Partnership should be $90, the sum of the partnership's original $60 basis for an undivided two-thirds of Whiteacre, plus the $30 paid for A's one-third interest. But the remaining partners also realized, but did not recognize, a $60 gain when they transferred their two-thirds interest in Blackacre, which had a basis of zero, and received $60 of value. Reducing the basis of Whiteacre by $60, leaving the partnership a $30 basis, reflects the postponed recognition of this $60 gain. The BC Partnership's balance sheet will be as follows:

	Assets				Partners' Capital Accounts		
		Book	Tax Basis			Book	Tax Basis
Cash		$ 90	$ 90	B		$ 90	$ 60
Whiteacre		$ 90	$ 30	C		$ 90	$ 60
		$180	$120			$180	$120

Example (2)

Suppose, instead, that Whiteacre had been distributed to partner A. A's exchanged basis in Whiteacre is $60 under § 732(b). This exchanged basis in Whiteacre is $30 less than the partnership's $90 basis. Section 734(b)(1)(B) provides for a $30 increase in the bases of the partnership's remaining assets to reflect the excess of the partnership's basis in Whiteacre over A's basis. Here the remaining partners transferred $60 worth of property (their two-thirds interest in Whiteacre having a basis to them of $60) in exchange for $30 cash (the distributee partner's interest in the $90 partnership cash) and A's interest in Blackacre, worth $30. Hence, they paid $30 value for the distributee partner's one-third interest in Blackacre. The zero basis of Blackacre, therefore, should be increased by the $30 cost of that one-third interest. It need not then be reduced since the remaining partners' original basis for their two-thirds interest in Whiteacre, $60, was exactly equal to the amount they realized on the exchange and they therefore had no gain on the exchange. Here again, § 734(b) produces the correct result since the $90 partnership basis for Whiteacre exceeds by $30 the $60 basis that A takes in Whiteacre under § 732(b).[7] The BC Partnership's balance sheet would be as follows:

	Assets				Partners' Capital Accounts		
		Book	Tax Basis			Book	Tax Basis
Cash		$ 90	$ 90	B		$ 90	$ 60
Blackacre		$ 90	$ 30	C		$ 90	$ 60
		$180	$120			$180	$120

Example (3)

Finally, suppose the $90 cash had been distributed to partner A. A recognizes $30 of gain under § 731(a)(1) and § 734(b)(1)(A) provides for a

7. In determining whether the basis of Blackacre is increased to reflect its acquisition cost, the character of the distributed asset theoretically should be immaterial. Under Treas. Reg. § 1.755–1(b), however, if Whiteacre were inventory and Blackacre were a § 1231 asset, no adjustment would be made at the time of the distribution, but one could be made when the partnership later acquired an asset other than a capital or § 1231 asset. If, on the other hand, Whiteacre were a capital asset and Blackacre were neither a capital asset nor a § 1231 asset (and assuming, somewhat unrealistically that § 751(b) did not apply), then the $30 basis adjustment would be totally lost to the partnership. See page 363.

$30 increase in the basis of the remaining partnership assets. Here the remaining partners have transferred $60 (their two-thirds interest in the cash) in exchange for the distributee partner's one-third interest in each of Blackacre and Whiteacre. Since the partnership's basis in the one-third interest in Whiteacre acquired from A already was $30, no adjustment is necessary. The cost of Whiteacre is $60, the remaining partners' original basis, plus the $30 paid for A's interest, or $90. But the partnership's basis in the one-third interest in Blackacre purchased from A was zero. Thus the basis of Blackacre should be increased by $30. The BC Partnership's balance sheet is as follows:

Assets				Partners' Capital Accounts		
	Book	Tax Basis			Book	Tax Basis
Whiteacre	$ 90	$ 90	B		$ 90	$ 60
Blackacre	$ 90	$ 30	C		$ 90	$ 60
	$180	$120			$180	$120

After A's retirement, B's and C's aggregate basis for their partnership interests will be $120, and by virtue of the foregoing basis adjustments, the aggregate basis for all of the partnership's assets also will be $120. Thus, the partners could still apply the alternative rule of § 705(b) and compute the basis for their partnership interests with reference to their pro rata share of the partnership's basis for its assets. If the partners' aggregate outside basis equals the aggregate basis for partnership assets prior to the distribution, the § 734(b) adjustment works to maintain that equality after the distribution. But if outside basis and inside basis are not equal prior to the distribution (e.g., due to distributions at a time when there was not a § 754 election in effect) the § 734(b) adjustment cannot restore that equality.

In the long run the difference between the general rule of § 734(a), under which the basis of partnership assets is not adjusted, and the optional rule of § 734(b), under which the basis of partnership assets is adjusted, is primarily one of timing, although some character differences may result if depreciable assets are involved. If an upward adjustment is appropriate, but is not made, the partners will recognize greater current income (greater gains and smaller depreciation deductions) during the life of the partnership than they would have recognized if a basis adjustment had been made. On liquidation of their interests, however, due to a higher basis in their partnership interests resulting from the relatively larger basis adjustments under § 705, the partners will recognize relatively less capital gain or greater capital loss if no basis adjustments were made than if basis adjustments had been made. (Or, if liquidating distributions were in kind, the partners would have a greater basis in the distributed assets). In other words, an upwards basis adjustment reduces gain in early years and increases gain (or reduces loss) in later years. If a downward adjustment is appropriate, but is not made, the partners will recognize less current income (smaller gains and greater depreciation deductions) during the life of the partnership than they would have recognized if a basis adjustment had been made. On liquidation of their interests, however, they correspondingly will have a lower basis in their partnership interests and will recognize relatively more gain or smaller losses than if no basis adjustments were made than if basis adjustments had been made (or, if liquidating distributions were in kind, lower basis in the distributed assets).

These tradeoffs, less current income for more future income or more current income for less future income, obviously can be important if the future is many years down the line. If a partner dies while still holding the partnership interest, § 1014, which provides the partner's successor in interest with a basis for the partnership interest equal to its fair market value at the date of the partner's death, will eliminate the future gain or loss, leaving the distortions permanent. In addition, because gain or loss on liquidation of a partnership interest always is capital gain or loss, but the affected current income could be ordinary, rate arbitrage, either to the taxpayer's advantage or disadvantage, may occur. Finally, even apart from time value of money and rate arbitrage considerations, a partner who receives lesser depreciation deductions, thereby recognizing greater current income, is not made whole by an offsetting future capital loss due to the limitations of § 1211.

The § 734(b) basis adjustment is one of the few instances in the Code providing a current basis step-up without current recognition of gain. It is premised on the idea that both the distributing partnership and the distributee partner will recognize gains and losses on the distributed and undistributed property contemporaneously, and in this situation produces the correct result. Because these events may be widely separated in time, however, § 734 presents the potential for abusive transactions.

2. ALLOCATION OF BASIS ADJUSTMENT UNDER SECTION 755

2.1. *General Rules*

As is the case with § 743(b) adjustments, discussed at page 296, under § 755(b) any overall § 734(b) adjustment first is divided into an adjustment attributable to § 1231 assets and capital assets and an adjustment attributable to all other assets. The regulations interpret this provision to require adjustments to remaining partnership property having the same character as that of the distributed assets that have a basis in the hands of the distributee different from the basis the partnership had in those assets. Treas. Reg. § 1.755–1(c)(1)(i). The overall adjustment then is allocated to property of each class so as to reduce differences between basis and value. Treas. Reg. § 1.755–1(c)(2). Whether the adjustment is positive or negative, the allocation process involves two steps.

A positive § 734(b) basis adjustment is first allocated among appreciated partnership assets (in the class of assets subject to a basis adjustment) in proportion to their respective unrealized appreciation, but only to the extent of each property's unrealized appreciation. Second, any remaining positive adjustment is then allocated among the assets within the class in proportion to their respective fair market values. Treas. Reg. § 1.755–1(c)(2)(i).

If the assets of the partnership constitute a trade or business, a portion of the basis adjustment usually will have to be allocated to partnership goodwill and other § 197 intangibles, (e.g., customer lists, licenses, franchises, trademarks, trade names, advantageous contracts, etc.). In applying the apportionment rules of Treas. Reg. § 1.755–1, the fair market value of the partnership's § 197 intangibles, including goodwill and going concern value, must be determined using the residual method required by § 1060 for applicable asset acquisitions. Pursuant to Treas. Reg. § 1.755–1(a), § 197 intangibles are valued by applying the following procedure. First, the partnership determines the value of all of its assets other than § 197 intangibles. Second, the partnership determines the "partnership gross value." Generally speaking, "partnership gross value" is the amount that, if assigned to all partnership property, would result in a liquidating distribution to the transferee partner equal to that partner's basis (reduced by the amount, if any, of the partner's basis that is attributable to partnership liabilities) in the transferred partnership interest immediately following the acquisition. Third, the partnership determines the value of its § 197 intangibles under the residual method, i.e. the value of § 197 intangibles equals the partnership gross value minus the value of partnership assets other than § 197 intangibles. If the aggregate value of partnership property other than § 197 intangibles is equal to or greater than the partnership gross value, all § 197 intangibles are treated has having zero value. If there is any value assigned to the § 197 intangibles, that value is allocated among § 197 intangibles other than goodwill and going concern value before any value is assigned to goodwill and going concern value. In allocating values and basis to § 197 intangibles, value is assigned first to those § 197 intangibles (other than goodwill and going concern value) that would produce § 751(c) flush language unrealized receivables, i.e., those that have been previously amortized or depreciated, to the extent of their basis and the unrealized receivable amount; then among all § 197 intangibles (other than goodwill and going concern value) relative to fair market value.

Suppose the ABC Partnership (in which capital is a material income producing factor) has the following assets and partners' capital accounts, the book value of which has been adjusted to fair market value as allowed by Treas. Reg. § 1.704–1(b)(2)(iv)(f) in connection with a liquidating distribution to C.

Assets	Book	Tax Basis		Partners' Capital Accounts	Book	Tax Basis
Cash	$ 90	$ 90	A		$150	$ 60
Accounts			B		$150	$ 60
Receivable	$ 90	$ 0	C		$150	$ 60
Inventory	$ 90	$ 10				
§ 1231 Asset	$ 60	$ 50				
Capital Asset	$120	$ 30				
	$450	$180			$450	$180

The partnership distributes $60 worth of accounts receivable and $90 of cash to C in complete liquidation of C's interest. Neither § 736(a) nor § 751(b) applies on the facts. C recognizes a $30 gain on the distribution and takes a zero basis in the receivables. The § 734(b) adjustment, which is allocable to the class consisting of the capital asset and § 1231 asset, is $30. The capital asset is appreciated by $90 and the § 1231 asset is appreciated by $10. Thus, 90 percent ($90/($90 + $10)) of the $30 § 734(b) adjustment, or $27, is allocated to the capital asset, giving it a basis of $57, and ten percent ($10/($90 + $10)) of the of the $30 § 734(b) adjustment, or $3, is allocated to the § 1231 asset, giving it a basis of $53.

Now suppose that the partnership had distributed $60 worth of accounts receivable and $100 of cash to C, reflecting that the partnership had going concern value and goodwill worth $30, but with a zero basis. In this case, A would recognize a $40 gain on the distribution. The partnership's § 734(b) basis adjustment would be $40. The basis adjustments to the capital asset and the § 1231 asset remain the same, but the partnership increases its basis in goodwill to $10.

A negative § 734(b) basis adjustment is first allocated among depreciated partnership assets within the appropriate class in proportion to their respective amounts of unrealized depreciation, but only to the extent of each property's unrealized depreciation. Any excess negative adjustment is then allocated among the properties within the class in proportion to their remaining adjusted bases after taking into account the basis reduction in the first step. Treas. Reg. § 1.755–1(c)(2)(ii). Negative basis adjustments cannot reduce the basis of any partnership asset below zero. Treas. Reg. § 1.755–1(c)(3).

If the adjustment is attributable to the distributee partner recognizing either a gain or a loss, then the adjustment is allocated solely to capital and § 1231 assets. Treas. Reg. § 1.755–1(c)(1)(ii). Within that class of assets, the overall adjustment again is allocated among the assets in proportion to the difference between basis and fair market value, with all adjustments being required to decrease the difference. Treas. Reg. § 1.755–1(c)(2). Suppose the GHI Partnership, in which capital is a material income producing factor, has the following assets and partner's capital accounts, the book value of which has been adjusted to fair market value.

	Assets			Partners' Capital Accounts		
	Book	Tax Basis			Book	Tax Basis
Cash	$ 90	$ 90		G	$120	$ 50
Accounts Receivable	$ 90	$ 0		H	$120	$ 50
Inventory	$ 90	$ 30		I	$120	$ 50
Capital Asset	$ 90	$ 30				
	$360	$150			$360	$150

The partnership distributes $60 worth of accounts receivable and $60 of cash to G in complete liquidation of G's interest. Neither § 736(a) nor § 751(b) applies on the facts, and G recognizes a $10 gain on the distribution, taking a zero basis in the receivables. Section 734(b) calls for a $10 basis increase. In theory, $5 should be added to the basis of each of the inventory and capital asset, but under Treas. Reg. § 1.755–1(c)(1)(ii), only the basis of the capital asset can be adjusted.

From a theoretical perspective, the statutory rule that an adjustment must be allocated to property of each class so as to reduce differences between basis and value is a "fatal flaw" in the operation of the rules. As a result, § 734(b)(1) only roughly approximates the results achieved by applying pure aggregate theory. Suppose the DEF Partnership has the assets and partners' capital accounts shown on the following balance sheet (on which all assets and capital accounts have been revalued to reflect fair market value pursuant to Treas. Reg. § 1.704–1(b)(2)(iv)(f)):

Assets				Partners' Capital Accounts		
		Tax				Tax
	Book	Basis			Book	Basis
Cash	$ 300	$ 300	D		$ 600	$ 400
Inventory	$ 600	$ 700	E		$ 600	$ 400
Blackacre	$ 600	$ 100	F		$ 600	$ 400
Whiteacre	$ 300	$ 100				
	$1,800	$1,200			$1,800	$1,200

Blackacre and Whiteacre are both capital assets. D receives Blackacre as a distribution in liquidation of his interest in the partnership. Section 751(b) does not apply because the inventory is not substantially appreciated. D takes a $400 basis in Blackacre under § 732(b), and the partnership's § 734(b) adjustment should be negative $300 because D's basis in Blackacre is $300 more than the partnership's basis for Blackacre. Under the § 755 regulations, however, there is no property to which the basis decrease may be allocated. The basis of the inventory, which is higher than its fair market value, may not be decreased, because the distributed property, Blackacre, was a capital asset, and the basis of Whiteacre may not be decreased because any decrease in its basis would increase, not decrease, the difference between fair market value and basis.

If the partnership owns "no property of the character required to be adjusted", or a downward adjustment has been limited by the zero basis floor of Treas. Reg. § 1.755–1(c)(3), the remaining adjustment is held in suspense and applied when the partnership acquires property to which the adjustment can be applied. Treas. Reg. § 1.755–1(c)(4). For, example, if a partner recognizes gain as a result of a cash distribution in liquidation of her partnership interest from a partnership that holds only inventory that was not substantially appreciated (as defined in § 751(b)(3)), the partnership's § 734(b) basis adjustment will be held in suspense until the partnership acquires a capital or § 1231 asset. Immediately upon the acquisition of such an asset, its basis will be increased by the suspended adjustment, even if the adjustment results in a basis in excess of its fair market value. If an upward adjustment to the basis of capital and § 1231 assets is required, however, and the partnership owns such assets, but they are not appreciated sufficiently to utilize the entire adjustment, the Regulations do not provide for any carryover.

These rules present a problem because, as is illustrated in the examples involving the DEF and GHI Partnerships, the adjustment, in fact, may have been attributable to an increase or decrease in the value of a remaining asset having a character different from that of the distributed assets, or to a cash distribution which resulted in gain or loss to the distributee partner that was attributable to ordinary income assets of the partnership (although in most cases a cash distribution attributable to ordinary inventory will trigger the application of § 751(b), thereby obviating the need for a § 734(b) adjustment). In theory, in the example involving the DEF Partnership, the basis of both the inventory and Whiteacre should have been reduced. Under the regulations, however, no adjustment would be made at the time of the distribution, but one could be made when the partnership later acquired a capital or § 1231 asset, but only when the asset's basis exceeded its fair market value. These defects in the § 755 rules for allocating basis adjustments could be cured by providing that the adjustments be made to property of the same character as that to which the adjustment is attributable and not as that of the distributed property and by permitting basis adjustments that increase the disparity between fair market value and basis when consistent with the theoretical basis for allowing § 734(b) adjustments in the first place. See H. Rep. No. 86–1231, 86th Cong., 2d Sess. 98 (1960).

2.2. *Post-Adjustment Depreciation*

Treas. Reg. § 1.734–1(e) provides rules regarding the method for computing depreciation deductions with respect to increases and decreases in the basis of depreciable assets pursuant to § 734(b). If the basis of the partnership's depreciable property is increased under § 734(b), the increased portion of the basis must be depreciated as if it were newly-purchased property placed in service on the date the distribution occurred. The partnership's original basis in the property continues to be depreciated as before the distribution, as if there had been no basis increase. If § 734(b) requires a decrease in the basis of the partnership's depreciable property, the decrease in basis must be taken into account over the remaining recovery period of the property beginning with the recovery period in which the basis is decreased.

3. PROBLEMS IN THE SECTION 734(b) FORMULA

The formula in § 734(b) will provide the correct overall adjustment in most cases. But it appears inadequate in some instances because it is based on the distributee's basis for his partnership interest—which governs gain or loss to the distributee. The formula will not produce the correct result if the basis for the distributee partner's interest differs from his share of the partnership's basis for its assets. Thus, if in the ABC Partnership example, at page 357, A had purchased his interest from a previous partner, paying $90, or if A was an estate succeeding to a decedent partner's interest and having a $90 basis, there would be no adjustment under the formula.

This defect is most glaring in cases in which an estate's interest in a partnership is terminated by a distribution of cash and no gain is recognized to the estate to the extent § 1014 applies to give it a stepped-up basis for its partnership interest. No adjustment is allowed even though the partnership is paying for the estate's interest in assets that have increased in value. If the formula in § 734(b) related to the distributee's pro rata share of the partnership's aggregate basis for its assets (as is done in § 743(b)), the formula would work correctly. The obvious solution to this problem is for the partnership to make the § 754 election with respect to the transfer from the decedent partner to the successor partner. Under § 743(b), the bases of the partnership's assets are increased by an amount equal to the step-up in the basis of the partnership interest resulting from § 1014. Then, if the retiring partner who inherited the partnership interest receives a liquidating distribution of property in which it did not have a special basis adjustment in exchange for property in which it did have a special basis adjustment, under Treas. Reg. § 1.734–2(b) the basis adjustment is reallocated to the partnership's remaining property for the benefit of the continuing partners.

If a cash distribution to a retiring partner is attributable to unrealized receivables and is taxed under § 736(a), § 734(b) does not permit any increase in the basis of the retained unrealized receivables. In this case, however, a basis adjustment is unnecessary because the remaining partners have, in effect, received a deduction for the amount paid for the unrealized receivables. See Treas. Reg. § 1.736–1(a)(4). Therefore, it is appropriate that the partnership's basis in the receivables not be increased. See page 353.

4. APPLICATION OF SECTION 734(b) TO CURRENT DISTRIBUTIONS

Although all of the preceding examples involved liquidating distributions to a retiring partner, if a § 754 election is in effect, a current distribution to a partner will result in basis adjustments under § 734(b). Unlike the case under § 743(b), where the regulations provide that the basis adjustment under that section is special to the transferee partner, neither § 734(b) nor the regulations allocate the basis adjustment solely to the nondistributee partners. Thus a § 734(b) basis adjustment presumably applies for all partners.

Suppose the JKL Partnership has the following assets and partners' capital accounts, the book value of which has been adjusted to fair market value.

Assets	Book	Tax Basis		Partners' Capital Accounts	Book	Tax Basis
Whiteacre	$ 600	$ 900	J		$ 800	$ 700
Blackacre	$1,800	$1,200	K		$ 800	$ 700
			L		$ 800	$ 700
	$2,400	$2,100			$2,400	$2,100

To reduce J from a one-third partner to a one-ninth partner, the partnership distributes Whiteacre to J. Although the partnership's basis in Whiteacre is $900, because J's basis for the partnership interest is only $700, § 732(a)(2) limits J's basis for Blackacre to $700. (J has no remaining basis in the partnership interest.) Since J's basis for Whiteacre is $200 less than the partnership's basis, the partnership is entitled to increase the basis of Blackacre by $200, from $1,200 to $1,400 under § 734(b)(1)(B). Upon a subsequent sale of Blackacre for $1,800, the partnership recognizes a gain of $400, of which $44.44 is allocated to J and $177.78 is allocated to each of K and L. If J sold Whiteacre for $600, J would recognize a $100 loss. Thus, the income realized by each of the partners on the sale of the partnership's assets is as follows:

Partner	Whiteacre	Blackacre	Total
J	($100)	$ 44.44	($ 55.56)
K	0	$177.78	$177.78
L	0	$177.78	$177.78
			$300.00

Upon liquidation of the partnership following the sale of Blackacre, J receives $200 and K and L each receive $800 in liquidation of their partnership interests. J's gain under § 731 is $155.56, since J's basis in the partnership interest was increased from zero to $44.44 as a result of inclusion of that amount of gain on the sale of Blackacre. K and L each recognize a loss of $77.78 since their bases for their partnership interests were increased from $700 to $877.78 as a result of including the gain on the sale of Blackacre. The net result is that each partner recognizes the same $100 of net income that the partner would have recognized if the partnership had sold both properties and liquidated. The timing of the recognition, however, may be dramatically different.

This shifting of the timing of gains and losses recognized to the various partners as a result of the distribution of Whiteacre to J theoretically could be eliminated by special allocations of gain on the sale of Blackacre. The partners might agree that upon a sale of Blackacre, the first $400 of taxable gain would be allocated $200 to J and $100 to each of K and L, even though capital account adjustments would be $66.67 to J and $266.67 to each of K and L. However, there appears to be no authority in the § 704(b) regulations sanctioning such an allocation.

5. TIMING OF BASIS ADJUSTMENTS

Rev.Rul. 93–13, 1993–1 C.B. 126, held that if a partnership completely liquidates the interest of a retiring partner by making a series of cash payments treated as distributions under § 736(b)(1), the § 734(b) basis adjustments to the partnership property correspond in timing and amount with the recognition of gain or loss by the retiring partner under § 731. Assume that the GHI partnership has cash of $75,000 and a capital asset with a basis of $15,000 and a fair market value of $150,000. Retiring partner G has a $30,000 basis in her partnership interest and receives fixed-sum cash distributions of $25,000 per year for three years in liquidation of her partnership interest. In year 1, G recognizes no gain and the partnership has no basis adjustment; in year 2, G recognizes $20,000 of gain and the partnership increases its basis in the capital asset from $15,000 to $35,000; in year 3, G recognizes $25,000 of gain and the partnership increases its basis in the asset to $60,000.

If a § 734(b) basis adjustment increases the basis of depreciable property, the basis increase is treated as newly acquired property placed in service at the time of the adjustment. It has a class life and recovery method the same as the class life of the asset to which it relates. See Treas. Reg. § 1.734–1(e).

6. SPECIAL RULE FOR PARTNERSHIP HOLDING CORPORATE PARTNER'S STOCK

Section 755(c) provides that in applying the rules of § 755 for allocating a decrease in basis of the partnership's assets under § 734(b), the basis of stock of a partner that is a corporation (or a person related to the corporation under § 267(b) or § 707(b)(1)) will not be reduced. Any decrease in basis that otherwise would have been allocated to the stock must be allocated to other partnership assets. If the decrease in basis exceeds the basis of those other partnership assets, the partnership must recognize gain equal to the amount of the excess.

7. SPECIAL PROBLEM OF TIERED PARTNERSHIPS

Rev.Rul. 92–15, 1992–1 C.B. 215, holds that if an upper tier partnership and a lower tier partnership both have § 754 elections in effect, and the upper tier partnership distributes to a partner property other than an interest in the lower tier partnership and as a consequence adjusts its basis in the interest in the lower tier partnership, then the lower tier partnership also adjusts its basis in its own assets pursuant to § 734(b). Assume, for example, that A and B are each 50 percent partners in UTP, which owns a capital asset with a basis of $140 and a fair market value of $240 and a 10 percent interest in LTP, which has a basis of $30 and a fair market value of $80. LTP has a capital asset with a basis of $200 and a fair market value of $700 and a noncapital asset with a basis of $0 and a fair market value of $100. UTP's share of the basis of LTP's assets is $20. Partner A has a basis of $0 in his 50 percent interest in UTP, which has a fair market value of $160. To reduce A's interest in UTP to 20 percent, UTP distributes to A a one-half interest in the capital asset, worth $120, having a basis to the partnership of $70. Since A takes a $0 basis in the one-half of the capital asset, under § 734(b), UTP increases the basis of its assets by $70. The remaining one-half of the capital asset and UTP's interest in LTP each are appreciated in the amount of $50; thus under § 755(b), UTP's basis in each asset is increased by $35. UTP's basis increase for its interest in LTP is an event triggering a basis increase in UTP's share of the basis of LTP's property of a similar character to the distributed property. Accordingly, UTP increases the amount of its share of the basis of LTP's capital asset from $20 to $55.

Suppose that the AB Partnership holds two assets: Blackacre with a basis of zero and a fair market value of $100 and Whiteacre with a basis of

$100 and a fair market value of $100. If Whiteacre was distributed to A, who has a zero basis for her interest, she would take a zero basis for Whiteacre and, if a § 754 election was in effect, the partnership would increase its basis for Blackacre to $100. As a result, the $100 basis of Whiteacre has been transferred to Blackacre, and $100 of total gain will be recognized if they are both sold. Now suppose that instead the AB Partnership contributes Whiteacre to another partnership (LT) in which it has a 99 percent interest, following which it distributes its interest in the LT Partnership to A. She will take a zero basis for her interest in LT, but the basis of Whiteacre remains $100. If the AB Partnership can make a § 734(b) adjustment to the basis of Blackacre, then both assets can be sold without the recognition of any gain, although A would recognize gain if the proceeds were distributed to her by LT. Congress perceived this result as abusive, and in 1984 added the last sentence of § 734(b), disallowing an upward § 734 adjustment for the upper tier partnership, in this case AB, if the distributed property is an interest in another partnership, in this case LT, unless the other partnership also has a § 754 election in effect. Because § 761(e), also added in 1984, treats the distribution of a partnership interest as an exchange, Congress intended that § 734(b) require that the distributed partnership (LT) reduce the basis of its assets. See Staff of the Joint Committee on Taxation, 98th Cong., 2d Sess., General Explanation of the Tax Reform Act of 1984, at p. 249 (1984). See also Rev.Rul. 92–15, 1992–1 C.B. 215 (holding that § 734(b) required the distributed lower tier partnership to decrease the basis of its assets in such a case, but the predecessor of Treas. Reg. § 1.755–1(c)(4) could defer the date the required basis decrease was implemented).

As is apparent from the DEF and GHI Partnership examples at page 362, however, the adjustment allocation rules of Treas. Reg. § 1.755–1(c) may not produce the results intended by the 1984 legislation. Although A's basis for her interest in LT is zero, thereby requiring a § 734(b) adjustment reducing LT's basis for its assets by $100, the § 755 regulations require that this basis reduction be applied only to assets with a fair market value less than their basis. LT holds no such assets, so the basis of Whiteacre remains $100. Furthermore, the unused basis reduction is not held in suspense; it must be made at the time of the transfer or not at all. Thus, unless the distributed partnership holds depreciated property, the Congressional "solution" to this problem is not effective. The Treasury Department could remedy this problem by amending the § 755 Regulations under the authority in § 755(a)(2) to require under these circumstances that LT make a downward adjustment in the basis of its assets regardless of the value of those assets.

SECTION 4. SALE OF INTEREST TO OTHER PARTNERS VERSUS DISTRIBUTION

INTERNAL REVENUE CODE: Sections 731(a); 736(a) and (b); 741; 752(b) and (d).

REGULATIONS: Sections 1.736–1(b)(1); 1.741–1(a) and (b).

By its nature, a non pro-rata distribution to a partner that reduces the distributee's interest in the distributing partnership increases the partnership interests of the other partners. As discussed in the material beginning at page 355 relating to basis adjustments, under the distribution provisions a non pro-rata distribution that does not trigger application of § 751(b) and that changes a partner's interest may be viewed as an exchange in which the distributee partner may realize gain or loss, but the gain or loss is not recognized under the distribution rules of § 731(a) (except to the extent that cash distributions exceed basis). In contrast to the nonrecognition rule of § 731 applicable to non pro-rata distributions that exchange partnership interests, the sales rules of § 741 that provide for recognition of gain or loss on the sale or exchange of a partnership interest, including a sale to other partners. See Treas. Reg. § 1.741–1(b). The distinction between a distribution that restructures interests in a partnership, and a sale or exchange of partnership interests between partners is not always clear.

Colonnade Condominium, Inc. v. Commissioner

Tax Court of the United States, 1988.
91 T.C. 793.

■ WRIGHT, JUDGE: [Colonnade Condominium, Inc. ("Colonnade") was a general partner in Georgia King Associates ("Georgia King"), holding a 50.98 percent interest. There were three other unrelated partners. The shares of Colonnade were held equally by Bernstein, Feldman, and Mason. Prior to April 1978, Colonnade was obligated to make capital contributions to Georgia King in a series of installments in the total amount of $1,330,300. At that time it had actually contributed less than $400,000. Colonnade's basis in its partnership interest was $8,262,710. Its share of partnership liabilities was $10,074,456. Colonnade had a negative capital account balance. In April, 1978 the partnership agreement of Georgia King was amended to admit each of Bernstein, Feldman, and Mason as a 13.66 percent general partner. Colonnade's interest was reduced from 50.98 percent to 10 percent. Bernstein, Feldman, and Mason each assumed responsibility for contributing $272,000 of the future capital contribution previously required from Colonnade. * * * Colonnade did not treat the April 1, 1978 transfer of its 40.98 percent partnership interest to Bernstein, Feldman, and Mason as a taxable event. The Commissioner asserted that the transaction was a sale of a portion of Colonnade's partnership interest.]

OPINION

Respondent contends that Colonnade's transfer of a portion of its partnership interest in Georgia King Associates to its three shareholders pursuant to the April 1, 1978, amendment to the partnership agreement resulted in the sale of a 40.98–percent general partnership interest by Colonnade in return for the discharge of recourse and nonrecourse partnership liabilities. Accordingly, respondent argues that such disposition should be governed by sections 741 and 1001. * * * Petitioner, on the other hand, asserts that the April 1, 1978, amendment merely provided for the admission of new partners in an existing partnership and is a nontaxable event.

We agree with respondent.

* * *

The statutory scheme under subchapter K gives partners great latitude in selecting the form the partnership takes and in allocating economic benefits and tax burdens of partnership transactions among themselves. See, e.g., * * * Foxman v. Commissioner, 41 T.C. 535, 551 (1964), affd. 352 F.2d 466 (3d Cir.1965) * * *. Under the partnership provisions of the Code, this flexibility is achieved by, inter alia, allowing a partner to choose either to sell his partnership interest to a third person or to reorganize the partnership to allow the admission of the third person as a new partner.

This flexibility, however, is not unlimited. The form of the transaction must be in keeping with its true substance and the intent of the parties. See Commissioner v. Court Holding Co., 324 U.S. 331 (1945); Gregory v. Helvering, 293 U.S. 465 (1935)(the substance, rather than the form, of the transaction is controlling). In this regard, the provisions of written documents are not necessarily conclusive for tax purposes. * * * Nor will a "label" attached by a tax-conscious litigant control the proper characterization of a transaction involving the disposition of a partnership interest. * * * In short, "the legislative policy of flexibility does not permit a taxpayer to avoid the tax ramifications of a sale of a partnership interest simply by recasting the intended or constructive sale in the form of a reorganization to a partnership. Jupiter Corp. v. United States," 2 Cl.Ct. 58, 79 (1983).

Section 741 provides that in the case of the sale or exchange of a partnership interest, gain or loss shall be recognized to the transferor partner. The gain or loss, except to the extent that section 751 applies, is capital. Section 741 shall apply whether the partnership interest is sold to a member or nonmember of the partnership. Sec. 1.741–1(b), Income Tax Regs.

Section 721(a) states the general rule that gain or loss is not recognized through contributions of property to a partnership in exchange for partnership interests. Correspondingly, in a distribution by a partnership to a partner under section 731(a)(1), gain shall not be recognized except to the extent the distribution exceeds adjusted basis. Decreases in a partner's liabilities or share of the partnership's liabilities are considered distributions under section 752(b). Section 705(a)(2) provides that a partner's adjusted basis is decreased by his distributions from the partnership as well as the partner's distributive share of partnership losses. Petitioner argues that, as of April 1, 1978, three new partners were admitted to the partnership and, as a result, petitioner received a distribution as a result of being relieved of its share of partnership liabilities. Petitioner's basis in the partnership was reduced pursuant to section 705(a)(2).

The Code and regulations do not offer any guidance for distinguishing between an admission of new partners (pursuant to a contribution of property which is nontaxable under section 721), as petitioner contends is the correct characterization of the transaction before us, and a sale of a partnership interest under section 741, taxable as respondent urges. In one of the few cases addressing this issue, this Court in Richardson v. Commissioner, 76 T.C. 512 (1981), affd. 693 F.2d 1189 (5th Cir.1982), commented on the difference between the admission of a new partner into a partnership and the sale or exchange of a partnership interest:

> Admission of new partners is not in all respects identical to a sale or exchange of a partnership interest. In the former situation, the transaction is between the new partners and the partnership. The latter situation involves a transaction between a new partner and an existing partner. * * * [76 T.C. at 528.]

In *Richardson*, the taxpayers unsuccessfully maintained that they had sold their interest in three partnerships on December 30, 1974. 76 T.C. at 527–528. The admission of the new partners in *Richardson* corresponded with the infusion of large amounts of new capital into the partnership, although capital was not reduced with respect to the old partners. The transaction was essentially between the new partners and the partnership. Upon the admission of the new partners, the interests of all the original partners were reduced substantially. This Court viewed the transaction as an admission rather than a sale.

Unlike *Richardson*, the form and substance of the transaction at issue herein reflects transfers between an existing partner, Colonnade, and new partners, Bernstein, Feldman, and Mason and, therefore, was a sale of a partnership interest. The partnership as a whole was essentially unaffected. Prior to the April 1, 1978, amendment, Colonnade held a 50.98–percent partnership interest. As a result of the amendment, Colonnade divested itself of a 40.98–percent interest, which was acquired collectively by Bernstein, Feldman, and Mason at 13.66 percent each. Colonnade was left with a 10–percent interest, but together with its three shareholders, Colonnade still controlled the partnership as the majority general partner. The interests of the other partners in Georgia King were unchanged by the amendment.

Similarly, Colonnade divested itself of its rights under sections 10.03(c) and 10.05(a)(vi) of the partnership agreement (allocations of certain gains and losses) to the extent of 30 percent which were acquired collectively by Bernstein, Feldman, and Mason at 10 percent each. Again, the allocations under these two sections remained unchanged with respect to [the other partners]. Most notably, the aggregate capital contributions of Georgia King, $2,226,800, remained the same before and after the April 1, 1978, amendment. No additional contributions were required under the April 1, 1978, amendment to the partnership agreement. Colonnade, however, was discharged of its recourse obligation to contribute $816,060 in the future, an obligation which was acquired equally between Bernstein, Feldman, and Mason at $272,020 each. The total payment schedule for the contributions (in yearly installments) remained unchanged and continued to mirror the total equity payments required of the partnership. Colonnade was also discharged of 40.98 percent of its partnership nonrecourse liabilities, which were acquired by the three individual shareholders.

The fact that the three shareholders of Colonnade expressly assumed Colonnade's liabilities, in return for partnership interests which are capital assets under section 741, is especially significant. In determining whether an actual or constructive sale or exchange took place, we note that the touchstone for sale or exchange treatment is consideration. In LaRue v. Commissioner, 90 T.C. 465, 483–484 (1988), we noted that where liabilities are assumed as consideration for a partnership interest, a sale or exchange exists:

> If, in return for assets, any consideration is received, even if nominal in amount, the transaction will be classified as a sale or exchange. Blum v. Commissioner, 133 F.2d 447 (2d Cir.1943). * * * When the transferee of property assumes liabilities of the transferor encumbering the property, the liability is an amount realized by the transferor. Crane v. Commissioner, [331 U.S. 1 (1947)]; Commissioner v. Tufts, [461 U.S. 300 (1983)]. Assumption of liabilities by the transferee constitutes consideration making the transaction a sale or exchange. * * *

> * * * Where assets are transferred to third parties, assumption of liabilities constitutes consideration. * * *

> * * * [T]he assumption of liabilities by a third party transferee constitutes an amount realized, and this is consideration to the transferor. * * *

In arguing that the form of the arrangement reflects the substance, petitioner points out that the documents show that Bernstein, Feldman, and Mason were admitted to the partnership upon obtaining the required approval of [the New Jersey Housing Finance Agency], as well as * * * the managing general partner. Petitioner contends that the documents demonstrate an agreement between the partnership and the partners for the admission of new partners and do not reflect a transaction between petitioner and the new general partners. However, as we noted earlier, labels, semantics, technicalities, and formal documents do not necessarily control the tax consequences of a given transaction. * * * To look solely to the documents in this case and ignore the substance and reality of the transaction would exalt form over substance.

Aside from the transfer of a portion of Colonnade's partnership interest to the three new partners in return for a discharge of liabilities, there were no other changes in the structure or the operation of the Georgia King partnership as a result of the April 1, 1978, amendment. The substance of the transaction did not transpire between the partnership and the new partners, but rather, between Colonnade, an existing partner, and three new partners. Because there was no new or additional capital transferred to the partnership, there were no modifications of the partnership assets and liabilities. The only change was the transfers from the transferor partner's capital account to the transferees' capital accounts. As such, the transaction warrants sale and exchange treatment under section 741.

ILLUSTRATIVE MATERIAL

1. SALE VERSUS LIQUIDATION

The tension created by § 736 between the retiring partner and the continuing partners in a service partnership can lead to disputes among the partners unless the nature of payments is clearly spelled out by the partners. Under § 736(a) and (b), payments in excess of the value of the retiring partner's interest in partnership assets are ordinary income to the retiring partner and reduce the income of the continuing partners. Payments that are considered to be received in exchange for the retiring partner's interest in partnership assets are treated as capital gain after recovery of basis, or as a capital loss if basis is not recovered or exchanged into the basis of distributed property other than cash. I.R.C. § 731(a). In a service partnership (capital is not a material income producing factor) the partners are permitted a certain degree of latitude to treat liquidation payments as made for the retiring partner's interest in partnership property by designating in the partnership agreement that payments represent compensation for the retiring partner's interest in partnership goodwill. I.R.C. § 736(b)(2). Even where capital is a material income producing factor and § 736(b)(2) does not apply, the partners have a certain degree of flexibility by valuing goodwill on the partnership books to represent the full amount of any premium paid to a retiring partner over the value of the partner's interest in other assets, or to place a lower value on goodwill in order to create a premium that would be treated as a § 736(a) payment. See Treas.Reg. § 1.736–1(b)(1), discussed at page 349.

Alternatively, the partners may avoid § 736 entirely by structuring the transaction as a sale of the retiring partner's interest to the other partners, rather than as a liquidation distribution from the partnership. Under § 741 the selling partner receives capital gain or capital loss treatment for realized gain or loss on the disposition of the partnership interest. The purchasing partners increase their bases in their partnership interests, which may be reflected in an adjustment to the basis of partnership assets if an election under § 754 is in effect. Treas.Reg. § 1.741–1(b) expressly sanctions sales treatment with respect to the sale of a partnership interest to continuing partners. As indicated by the opinion in *Colonnade Condominium*, the substance of the transaction controls over its form. Distribution treatment requires a change in the partnership's internal capital accounts.

In Foxman v. Commissioner, 41 T.C. 535 (1964), referring to committee reports, the Tax Court recognized that the legislative scheme is intended to permit partners flexibility to arrange the tax consequence of partnership transactions. The court indicated that, "one of the underlying philosophic objectives of the 1954 Code was to permit the partners themselves to determine their tax burdens *inter sese* to a certain extent, and this is what the committee reports meant when they referred to 'flexibility.' The theory was that the partners would take their prospective tax liabilities into account in bargaining with one another. * * * " (551). See H.Rep. No. 1337, 83d Cong., 2d Sess., 65; S.Rep. No. 1622, 83d Cong., 2d Sess., 89.

Foxman is a good example of the conflict that can arise between the departing and continuing partners. Foxman, Grenell and Jacobowitz were one-third partners in a business that manufactured phonograph records. Because of conflicts among the partners, Foxman and Grenell agreed to continue the partnership business without Jacobowitz. The partners individually entered into an agreement for the purchase of Jacobowitz's interest for $242,550 plus an automobile that was in the name of the partnership and the stock of a related corporation called Sound Plastics owned individually by Foxman, Grenell and Jacobowitz. The cash was payable in installments over a period of approximately two years. The installment obligation was represented by a series of promissory notes on which the partnership appeared as the maker with the signatures of Foxman and Grenell on behalf of the partnership. The agreement described the transaction as a purchase of Jacobowitz's partnership interest, but also provided that Jacobowitz "hereby retires from the partnership." Foxman and Grenell agreed to continue the partnership business in substantially the same form. Foxman and Grenell also agreed to indemnify Jacobowitz from any liabilities arising out of the partnership business. On the advice of an attorney, the partnership was made a party to the agreement, but the court noted that there was no specific undertaking on the part of the partnership any place in the instrument. The first $67,500 payment to Jacobowitz was made by cashier's check. Foxman and Grenell decided to prepay the remaining installment notes due to Jacobowitz. The partnership borrowed the cash and distributed the money to Jacobowitz. On its tax return, the partnership treated the payment as a distribution of partnership earnings to Jacobowitz in the nature of a guaranteed payment. On his tax return, Jacobowitz treated the transaction as a sale and reported a long-term capital gain. The Commissioner, taking inconsistent positions, assessed a deficiency against Jacobowitz claiming that the transaction was a liquidation distribution resulting in ordinary income in part under § 736(a), and against Foxman and Grenell treating the transaction as a purchase of Jacobowitz's partnership interest, thereby disallowing deductions for the distribution as a guaranteed payment. The cases were consolidated before the Tax Court to allow the former partners to fight it out. The Tax Court sided with Jacobowitz finding that the partners intended to structure the transaction as a sale:

> The agreement of May 21, 1957, indicates a clear intention on the part of Jacobowitz to sell, and Foxman and Grenell to purchase, Jacobowitz's partnership interest. The * * * "whereas" clause refers to Jacobowitz as "selling" his interest and part "First" of the agreement explicitly states not only that the "sec-

ond parties [Foxman and Grenell] hereby purchase * * * the * * * interest of * * * [Jacobowitz] * * * in [the partnership]," but also that "the first party [Jacobowitz] does hereby sell" his interest in [the partnership]. Thus, Foxman and Grenell obligated themselves individually to purchase Jacobowitz's interest. Nowhere in the agreement was there any obligation on the part of [the partnership] to compensate Jacobowitz for withdrawing from the partnership. Indeed, a portion of the consideration received by him was the Sound Plastics stock, not a partnership asset at all. That stock was owned by Foxman and Grenell as individuals and their undertaking to turn it over to Jacobowitz as part of the consideration for Jacobowitz's partnership interest reinforces the conclusion that they as individuals were buying his interest, and that the transaction represented a "sale" of his interest to them rather than a "liquidation" of that interest by the partnership. Moreover, the chattel mortgage referred to in part "First" of the agreement of May 21, 1957, states that Jacobowitz "has sold * * * his * * * interest as a partner."

In addition to the foregoing, we are satisfied from the evidence before us that Foxman and Grenell knew that Jacobowitz was interested only in a sale of his partnership interest. The record convincingly establishes that the bargaining between them was consistently upon the basis of a proposed sale. And the agreement of May 21, 1957, which represents the culmination of that bargaining, reflects that understanding with unambiguous precision. The subsequent position of Foxman and Grenell, disavowing a "sale," indicates nothing more than an attempt at hindsight tax planning to the disadvantage of Jacobowitz.

Foxman and Grenell argue that Jacobowitz looked only to [the partnership] for payment, that he was in fact paid by [the partnership], that there was "in substance" a liquidation of his interest, and that these considerations should be controlling in determining whether section 736 or section 741 applies. But their contention is not well taken.

Jacobowitz distrusted Foxman and Grenell and wanted all the security he could get; he asked for, but did not receive, guarantees from their wives and mortgages on their homes. Obviously, the assets of [the partnership] and its future earnings were of the highest importance to Jacobowitz as security that Foxman and Grenell would carry out their part of the bargain. But the fact remains that the payments received by Jacobowitz were in discharge of their obligation under the agreement, and not that of [the partnership]. It was they who procured those payments in their own behalf from the assets of the partnership which they controlled. The use of [the partnership] to make payment was wholly within their discretion and of no concern to Jacobowitz; his only interest was payment. The terms of the May 21, 1957, agreement did not obligate [the partnership] to pay Jacobowitz.

Nor is their position measurably stronger by reason of the fact that Jacobowitz was given promissory notes signed in behalf of [the partnership]. These notes were endorsed by Foxman and Grenell individually, and the liability of [the partnership] thereon was merely in the nature of security for their primary obligation under the agreement of May 21, 1957. The fact that they utilized partnership resources to discharge their own individual liability in such manner can hardly convert into a section 736 "liquidation" what would otherwise qualify as a section 741 "sale." It is important to bear in mind the object of "flexibility" which Congress attempted to attain, and we should be slow to give a different meaning to the arrangement which the partners entered into among themselves than that which the words of their agreement fairly spell out. Otherwise, the reasonable expectations of the partners in arranging their tax burdens *inter sese* would come to naught, and the purpose of the statute would be defeated. While we do not suggest that it is never possible to look behind the words of an agreement in dealing with problems like the one before us, the considerations which Foxman and Grenell urge us to take into account here are at best of an ambiguous character and are in any event consistent with the words used. We hold that the Commissioner's determination in respect of this issue was in error in Jacobowitz's case but was correct in the cases involving Foxman and Grenell. * * * (552–553)

As the opinion in *Foxman* demonstrates, historically the real controversy in this area has been between the withdrawing partner, who preferred a sale classification with the resulting capital gain treatment, and the remaining partners, who preferred a "liquidation" classification since the payments would then reduce their distributive shares of partnership income. Section 736(b)(3) eliminated the ability of partnerships in which capital is a material income producing factor to classify payments to a retiring partner as § 736(a) payments that reduce the remaining partners' distributive shares of income. Thus, this tension under § 736 between the withdrawing partner and the continuing partnership is confined primarily to partnerships in which capital is not a material income producing factor. However, there remains the possibility, as in *Foxman*, to classify the transaction as a sale under § 741.

The Internal Revenue Service is, of course, concerned that, however characterized, the transaction be treated the same by both parties. It was able to obtain this result in *Foxman* by joining all of the parties in the same suit. The Service was not so fortunate, however, in another situation in which the same transaction was treated by the Tax Court as a capital gain—generating sale under § 741 for the withdrawing partner, Phillips v. Commissioner, 40 T.C. 157 (1963)(Nonacq.), while the remaining partners were allowed deductions under a § 736 liquidation theory by the Court of

Claims, Miller v. United States, 181 Ct.Cl. 331 (1967). The *Phillips–Miller* situation involved a two-person partnership and the Court of Claims, following Treas. Reg. § 1.736–1(b)(6), had no difficulty in treating the payments by the remaining partner as liquidation distributions by the partnership despite the fact that no partnership was actually in existence after the withdrawal. To the same effect is Stilwell v. Commissioner, 46 T.C. 247 (1966).

The taxpayer in Spector v. Commissioner, 71 T.C. 1017 (1979), rev'd and remanded, 641 F.2d 376 (5th Cir.1981), was a partner in an accounting partnership with Wilson.[8] To effect Spector's withdrawal from the partnership, the Spector–Wilson partnership was merged with another accounting partnership, following which Spector withdrew from the merged partnership in consideration of four equal annual payments. The withdrawal agreement specifically stated that one–half of each payment was a payment subject to § 736, none of which was for partnership property, and the other one half of the payment was for a covenant not to compete. Finding that the taxpayer had adduced "strong proof" that the form of the transaction did not reflect its substance, the Tax Court held that the payments were not controlled by § 736. Instead, the court concluded that in essence the partnership into which the Spector-Wilson partnership had merged had purchased the taxpayer's share of the goodwill of the Spector–Wilson partnership, and it allowed the taxpayer capital gains treatment. The Court of Appeals reversed the Tax Court, on the ground that it had applied an erroneous standard. Economic reality does not provide a ground to set aside the structure chosen to effect a partner's withdrawal. The court explained that the fundamental theory underlying Subchapter K is that given the substantial, if not total, identity in terms of economic net result between a sale and a liquidation, the withdrawing and continuing partners should be allowed to allocate the tax benefits and burdens as they see fit. It then remanded the case for a determination of whether the taxpayer had adduced proof of mistake, fraud, undue influence, or any other ground that in an action between the parties to the agreement would be sufficient to set it aside or alter its construction. On remand, the Tax Court concluded that this burden had not been met. Accordingly, § 736 controlled treatment of the payments. T.C. Memo. 1982–433.

In Crenshaw v. United States, 450 F.2d 472 (5th Cir.1971), the taxpayer desired to sell her interest in a partnership. A transaction was arranged whereby she received a distribution of real property from the partnership, which she then transferred to the estate of her deceased husband in exchange for another parcel of real estate. The estate subsequently sold the property back to the original partners for cash, after which it was recontributed to the old partnership. The taxpayer argued that the transaction should be treated as a liquidating distribution under § 736

---

8. Before 1993, all partnerships were allowed under § 736(b)(2)(B) to designate a portion of liquidation distributions as in exchange for the retiring partner's interest in partnership goodwill, regardless of whether capital was a material income producing factor in the partnership.

followed by a tax-free like-kind exchange under § 1031. The Court of Appeals, reversing the District Court, applied the step transaction doctrine and held that the net result of the various exchanges was in effect a sale of her partnership interest for cash which was taxable under § 741.

In contrast, Harris v. Commissioner, 61 T.C. 770 (1974), declined to recharacterize as a sale a transaction carefully structured to produce a § 1231 loss rather than a capital loss on the disposition of a partnership interest. To effect the taxpayer's withdrawal from a partnership in which he held a forty percent interest, the partnership first sold to a trust for the benefit of children of another partner an undivided ten percent interest in the real estate which was its principal asset. The trust immediately leased its undivided interest back to the partnership. The loss on the sale was specially allocated to the taxpayer, and the sales proceeds were distributed to him; his capital account was reduced by the loss and the distribution, and his partnership interest was reduced to thirty-three percent. The following year, the partnership distributed to the taxpayer in full liquidation of his partnership interest an undivided thirty percent interest in the real estate, which the taxpayer immediately leased back to the partnership. About two months later the taxpayer sold the undivided thirty percent interest to the trust which had purchased the ten percent interest the prior year. Because the trust did not become a partner and the taxpayer's partnership interest did not survive the transaction, the court distinguished *Crenshaw* and allowed the taxpayer a § 1231 loss on the sale of the real estate.

The problem of the retiring partner and the partnership taking inconsistent positions regarding characterization of a transaction as a sale versus the liquidation of a partnership interest in many cases may be solved by application of the partnership level audit rules. See page 94.

2. PROPOSED DISGUISED SALE REGULATIONS

Proposed Regulations § 1.707–7 (2004) would apply § 707(a)(2)(B) to treat a distribution to a partner as a disguised sale of a partnership interest under principles similar to the disguised sales rules of Treas. Reg. §§ 1.707–3 through 1.707–6, discussed at page 234. Prop. Reg. § 1.707–7(b) (2004) would provide that "a transfer of money, property or other consideration (including the assumption of a liability) * * * by a purchasing partner to a partnership and a transfer of consideration by the partnership to a selling partner constitute a sale, in whole or in part, of the selling partner's interest in the partnership to the purchasing partner only if, based on all the facts and circumstances, the transfer by the partnership would not have been made but for the transfer to the partnership, and, in cases in which the transfers are not made simultaneously, the subsequent transfer is not dependent on the entrepreneurial risks of partnership operations." Notice of Proposed Rulemaking, Section 707 Regarding Disguised Sales, Generally, REG–149519–03, 69 F.R. 68838 (Nov. 26, 2004). With some exceptions, Prop. Reg. § 1.707–7(k) (2004) would require disclosure under Treas. Reg. § 1.707–8 of any transfer of consideration to a partnership by a partner and a partnership transfer of consideration to another partner that occur within a seven year period.

Rather than following the relatively straight-forward approach of *Colonnade Condominium*, which looks to whether there is a change in partnership capital to distinguish a distribution from an exchange of interests, the proposed regulations list in Prop. Reg. § 1.707–7(b)(2) (2004) the facts and circumstances that "*may* tend to prove the existence of a sale." These factors, based on the facts and circumstances in Prop. Reg. § 1.707–7(b)(2) (2004), include the following—

(i)   That at timing and amount of the transfer of consideration to one partner and the contribution of consideration by another are determinable with reasonable certainty at the time of the transfer;

(ii) That the person receiving the second transfer has a legally enforceable right or a secured right to the subsequent transfer;

(iii) That the same property (other than money or marketable securities) treated as money under § 731(c), is received by the partnership from one party and transferred to the other;

(iv) That partnership distributions and allocations of control are designed to effect an exchange the benefits and burdens of property ownership, including partnership interests;

(v)   That the partnership holds property for a limited period of time;

(vi) That the transfer of property to the selling partner is disproportionately large in relation to the selling partner's interest in partnership interest in partnership profits;

(vii) That the selling partner has no obligation to return or repay transferred property;

(viii) That the transfer of consideration by the selling or purchasing partner is not pro-rata;

(ix) That there were negotiations (either directly or through the partnership) between the selling and purchasing partners; and

(x)   That the selling and purchasing partners enter into agreements, including an amendment to the partnership agreement (other than for admitting the purchasing partner) relating to the transfer.

The facts and circumstances inquiry is partially avoided under presumptions in Prop. Reg. § 7.707–7(c) and (d) (2004) that would provide that transfers to and from a partnership within two years would be presumed to be a sale, and that transfers more than two years apart would be presumed not to constitute a sale of a partnership interest. The proposed regulations contain a caveat that these presumptions would apply unless the facts and circumstances "clearly establish" that the transfers should or should not be treated as a sale, as the case may be. Prop. Reg. § 1.707–7(e) (2004) would add an additional presumption that transfers of money (or marketable securities treated as money by § 731(c)) in complete liquidation of a partner's partnership interest will not be treated as a sale unless the facts and circumstances "clearly establish" that the transfer is part of a sale. Also, transfers of money to and by service partnerships would not be subject to the disguised sales rules. Prop. Reg. § 1.707–7(g) (2004).

Where the consideration paid to the selling partner and the consideration transferred to the partnership by the purchasing partner are in different amounts, the lower of the two considerations is treated as price paid for the sold partnership interest. Prop. Reg. § 1.707–7(a)(3) (2004). The remainder is subject to the contribution or distribution rules of §§ 721 or 731. Under Prop. Reg. § 1.707–7(a)(2)(ii) (2004), the sale is deemed to occur on the earliest of the transfer to the selling shareholder or the transfer of consideration by the purchasing shareholder. These concepts are illustrated by the following example based on Prop. Reg. § 1.707–7(*l*), Ex. (2) (2004). A and B are 50 percent partners in the AB partnership, which holds Blackacre worth $400x. Suppose that A's basis in the partnership interest is $40x. On March 25, 2008, AB transfers $100x to A. On May 25, 2008, C transfers $50x to the AB partnership. Assume that the transaction would be treated as a sale under the proposed regulations. A is treated as selling a partnership interest worth $50x to C on March 25, 2008, the date of the earliest of the two transfers. A recognizes $40 of gain on the sale of one-half of A's partnership interest ($50 – [$40 × $50/$100]). C is treated as transferring an obligation to pay $50x to C on March 25, and as satisfying that obligation on May 25. A also is treated as receiving in A's capacity as a partner a distribution of $50x from AB that is subject to § 731. The distribution is treated as occurring immediately following the sale so that A's basis is first reduced by the basis of A's transferred interest. Thus, A's basis remaining after the sale is $30 ($40 – $10) and A recognizes $20 of gain on the distribution under § 731(a)(1). If the consideration provided by the purchasing partner is greater than the consideration transferred to the selling partner, the purchasing partner is treated as making a contribution to the partnership in the amount of the excess. See Prop. Reg. § 1.707–7(*l*), Ex. (3).

With respect to the treatment of liabilities, the proposed regulations adopt the rules of *Colonnade Condominium* and Rev. Rul. 84–53, page 271, which include a reduction of liabilities of the selling partner in amount realized on disposition of the partnership interest and treat the purchasing partner as providing consideration with respect to an increase of liabilities of the purchasing partner. Prop. Reg. 1.707–7(j) (2004). A partner's share of recourse liability is determined under the principles of Treas. Reg. § 1.752–1(a)(1), discussed at page 185. Prop. Reg. § 1.707–7(j)(4)(i) (2004). A partner's share of nonrecourse liability for this purpose is determined from the partner's percentage residual profit share that is used for allocating nonrecourse liabilities under Treas. Reg. § 1.752–3(a)(3), discussed at page 197. Prop. Reg. § 1.707–7(j)(4)(ii) (2004). Deemed contributions and deemed distributions under § 752(a) and (b) which result from reallocations of partnership liabilities that are not related to a transfer of partnership interests would not be treated as transfers of consideration under Prop. Reg. § 1.707–7(j)(1) (2004). Also, under Prop. Reg. § 7.707–7(j)(6) (2004), a transfer of encumbered property to a partnership will not be treated as a disguised sale of a partnership interest unless the transfer of encumbered property is related to a transfer of consideration by another partner for a partnership interest. Finally, Prop. Reg. § 1.707–7(j)(8) (2004) contains an anti-abuse rule that would treat a decrease in a partner's share of liabilities as consideration in a disguised sale of a partnership interest if the proposed regulations do not otherwise "adequately capture" an integrated set of transactions that revise partners' liabilities in a manner that is disproportionate to the partners' interests in partnership profits or capital where, "the transactions are undertaken pursuant to a plan that has as one of its principal purposes minimizing the extent to which the partner is treated as making a transfer of consideration to the partnership that may be treated as part of a sale * * * ." See Notice of Proposed Rulemaking, Section 707 Regarding Disguised Sales, Generally, REG–149519–03, 69 F.R. 68838 (Nov. 26, 2004).

If a transaction might be treated both as a disguised sale of property and a disguised sale of a partnership interest, the disguised property rules of Treas. Reg. § 1.707–3(a) apply to the property sale before the disguised partnership sales rules of Prop. Reg. § 1.707–7 (2004) would be applied to the sale of a partnership interest. Prop. Reg. § 1.707–7(a)(6) (2004); see also Prop. Reg. § 1.707–7(*l*), Ex. (7).

SECTION 5.   COMPLETE LIQUIDATION OF THE PARTNERSHIP

INTERNAL REVENUE CODE: Sections 708; 731(a), (b); 732(b)–(e); 735; 741; 751(b); 752(a)–(c).

REGULATIONS: Sections 1.708–1(b)(1); 1.736–1(a)(1)(ii).

Complete liquidation of a partnership is governed by the same provisions that govern liquidation of a partner's interest, except that § 736 usually is inapplicable because, other than in very narrow circumstances, there is no continuing partnership. Generally speaking, the tax consequences of the complete liquidation of a partnership are the sum of the consequences to the individual partners. A partner does not recognize any gain unless the partner receives a cash distribution (including net debt relief under §§ 752(a) and (b) if the other partners assume a disproportionate share of the partnership's liabilities) in excess of the partner's basis for the partnership interest. I.R.C. § 731(a)(1). Any gain that is recognized is a capital gain under § 741. Property received in the liquidation generally will take an exchanged basis equal to the partner's basis for the partnership interest less any cash received. I.R.C. § 732(b). The exchanged basis, i.e., partnership interest basis less cash received, is then allocated among the distributed assets according to the formula of § 732(c), discussed at page 347. A partner may recognize a loss upon liquidation of the partnership if (1) a distribution consists solely of cash that is less than the partner's basis for the partnership interest, or (2) the partner receives only cash, unrealized receivables, and inventory, *and* the sum of the amount of the cash and the partner's basis under § 732(a)(2) for the unrealized receivables and inventory—which cannot exceed the partnership's basis therefor—is less than the partner's basis for the partnership interest. I.R.C. § 731(a)(2). Any loss recognized under § 731(a) is a capital loss under § 741.

In the simple case of a complete dissolution in which the distribution is pro rata and the partners' bases do not differ from their pro rata share of the aggregate partnership basis for its assets (e.g., there were no contributions of assets having differing bases and credited value, and no transfers of partnership interests or non-pro rata distributions without basis adjustments being made), the dissolution results in no alteration of the bases of the properties involved and no gain or loss consequences. In more complex cases, however, the basis limitation rules in § 732(b) and (c) may affect the result. If the distribution does not involve a pro rata interest in each partnership asset, the deemed exchange rules of § 751(b) also may be applicable.

Finally, under § 708(b)(1)(B) there is a forced termination of a partnership if more than 50 percent of the interests in profits or capital are sold within twelve months. This transaction constitutes a liquidation of the old partnership and formation of a new partnership. Among other issues, this transaction raises questions regarding the applicability of the basis adjustment rules of § 743(b).

Revenue Ruling 84–111

1984–2 C.B. 88.

* * *

FACTS

The three situations described in Rev. Rul. 70–239 involve partnerships X, Y, and Z, respectively. Each partnership used the accrual method of accounting and had assets and liabilities consisting of cash, equipment, and accounts payable. The liabilities of each partnership did not exceed the adjusted basis of its assets. The three situations are as follows:

Situation 1

X transferred all of its assets to newly-formed corporation R in exchange for all the outstanding stock of R and the assumption by R of X's liabilities. X then terminated by distributing all the stock of R to X's partners in proportion to their partnership interests.

Situation 2

Y distributed all of its assets and liabilities to its partners in proportion to their partnership interests in a transaction that constituted a termination of Y under section 708(b)(1)(A) of the Code. The partners then transferred all the assets received from Y to newly-formed corporation S in exchange for all the outstanding stock of S and the assumption by S of Y's liabilities that had been assumed by the partners.

Situation 3

The partners of Z transferred their partnership interests in Z to newly-formed corporation T in exchange for all the outstanding stock of T. This exchange terminated Z and all of its assets and liabilities became assets and liabilities of T.

In each situation, the steps taken by X, Y, and Z, and the partners of X, Y, and Z, were parts of a plan to transfer the partnership operations to a corporation organized for valid business reasons in exchange for its stock and were not devices to avoid or evade recognition of gain. Rev. Rul. 70–239 holds that because the federal income tax consequences of the three situations are the same, each partnership is considered to have transferred its assets and liabilities to a corporation in exchange for its stock under section 351 of the Internal Revenue Code, followed by a distribution of the stock to the partners in liquidation of the partnership.

LAW AND ANALYSIS

* * *

Section 351(a) of the Code provides that no gain or loss will be recognized if property is transferred to a corporation by one or more persons solely in exchange for stock or securities in such corporation and immediately after the exchange such person or persons are in control (as defined in section 368(c)) of the corporation.

Section 1.351–1(a)(1) of the Income Tax Regulations provides that, as used in section 351 of the Code, the phrase "one or more persons" includes individuals, trusts, estates, partnerships, associations, companies, or corporations. To be in control of the transferee corporation, such person or persons must own immediately after the transfer stock possessing at least 80 percent of the total combined voting power of all classes of stock entitled to vote and at least 80 percent of the total number of shares of all other classes of stock of such corporation.

Section 358(a) of the Code provides that in the case of an exchange to which section 351 applies, the basis of the property permitted to be received under such section without the recognition of gain or loss will be the same as that of the property exchanged, decreased by the amount of any money received by the taxpayer.

Section 358(d) of the Code provides that where, as part of the consideration to the taxpayer, another party to the exchange assumed a liability of the taxpayer or acquired from the taxpayer property subject to a liability, such assumption or acquisition (in the amount of the liability) will, for purposes of section 358, be treated as money received by the taxpayer on the exchange.

Section 362(a) of the Code provides that a corporation's basis in property acquired in a transaction to which section 351 applies will be the same as it would be in the hands of the transferor.

Under section 708(b)(1)(A) of the Code, a partnership is terminated if no part of any business, financial operation, or venture of the partnership continues to be carried on by any of its partners in a partnership. Under section 708(b)(1)(B), a partnership terminates if within a 12–month period there is a sale or exchange of 50 percent or more of the total interest in partnership capital and profits.

Section 732(b) of the Code provides that the basis of property other than money distributed by a partnership in a liquidation of a partner's interest shall be an amount equal to the adjusted basis of the partner's interest in the partnership reduced by any money distributed. Section 732(c) of the Code provides rules for the allocation of a partner's basis in a partnership interest among the assets received in a liquidating distribution.

Section 735(b) of the Code provides that a partner's holding period for property received in a distribution from a partnership (other than with respect to certain inventory items defined in section 751(d)(2)) includes the partnership's holding period, as determined under section 1223, with respect to such property.

Section 1223(1) of the Code provides that where property received in an exchange acquires the same basis, in whole or in part, as the property surrendered in the exchange, the holding period of the property received includes the holding period of the property surrendered to the extent such surrendered property was a capital asset or property described in section 1231. Under section 1223(2), the holding period of a taxpayer's property, however acquired, includes the period during which the property was held by any other person if that property has the same basis, in whole or in part, in the taxpayer's hands as it would have in the hands of such other person.

Section 741 of the Code provides that in the case of a sale or exchange of an interest in a partnership, gain or loss shall be recognized to the transferor partner. Such gain or loss shall be considered as a gain or loss from the sale or exchange of a capital asset, except as otherwise provided in section 751.

Section 751(a) of the Code provides that the amount of money or the fair value of property received by a transferor partner in exchange for all or part of such partner's interest in the partnership attributable to unrealized receivables of the partnership, or to inventory items of the partnership that have appreciated substantially in value, shall be considered as an amount realized from the sale or exchange of property other than a capital asset.

Section 752(a) of the Code provides that any increase in a partner's share of the liabilities of a partnership, or any increase in a partner's individual liabilities by reason of the assumption by the partner of partnership liabilities, will be considered as a contribution of money by such partner to the partnership.

Section 752(b) of the Code provides that any decrease in a partner's share of the liabilities of a partnership, or any decrease in a partner's individual liabilities by reason of the assumption by the partnership of such individual liabilities, will be considered as a distribution of money to the partner by the partnership. Under section 733(1) of the Code, the basis of a partner's interest in the partnership is reduced by the amount of money received in a distribution that is not in liquidation of the partnership.

Section 752(d) of the Code provides that in the case of a sale or exchange of an interest in a partnership, liabilities shall be treated in the same manner as liabilities in connection with the sale or exchange of property not associated with partnerships.

The premise in Rev. Rul. 70–239 that the federal income tax consequences of the three situations described therein would be the same, without regard to which of the three transactions was entered into, is incorrect. As described below, depending on the format chosen for the transfer to a controlled corporation, the basis and holding periods of the various assets received by the corporation and the basis and holding periods of the stock received by the former partners can vary.

* * * Recognition of the three possible methods to incorporate a partnership will enable taxpayers to avoid the above potential pitfalls and will facilitate flexibility with respect to the basis and holding periods of the assets received in the exchange.

HOLDING

Rev. Rul. 70–239 no longer represents the Service's position. The Service's current position is set forth below, and for each situation, the methods described and the underlying assumptions and purposes must be satisfied for the conclusions of this revenue ruling to be applicable.

Situation 1

Under section 351 of the Code, gain or loss is not recognized by X on the transfer by X of all of its assets to R in exchange for R's stock and the assumption by R of X's liabilities.

Under section 362(a) of the Code, R's basis in the assets received from X equals their basis to X immediately before their transfer to R. Under section 358(a), the basis to X of the stock received from R is the same as the basis to X of the assets transferred to R, reduced by the liabilities assumed by R, which assumption is treated as a payment of money to X under section 358(d). In addition, the assumption by R of X's liabilities decreased each partner's share of the partnership liabilities, thus, decreasing the basis of each partner's partnership interest pursuant to sections 752 and 733.

On distribution of the stock to X's partners, X terminated under section 708(b)(1)(A) of the Code. Pursuant to section 732(b), the basis of the stock distributed to the partners in liquidation of their partnership interests is, with respect to each partner, equal to the adjusted basis of the partner's interest in the partnership.

Under section 1223(1) of the Code, X's holding period for the stock received in the exchange includes its holding period in the capital assets and section 1231 assets transferred (to the extent that the stock was received in exchange for such assets). To the extent the stock was received in exchange for neither capital nor section 1231 assets, X's holding period for such stock begins on the day following the date of the exchange. See Rev. Rul. 70–598, 1970–2 C.B. 168. Under section 1223(2), R's holding period in the assets transferred to it includes X's holding period. When X distributed the R stock to its partners, under sections 735(b) and 1223, the partners' holding periods included X's holding period of the stock. Furthermore, such distribution will not violate the control requirement of section 368(c) of the Code.

Situation 2

On the transfer of all of Y's assets to its partners, Y terminated under section 708(b)(1)(A) of the Code, and, pursuant to section 732(b), the basis of the assets (other than money) distributed to the partners in liquidation of their partnership interests in Y was, with respect to each partner, equal to the adjusted basis of the partner's interest in Y, reduced by the money distributed. Under section 752, the decrease in Y's liabilities resulting from the transfer to Y's partners was offset by the partners' corresponding assumption of such liabilities so that the net effect on the basis of each partner's interest in Y, with respect to the liabilities transferred, was zero.

Under section 351 of the Code, gain or loss is not recognized by Y's former partners on the transfer to S in exchange for its stock and the assumption of Y's liabilities, of the assets of Y received by Y's partners in liquidation of Y.

Under section 358(a) of the Code, the basis to the former partners of Y in the stock received from S is the same as the section 732(b) basis to the former partners of Y in the assets received in liquidation of Y and transferred to S, reduced by the liabilities assumed by S, which assumption is treated as a payment of money to the partners under section 358(d).

Under section 362(a) of the Code, S's basis in the assets received from Y's former partners equals their basis to the former partners as determined under section 732(c) immediately before the transfer to S.

Under section 735(b) of the Code, the partners' holding periods for the assets distributed to them by Y includes Y's holding period. Under section 1223(1), the partners' holding periods for the stock received in the exchange includes the partners' holding periods in the capital assets and section 1231 assets transferred to S (to the extent that the stock was received in exchange for such assets). However, to the extent that the stock received was in exchange for neither capital nor section 1231 assets, the holding period of the stock began on the day following the date of the exchange. Under section 1223(2), S's holding period of the Y assets received in the exchange includes the partner's holding periods.

Situation 3

Under section 351 of the Code, gain or loss is not recognized by Z's partners on the transfer of the partnership interests to T in exchange for T's stock.

On the transfer of the partnership interests to the corporation, Z terminated under section 708(b)(1)(A) of the Code.

Under section 358(a) of the Code, the basis to the partners of Z of the stock received from T in exchange for their partnership interests equals the basis of their partnership interests transferred to T, reduced by Z's liabilities assumed by T, the release from which is treated as a payment of money to Z's partners under sections 752(d) and 358(d).

T's basis for the assets received in the exchange equals the basis of the partners in their partnership interests allocated in accordance with section 732(c). T's holding period includes Z's holding period in the assets.

Under section 1223(1) of the Code, the holding period of the T stock received by the former partners of Z includes each respective partner's holding period for the partnership interest transferred, except that the holding period of the T stock that was received by the partners of Z in exchange for their interests in section 751 assets of Z that are neither capital assets nor section 1231 assets begins on the day following the date of the exchange.

* * *

ILLUSTRATIVE MATERIAL

1.   PURCHASE OF PARTNERSHIP INTEREST VERSUS PURCHASE OF PARTNERSHIP ASSETS

Suppose that A and B are partners and that A purchases B's entire partnership interest. Since the purchase results in the termination of the partnership, A could either take a cost basis in an undivided one-half of the partnership assets, as if she purchased them directly from B, and a basis in the other half determined under § 732, or she could take a basis in the assets determined by treating the transaction first as the purchase of a partnership interest to which § 742 and § 743 apply, followed by the liquidation of the partnership, in which A's basis in all of the assets is determined under § 732. McCauslen v. Commissioner, 45 T.C. 588 (1966), held that the purchaser is treated as having acquired by direct purchase the portion of partnership assets attributable to the acquired partnership interest. Rev.Rul. 67–65, 1967–1 C.B. 168, followed *McCauslen*. For the seller, however, Treas. Reg. § 1.741–1(b) provides that the transferor partner is treated as selling his partnership interest, not an undivided share of the partnership assets. This same rule would apply whenever all of the interests in a partnership are sold to one or more purchasers in an integrated transaction.

Although Rev.Rul. 67–65 has not been revoked, Rev.Rul. 84–111, indicates that the Internal Revenue Service might not follow *McCauslen* if the issue were raised currently. Rev.Rul. 84–111 respected the form of each alternative transaction by which the same end result was reached. In the third situation the partners were treated as exchanging their partnership interests for stock in a transaction governed by § 351. Although the partnership was terminated under § 708(b)(1)(A) upon the transfer of the partnership interests, the corporation was held to have acquired the partnership assets by virtue of liquidation of the partnership. If *McCauslen* were followed, the assets would have been acquired in exchange for stock.

Rev. Rul. 2004–59, 2004–1 C.B. 1050, held that when a partnership converts into a state law corporation under a state law formless conversion statute, the partnership contributes all its assets and liabilities to the corporation in exchange for stock in such corporation, and immediately thereafter, the partnership liquidates distributing the stock of the corporation to its partners. Rev. Rul. 84–111 does not apply

2. LIQUIDATION OF LIMITED LIABILITY COMPANY

The form of the transaction also is important when a limited liability company with two or more members becomes a single member limited liability company, as is permitted under the laws of many states. A single member limited liability company that has not elected to be taxed as a corporation is not recognized as a separate business entity for tax purposes. See Treas. Reg. § 301.7701–2(c)(1) and (2), discussed at page 24. In Rev. Rul. 99–6, 1999–1 C.B. 432, the Internal Revenue Service applied the *McCauslen* analysis to hold that termination of the partnership on sale of a membership interest by one member of a two-member limited liability company to the other member will be treated by the selling member as the sale of a partnership interest under § 741. With respect to the purchasing member, the transaction is treated as a liquidation distribution to the selling member followed by the purchase of the selling member's interest in the former partnership assets with respect to the purchasing member. The purchasing member may recognize gain under § 731(a) with respect to the liquidation distribution of the purchasing member's interest in the pre-sale partnership interest if there is a distribution of cash in excess of the purchasing member's basis in the membership interest. As in *McCauslen*, the purchasing member acquires a cost basis in the purchased portion of the acquired assets.

Rev. Rul. 99–6 also holds that the sale of membership interests by both of the members of a two-member limited liability company to a single purchaser will be treated as the sale of their partnership interests that is governed by § 741 with respect to each of the selling members. The purchaser, however, is treated as acquiring an undivided interest in each of the limited liability company's assets. Rev. Rul. 99–6 takes note, without comment, of the contrary result in the third situation of Rev. Rul. 84–111.

3. APPLICABILITY OF SECTION 751(b)

It is not clear on the face of § 751 and the regulations thereunder whether § 751 applies to disproportionate distributions on dissolution of the partnership. This ambiguity arises because § 751(b) requires distributions representing an exchange of a distributee's interest in § 751 assets for other partnership property (or vice versa) "to be considered as a sale or exchange of such property between the distributee and the partnership (as constituted after the distribution)." In a complete liquidation no partnership would exist after the distribution and the exchange would have to be between the distributee and the other partners. Yourman v. United States, 277 F.Supp. 818 (S.D.Cal.1967), held that § 751(b) was applicable to a non-pro rata distribution of assets on the dissolution of a partnership. Rev.Rul.

77–412, 1977–2 C.B. 223, is to the same effect, holding that each partner can be treated as a distributee partner in determining gain or loss recognized under § 751(b), and in the case of a two person partnership, the other partner can be treated as the continuing partnership. See also Wolcott v. Commissioner, 39 T.C. 538 (1962).

Assume, for example, that the AB Partnership has two assets, Blackacre, a § 1231 asset (that is not subject to any depreciation recapture), with a basis of $500 and a fair market value of $1,000, and inventory, with a basis of $600 and a fair market value of $1,000. A and B each have a basis of $550 in their respective partnership interests. The partnership liquidates by distributing the inventory to A and Blackacre to B. Each of A and B are treated as receiving a pro rata share of each of Blackacre and the inventory, taking a $300 basis in the inventory and a $250 basis in the undivided one-half interest in Blackacre, following which A exchanges one–half of the inventory to B for an undivided one half interest in Blackacre. On the exchange, A recognizes ordinary income of $200, and B recognizes $250 of § 1231 gain. A's basis in Blackacre is $750, a $500 cost basis in the undivided one–half received in the deemed § 751(b) exchange plus $250 for the other one–half under § 732(b). B's basis in the inventory is $800, a $500 cost basis in the inventory received in the deemed § 751(b) exchange plus $300 for the remaining portion.

4. WHEN IS A PARTNERSHIP "LIQUIDATED"

The exact time and method of liquidation of a partnership may be ambiguous. A partnership is not necessarily terminated for federal income tax purposes merely because it has dissolved under state law. For example, Sirrine Building No. 1 v. Commissioner, T.C. Memo, 1995–185, held that a partnership that under state law dissolved more than six years earlier did not terminate prior to the year it was required to report gain from the sale of land on the installment method.

Tapper v. Commissioner, T.C. Memo. 1986–597, held that a partnership organized to construct and sell a particular building was liquidated upon the sale of the building even though no actual distribution of cash or property was received by the partners; the taxpayer received a distribution equal to his share of the mortgage assumed by the buyer. This result presumably occurs whenever a partnership sells all of its assets and receives no net cash because encumbrances equal or exceed the fair market value of its assets.

In Goulder v. United States, 64 F.3d 663 (6th Cir.1995), a partnership that owned a single apartment building defaulted on the mortgage loan. The loan was foreclosed in 1980 and the property sold, without any distribution of proceeds to the partnership. The partnership ceased rental activities, but still held some tenant security deposits. In 1981, the partnership determined that the lender was not claiming the security deposits and distributed them to the partners. The court allowed the taxpayer-partner to claim a loss on the liquidation of his partnership interest in 1980, even though all assets were not distributed until 1981. The decision may be based more on the government's stipulation that the partnership ceased all activities in 1980 rather than on the actual facts.

5. APPLICATION OF SECTION 736(a)

In most partnership liquidations, § 736 is not relevant because there is no continuing partnership. The exception is the termination of a two person partnership in which one partner retires and the other partner agrees to make payments to the retired partner over a period of years. If any of these payments are classified as § 736(a) payments under the standards discussed at page 349, the partnership continues in existence as long as such payments are due. Treas. Reg. §§ 1.736–1(a)(1)(ii) and (6); 1.708–1(b)(1)(i)(b). This situation most frequently will occur where a member of a two person professional practice retires and the partner who continues the practice as a sole proprietor makes continuing payments of either a fixed amount or a share of profits from the practice to the retired partner.

6. SPECIAL ALLOCATION OF BASIS UNDER SECTION 732(d)

Section 732(d) applies a special basis allocation rule where the retiring partner obtained the partnership interest by purchase, death, or other transfer within the prior two years of the partnership liquidation. In Rudd v. Commissioner, 79 T.C. 225 (1982) (Acq.), § 732(d) was applied to give a partner a substantial basis in partnership goodwill, which was found to have been distributed to the partners in liquidation of a professional accounting partnership. Upon abandonment of the use of the partnership name following the liquidation of the partnership, the individual partner who had succeeded to the right to use the name was allowed an ordinary loss under § 165 for the portion of the basis of the goodwill allocated to the partnership name. Because the business of the partnership was continued by a new partnership, no loss was allowed with respect to the remaining partnership goodwill.

7. SALES OF PARTNERSHIP INTERESTS CAUSING CONSTRUCTIVE TERMINATIONS

7.1. *General*

Section 708(b)(1)(B) treats a partnership as terminated if 50 percent or more of the total interest in partnership profits and capital is sold or exchanged within a twelve month period.[9] The Internal Revenue Service applies § 708(b)(1)(B) to all exchanges, even though the exchange itself may be subject to a nonrecognition provision. See Rev.Rul. 81–38, 1981–1 C.B. 386 (transfer of 50 percent partnership interest to wholly owned subsidiary in transaction entitled to nonrecognition under § 351); Rev.Rul. 87–110, 1987–2 C.B. 159 (acquisition of corporate 50 percent partner in corporate reorganization entitled to nonrecognition under § 368). Treas. Reg. § 1.708–1(c) and (d), discussed in Section 7 of this chapter, provide

---

9. The partnership termination rule of § 708(b)(1)(B) does not apply however, to "electing large partnerships," discussed at page 92. I.R.C. § 774(c).

rules regarding the termination of a partnership in the case of merger of two or more partnerships or the division of one partnership into two or more partnerships, respectively.

Rev.Rul. 84–52, 1984–1 C.B. 157, held that the transfer of 50 percent of the interests in a general partnership to effect the conversion of those interests to limited partnership interests, pursuant to an amendment to the partnership agreement, did not result in termination of the partnership under § 708(b)(1)(B). The Ruling also held that the exchange is accorded nonrecognition by § 721. Rev. Rul. 95–37, 1995–1 C.B. 130, reached the same conclusions with respect to the conversion of a partnership into a limited liability company classified as a partnership for tax purposes. Do these rulings mean that no transfer of a partnership interest that is governed by § 721 is an exchange for purposes of § 708(b)(1)(B)? Suppose that A is a 50 percent partner in the AB Partnership and he contributes his interest to the DEF Partnership in exchange for a 10 percent partnership interest in DEF. (This transaction is governed by § 721, see Rev. Rul. 84–115, 1984–2 C.B. 118.) If an entity theory of partnership taxation is applied, the AB partnership is terminated. If the aggregate theory is applied to look through the DEF partnership, A has retained a 5 percent interest in the AB partnership, with the result that there has been an exchange of only 45 percent of the interests of the AB partnership. Accordingly, the AB partnership does not terminate. If, however, A held a 60 percent interest in the AB partnership, which he exchanged for a 10 percent interest in the DEF partnership, A has retained a six percent interest in the AB partnership and a 54 percent interest in the AB partnership has been exchanged. In this case, the AB partnership terminates. In Private Letter Ruling 8116041 (Jan. 21, 1981) the Service treated contributions of partnership interests to another partnership as exchanges that counted against the limit in § 708(b)(1)(B) without discussion of aggregate versus entity theory, but Private Letter Ruling 8819083 (Jan. 12, 1988) did not apply § 708(b)(1)(B) in a case in which ninety-nine percent of the interests in a partnership were contributed to a new partnership in exchange for all of the interests in the new partnership. The ruling states that "the purpose of [§ 708(b)(1)(B)] is to cause a termination only when, in fact, a substantial portion of the ownership of a partnership shifts."

In contrast to the sale of a partnership interest, when a new partner is admitted and acquires a 50 percent (or more) interest by virtue of a contribution to the partnership, § 708(b)(1)(B) does not apply. Rev.Rul. 75–423, 1975–2 C.B. 260. As in the sale versus liquidation area, the line between a purchase of a partnership interest versus admission of a new partner may be difficult to draw.

7.2. *Effect of a § 708(b) Termination*

Treas. Reg. § 1.708–1(b)(4) provides that the terminating partnership is deemed to have transferred all of its assets and liabilities to a new partnership in exchange for an interest in the new partnership, and immediately thereafter the terminating partnership (which now includes the purchasing partner rather than the selling partner) is deemed to have liquidated by distributing interests in the new partnership to the purchaser and the other remaining partners in proportion to their respective interests. The new partnership is treated as continuing the old partnership's business (or, if the facts warrant, as dissolving and winding up).

This treatment limits the effect of the constructive termination in a number of important respects. First, it generally prevents any partner from recognizing gain under § 731 as a result of a constructive cash distribution. Second, it generally prevents any reallocation of the basis of the partnership's assets, although the partners can obtain special basis adjustments under § 743(b). Finally, under Treas. Reg. § 1.704–1(b)(2)(iv)(*l*), the deemed contribution of assets to the new partnership and the distribution of the new partnership interests to the partners of the old partnership are disregarded for purposes of maintaining capital accounts. As a result, a § 708(b) termination does not change the capital accounts of the partners or the books of the partnership, and the deemed contribution of assets to a new partnership thus does not create additional § 704(c) property. In addition, Treas. Reg. § 1.731–2(g)(2) provides that the deemed distribution of partnership interests under Treas. Reg. § 1.708–1(b)(1)(iv) does not trigger the application of § 731(c), relating to gain recognition on the distribution of marketable securities.

Nevertheless, a § 708(b) termination can have some important implications. As discussed at page 90, the "new" partnership may be required to change its taxable year to comport with the taxable years of the "new" partners. Elections made by the "old" partnership are no longer in effect, and new elections must be made. But see Rev.Rul. 86–73, 1986–1 C.B. 282 (§ 754 election of "old" partnership applies to adjust basis of assets under § 743(b) immediately prior to deemed liquidating distribution). In addition, the new partnership is not bound by the § 704(c) method, i.e., ceiling method, curative allocations, or remedial allocations, used by the terminated partnership.

7.3.   *Availability of Section 754 Election*

Treas.Reg. § 1.708–1(b)(5) provides that a § 754 election of the terminated partnership applies to the purchase of a partnership interest in a transaction that caused a constructive termination of the partnership under § 708(b)(1)(B). The regulation also permits a partnership to make a § 754 election on its final return when a sale of a partnership interest causes a constructive termination of the partnership. As a result, the basis of the partnership's assets is adjusted under § 743(b) prior to the deemed distribution, and the purchasing partner's basis in the assets, determined under § 732, will take into account the adjustment. Similarly, the reconstituted partnership's basis in the assets under § 723 will reflect the adjustment. The same result would be effected by a valid § 732(d) election by the purchasing partner, but the Service has not ruled on whether § 732(d) elections are available with respect to deemed distributions under § 708.

If the "old" partnership has a § 754 election in effect, or it makes a § 754 election for its final year in connection with the purchase of the more than 50 percent interest, only the purchasing partner receives the benefit of special basis adjustments under § 743(b). But Treas. Reg. § 1.761–1(e) treats the distribution of interests in the "new" partnership as an exchange for purposes of § 743(b). The apparent effect of this provision is to permit the new partnership to make a § 754 election for its first year thereby according § 743(b) basis adjustments to all of the partners.

7.4.   *Tiered Partnerships*

Under Treas.Reg. § 1.708–1(b)(2), the sale of an interest in an upper tier partnership (UTP) is treated as a sale of an interest in the lower tier partnership (LTP) only if the sale of the upper tier partnership causes its termination under § 708(b)(1)(B). Thus, if G sells his 40 percent interest in the LTP Partnership to H, and I sells to J his 40 percent interest in UTP Partnership, which is a 40 percent partner of LTP, the LTP Partnership does not terminate, even though, in effect, there has been a sale of 56 percent of beneficial interest in the partnership. The regulation does provide, however, that if the upper-tier partnership is terminated under § 708(b)(1)(B), the upper-tier partnership's entire interest in a lower-tier partnership is treated as sold. Thus, if I had owned and sold a 50 percent interest in UTP, then UTP would have terminated, and its 40 percent interest in LTP would be treated as sold. As a result, LTP would terminate. This result would be true even if G had owned and sold only 10 percent of UTP, notwithstanding that, in effect, the beneficial interest in only 30 percent of the interests in LTP had been sold.

SECTION 6.   "MIXING BOWL" TRANSACTIONS

INTERNAL REVENUE CODE: Sections 704(c)(1)(B) and (c)(2); 737.

Section 704(c)(1)(A), discussed at page 154, requires the partnership to allocate gain or loss on the sale of contributed property to the contributing partner to the extent of the built-in gain or loss at the time of the contribution of the property. To prevent avoidance of such an allocation through the subsequent distribution to a different partner of contributed property having a built-in gain or loss, § 704(c)(1)(B) treats the distribution of such property within seven years of its contribution to the partnership as a recognition event to the contributing partner. The amount of the gain or loss is the same amount as would have been allocated to the contributing partner by reason of § 704(c)(1)(A) if the partnership had sold the property to the distributee partner at its fair market value on the date of the distribution. Thus, the contributing partner must recognize the built-in gain that existed on the date the property was contributed to the partnership. Even though the gain or loss is recognized directly by the contributing partner, and not as a distributive share of partnership income, § 704(c)(1)(B)(iii) requires that the contributing partner's basis in her partnership interest be increased or decreased appropriately. Similarly, in applying § 732 and § 705 to determine the distributee partner's basis for the property and her partnership interest after the distribution, the partnership's basis in the property immediately before the distribution is increased by the gain (or decreased by the loss) recognized by the contributing partner.

Assume that A contributes $100 cash and Blackacre, with an adjusted basis of $100 and a fair market value of $400, to the AB Partnership. B contributes $500 cash. Four years later (thereby avoiding § 707(a)(2)(B)), when Blackacre is worth $450 and the partnership has total assets of $1,100, the partnership distributes Blackacre to B and reduces B's interest in the partnership commensurately. Section 704(c)(1)(B) taxes A in the year of the distribution on the entire $300 gain that was inherent in Blackacre at the time of its contribution. In determining B's basis in Blackacre under § 732(a), the partnership adds the $300 recognized by A to its original basis of $100, so that B takes a $400 basis in Blackacre.

Section 704(c)(2) authorizes regulations to carve out an exception to § 704(c)(1)(B) in cases in which two partners each contribute § 704(c) property that is like–kind property within the meaning of § 1031 to a partnership and within 180 days (or prior to the due date of the partnership's return, if sooner) of the distribution to one partner of the property contributed by the other partner, the property contributed by the partner who received the first distribution is distributed to the other partner. For example, C and D form the CD partnership to which C contributes Blackacre, with a basis of $100 and a fair market value of $500, and D contributes Whiteacre, with a basis of $200 and a fair market value of $500. Two years later, the partnership liquidates and distributes Blackacre to D and Whiteacre to C. Since the same end result could have been achieved through a § 1031 like-kind exchange without the recognition of gain by either C or D, § 704(c)(1)(B) does not apply, and the normal partnership distribution rules do apply. See Treas. Reg. § 1.704–4(d)(3).

Section 704(c)(1)(B) does not apply at all if the contributing partner's interest in the partnership is completely liquidated before the contributed property is distributed to another partner. This situation is governed by § 737, which is designed to prevent avoidance of § 704(c)(1)(B). Suppose, for example, that D contributed Capital Asset #1, with a basis of $200 and a fair market value of $1,000, to the ABCD partnership in year 1; in year 3, the partnership distributed Capital Asset #2 to D in complete liquidation of D's partnership interest; and in year 5 the partnership distributed Capital Asset #1 to A. Since D is not a partner in year 5, § 704(c)(1)(B) does not apply. Apart from § 737, D simply would take Capital Asset #2 with a basis of $200 and would not recognize gain or loss. I.R.C. §§ 731 and 732(b). To prevent such avoidance of § 704(c)(1)(B), § 737 taxes D on the receipt of Capital Asset #2 in year 3 in an amount equal to the gain that would have been recognized if Capital Asset #1 had been distributed to another partner in year 3. The partner's basis in the partnership interest is increased by the amount of the gain recognized. This increase is deemed to occur immediately before the distribution. Thus, for example, if the fair market value of Capital Asset #1 were $800 at the time Capital Asset #2 was distributed, D would recognize a $600 gain. The basis of D's partnership interest would be increased to $800 ($200 + $600), and D's basis in Capital Asset #2 would be $800.

Section 737 applies only if the partner receiving the distribution contributed appreciated property to the partnership within seven years of receiving the distribution. Thus, for example, if D had not received Capital Asset #2 until year 8 (and A did not receive Capital Asset #1 until year 10) neither § 704(c)(1)(B) nor § 737 would have required any gain to be recognized to D by virtue of the distributions. Furthermore, § 737 does not apply to the extent § 751(b) applies to the distribution. Nor does § 737 apply to distributions of property previously contributed to the partnership by the partner receiving the distribution.

Although § 737 is designed primarily to cover situations that § 704(c)(1)(B) does not reach, it is possible for both § 704(c)(1)(B) and § 737 to be triggered by the same distribution. Suppose that E, F, and G form a partnership to which E contributed Greenacre, with a basis of $100 and a fair market value of $500, F contributed stock of a closely held corporation, with a basis of $150 and a fair market value of $500, and G contributed $500 cash. The distribution of Greenacre to F in complete liquidation of F's interest triggers § 704(c)(1)(B) with respect to E's $400 built-in gain in Greenacre at the time it was contributed, as well as triggering § 737 with respect to F's built-in gain in the corporate stock.

ILLUSTRATIVE MATERIAL

1.   DISTRIBUTIONS OF SECTION 704(c) PROPERTY

Treas. Reg. § 1.704–4 provides technical details regarding the operation of § 704(c)(1)(B). The regulations make it clear that the amount of gain or loss recognized may depend on the method used by the partnership in making allocations under § 704(c)(1)(A) and Treas. Reg. § 1.704–3, see page 395, because the amount of built-in gain or loss remaining on the date the property is distributed may depend on the particular allocation method adopted by the partnership, e.g., traditional method with the ceiling rule versus remedial allocations. See Treas. Reg. § 1.704–4(a)(5), Ex. (1)–(3). Because § 704(c)(1)(B) treats the property as having been sold by the partnership to the distributee partner, any loss that would have been disallowed by § 707(b)(1) if the distributed property actually had been sold to the distributee partner is disallowed. Similarly, the character of the contributing partner's gain or loss is the same as it would have been if the property had been sold by the partnership to the distributee partner. Treas. Reg. § 1.704–4(b). As a result of this rule, if the distributee partner holds more than a 50 percent capital or profits interest in the partnership, the contributing partner's gain recognized on a distribution of depreciable § 1231 property may be ordinary income pursuant to § 707(b)(2). Property received by a partnership in exchange for contributed property in a nonrecognition transaction, e.g., in a § 1031 like-kind exchange, is treated as the contributed property upon a subsequent distribution. Treas. Reg. § 1.704–4(d)(1).

The regulations provide several exceptions to § 704(c)(1)(B). First, § 704(c)(1)(B) does not apply to a distribution of property in connection with a termination of the partnership under § 708(b)(1)(B), discussed at page 390. Treas. Reg. § 1.704–4(c)(3). Termination under § 708(b)(1)(B) does not cause a new seven year period to begin running and the period is counted from the date the property was contributed to the terminated partnership. See Treas. Reg. § 1.704–4(a)(4)(ii). Second, § 704(c)(1)(B) does not apply to a distribution in a complete liquidation of the partnership if a portion of the contributed property is distributed to the contributing partner and that portion has unrecognized gain or loss in the hands of the contributing partner, determined immediately after the distribution, that equals the built-in gain or loss that would have been allocated to the contributing partner under § 704(c)(1)(A) on a sale of the contributed property by the partnership at the time of the distribution. Treas. Reg. § 1.704–4(c)(2). In such a case there has been no shifting of built-in gain or loss among partners and the abuse at which § 704(c)(1)(B) is aimed is not present. Third, Treas. Reg. § 1.704–4(d)(3) provides a special rule that limits the gain recognized under § 704(c)(1)(B) if property of like kind to the distributed § 704(c) property is distributed to the contributing partner within 180 days (or, if earlier, the due date of the partnership's tax return) of the distribution of the § 704(c) property. The reason for this exception is that the two transactions are in substance akin to a like kind exchange that could have qualified for nonrecognition under § 1031 if they had been done directly.

Under the regulations, the adjustments to the contributing partner's basis for her partnership interest, required by § 704(c)(1)(B)(iii), are taken into account in determining: (1) the noncontributing partner's basis in the property distributed to that partner, (2) the contributing partner's basis in any property distributed to that partner in the same transaction, (3) any basis adjustments to partnership property as a result of a § 754 election, and (4) the amount of the contributing partner's gain under § 731 or § 737 on a related distribution of money or property to the contributing partner. Treas. Reg. § 1.704–4(e). The partnership's basis in the distributed § 704(c) property immediately before the distribution is increased or decreased by the gain or loss recognized to the contributing partner. This adjustment in turn affects the distributee partner's basis under § 732.

2.   DISTRIBUTIONS SUBJECT TO SECTION 737

The statutory formula for the application of § 737 requires recognition by the distributee partner of gain in an amount equal to the lesser of (1) the excess, if any, of the fair market value of the distributed property received by the partner over the adjusted basis of the partner's interest in the partnership, the so called "excess distribution" or (2) the gain that would have been recognized to the partner under § 704(c)(1)(B) if, at the time of the distribution, the built-in gain property that had been contributed by the partner had been distributed by the partnership to another partner, the "net precontribution gain." Treas. Reg. § 1.737–1(a)–(c). For an example of the application of the general rule, see Treas. Reg. § 1.737–1(e), Ex. (1).

In determining the amount of the excess distribution, the distributee partner's adjusted basis in her partnership interest is adjusted for all basis adjustments resulting from the distribution subject to § 737 as well as any basis adjustments resulting from any other distribution that is part of the same plan or arrangement, for example, adjustments required under § 704(c)(1)(B) and § 751(b). For this purpose, however, basis is neither increased for any gain recognized under § 737 nor decreased under § 733 for property distributed to the distributee partner in the transaction, other than for property previously contributed to the partnership by the partner. Treas. Reg. § 1.737–1(b)(3). Reducing the partner's basis in the partnership interest for distributions of previously contributed property assures that gain built into previously contributed property that is returned to the contributing partner is not taken into account in determining the excess distribution. The distributee partner takes a transferred basis from the partnership in the distributed previously contributed property. Treas.Reg. § 1.737–3(b)(2). In calculating the excess distribution, the fair market value of distributed property is not reduced by any liabilities assumed (or taken subject to) by the distributee partner, but the partner's basis in the partnership interest is increased by the amount of any such liability. Accordingly, the amount of the excess distribution is limited to the net value of the distributed property. Any distribution of property previously contributed to the partnership by the distributee partner is not taken into account in determining the amount of the excess distribution or the partner's net precontribution gain. Treas. Reg. § 1.737–2(d). For an example of the application of these rules, see Treas. Reg. § 1.737–2(e), Ex. (1).

Treas. Reg. § 1.737–1(c)(2)(ii) provides that net precontribution gain is reduced as a result of a basis increase to the contributed property under § 734(b)(1)(A) to reflect gain recognized by the partner under § 731 on a distribution of money in the same plan or arrangement as the distribution of property subject to § 737. This adjustment is appropriate because under § 731 some or all of the precontribution gain would be recognized by the contributing partner on the distribution.

Net precontribution gain is also reduced by the amount of gain recognized by the contributing partner under § 704(c)(1)(B) in a distribution of contributed property in a related distribution to another partner, and by the amount of gain that the partner would have recognized under § 704(c)(1)(B) on the distribution of contributed property to another partner but for the exception of § 704(c)(2). Treas. Reg. § 1.737–1(c)(2)(iv). This reduction avoids recognizing the same built-in gain under both § 704(c)(1)(B) and § 737. For an example of the application of this rule, see Treas. Reg. § 1.737–1(e), Ex. (3).

Treas. Reg. § 1.737–1(d) provides that the character of the contributing partner's gain is the same (and in the same proportion) as the character of any net positive amounts resulting from the netting of precontribution gains and losses. Character is determined at the partnership level. Because the contributed property is not actually transferred by the partnership to anyone, unlike the situations to which § 704(c)(1)(B) applies, the character conversion rule of § 707(b)(2) does not apply in determining the character of the distributee partner's gain under § 737.

Treas. Reg. § 1.737–2(a) provides that § 737 does not apply to a deemed distribution of property on a constructive termination of the partnership under § 708(b)(1)(B). As in the case of § 704(c)(1)(B), however, a new seven-year period begins for property to the extent that the pre-termination gains and losses, if any, had not previously been allocated to the original contributing partner under § 704(c)(1)(A).[9]

A transferee partner in a transfer causing a deemed termination of the partnership under § 708(b)(1)(B) generally will not have any net precontribution gain immediately after the deemed formation of the new partnership. The basis of the property deemed to have been contributed to the new partnership by the transferee partner is determined under § 732; although on an individual basis the transferee partner may be treated as having contributed built-in gain and built-in loss property to the new partnership, on an aggregate basis these built-in gain and loss properties generally should net to zero. Nevertheless, the transferee partner subsequently could have a net precontribution gain on a distribution if, for example, the partnership sold some of the built-in loss property that was deemed to have been contributed to the new partnership as a result of the § 708(b)(1)(B) termination but retains the built-in gain property.

Treas. Reg. § 1.737–2(b) also excludes from the ambit of § 737 partnership mergers and similar transactions (including partnership divisions) in which the partners merely have converted interests in the transferor partnership to an interest in the transferee partnership. Section 737 does apply, however, upon incorporation of a partnership involving an actual distribution of property by the partnership to the partners followed by a contribution to a corporation. Treas. Reg. § 1.737–2(c).

Section 737(c)(1) provides that a contributing partner's basis in his partnership interest is increased by the amount of gain recognized to the partner under § 737(a). Treas. Reg. § 1.737–3(a) and (b) provide that this basis increase is taken into account when determining the partner's basis for property received by that partner, but not in determining the amount of gain recognized by the partner under § 737 or under § 731 on any distribution of money in the same distribution.

Treas. Reg. § 1.737–3(c) limits the partnership's increase in basis of the contributed property under § 737(c)(2) to built-in gain property held by the partnership after the distribution with the same character as the gain recognized by the contributing partner under § 737. The basis increase is

---

9. Treas. Reg. § 1.737–2(a) provides that a new seven year period is not started, and § 737 applies to the reconstituted part-nership only to the extent it would have applied if the original partnership had continued.

allocated to property in the order it was contributed to the partnership, thereby preserving the effect of the seven-year rule. No basis increase is allocated to any property distributed to another partner in a related distribution to which § 704(c)(1)(B) applies; in such a case, the basis of the distributed property is adjusted for any gain or loss recognized by the contributing partner under § 704(c)(1)(B).

SECTION 7. PARTNERSHIP MERGERS AND DIVISIONS

REGULATIONS: Sections 1.708–1(c), (d); 1.752–1(g), Ex. (2).

In 2001, the Treasury Department promulgated regulations dealing specifically with mergers and divisions of partnerships. T.D. 8925, Partnership Mergers and Divisions, 2001–1 C.B. 496. These regulations were issued in proposed form in 2000. The preamble to the proposed regulations, which follows, generally describes the purpose and operation of the final regulations.

Notice of Proposed Rulemaking, Partnership Mergers and Divisions, REG–111119–99

2000–1 C.B. 455.

Partnership Mergers

Background

Section 708(b)(2)(A) provides that in the case of a merger or consolidation of two or more partnerships, the resulting partnership is, for purposes of section 708, considered the continuation of any merging or consolidating partnership whose members own an interest of more than 50 percent in the capital and profits of the resulting partnership. Section 1.708–1(b)(2)(i) of the Income Tax Regulations provides that if the resulting partnership can be considered a continuation of more than one of the merging partnerships, the resulting partnership is the continuation of the partnership that is credited with the contribution of the greatest dollar value of assets to the resulting partnership. If none of the members of the merging partnerships own more than a 50 percent interest in the capital and profits of the resulting partnership, all of the merged partnerships are considered terminated, and a new partnership results. The taxable years of the merging partnerships that are considered terminated are closed under section 706(c).

Although section 708 and the applicable regulations provide which partnership continues when two or more partnerships merge, the statute and regulations do not prescribe a form for the partnership merger. (Often, state merger statutes do not provide a particular form for a partnership merger.) In revenue rulings, however, the IRS has prescribed the form of a partnership merger for Federal income tax purposes.

In Rev. Rul. 68–289 (1968–1 C.B. 314), three existing partnerships (P1, P2, and P3) merged into one partnership with P3 continuing under section 708(b)(2)(A). The revenue ruling holds that P1 and P2, the two terminating partnerships, are treated as having contributed all of their respective assets and liabilities to P3, the resulting partnership, in exchange for a partnership interest in P3. P1 and P2 are considered terminated and the partners of P1 and P2 receive interests in P3 with a basis under section 732(b) in liquidation of P1 and P2 (Assets–Over Form). Rev. Rul. 77–458 (1977–2 C.B. 220), and Rev. Rul. 90–17 (1990–1 C.B. 119), also follow the Assets–Over Form for a partnership merger.

Explanation of Provisions

A.   *Form of a Partnership Merger*

The IRS and Treasury are aware that taxpayers may accomplish a partnership merger by undertaking transactions in accordance with jurisdictional laws that follow a form other than the Assets–Over Form. For example, the terminating partnership could liquidate by distributing its assets and liabilities to its partners who then contribute the assets and liabilities to the resulting partnership (Assets–Up Form). In addition, the partners in the terminating partnership could transfer their terminating partnership interests to the resulting partnership in exchange for resulting partnership interests, and the terminating partnership could liquidate into the resulting partnership (Interest–Over Form).

In the partnership incorporation area, a taxpayer's form generally is respected if the taxpayer actually undertakes, under the relevant jurisdictional law, all the steps of a form that is set forth in one of three situations provided in Rev. Rul. 84–111 (1984–2 C.B. 88). The three situations that Rev. Rul. 84–111 sets forth are the Assets–Over Form, Assets–Up Form, and Interest–Over Form. Rev. Rul. 84–111 explains that, depending on the form chosen to incorporate the partnership, the adjusted basis and holding periods of the various assets received by the corporation and the adjusted basis and holding periods of the stock received by the former partners can vary. Like partnership incorporations, each form of a partnership merger has potentially different tax consequences.

Under the Assets–Up Form, partners could recognize gain under sections 704(c)(1)(B) and 737 (and incur state or local transfer taxes) when the terminating partnership distributes the assets to the partners. However, under the Assets–Over Form, gain under sections 704(c)(1)(B) and 737 is not triggered. See §§ 1.704–4(c)(4) and 1.737–2(b). Additionally, under the Assets–Up Form, because the adjusted basis of the assets contributed to the resulting partnership is determined first by reference to section 732 (as a result of the liquidation) and then section 723 (by virtue of the contribution), in certain circumstances, the adjusted basis of the assets contributed may not be the same as the adjusted basis of the assets in the terminating partnership. These circumstances occur if the partners' aggregate adjusted basis of their interests in the terminating partnership does not equal the terminating partnership's adjusted basis in its assets.

Under the Assets–Over Form, because the resulting partnership's adjusted basis in the assets it receives is determined solely under section 723, the adjusted basis of the assets in the resulting partnership is the same as the adjusted basis of the assets in the terminating partnership.

The regulations propose to respect the form of a partnership merger for Federal income tax purposes if the partnerships undertake, pursuant to the laws of the applicable jurisdiction, the steps of either the Assets–Over Form or the Assets–Up Form. (This rule applies even if none of the merged partnerships are treated as continuing for Federal income tax purposes.) Generally, when partnerships merge, the assets move from one partnership to another at the entity level, or in other words, like the Assets–Over Form. However, if as part of the merger, the partnership titles the assets in the partners' names, the proposed regulations treat the transaction under the Assets–Up Form. If partnerships use the Interest–Over Form to accomplish the result of a merger, the partnerships will be treated as following the Assets–Over Form for Federal income tax purposes.

In the context of partnership incorporations, Rev. Rul. 84–111 distinguishes among all three forms of incorporation. However, with respect to the Interest–Over Form, the revenue ruling respects only the transferors' conveyances of partnership interests, while treating the receipt of the partnership interests by the transferee corporation as the receipt of the partnership's assets (i.e., the Assets–Up Form). The theory for this result, based largely on McCauslen v. Commissioner, 45 T.C. 588 (1966), is that the transferee corporation can only receive assets since it is not possible, as a sole member, for it to receive and hold interests in a partnership (i.e., a partnership cannot have only one member; so, the entity is never a partnership in the hands of the transferee corporation).

Adherence to the approach followed in Rev. Rul. 84–111 creates problems in the context of partnership mergers that are not present with respect to partnership incorporations. Unlike the corporate rules, the partnership rules impose certain tax results on partners based upon a concept that matches a contributed asset to the partner that contributed the asset. Sections 704(c) and 737 are examples of such rules. The operation of these rules breaks down if the partner is treated as contributing an asset that is different from the asset that the partnership is treated as receiving.

Given that the hybrid treatment of the Interest–Over Form transactions utilized in Rev. Rul. 84–111 is difficult to apply in the context of partnership mergers, another characterization will be applied to such transactions. The Assets–Over Form generally will be preferable for both the IRS and taxpayers. For example, when partnerships merge under the Assets–Over Form, gain under sections 704(c)(1)(B) and 737 is not triggered. Moreover, the basis of the assets in the resulting partnership is the same as the basis of the assets in the terminating partnership, even if the partners' aggregate adjusted basis of their interests in the terminating partnership does not equal the terminating partnership's adjusted basis in its assets.

If partnerships merge under applicable law without implementing a form, the proposed regulations treat the partnerships as following the Assets–Over Form. This approach is consistent with the treatment of partnership to corporation elective conversions under the check-the-box regulations and technical terminations under section 708(b)(1)(B), other formless movements of a partnership's assets.

B.   Adverse Tax Consequences of the Assets–Over Form

The IRS and Treasury are aware that certain adverse tax consequences may occur for partnerships that merge in a transaction that will be taxed in accordance with the Assets–Over Form. These proposed regulations address some of the adverse tax consequences regarding section 752 liability shifts and buyouts of exiting partners.

1.   Section 752 Revisions

If a highly leveraged partnership (the terminating partnership) merges with another partnership (the resulting partnership), all of the partners in the terminating partnership could recognize gain because of section 752 liability shifts. Under the Assets–Over Form, the terminating partnership becomes a momentary partner in the resulting partnership when the terminating partnership contributes its assets and liabilities to the resulting partnership in exchange for interests in the resulting partnership. If the terminating partnership (as a momentary partner in the resulting partnership) is considered to receive a deemed distribution under section 752 (after netting increases and decreases in liabilities under § 1.752–1(f)) that exceeds the terminating partnership's adjusted basis of its interests in the resulting partnership, the terminating partnership would recognize gain under section 731. The terminating partnership's gain then would be allocated to each partner in the terminating partnership under section 704(b). In this situation, a partner in the terminating partnership could recognize gain even though the partner's adjusted basis in its resulting partnership interest or its share of partnership liabilities in the resulting partnership is large enough to avoid the recognition of gain, provided that the decreases in liabilities in the terminating partnership are netted against the increases in liabilities in the resulting partnership.

The proposed regulations clarify that when two or more partnerships merge under the Assets–Over Form, increases or decreases in partnership liabilities associated with the merger are netted by the partners in the terminating partnership and the resulting partnership to determine the effect of the merger under section 752. The IRS and Treasury consider it appropriate to treat the merger as a single transaction for determining the net liability shifts under section 752. Therefore, a partner in the terminating partnership will recognize gain on the contribution under section 731 only if the net section 752 deemed distribution exceeds that partner's adjusted basis of its interest in the resulting partnership.

2. Buyout of a Partner

Another adverse tax consequence may occur when a partner in the terminating partnership does not want to become a partner in the resulting partnership and would like to receive money or property instead of an interest in the resulting partnership. Under the Assets–Over Form, the terminating partnership will not recognize gain or loss under section 721 when it contributes its property to the resulting partnership in exchange for interests in the resulting partnership. However, if, in order to facilitate the buyout of the exiting partner, the resulting partnership transfers money or other consideration to the terminating partnership in addition to the resulting partnership interests, the terminating partnership may be treated as selling part of its property to the resulting partnership under section 707(a)(2)(B). Any gain or loss recognized by the terminating partnership generally would be allocated to all the partners in the terminating partnership even though only the exiting partner would receive the consideration.

The IRS and Treasury believe that, under certain circumstances, when partnerships merge and one partner does not become a partner in the resulting partnership, the receipt of cash or property by that partner should be treated as a sale of that partner's interest in the terminating partnership to the resulting partnership, not a disguised sale of the terminating partnership's assets. Accordingly, the proposed regulations provide that if the merger agreement (or similar document) specifies that the resulting partnership is purchasing the exiting partner's interest in the terminating partnership and the amount paid for the interest, the transaction will be treated as a sale of the exiting partner's interest to the resulting partnership. This treatment will apply even if the resulting partnership sends the consideration to the terminating partnership on behalf of the exiting partner, so long as the designated language is used in the relevant document. [Ed.: The final regulations provide that sale treatment will be accorded to the transaction under this special rule only if the exiting partner consents to sale treatment prior to or contemporaneously with the transfer.]

In this situation, the exiting partner is treated as selling a partnership interest in the terminating partnership to the resulting partnership (and the resulting partnership is treated as purchasing the partner's interest in the terminating partnership) immediately prior to the merger. Immediately after the sale, the resulting partnership becomes a momentary partner in the terminating partnership. Consequently, the resulting partnership and ultimately its partners (determined prior to the merger) inherit the exiting partner's capital account in the terminating partnership and any section 704(c) liability of the exiting partner. If the terminating partnership has an election in effect under section 754 (or makes an election under section 754), the resulting partnership will have a special basis adjustment regarding the terminating partnership's property under section 743. * * * [Ed.: Where the resulting partnership, as part of the merger, has acquired an interest in the terminating partnership in accordance with the special buyout rule, the terminating partnership is treated as distributing its assets to the resulting partnership in liquidation of the resulting partnership's interest in the terminating partnership. Accordingly, the resulting partnership takes an exchanged basis in the distributed assets under section 732(b).]

C. Merger as Part of a Larger Transaction

The proposed regulations provide that if the merger is part of a larger series of transactions, and the substance of the larger series of transactions is inconsistent with following the form prescribed for the merger, the form may not be respected, and the larger series of transactions may be recast in accordance with their substance. An example illustrating the application of this rule is included in the proposed regulations.

D. Measurement of Dollar Value of Assets

As discussed above, the regulations currently provide that in a merger of partnerships, if the resulting partnership can be considered a continuation of more than one of the merging partnerships, the resulting partnership is the continuation of the partnership that is credited with the contribution of the greatest dollar value of assets to the resulting partnership. Commentators have questioned whether this rule refers to the gross or net value of the assets of a partnership. The proposed regulations provide that the value of assets of a partnership is determined net of the partnership's liabilities.

* * *

Partnership Divisions

Background

Section 708(b)(2)(B) provides that, in the case of a division of a partnership into two or more partnerships, the resulting partnerships (other than any resulting partnership the members of which had an interest of 50 percent or less in the capital and profits of the prior partnership) are considered a continuation of the prior partnership. Section 1.708–1(b)(2)(ii) provides that any other resulting partnership is not considered a continuation of the prior partnership but is considered a new partnership. If the members of none of the resulting partnerships owned an interest of more than 50 percent in the capital and profits of the prior partnership, the prior partnership is terminated. Where members of a partnership that has been divided do not become members of a resulting partnership that is considered a continuation of the prior partnership, such partner's interest is considered liquidated as of the date of the division.

Section 708(b)(2)(B) and the applicable regulations do not prescribe a particular form for the division involving continuing partnerships. The IRS has not addressed in published guidance how the assets and liabilities of the prior partnership move into the resulting partnerships. Taxpayers generally have followed either the Assets–Over Form or the Assets–Up Form for partnership divisions.

Under the Assets–Over Form, the prior partnership transfers certain assets to a resulting partnership in exchange for interests in the resulting partnership. The prior partnership then immediately distributes the resulting partnership interests to partners who are designated to receive interests in the resulting partnership.

Under the Assets–Up Form, the prior partnership distributes certain assets to some or all of its partners who then contribute the assets to a resulting partnership in exchange for interests in the resulting partnership.

Explanation of Provisions

A. *Form of a Partnership Division*

As with partnership mergers, the IRS and Treasury recognize that different tax consequences can arise depending on the form of the partnership division. Because of the potential different tax results that could occur depending on the form followed by the partnership, the regulations propose to respect for Federal income tax purposes the form of a partnership division accomplished under laws of the applicable jurisdiction if the partnership undertakes the steps of either the Assets–Over Form or the Assets–Up Form. Thus, the same forms allowed for partnership mergers will be allowed for partnership divisions.

Generally, an entity cannot be classified as a partnership if it has only one member. This universally has been held to be the case in classifying transactions where interests in a partnership are transferred to a single person, so that the partnership goes out of existence. McCauslen v. Commissioner, 45 T.C. 588 (1966); Rev. Rul. 99–6, 1999–1 C.B. 432; Rev. Rul. 67–65, 1967–1 C.B. 168; Rev. Rul. 55–68, 1955–1 C.B. 372. However, in at least one instance involving the contribution of assets by an existing partnership to a newly-formed partnership, regulations have provided that the momentary existence of the new partnership will be respected for Federal income tax purposes. See § 1.708–1(b)(1)(iv). Pursuant to the proposed regulations, under the Assets–Over Form of a partnership division, the prior partnership's momentary ownership of all the interests in a resulting partnership will not prevent the resulting partnership from being classified as a partnership on formation.

The example in current § 1.708–1(b)(2)(ii) indicates that when a partnership is not considered a continuation of the prior partnership under section 708(b)(2)(B) (partnership considered a new partnership under current § 1.708–1(b)(2)(ii)), the new partnership is created under the Assets–Up Form. The regulations propose to modify this result and provide examples illustrating that partnerships can divide and create a new partnership under either the Assets–Over Form or the Assets–Up Form.

Consistent with partnership mergers, if a partnership divides using a form other than the two prescribed, it will be treated as undertaking the Assets–Over Form.

These proposed regulations use four terms to describe the form of a partnership division. Two of these terms, prior partnership and resulting partnership, describe partnerships that exist under the applicable jurisdictional law. The prior partnership is the partnership that exists under the applicable jurisdictional law before the division, and the resulting partnerships are the partnerships that exist under the applicable jurisdictional law after the division. The other two terms, divided partnership and recipient partnership, are Federal tax concepts. A divided partnership is a partnership that is treated, for Federal income tax purposes, as transferring assets in connection with a division, and a recipient partnership is a partnership that is treated, for Federal income tax purposes, as receiving assets in connection with a division. The divided partnership must be a continuation of the prior partnership. Although the divided partnership is considered one continuing partnership for Federal income tax purposes, it may actually be two different partnerships under the applicable jurisdictional law (i.e., the prior partnership and a different resulting partnership that is considered a continuation of the prior partnership for Federal income tax purposes).

Finally, because in a formless division it generally will be unclear which partnership should be treated, for Federal income tax purposes, as transferring assets (i.e., the divided partnership) to another partnership (i.e., the recipient partnership) where more than one partnership is a continuation of the prior partnership, the proposed regulations provide that the continuing resulting partnership with the assets having the greatest fair market value (net of liabilities) will be treated as the divided partnership. This issue also is present where the partnership that, in form, transfers assets is not a continuation of the prior partnership, but more than one of the other resulting partnerships are continuations of the prior partnership. The same rule applies to these situations.

B. Consequences under Sections 704(c)(1)(B) and 737

Gain under sections 704(c)(1)(B) and 737 may be triggered when section 704(c) property or substituted section 704(c) property is distributed to certain partners. These rules often will be implicated in the context of partnership divisions.

Where a division is accomplished in a transaction that is taxed in accordance with the Assets–Over Form, the partnership interest in the recipient partnership will be treated as a section 704(c) asset to the extent that the interest is received by the divided partnership in exchange for section 704(c) property. Section 1.704–4(d)(1). Accordingly, the distribution of the partnership interests in the recipient partnership by the divided partnership generally will trigger section 704(c)(1)(B) where the interests in the recipient partnership are received by a partner of the divided partnership other than the partner who contributed the section 704(c) property to the divided partnership. In addition, section 737 may be triggered if a partner who contributed section 704(c) property to the divided partnership receives an interest in the recipient partnership that is not attributable to the section 704(c) property.

Where a division is accomplished under the Assets–Up Form, assets are distributed directly to the partners who will hold interests in the recipient partnership. The distribution could trigger section 704(c)(1)(B) or 737 depending on the identity of the distributed asset and the distributee partner.

The regulations under section 737 provide an exception for certain partnership divisions. Section 737 does not apply when a transferor partnership transfers all the section 704(c) property contributed by a partner to a second partnership in a section 721 exchange, followed by a distribution of an interest in the transferee partnership in complete liquidation of the interest of the partner that originally contributed the section 704(c) property to the transferor partnership. Section 1.737–2(b)(2). This rule, however, may not apply to many partnership divisions because the original contributing partner often remains a partner in the divided partnership. No similar rule is provided under section 704(c)(1)(B).

In many instances, the application of sections 704(c)(1)(B) and 737 will be appropriate when a partnership divides under either the Assets–Over Form or the Assets–Up Form. Consider the following example: A, B, C, and D form a partnership. A contributes appreciated property X ($0 basis and $200 value), B contributes property Y ($200 basis and $200 value), and C and D each contribute $200 cash. The partnership subsequently divides into two partnerships using the Assets–Over Form, distributing interests in the recipient partnership in accordance with each partner's pro rata interest in the prior partnership. Property X remains in the prior partnership, and property Y is contributed to the recipient partnership. Under these facts, section 737 could be avoided if an exception were created for the distribution of the recipient partnership interests. If, subsequent to the division, half of property Y is distributed to A, section 737 would not be triggered because property X (the section 704(c) property) is no longer in the same partnership as property Y.

* * *

C. *Division as Part of a Larger Transaction*

The proposed regulations provide the same rule for partnership divisions that applies to partnership mergers.

ILLUSTRATIVE MATERIAL

1. PARTNERSHIP MERGERS

Generally, the regulations require that the partnership actually convey ownership of its assets to the partners under the law of the applicable jurisdiction for the "assets-up form" to be respected. The preamble to the final regulations notes that it should not be necessary for the partners actually to assume the liabilities of the partnership in order to follow that form. T.D. 8925, Partnership Mergers and Divisions, 2001–1 C.B. 496, 497. The preamble also explains that an actual transfer and recording of the deed or certificate of title will not be required if local law allows ownership to be conveyed without the actual transfer and recording of a deed or certificate of title. Thus, it might be said that *"form lite"* controls in this regard.

Under the regulations, a partnership cannot pick and choose among its assets and treat some as having been conveyed under the "assets-over form" and others as having been conveyed under the "assets-up form." If a partnership wants to adopt the assets-up form, that form must be followed with respect to all of its assets and all of its partners. If the partnership attempts to bifurcate the merger between the assets-over form and the assets-up form, the entire merger will be treated as an assets-over form of merger.

Rev. Rul. 2004–43, 2004–1 C.B. 842, dealt with the application of §§ 704(c)(1)(B) and 737(b) in partnership mergers. The ruling held that § 704(c)(1)(B) applies to newly created § 704(c) gain or loss in property contributed by the transferor partnership to the continuing partnership in an assets-over partnership merger, but does not apply to newly created reverse § 704(c) gain or loss resulting from a revaluation of property in the continuing partnership. Likewise, for purposes of § 737(b) (discussed in Section 8 of this chapter), net precontribution gain includes newly created § 704(c) gain or loss in property contributed by the transferor partnership to the continuing partnership in an assets-over partnership merger, but does not include newly created reverse § 704(c) gain or loss resulting from a revaluation of property in the continuing partnership. Thus, a distribution within seven years after the merger of property previously held by the disappearing partnership will trigger gain recognition. In Rev. Rul. 2005–10, 2005–7 I.R.B. 492, the Service revoked Rev. Rul. 2004–43 and announced that it intended to promulgate regulations implementing the principles of Rev. Rul. 2004–43, which will be effective after January 19, 2005.

2. PARTNERSHIP DIVISIONS

When a partnership divides into two or more partnerships, a resulting partnership will be a continuation of the original partnership if the partners of the continuing partnership owned more than 50 percent of the capital and profits of the original partnership. Other partnerships are new partnerships, and their partners are treated as having had their original partnership interests liquidated in the division. Treas. Reg. § 1.708–1(d)(1).

Consider the following situation. The ABC Partnership owns an apartment building and an office building. A and B each own a 15 percent interest and C owns a 70 percent interest in the Partnership. C does not want to continue in the partnership with A and B and would like to operate the office building with D. To this end, the ABC Partnership distributes the office building to C in liquidation of C's interest in partnership ABC. Immediately thereafter, C forms a partnership with D and contributes the office building to the CD Partnership. After the distribution and contribution of the office building, the AB Partnership owns the apartment building and the CD Partnership owns the office building. Despite appearances, this transaction is not a partnership division under the regulations. To have a division, at least two members of the prior partnership must be members of each resulting partnership that exists after the transaction. Treas. Reg. § 1.708–1(d)(4)(iv). C is the only member of the ABC Partnership in the CD Partnership. This transaction would be treated as a liquidation distribution from the ABC partnership to C, followed by a contribution of the office building to the new CD Partnership, with the ABC Partnership continuing as the AB Partnership.

In the case of partnership divisions, the treatment of the transfer of assets to any particular resulting partnership must consistently follow the assets-over form or the asset-up form, as with partnership mergers. But where the transfer to each of two or more successor partnerships is considered separately, the transfer to one may follow the assets-over form while the transfer to another follows the assets up-form. See Treas. Reg. § 1.708–1(d)(5), Ex. (7).

SECTION 8. SPECIAL PROBLEMS OF THE LIQUIDATION OF A PARTNERSHIP INTEREST FOLLOWING THE DEATH OF A PARTNER

INTERNAL REVENUE CODE: Sections 706(c); 731(a)–(c); 732(a)–(e); 734; 735; 736(a); 741; 742; 743(a)–(d); 751(c), (d)(2); 753; 754; 755(a) and (b); 761(d).

REGULATIONS: Sections 1.708–1(b)(1)(i); 1.732–1(d); 1.734–2; 1.736–1; 1.742–1; 1.743–1(b); 1.753–1; 1.754–1; 1.755–1.

Under state law a partnership technically is dissolved on the death of a general partner. However, under § 708 the partnership continues for federal tax purposes as long as the business of the partnership is continued, unless the partnership had only two partners. The deceased partner's interest in the partnership typically is disposed of in one of three ways: his estate (or other designated successor in interest) may receive a liquidating distribution; his interest may be purchased by the surviving partners, frequently pursuant to a prearranged agreement; or his designated successor may be substituted as a partner. Limited partnership interests are generally subject to the same treatment, but a limited partnership ordinarily is not automatically dissolved under state law by the death of a limited partner. Limited liability companies taxed as partnerships also ordinarily do not dissolve on the death of a member, and the tax treatment of the interest of a deceased member of a limited liability company taxed as a partnership raises the same issues.

When a deceased partner's interest is liquidated, the rules regarding distributions in liquidation generally govern the taxation of the liquidating distributions and their effect on the partnership. Similarly, if the interest is sold to the remaining partners, the rules governing sales of partnership interests, discussed in Chapter 8, generally govern. In both cases, however, either § 1014, providing that the basis of property acquired by bequest or inheritance is the fair market value at the decedent's date of death, or § 691, which denies a date of death basis to "income in respect of a decedent," must be taken into account. Where the deceased partner's successor in interest is substituted as a partner, there is no distribution or taxable transfer, but the transfer nevertheless has important effects. For example, if a § 754 election is in effect, a § 743(b) adjustment to the basis of partnership property is required.

In all three cases consideration must be given to the effect of the partner's death on the taxable year of the partner and of the partnership. Section 443(a)(2) closes the deceased partner's taxable year on the date of death. Section 706, however, not only provides the rules governing the partnership's taxable year, but modifies the application of § 443(a)(2) with respect to the deceased partner's distributive share of partnership items. Most controversy in this area involves the allocation of partnership income or loss between the decedent's final return and the income tax return of the decedent's estate.

ILLUSTRATIVE MATERIAL

1. ALLOCATION OF PARTNERSHIP INCOME BETWEEN THE DE-CEASED PARTNER AND THE ESTATE

Suppose that a partnership is on a February 1–January 31 fiscal year and a partner who is on a calendar year dies on November 30, 2005. Under § 443(a)(2) the deceased partner's executor must file an income tax return for the decedent partner for the period January 1–November 30, 2005, including therein income of the decedent allocable to that period under the decedent's method of accounting. The executor must therefore include the decedent's distributive share of the partnership income for the previous February 1, 2004–January 31, 2005 fiscal year. In addition, under § 706(c)(2)(A) the death of the partner is a disposition of the partner's entire interest in the partnership, which requires that the partnership year be closed with respect the deceased partner. Thus the partnership income for the period February 1, 2005–November 30, 2005 also must be included in the decedent's final return. As a consequence, twenty-two months of income will be bunched in the decedent's final return.

Before 1997, this bunching of income was avoided by former § 706(c)(2)(A)(ii), which provided that the partnership year did not close for the decedent partner, or for the partnership, unless the partnership actually terminated on the decedent's death. Thus all partnership items for the year of the death of a partner were allocated to the decedent's estate. This provision was not always beneficial. If the partnership had a loss in the year of a partner's death, all of the loss was allocated to the decedent's estate and none of the loss was available to reduce income on the decedent's final tax return.[11] See e.g. Estate of Applebaum v. Commissioner, 724 F.2d 375 (3d Cir.1983). Section 706(c)(2)(A)(ii) was inconsistent with the rules of § 706(d), discussed at page 173, which require that a partner's distributive share take into account his varying interests during the year. In addition, because § 706(b), discussed at page 90, limits the situations in which a partnership may have a taxable year that differs from those of the partners, the bunching problem to which former § 706(c)(2)(A)(ii) originally was addressed was largely eliminated by changes to other provisions of Subchapter K.

2.   TWO–PERSON PARTNERSHIPS

A special problem arises in the case of a two-person partnership. If a partner of a two-person partnership dies, and his interest is purchased by the surviving partner who continues the business as a sole proprietor, the partnership is terminated because no part of its operations continues to be carried on "in a partnership." However, the partnership continues for tax purposes so long as the estate or other successor in interest continues to share in the profits or losses of the partnership business or receives payments under § 736. Treas. Regs. §§ 1.708–1(b)(1)(i), 1.736–1(a)(6); see also Rev.Rul. 66–325, 1966–2 C.B. 249; Estate of Skaggs v. Commissioner, 672 F.2d 756 (9th Cir.1982).

3.   TREATMENT OF DECEASED PARTNER'S SUCCESSOR IN INTEREST

3.1.   *Basis of Partnership Assets*

The basis problems and the Subchapter K solutions to those problems on the death of a partner are essentially the same as in the case of the sale of a partnership interest, see Chapter 8, Section 2. In the case of the death of a partner, § 742 refers to the general basis rules of § 1011, et seq. for determining the basis of a partnership interest acquired at death. Thus, under § 1014 the successor's basis for the partnership interest is the fair market value of the partnership interest at the deceased partner's date of death. Under § 743(a), the basis of partnership assets is not affected. However, if the estate or successor continues as a partner and a § 754 election has been made, then the basis of the partnership assets will be adjusted under § 743(b) to eliminate any difference between the basis in the partnership interest and the new partner's share of the basis in the partnership assets.

3.2.   *Transferees Eligible for Basis Adjustments*

Under § 761(e) the distribution of a partnership interest from an estate to the beneficiary may be an exchange for purposes of § 743(b), and

---

11. If partnership losses allocated to the decedent's final return exceed income shown on the return, the losses may be carried back to the two preceding years under § 172. If partnership losses are in excess of income on the estate's return for the year in which the partnership's taxable year is closed, the losses can only be carried forward. Under § 642(h), the beneficiaries of the estate are entitled to deduct in their returns the estate's unused net operating losses when the estate terminates.

if a § 754 election is in effect, a basis adjustment may be required. However, since the distribution is a nonrecognition event to the estate and under § 643(e)(1) the distributee takes a transferred basis, unless the estate elects under § 643(e)(3) to treat the distribution as a recognition event, a second adjustment will not be made.

Rev.Rul. 79–124, 1979–1 C.B. 224, held that an adjustment to the basis of partnership assets under § 743(b) is to be made with respect to the partnership property attributable to the entire interest of a deceased partner which was held as community property if pursuant to § 1014(b)(6) the entire interest is treated as received by the surviving spouse from the decedent.

3.3. *Income In Respect of a Decedent: Partnerships Holding Unrealized Receivables*

The basis rules of § 1014 and § 743(b) present problems if the assets of the partnership include accounts receivable with a zero basis. If the basis for such a partnership interest were the estate tax value determined under § 1014(a), it would be attributable in part to a value represented by the accounts receivable. Ordinarily, however, accounts receivable of a decedent take a carryover basis under § 691, thereby preserving their inherent ordinary income. In the case of a partnership holding accounts receivable, if a basis adjustment under § 743(b) were allowed to the decedent's successor, then realization of the potential ordinary income in the accounts receivable could be permanently avoided. The regulations attempt to close this obvious loophole by providing that the basis of the partnership interest acquired from a decedent is the fair market value of the interest reduced to the extent that such value is attributable to items constituting income in respect of a decedent under § 691. Treas. Reg. § 1.742–1. Assuming that this is a fair interpretation of the reference in § 742 to the general basis provisions, the question remains whether accounts receivable in this situation would constitute income in respect of a decedent. Clearly, if the accounts receivable had been held by the partner individually, they would have represented income in respect of a decedent in the hands of his estate or heirs. Here, however, the receivables are technically property of the partnership, and not of the individual partner. Section 691(e) refers to § 753 for the application of § 691 to income in respect of a deceased partner and that section merely provides that § 736(a) payments in liquidation of the deceased partner's interest are to be treated as income in respect of a decedent.

The obvious inadequacy of the statutory treatment of the problem has not prevented the courts from achieving the correct result. In Quick's Trust v. Commissioner, 54 T.C. 1336 (1970), aff'd per curiam, 444 F.2d 90 (8th Cir.1971), the court held that the right of a successor partner to share in the collection of accounts receivable could be separated from the general "bundle of rights" represented by the partnership interest and such right was covered by § 691. The reference in § 753 to § 736(a) payments was not to be treated as exclusive. As a result, the new basis of the partnership interest was reduced by the fair market value of the accounts receivable and the increase in the basis of the accounts receivable under § 743(b) was eliminated. A similar analysis was applied in Woodhall v. Commissioner, 454 F.2d 226 (9th Cir.1972), involving the sale of a partnership interest received from a decedent partner in a situation in which the partnership held unrealized receivables at the time of the partner's death.

4.   PAYMENTS OR DISTRIBUTIONS

When a general partner dies, under state law the partnership is dissolved, and his estate is entitled to distribution of his capital account, unless the partnership agreement provides otherwise. Limited liability company agreements may call for a liquidation distribution to the successor in interest of a deceased limited liability company member. If such a liquidating distribution is made, the general rules governing liquidating distributions under §§ 731–736 and 751(b) control. See Section 2. Of course, due to the change in basis to fair market value under § 1014, gain or loss generally will not be recognized under § 731(a), even if the entire distribution is in cash. Nevertheless, §§ 736(a) and 751(b) may result in ordinary income treatment.

4.11.   *Cash Payments*

4.1.1.   *Initial Classification of Payments*

Partnership agreements often provide that the estate of a deceased partner will receive a percentage of the profits for several years or a fixed annual amount, or some combination of the various alternatives. These payments are in liquidation of the decedent's interest in the partnership assets and goodwill, or in the nature of mutual insurance. These classification problems are identical with those considered earlier on the retirement of a partner, and the Subchapter K solution is the same. Section 736(a), discussed in Section 2, classifies these payments between those considered as in exchange for the estate's interest in partnership property and those considered to be the estate's distributive share of partnership income or a guaranteed payment to the estate. See Treas. Regs. §§ 1.736–1(a)(2) and 1.736–1(b). While a payment made for a decedent's share of substantially appreciated inventory is treated as a § 736(b) distribution, § 751(b) applies and results in ordinary income unless basis adjustments under §§ 754 and 743(b) have been made.

4.1.2.   *Income in Respect of a Decedent*

Section 753 provides that the amounts classified under § 736(a) are considered income in respect of a decedent under § 691. The regulations also include as § 691 income any amounts paid by a third party in exchange for rights to future partnership § 736(a) payments. Treas. Reg. § 1.753–1(a). *Quick's Trust* and *Woodhall*, supra, indicate that the statutory reference to § 736(a) in § 753 is not exclusive.

If the estate receives § 736(a) payments that are treated as income in respect of a decedent, Treas. Reg. § 1.742–1 requires any § 1014 basis of the partnership interest to be reduced by the amount of the payments, thus preventing the estate from realizing a loss equal to the amount of the § 736(a) payments, i.e., the difference between any § 1014 basis and the § 736(b) payments.

The income in respect of a decedent treatment provided by § 753 implies that the value of the § 736(a) payments, e.g., for unrealized receivables and goodwill in the absence of an agreement in the case of a general partner in a partnership in which capital is not a material income producing factor, will be subject to estate tax and, consequently, will qualify for the deduction under § 691 for estate tax paid. See Rev.Rul. 71–507, 1971–2 C.B. 331.

Only the value of the decedent's distributive share as of the date of death is an asset of the estate for estate tax purposes. The regulations provide that the amount of the estate's distributive share included in its income will be treated as income in respect of a decedent. Treas. Reg. § 1.753–1(b).

4.2.   *Property Distributions*

Property distributions to an estate in liquidation of the interest of a deceased partner are subject to the general rules governing recognition of gain or loss by the distributee, the basis of property distributed, and the disposition of the property by the distributee discussed in Section 2. The § 1014 date of death value basis of the partnership interest is used in assigning basis to the distributed property under § 732(b) and (c).

5.   TREATMENT OF REMAINING PARTNERS

The rules applicable to the treatment of the remaining partners on the retirement of a partner are equally applicable to the liquidation of a deceased partner's interest. These rules are discussed in Section 3.

If as a result of an election under § 754, the partnership must adjust the bases of the partnership assets, the formula of § 734(b) does not provide the correct result. The gain or loss to the estate is affected by the application of § 1014(a). To the extent that § 1014 produces a step-up in basis for the estate, gain that would otherwise be recognized on a liquidating distribution of cash is reduced pro tanto and hence the premise of the formula of § 734(b) is not satisfied. Conversely, if basis is stepped down, loss that otherwise would be recognized is eliminated. This problem is corrected to some extent by the regulations in allowing any unused special basis adjustment the estate may have by virtue of § 743(b) or 732(d) to shift to the remaining assets for the benefit of the remaining partners. Treas. Reg. § 1.734–2(b)(1). But this is not a principled compensation and the results are not theoretically correct.

In Estate of Skaggs v. Commissioner, 672 F.2d 756 (9th Cir.1982), the surviving partner of a husband-wife partnership, who inherited the deceased partner's interest, unsuccessfully asserted that the partnership automatically terminated upon the death of the deceased partner and that under § 1014 the basis of an undivided one-half of the partnership's assets should be increased to the fair market value on the date of death. The court found that the partnership continued for purposes of paying its debts and winding up its affairs, and that absent a valid § 754 election, no basis adjustment was allowable with respect to the partnership assets. For the possibility of filing a § 754 election on an amended partnership return for the year of the partner's death on facts similar to *Estate of Skaggs*, see Rev.Rul. 86–139, 1986–2 C.B. 95.

*

PART II

ELECTIVE PASSTHROUGH TAX TREATMENT

CHAPTER 10

S CORPORATIONS

INTERNAL REVENUE CODE: Sections 1361–1378.

SECTION 1. INTRODUCTION

Overview. Subchapter S was enacted in 1958 to make it possible for "businesses to select the form of business organization desired, without the necessity of taking into account major differences in tax consequence." S.Rep. No. 85–1983, 85th Cong., 2d Sess. 87 (1958). As originally enacted, Subchapter S status was available only for corporations that had no more than ten individual shareholders. Although shareholders were taxed on undistributed corporate profits in addition to actual dividend distributions, except for capital gains, the character of items did not pass through to the shareholders as in the case of partnerships. If the corporation had a net operating loss, it also passed through to stockholders. A stockholder's stock basis was increased by undistributed taxable income and decreased by pass-through net operating losses. An electing corporation was not subject to tax unless it realized extraordinary capital gains.[1]

In 1969 the Treasury Department, in conjunction with the Tax Section of the American Bar Association, proposed revising Subchapter S to conform more closely to the complete pass-through model of the partnership rules.[2] To alleviate problems caused by the hybrid nature of the S corpora-

---

1. The corporate level tax was designed to discourage a "one-shot" election by a corporation anticipating gain on the disposition of capital (or § 1231) assets.

2. U.S. Treasury Dept. Tax Reform Studies and Proposals, House Ways and Means Committee and Senate Finance Committee, 91st Cong., 1st Sess. (1969).

tion under then current law, "not quite a corporation and not quite a partnership," the Treasury study recommended adoption of complete pass-through taxation of the entity's tax-significant items under the partnership rules plus a number of other changes to simplify Subchapter S. The 1969 proposal was adopted, generally intact, in 1982. Thus, while the detailed rules of Subchapter S have metamorphosed over the years, the fundamental purpose of Subchapter S—to eliminate the corporation as a taxable entity and provide a system under which the operating profits of qualifying corporations are taxed directly to the shareholders—remains unchanged.[3]

Prior to the mid–1980's, only a relatively small number of corporations elected Subchapter S status. One reason was that prior to 1982, Subchapter S status could not be maintained if more than 20 percent of the corporation's gross receipts were derived from passive investments such as interest, dividends, rents and royalties. In many other cases, closely held corporations simply did not show a profit after paying shareholder-employees salaries. The election was mostly valuable during the early years of a venture when the corporation produced losses that could be passed through to the stockholders.

After 1986, however, Subchapter S elections by eligible corporations became vastly more popular than previously. This result occurred because, taking into account the double taxation of distributed earnings of a C corporation, the maximum effective rate of taxation of distributed C corporation income in 1987 was significantly higher than on S corporation income, 52.4 percent for C corporation shareholders compared to 28 percent for S corporation shareholders. This fact, coupled with the reduction of preferential treatment accorded long-term capital gains in the 1986 Act, resulted in the pass-through entity being the preferred form of business organization from a tax perspective.[4] But subsequent changes in the tax rate schedules, the reemergence of a significant capital gains preference, and the widespread enactment by states of limited liability company statutes may reduce the attractiveness of S corporations. In the 1990s, virtually every state enacted a limited liability company (LLC) statute. Generally, LLCs are formed so as to be taxed as partnerships, even though

---

3. Technical aspects of Subchapter S in all likelihood will continue to evolve.

4. For 1986 24.1 percent of all corporations, 826,214 out of 3,428,515 corporations, filed S corporation returns. Staff of the Joint Committee on Taxation, Present Laws and Proposals Relating to Subchapter S Corporations and Home Office Deductions, p.16 (JCS–16–95, May 24, 1995). By 2002, the percentage of corporations electing S status had climbed to 58.9 percent, representing approximately 3.2 million S corporations out of approximately 5.3 million total corpora-

tions. Kelly Luttrell, S Corporation Returns, 2002, 24 Statistics of Income Bulletin 59 (Spring 2005). In recent years most new S corporation elections are by corporations engaged in professional, technical, scientific, and construction businesses, but the largest single business sector represented is wholesale and retail trade. In any event, S corporations, are primarily small enterprises. The 59 percent of all corporations electing S status held approximately 4 percent of all corporate assets and collected less than 20 percent of the gross receipts for all corporations in 2002. Id.

they confer limited liability on every member. From both the tax and nontax points of view, the LLC is a more flexible form of business organization than a corporation that makes a Subchapter S election. Nevertheless, whether a partnership, an S corporation, or a limited liability company that is taxed as a partnership is the more desirable form depends on a broad range of factors.

The Basic Framework of Subchapter S. To be eligible to make a Subchapter S election, a corporation must meet a number of requirements, including limitations on the number and identity of its shareholders. First, an electing corporation, referred to as an "S corporation," may have no more than 100 stockholders. I.R.C. § 1361(b)(1)(A). The 100 shareholder limit is somewhat illusory, however, because § 1361(c)(1) treats as a single shareholder all of the members of a family traced to a common ancestor no more than six generations removed from the youngest family member who is a shareholder. Qualifying stockholders include only individuals, grantor trusts, voting trusts, "qualified Subchapter S trusts" (QSSTs), "electing small business trusts," tax exempt charitable organizations, and certain retirement pension trusts. It cannot have a stockholder who is a nonresident alien individual, a corporation (other than a tax exempt charitable organization), partnership, or LLC, and it may issue only one class of stock (although there is an exception for stock that varies in voting rights). I.R.C. § 1361(b) and (c). An S corporation may hold stock in a controlled subsidiary corporation, but may not be a subsidiary of another corporation unless it is 100 percent owned by a parent S corporation that has elected to treat the subsidiary, in effect, as an operating division rather than a separate corporation. I.R.C. § 1361(b)(3).

S corporation status may be elected only with the consent of all stockholders at the time the election is filed. An election is effective on the first day of the taxable year following the filing of the election, except that an election filed within the first two and one-half months of the taxable year may be retroactive to the first day of the taxable year. In the latter case, the corporation must have satisfied all of the requirements for S corporation status since the first day of the taxable year. I.R.C. § 1362(b). Once made, an election continues in effect until it is revoked by a majority of the stockholders, the corporation ceases to meet the qualifications as an S corporation, or the corporation has accumulated earnings and profits[5] and earns passive investment income in excess of 25 percent of gross receipts for three consecutive taxable years. I.R.C. § 1362(d).

Generally an S corporation is not subject to corporate tax. I.R.C. § 1363(a). There are two exceptions. Under § 1374, S corporations are taxable on certain gain recognized on disposition of appreciated assets or income items generated while the corporation was a C corporation, or acquired from a C corporation in a nonrecognition transaction. In addition, under § 1375, an S corporation with accumulated earnings and profits is

---

5. A corporation will accumulate earnings and profits only in years it is a C corporation. Thus, this restriction does not apply to a corporation that has no tax history as a C corporation.

taxable at regular corporate rates to the extent that passive investment income exceeds 25 percent of its gross receipts.

S corporation items of income, loss or deduction are passed through the entity to the stockholders, and retain their character in the stockholder's hands, in the same manner that partnership items are passed through to partners under Subchapter K. I.R.C. § 1366. Thus each item of income or deduction that may affect stockholders differently must be separately stated and reported to the stockholders. For example, tax exempt interest income retains its exemption under § 103, and interest expense must be categorized under the complex interest allocation rules to determine its deductibility by the individual stockholders. Each stockholder reports the item on his return as if the item were derived by the stockholder directly. The character of items, such as capital gain, is based on the character of income at the corporate level. The stockholder's basis in S corporation stock is increased for income items and decreased for deduction or loss items passed through to the stockholder from the corporation. I.R.C. § 1367. As under the partnership model, the stockholder's deductible loss is limited to the stockholder's basis in stock, but S corporation shareholders who lend money to the corporation may deduct losses up to their basis in the debt of the S corporation as well. I.R.C. § 1366(d)(1).

Since S corporation income is taxed to the stockholders when realized by the corporation, subsequent distributions of the previously taxed income are received by stockholders without additional tax. I.R.C. § 1368. Distributions reduce the stockholder's basis in stock of the corporation. Distributions in excess of basis result in recognition of capital gain.

A second tier of distribution rules applies to an S corporation that has accumulated earnings and profits from taxable years in which it was a C corporation. The corporation must maintain an "accumulated adjustments account" that reflects net corporate income items that have been passed through to stockholders. Distributions to the extent of this accumulated adjustments account are received by the stockholders without tax. I.R.C. § 1368(b). To the extent that distributions exceed the accumulated adjustments account, the distributions are treated as distributions of earnings and profits, to the extent thereof, and are taxed to the stockholders as dividends. Thus a "double" tax pattern is preserved for earnings originally generated in a C corporation. Any further distributions are received by the stockholders as a reduction of basis, then as capital gain to the extent that a distribution exceeds the recipient stockholder's basis.

Comparison of S Corporations and Partnerships (Including LLCs). Although Subchapter S in general adopts the partnership model for taxing S corporations, there are significant differences between the taxation of S corporations and partnerships that affect a taxpayer's choice between the two entities. (Since an LLC almost always will elect to be taxed as a partnership, the following considerations are applicable to LLCs as well.) As discussed previously, beneficial ownership of an S corporation nominally is limited to 100 stockholders, while there is no limit on the number of persons who may be partners in a partnership. Nor is there any restriction upon the types of entities that may be partners. The partnership form provides a significant advantage in the case of leveraged investments if losses are anticipated. Partners are allowed to include their shares of partnership debt in the bases of their partnership interests, which in turn allows partners to deduct partnership losses attributable to partnership level debt. In contrast, the stockholder's basis in Subchapter S stock or debt is limited to the stockholder's actual investment in the corporation. This limitation also means that while untaxed entity level cash, e.g., from a refinancing, can be distributed by a partnership free of tax, the same distribution by an S corporation may trigger gain recognition. For these reasons, S corporations have not been used for leveraged investments such as real estate.

Subchapter S also differs from Subchapter K in its treatment of distributions of appreciated property. An S corporation is required by §§ 311(b) and 336 to recognize gain on a distribution of appreciated property to stockholders. The recognized gain is passed through to the stockholders, who increase the basis of their stock accordingly. The distributee stockholder obtains a fair market value basis in the distributed property, and decreases the basis of the S corporation stock by the same amount. Subject to some exceptions, distributions of appreciated property by a partnership generally do not trigger recognition of gain. Instead, the distributee partner takes the partnership's basis in the property and recognition of gain is deferred until the distributee disposes of the property. The Code is thus not completely neutral as to the choice between a Subchapter S corporation and a partnership.

As the following material indicates, the tax treatment of S corporations that have always been S corporations is relatively straight-forward. Technical complexities, of course, are encountered. But for such corporations, the governing provisions are not particularly difficult either in concept or in practice. Section 3 discusses Subchapter S in the context of a corporation that was formed as an S corporation and never changed that status.

While a corporation that has a C corporation history can elect S corporation status, the rules governing such corporations are much more complex than those applicable to S corporations with no C corporation history. These rules are discussed in Section 4.

Subchapter S represents one way of integrating the corporate and personal income taxes. At the end of Section 3, consider whether the S corporation regime can be applied to corporations such as General Motors or Exxon. At the end of Section 4, consider whether the rules adopted for corporations with a C corporation history can or should be used as transition rules to a fully integrated corporate and individual tax system.

SECTION 2.   ELIGIBILITY, ELECTION AND TERMINATION

A.   STOCKHOLDER RULES

INTERNAL REVENUE CODE: Section 1361(b)(1), (c)(1)–(3), (d), (e).

REGULATIONS: Section 1.1361–1(e), (f).

Section 1361(b)(1) requires that the electing corporation have no more than 100 stockholders (treating as a single shareholder all of the members of a family traced to a common ancestor no more than six generations removed from the youngest family member who is a shareholder) and that it have no stockholder who is not an individual, an estate, a grantor trust, a "qualified Subchapter S trust" (QSST), an "electing small business trust," a tax exempt charitable organization, or a qualified retirement pension trust. When stock is held by a nominee, guardian, or custodian, the beneficial owner is treated as the shareholder. Treas. Reg. § 1.1361–1(e). A corporation, partnership, or LLC may not be a shareholder in an S corporation other than as a nominee for the beneficial owner. See Treas. Reg. § 1.1361–1(e)(1).

Section 1361(c)(2) permits five types of domestic trusts as stockholders of an S corporation: trusts treated as owned by a United States citizen or resident (grantor trusts), grantor trusts that survive the death of the grantor (but only for a limited period), testamentary trusts (again only for a limited period), voting trusts, and "electing small business trusts" (as defined in § 1361(e)). Section 1361(d) further provides that a "qualified Subchapter S trust" (QSST), a trust with a single income beneficiary who has elected to be treated as the owner of S corporation stock held by the trust, is a qualified shareholder; S corporation items of income and loss pass through the trust to the beneficiary. With the exception of these permitted trusts, trusts are ineligible shareholders.

Is any significant policy goal served by limiting the number of shareholders permitted in an S corporation? Consider the following Revenue Ruling, which was promulgated when the ceiling was thirty-five shareholders.

Revenue Ruling 94–43

1994–2 C.B. 198.

In Rev. Rul. 77–220, 1977–1 C.B. 263, thirty unrelated individuals entered into the joint operation of a single business. The individuals divided into three equal groups of ten individuals and each group formed a separate corporation. The three corporations then organized a partnership for the joint operation of the business. The principal purpose for forming three separate corporations instead of one corporation was to avoid the 10 shareholder limitation of § 1371 of the Internal Revenue Code of 1954 (the predecessor of § 1361) and thereby allow the corporations to elect to be treated as S corporations under Subchapter S.

Rev. Rul. 77–220 concluded that the three corporations should be considered to be a single corporation, solely for purposes of making the election, because the principal purpose for organizing the separate corporations was to make the election. Under this approach, there would be 30 shareholders in one corporation and the election made by this corporation would not be valid because the 10 shareholder limitation would be violated.

The Service has reconsidered Rev. Rul. 77–220 and concluded that the election of the separate corporations should be respected. The purpose of the number of shareholders requirement is to restrict S corporation status to corporations with a limited number of shareholders so as to obtain administrative simplicity in the administration of the corporation's tax affairs. In this context, administrative simplicity is not affected by the corporation's participation in a partnership with other S corporation partners; nor should a shareholder of one S corporation be considered a shareholder of another S corporation because the S corporations are partners in a partnership. Thus, the fact that several S corporations are partners in a single partnership does not increase the administrative complexity at the S corporation level. As a result, the purpose of the number of shareholders requirement is not avoided by the structure in Rev. Rul. 77–220 and, therefore, the election of the corporations should be respected.

ILLUSTRATIVE MATERIAL

1.   FAMILY MEMBERS AS SHAREHOLDERS

1.1.   *Husband and Wife Shareholders*

In counting the number of stockholders, a husband and wife (and their respective estates) are treated as a single stockholder regardless of the form of ownership in which the stock is held. I.R.C. § 1361(c)(1)(A)(i). Under § 1361(b)(1)(C) an S corporation may not have a nonresident alien stockholder. In Ward v. United States, 661 F.2d 226 (Ct.Cl.1981), a corporation's Subchapter S election was held invalid because the taxpayer's nonresident alien wife was the beneficial owner of the corporation's stock under community property laws.

1.2.   *Family Members*

Prior to 2004, each family member, other than husband and wife, counted as a separate shareholder. In 2004, § 1361(c)(1) was amended to provide that all of the members of a family traced to a common ancestor no more than six generations removed from the youngest family member who is a shareholder will be treated as a single shareholder. See I.R.C. § 1361(c)(1)(B). As a result of this rule, hundreds of members of a family might count as a single shareholder, and thousands of individuals who are members of up to 100 families might own an S corporation

2.   ESTATES AND TRUSTS AS ELIGIBLE STOCKHOLDERS

2.1.   *General*

Section 1361 permits the estate of a deceased stockholder, the estate of an individual in bankruptcy, and certain trusts, including "grantor trusts" if the grantor is a United States citizen or resident, voting trusts, and, for a limited period of time, testamentary trusts to be S corporation stockholders. In the case of a grantor trust, the grantor is treated as the stockholder and in the case of voting trusts, each beneficiary of the trust is treated as a stockholder. See generally Treas. Reg. § 1.1361–1(h)(1)(i), (v). Rev. Rul. 92–73, 1992–2 C.B. 224, held that a trust qualified as an individual retirement account is not a permitted Subchapter S corporation shareholder because its income is not currently taxed to the beneficiary. Mourad v. Commissioner, 387 F.3d 27 (1st Cir. 2004), aff'g 121 T.C. 1 (2003), held that the filing of a bankruptcy petition by an S corporation for a Chapter 11 plan of reorganization neither terminates an S election nor creates a separate taxable entity. Accordingly, even though an independent trustee was appointed, the shareholder remained liable for the taxes on the sale of the S corporation's principal assets by the trustee.

A testamentary trust to which stock of an S corporation has been transferred is an eligible S corporation stockholder for only two years following the day on which the stock is transferred. I.R.C. § 1361(c)(2)(A)(iii). Similarly, under § 1361(c)(2)(A), a grantor trust may continue as an S corporation stockholder for 60 days following the death of the grantor or, if the corpus of the trust is includable in the gross estate of the grantor for estate tax purposes, the trust may continue as a stockholder for two years. Treas. Reg. § 1.1361–1(h)(1)(ii). In a community property state, the grantor trust of a decedent is treated as the S corporation shareholder only for that portion of the trust that is included in the decedent's gross estate. The surviving spouse is treated as the shareholder of the remaining portion of the S corporation stock. Treas. Reg. § 1.1361–1(h)(3)(i)(B). If grantor trust status terminates for some reason other than the death of the grantor—for example, if the grantor relinquishes the powers that make the trust a grantor trust—the trust becomes an ineligible stockholder and the corporation's S corporation status is terminated immediately.

There is no statutory limit on the length of time that an estate may remain a qualified stockholder. However, Old Virginia Brick Co. v. Commissioner, 367 F.2d 276 (4th Cir.1966), held that an estate that was one of the stockholders of an S corporation and which was kept open substantially beyond the period necessary for the performance of administrative duties became in effect an ineligible testamentary trust; accordingly the corporation was disqualified from S corporation status.[6] But Rev. Rul. 76–23, 1976–1 C.B. 264, allowed retention of S corporation stock by an estate for purposes of the ten year installment payment of estate taxes in § 6166.

2.2. *Qualified Subchapter S Trusts*

Section 1361(d) permits a "qualified Subchapter S trust" (QSST) to be an S corporation stockholder. A QSST is a trust that, by its terms, has only one current income beneficiary who will be the sole income beneficiary

---

6. See also Treas. Reg. § 1.641(b)–3(a) (an estate is deemed terminated for federal tax purposes after the expiration of a reason-able period for the performance by the executor of the duties of administration).

during the beneficiary's life or for the term of the trust.[7] I.R.C. § 1361(d)(3). See Rev. Rul. 93–31, 1993–1 C.B. 186 (separate and independent share of a trust within the meaning of § 663(c) cannot be a QSST if there is any possibility, however remote, that during the income beneficiary's lifetime the corpus will be distributed to someone other than the income beneficiary). To avoid any possibility of splitting S corporation income and deductions between the trust and the beneficiary, a QSST is an eligible stockholder only if the beneficiary elects in effect to treat the trust as a grantor trust with respect to the S corporation stock. Thus the income beneficiary is treated as the owner of the portion of the trust that consists of S corporation stock. The beneficiary is taxed on the income and receives the deductions allocable to the S corporation stock without regard to the normal rules of trust taxation. I.R.C. § 1361(d)(1)(B). See generally Treas. Reg. § 1.1361–1(j). However, gain from the sale of stock by a QSST trust is not taxable to the beneficiary of the trust; instead, the trust itself is taxed on any such gain. Treas. Reg. § 1.1361–1(j)(8).

The strict requirements of § 1361(d) apparently were designed to prevent the use of trusts to avoid the 35 shareholder limitation that was in force prior to 1996, while facilitating pass-through taxation of the trust beneficiary as the ultimate recipient of the S corporation income. In light of subsequent amendments (1) increasing the number of permitted shareholders to 100, and (2) counting as a single shareholder all of the members of a family traced to a common ancestor no more than six generations removed from the youngest family member who is a shareholder, any valid policy-based purpose for the limitations in § 1361(d) is difficult to discern.

A trust is a QSST only if a timely election is filed with the Internal Revenue Service by the beneficiary (or the beneficiary's legal representative or parent if there is no legal representative appointed). A separate election is required with respect to the stock of each S corporation owned by a QSST. Failure to file the election for a trust that becomes an S corporation stockholder will result in revocation of the corporation's status as an S corporation. See Rev. Rul. 93–79, 1993–2 C.B. 269 (retroactive judicial reformation of trust to conform to requirements for a QSST was not effective to validate S corporation election prior to reformation at a time when the trust did not qualify).

Section 1361(d)(2)(D) provides that an election to be a QSST is retroactively effective for the two month and fifteen day period preceding

---

7. In Rev. Rul. 92–64, 1992–2 C.B. 214, the QSST provided for distributions of trust income in December and June of each year. The income beneficiary died on May 1. The ruling allowed distributions of trust income accumulated between the last distribution and the date of the beneficiary's death to be made to either the deceased beneficiary's estate under state law or the successor beneficiary under a provision of the trust. The Ruling concluded that after the date of death, the successor income beneficiary is the only income beneficiary of the trust, even though the estate may become entitled to a distribution.

In Rev. Rul. 92–48, 1992–1 C.B. 301, the Service ruled that a charitable remainder trust, qualified under § 664, cannot be qualified as a QSST. The ruling concluded that the scheme for the taxation of charitable remainder trusts is incompatible with the requirements of the QSST rules.

the filing of the election. See Treas. Reg. § 1.1361–1(j)(6) for the detailed procedural rules respecting the election.

If it meets the requirements, a testamentary trust or a grantor trust can continue as an eligible S corporation stockholder by electing to be a QSST. See Treas. Reg. § 1.1361–1(h)(3)(i)(B). Treas. Reg. § 1.1361–1(j)(6)(iii)(C) provides that an estate or grantor trust can elect to become a QSST at any time during the two year period of eligibility as an S corporation stockholder provided by § 1361(c)(2)(A)(ii) and (iii), but no later than the sixteen month and two day period following the date on which the testamentary or grantor trust ceases to qualify as an eligible stockholder. As of the effective date of the election, the beneficiary of the QSST becomes the eligible shareholder instead of the trust or estate. Treas. Reg. § 1.1361–1(h)(3)(i)(B) & (D).

2.3. *Electing Small Business Trusts*

Under § 1361(e), a trust may elect to be a "small business trust" (ESBT) if the only current beneficiaries of the trust are individuals, estates eligible to own S corporation stock, and tax exempt charitable organizations, and none of the beneficiaries has purchased the interest in the trust.

The election is made by the trustee of the trust. Treas. Reg. § 1.1361–1(m)(2). If an election is made, the portion of the trust consisting of the S corporation stock is treated as a separate trust and trust income attributable to the S corporation stock, including gain on the sale of the stock, is taxed to the trust at the highest individual rate, whether or not the income is distributed. The beneficiaries, in turn, are not taxed on any trust distributions attributable to the stock. See I.R.C. § 641(c). This provision is designed to permit discretionary, or "spray" trusts to be S corporation shareholders, which may be desired by shareholders for estate planning purposes. Since each potential current beneficiary of the trust is counted against the shareholder limit, I.R.C. § 1361(c)(2)(B)(v), however, the use of this provision may conceivably result in termination of S corporation status if several trusts with a large number of beneficiaries who are not members of the same family make an election.

The literal language of § 1361(e)(1)(A)(i) appears to permit individuals as beneficiaries of an ESBT without qualification. However, § 1361(c)(2)(B)(v) states that each potential current beneficiary of an electing small business trust shall be treated as a shareholder of the S corporation. Treas. Reg. § 1.1361–1(m)(4)(i) treats each potential income current beneficiary of an ESBT as a shareholder of the corporation, and Treas. Reg. § 1.1361–1(m)(1)(ii)(D) warns that if a nonresident alien is a potential current income beneficiary of an ESBT, the corporation's S election will be terminated.

Treas. Reg. § 1.1361–1(m) contains specific rules regarding the identification of the beneficiaries of an ESBT. A person whose entitlement to a distribution is contingent on a specified event or a specified time is not treated as a current beneficiary until occurrence of the event or passage of the time. Treas. Reg. § 1.1361–1(m)(4)(v). A person in whose favor a power of appointment may be exercised is not counted as a current beneficiary until the power is exercised. Treas. Reg. § 1.1361–1(m)(1)(ii)(C). A trust that is a beneficiary of an ESBT is not itself treated as a beneficiary of the ESBT.[8] Instead, the current income beneficiaries of the beneficiary trust are treated as beneficiaries of the ESBT. Treas. Reg. § 1.1361–1(m)(1)(ii)(B). However, a distributee trust that is entitled to a distribution of income or principal from an ESBT must itself be qualified to be a shareholder of an S corporation or the Subchapter S election will terminate. Treas. Reg. § 1.1361–1(m)(4)(iv)(B).

Treas. Reg. § 1.1361–1(m)(2)(iv) provides that a grantor trust may elect to be an ESBT, if it qualifies, after the death of the person treated as the owner of the trust. Treas. Reg. § 1.1361–1(j)(12) provides that a QSST may convert to an ESBT. Treas. Reg. § 1.1361–1(m)(7) provides that an electing small business trust may convert to a QSST. Thus, a trust with a single current beneficiary that becomes a spray trust for multiple beneficiaries upon the death of the first beneficiary can successively be a QSST and then an ESBT.

3. POLICY ASPECTS OF THE 100 SHAREHOLDER LIMITATION

The legislative history of the Subchapter S Revision Act of 1982, which increased the number of permitted shareholders from 10 to 35, indicated that the 35 stockholder limit was intended to correspond to the private placement exemption of federal securities law.[9] When the ceiling on the number of shareholders was increased from 35 to 75 in 1996, the reason given was to "facilitate corporate ownership by additional family members, employees and capital investors." H.R. Rep. No. 104–586, 104th Cong., 2d Sess. 82 (1996). When in 2004 the ceiling was increased to 100 shareholders, treating as a single shareholder all of the members of a family traced to a common ancestor no more than six generations removed from the youngest family member who is a shareholder, the stated reason was to "modernize the S corporation rules and eliminate undue restrictions on S corporations in order to expand the application of the S corporation provisions so that more corporations and their shareholders will be able to enjoy the benefits of subchapter S status." H.R. Rep. No. 108–548, 108th Cong, 2d Sess. (2004). There is, however, no inherent tax policy rationale for limiting pass through tax treatment to any particular number of stockholders, as long as the corporation is not publicly traded.[10] If there are too many stockholders, however, administrative problems may arise because audits are conducted and tax deficiencies are assessed and collected at the shareholder level. Although limiting the number of stockholders

---

8. A trust that is the beneficiary of an ESBT that is a charitable organization qualified to be an S Corporation shareholder is treated as a beneficiary of the ESBT. Treas. Reg. § 1.1361–1(m)(1)(ii)(B).

9. S.Rep. No. 97–640, 97th Cong. 2d Sess. 7 (1982).

10. Section 7704, which treats any partnership that is publicly traded as an association, subject to the corporate income tax, evidences a Congressional intent that pass-through taxation is not appropriate for publicly traded businesses regardless of the form of organization.

allowed to an S corporation reduces the complexity of accounting for allocations of corporate items to the stockholders, experience with Subchapter K demonstrates that pass-through accounting on a large scale is possible.

4.   TAX EXEMPT ENTITIES AS ELIGIBLE SHAREHOLDERS

Section 1361(c)(6) permits tax-exempt charities under § 501(c)(3) and tax-exempt employee benefit trusts under § 401(a) as shareholders of an S corporation. This provision allows an Employee Stock Ownership Plan (ESOP) to hold the stock of an S corporation. An ESOP is designed to invest primarily in securities of the employer of the beneficiaries of the plan. See I.R.C. § 409. As a consequence, S corporation income that is passed-through to the ESOP is not subject to tax until the income is withdrawn from the ESOP by employees on retirement. An ESOP as the holder of S corporation stock (which may constitute 100 percent of the stock) allows deferral of unlimited amounts of income on behalf of the employees of an S corporation. See Simmons and DeAngelis, ESOP–Owned Subchapter S Corporations: A Mistake in Need of a Fix, 82 Tax Notes 1325 (1999).

Section 409(p) limits the use of an ESOP to defer S corporation income to an ESOP that provides broad coverage to employees. Qualification as an ESOP for a plan that holds S corporation stock requires that benefits do not accrue to a "disqualified person," defined as a person who is entitled to the benefit of 10 percent or more of the shares of the S corporation (or 20 percent of the shares of such person and members of the person's family) where disqualified persons own 50 percent or more of the total shares of the stock of the S corporation (including portions of stock attributed to disqualified persons from the ESOP). I.R.C. § 409(p)(3) and (4). In order to avoid an end-run around these limitations with devices to provide additional compensation to highly compensated employees and managers, § 409(p)(5) provides that a person's shares in an S corporation include "synthetic equity," which is a right to receive stock of the S corporation in the future, or a right to compensation based on the value of S corporation stock. Temp. Reg. § 1.409(p)–1T, and Prop. Reg. § 1.409(p)–1 (2003), expand the definition of synthetic equity to include nonqualified deferred compensation plans and rights to acquire stock in related entities.

B.   CORPORATE ELIGIBILITY

INTERNAL REVENUE CODE: Section 1361(a),(b)(1)(D), (b)(2)–(3), (c)(4).

REGULATIONS: Sections 1.1361–1(b), (*l*).

Only a domestic corporation may elect to be an S corporation. A controlled subsidiary of an S corporation cannot itself make an S election because its parent corporation is an ineligible shareholder. Thus, the subsidiary is a C corporation. If, however, the subsidiary is wholly owned by the parent S corporation and the subsidiary would be eligible to be an S corporation if the stock of the corporation were held directly by the shareholders of its parent S corporation, § 1361(b)(3) allows the parent S corporation to elect to ignore the separate existence of its subsidiary for tax purposes and to treat its subsidiary's assets, liabilities, income, and deduction items as its own.

Certain corporations are ineligible for S corporation status. These include small (but not large) banks, insurance companies, and other corporations subject to a special tax regime. I.R.C. § 1362(b)(2).

Under § 1361(b)(1)(D), an S corporation is allowed to have only one class of stock. The purpose of this requirement is to avoid accounting difficulties that would arise if the corporation were permitted to create different interests in income and loss in different classes of stock. Thus, unlike partnerships, S corporations are not allowed to make special allocations of income and loss among S corporation stockholders.

Section 1361(c)(4) allows differences in voting rights without violating the one-class-of-stock rule so long as the outstanding shares are identical with respect to the rights of the holders in the profits and in the assets of the corporation. The existence of debt of an S corporation that might be classified as equity creates a risk that the re-classified equity interests will be treated as a prohibited second class of stock. To reduce this risk, § 1361(c)(5) provides a safe-harbor in which certain "straight debt" will not be considered a second class of stock.

ILLUSTRATIVE MATERIAL

1.   ONE CLASS OF STOCK

1.1.   *General*

Treas. Reg. § 1.1361–1(*l*)(1) provides that a corporation has one class of stock if all of the outstanding shares of stock of the corporation confer identical rights to current distributions and liquidation proceeds. Differences in voting rights are disregarded. The determination of whether stock possesses identical distribution and liquidation rights is made under the formal governing provisions applicable to the corporation, including state law, the corporate charter, articles of incorporation, bylaws, and binding agreements relating to distributions and liquidation proceeds. Treas. Reg. § 1.1361–1(*l*)(2)(i). Contractual arrangements, such as a lease or a loan, will not be treated as a binding agreement regarding distributions or liquidation proceeds, and thus not a governing instrument, unless the principal purpose of the agreement is to circumvent the one class of stock requirement. Treas. Reg. § 1.1361–1(*l*)(2)(i) provides that "distributions * * * that differ with respect to either timing or amount are to be given appropriate tax effect in accordance with the facts and circumstances." Treas. Reg. § 1.1361–1(*l*)(2)(vi), Ex. (3)–(5), indicates that an agreement (that is not included in the corporate governing provisions) that results in payments to shareholder-employees of excessive compensation that are not allowed as a deduction, makes fringe benefits available to employee-shareholders, or provides below market-rate loans to shareholders, will not be treated as creating a second class of stock if the arrangement is not entered into to circumvent the one class of stock requirement.

Historically, the single class of stock limitation had been interpreted strictly. In Paige v. United States, 580 F.2d 960 (9th Cir.1978), a second class of stock was created as a result of conditions imposed by the California Department of Corporations on stock held by stockholders transferring property to the corporation. Similar conditions were not imposed on stockholders who had transferred cash to the corporation. Among the conditions were restrictions preventing dividend or liquidation distributions to the property stockholders until the cash stockholders received cumulative dividends equal to 5 percent of the purchase price. The result in *Paige* has been incorporated in Treas. Reg. § 1.1361–1(*l*)(2)(vi), Ex. (1).

Treas. Reg. § 1.1361–1(*l*)(2)(i) refers to "outstanding shares of stock" for purposes of the one-class of stock rules, and Treas. Reg. § 1.1371–1(*l*)(3) provides that except as otherwise provided (for restricted stock, deferred compensation plans, and "straight-debt") all "outstanding" stock is taken into account in determining whether the single class of stock requirement has been met. This infers that unissued or treasury stock of a different class than the outstanding stock should not create a second class of stock. In addition, Treas. Reg. § 1.1361–1(b)(3) provides that stock which has not been included in income by the holder under § 83 because it is substantially nonvested will not be treated as outstanding stock. However, restricted stock for which an election has been made under § 83(b) is taken into account in determining whether there is a second class of stock, but the stock will not be treated as a second class if rights to distributions and liquidation proceeds are identical to unrestricted stock. Treas. Reg. § 1.1361–1(*l*)(3). Instruments held as part of a deferred compensation plan that are not required to be taken into income by beneficiaries of the plan (e.g., stock appreciation rights) are not treated as a second class of stock. Treas. Reg. § 1.1361–1(b)(4).

1.2. *Voting Rights*

Section 1361(c)(4) allows variations in voting rights among the shares of common stock, including the issuance of nonvoting common stock, without creating a second class of stock. This provision settled an issue that also gave rise to litigation under the pre–1983 Subchapter S provisions. See e.g. Parker Oil Co. v. Commissioner, 58 T.C. 985 (1972) (Acq.) (stockholders' agreement providing that the right to vote certain shares was irrevocably granted by proxy to an unrelated third party did not create a second class of stock).

1.3. *Options*

Call options, warrants and similar instruments will be treated as a second class of stock if, under the facts and circumstances, (1) the option is substantially certain to be exercised and (2) has an exercise price substantially below the fair market value of the underlying stock on the date the option is (a) issued (unless fair market value at exercise is used), (b) transferred by a person who is an eligible shareholder to a person who is not an eligible shareholder, or (c) materially modified. Treas. Reg. § 1.1361–1(*l*)(4)(iii)(A). A safe harbor exception applies if the exercise price is at least 90 percent of the fair market value of the underlying stock on the date the option is issued, transferred to an ineligible shareholder, or modified. Treas. Reg. § 1.1361–1(*l*)(4)(iii)(C). Additional exceptions are provided for call options issued in connection with a loan to the corporation by a person regularly engaged in the business of lending, or issued to an employee or independent contractor in connection with the performance of services if the call option is nontransferable and does not have a readily ascertainable fair market value at the time the option is issued. Treas. Reg. § 1.1361–1(*l*)(4)(iii)(B).

1.4. *Debt Reclassified as Equity*

The one class of stock requirement was the subject of considerable litigation for years prior to 1983, but the straight debt safe harbor of § 1361(c)(5), enacted in 1982, has reduced the tension in this area. The Senate Finance Committee Report explained the provision as follows:

> In order to insure that the corporation's election will not terminate in certain situations where the existence of a purported debt instrument (that otherwise would be classified as stock) may not lead to tax avoidance and does not cause undue complexity, the bill provides that an instrument which is straight debt will not be treated as a second class of stock (within the meaning of sec. 1361(b)(1)(D)), and therefore cannot disqualify a Subchapter S election. For this purpose, a straight debt instrument means a written unconditional promise to pay on demand or on a specified date a sum certain in money so long as the interest rate, and payment date are fixed. For this purpose these factors are fixed if they are not contingent on the profits of the corporation, the discretion of the corporation, or other similar factors. However, the fact that the interest rate is dependent upon the prime rate or a similar factor not related to the debtor corporation will not disqualify the instrument from being treated under the safe harbor. In order for the "safe harbor" to apply, the instrument must not be convertible into stock, and must be held by a person eligible to hold Subchapter S stock.

S.Rep. No. 97–640, 97th Cong., 2d Sess. 8 (1982).

Section 1361(c)(5) was amended in 1996 to add to the list of eligible holders of straight debt "a person which is actively and regularly engaged in the business of lending money." This amendment was intended to extend the straight debt safe harbor to loans from financial institutions, even though most financial institutions are not eligible to be shareholders. The rationale for this provision is that it generally is unlikely that a loan from a financial institution in the business of lending money is a disguised equity interest.

Treas. Reg. § 1.1361–1(*l*)(5)(i) provides that for debt to qualify for the straight debt safe harbor it must be: (1) an unconditional written obligation to pay a sum certain on demand or on a specified date, that is not convertible into an equity interest; (2) held by a person or trust eligible to be an S corporation shareholder (a limitation that must be qualified by the subsequent amendment to § 1361(c)(5) permitting financial institutions to hold straight debt); and (3) neither the timing nor amount of payments of interest and principal can be contingent on the corporation's profits. Subordination of the debt to other corporate debt does not prevent its treatment as straight debt. Treas. Reg. § 1.1361–1(*l*)(5)(ii). Although instruments qualifying as straight debt are treated as debt for tax purposes, Treas. Reg. § 1.1361–1(*l*)(5)(iv) provides that the payment of an unreasonably high rate of interest may be classified as a payment that is not interest. The regulations add, however, that the payment will not be treated as creating a second class of stock.

Treas. Reg. § 1.1361–1(*l*)(4)(ii)(B)(2) provides that proportionately held debt reclassified as equity will not constitute a second class of stock. In a somewhat similar vein, Treas. Reg. § 1.1361–1(*l*)(4)(ii)(A) provides that debt reclassified as equity will not be treated as a second class of stock unless a principal purpose of issuing the instrument was to circumvent the rights to distribution or liquidation proceeds conferred by the outstanding shares of stock or to circumvent the limitations on eligible shareholders. Furthermore, unwritten advances from a shareholder that are reclassified as equity and that do not exceed $10,000 in the aggregate, are treated by the parties as debt, and are expected to be repaid within a reasonable period of time, will not be treated as a second class of stock. Treas. Reg. § 1.1361–1(*l*)(4)(ii)(B)(1). Failure of an unwritten advance to comply with the safe harbor will not create a second class unless the advance is reclassified as equity *and* a principal purpose of making the advance was to circumvent the rights to distribution or liquidation proceeds conferred by the outstanding shares of stock or to circumvent the limitations on eligible shareholders.

The potential classification of purported debt instruments as a second class of stock remains a problem if debt is convertible, held by a corporation related to a shareholder, or otherwise falls outside of the safe harbors. Treas. Reg. § 1.1361–1(*l*)(4)(iv) provides that debt convertible into equity will be treated as a second class of stock if the debt is reclassified as equity and a principal purpose of issuing the instrument was to circumvent the rights to distributions or liquidation proceeds conferred by the outstanding shares of stock or to circumvent the limitations on eligible shareholders. Convertible debt will also be classified as a second class of stock if it embodies rights equivalent to a call option that is substantially certain to be exercised and which has a conversion price that is substantially below the fair market value of the underlying stock on the date of issuance, on the date of transfer to a person who is not an eligible shareholder, or on the date of a material modification.

1.5. *Policy Analysis*

There is no strong policy or administrative reason for prohibiting S corporations from issuing nonparticipating preferred stock. In 1995, legislation that would have permitted S corporations to issue nonparticipating preferred stock was considered, but not enacted. Dividends paid with respect to such stock would have been treated as interest, deductible to the corporation, i.e., the deduction would pass through to the common shareholders and the dividends would be includable by the preferred shareholders without regard to corporate earnings. S. 758, 104th Cong., 1st Sess. § 201. See Staff of the Joint Committee on Taxation, Present Laws and Proposals Relating to Subchapter S Corporations and Home Office Deductions, p.29 (JCS–16–95, May 24, 1995).

C. S Corporation Election Procedures

Internal Revenue Code: Section 1362(a), (b), (c), and (f).

Regulations: Sections 1.1362–1, –6.

A Subchapter S election is made by the corporation, but the election is valid only if all of the stockholders file consents to this election. I.R.C. § 1362(a). After an election has been made, new stockholders are not required to consent. A stockholder individually cannot directly revoke or terminate an election, but undertaking a transaction that causes the corporation no longer to qualify for S corporation status may have that effect. See page 436.

An election made any time during the taxable year will be effective for the corporation's next succeeding taxable year. I.R.C. § 1362(b)(1)(A). Section 1362(b)(1)(B) provides for an election retroactive to the first day of the taxable year if the election is made on or before the fifteenth day of the third month of the taxable year. However, a retroactive election is effective for the taxable year in which made only if the corporation meets all of the requirements for S corporation status during the portion of the taxable year preceding the filing of the election and all of the stockholders consent to the election, including stockholders who were stockholders before the election was filed but who are no longer stockholders at the time of the election. I.R.C. § 1362(b)(2); Treas. Reg. § 1.1362–6(a)(2)(ii)(B). This requirement is intended to avoid an allocation of income and loss to pre-election stockholders who were either ineligible to hold S corporation stock or who did not consent to the election.[11] If the corporation and its stockholders were not qualified to elect S corporation status during each day of the portion of the taxable year preceding a retroactive election, the election will be effective on the first day of the next taxable year. I.R.C. § 1362(b)(3).

ILLUSTRATIVE MATERIAL

1. STOCKHOLDER CONSENTS

Section 1362(a)(2) requires the consent of all stockholders of the corporation as of the day of the election. See Kean v. Commissioner, 469

---

11. S.Rep. No. 97–640, 97th Cong., 2d Sess. 11 (1982).

F.2d 1183 (9th Cir.1972) (consent was required from the beneficial owner of stock of an electing corporation even though the person was not included on the corporate books as a stockholder of record); Cabintaxi Corp. v. Commissioner, T.C. Memo. 1994–316, aff'd, 63 F.3d 614 (7th Cir.1995) (election must be joined in by all persons who have contributed equity capital, not merely those to whom stock certificates have been issued; whether a person is a shareholder for this purpose depends on whether the person would have been required to report income from the S corporation if it were profitable and a valid election had been made). See Treas. Reg. § 1.1362–6 for procedural aspects of shareholder consents and extensions of time for filing consents.

Although husband and wife are treated as a single stockholder, Treas. Reg. § 1.1362–6(b)(2)(i) requires that both consent to the election if they own the stock as community property, tenants in common, joint tenants, or as tenants by the entirety. In Wilson v. Commissioner, 560 F.2d 687 (5th Cir.1977), the record owner of a single share of stock who lived in a community property state, held the stock as an accommodation to other stockholders. He filed a consent to the corporation's S election but his wife did not. The court held that the husband had no beneficial interest in the stock and was therefore not required to consent to the corporation's S election. Thus his wife's consent was also unnecessary.

Section 1362(f) authorizes the Commissioner to waive a defect rendering an election ineffective because all of the required shareholder consents (including QSST elections) were not obtained in a timely manner if (1) the defect was inadvertent, (2) within a reasonable period of time the corporation obtains the shareholder consents, and (3) the corporation and the shareholders all agree to report as if the S corporation had been effective originally. See also Treas. Reg. § 1.1362–6(b)(3)(iii), providing for a waiver of the timely shareholder consent requirement in certain circumstances for years prior to the amendment of § 1362(f) to deal with this problem.

2.   CORPORATE ELECTION

With respect to a newly formed corporation, it is necessary to identify the date on which the taxable year begins in order to determine whether an election has been filed on or before the fifteenth day of the third month of the taxable year. Treas. Reg. § 1.1362–6(a)(2)(ii)(C) provides that the taxable year of a new corporation begins on the date the corporation has stockholders, acquires assets, or begins doing business, whichever is the first to occur. See Bone v. Commissioner, 52 T.C. 913 (1969) (first taxable year had begun when the corporation acquired assets and engaged in business even though no stock had been issued to stockholders; under state law the issuance of stock was not a prerequisite to corporate existence).

Treas. Reg. § 1.1362–6(a)(2)(ii)(C) provides that a month is measured from the first day of the corporation's taxable year to the day preceding the same numerical date of the following month, or the last day of the month if there is no corresponding date in the succeeding month. Treas. Reg. § 1.1362–6(a)(2)(iii), Ex. (1), promulgated before the 1996 amendments to

§ 1362(f), indicates that an election filed before the corporation begins its first taxable year will not be valid. Presumably, the 1996 amendments to § 1362(f) now permit the Service to treat such a premature election as an effective election.

Section 1362(b)(5) permits the Commissioner to waive a late election for "reasonable cause." Rev.Proc. 98–55, 1998–2 C.B. 643, provides detailed procedures for seeking relief from a late election under § 1362(b)(5). If the only defect was a late filed Form 2553 (the corporate election itself) and the due date for the first corporate tax return (excluding extensions) has not passed, relief is virtually automatic if the election is filed within twelve months of the original due date and there was reasonable cause for the failure to file a timely S Corporation election. Otherwise, a private letter ruling seeking relief under § 1362(b)(5) must be requested.

Under Rev.Proc. 97–48, 1997–2 C.B. 521, later is better. Rev.Proc. 97–48 provides automatic relief for late filed elections that are made at least six months after the date on which the corporation filed its tax return for the first year the corporation intended to be treated as an S corporation. Automatic relief is provided under Rev.Proc. 97–48 if the corporation fails to qualify as an S corporation because its election was not timely, the corporation and all of its shareholders reported their income consistent with S corporation status for the year in which the election should have been made and for all subsequent years. Automatic relief is available to the corporation and its shareholders even where the Internal Revenue Service has notified the corporation of an invalid election and has indicated that the corporation must file as a C corporation, as long as the statute of limitations has not lapsed with respect to either the corporation or any of its shareholders for years that the corporation intended to be treated as an S corporation. In order to seek automatic relief from a late filed election, the election must be signed by a corporate officer and all persons who were shareholders during the period the corporation is to be treated as an S corporation. The corporation and the shareholders must certify that returns were filed consistent with S corporation status, or in the case of a corporation notified by the Service that its S status in invalid, the corporation and shareholders must agree to amend their returns to reflect S corporation status.

Rev. Proc. 2003–43, 2003–1 C.B. 998, provides a simplified procedure for relief from late Subchapter S elections, QSST elections, and Electing Small Business Trust elections. Relief is available if the request is filed within 24 months of the original due date of the election and there is a showing that a late S Corporation election was due to reasonable cause, or the failure to make a valid S Corporation election, an inadvertent termination of an S Corporation election, or failure to make a timely ESBT or QSST election was inadvertent. In addition to other requirements, the application for relief must be filed no later than six months after the due date of a tax return for the year of the election, and all shareholders must report their taxes consistent with a valid election. If the conditions for relief under Rev. Proc. 2003–23 are not met, the taxpayer may seek relief through application for a private letter ruling.

D.   REVOCATION OR TERMINATION OF S CORPORATION STATUS

INTERNAL REVENUE CODE: Section 1362(d), (e), (f) and (g).

REGULATIONS: Section 1.1362–2(a) and (b), –3 (omitting –3(c)), –4, –5.

An S corporation election is effective for the taxable year to which it first applies and all succeeding taxable years until revoked or terminated. S corporation status may be ended in three ways: voluntary revocation by stockholders holding a majority of the S corporation stock, failure to comply with the requirements for S corporation status, or receipt of passive investment income in excess of 25 percent of gross income for three consecutive years if the corporation has Subchapter C previously accumulated and undistributed earnings and profits in those years.[12] Section 1362(d)(1) provides that a voluntary revocation of S corporation status by stockholders can be effective on the date specified by the revocation. Termination of S corporation status because the corporation or its stockholders subsequently fail to meet the initial requirements for eligibility is effective on the date the corporation ceases to qualify as an S corporation. I.R.C. § 1362(d)(2). The S corporation's taxable year ends on the day preceding the effective date of a revocation or termination and a new taxable year begins for the corporation as a C corporation on the following day. I.R.C. § 1362(e). Items of income and deduction must be allocated between the corporation's short Subchapter S and Subchapter C taxable years.

ILLUSTRATIVE MATERIAL

1.   TERMINATION BY VOLUNTARY REVOCATION

Section 1362(d)(1) allows revocation of an S election by stockholders owning a majority of outstanding stock. A revocation made on or before the fifteenth day of the third month of the taxable year will be retroactively effective as of the first day of the taxable year. Otherwise, a revocation is effective on the first day of the next taxable year. Alternatively, the revocation may specify an effective date as long as the date specified is subsequent to the date of the revocation. Treas. Reg. § 1.1362–2(a)(2)(ii) requires that the date be specified in terms of a day, month, and year, rather than in terms of a particular event. Treas. Reg. § 1.1362–2(a)(4) also allows rescission of a voluntary prospective revocation at any time before the revocation becomes effective. Rescission requires the consent of any person who consented to the revocation and any person who became a stockholder of the corporation after the revocation was filed.

Section 1362(e) requires that in any taxable year in which the S corporation election terminates effective on a date other than the first day

---

12.   The rules governing an S corporation with a prior history as a C corporation are discussed in Section 4 of this Chapter.

of the taxable year, income and deduction items must be allocated between the portion of the year the corporation is qualified as an S corporation and the portion of the year the corporation is treated as a C corporation. This rule is discussed at page 454.

2.   INADVERTENT TERMINATION

A corporation's S election terminates immediately upon an event that disqualifies the corporation or one of its stockholders under the initial requirements for S corporation status. I.R.C. § 1361(d)(2). However, the savings clause of § 1362(f) allows the Commissioner to overlook an inadvertent termination if (1) the Commissioner determines that disqualification was inadvertent, (2) the corporation and/or its stockholders take steps to remedy the disqualifying event within a reasonable period after discovery, and (3) the corporation and each stockholder agree to such adjustments as the Commissioner may prescribe. The Senate Finance Committee indicated that it "intends that the Internal Revenue Service be reasonable in granting waivers, so that corporations whose Subchapter S eligibility requirements have been inadvertently violated do not suffer the tax consequences of a termination if no tax avoidance would result from the continued Subchapter S treatment."[13]

Treas. Reg. § 1.1362–4(b) provides that the burden of establishing that termination is inadvertent under the facts and circumstances is on the corporation. The regulations add: "The fact that the terminating event was not reasonably within the control of the corporation and was not part of a plan to terminate the election, or the fact that the event took place without the knowledge of the corporation notwithstanding its due diligence in the course of its business to safeguard itself against such an event, tends to establish that the termination was inadvertent." See Rev. Proc. 98–55, 1998–2 C.B. 645 (granting automatic inadvertent termination relief to S corporations when stock is transferred to a QSST whose beneficiary inadvertently fails to file a timely election or an ESBT whose trustee fails to file a timely election, if the beneficiary or trustee files the election within 24 months of the original due date and the corporation and all shareholders report income as if a timely election had been filed). Rev.Rul. 86–110, 1986–2 C.B. 150, granted inadvertent termination relief to an S corporation that lost its eligibility because the majority stockholders transferred stock to trusts for the stockholder's children. The stockholder acted on the advice of counsel that the transfer would not disqualify the corporation's S election and would not have made the transfer but for the advice of counsel. Private letter rulings issued by the Internal Revenue Service indicate that it is quite lenient in applying the authority granted under § 1362(f).

3.   TRANSFER TO INELIGIBLE OWNER BY MINORITY STOCKHOLDER

May a minority stockholder intentionally and unilaterally, to the detriment of other shareholders, terminate an S election by transferring

---

13.   S.Rep. No. 97–640, 97th Cong., 2d Sess. 12 (1982).

stock to a disqualified person or by otherwise taking action to fail the initial requirements for S corporation status? In T.J. Henry Associates, Inc. v. Commissioner, 80 T.C. 886 (1983)(Acq.), the controlling stockholder of a Subchapter S corporation transferred a single share of stock to himself as custodian for his children under a Uniform Gifts to Minors statute. The transfer was intended to terminate the corporation's S election.[14] The Tax Court rejected the Commissioner's assertion that the transfer was not a bona fide transfer of beneficial ownership of the stock and that the stockholder acted as a custodian for his children merely as an accommodation. The Tax Court further held that, so long as there is a bona fide transfer of beneficial ownership, a transfer deliberately made to disqualify an S election should be recognized. The Internal Revenue Service has acquiesced in this result. 1984–1 C.B. 1.

The result in *T.J. Henry Associates, Inc.* permits a single shareholder to terminate an S election without the consent of majority stockholders, which otherwise is required for voluntary revocation under § 1361(d)(1). Provisions in corporate documents and shareholder agreements often seek to limit the shareholder's ability to make a stock transfer that would terminate the corporation's S election. While not always effective to prevent termination, such provisions might give rise to civil liability for shareholders undertaking disqualifying events.

4.   ELECTION FOLLOWING REVOCATION OR TERMINATION OF S CORPORATION STATUS

Under § 1362(g), if an S corporation election is revoked or terminated the corporation or its successor is not eligible to make a new election for five years unless the Commissioner consents to an earlier election. Treas. Reg. § 1.1362–5(a) provides that consent ordinarily will be denied unless it can be shown that the event causing termination was not reasonably within the control of the corporation or stockholders having a substantial interest in the corporation and was not part of a plan to terminate the election. The regulations also provide that consent should be granted if more than 50 percent of the corporation's stock is owned by persons who were not stockholders at the time the election was terminated. Private letter rulings reflect a rather relaxed approach on the part of the Commissioner in granting the requisite consent.

E.   COORDINATION WITH SUBCHAPTER C

INTERNAL REVENUE CODE: Section 1371.

Section 1371 contains rules coordinating the treatment of items that affect both Subchapter S and Subchapter C years when a former C corporation elects S corporation status or an S corporation revokes or terminates its Subchapter S election.

---

14. With respect to the taxable year involved, § 1372(e)(1) required an affirmative consent to the election by a new stockholder in order to maintain S corporation status. The stockholder in *T.J. Henry Assoc., Inc.* did not file the requisite consent.

There are no carrybacks or carryovers of loss or other items from Subchapter C years to Subchapter S years and vice versa. I.R.C. § 1371(b). Thus, a carryover of net operating losses incurred in a Subchapter C year will not be available to reduce S corporation income taxable to the stockholders. See Rosenberg v. Commissioner, 96 T.C. 451 (1991) (shareholders of former C corporation that elected S corporation status when it had unused net operating loss carryovers attributable to the development of condominiums could not exclude gain from the subsequent sale of the condominium units under the tax benefit rule). See also Frederick v. Commissioner, 101 T.C. 35 (1993) (shareholders of an S corporation were required to include under the tax benefit rule of § 111 a "recovery" of accrued but unpaid interest expense by an S corporation deducted in a prior year when the corporation was a C corporation).

The period during which the S election is in effect will be counted in determining the number of years during which a carryforward or carryback is available. I.R.C. § 1371(b)(3). In the case of a former S corporation, however, losses will have passed through to stockholders who may carryover losses on their individual returns to a year following revocation of the S election.

SECTION 3. EFFECT OF THE SUBCHAPTER S ELECTION BY A CORPORATION WITH NO C CORPORATION HISTORY

A. PASSTHROUGH OF INCOME AND LOSS

(1) GENERAL PRINCIPLES

INTERNAL REVENUE CODE: Sections 1363; 1366(a)–(e); 1367; 1378; 444.

REGULATIONS: Sections 1.1366–1, –2, 1.1367–1, –2, 1.1368–1(e)(2) and (g).

Senate Finance Committee Report, Subchapter S Revision Act of 1982

S.Rep. No. 97–640, 97th Cong., 2d Sess. 15–18 (1982).

2. Treatment of shareholders (secs. 1363(b) and (c), 1366, 1367, 1371(b) and 1373)

In general

The bill sets forth new rules for the taxation of income earned by, and the allowance of losses incurred by, subchapter S corporations. These rules generally follow the * * * rules governing the taxation of partners with respect to items of partnership income and loss.

Computation of corporate items

A subchapter S corporation's taxable income will be computed under the same rules presently applicable to partnerships under section 703, except that the amortization of organization expenditures under section

248 will be an allowable deduction. As in the case of partnerships, deductions generally allowable to individuals will be allowed to subchapter S corporations, but provisions of the Code governing the computation of taxable income which are applicable only to corporations, such as the dividends received deduction (sec. 243) or the special rules relating to corporate tax preferences (sec. 291), will not apply. Items, the separate treatment which could affect the liability of any shareholder (such as investment interest) will be treated separately. Elections will generally be made at the corporate level, except for those elections which the partners of a partnership may make separately (such as the election to claim the foreign tax credit).

Generally subchapter C will apply, except that a subchapter S corporation will be treated in the same manner as an individual in transactions, such as the treatment of dividends received under section 301, where the corporation is a shareholder in a regular corporation. Provisions relating to transactions by a subchapter S corporation with respect to its own stock will be treated as if the S corporation were a regular corporation. However, the subchapter C rules are not to apply where the result would be inconsistent with the purpose of the subchapter S rules which treat the corporation as a passthrough entity.

Passthrough of items

The following examples illustrate the operation of the bill's passthrough rules:

a. *Capital gains and losses.*—Gains or losses from sales or exchanges of capital assets will pass through to the shareholders as capital gains or losses. Net capital gains will no longer be offset by ordinary losses at the corporate level.

b. *Section 1231 gains and losses.*—The gains and losses on certain property used in a trade or business will be passed through separately and will be aggregated with the shareholder's other section 1231 gains and losses. Thus, section 1231 gains will no longer be aggregated with capital gains at the corporate level and passed through as capital gains.

c. *Charitable contributions.*—The corporate 10–percent limitation will no longer apply to contributions by the corporation. As in the case of partnerships, the contributions will pass through to the shareholders, at which level they will be subject to the individual limitations on deductibility.

d. *Tax-exempt interest.*—Tax-exempt interest will pass through to the shareholders as such and will increase the shareholders' basis in their subchapter S stock. Subsequent distributions by a corporation will not result in taxation of the tax-exempt income. (See discussion below for rules relating to corporate distributions.)

* * *

f. *Credits.*—As with partnerships, items involved in the determination of credits, * * * will pass through to the subchapter S corporation's shareholders.

* * *

i. *Other items.*—Limitations on the * * * expensing of certain depreciable business assets (sec. 179), and the amortization of reforestation expenditures (sec. 194) will apply at both the corporate level and shareholder level, as in the case of partnerships. * * *

Carryovers from years in which the corporation was not a subchapter S corporation will not be allowed to the corporation while in subchapter S status.

Shareholders treatment of items

In general.—As with the partners of a partnership, each shareholder of a subchapter S corporation will take into account separately his or her pro rata share of items of income, deduction, credit, etc., of the corporation. These rules parallel the partnership rules under section 702.

Each shareholder's share of the items will be taken into account in the shareholder's taxable year in which the corporation's year ends. In the case of the death of a shareholder, the shareholder's portion of subchapter S items will be taken into account on the shareholder's final income tax return. Items from the portion of the corporation's taxable year after the shareholder's death will be taken into account by the estate or other person acquiring the stock.

* * * In cases of transfers of subchapter S stock during the taxable year, income, losses, and credits will be allocated in essentially the same manner as when the election terminates during the year. Thus, the allocation generally will be made on a per-share, per-day basis unless the corporation, with the consent of its shareholders, elected to allocate according to its permanent records (including work papers).

A "conduit" rule for determining the character of items realized by the corporation and included in the shareholder's pro rata share will be the same as the partnership rule (sec. 702(b)). Under the partnership rules, this has generally resulted in an entity level characterization. Also, the "gross income" determinations made by a shareholder will parallel the partnership rule (sec. 702(c)).

Worthless stock.—If the corporation's stock becomes worthless in any taxable year of the corporation or shareholder, the corporate items for that year will be taken into account by the shareholders and the adjustments to the stock's basis will be made before the stock's worthlessness is taken into account under section 165(g).

Family members.—Under [section 1366(e)], items taken into account by members of the family (whether or not themselves shareholders) wherever it is necessary to reflect reasonable compensation to the shareholder for services rendered or capital furnished to the corporation may be properly adjusted. Both the amount of compensation and the timing of the compensation can be so adjusted.

Loss limitations.—As under [pre–1983] law, a shareholder's allowable pro rata share of the corporation's loss will be limited to the sum of the shareholder's adjusted basis in the stock of the corporation plus the shareholder's adjusted basis of any indebtedness of the corporation to the shareholder. However, unlike [pre–1983] law, disallowed losses can be carried forward or allowed in any subsequent year in which the shareholder has adequate basis in such stock or debt.

* * *

Terminated election.—Subsequent to a termination of a subchapter S election, these disallowed losses will be allowed if the shareholder's basis in his stock in the corporation is restored by the later of the following dates:

(1) One year after the effective date of the termination, or the due date for the last subchapter S return, whichever is later; or

(2) 120 days after a determination that the corporation's subchapter S election had terminated for a previous year. (A determination will be defined as a court decision which becomes final, a closing agreement, or an agreement between the corporation and the Internal Revenue Service that the corporation failed to qualify.)

3. Basis adjustment (sec. 1367)

Under [section 1367(a)], both taxable and nontaxable income and deductible and nondeductible expenses will serve, respectively, to increase and decrease a subchapter S shareholder's basis in the stock of the corporation. These rules generally will be analogous to those provided for partnerships under section 705. [Section 1368(d) requires that adjustments to basis as a result of distributions be taken into account under section 1367(a) prior to applying the rule of section 1366(d) limiting shareholder loss deductions to basis.]* Unlike the partnership rules, however, to the extent property distributions are treated as a return of basis, basis will be reduced by the fair market value of these properties * * *. Any passthrough of income for a particular year (allocated according to the proportion of stock held in the corporation) will first increase the shareholder's basis in loans to the corporation to the extent the basis was previously reduced by the passthrough of losses.

ILLUSTRATIVE MATERIAL

1. PASS THROUGH OF CHARACTER OF INCOME AND LOSS

Although the individual shareholders report the items of gain or loss on their own returns, the character of items is determined at the corporate

---

* [Ed.: The material in brackets reflects amendments to §§ 1366 and 1368 made in   the Small Business Job Protection Act of 1996.]

level and passed through to the shareholders pursuant to § 1366(b), a provision analogous to § 702(b), which requires that partnership items be characterized at the partnership level. In Rath v. Commissioner, 101 T.C. 196 (1993), the Tax Court held that § 1244, cannot apply to allow an ordinary loss to be recognized on the sale of stock in another corporation held by an S corporation. Even though the loss ultimately will be reported by individuals, under § 1366(b) the character of the loss is determined at the corporate level. An S corporation shareholder does not "step into the shoes of the corporation for purposes of determining the character of a loss." Since Treas. Reg. § 1.1244(a)–1(b) provides that a corporation cannot claim an ordinary loss for § 1244 stock, the loss passes through to the shareholders as a capital loss. On the other hand, Rev. Rul. 2000–43, 2000–2 C.B. 333, held that an accrual-method S corporation could not elect under § 170(a)(2) to treat a charitable contribution as paid in the year that it was authorized by its board of directors when the contribution was paid by the S corporation after the close of the taxable year. This result was required because § 1363(b) requires S corporations to compute their taxable income in the same manner as individuals.

After the character of an item is determined at the corporate level, whether it must be separately stated depends on whether the characterization may affect the computation of tax at the shareholder level. Thus, Rev.Rul. 93–36, 1993–1 C.B. 187, held that a nonbusiness bad debt must be separately stated as a short term capital loss under § 166(d) and passed through to its shareholders as such. Because § 166 is not an enumerated exception to § 1363(b), § 166 applies in the same manner as it does for an individual in computing the taxable income of an S corporation.

Treas. Reg. § 1.1366–1(b)(2) and (3) contain exceptions to the general rule that gains and losses are characterized at the corporate level in cases where the corporation is formed or availed of by any shareholder, or group of shareholders, for the purpose of converting ordinary gain at the shareholder level on property contributed to the corporation, which holds the property as a capital asset, or, conversely, converting a capital loss at the shareholder level on contributed property to an ordinary loss on sale of the property by the corporation.

2. PERMITTED TAXABLE YEAR

Before the enactment of § 1378 in 1982, calendar year stockholders of a profitable S corporation generally preferred a taxable year for the corporation ending on January 31. Under § 1366(a), stockholders account for their share of an S corporation's items in the taxable year of the stockholder in which the taxable year of the S corporation ends. A January 31 year-end permitted calendar year stockholders to defer income for up to eleven months. If, on the other hand, the S corporation was passing through losses to the stockholders, the stockholders preferred a calendar year so as to avoid any deferral of deductions.

Section 1378(b)(1) generally requires an S corporation to report on the calendar year. Although § 1378(b) allows an S corporation to adopt a different taxable year with the permission of the Internal Revenue Service if the corporation can establish a business purpose for the fiscal year, the last sentence of 1378(b) prohibits stockholder tax deferral from being treated as a business purpose for adopting a fiscal year.

Rev.Proc. 87–32, 1987–2 C.B. 396, modified by Rev.Proc. 92–85, 1992–2 C.B. 490, and Rev.Proc. 93–28, 1993–2 C.B. 344, set forth procedures to obtain the Service's approval of a different taxable year that coincides with the S corporation's "natural business year." An S corporation's natural business year is any twelve month period in the last two months of which the corporation realizes twenty-five percent of its gross receipts (under the method of accounting used to prepare its tax returns) for three consecutive years. If the corporation has more than one natural business year, it may only adopt the one in which the highest percentage of gross receipts are received in the last two months. Rev.Rul. 87–57, 1987–2 C.B. 117, explains the factors to be considered and deals with eight fact patterns in which the corporation does not have a natural business year under Rev.Proc. 87–32 or desires a taxable year different from its natural business year. Under the facts and circumstances test of Rev.Rul. 87–57, a business purpose for a particular year is not established merely by the use of a particular year for regulatory, financial accounting, or administrative purposes. If the desired taxable year creates deferral or distortion, which according to the ruling always occurs if the requested year differs from the calendar year, the corporation "must demonstrate compelling reasons for the requested tax year."

The rigid rules of § 1378, limiting flexibility in choosing the S corporation's taxable year, are ameliorated by § 444. This provision allows an S corporation to elect a taxable year other than that required by § 1378, provided that the selected year does not end more than three months before the end of the required year, even if there is no business purpose for the selected year. Thus, for example, if an S corporation otherwise is required to use the calendar year because it either has no natural business year or no business purpose for a different year, it nevertheless may elect to adopt a fiscal year ending in September, October, or November. If an election is made under § 444, the partnership must make a payment computed under § 7519 to compensate the Treasury for the deferral of taxes. This is a nondeductible entity level payment which is not credited against the partners' individual tax liabilities. (This payment in effect converts the interest free loan generated by any tax deferral resulting from the use of a fiscal year into an interest-bearing loan.)

3. STOCKHOLDER'S BASIS

3.1. *General*

The stockholder's basis in S corporation stock initially is determined in the same manner as the basis of any other stock. Thereafter, in general, the stockholder's basis is increased by items included in the stockholder's income (and the stockholder's share of the corporation's tax exempt income) and reduced by deductions allocated and distributions made to the stockholder. I.R.C. § 1367. Treas. Regs. §§ 1.1367–1(b)(2) and (c)(3) pro-vide that increases and decreases to the basis of Subchapter S stock are determined on a per share per day basis. Basis adjustments generally are made at the close of the taxable year, Treas. Reg. § 1.1367–1(d)(1), but if a shareholder sells stock during the year, the adjustment to the basis of the stock sold is effective immediately prior to the disposition. Treas. Reg. § 1.1367–1(d)(1). Adjustments to the basis of the stock are made in the following order: (1) increases for income items; (2) decreases for distribu-tions; (3) decreases for noncapital nondeductible expenses; and (4) decreas-es for losses. See Treas. Reg. § 1.1367–1(f).

Section 1367(a)(2)(D) requires a reduction in basis for expenses that are neither deductible nor chargeable to capital account. Treas. Reg. § 1.1367–1(c)(2) clarifies this language as applying only to expenses for which no loss or deduction is allowable, and as not applying to expenses that are deferred to a later taxable year. The regulations describe expenses to which § 1367(a)(2)(D) apply as including such things as fines, penalties, illegal bribes and kickbacks and other items disallowed under § 162(c) and (f); expenses incurred to earn tax exempt income disallowed under § 265; losses disallowed under § 267 relating to related party transactions; and the nondeductible portion of meal and entertainment expenses under § 274. This adjustment is necessary to prevent the shareholder from in effect recognizing the disallowed deduction by realizing less gain or greater loss on the subsequent sale of the stock.

3.2.   *Effect of Corporate Level Cancellation of Indebtedness Income*

Because § 1367 provides for a stockholder basis increase with respect to the stockholder's separately stated income items in § 1366(a)(1)(A), as well as with respect to the stockholder's share of the corporation's nonsepa-rately stated income, and § 1366(a)(1)(A) refers to "tax-exempt income," a stockholders's basis in stock of an S corporation is increased by the stockholder's share of tax exempt income. The committee reports accompa-nying the enactment of these rules give as an example of tax exempt income interest excluded under § 103. See S. Rep. No.97–640, page 439. Neither the Code nor the regulations, however, clearly define "tax exempt" income for this purpose, and the question arises regarding what is "tax-exempt income," which results in a current basis adjustment, versus what is "tax deferred income," which does not result in a current basis increase.

In Gitlitz v. Commissioner, 531 U.S. 206 (2001), the taxpayer was the sole shareholder of an S corporation that realized cancellation of indebted-ness (COD) income while it was insolvent. Under § 108(a), the corporation properly excluded the COD income. Upon the subsequent disposition of the stock (in the same year) the taxpayer shareholder claimed an increase in the basis of his stock in the corporation pursuant to §§ 1367(a)(1)(A) and 1366(a)(1)(A) on the theory that the COD income was passed-through "exempt" income, and reported a long-term capital loss. The Commissioner disallowed the portion of the loss attributable to the untaxed COD income. The Tax Court, 110 T.C. 114 (1998), and the Court of Appeals, 182 F.3d

1143 (10th Cir. 1999), upheld the Commissioner's position and denied the basis increase. The Supreme Court reversed on the basis of its reading of the "plain meaning" of the statutory scheme. First, the Court concluded that COD was "income" within the meaning of § 1366(a)(1)(A), which increases shareholder basis under § 1367(a)(1)(A). The fact that COD may be "tax-deferred" because of the insolvency exclusion of § 108(a)(1)(B) does not take the income out of the definition of income under § 1366(a)(1)(A). In addition, although § 108(d)(7)(A), as in effect for the year in question, provided that the exclusions of § 108(a) and the attribute reductions required by § 108(b) were to be applied to an S corporation at the corporate level, the Court concluded that § 108(b)(4)(A), which provides that attribute reduction under § 108(b)(2) takes place "after the determination of the tax imposed by this chapter," expressly requires that the S corporation's shareholder's pass-through of income and basis adjustment must be taken into account before the COD income is reduced by corporate level net operating losses. As a result of this reasoning, the S corporation shareholder in *Gitlitz* received a tax-free step-up in basis, which he was able to convert into a deductible capital loss. The Court addressed this concern by stating:

> Second, courts have discussed the policy concern that, if shareholders were permitted to pass through the discharge of indebtedness before reducing any tax attributes, the shareholders would wrongly experience a "double windfall": They would be exempted from paying taxes on the full amount of the discharge of indebtedness, and they would be able to increase basis and deduct their previously suspended losses. See, e.g., 182 F.3d at 1147–1148. Because the Code's plain text permits the taxpayers here to receive these benefits, we need not address this policy concern.

Gitlitz was overruled by a 2002 Act amendment to § 108(d)(7) providing that amounts excluded under § 108(a) will not be taken into account under § 1366(a). See also, Treas. Reg. § 1.1366–1(a)(2)(viii), promulgated in 1999 before *Gitlitz* was decided by the Supreme Court, providing that cancellation of indebtedness income excluded at the corporate level under § 108(d)(7)(A) is not "tax exempt" income for purposes of §§ 1366 and 1367. Although the validity of the regulation was questionable after *Gitlitz*, the regulation is consistent with the 2002 statutory change.

4.   LIMITATION OF LOSS DEDUCTIONS TO BASIS

4.1.   *General*

When net losses have reduced a stockholder's basis to zero, additional allocations of deduction and loss items reduce the basis of any indebtedness of the S corporation held by the stockholder. I.R.C. § 1367(b)(2)(A). See also Treas. Reg. § 1.1366–2. (If an S corporation has a qualified S corporation subsidiary, any indebtedness of the subsidiary to a shareholder of the parent is treated as indebtedness of the parent S corporation to the shareholder for this purpose. I.R.C. § 1361(b)(3)(A)(ii); H.R. Rep. No. 104–586, 104th Cong., 2d Sess. 89 (1996).) When the basis of both the stockholder's stock and corporate indebtedness have been reduced to zero, passed through losses no longer can be deducted by the stockholder. The losses are suspended and may be deducted in a later year in which the stockholder acquires basis. I.R.C. § 1366(d). Treas. Reg. § 1.1367–2(b)(3) provides that if the shareholder holds multiple indebtedness of the S Corporation, the reduction in basis is applied to each indebtedness in proportion to the relative bases of the indebtedness. The legislative history of the Small Business Job Protection Act directs the Service to promulgate regulations governing the order in which the basis of indebtedness is reduced if a shareholder holds indebtedness of both an S corporation and the corporation's qualified Subchapter S subsidiary. H.R. Rep. No. 104–586, 104th Cong., 2d Sess. 89 (1996).

The reduction in basis occurs notwithstanding the taxpayer's inability to use the losses on his own tax return. In Hudspeth v. Commissioner, 914 F.2d 1207 (9th Cir.1990), the stockholders were required to reduce the basis of bonds because of the corporation's net operating losses. However, because the stockholders' shares of losses exceeded their incomes in the taxable year of the losses and in subsequent years, they received no tax benefit with respect to the losses. The court rejected the stockholders' assertion that under the tax benefit rule the basis of the bonds should not be reduced to the extent that the corporation's losses did not produce a tax benefit. The court indicated that to so hold would nullify the limited carryback and carryforward provisions of § 172.

For purposes of the loss limitation of § 1366(d), the basis of stock received as a gift is limited under the transferred basis rules of § 1015(a) for determining loss. Treas. Reg. § 1.1366–2(a)(6). Thus the transferee's basis for purposes of § 1366(d) is the lesser of the fair market value or adjusted basis of the stock at the time of the gift.

4.2.   *Restoration of Basis*

If a stockholder has reduced the basis in her stock to zero and also has reduced the basis of corporate indebtedness by any amount, any "net increase in basis" attributable to passed-through income in a subsequent year (i.e., basis increase minus distributions for the year) will be applied to restore the basis of indebtedness before there is any increase in the basis of stock. I.R.C. § 1367(b)(2)(B); Treas. Reg. § 1.1367–2(c). Assume for example, that A is the sole shareholder of X Corp., which has an S election in effect. The basis of A's stock in X Corp. is $10,000 and A holds a $5,000 promissory note from X Corp. In 2005, X Corp. passes through to A a $14,000 loss, and A reduces the basis of the X Corp. stock to zero and the basis of the promissory note to $1,000. In 2006, X Corp. has $6,500 of income and distributes $3,000 to A. To the extent of the $3,000 distribution, the passed through income is allocated to increase the basis of A's stock, and because the positive and negative adjustments to the stock basis offset, its basis remains zero. The remaining $3,500 of passed-through income increases the basis of the debt to $4,500. See Treas. Reg. § 1.1367–2(e), Ex. (2).

Nevertheless, § 1367(b)(2)(B) can produce an unexpected consequence to the stockholder. To the extent that corporate earnings passed through to the stockholder under § 1366 are allocated to increase the basis of stockholder debt, the stockholder's stock basis will not be adjusted to reflect income previously taxed to the stockholder. Distributions of these earnings in a subsequent year might be taxed to the stockholder to the extent distributions exceed the stockholder's stock basis even though the stockholder has basis in the debt. Thus, if in the immediately preceding example, in 2007 X Corp. realized neither income nor loss and distributed $2,000 to A, A would recognize a $2,000 gain under § 1368. (But if X Corp. had distributed $5,000 to A in 2006, A would have recognized no gain under § 1368 and the basis of the debt would have been increased to only $2,500.) As a consequence, the stockholder appears to be taxed twice on the same income; once as the stockholder is allocated a proportionate share of the income under § 1366, and a second time to the extent the distribution of that income exceeds the stockholder's stock basis. The "second" tax, however, can be viewed as a consequence of the pass through of losses in excess of stock basis, which has reduced the basis in the debt; the statute in effect requires those losses to be "recaptured" when distributions are made on the stock before the full basis of the debt has been accounted for.

Treas. Reg. § 1.1367–2(d) provides that adjustments to debt obligations held by shareholders are generally determined at the close of the taxable year, but if the debt is repaid during the year, its basis is adjusted immediately before the repayment. Suppose, for example, that in 2005 a shareholder-creditor is allocated a loss that exceeds the basis of her stock by $600, and as a result reduces the basis of a $1,000 corporate debt obligation to $400. In July 2006, the corporation repays the debt and for 2006, the shareholder's share of the S corporation's income is $700. If the debt had not been repaid until January 1, 2007, its basis would have been increased from $400 to $1,000 as a result of the 2006 income, and no gain would have been recognized upon repayment. Under Treas. Reg. § 1.1367–2(d), the shareholder's basis in the debt obligation is adjusted immediately before repayment to reflect the shareholder's share of the corporation's 2006 income As a result, the shareholder realizes no gain in 2006.

4.3. *Carryover of Disallowed Losses*

The loss limitation of § 1366(d)(1) prevents a stockholder from claiming losses in excess of the stockholder's investment in the S corporation. Losses disallowed by § 1366(d)(1) may be carried over indefinitely to future years and deducted whenever the stockholder has sufficient basis to support the deduction. I.R.C. § 1366(d)(2). The loss carryover is personal to each individual stockholder and is not a loss carryover to the corporation. I.R.C. § 1366(d)(2); Treas. Reg. § 1.1366–2(a)(5). Thus, disposition of S corporation stock by the stockholder, including a disposition by gift that has a transferred basis to the donee under § 1015, generally terminates the loss carryforward attributable to that stock. However, § 1366(d)(2)(B) provides that if stock of an S corporation with respect to which there is a suspended loss is transferred between spouses pursuant to a divorce, the suspended loss follows the stock and is available to the transferee spouse.

A stockholder may have losses carried into the last taxable year of the S corporation. In such a case, the loss is treated as a loss incurred by the stockholder on the last day of a "post-termination transition period." The post-termination transition period is defined in § 1377(b) as the period beginning on the last day of the corporation's taxable year as an S corporation and ending on the later of (1) one year after the last day of the S corporation taxable year, (2) the due date for the tax return for the last taxable year as an S corporation (including extensions), (3) 120 days after any determination pursuant to a post-termination audit of a shareholder that adjusts any item of S corporation income, loss, or deduction for the period the corporation was an S corporation, or (4) if there is a judicial determination or administrative agreement that the corporation's S election terminated in an earlier taxable year, 120 days after the date of the determination. See also Treas. Reg. § 1.1377–2.

4.4. *Additional Shareholder Contributions to Capital*

Cash or property contributions to capital will increase the shareholder's stock basis, thereby allowing the shareholder to deduct losses otherwise in excess of basis. In Rev.Rul. 81–187, 1981–2 C.B. 167, the stockholder of an S corporation attempted to increase basis for purposes of deducting a net operating loss by transferring the stockholder's own promissory note to the corporation. The Internal Revenue Service ruled that the note did not increase the stockholder's basis because the stockholder incurred no cost in executing the note; the stockholder's basis in the note was zero. But see Peracchi v. Commissioner, 143 F.3d 487 (9th Cir.1998); Lessinger v. Commissioner, 872 F.2d 519 (2d Cir.1989).

A contribution of additional assets will not necessarily increase basis, however, if the assets are encumbered or the corporation assumes liabilities of the shareholder in connection with the transfer. In Wiebusch v. Commissioner, 59 T.C. 777 (1973), aff'd per curiam, 487 F.2d 515 (8th Cir.1973), the taxpayer transferred the assets of a sole proprietorship to an existing S corporation that also assumed certain of the transferor's liabilities. The liabilities exceeded the taxpayer's basis for the assets, which resulted in gain to the taxpayer under § 357(c) and, as a result of § 358(d)(1), the taxpayer's basis in the stock was reduced to zero. Accordingly, the corporation's current losses could not be deducted by the taxpayer. As a result of the contribution, the taxpayer recognized gain and lost the benefit of a current loss deduction, neither of which would have occurred had the business continued to be operated in a sole proprietorship form.

5. ALLOCATIONS IF STOCK OWNERSHIP CHANGES DURING THE YEAR

5.1. *In General*

Section 1377(a) provides that each shareholder's pro rata share of an S corporation's items passed through under § 1366 is determined on a day-by-day, share-by-share method if the ownership of shares changes during the year. See Treas. Reg. § 1.1377–1(a), (c), Ex. (1). This rule is similar to the proration method available to partnerships under § 706(d), except that in the case of an S corporation, the proration method is the normal rule. Pursuant to authority granted in § 1377(a)(2), Treas. Reg. § 1.1377–1(b) allows an S corporation to close its year for purposes of allocating income among shareholders if a shareholder completely terminates his interest and the corporation and all of the shareholders who are affected consent. If stock is sold, the affected shareholders are the seller and the purchaser(s); if stock is redeemed by the corporation, however, all shareholders are affected and must consent. I.R.C. § 1377(a)(2)(B); Treas. Reg. § 1.1377–1(b)(2). Treas. Reg. § 1.1368–1(g) provides a similar election if any shareholder disposes of more than 20 percent of the outstanding stock of the corporation during the taxable year but has not disposed of all of her stock. Treas. Reg. § 1.1368–1(g) requires consent of all shareholders, not just the "affected shareholders." The Treasury has not amended Treas. Reg. § 1.1368–1(g) to conform to the consent requirements in § 1377(a)(2), apparently because it was not promulgated under authority of that Code section, although the policy considerations are identical. The proration method is not applicable, however, and allocations based on the closing corporate books method are required if there is a sale or exchange of more than 50 percent of the corporation's stock during a year in which the corporation's S election terminates. I.R.C. § 1362(e)(6)(D).

If items are allocated by closing the corporation's books, the corporation prorates its income within each segment of the year among the shareholders in proportion to their ownership during that segment of the year and then cumulates the share of items for each shareholder for all of the segments of the year.[15] If two or more qualifying dispositions occur during the year, it apparently would be possible for the corporation to terminate its year with respect to one but to pro rate income with respect to the other.

These principles are illustrated by the following example. Assume that A, B, C, D, and E each owned 100 shares of stock of X Corp., which had made an S election. X Corp.'s income for the year was $182,500, but by quarters it was as follows: 1st quarter, ($90,000); 2nd quarter, $90,000; 3rd quarter, $229,000; 4th quarter, ($46,500). On March 31st, A sold his stock to F, and on September 30, B sold her stock to G.[16]

Under the normal method in § 1377(a), $500 of the corporation's $182,500 of income would be allocated to each day, and then $1 would be allocated to each share. The shareholders' income would be as follows:

---

15. See Treas. Reg. § 1.1377–1(b), (c)(2) (method of making the election to allocate items under this method; illustrating method of making computations).

16. On the day of the sale the selling shareholder rather than the purchaser is counted as the shareholder. Treas. Reg. § 1.1377–1(a)(2)(ii).

Shareholder	Days	Shares	Income/Share/Day	Total
A	90	100	$1	$ 9,000
B	273	100	$1	$27,300
C	365	100	$1	$36,500
D	365	100	$1	$36,500
E	365	100	$1	$36,500
F	275	100	$1	$27,500
G	92	100	$1	$ 9,200

If, however, all affected shareholders consented to closing the books as of March 31, $18,000 of the corporation's $90,000 loss for the first quarter would be allocated to A and $54,450 of the corporation's $272,500 income for the last three quarters (rounded off to $2.00 per share-per day) would be allocated to F. Section 1377(a)(2)(B) and Treas. Reg. § 1.1377–1(b)(2) define affected shareholders as including only the seller and purchaser. Thus, A and F are the only affected shareholders with respect to the March 31 sale and only A and F need consent to closing the books on March 31. The overall annual $1 per share per day profit would be allocated among B, C, D, E, and G without regard to the closing of the books with respect to A and F. The results are as follows:

Shareholder	Days	Shares	Income/Share/Day	Total
A	90	100	($2)	($18,000)
B	273	100	$1	$27,300
C	365	100	$1	$36,500
D	365	100	$1	$36,500
E	365	100	$1	$36,500
F	275	100	$2	$54,500
G	92	100	$1	$ 9,200

Since F realizes significantly greater income by closing the books at the end of the first quarter than under the proration method, F is not likely to consent unless F is compensated in some manner. B's and G's shares are computed without reference to the March 31 closing of the books, which applies only to A and F. B and G could, however, make their own election to close the books with respect to their shares on September 30.

5.2. *Bankruptcy Situations*

In Williams v. Commissioner, 123 T.C. 144 (2004), the taxpayer owned all of the stock of two S corporations that incurred losses for the year. He filed a personal bankruptcy petition at the beginning of December and reported a pro rata share of the losses on his personal return. The court disallowed the passed-through losses on the grounds that § 1377(a) did not apply and that § 1398 allocated all of the losses to the bankruptcy estate. It reasoned that under § 1398(f)(1) "a transfer of an asset from the debtor to the bankruptcy estate when the debtor files for bankruptcy is not a disposition triggering tax consequences, and the estate is treated as the debtor would be treated with respect to that asset." Thus the bankruptcy estate was treated as if it had owned all of the shares of the S corporations for the entire year and was entitled to all of the passed-through losses.

In contrast, Mourad v. Commissioner, 387 F.3d 27 (1st Cir. 2004), aff'g 121 T.C. 1 (2003), held that when an individual's wholly-owned S corporation filed for a bankruptcy chapter 11 plan of reorganization and an independent trustee was appointed by the Bankruptcy Court, the individual remained liable for the tax on any income or gain recognized by the S corporation.

6.   ALLOCATIONS AMONG FAMILY GROUPS

The Commissioner is given authority to allocate items described in § 1366 among those stockholders who are members of the stockholder's family (spouse, ancestors, and lineal descendants) if he determines that reallocation is necessary to reflect the value of services rendered by any of those persons. I.R.C. § 1366(e). See also Treas. Reg. § 1.1366–3. Thus, if a parent works for a low salary in an effort to shift income to the parent's stockholder-children, the Commissioner may allocate additional income to the parent or reduce the deduction for salary allocable to the parent. Unlike § 704(e)(3), discussed at page 180, which reallocates partnership income in the case of an interest purchased from a related person, § 1366(e) permits reallocation of S corporation income among family members who purchased their stock from the corporation or from an outsider in an arm's length transaction. On the other hand, § 1366(e) is more restrictive than § 704(e)(1) and (2) (which provide for reallocation of partnership income in the case of transfers by gift) in the sense that it permits reallocation only among family members.

In Davis v. Commissioner, 64 T.C. 1034 (1975), the Tax Court held that the Commissioner abused his discretion under the predecessor to § 1366(e) by allocating 100 percent of the income of two S corporations to the taxpayer. The taxpayer was an orthopedic surgeon who organized two corporations to perform X-ray and physical therapy services related to his medical practice. Ninety percent of the stock of each corporation was owned by the taxpayer's three minor children. The Tax Court indicated that the value of the taxpayer's services depended upon factors such as the nature of the services, the responsibilities involved, the time spent, the size and complexity of the business, economic conditions, compensation paid by others for comparable services, and salary paid to company officers in prior years. The court held that the 20 or so hours per year that the taxpayer spent directly performing services for the corporations was minimal and rejected the Commissioner's argument that the taxpayer's referral of patients to the corporations was personal service rendered by him to the corporations. Thus, the fees earned by the corporations were the result of the use of equipment owned by the corporations and the services of corporate employees, and not the result of services rendered by the taxpayer. The Tax Court also rejected the Commissioner's claim that income was allocable to the taxpayer under § 482 and assignment of income principles.

7.   APPLICABILITY OF AT RISK AND PASSIVE ACTIVITY LOSS LIMITATION RULES

The at risk rules of § 465, discussed at page 244, apply to the stockholder of an S corporation. As a result, a loss that is passed through to a stockholder may be deducted only to the extent that the stockholder is at risk with respect to the activities that generated the loss. Under the aggregation rules of § 465(c)(3)(B), an S corporation may be treated as engaged in a single activity if its activities constitute a trade or business and 65 percent or more of the losses are allocable to persons who actively participate in the management of the trade or business. If passed through losses have been suspended by the at-risk rules and they have not been used by the shareholder prior to the termination of the corporation's S election, the suspended losses may be carried forward to the post-termination transition period (as defined in § 1377(b)) and can be deducted in the year or years within the post-termination transition period to the extent the taxpayer's at-risk amount is increased.

In Van Wyk v. Commissioner, 113 T.C. 440 (1999), the taxpayer together with another person each owned 50 percent of the stock of an S corporation engaged in the farming business. The taxpayer and his wife borrowed funds from the other shareholder and his wife and re-lent them to the corporation, after which taxpayer attempted to claim passed-through losses against the debt basis under § 1366(d)(1)(B). The court held that pursuant to § 465(b)(3), the taxpayer shareholder was not at risk for amounts lent to the corporation because he borrowed the funds from another shareholder (and that shareholder's spouse, from whom borrowing is treated in the same manner as borrowing from the husband under § 465(b)(3)(c)) to re-lend them to the corporation. The taxpayer was thus denied a current deduction for losses passed through under § 1366. Money that is borrowed from a third party by the taxpayer on his own credit and then invested or contributed by the taxpayer to an activity is not governed by § 465(b)(1)(A), but rather is treated as borrowing with respect to the activity and will be considered to be at risk only if the borrowing transaction passes muster under the several other subsections of § 465 dealing with the treatment of borrowed funds. Treas. Regs. § 1.465–8 and 1.465–20, promulgated in 2004, extend to all activities the rule that amounts borrowed from another party with an interest in the activity (other than a creditor) are not at risk, even if the borrowing is with full recourse. This rule does not apply, however, to amounts that are qualified nonrecourse borrowing under § 465(b)(6), or that would have been qualified nonrecourse borrowing if the debt had been nonrecourse.

The passive activity loss limitation of § 469 applies to losses passed through to S corporation stockholders in the same manner as to partners. Thus net losses of an activity operated by an S corporation in which the stockholder does not materially participate are deductible by the stockholder only to the extent of the stockholder's passive activity income. Disallowed losses are carried forward and treated as passive activity deductions in the next succeeding year until offset by the taxpayer's passive activity income. Complete disposition of the activity of the S corporation allows the taxpayer to deduct the unused loss attributable to the specific activity.

St. Charles Investment Co. v. Commissioner, 110 T.C. 46 (1998), rev'd 232 F.3d 773 (10th Cir. 2000), involved an S corporation that prior to making its S election had been subject to § 469 as a closely held C corporation. The corporation had unused passive activity loss carryovers from the period that it had been a C corporation. The Tax Court held that under § 1371(b)(1), the passive activity loss carryovers from C corporation years could not be claimed against passive activity income recognized in S corporation years. The court of appeals reversed and allowed the suspended losses to be carried over and applied to reduce the passive activity income passed through to the shareholders in years for which the S election was in effect.

8.   SHORT SUBCHAPTER S AND SUBCHAPTER C TAXABLE YEARS ON TERMINATION

Section 1362(e) requires that in any taxable year in which the S corporation election terminates effective on a date other than the first day of the taxable year, income and deduction items must be allocated between the portion of the year the corporation is qualified as an S corporation and the portion of the year the corporation is treated as a C corporation.[17] The Senate Finance Committee Report explained the allocation rule as follows:

> The day before the day on which the terminating event occurs will be treated as the last day of a short Subchapter S taxable year, and the day on which the terminating event occurs will be treated as the first day of a short regular (i.e., Subchapter C) taxable year. There will be no requirement that the books of a corporation be closed as of the termination date. Instead the corporation will allocate the income or loss for the entire year (i.e., both short years) on a proration basis.

S.Rep. No. 97–640, 97th Cong., 2d Sess. 11 (1982).

Each separately stated item of the corporation's income and loss during the short Subchapter S year must be allocated to each day of the short taxable year and taken into account by the stockholders. I.R.C. § 1362(e)(2). The remaining taxable income for the taxable year is allocated to the short C corporation year. Taxable income for the short Subchapter C year is then annualized for purposes of computing the tax under § 11. First, the corporation's tax for the short Subchapter C year is determined as if it had earned a proportionate amount of taxable income for a full taxable year; then the corporation pays only the proportionate amount of the tax that corresponds to the portion of a full taxable year that it is deemed a C corporation. See Treas. Reg. § 1.1362–3(a) and (c)(2). For example, suppose S Corporation has taxable income of $100,000 in 2006. Its Subchapter S election terminates effective April 1, 2006. There have been 90 days in S Corporation's short taxable year ending on March 31, 2006, and there are 275 days in S Corporation's short Subchapter C year beginning on April 1, 2006. As a result, $24,658 of S Corporation's $100,000 taxable income is allocated to the short S corporation year ($100,000 × 90/365) and the remaining $75,342 of taxable income is allocated to S Corporation's Subchapter C year. The $75,342 of taxable

---

17.   Section 1362(e)(6)(A) provides that the short taxable years required by § 1362(e) shall be treated as only one year for purposes of the carryback and carryforward of corporate items such as net operating losses.

income is annualized so that S Corp. is deemed to have $100,000 of taxable income for purposes of determining its corporate tax for the short Subchapter C year ($75,342 × 365/275). The tax under § 11 on $100,000 of taxable income is $22,250. S Corporation's actual tax liability for the short Subchapter C year then is calculated to be $16,764 ($22,250 × 275/365).

In lieu of a pro rata allocation of income between the short Subchapter S and C years, the corporation may elect, with the consent of *all* stockholders at any time during the S year and all shareholders on the first day of the C year, to report income and deductions on the basis of actual amounts shown on the corporate books. I.R.C. § 1362(e)(3). Allocation of amounts based on the corporate books is required if the corporation's stock is acquired by a corporation, thereby terminating the S election, if the acquiring corporation elects to treat the acquisition as an asset purchase under § 338. I.R.C. § 1362(e)(6)(C). The "closing of the books" method may be desirable in situations in which the parties do not want events occurring after termination to affect income determination for the S corporation portion of the year. Note, however, that a single shareholder, who may be adversely affected, can prevent the use of the closing of the books method.

(2) EFFECT OF INDIRECT CONTRIBUTIONS ON LIMITATION OF LOSS DEDUCTIONS TO SHAREHOLDER BASIS

Estate of Leavitt v. Commissioner

Court of Appeals, United States, Fourth Circuit, 1989.
875 F.2d 420.

■ MURNAGHAN, CIRCUIT JUDGE:

The appellants, Anthony D. and Marjorie F. Cuzzocrea and the Estate of Daniel Leavitt, Deceased, et al., appeal the Tax Court's decision holding them liable for tax deficiencies for the tax years 1979, 1980 and 1981. Finding the appellants' arguments unpersuasive, we affirm the Tax Court.

I.

As shareholders of VAFLA Corporation,[1] a subchapter S corporation during the years at issue, the appellants claimed deductions under § 1374 of the Internal Revenue Code of 1954 to reflect the corporation's operating losses during the three years in question. The Commissioner disallowed deductions above the $10,000 bases each appellant had from their original investments.

The appellants contend, however, that the adjusted bases in their stock should be increased to reflect a $300,000 loan which VAFLA obtained from

---

1. VAFLA is a Virginia corporation incorporated in February 1979 to acquire and operate the Six–Gun Territory Amusement Park near Tampa, Florida. At that time, both Cuzzocrea and Leavitt each paid $10,000 for their respective shares of VAFLA. Therefore, the adjusted bases of their stock amounted to $10,000 each, the cost of the stock.

the Bank of Virginia ("Bank") on September 12, 1979, after the appellants, along with five other shareholders ("Shareholders–Guarantors"), had signed guarantee agreements whereby each agreed to be jointly and severally liable for all indebtedness of the corporation to the Bank.[5] At the time of the loan, VAFLA's liability exceeded its assets, it could not meet its cash flow requirements and it had virtually no assets to use as collateral. The appellants assert that the Bank would not have lent the $300,000 without their personal guarantees.

VAFLA's financial statements and tax returns indicated that the bank loan was a loan from the Shareholders–Guarantors. Despite the representation to that effect, VAFLA made all of the loan payments, principal and interest, to the Bank. The appellants made no such payments. In addition, neither VAFLA nor the Shareholders–Guarantors treated the corporate payments on the loan as constructive income taxable to the Shareholders–Guarantors.

The appellants present the question whether the $300,000 bank loan is really, despite its form as a borrowing from the Bank, a capital contribution from the appellants to VAFLA. They contend that if the bank loan is characterized as equity, they are entitled to add a *pro rata* share of the $300,000 bank loan to their adjusted bases, thereby increasing the size of their operating loss deductions.[7] Implicit in the appellants' characterization of the bank loan as equity in VAFLA is a determination that the Bank lent the $300,000 to the Shareholders–Guarantors who then contributed the funds to the corporation. The appellants' approach fails to realize that the $300,000 transaction, regardless of whether it is equity or debt, would permit them to adjust the bases in their stock if, indeed, the appellants, and not the Bank, had advanced VAFLA the money. The more precise question, which the appellants fail initially to ask, is whether the guaranteed loan from the Bank to VAFLA is an economic outlay of any kind by the Shareholders–Guarantors. To decide this question, we must determine whether the transaction involving the $300,000 was a loan from the Bank to VAFLA or was it instead a loan to the Shareholders–Guarantors who then gave it to VAFLA, as either a loan or a capital contribution.

Finding no economic outlay, we need not address the question, which is extensively addressed in the briefs, of whether the characterization of the $300,000 was debt or equity.

---

5. All the guarantees to the Bank were unlimited except the guarantee of Cuzzocrea which was limited to $300,000. The Shareholders–Guarantors had an aggregate net worth of $3,407,286 and immediate liquidity of $382,542.

7. Former § 1374 of the 1954 tax code which was in effect during the years in issue provides that a shareholder of an electing small business corporation may deduct from gross income an amount equal to his or her portion of the corporation's net operating loss to the extent provided for in § 1374(c)(2). Such deduction is limited, however, to the sum of (a) the adjusted basis of the shareholder's stock in the corporation, and (b) the adjusted basis of any indebtedness of the corporation to the shareholder, as determined as of the close of the corporation's taxable year.

II.

To increase the basis in the stock of a subchapter S corporation, there must be an economic outlay on the part of the shareholder. See Brown v. Commissioner, 706 F.2d 755, 756 (6th Cir.1983), affg. T.C. Memo. 1981–608("In similar cases, the courts have consistently required some economic outlay by the guarantor in order to convert a mere loan guarantee into an investment."); Blum v. Commissioner, 59 T.C. 436, 440 (1972)(bank expected repayment of its loan from the corporation and not the taxpayers, i.e., no economic outlay from taxpayers).[8] A guarantee, in and of itself, cannot fulfill that requirement. The guarantee is merely a promise to pay in the future if certain unfortunate events should occur. At the present time, the appellants have experienced no such call as guarantors, have engaged in no economic outlay, and have suffered no cost.

The situation would be different if VAFLA had defaulted on the loan payments and the Shareholders–Guarantors had made actual disbursements on the corporate indebtedness. Those payments would represent corporate indebtedness to the shareholders which would increase their bases for the purpose of deducting net operating losses under § 1374(c)(2)(B). Brown, 706 F.2d at 757. See also Raynor v. Commissioner, 50 T.C. 762, 770–71 (1968)("No form of indirect borrowing, be it guaranty, surety, accommodation, co-making or otherwise, gives rise to indebtedness from the corporation to the shareholders until and unless the shareholders pay part or all of the obligation.").

The appellants accuse the Tax Court of not recognizing the critical distinction between § [1366(d)(1)(A)] (adjusted basis in stock) and § [1366(d)(1)(B)] (adjusted basis in indebtedness of corporation to shareholder). They argue that the "loan" is not really a loan, but is a capital contribution (equity). Therefore, they conclude, § [1366(d)(1)(A)] applies and § [1366(d)(1)(B)] is irrelevant. However, the appellants once again fail to distinguish between the initial question of economic outlay and the secondary issue of debt or equity. Only if the first question had an affirmative answer, would the second arise.

The majority opinion of the Tax Court, focusing on the first issue of economic outlay, determined that a guarantee, in and of itself, is not an event for which basis can be adjusted. It distinguished the situation presented to it from one where the guarantee is triggered *and actual payments are made.* In the latter scenario, the first question of economic outlay is answered affirmatively (and the second issue is apparent on its face, i.e., the payments represent indebtedness from the corporation to the shareholder as opposed to capital contribution from the shareholder to the corporation). To the contrary is the situation presented here. The Tax Court, far from confusing the issue by discussing irrelevant matters, was

---

8. Even the Eleventh Circuit case on which the appellants heavily rely applies this first step. See Selfe v. United States, 778 F.2d 769, 772 (11th Cir.1985)("We agree with *Brown* inasmuch as that court reaffirms that economic outlay is required before a stockholder in a Subchapter S corporation may increase her basis.").

comprehensively explaining why the transaction before it could not represent any kind of economic outlay by the appellants.

The Tax Court correctly determined that the appellants' guarantees, unaccompanied by further acts, in and of themselves, have not constituted contributions of cash or other property which might increase the bases of the appellants' stock in the corporation.

The appellants, while they do not disagree with the Tax Court that the guarantees, standing alone, cannot adjust their bases in the stock, nevertheless argue that the "loan" to VAFLA was in its "true sense" a loan to the Shareholders–Guarantors who then theoretically advanced the $300,000 to the corporation as a capital contribution. The Tax Court declined the invitation to treat a loan and its uncalled-on security, the guarantee, as identical and to adopt the appellants' view of the "substance" of the transaction over the "form" of the transaction they took. The Tax Court did not err in doing so.

Generally, taxpayers are liable for the tax consequences of the transaction they actually execute and may not reap the benefit of recasting the transaction into another one substantially different in economic effect that they might have made. They are bound by the "form" of their transaction and may not argue that the "substance" of their transaction triggers different tax consequences. Don E. Williams Co. v. Commissioner, 429 U.S. 569, 579–80, 97 S.Ct. 850, 856–57, 51 L.Ed.2d 48 (1977) * * *.[10] In the situation of guaranteed corporate debt, where the form of the transaction may not be so clear, courts have permitted the taxpayer to argue that the substance of the transaction was in actuality a loan to the shareholder. See Blum, 59 T.C. at 440. However, the burden is on the taxpayer and it has been a difficult one to meet. That is especially so where, as here, the transaction is cast in sufficiently ambiguous terms to permit an argument either way depending on which is subsequently advantageous from a tax point of view.

In the case before us, the Tax Court found that the "form" and "substance" of the transaction was a loan from the Bank to VAFLA and not to the appellants:

---

10. On the other hand, the Commissioner is not so bound and may recharacterize the nature of the transaction according to its substance while overlooking the form selected by the taxpayer. Higgins v. Smith, 308 U.S. 473, 477, 60 S.Ct. 355, 357, 84 L.Ed. 406 (1940). In doing so, the Commissioner usually applies debt-equity principles to determine the true *nature* of the transaction. As the *Selfe* court noted:

> This principle is particularly evident where characterization of capital as debt or equity will have different tax consequences. Thus in Plantation Patterns [462 F.2d 712 (5th Cir.1972)] the court

held that interest payments by a corporation on debentures were constructive stockholder dividends and could not be deducted by the corporation as interest payments. There, the former Fifth Circuit recharacterized debt as equity at the insistence of the Commissioner.

Selfe, 778 F.2d at 773.

It is important to note that those cases did not involve the question posed here of whether an economic outlay existed because it clearly did. Actual payments were made. The only question was what was the nature of the payments, debt or equity.

The Bank of Virginia loaned the money to the corporation and not to petitioners. The proceeds of the loan were to be used in the operation of the corporation's business. Petitioners submitted no evidence that they were free to dispose of the proceeds of the loan as they wished. Nor were the payments on the loan reported as constructive dividends on the corporation's Federal income tax returns or on the petitioners' Federal income tax returns during the years in issue. Accordingly, we find that the transaction was in fact a loan by the bank to the corporation guaranteed by the shareholders.

Whether the $300,000 was lent to the corporation or to the Shareholders/Guarantors is a factual issue which should not be disturbed unless clearly erroneous. Finding no error, we affirm.

It must be borne in mind that we do not merely encounter naive taxpayers caught in a complex trap for the unwary. They sought to claim deductions because the corporation lost money. If, however, VAFLA had been profitable, they would be arguing that the loan was in reality from the Bank to the corporation, and not to them, for that would then lessen their taxes. Under that description of the transaction, the loan repayments made by VAFLA would not be on the appellants' behalf, and, consequently, would not be taxed as constructive income to them. See Old Colony Trust Co. v. Commissioner, 279 U.S. 716, 49 S.Ct. 499, 73 L.Ed. 918 (1929) (payment by a corporation of a personal expense or debt of a shareholder is considered as the receipt of a taxable benefit). It came down in effect to an ambiguity as to which way the appellants would jump, an effort to play both ends against the middle, until it should be determined whether VAFLA was a profitable or money-losing proposition. At that point, the appellants attempted to treat the transaction as cloaked in the guise having the more beneficial tax consequences for them.

Finally, the appellants complain that the Tax Court erred by failing to apply debt-equity principles to determine the "form" of the loan. We believe that the Tax Court correctly refused to apply debt-equity principles here, a methodology which is only relevant, if at all,[12] to resolution of the second inquiry—what is the nature of the economic outlay. Of course, the second inquiry cannot be reached unless the first question concerning whether an economic outlay exists is answered affirmatively. Here it is not.

The appellants, in effect, attempt to collapse a two-step analysis into a one-step inquiry which would eliminate the initial determination of eco-

12. In a § [1366(d)] subchapter S corporation case, the inquiry whether or not the economic outlay, assuming there is one, is debt or equity appears not to matter since the economic outlay, regardless of its characterization as debt or equity, will increase the adjusted basis. * * * There are no different tax consequences from the point of view of the taxpayer on the narrow issue of what amount of net operating losses may be deducted. Therefore, application of debt-equity principles in a case such as this one appears to be a red herring. However, we do not reach that issue because the Tax Court's factual finding that the appellants have shown no economic outlay on their part is not clearly erroneous.

nomic outlay by first concluding that the proceeds were a capital contribution (equity). Obviously, a capital contribution is an economic outlay so the basis in the stock would be adjusted accordingly. But such an approach simply ignores the factual determination by the Tax Court that the Bank lent the $300,000 to the corporation and not to the Shareholders–Guarantors.

The appellants rely on Blum v. Commissioner, 59 T.C. 436 (1972), and Selfe v. United States, 778 F.2d 769 (11th Cir.1985), to support their position. However, the appellants have misread those cases. In *Blum,* the Tax Court declined to apply debt-equity principles to determine whether the taxpayer's guarantee of a loan from a bank to a corporation was an indirect capital contribution.[13] The Tax Court held that the taxpayer had failed to carry his burden of proving that the transaction was in "substance" a loan from the bank to the shareholder rather than a loan to the corporation. The *Blum* court found dispositive the fact that "the bank expected repayment of its loan from the corporation and not the petitioner." Blum, 59 T.C. at 440.

With regard to *Selfe,* the Tax Court stated:

the Eleventh Circuit applied a debt-equity analysis and held that a shareholder's guarantee of a loan made to a subchapter S corporation may be treated for tax purposes as an equity investment in the corporation where the lender looks to the shareholder as the primary obligor. We respectfully disagree with the Eleventh Circuit and hold that a shareholder's guarantee of a loan to a subchapter S corporation may not be treated as an equity investment in the corporation absent an economic outlay by the shareholder.[15]

The Tax Court then distinguished Plantation Patterns, 462 F.2d 712 (5th Cir.1972), relied on by *Selfe,* because that case involved a C corporation, reasoning that the application of debt-equity principles to subchapter S corporations would defeat Congress' intent to limit a shareholder's pass-

---

13. The *Blum* court stated:

The respondent [Commissioner] has argued that the entire equity-contribution argument espoused by petitioner is inimical to the subch. S area. Because of our holding that the facts do not warrant the applicability of this doctrine to the present case we will not consider this rather fascinating question.

Blum, 59 T.C. at 439 n. 4. In other words, the *Blum* court never reached the second step of the analysis, if there is a second step, because it found that there was no economic outlay. The Tax Court focused on the first inquiry: "we must find that the bank in substance

loaned the sums to petitioner, not the corporation, and that petitioner then proceeded to advance such funds to the corporation." Id. at 440. The court found that "there is no evidence to refute the fact that the bank expected repayment of its loan from the corporation and not the petitioner." Id.

* * *

15. Our reading of the *Selfe* opinion, as explained below, does not require us to reject the case completely. In this respect we disagree with the Tax Court's interpretation of Selfe in the present case and in Erwin v. Commissioner, 56 T.C.M. (CCH) 1343 (1989).

through deduction to the amount he or she has actually invested in the corporation.[16]

The Tax Court also distinguished In re Lane, 742 F.2d 1311 (11th Cir.1984), relied on by the *Selfe* court, on the basis that the shareholder had actually paid the amounts he had guaranteed, i.e., there was an economic outlay. In Lane, which involved a subchapter S corporation, the issue was "whether advances made by a shareholder to a corporation constitute debt or equity * * *." Id. at 1313. If the advances were debt, then Lane could deduct them as bad debts. On the other hand, if the advances were capital, no bad debt deduction would be permitted. Thus, the issue of adjusted basis for purposes of flow-through deductions from net operating losses of the corporation was not at issue. There was no question of whether there had been an economic outlay.

Although *Selfe* does refer to debt-equity principles, the specific issue before it was whether any material facts existed making summary judgment inappropriate. The Eleventh Circuit said:

> At issue here, however, is not whether the taxpayer's contribution was either a loan to or an equity investment in Jane Simon, Inc. The issue is whether the taxpayer's guarantee of the corporate loan was in itself a contribution to the corporation [as opposed to a loan from the bank] sufficient to increase the taxpayer's basis in the corporation.

The *Selfe* court found that there was evidence that the bank primarily looked to the taxpayer and not the corporation for repayment of the loan.[17] Therefore, it remanded for "a determination of whether or not the bank primarily looked to Jane Selfe [taxpayer] for repayment [the first inquiry]

---

16. The Committee on Finance of the Senate stated in its report:

> The amount of the net operating loss apportioned to any shareholder pursuant to the above rule is limited under § [1366(d)(1)] to the adjusted basis of the shareholder's investment in the corporation; that is, to the adjusted basis of the stock in the corporation owned by the shareholder and the adjusted basis of any indebtedness of the corporation to the shareholder.

S.Rep. No. 1983, 85th Cong., 2d Sess. at 220, (1958–3 Cum.Bull. at 1141). The word "investment" was construed to mean the actual economic outlay of the shareholder in question. Perry v. Commissioner, 54 T.C. 1293, 1296 (1970).

In other words, the economic outlay must be found to exist first.

17. The loan officer so stated during deposition testimony. Furthermore, the bank originally extended a credit line to the taxpayer in consideration of her pledge of 4500 shares of stock in another corporation. When her business was later incorporated, the bank converted the loans made on the existing credit line to corporate loans, accompanied by taxpayer's agreement guaranteeing the corporation's indebtedness to the bank. The Eleventh Circuit noted that "a guarantor who has pledged stock to secure a loan has experienced an economic outlay to the extent that the pledged stock is not available as collateral for other investments." Id. at 772 n. 7. Thus, upon remand, the district court could determine that there was an economic outlay on that basis alone, before deciding whether the form of the loan was to the taxpayer or to the corporation.

This particular situation is not before us and we decline to address the question of whether a guarantee can be an economic outlay when accompanied by pledged collateral.

and for the court to apply the factors set out in In re Lane and I.R.C. section 385 to determine if the taxpayer's guarantee amounted to either an equity investment in or shareholder loan to Jane Simon, Inc. [the second inquiry]." Id. at 775. The implications are that there is still a two-step analysis and that the debt-equity principles apply only to the determination of the characterization of the economic outlay, once one is found.

Granted, that conclusion is clouded by the next and final statement of the *Selfe* court: "In short, we remand for the district court to apply Plantation Patterns and determine if the bank loan to Jane Simon, Inc. was in reality a loan to the taxpayer." Id.[18] To the degree that the *Selfe* court agreed with Brown that an economic outlay is required before a shareholder may increase her basis in a subchapter S corporation, *Selfe* does not contradict current law or our resolution of the case before us. Furthermore, to the extent that the *Selfe* court remanded because material facts existed by which the taxpayer could show that the bank actually lent the money to her rather than the corporation, we are still able to agree.[19] It is because of the *Selfe* court's suggestion that debt-equity principles must be applied to resolve the question of whether the bank actually lent the money to the taxpayer/shareholder or the corporation, that we must part company with the Eleventh Circuit for the reasons stated above.

In conclusion, the Tax Court correctly focused on the initial inquiry of whether an economic outlay existed. Finding none, the issue of whether debt-equity principles ought to apply to determine the nature of the economic outlay was not before the Tax Court. * * *

ILLUSTRATIVE MATERIAL

1. DETERMINING A SHAREHOLDER'S "ACTUAL" INVESTMENT IN THE CORPORATION

1.1. *General*

As *Leavitt* indicates, the nature of a shareholder's investment in a Subchapter S corporation can be crucially important. The taxpayers in *Leavitt* could have increased their stock bases by borrowing directly from the bank and contributing or lending the proceeds to the corporation, transactions which are economically essentially the same as the one which

---

18. It is unclear whether the reference to *Plantation Patterns* means that debt-equity principles should be applied or refers back to an earlier statement in the *Selfe* court's opinion which related to the initial inquiry:

> In Plantation Patterns, the Fifth Circuit held that a loan is deemed to be made to a stockholder who has guaranteed a corporate note when the facts indicate that the lender is looking primarily to the stockholder for repayment.

Selfe, 778 F.2d at 771.

19. We note, however, that under the circumstances presented here, the Tax Court resolved that factual determination against the appellants because they could not overcome the uncontradicted fact that they did not treat the loan repayments made by VAF-LA as constructive income to them. Such a position was inconsistent with their claim that the transaction was in actuality a loan from the Bank to them followed by their contribution of the $300,000 to the corporation.

was actually carried out. The *Selfe* case, discussed in the *Leavitt* opinion, represented a rare taxpayer victory in the guaranty context. *Estate of Leavitt* was followed in Harris v. United States, 902 F.2d 439 (5th Cir. 1990); Goatcher v. United States, 944 F.2d 747 (10th Cir.1991); Uri v. Commissioner, 949 F.2d 371 (10th Cir.1991). In a wide variety of fact patterns, the courts have uniformly required a direct investment in the S corporation in the form of stock ownership or a loan to find that the shareholder had the requisite basis.

In Oren v. Commissioner, 357 F.3d 854 (8th Cir. 2004), the taxpayer was the controlling shareholder of three S corporations, one of which (Dart) passed-through substantial income, and the others of which (Highway Leasing and Highway Sales) passed-through losses that exceeded the taxpayer's basis for his stock. He sought to utilize the losses by creating basis in loans to Highway Leasing and Highway Sales through a series of circular loan transactions. He borrowed money from Dart, which he lent to Highway Leasing and Highway Sales on terms identical to the terms of the loans from Dart to him, following which Highway Leasing and Highway Sales lent the funds to Dart. The court of appeals affirmed the Tax Court's holding that Oren's loans to Highway Leasing and Highway Sales had no economic substance and, thus, were not real economic outlays, even though all of the formalities necessary to create legal obligations were followed. No external parties were involved and the transactions were not at arm's length. Oren was in the same position after the transactions as before. The transactions resembled offsetting book entries or loan guarantees more than substantive investments.

The taxpayers in Sleiman v. Commissioner, 187 F.3d 1352 (11th Cir. 1999), owned the stock of two S Corporations that obtained bank loans, secured by mortgages on their rental real estate. The shareholder-taxpayers personally guaranteed the corporations' debts, but the bank never called on the taxpayers for repayment. In 1992 the taxpayers received distributions from each of the corporations that exceeded the basis of their stock in the respective corporations, as computed without regard to the effect, if any, of their guarantees of the corporations' debts on their stock basis. The taxpayers claimed that none of the distributions were taxable under § 1368 because their adjusted bases in the corporations included the amount of the bank loans they personally guaranteed and, with that adjustment, the basis of their stock before the distributions exceeded the amount of the distributions. The Court of Appeals denied the basis increase, distinguishing the Eleventh Circuit's prior decision in Selfe v. United States, 778 F.2d 769 (11th Cir. 1985), discussed in *Leavitt* (page 455), which held that an S corporation shareholder who personally guaranteed corporate debt may increase the stock basis by the amount of the debt if the facts and circumstances establish that the substance of the transaction was a loan to the shareholder followed by a capital contribution by the shareholder to the corporation. In *Sleiman*, the Court of Appeals held that the Tax Court's findings that the substance of the bank loans was the same as their form, and that they were not in effect loans to the shareholders followed by capital contributions to the S corporations (Sleiman v. Commissioner, T.C.

Memo. 1997–530), were not erroneous. Because the corporations mortgaged valuable collateral and had ample cash flow, the loans had economic substance—the bank looked to the corporations as the primary obligors. Although the bank required the shareholders' guarantees, they did not pledge any personal assets to secure the guarantees, and the guarantees did not alone indicate that the bank looked to the shareholders for repayment.

In Grojean v. Commissioner, 248 F.3d 572 (7th Cir. 2001), an S corporation shareholder, rather than guaranteeing a loan from a bank to his wholly-owned S corporation, as initially demanded by the bank, acquired a $1.8 million loan participation interest in the bank's $10 million loan to the corporation. The loan participation was financed by borrowing the amount from the bank at an interest rate identical to the interest rate on the loan to the corporation. The participation was subordinated to the bank's interest. The shareholder's note and the corporation's note had identical terms. The bank automatically credited payments on the corporation's note against the shareholder's note. No cash passed hands between the shareholder and the bank in the circular transaction, and the shareholder made no economic outlay. If the loan was repaid, the two loans would cancel out and the taxpayer never would receive or be out any cash. If the S corporation defaulted, the shareholder would have to make good to the bank a portion of its loss equal to the loan to the shareholder. According to the court, " 'Business realities' cast Grojean in the role of guarantor rather than lender; no business realities compelled him to recharacterize his guarantee as a loan participation." The shareholder thus acquired no additional basis to support passed-through losses. In the course of it's analysis the court explained:

> The difference between a loan and a guaranty may seem a fine one, since, when the amount is the same, the lender and guarantor assume the same risk (subject to a possible wrinkle, concerning bankruptcy). The difference between the two transactional forms may seem to amount only to this: the loan supplies funds to the borrower, and the guaranty enables funds to be supplied to the borrower. That is indeed the main difference, but it is not trivial or nominal ("formal").
> * * *
>
> At a high enough level of abstraction, it is true, the difference between providing and enabling the provision of funding may disappear. Indeed, at that level, the difference between equity and debt, as methods of corporate financing, disappears. * * * But at the operational level, because of various frictions that some economic models disregard, such as transaction and liquidity costs, there really is a substantive and not merely a formal difference between lending and guaranteeing. In contrast, the difference between a guaranty and the form that Grojean's loan participation assumed was nothing but the label. It was a purely formal difference, and in federal taxation substance prevails over form. * * *

In Bolding v. Commissioner, 117 F.3d 270 (5th Cir.1997), the shareholder of an S corporation successfully argued that a bank loan was made to the shareholder who then re-lent the proceeds to his S corporation. The taxpayer conducted a cattle ranching business through an S corporation, "Three Forks Land & Cattle Co." The taxpayer arranged a line of credit from a bank, signing the note and security agreement "Dennis E. Bolding d/b/a Three Forks Land & Cattle Co." The taxpayer signed a UCC-1 using his name only. The bank disbursed the loan proceeds directly to the corporation's bank account and the corporation made loan payments directly to the bank. When the corporation incurred losses in excess of the taxpayer's basis in his stock, the taxpayer claimed losses against the amount of the loan. The corporation's return showed the loan as a loan from stockholders. The court upheld the taxpayer's contention because the transaction followed the form of a loan from the bank to the taxpayer individually, and rejected the Commissioner's argument that the loan was in substance made to the corporation. The taxpayer's failure to report interest income from the corporation and to claim interest deductions for payments to the bank was not contrary to the taxpayer's characterization because at the same interest rate these items were a wash.

1.2. *Shareholder Satisfaction of Guarantee*

If a stockholder is required to satisfy a corporate liability pursuant to a guarantee of the corporation's note, an obligation from the corporation to the stockholder is created as a result of the subrogation doctrine[18] with a basis equal to the amount paid on the guaranty. Rev.Rul. 70–50, 1970–1 C.B. 178 (holding that basis arises only in the year of payment under the guaranty); Rev.Rul. 75–144, 1975–1 C.B. 277 (same result in case in which the stockholder executed a personal note that the creditor accepted in satisfaction of the corporate obligation); but see Underwood v. Commissioner, 535 F.2d 309 (5th Cir.1976) (substitution of stockholder note for note of S corporation to another corporation controlled by the stockholder merely amounted to a guaranty since, unlike Rev.Rul. 75–144, the creditor was not an independent third party and there was no likelihood the payment would ever be required under the note; as a result no basis was acquired in the indebtedness of the S corporation until payments were actually made on the note to the creditor corporation); Brown v. Commissioner, 706 F.2d 755 (6th Cir.1983) (guaranteeing stockholders must make actual disbursements on the corporate indebtedness before they can increase basis).

1.3. *Indirect Corporate Obligations*

In Hitchins v. Commissioner, 103 T.C. 711 (1994), the taxpayer lent money to CCC Corp., a C corporation formed to develop a database for a corporation subsequently to be formed. CMB Corp. subsequently was formed with the taxpayer as a shareholder, and CMB Corp. validly elected to be an S corporation. CMB Corp. gave a note to CCC Corp. for the amount the latter had expended in developing the database. Subsequently,

---

18. See Putnam v. Commissioner, 352 U.S. 82 (1956), holding that the debt of a C corporation paid by a stockholder is deductible as a bad debt upon failure of the corpora-tion to pay the shareholder's subrogation claim because the stockholder steps into the shoes of the original creditor and becomes a creditor of the corporation.

in partial payment of the note, CMB Corp assumed CCC Corp.'s indebtedness to the taxpayer, but CCC Corp.'s promissory note to the taxpayer was not canceled and CMB Corp. did not issue its own promissory note to the taxpayer. The court held that the amount lent by the taxpayer to CCC Corp. could not be included in his basis in the stock and indebtedness of CMB Corp. when determining the amount of CMB Corp. losses the taxpayer could deduct under § 1366(d)(1):

> There is no question that there was an economic outlay by [the taxpayer]. Nor is there any question that, by virtue of the assumption, CMB became obligated to pay to petitioner the amount owed him on the note from CCC representing his loan to it. * * *

> [The taxpayer] argue[s] that, because section 1366(d)(1)(B) refers to *"any indebtedness"* (emphasis added), without qualifying language, the debt assumed by CMB should be considered an indebtedness to petitioners.

> [The Commissioner] counters that, because of the words *"of"* and *"to"* in section 1366(d)(1)(B) (emphasis added), the indebtedness must represent an outlay from the taxpayer directly to the S corporation incurring the loss and that CMB's assumption of CCC's liability does not constitute such an outlay. * * *

> In the absence of any evidence of a direct obligation from CMB to him, [taxpayer] was simply a creditor beneficiary of CMB whose rights against it were derivative through CCC, albeit that he could probably sue CMB without joining CCC. * * * We think it significant that, as between CCC and CMB, CCC remained liable as a surety of the obligation of CMB to [taxpayer]; there was no novation relieving CCC of its liability to [taxpayer] as a primary obligor. * * * Thus, if CMB failed to pay its obligation, petitioner would have had recourse against CCC. * * * The continued obligation of CCC to [taxpayer] would, if CMB defaulted, provide a remedy to [taxpayer] which would in effect produce a reimbursement of his initial outlay by way of his loan to CCC. * * * Thus, [taxpayer's] position ultimately depended upon his status as a creditor and shareholder of CCC, and not as an investor in CMB. * * * We are satisfied that, under these circumstances, there was no "investment" by [taxpayer] in CMB * * *.

In Frankel v. Commissioner, 61 T.C. 343 (1973), aff'd by order, 506 F.2d 1051 (3d Cir. 1974), taxpayers were stockholders of an S corporation that operated a restaurant located in a building owned by a partnership in which the taxpayers were partners. The taxpayers' interests in the corporation and the partnership were identical. The partnership loaned funds to the corporation and the taxpayers asserted that their bases for purposes of passing through a net operating loss should include the partnership loans on the theory that loans from the partnership constituted loans made by the individual partners. The court held, however, that the debt ran to the partnership and the stockholders were not entitled to reflect the loans in their bases.

2.   COMPARISON OF SUBCHAPTER S AND PARTNERSHIP TREAT-MENT OF ENTITY–LEVEL DEBT

The requirement that only actual investment in the corporation, however determined, is included in the S corporation stockholder's stock and debt basis precludes the kind of pass through treatment provided to debt incurred by a partnership. In the case of a partnership, each partner is deemed to contribute money to the partnership to the extent of the partner's share of partnership liabilities, including nonrecourse liabilities. This deemed contribution increases the partner's basis in the partner's partnership interest. I.R.C. §§ 752(a) and 722. In this sense, a partnership is treated as an aggregate of the partners' interests with each partner sharing in the partnership's liabilities. The S corporation is treated as an entity separate from the stockholders, who do not share corporate debt as a pass through attribute. Why should the S corporation be treated differently? One possible answer is that, unlike general partners, S corporation stockholders are not responsible for corporate debt by virtue of their corporate limited liability. However, this protection is often eliminated by stockholder guarantees, as in *Leavitt*. In addition, nonrecourse partnership debt for which no partner is subject to an economic risk of loss is allocated to the partners and increases their basis in their partnership interests. However, the partnership rules also require a matching allocation of partnership income to partners who receive credit for nonrecourse partnership debt so that, as the debt is repaid, the partner whose basis was increased by the debt is charged with partnership income equivalent to the debt principal. See page 197. The same matching of income allocations with payments of debt may occur in a partnership with respect to partner guarantees of partnership debt and partnership debt for which a partner is personally liable. In addition, a partner who personally assumes a non-pro rata share of partnership debt may be specially allocated the partnership income used to satisfy debt principal (as long as the allocation satisfies the substantial economic effect requirement of § 704(b)) so that the partner's basis increase and deductions claimed by the partner based on the debt are matched with an offsetting income allocation. There is no equivalent vehicle for such an allocation of S corporation income, which is shared pro rata among stockholders in proportion to stock ownership. An allocation of corporate debt to stockholders of an S corporation could be unsatisfactory because the allocation would not be adjusted to account for a particular stockholder's secondary liability through guarantees or other devices. Although these problems can be resolved with provisions similar to the partnership rules providing for adjustable allocations to S corporation stockholders, the change would add substantial complexity to Subchapter S.

B.   DISTRIBUTIONS

INTERNAL REVENUE CODE: Sections 1368, 1371(c) and (e); 453B(h).

REGULATIONS: Sections 1.1367–1(d)(1), (f), (h), Ex. (2); 1.1368–1(a)–(c), (e)(2), –3, Ex. (1).

Senate Finance Committee Report, Subchapter S Revision Act of 1982

S.Rep. No. 97–640, 97th Cong., 2d Sess. 20 (1982).

Explanation of Provisions

1.   Taxation of shareholders (secs. 1368 and 1371(c))

Under [section 1368(a)], the amount of any distribution to a shareholder will equal the amount of cash distributed plus the fair market value of any property distributed * * *.

The amount of a distribution by a corporation without accumulated earnings and profits will be tax-free to the extent of the shareholder's basis in the stock. The distribution will be applied to reduce the shareholder's basis in his stock. To the extent the amount of the distribution exceeds basis, capital gains generally will result.

No post–1982 earnings of a subchapter S corporation will be considered earnings and profits for this purpose. Thus, under [section 1371(c)(1)], a corporation will not have earnings and profits attributable to any taxable year beginning after 1982 if a subchapter S election was in effect for that year.

* * *

2.   Treatment of corporation [sec. 311]

Gain will be recognized by a subchapter S corporation on a distribution of appreciated property, other than distributions [of property permitted to be received without recognition of gain under sections 354, 355 or 356], in the same manner as if the property had been sold to the shareholder as its fair market value. Like other corporate gain, it will pass-thru to the shareholders.

Without this rule, assets could be distributed tax-free (except for recapture in certain instances) and subsequently sold without income recognition to the selling shareholder because of the stepped-up fair market value basis.

ILLUSTRATIVE MATERIAL

1.   DISTRIBUTIONS OF APPRECIATED PROPERTY

1.1.   *Generally*

In a significant departure from the partnership provisions on which treatment of S corporation distributions is generally based, § 311(b) requires recognition of gain at the corporate level on the distribution of appreciated property to stockholders. In the corresponding partnership situation, gain recognition is postponed through the rules on basis adjustments.[19] Presumably, Congress believed that the partnership approach

---

19. Except to the extent required by § 751, no gain is recognized by a partnership on a distribution of appreciated property. The partnership basis carries over to the distribu-

would have been too complex to apply in a corporate context. Technically, this result is reached under § 1371(a), which provides that, except when specifically displaced, the normal Subchapter C rules, including the rules governing corporate distributions, are applicable to Subchapter S corporations. Thus, § 311(b) requires recognition of corporate level gain on the distribution of appreciated property as if the property were sold for its fair market value.[20] The recognized gain is passed through to stockholders who report the gain as income under § 1366. Under § 1368, the distribution of the property itself is tax-free to the stockholder to the extent of the stockholder's basis in his stock. The stockholder's basis in the property received is its fair market value, I.R.C. § 301(d), and the shareholder reduces by a like amount the basis of the stock with respect to which the distribution was made. Thus, in comparison to the treatment accorded distributions by a partnership, the distribution of appreciated property by an S corporation accelerates the payment of tax, although there is still only one level of tax.

1.2. *Liquidating Distributions*

Liquidating distributions by an S corporation are also subject to the liquidation rules of Subchapter C. Section 336 requires recognition of gain or loss at the corporate level as if the property were sold for its fair market value. The gain or loss is passed through to stockholders under § 1366 and their bases in their stock are adjusted accordingly pursuant to § 1367. Under § 331 liquidating distributions are treated as received by the stockholders in exchange for their stock; gain is recognized to the extent the distribution exceeds basis, or loss is recognized if the distribution is less than the stockholder's basis. Stock gain or loss is recognized in situations where the stockholder's stock basis is not the same as the stockholder's ratable share of the corporation's asset bases, e.g., where the stockholder acquired the stock by purchase or bequest.

Distribution of a § 453 installment obligation generally results in immediate recognition, under either or both of §§ 311 and 453B, of gain to the corporation, which will be passed through to the shareholders. Section 453B(h), however, provides a very narrow exception for the distribution of an installment obligation acquired by an S corporation on the sale of its assets within twelve months preceding complete liquidation of the corporation. Corporate level gain is not triggered by the distribution in liquidation of the installment obligation,[21] and the shareholder does not treat receipt of the installment obligation itself as a payment in exchange for the stockholder's stock in the liquidation. I.R.C. § 453(h). Instead, the receipt of

tee partner to the extent of the partner's basis in the partner's partnership interest.

20. H.Rep.No. 100–795, 100th Cong., 2d Sess. 64 (1988).

21. Section 453B(h) does not apply for purposes of determining the corporation's tax

liability under Subchapter S. Thus the corporation is not relieved from recognition of gain on the distribution of an installment obligation that triggers the built-in gain tax of § 1374, discussed at page 481, or the tax on passive investment income of § 1375, discussed at page 478.

each installment payment by the stockholder is a taxable event. Thus, S corporation stockholders are permitted to defer recognition of liquidation gain in the same manner that § 453(h) permits deferral of recognition by C corporation stockholders. But § 453B(h) requires that the character of the stockholder's gain be determined as if the corporation had recognized the gain and the gain had passed through to the stockholders under § 1366.

2. TIMING OF BASIS ADJUSTMENTS FOR GAIN AND LOSS AND DISTRIBUTIONS

Section 1368(d) requires that positive adjustments to a stockholder's stock basis under § 1367(a)(1), reflecting the stockholder's share of corporate income, be taken into account before applying the distribution rules of § 1368(b), but that distributions be taken into account before negative adjustments to a stockholder's stock basis are made under § 1367(a)(2), reflecting the stockholder's share of corporate loss. See also Treas. Reg. § 1.1367–1(f), (h), Ex. (2). This asymmetrical rule works to the shareholder's advantage by preventing interim distributions of profits during the year from being treated as distributions in excess of basis, thereby triggering gain under § 1368(b)(2). Conversely, if the corporation loses money, distributions will not be taxed to the extent they did not exceed the shareholder's basis at the beginning of the year (subject to adjustment for items other than passed-through corporate losses).

Prior to 1997, adjustments to stock basis to reflect passed-through losses were taken into account before the distribution rules were applied. Thus, if the corporation lost money, distributions that did not exceed basis on the date of the distribution could result in recognition of capital gain when taken into account after the stockholder's basis had been reduced by the loss for the year. While this result may appear to have been detrimental to the shareholder, it was in some cases quite beneficial because it could create capital gains and ordinary losses that offset in amounts but not in character.

Suppose that A is a fifty percent shareholder of X Corp., an S Corporation. A's adjusted basis in the X Corp. stock on January 1, 1996, was $1,000. During 1996, A's share of X Corp.'s items of income and loss were a capital gain of $200 and an operating loss of $900, and during the year X Corp. distributed $700 to A. Under the pre–1997 rules, A would have recognized both the $200 capital gain and the $900 ordinary loss under § 1366; as a result A's stock basis would be reduced to $300 under § 1367. A also would have recognized a $400 gain on the distribution. The net result would have been that A recognized $600 of capital gain and $900 of ordinary loss.

Under the post–1996 rules, the loss is taken into account last. A's basis in the X Corp. stock first is increased to $1,200 ($1,000 plus $200 capital gain). The distribution then reduces A's stock basis to $500, with no gain being recognized. Finally, A is able to deduct currently $500 of the $900 loss that passed through, reducing A's basis to zero. The remaining $400 loss is carried forward pursuant to § 1366(d)(2). The net result is that A recognizes currently $200 of capital gain and $500 of ordinary loss. See Staff of the Joint Committee on Taxation, General Explanation of Tax Legislation Enacted in the 104th Congress 122–124 (Comm. Prt. 1996).

3. DISTRIBUTIONS FOLLOWING TERMINATION OF S CORPORATION STATUS

Following termination of an S election, distributions of money may be received by stockholders as a tax-free reduction of basis to the extent of the undistributed taxable income of the S corporation that has been passed through to the stockholders. I.R.C. § 1371(e)(1). The distribution must be made within the "post-termination transition period" as defined in § 1377(b), generally at least a one year period after termination of S corporation status, although the period may differ in certain specified circumstances. See Treas. Reg. § 1.1377–2. If the stockholders fail to withdraw previously taxed income from the corporation within the applicable period, the privilege of tax-free distribution under § 1368 is lost and subsequent corporate distributions are taxable under § 301, i.e., subsequent distributions are taxable dividends if supported by sufficient earnings and profits. (If the corporation has always been an S corporation, earnings and profits will arise only in the period following termination of the election.)

Section 1371(e)(1) prescribes that only distributions of "money" may be tax-free during the post-termination transition period. Under a requirement of the pre–1983 Subchapter S rules, distributions of money during the first two and one-half months of the taxable year were received tax-free by the stockholders as distributions of previously taxed income of the prior taxable year.[22] Taxpayers attempted various devices to circumvent this "money" distribution requirement, but with a marked lack of success. This case law remains relevant under § 1371(e)(1). See, e.g., Roesel v. Commissioner, 56 T.C. 14 (1971) (Nonacq.) (cash distribution and subsequent loan to corporation by stockholders were disregarded and the transaction was treated as a taxable distribution of the debt obligations); DeTreville v. United States, 445 F.2d 1306 (4th Cir.1971) (two transactions treated as one because the stockholders purported to receive cash distributions and immediately purchased property from the corporation; the transactions were in substance a distribution of property); Stein v. Commissioner, 65 T.C. 336 (1975) (fact that stockholders were in constructive receipt of amounts credited to their accounts on the books of the corporation did not satisfy the money requirement).

4. SHAREHOLDER–EMPLOYEE FRINGE BENEFITS

For purposes of employee fringe benefit provisions, § 1372 treats an S corporation as a partnership and each more than 2 percent stockholder as a

---

22. Otherwise, distributions during the taxable year were taxed as dividends to the extent of the current year's earnings and profits. After current earnings were distributed, distributions of prior years' undistributed taxable income were also received tax-free by stockholders.

partner. As a result, S corporation stockholders holding more than 2 percent of the stock are not eligible for employee fringe benefits. Revenue Ruling 91–26, 1991–1 C.B. 184, holds that payments of health and accident insurance premiums with respect to a more than two percent shareholder/employee of an S corporation must be included in income by the shareholder/employee and are not subject to exclusion from gross income under § 106. The corporation may deduct the premiums under § 162 and is required to report the premiums as compensation to the employee/shareholder on a Form W–2.

Section 1372 does not affect the treatment of a qualified pension plan maintained by an S corporation. If an S corporation had a qualified pension plan, a shareholder of the corporation who is also an employee may participate in the corporation's qualified pension plan regardless of the amount of stock that the shareholder–employee owns. But if the shareholder is not also an employee, the shareholder may not participate in the qualified pension plan. Passed through S corporation income is not self–employment income for purposes of maintaining an H.R. 10 Plan.

SECTION 4.   QUALIFIED SUBCHAPTER S SUBSIDIARIES

INTERNAL REVENUE CODE: Sections 1361(b)(3).

REGULATIONS: Sections 1.1361–3, –4.

Prior to 1997, an S corporation could not be part of an affiliated group of corporations as defined in § 1504. This meant that an S corporation could not own stock of an 80 percent or more controlled subsidiary. The limitation was repealed by the 1996 Act, thereby permitting an S corporation to own 80 percent or more of the stock of a subsidiary that is a C corporation. Such a C corporation subsidiary may elect to join in the filing of a consolidated return, with its affiliated C corporations (chains of controlled corporations of which the subsidiary is the common parent), but the S corporation parent is not allowed to join in the consolidated return. See I.R.C. § 1504(b)(8). On the other hand, because a corporation that has another corporation as a shareholder is not eligible to make an S election, a subsidiary of another corporation may not be an S corporation. However, § 1361(b)(3) provides a special rule for "qualified Subchapter S subsidiaries".

A qualified subchapter S subsidiary (QSub) is any domestic corporation that (1) is not an ineligible corporation, (2) is wholly owned by an S corporation, and (3) for which the parent S corporation elects to treat as a QSub. I.R.C. § 1361(b)(3)(B). Election procedures are described in Treas. Reg. § 1.1361–3(a). A corporation for which a QSub election is made is not treated as a separate corporation. The existence of the stock of a QSub is ignored for tax purposes. Treas. Reg. § 1.1361–4(a)(4). All assets, liabilities, and items of income, deduction, and credit of the QSub are treated as assets, liabilities, and items of income, deduction, and credit of the parent S corporation. Treas. Reg. § 1.1361–4(a)(1). Transactions between the S corporation parent and the qualified S corporation subsidiary are not taken into account for tax purposes.

ILLUSTRATIVE MATERIAL

1.   ELECTIONS AND REVOCATIONS

1.1.   *Procedures*

Treas. Reg. § 1.1361–3(a)(4) allows the effective date of a QSub election to be any specified date within 2 months and 15 days prior to, or not more than 12 months after, the date the election is made. Unlike an S election, a QSub election does not have to be made within 2 months and 15 days of the beginning of a taxable year to be retroactive, although if the election is made more than 2 months and 15 days after the beginning of a taxable year it cannot be retroactive for the entire year.

A QSub election may be revoked as of any specified date within 2 months and 15 days prior to, or not more than 12 months after, the date of the revocation. Treas. Reg. § 1.1361–3(b)(2). A QSub that ceases to qualify under § 1361(b)(3)(B) or whose election has been revoked is treated as a new corporation that has acquired all of its assets and assumed all of its liabilities from its S corporation parent in exchange for the subsidiary's stock immediately before the cessation of QSub status. I.R.C. § 1361(b)(3)(C); Treas. Reg. § 1.1361–5(b)(1). This hypothetical transaction is governed by general income tax principles, including § 351 and its associated sections. For purposes of determining control under § 351, equity instruments that are not treated as a second class of stock under § 1361(b)(2)(D) are disregarded. The regulations also provide that the step transaction doctrine is applicable. Thus a disposition of the stock of the former QSub will affect application of § 351. Treas. Reg. § 1.1361–5(b)(3), Ex. (1).

A QSub whose election has terminated may not have a QSub election made with respect to it (or, if its stock is acquired by eligible shareholders, make an S election itself) before its fifth taxable year that begins after the first taxable year for which the termination is effective without the Service's consent. I.R.C. § 1361(b)(3)(D); Treas. Reg. § 1.1361–5(c). If a QSub election is terminated by reason of the disposition of the stock of the subsidiary by the parent, the new owners may make an immediate S election, without the consent of the Internal Revenue Service, provided that there has been no intervening period in which the corporation was a C corporation. Treas. Reg. § 1.1361–5(c)(2).

Section 1362(f) permits the Service to grant relief from inadvertently invalid QSub elections and inadvertent terminations of QSub elections. Rev. Proc. 2003–43, 2003–1 C.B. 998, provides a simplified procedure for relief from late QSub elections. Relief is available if the request if filed within 24 months of the original due date of the election and there is a showing that the late election was due to reasonable cause. The application for relief must be filed no later than six months after the due date of a tax return for the year of the election, and all shareholders must report their taxes consistent with a valid election.

1.2.   *Treatment of Transition*

If a QSub election is made for a newly formed subsidiary, the subsidiary is treated as a QSub from its inception—the parent and subsidiary both are treated as if the subsidiary never had been formed. Treas. Reg. § 1.1361–4(a)(2)(i). In the case of a preexisting subsidiary, as a result of a QSub election the subsidiary is deemed to have liquidated under §§ 332 and 337 immediately before the election is effective. Treas. Reg. § 1.1361–4(a)(2), (b).

SECTION 5.   S CORPORATIONS THAT HAVE A C CORPORATION HISTORY

A.   DISTRIBUTIONS FROM AN S CORPORATION WITH EARNINGS AND PROFITS ACCUMULATED FROM SUBCHAPTER C YEARS

INTERNAL REVENUE CODE: Section 1368(a), (c)–(e).

REGULATIONS: Sections 1.1368–1(d)–(f), –2, –3.

Conversion of an existing C corporation to S corporation status raises several problems that are related to the double tax regime of Subchapter C.[23] The Subchapter S rules are structured to maintain the possibility of a second layer of tax on income earned or appreciation in assets occurring while the Subchapter S corporation was subject to Subchapter C. Thus, under § 1368(c)(1), distributions by an S corporation that has accumulated earnings and profits from its C corporation years are tax-free to stockholders only to the extent of an "accumulated adjustments account." The accumulated adjustments account, as defined in § 1368(e)(1), reflects the S corporation's taxable income that has been passed through and taxed to shareholders under § 1368 while the corporation has been subject to Subchapter S. Distributions in excess of the accumulated adjustments account are treated as taxable dividends to the stockholders to the extent of the corporation's accumulated earnings and profits. I.R.C. § 1368(c)(2). Distributions in excess of both the accumulated adjustments account and accumulated earnings and profits are treated the same as distributions from a corporation with no earnings and profits; distributions are not included in the stockholder's gross income to the extent of the stockholder's basis in the S corporation's stock, and any excess is capital gain.

ILLUSTRATIVE MATERIAL

1.   SOURCES OF S CORPORATION EARNINGS AND PROFITS

Generally, corporate activities during the period when a Subchapter S election is in effect have no impact on the corporation's earnings and

---

23. For tax year 2002, approximately 333,600 corporations elected S status for the first time; of those, 242,800 were newly formed corporations and 97,000 converted from C corporation status. Kelly Luttrell, S Corporation Returns, 2002, 24 Statistics of Income Bulletin 59 (Spring 2005).

profits. I.R.C. § 1371(c)(1). An S corporation will have earnings and profits only (1) if it has accumulated earnings from a period before its S election during which it was a C corporation, or (2) if it succeeded to the earnings and profits account of a C corporation that was acquired in a merger or other transaction to which § 381 applies.

2. ACCUMULATED ADJUSTMENTS ACCOUNT

2.1. *General*

Distributions to stockholders from an S corporation with earnings and profits are excluded from the stockholders' gross incomes only to the extent of the corporation's accumulated adjustments account. I.R.C. § 1368(c)(1). The accumulated adjustments account is basically a running total of the corporation's net taxable income while operating as an S corporation. The account is based on adjustments to the stockholders' basis under § 1367 except that the accumulated adjustments account does not include tax-exempt income, nor is it reduced by deductions not allowed in computing the corporation's taxable income. I.R.C. § 1368(e)(1); Treas. Reg. § 1.1368–2(a)(2) and (3). The exclusion of tax-exempt items from the accumulated adjustments account means that tax-exempt income of the S corporation may not be distributed tax-free to stockholders until after the taxable distributions of accumulated earnings and profits from the Subchapter C period have been made.

Operation of the stacking principle used in § 1368(c) is illustrated as follows: As of January 1, 2005, the effective date of its Subchapter S election, Y Corporation had $50,000 of Subchapter C accumulated earnings and profits. Y Corporation's sole shareholder, A, had a basis in her stock of $6,000. For 2005, Y Corporation had taxable income of $30,000 and made a cash distribution to A of $100,000. Before taking into account the effect of the distribution, the $30,000 of current taxable income generates an increase in the basis of A's stock in Y Corporation from $6,000 to $36,000 and the balance in the accumulated adjustments account is increased from zero to $30,000. The distribution is treated as follows: Pursuant to § 1368(c)(1), the first $30,000, attributable to the accumulated adjustments account, is applied against the basis of the stock, reducing A's basis in the stock to $6,000; and the balance in the accumulated adjustments account is reduced to zero. Under § 1368(c)(2), the next $50,000, attributable to the accumulated earnings and profits, is taxed as a dividend. Once accumulated earnings and profits are exhausted, § 1368(c)(3) brings § 1368(b) into play and the next $6,000 is applied against basis, reducing A's basis in the stock to zero. The final $14,000 is treated as gain from the sale or exchange of the stock.

The accumulated adjustments account is a corporate account that is not apportioned among the shareholders. Treas. Reg. § 1.1368–2(a)(1). If an S corporation makes two or more distributions during the taxable year that in the aggregate exceed the accumulated adjustments account, the accumulated adjustments account determined as of the end of the year without regard to distributions during the year, is allocated among the distributions pro rata. Treas. Reg. § 1.1368–2(b). Application of this rule is illustrated by the following example, derived from Treas. Reg. § 1.1368–3, Ex. (5). Assume that the stock of X Corporation, which as of December 31, 2005 has earnings and profits of $1,000 and an accumulated adjustments account of $400, is owned 40 percent by A and 60 percent by B. For 2006, X Corp. has taxable income of $120, which increases its accumulated adjustments account to $520. On January 31, 2006, X Corp. distributes $240 to A and $360 to B. On October 31, 2006, X Corp. distributes $80 to A and $120 to B. During the year, X Corp. distributed $800, which exceeded its $520 accumulated adjustments account by $280. A's January distribution was 30 percent of the total distributions (240/800), so thirty percent of the accumulated adjustments account as of December 31, 2006, or $156 is allocated to A's January distribution. B's January distribution was 45 percent of the total distributions for the year, so $234 of the accumulated adjustments account is allocated to that distribution. A's October distribution was 10 percent of the total distributions, so $52 of the accumulated adjustments account is allocated to that distribution; likewise 15 percent of the accumulated adjustments account, or $78 is allocated to B's October distribution. A has received a total of $208 ($156 + $52) tax–free under § 1368(c)(1) and $112 taxed as a dividend; B has received $312 ($234 + 78) tax–free and a dividend of $168. Earnings and profits are reduced to $720 to reflect the $280 of dividends.

2.2. *Distributions in Loss Years*

Although positive adjustments to a shareholder's stock basis under § 1367(a)(1) to reflect the stockholder's share of corporate income are taken into account before applying the distribution rules of § 1368(c), if the corporation incurs a loss, § 1368(d) directs that distributions be taken into account first. Consonantly, § 1368(e)(1)(C) directs that negative adjustments to the accumulated adjustments account to reflect losses incurred by the corporation be taken into account after distributions. The operation of this rule is illustrated by the following example derived from H.R. Rep. No. 104–586, 104th Cong., 2d Sess. 90–91 (1996):

> B is the sole shareholder of X Corp., an S corporation with $500 of accumulated earnings and profits and an accumulated adjustments account of $200. B's adjusted basis in the X Corp. stock on January 1, 2000, is $1,000. During 2000, X Corp. recognizes a capital gain of $200, incurs an operating loss of $900, and distributes $600 to B. Because there is a net negative adjustment for the year, no adjustment is made to the accumulated adjustments account before determining the effect of the distribution under § 1368(c). First, B's adjusted basis in the X Corp. stock is increased from $1,000 to $1,200 to reflect the capital gain. Second, $200 of the $600 distribution to B is a distribution from X Corp.'s accumulated adjustments account, reducing the accumulated adjustments account to zero. This $200 is applied against B's adjusted basis of $1,200, reducing B's basis in the stock to $1,000. The remaining $400 of the distribution is a distribution of accumulated earnings

and profits. It is taxable as a dividend to B and does not reduce B's basis in the X Corp. stock. X Corp.'s earnings and profits account is reduced by $400, to $100. X Corp.'s accumulated adjustments account is then increased by $200 to reflect the recognized capital gain and reduced by $900 to reflect the operating loss, leaving a negative balance in the accumulated adjustments account on January 1, 2001, of $700. Because B's adjusted basis is $1,000, the § 1366(d) loss limitation does not apply, and B may deduct the entire $900 operating loss. As a result, B's basis in the X Corp. stock is decreased by $900, and B's basis in the stock on January 1, 2001, is $100 ($1,000 plus $200 less $200 less $900).

See Staff of the Joint Committee on Taxation, General Explanation of Tax Legislation Enacted in the 104th Congress 122–124 (Comm. Prt. 1996).

3. REDEMPTIONS

Section 1371(c) applies to redemptions by an S corporation with earnings and profits that are treated as a § 301 distribution because none of the tests for redemption treatment in § 302 or § 304 have been met. If a distribution is received by a stockholder as a redemption in exchange for stock under § 302(a) or § 303, a pro rata portion of the distribution is deemed to reduce the accumulated adjustments account. I.R.C. § 1368(e)(1)(B).[24] Rev. Rul. 95–14, 1995–1 C.B. 169, involved a redemption subject to § 1368(c) rather than § 302(a) where both the shareholder's basis in her stock and the corporation's accumulated adjustments account exceeded the amount of the distribution. Under § 1368(c), none of the distribution was included in income, and under § 1368(e)(1)(A), the accumulated adjustments account was reduced by an amount equal to the distribution. Section 1368(e)(1)(B) was not applicable because the redemption did not qualify under either § 302(a) or § 303.

4. ELECTIONS

Section 1368(e)(3) provides an election, with the consent of all stockholders, to treat distributions as dividends from accumulated earnings and profits before reducing the accumulated adjustments account. The election may be used to prevent termination for excess passive investment income under § 1362(d)(3), or to avoid the § 1375 tax on passive investment income of an S corporation with accumulated earnings and profits, discussed below. Treas. Reg. § 1.1368–1(f)(3) also provides for an election to reduce Subchapter C earnings and profits by a deemed dividend. The amount deemed to be received as a dividend by shareholders is treated as a cash contribution back to the corporation.

---

24. Section 1371(c)(2) requires adjustments to the earnings and profits account in the case of redemptions, liquidations, reorganizations and other transactions to which Subchapter C is applicable. Section 1371(c)(3) provides for an adjustment to earnings and profits in the case of distributions treated as dividends under § 1368(c)(2). See Treas. Reg. § 1.1368–2(d).

B.   PASSIVE INVESTMENT INCOME OF AN S CORPORATION WITH ACCUMULATED EARNINGS AND PROFITS

INTERNAL REVENUE CODE: Sections 1362(d)(3); 1375.

REGULATIONS: Section 1.1362–2, –3(b).

There are no limitations on the type of income, e.g., passive versus active, that can be earned by an S corporation with no C corporation history.[25] On the other hand, § 1375 imposes a tax on an S corporation with accumulated Subchapter C earnings and profits in any year in which the corporation has passive investment income in excess of 25 percent of gross receipts. The tax is imposed at the highest rate under § 11(b) on "excess net passive income," which is defined in § 1375(b) as an amount that bears the same ratio to net passive income as the passive investment income in excess of 25 percent of gross receipts bears to the passive investment income for the taxable year. In other words, the taxable amount is determined from the formula—

$$\text{Net Passive Investment Income} \times \frac{\text{Passive Investment Income minus 25 percent of Gross Receipts}}{\text{Passive Investment Income}}$$

"Net passive investment income" is defined as passive income (defined below) less deductible expenses incurred to produce the passive investment income. By virtue of this definition, the apportionment formula allocates expenses between the passive investment income in excess of 25 percent of gross receipts, which is subject to the tax, and the passive investment income that is less than 25 percent of gross receipts, which is not taxed. Finally, the amount subject to tax as net passive investment income is limited to the corporation's regular taxable income for the year. I.R.C. § 1375(b)(1)(B).

Suppose, for example, that an S corporation with earnings and profits from its C corporation history had gross receipts from an active business of $600,000, dividend income of $360,000, and expenses to earn the dividend income of $60,000. The formula in § 1375(b) is as follows:

$$(\$360{,}000 - \$60{,}000) \times \frac{(\$360{,}000 - [0.25 \times (\$600{,}000 + \$360{,}000)])}{\$360{,}000} = \$100{,}000$$

Thus, the § 1375(a) tax is levied on the amount of $100,000, which under the formula is the corporation's "excess net passive investment income." Applying the highest rate under § 11, 35 percent, the tax is $35,000. Pursuant to § 1366(f)(3), the amount of dividend income passed through to

---

25. Before 1982, former § 1375(e)(5) provided for termination of an S election for any corporation if more than 20 percent of its gross receipts constituted passive investment income, without regard to whether the corpo- ration also had Subchapter C earnings and profits. The definition of passive investment income under this now repealed provision raised interpretive issues that continue to be important under current law.

the shareholders will be reduced by the tax imposed on the corporation with respect to that income.

The Commissioner may waive imposition of the passive investment income tax if the corporation establishes that it determined in good faith that it had no Subchapter C earnings and profits and within a reasonable period of time the corporation distributed its earnings and profits to stockholders. I.R.C. § 1375(d).

In addition, pursuant to § 1362(d)(3), an S election is terminated if the corporation has Subchapter C earnings and profits at the close of each of three consecutive taxable years following the election and during each of the three years more than 25 percent of the corporation's gross receipts are passive investment income.[26] This provision is intended to prevent an S corporation from utilizing accumulated C corporation earnings and profits for passive investment purposes.

A termination because of excess passive investment income is effective on the first day of the taxable year following the third consecutive year in which the corporation has disqualifying earnings and profits and investment income. Termination may be avoided if the Internal Revenue Service determines that the termination is inadvertent under the standards of § 1362(f), see page 437.

Both the tax on passive investment income and termination of S status can be avoided either by distributing accumulated earnings and profits to stockholders as a taxable dividend prior to making the S election or by making a deemed dividend and recontribution election under Treas. Reg. § 1.1368–1(f)(3).

ILLUSTRATIVE MATERIAL

1. PASSIVE INVESTMENT INCOME

For purposes of §§ 1362(d)(3) and 1375, passive investment income is defined as income from royalties, rents, dividends, interest, annuities and sales or exchanges of stock or securities (but only to the extent of gains). Passive investment income, however, does not include interest on notes acquired in the ordinary course of business on the sale of inventory, or gross receipts from the regular conduct of a lending or finance business. I.R.C. § 1362(d)(3)(C). In addition, § 1362(d)(3)(E) excludes from passive investment income dividends that are attributable to the active conduct of a trade or business of a C corporation in which the S corporation has an 80 percent or greater ownership interest (as defined in § 1504(a)(2)). Treas. Reg. § 1.1362–8 (1998) provides rules for determining whether the earnings and profits of the subsidiary are "active" or "passive."

---

26. The termination rule does not apply with respect to earnings and profits accumulated before the effective date of the 1982 Act. Prior to 1983 it was possible for an S corporation to accumulate earnings and profits because earnings and profits could exceed pass-through taxable income.

Treas. Reg. § 1.1362–2(c)(5)(ii)(B)(2) provides that the term "rents" does not include rents derived in an active trade or business of renting property if the corporation provides significant services or incurs substantial costs in the rental business. Thus, for example the income from hotel and motel operations is not rent. However, Feingold v. Commissioner, 49 T.C. 461 (1968), held under predecessor Regulations that rental income from summer bungalows did not fall within the "significant services" exception and constituted disqualifying income.

The list of passive interest income items in the predecessor to § 1362(d)(3)(C)(i) was held to be exclusive, so that gains from the sale of unimproved real estate did not constitute passive investment income for purposes of the limitation. Howell v. Commissioner, 57 T.C. 546 (1972)(Acq.); Rev.Rul. 75–188, 1975–1 C.B. 276.

If an S corporation receives passive investment income specified in § 1362(d)(3)(C), the fact that it is an active operating company with respect to such income does not prevent application of the disqualification rule. See Zychinski v. Commissioner, 506 F.2d 637 (8th Cir.1974), in which a corporation's Subchapter S status was terminated because too high a percentage of its income was gains on sales of stocks and securities; that the corporation was a dealer did not change the result. This result is mitigated for lending and financing businesses, however, by § 1362(d)(3)(C)(iii), which excludes the interest received in the ordinary course by S corporations engaged in such a business from investment income for purposes of the termination rule. In a similar vein, § 1362(d)(3)(D) provides that gains or losses on certain futures contracts and options derived by commodities and options dealers will not be taken into account in determining passive investment income. There is no corresponding relief for rental income derived in the ordinary course of a business. Thus a corporation with Subchapter C earnings and profits still cannot conduct rental operations yielding rents in excess of 25 percent of its gross receipts for more than three years and retain S corporation status.

2. GROSS RECEIPTS

Treas. Reg. § 1.1362–2(c)(4)(i) provides that gross receipts are not the same as gross income. A corporation operating at a loss because its cost of goods sold exceeds its receipts will still have gross receipts. In contrast, proceeds from the sale or exchange of capital assets (except for stocks or securities) are taken into account in computing gross receipts only to the extent that gains from the sale or exchange of capital assets exceed losses from the sale or exchange of capital assets. I.R.C. § 1362(d)(3)(B). Gross receipts from the sale of stock or securities are taken into account only to the extent of gains. Losses from the sale of stock or securities do not offset the gains for this purpose. See Treas. Reg. § 1.1362–2(c)(4)(ii)(B). This rule prevents the corporation from acquiring and selling stocks to enhance artificially the amount of its gross receipts. Receipts that are not included in gross income because the corporation is a mere conduit are not included in gross receipts. See Kaiser's Estate v. Commissioner, T.C. Memo. 1997–88

62-64

(an insurance agency's gross receipts from its insurance business included only commissions received with respect to policies written by it; gross receipts did not include premiums collected from customers on behalf of the insurance company and remitted to the company).

C.   BUILT-IN GAIN TAX

INTERNAL REVENUE CODE: Section 1374. See also section 1363(d).

REGULATIONS: Section 1.1374–1, –2, –3, –4(a), (b), (h)(1) and (2), –7, and –9.

Technical and Miscellaneous Revenue Act of 1988, Report of the Committee on Ways and Means, House of Representatives

H.Rep. No. 100–795, 100Th Cong., 2D Sess. 62–64 (1988).

A corporate level tax is imposed [by section 1374] on gain that arose prior to the conversion of a C corporation to an S corporation ("built-in gain") that is recognized by the S corporation through sale, distribution, or other disposition within 10 years after the date on which the S election took effect. The total amount of gain that must be recognized by the corporation, however, is limited to the aggregate net built-in gain of the corporation at the time of conversion to S status.

The 1986 Act [section 1374(c)(2)] provided that the amount of recognized built-in gains taken into account for any taxable year shall not exceed the excess (if any) of 1) the net unrealized built-in gain, over 2) the recognized built-in gains for prior years beginning in the 10–year recognition period. Also, recognized built-in gain is not taxed in a year to the extent that it exceeds the taxable income of the corporation for the year computed as if the corporation were a C corporation.

Under [section 1374(b)(2) and (3)], the corporation may take into account certain subchapter C tax attributes in computing the amount of tax on recognized built-in gains. Thus, for example, it may use unexpired net operating losses to offset the gain and may use business credit carryforwards to offset the tax.

The [1988 Act] modifies the operation of the built-in gains tax. [Section 1374(d)(2)(A)(ii)] retains the net income limitation of the [1986] Act by providing that a net recognized built-in gain for a year will not be taxed to the extent the corporation would not otherwise have taxable income for the year if it were a C corporation (determined in accordance with section 1375(b)(1)(B)). Under [section 1374(d)(2)(A)(ii)], therefore, recognized built-in gain in any post-conversion year is reduced for purposes of the built-in gains tax by any recognized built-in loss for that year, and also by any other post-conversion losses for that year.

Although the committee believes it is appropriate not to impose the built-in gains tax in a year in which the taxpayer experiences losses, the committee also believes it is appropriate to reduce the potential for taxpayers to manipulate the timing of post-conversion losses in a manner that might entirely avoid the built-in gains tax on the net unrealized built-in gain of the former C corporation. Accordingly, [section 1374(d)(2)(B)] provides that any net recognized built-in gain that is not subject to the built-in gains tax due to the net income limitation will be carried forward.

Thus, an amount equal to any net recognized built-in gain that is not subject to the built-in gains tax because of the net income limitation will be carried forward and will be subject to the built-in gains tax to the extent the corporation subsequently has other taxable income (that is not already otherwise subject to the built-in gains tax) for any taxable year within the 10 year recognition period. * * *

The provision is illustrated by the following example: Corporation A elects S status on March 31, 1988. The corporation has two assets, one with a value of $200 and an adjusted basis of $0 and the other with a value of $0 and an adjusted basis of $100. It has no other items of built-in gain or loss. The corporation thus has a net unrealized built-in gain of $100. In its first taxable year for which it is an S corporation, the corporation sells both assets for their fair market value and has a net recognized built-in gain of $100. It also has an additional $100 loss from other post-conversion activities. The corporation is not subject to any built-in gains tax in that year because its net recognized built-in gain ($100) exceeds its net income determined in accordance with section 1375(b)(1)(B) ($0). In its next taxable year, the corporation has $200 of taxable income. $100 is subject to the built-in gains tax in that year, because of the carryforward of the $100 of net unrecognized built-in gain that had been untaxed due to the net income limitation.

[Section 1374(d)(8)] clarifies that the built-in gain provision applies not only when a C corporation converts to S status but also in any case in which an S corporation acquires an asset and the basis of such asset in the hands of the S corporation is determined (in whole or in part) by reference to the basis of such asset (or any other property) in the hands of the C corporation. In such cases, each acquisition of assets from a C corporation is subject to a separate determination of the amount of net built-in gain, and is subject to the provision for a separate 10–year recognition period. * * *

[Section 1374(d)(5)(A)] clarifies that, for purposes of this built-in gains tax under section 1374, any item of income which is properly taken into account for any taxable year in the recognition period but which is attributable to periods before the first taxable year for which the corporation was an S corporation is treated as a recognized built-in gain for the taxable year in which it is properly taken into account. Thus, the term "disposition of any asset" includes not only sales or exchanges but other income recognition events that effectively dispose of or relinquish a taxpayer's right to claim or receive income. For example, the term "disposition of any asset" for purposes of this provision also includes the collection of accounts receivable by a cash method taxpayer and the completion of a long-term contract performed by a taxpayer using the completed contract method of accounting.

Similarly, [section 1374(d)(5)(B)] clarifies that amounts that are allowable as a deduction during the recognition period but that are attributable to periods before the first S corporation taxable year are thus treated as recognized built-in losses in the year of the deduction.

As an example of these built-in gain and loss provisions, in the case of a cash basis personal service corporation that converts to S status and that has receivables at the time of the conversion, the receivables, when received, are built-in gain items. At the same time, built-in losses would include otherwise deductible compensation paid after the conversion to the persons who performed the services that produced the receivables, to the extent such compensation is attributable to such pre-conversion services. To the extent such built-in loss items offset the built-in gains from the receivables, there would be no amount subject to the built-in gains tax.

[Section 1374(b)(2)] clarifies that capital loss carryforwards may also be used to offset recognized built-in gains.

ILLUSTRATIVE MATERIAL

1. SCOPE OF SECTION 1374: DOUBLE TAXATION OF GAIN ECONOMICALLY ACCRUING DURING S CORPORATION'S PRIOR C CORPORATION HISTORY

Section 1374 is intended to impose double taxation of appreciation that occurred while assets were held by a C corporation that subsequently made an S election if the corporation does not continue to hold the assets for a substantial period of time after making the S election. Double taxation is achieved by imposing a corporate level tax on recognized built-in gain with respect to assets held by the corporation at the time of conversion from C to S corporation status in addition to taxing the shareholders on the gain under § 1366. The tax also applies to built-in gain recognized on the disposition of an asset acquired from a C corporation in a nonrecognition transaction with a transferred basis to the acquiring S corporation. Section 1374 is not applicable to an S corporation that was never a C corporation or to an S corporation that has no assets that it acquired from a C corporation in a nonrecognition transaction. I.R.C. § 1374(c)(1). Nor is § 1374 applicable to assets purchased by the corporation or contributed to it during the period an S election is in effect.

Built-in gain recognized by an S corporation during the ten year recognition period[27] is subject to tax at the highest corporate tax rate under § 11(b), currently 35 percent. Recognized built-in gain is then subject to a

---

27. Treas. Reg. § 1.1374–1(d) provides that the "recognition period" during which the § 1374 tax applies is the 120 month period beginning on the first day that the corporation is an S corporation (or acquires an asset from a C corporation in a transferred basis transaction), and provides rules for determining taxable recognized built-in gain when the recognition period ends within the corporation's taxable year.

second tax at the stockholder level as the recognized gain is passed through to stockholders under § 1366. Each stockholder's proportionate share of recognized built-in gain is reduced by the stockholder's proportionate share of the § 1374 tax. I.R.C. § 1366(f)(2). For example, if S Corporation sells a built-in gain asset with a basis of $10 for $110, the corporation's recognized gain of $100 is subject to tax of 35 percent. Stockholders are allocated their proportionate share of the $100 of gain, less the tax of $35, or a net taxable gain of $65. Then the stockholders pay a tax equal to 35 percent of $65. Before the introduction in 2003 of the 15 percent preferential rate for dividends, the total taxes of $57.75 would have been the same as would have been imposed on a C corporation selling the assets and distributing the after-tax proceeds as a dividend, thus preserving the effects of the double tax regime. Since 2003, when an S corporation that formerly was a C corporation sells assets with a built-in gain, the effect of the § 1374 tax is to impose a higher total tax burden than is imposed on a C corporation selling assets and distributing the after-tax proceeds as a dividend.

Section 1374(e) grants to the Treasury Department broad authority to promulgate regulations to ensure that the double tax on assets that were appreciated at the time the corporation converted from C to S corporation status is not circumvented. Treas. Regs. §§ 1.1374–1 through 1.1374–10 provide detailed rules governing the application of § 1374.

2.   AMOUNT OF GAIN SUBJECT TO THE BUILT–IN GAIN TAX

The technical operation of § 1374 is somewhat convoluted. Section 1374(a) imposes the tax on the corporation's "net recognized built-in gain." The term net recognized built-in gain is, in turn, defined in § 1374(d)(2)(A) as the amount that would be the corporation's taxable income for the year if only "recognized built-in gains" and "recognized built-in losses" were taken into account (but not more than the corporation's actual taxable income for the year). "Recognized built-in gain" is defined in § 1374(d)(3) as the amount of the gain recognized with respect to any asset disposed of during the year that was held by the corporation on the first day of its first taxable year as an S corporation to the extent the property's fair market value exceeded its basis on that day. Similarly, recognized built-in loss is defined in § 1374(d)(4) as the loss recognized with respect to any asset disposed of during the year that was held by the corporation on the first day of its first taxable year as an S corporation to the extent the fair market value of the property was less than its basis on that day. Section 1374(c)(2) then limits the net recognized built-in gain taxable under § 1374(a) for the year to the excess of the corporation's "net unrealized built-in gain" over the net recognized built-in gain for previous years. "Net unrealized built-in gain" is defined in § 1374(d)(1) as the excess of the fair market value of the corporation's assets on the first day of its first taxable year as an S corporation over the aggregate basis of those assets on that day.

The purpose of this maze of statutory rules is to assure that the aggregate amount taxed under § 1374 if assets held on the day the S election was made are sold over a number of years does not exceed the gain that would have been recognized if the corporation had sold all of its assets immediately before making the S election. Furthermore, since the precise wording of § 1374(d)(3) creates rebuttable presumptions that all recognized gain on any asset sold during the ten year recognition period is built-in gain and that no loss recognized during the period is built-in loss, it is incumbent on the corporation to appraise all of its assets as of the effective date of an S election.

The limitation in § 1374(c) is illustrated in the following example. Assume that X Corporation made an S election on July 1, 2003. At that time X Corporation had the following assets:

Asset	Basis	Fair Market Value	Built-in Gain/Loss
Blackacre	$150	$225	$ 75
Whiteacre	$300	$550	$250
Greenacre	$450	$350	($100)
			$225

In 2005, when it has operating profits of $500, X Corporation sells Whiteacre for $650 and Greenacre for $300. The corporation recognizes a gain of $350 on Whiteacre and a loss of $150 on Greenacre. Assuming that X Corporation satisfies its burden of proof as to the properties' fair market values on July 1, 2003, the recognized built-in gain on Whiteacre is $250 and the recognized built-in loss on Greenacre is $100. The net recognized built-in gain for the year is $150. Since the corporation's net unrealized built-in gain with respect to all of its assets is $225, the entire net recognized built-in gain is taxed under § 1374(a) in 2005. If Blackacre is sold the following year for $225, the entire gain is net recognized built-in gain, and since the ceiling in § 1374(c)(2) is $75 ($225 net unrealized built-in gain minus $150 net recognized built-in gain from 2005), the entire $75 gain is taxed at the corporate level under § 1374(a).

Now assume alternatively that in 2005, X Corporation sells Blackacre for $225 and Greenacre for $300. X Corporation recognizes a gain of $75 on Blackacre and a loss of $150 on Greenacre. Assuming that X Corporation satisfies its burden of proof as to the properties' fair market values on July 1, 2003, the recognized built-in gain on Blackacre is $75 and the recognized built-in loss on Greenacre is $100. Its net recognized built-in loss for the year is $25, and no tax is due under § 1374(a). If Whiteacre is sold the following year for $650, the corporation recognizes a gain of $350, of which $250 is net recognized built-in gain. But since the corporation's net unrealized built-in gain is only $225, only $225 of that gain is subject to corporate level tax under § 1374(a).

Although § 1371(b) generally proscribes the use by an S corporation of net operating loss carryovers from years when it was a C corporation, there is an exception if built-in gains are required to be recognized and taxed to the S corporation under § 1374. Section 1374(b) permits Subchapter C

NOL carryovers to offset net recognized built-in gain for a Subchapter S year solely for the purpose of computing the § 1374 tax.

Treas. Regs. §§ 1.1374–9 and 1.1374–10(b)(3) provide anti-abuse rules directed to the acquisition of property for the purpose of avoiding the § 1374 tax.

3.   EFFECT OF ACCOUNTING METHOD ON APPLICATION OF SECTION 1374 TO GAINS FROM PROPERTY

Treas. Reg. § 1.1374–7 provides that the inventory method maintained by a corporation will be used to determine whether goods required to be included in inventory were on hand with built-in gain at the time of conversion to S corporation status. Reliable Steel Fabricators, Inc. v. Commissioner, T.C. Memo. 1995–293, held that the valuation of inventory work in progress on the effective date of an S election must include some profit margin for completed work, but not for raw materials.

Treas. Reg. § 1.1374–4(h) imposes the tax under § 1374 on all gains from an installment sale under § 453 recognized during or after the 120 month recognition period if the sale occurred prior to or during the 120 month recognition period. Tax is imposed under this provision, however, only to the extent that the gain would have been included in net recognized built-in gain if the entire gain had been recognized in the year of sale, taking into account the taxable income limitation. In determining the limitation, if the sale occurred before commencement of the recognition period (generally speaking, while the corporation was still a C Corporation), the sale is deemed to have occurred in the first year of the recognition period.

4.   INCOME ITEMS OTHER THAN GAIN FROM THE SALE OF PROPERTY SUBJECT TO SECTION 1374

Section 1374(d)(3) and (4) defines built-in gain and loss as gain or loss "from the disposition of any asset." Treas. Reg. § 1.1374–4(a)(3), Ex. (1), states that income from the sale of oil under a working interest in oil and gas property held by a corporation at the time of its conversion to S corporation status is not recognized built-in gain. The example reasons that at the time of conversion to S status the corporation held a working interest in oil in place, and not the oil itself. By analogy to the example in the regulations, Rev. Rul. 2001–50, 2001–23 C.B. 343, held that income from the sale of standing timber, or from the sale of coal or iron ore, owned by a corporation at the time of its S corporation election likewise is not recognized built-in gain under § 1374. (The ruling applies both to gains that are treated as capital gains under the special rules of § 631, and gains that are not subject to § 631.) The ruling indicates that timber cut and sold during the recognition period is sold as inventory that "did not constitute separate assets held by the S corporation on the conversion date." The ruling also states that even though some income from the disposition of timber or coal and iron ore receives capital gains treatment under § 631, "the income received from the sale of the resulting wood product, produced coal, or produced iron ore involves the receipt of normal operating business income in the nature of rent or royalties" that is not subject to tax under § 1374. Both the regulations' example and the revenue ruling avoid the very difficult valuation problem that would exist in attempting to determine built-in gain or loss of natural resources at the time of conversion to S status.

Under Treas. Reg. § 1.1374–4(b)(1) and (2), items of income and deduction attributable to prior periods that are taken into account as built-in gain items under § 1374(d)(5) include items that would have been taken into account before the beginning of the recognition period if the corporation had used the accrual method of accounting. Thus, for example, accounts receivable accrued before conversion to S Corporation status, but collected by a cash method S corporation after conversion, are treated as built-in gain items. See Treas. Reg. § 1.1374–4(b)(3), Ex. (1); Leou, M.D., P.A. v. Commissioner, T.C. Memo. 1994–393 (§ 1374 built-in gains tax applied to collection of cash method accounts receivable of a corporation that elected S status in 1988 and previously had been a C corporation).

Treas. Reg. § 1.1374–4(f) provides that discharge of indebtedness income or bad debt deductions attributable to indebtedness that exists prior to the beginning of the recognition period will be treated as built-in gain or loss. In addition, built-in gain or loss includes adjustments to income required under § 481 as a result of a change in accounting method effective before the beginning of the second year of the recognition period. Treas. Reg. § 1.1374–4(d).

Under Treas. Reg. § 1.1374–4(i)(1), an S corporation's distributive share of income or loss from a partnership interest owned by the S corporation will be treated as built-in gain or loss to the extent that the item would have been so treated if it had been taken into account directly by the corporation. Among other limitations, the amount of built-in gain or loss recognized by an S corporation as its distributive share of partnership items will be limited to the corporation's built-in gain or loss in the partnership interest itself. Treas. Reg. § 1.1374–4(i)(4). Subject to an anti-abuse rule, these partnership rules do not apply if the fair market value of an S corporation's partnership interest is less than $100,000 and represents less than 10 percent of the partnership capital and profits. Treas. Reg. § 1.1374–4(i)(5).

5.   LIFO RECAPTURE

Section 1363(d) requires a corporation that makes a Subchapter S election and which has used the last-in-first-out (LIFO) method of inventory accounting to include in gross income for its last year as a C corporation the amount by which its "inventory amount" (i.e., the basis in its inventory) would have been if it had used the first-in-first-out (FIFO) method of inventory accounting exceeds its inventory amount under the LIFO inventory accounting method. Because the FIFO inventory amount often significantly exceeds the LIFO inventory amount, § 1363(d) frequently imposes a significant impediment to an existing corporation that maintains inventory making an S election.

In Coggin Automotive Corp. v. Commissioner, 292 F.3d 1326 (11th Cir. 2002), rev'g 115 T.C. 349 (2000), the taxpayer originally was a C corporation with a number of subsidiaries that owned automobile dealerships and used the LIFO method of inventory accounting. To facilitate making a Subchapter S election, the taxpayer restructured the group. The owners of the taxpayer formed six new S corporations that became the general partners in six limited partnerships. Each subsidiary contributed its dealership assets to a limited partnership in exchange for a limited partnership interest, following which the subsidiaries were liquidated and the taxpayer became the limited partner in each partnership. The taxpayer then made a Subchapter S election. The Commissioner asserted that by applying the aggregate approach to partnership taxation, the taxpayer's conversion to an S corporation triggered the inclusion in the year of the election of the subsidiaries' pre-S-election LIFO reserves under § 1363(d). The Tax Court agreed with the Commissioner because it concluded that application of the aggregate approach to partnership taxation furthered the purpose of § 1363(d). Under this approach, the taxpayer was treated as owning a pro rata share of the partnerships' inventories and as a result of the Subchapter S election it was required to include the LIFO recapture in gross income. On appeal, the Eleventh Circuit Court of Appeals reversed, expressly applying the *Gitlitz* "plain language" principle, discussed at, page 445. The Court of Appeals held that § 1363(d) LIFO recapture is triggered only if the corporation electing Subchapter S status itself directly owned the LIFO inventory.

Treas. Reg. § 1.1363–2(b)–(d), promulgated in 2005 reverses the rule in *Coggin Automotive* for Subchapter S elections after its promulgation. The regulation requires LIFO recapture when a corporation that conducts business through an interest in a partnership makes a Subchapter S election.

6. APPLICATION OF BUILT–IN GAINS TAX TO QUALIFIED SUBCHAPTER S SUBSIDIARY

If an election is made under § 1361(b)(3) to treat an existing wholly owned subsidiary corporation as a qualified Subchapter S subsidiary, the subsidiary is treated as having been liquidated immediately before the election is effective. Section 332 provides nonrecognition to the parent S corporation, and § 337 provides nonrecognition to the subsidiary. The basis of the subsidiary's assets remains the same under § 334(b). Pursuant to § 381, the S corporation parent also inherits any earnings and profits of its subsidiary. If the subsidiary previously was a C corporation, the § 1374 built-in gains tax will apply to the subsidiary's assets as if the subsidiary had made a Subchapter S election. (The LIFO recapture tax under § 1363(d), if applicable, will apply immediately.) H.R. Rep. No. 104–586, 104th Cong., 2d Sess. 89 (1996).

7.   BUILT–IN GAINS ATTRIBUTABLE TO A SUBCHAPTER C SUBSID-
     IARY

If, at the time a corporation elects Subchapter S status, it owns all of
the stock of a subsidiary Subchapter C corporation, built-in gain or loss
attributable to the stock will be reflected in the S corporation's net
unrealized built-in gain or loss. If the subsidiary is subsequently liquidated
in a transaction for which §§ 332 and 337 provide nonrecognition of gain to
the parent and liquidated subsidiary corporations, net unrealized built-in
gain or loss attributable to the subsidiary's assets will again be added to the
net unrealized built-in gain or loss of the parent, thereby potentially
double-counting unrealized appreciation or depreciation attributable to the
subsidiary. Treas. Reg. § 1.1374–3(b) provides an adjustment to the net
unrealized built-in gain or loss of the parent S corporation to eliminate the
effect or any built-in gain or loss attributable to the stock of the subsidiary
that is redeemed or cancelled. The adjustment reflects only net unrealized
built-in gain or loss attributable to the subsidiary stock at the time the
parent corporation first became subject to the tax of § 1374 that has not
resulted in recognized built-in gain or loss. The regulations also disallow an
adjustment that is duplicative of an adjustment that has been made to the
pool of assets reflected in the subsidiary and its stock. Treas. Reg.
§ 1.1374–3(b)(2).

D.   POLICY ASPECTS OF THE TREATMENT OF SUBCHAPTER S CORPORATIONS WITH A SUBCHAPTER C HISTORY

The policy basis of the various rules dealing with Subchapter S
corporations that have previously operated as C corporations is not clearly
articulated in the legislative history of the provisions. With respect to the
built-in gain rules, the provisions can perhaps best be understood as a
variation on the *General Utilities* problem. The conversion from C status to
S status and the consequent move to a single tax regime is in many ways
like a liquidation of the corporation and a transfer of the assets out of
corporate solution. If this change in taxing pattern had been achieved
through a liquidation, § 336 would have required recognition of gain at the
corporate level, followed by a shareholder level gain. In the Subchapter S
situation, rather than impose an immediate tax at the time of conversion,
the statute defers the tax until a sale of the assets and in effect turns that
deferral into an exemption if the assets are held for ten years.

As to the passive income limitations, if the liquidation model is
continued, on a liquidation the accumulated but undistributed corporate
level earnings would not be subject to dividend taxation when distributed
in liquidation, but would incur a shareholder level capital gains tax, the
size of which would depend on the stock basis. Since the conversion to S
status does not result in any shareholder level tax, Congress apparently felt
that it was inappropriate to allow those earnings, unreduced by any second
level tax, to be reinvested in assets generating passive income unrelated to
the basic business operations of the corporation. Initially the sanction is an

additional level of tax, with the corporation ultimately losing its S status if the situation goes on for too long.

If conversion from C to S status were treated as a liquidation of the old corporation and formation of a new corporation, the rules designed to safeguard the double tax regime with respect to gains accrued during the time the corporation was a C corporation could be eliminated and Subchapter S simplified. The Treasury Department advanced such a proposal in 1995 as part of a broader debate on the extent to which pass-through treatment should be available to small businesses, however organized, in light of the phenomenal growth in the popularity of limited liability companies, which provide limited liability for all members under state law but, if properly organized, partnership taxation under federal tax laws. The Treasury Department recommended to Congress that S corporations generally should be permitted to elect to be taxed as a partnership notwithstanding that the corporation was organized as such under state law. Furthermore, the election would not be treated as a liquidation and accrued gains would not be taxed at that time. To offset the revenue loss from this proposal, the Treasury Department further recommended that Congress should consider treating an S election by an existing C corporation as a constructive liquidation. This proposal mirrored a recommendation of the Joint Committee on Taxation in 1990. See Statement of Leslie B. Samuels, Assistant Secretary (Tax Policy), Department of the Treasury, Before the House Committee on Ways and Means (July 28, 1995).

SECTION 6. POLICY ASPECTS OF SUBCHAPTER S

Subchapter S raises significant questions both in theory and in practice. Given the fundamental decision to have a separate corporate income tax, the question is whether there are situations that justify departure from that model. The argument in favor of Subchapter S is that taxes should be as neutral as possible as respects the form of doing business for a closely held enterprise. That argument may justify the special pass-through treatment of S corporations. On the other hand, Subchapter S contains significant differences from the other major form of pass-through enterprise, the partnership, which create significant advantages and disadvantages depending upon particular circumstances. Compared to partnerships, Subchapter S provides a less complex device for pass-through taxation of a joint enterprise. The differences between Subchapters K and S are substantial, however, and require tax motivated choices between the forms of doing business. Does the reduced complexity of Subchapter S justify its variations from the partnership model?

While the partnership rules of Subchapter K adopt an aggregate approach to many issues, with attendant complexity attributable to the aggregate treatment of liabilities and the partners' aggregate shares of the partnership's inside basis if they so elect, the S corporation can be characterized as an entity with a specific pass-through of designated income and loss items. The aggregate versus entity distinction is apparent in the divergent treatment of distributions of appreciated property; distributions by partnerships do not trigger recognition by the partnership and the partners take a carryover basis; and distributions of appreciated property by an S corporation require recognition of gain by all the stockholders and the recipient stockholder receives a step-up in basis to fair market value. Entity level recognition by the S corporation avoids the partnership problems addressed in § 751(b) and the need for adjustments to aggregate basis provided for in § 734, both highly complex provisions. On the other hand, the entity level recognition operates as a disincentive to non-pro rata distributions since the non-recipient shareholders recognize current gain and the tax effect of that recognition may not be reversible until liquidation (by means of a capital loss deduction).

These disparate distribution rules also affect liquidations. Subject to the exceptions of § 751(b), a partnership can be liquidated and assets distributed to the partners without current taxation. The partners substitute their outside basis in their partnership interests for the partnership's basis in the assets distributed to them. The liquidation of an S corporation is subject to the normal rules of Subchapter C (§§ 331 and 336), which require recognition of gain at the corporate level. In tandem, these provisions require recognition of at least corporate level gain on distributed appreciated assets, and perhaps additional gain at the stockholder level depending upon the relationship between the stockholders' stock bases and the value of distributed property. As a result of the taxable nature of the transaction, the stockholders take a fair market value basis in the distributed assets.

Similar disparities exist in comparing the redemption (under § 302) of an S corporation stockholder with the retirement of a partner. A distribution of appreciated property to an S corporation stockholder in a stock redemption will result in recognition of gain by the corporation. The gain is passed through to all shareholders in proportion to stockholdings, while only the redeemed stockholder receives the distributed property. The redeemed stockholder may or may not recognize gain depending on the basis of redeemed stock. A distribution of appreciated property in retirement of a partner's partnership interest will not trigger partnership level recognition of gain or loss, unless § 751 assets are involved. The distributee partner will recognize gain, loss, or in some cases (if § 736(a) is involved) both ordinary gain and a capital loss.

The entity approach to Subchapter S also affects the potential for shifting income from one stockholder to another as a result of a contribution of appreciated property to the corporation. Section 704(c) operates in Subchapter K to prevent a shift of pre-contribution appreciation or losses to the non-contributing partners by requiring that the difference between basis and fair market value at the time of contribution be reflected in allocations to the partners. There is no provision for equivalent adjustments under Subchapter S where each stockholder is required to report the stockholder's proportionate share of corporate income and loss items.

The restrictions of Subchapter S on the number and types of S corporation stockholders may also be analyzed as a response to perceived problems of complexity. Although Subchapter K demonstrates that pass-through accounting on a large scale is a possible alternative for income tax purposes, the limited number of permissible stockholders of an S corporation and the restrictions on the types of permissible stockholders, excluding other pass-through entities and corporations, substantially reduces the burden of accounting for the pass-through of S corporation income.

However, the goal of simplicity in Subchapter S creates its own complexity. Differences in the pass-through treatment under Subchapters K and S require careful planning choices regarding the choice of entity. The flexibility permitted by Subchapter K with respect to allocations of income and loss items can be contrasted with the rather rigid requirements of a single class of stock under Subchapter S. Stockholder attempts to create preferential interests in an S corporation through the use of purported debt instruments have been a source of considerable litigation. Additional difficulty is created by the detailed requirements for electing S corporation status. Failure to comply with the statutory requirements regarding timing and form can defeat the attempts of well-intentioned taxpayers to elect S corporation status. No such requirements are imposed on operation as a partnership, an entity also requiring participants to report their share of entity level income and loss, though the question of entity classification represents a somewhat similar problem. Nevertheless, provisions for notifying the Internal Revenue Service of an intent to operate a corporation as a pass-through entity and requiring stockholders to consent to the pass-through of tax significant items are warranted.

Beyond the question of the relationship between Subchapter S and partnership taxation, the Subchapter S provisions raise the more fundamental issue of the extent to which operation in corporate form should be coupled with a double level of tax on distributions. Absent a decision to adopt some general form of integration of corporate and individual taxes, why should closely held corporations with only common stock be subject to a single level of tax while all other corporate entities operate in a two tax world? Do these characteristics have any bearing on whether double tax or single tax is appropriate?

INDEX

†